Leadership, Social Memory and Judean Discourse
in the Fifth–Second Centuries BCE

Worlds of the Ancient Near East and Mediterranean

Series editor: Diana V. Edelman, University of Oslo

Worlds of the Ancient Near East and Ancient Mediterranean brings alive the texts, archaeology and history of the cultures of the regions around the Mediterranean Sea and eastward to ancient Iran and Iraq, from the Neolithic through the Roman periods (ca 10,000 BCE–393 CE). Studies of one or more aspects of a single culture or of a subject across cultures in the regions outlined will form the foundation of this series, in which interdisciplinary approaches are encouraged. Studies can be based on texts, on material remains, or a combination of the two, where appropriate. In the case of a project that focuses on either the memory or the reception history of a place, person, myth, practice, or idea that arose or existed within the prescribed time, chapters that trace ongoing relevance to the present are welcome. The volumes are meant to be accessible to a wide audience interested in how the inhabitants of these parts of the world lived or how they understood their own pasts, presents, and futures, as well as how current scholars are understanding and recreating their pasts or their future aspirations.

Published titles

A History of Biblical Israel:
The Fate of the Tribes and Kingdoms from Merenptah to Bar Kochba

Axel Knauf and Philippe Guillaume

Ancient Cookware from the Levant: An Ethnoarchaeological Perspective

Gloria London

Forthcoming titles

Burial Practices in Ancient Israel and the Neighboring Cultures (c. 1500–330 BCE)

Jürg Hutzli and Stefan Münger

Recovering Women's Rituals in the Ancient Near East

Julye Bidmead

Leadership, Social Memory and Judean Discourse in the Fifth–Second Centuries BCE

edited by

Diana V. Edelman and Ehud Ben Zvi

Published by Equinox Publishing Ltd.

UK: Office 415, The Workstation, 15 Paternoster Row, Sheffield, South Yorkshire S1 2BX
USA: ISD, 70 Enterprise Drive, Bristol, CT 06010

www.equinoxpub.com

First published 2016

© Diana V. Edelman and Ehud Ben Zvi and individual authors, 2016

All rights reserved. No part of this publication may be reproduced or transmitted in any form or by any means, electronic or mechanical, including photocopying, recording or any information storage or retrieval system, without prior permission in writing from the publishers.

British Library Cataloguing-in-Publication Data

A catalogue record for this book is available from the British Library.

ISBN 9781781792681 (hardback)
ISBN 9781781792698 (paperback)

Library of Congress Cataloging-in-Publication Data

Edelman, Diana Vikander, 1954— editor.
Leadership, social memory, and Judean discourse in the fifth-second centuries BCE / edited by Diana V. Edelman and Ehud Ben Zvi.
   pages cm.—(Worlds of the ancient Near East and Mediterranean)
Includes bibliographical references and index.
LCCN 2015031545| ISBN 9781781792681 (hb) | ISBN 9781781792698 (pb)
LCSH: Leadership—Biblical teaching. | Leadership in the Bible. | Judaism—History—Post-exilic period, 586 B.C.–210 A.D. | Palestine—History—To 70 A.D. | Bible. Old Testament—Criticism, interpretation, etc.
Classification: LCC BS1199.L4 L43 2016 | DDC 221.8/30334—dc23

LC record available at https://lccn.loc.gov/2015031545

Typeset by Queenston Publishing, Hamilton, Ontario, Canada

Printed and bound in Great Britain by
Lightning Source Inc. (La Vergne, TN), and Lightning Source UK Ltd. (Milton Keynes)

Contents

List of contributors	vii
Abbreviations	viii

1. Introduction
   Diana V. Edelman — 1

2. Memory and Political Thought in the Late Persian/Early Hellenistic Yehud/Judah: Some Observations
   Ehud Ben Zvi — 9

3. Memories of Judah's Past Leaders Utilized as Propaganda in Yehud
   James M. Bos — 27

4. Mystified Authority: Legitimating Leadership Through "Lost Books"
   Kåre Berge — 41

5. Israel's King as Primus Inter Pares: The "Democratic" Re-conceptualization of Monarchy in Deut 17:14–20
   Reinhard Müller — 57

6. The Kingdom of God in Samuel
   Geoffrey P. Miller — 77

7. Reconsidering Davidic Kingship in Ezekiel
   Christophe Nihan — 89

8. Imagining the Memory of an Elder: Job 29–30
   Terje Stordalen — 111

9. At the Hands of Foreign Kings: Divine Endorsement of Foreign Rulers in the Hebrew Bible in the Memory of Persian and Hellenistic Yehud
   Thomas M. Bolin — 127

10. At the Crossroads of Persian and Hellenistic Ideology: The Book of Esther as "Political Theology" Beate Ego	147
11. Models of Local Political Leadership in the Nehemiah Memoir Anne Fitzpatrick-McKinley	165
12. The Three Constitutions in Greek Political Thought Lynette Mitchell	201
13. Monarchy, Oligarchy, and Democracy in the Constitutional Debate in Herodotus and in 1 Samuel 8 Wolfgang Oswald	219
14. Remembering Samson in a Hellenized Jewish Context (Judges 13–16) Diana V. Edelman	231
15. Judith Maccabee? On Leadership, Resistance, and the Great Deeds of Little People Anne-Mareike Schol-Wetter	249
INDEX OF ANCIENT SOURCES	263
AUTHOR INDEX	278

Contributors

James M. Bos is Assistant Professor of Religion at the University of Mississippi.

Diana V. Edelman is Pofessor of Hebrew Bible/Old Testament in the Faculty of Theology at the University of Oslo.

Ehud Ben Zvi is Professor emeritus in the Department of History and Classics at the University of Alberta.

Kåre Berge is Professor of Old Testament Studies at NLA University College, Bergen.

Reinhard Müller is Professor of the Old Testament at the University of Münster.

Geoffrey P. Miller is Stuyvesant P. Comfort Professor of Law at New York University.

Christophe Nihan is Associate Professor of the Hebrew Bible and History of Ancient Israel at the University of Lausanne.

Terje Stordalen is Professor in the Faculty of Theology at the University of Oslo.

Thomas M. Bolin is Professor of Theology and Religious Studies at St. Norbert College in De Pere, Wisconsin.

Beate Ego is Professor of Exegesis and Theology of the Old Testament at Ruhr-Universität Bochum.

Anne Fitzpatrick-McKinley is Lecturer in Biblical Studies at Trinity College, Dublin.

Lynette Mitchell is Professor in Greek History and Politics at the University of Exeter.

Wolfgang Oswald is Adjunct Professor of Old Testament in the Faculty of Protestant Theology at the University of Tübingen.

Anne-Mareike Schol-Wetter is head of the department of Bible Advocacy of the Dutch Bible Society and associated researcher at the Center for Contextual Biblical Interpretation (Free University Amsterdam/Protestant Theological University).

ABBREVIATIONS

AB	Anchor Bible
ANEM	Ancient Near Eastern Monographs
ANES	*Ancient Near Eastern Studies*
ATD	Das Alte Testament Deutsch
BBB	Bonner biblische Beiträge
BETL	Bibliotheca ephemeridum theologicarum lovaniensium
BibInt	Biblical Interpretation Series
BibInt	*Biblical Interpretation*
BWANT	Beiträge zur Wissenschaft vom Alten und Neuen Testament
BZAR	Beihefte zur Zeitschrift für altorientalische und biblische Rechtsgeschichte
BZAW	Beihefte zur Zeitschrift für die alttestamentliche Wissenschaft
CBQ	*Catholic Biblical Quarterly*
FAT	Forschungen zum Alten Testament
FRLANT	Forschungen zur Religion und Literatur des Alten und Neuen Testaments
HANEM	History of Ancient Near East/Monographs
HeBAI	*Hebrew Bible and Ancient Israel*
HCS	Hellenistic Culture and Society
Historia	*Historia: Zeitschrift für Alte Geschichte*
HSM	Harvard Semitic Monographs
HThKAT	Herders Theologischer Kommentar zum Alten Testament
HTR	*Harvard Theological Review*
ICC	International Critical Commentary
IEJ	*Israel Exploration Journal*
JBL	*Journal of Biblical Literature*
JESHO	*Journal of the Economic and Social History of the Orient*
JHebS	*Journal of Hebrew Scriptures*
JHS	*Journal of Hellenic Studies*
JQR	*Jewish Quarterly Review*

Abbreviations

JNES	*Journal of Near Eastern Studies*
JSOT	*Journal for the Study of the Old Testament*
JSOTSup	Journal for the Study of the Old Testament: Supplement Series
JSP	*Journal for the Study of the Pseudepigrapha*
JTS	*Journal of Theological Studies*
KAT	Kommentar zum Alten Testament
LCL	Loeb Classical Library
LHBOTS	Library of Hebrew Bible / Old Testament Studies
NICOT	New International Commentary on the Old Testament
OBO	Orbis biblicus et orientalis
OTL	Old Testament Library
RAr	*Revue archéologique*
SBAB	Stuttgarter biblische Aufsatzbände
SBL	Society of Biblical Literature
SBLAIL	Society of Biblical Literature Ancient Israel and Its Literature
SBLDS	Society of Biblical Literature Dissertation Series
SJOT	*Scandinavian Journal of the Old Testament*
TSAJ	Texte und Studien zum antiken Judentum
VT	*Vetus Testamentum*
VTSup	Supplements to Vetus Testamentum
WBC	Word Biblical Commentary
WMANT	Wissenschaftliche Monographien zum Alten und Neuen Testament
WUNT	*Wissenschaftliche Untersuchungen zum Neuen Testament*
ZABR	*Zeitschrift für altorientalische und biblische Rechtgeschichte*
ZAW	*Zeitschrift für die alttestamentliche Wissenschaft*
ZBK	Zürcher Bibelkommentare

— 1 —

Introduction

Diana V. Edelman

In this volume, fifteen scholars explore the various ways in which types of political leadership were remembered and evaluated by readers (and hearers) of texts that were eventually included in the Hebrew Bible. These texts often carried implicit or explicit responses to different types of regimes imagined for the religious community called Israel, with which the readers (and hearers) identified. As a collection, the essays assume audiences living in the fifth through second centuries BCE, though a more specific time frame within that wider chronology is often explored in each essay. Some essays focus more on the commitment of these memories to writing and others more on the reception of memories already encoded in texts. The issue of their historicity is not part of the intended purview addressed in this volume.

The five papers by E. Ben Zvi, G. P. Miller, R. Müller, C. Nihan, and A.-M. Schol-Wetter were presented in the final two sessions jointly chaired by Ehud and me as part of the working group "Israel and the Production and Reception of Authoritative Books in the Persian and Hellenistic Periods" at the annual meeting of the European Association of Biblical Studies in Leipzig in 2013. The group continues under the capable leadership of Susanne Gillmayr-Bucher and Maria Häusl. The announced theme for our final sessions was "Monarchy, Oligarchy and 'Democracy' in Yehudite Discourse: Political Thought, Social Memory, and Imagination." The remaining papers have been invited by the editors with an eye toward covering a range of topics and approaches. The papers by G. P. Miller and L. G. Mitchell are intended to provide an interdisciplinary examination of leadership from the fields of Law and Classics, respectively. All papers were peer-vetted, including the contributions written by the editors.

In the end, a surprising range of political forms has been covered in the volume: monarchy, both absolute and constitutional, leadership involving councils, assemblies, and elders as part of shared or delegated power; imperialism; tyranny; democracy; oligarchy; autocracy; theocracy, both absolute and with a human intermediary; rule by a *primus inter pares*, temporary grass-roots leadership; and other informal authority systems, including the priestly Levites in charge of Torah, an unofficial institution for the prophetic guardianship of *tôrâ* by an individual or group, and patron-client relationships. Anyone who has put together a collection of essays will know how hard it is to get commitments from colleagues to write on specifically designated topics; we were fortunate in this regard in more than one instance and appreciate our colleagues' willing cooperation.

We also have been pleasantly surprised at a number of serendipitous overlaps and dialogues that have emerged among the papers. Four essays, for example, explore the role, social setting, and motivations of the literati who produced the texts (Ben Zvi, Bos, Berge, and Bolin), and two examine the significance of the act of obeisance in biblical texts (Ego and Edelman). The Greek constitutional debate in Herodotus is discussed at length also in two papers (Mitchell and Oswald). Various aspects of David's kingship and a future Davidic leader are explored in a number of the essays (Ben Zvi, Bos, Nihan, Bolin, Oswald, and Schol-Wetter) and, to a lesser degree, the figure of Solomon, the other founding king of the "Golden Age" (Ben Zvi, Müller, and Ego). Four engage with the multi-faceted figure of Moses in memory (Ben Zvi, Berge, Müller, and Miller), and three discuss the "law of the king" in the book of Deuteronomy (Müller, Berge, and Oswald). Three consider the role of elders (Stordalen, Müller, Oswald), two the role of prophets (Ben Zvi and Bos), and four the figure of Moses (Ben Zvi, Berge, Müller, and Miller). Six discuss the role of Torah in ensuring successful leadership in Israel or in indicating that no human political organization ensures lasting stability and happiness for those governed by it (Ben Zvi, Bos, Berge, Müller, Oswald, Edelman), and a number deal with unofficial forms of leadership (Ben Zvi, Berge, Fitzpatrick-McKinley, Schol-Wetter, and Ego, in some respects). Six provide examples of Othering (Ben Zvi, Bos, Berge, Bolin, Mitchell, and Schol-Wetter), and there are three engagements with utopian and eschatological concepts (Ben Zvi, Nihan, and Ego).

The range of biblical and early Jewish literature used in the various studies is wide. Three studies focus on Deuteronomy (Berge, Müller, and Oswald), of which two discuss the law of the king in ch. 17 and the other deals with many passages in the book. Other narratives addressed include the garden of Eden (Miller) and the rape of Dinah (Schol-Wetter) in Genesis, the golden calf incident in Exodus (Miller), Pinehas in Numbers (Schol-Wetter), Joshua in the book of Joshua (Ben Zvi), the stories of Gideon/Abimelech (Ben Zvi, Müller, and Miller) and Samson (Edelman) in Judges, aspects of the stories of Samuel (Ben Zvi, Müller, Miller, Oswald), Saul (Bos, Müller, Ego), and David (Nihan, Schol-Wetter) in the books of Samuel, of Solomon (Müller and Ego), Shishak (Bolin), Jeroboam (Ben Zvi and Bos), Hezekiah (Müller and Bolin), Sennacherib (Bolin), Josiah (Bos, Bolin), Necho (Bolin), Zedekiah (Nihan), and Jehoiachin (Nihan) in the books of Kings, Cyrus in Isaiah (Bolin), the *nagid* and lion and tree metaphors in Ezekiel (Nihan), Zerubbabel in Haggai (Ben Zvi, Bos and Fitzpatrick-McKinley), the elders in Job 29–30 (Stordalen), Nebuchadnezzar in Daniel (Bolin and Edelman), the Nehemiah Memoir (Fitzpatrick), the book of Judith (Schol-Wetter), the Maccabees, Achior, and Holofernes in 1 Maccabees (Schol-Wetter), Nehemiah in 2 Maccabees (Ben Zvi and Fitzpatrick-McKinley) and Chronicles (Ben Zvi), and Josephus (Ben Zvi, Berge, Ego, Fitzpatrick-McKinley and Edelman).

The range of classical authors includes Homer (Bolin and Mitchell), Tyrtaeus (Mitchell), Pindar (Mitchell and Edelman), Aeschylus (Mitchell, Edelman), Baccylides (Edelman), Herodotus (Ben Zvi, Bolin, Ego, Mitchell and Oswald), Hesiod (Mitchell), Thucydides (Mitchell), Euripides (Mitchell, Edelman), Xenophon (Ben Zvi, Mitchell), Socrates (Edelman), Plato (Mitchell and Edelman), Aristotle (Bolin, Mitchell, and Oswald), Plutarch (Ego and Mitchell), Diodorus (Mitchell and Edelman), Polybius (Ben Zvi), Arrian (Ego, Edelman), Curtius Rufus (Ego), Old Oligarch (Mitchell), Isocrates (Mitchell and Edelman), Apollodorus (Edelman), and Ovid (Edelman). Not all the engagements with Greek texts deal explicitly with passages that focus on discussions of forms of political leadership or which would be best, but many do. As noted by E. Ben Zvi in his contribution,[1] Western society has been so heavily influenced by debates over the pros and cons of various kinds of political leadership in classical Greek literature that it has tended to overlook discussions in other ancient cultures. Our invitation to L. G. Mitchell to write specifically on the Constitutional Debate from the perspective of a classicist derives from this trend, but at the same time, is designed to allow readers of this volume to get a better sense of both how widespread such debate is in the biblical and early Jewish literature and how it usually takes place in a different format, using different literary genres.

Different methodological and theoretical approaches used among the essays in the volume include memory studies, propaganda theory, anthropological theory of informal authority systems, anthropological theories of mimesis and alterity, critical social analysis of the Moroccan Kabyle tribe by P. Bourdieu and of a traditional village in China by X. Fei, alongside more familiar methods of text criticism, literary criticism, narrative criticism, and synchronic reading. While the biblical texts of the Hebrew Bible form the main source of analysis, comparative ancient Near Eastern literature, epigraphic evidence and many classical Greek writers, early Jewish writings, and archaeological remains are also cited in various discussions and used as corroborating evidence.

In his contribution, Ben Zvi also has drawn attention to the role historical context played in stimulating political reflection in Greece and in Israel.[2] As demonstrated in this volume, the biblical texts reflect extensive debate over the pros and cons of various forms of leadership that took place after the loss of political independence. In contrast, the heyday of the initial Greek debate took place during a period when Greece was still independent but threatened by conquest and absorption into the imperial Achaemenid Empire. Once it had become part of the Empire of Alexander the Great and his successors, such discussion abated considerably. L. G. Mitchell notes in her chapter that Greek abstract and analytical thinking about constitutional forms of leadership emerged in the fourth century BCE in a process of reflecting over the memory of selected past events, including the Spartan constitution of Lycurgus and the Persian attack on Athenian soil and the expulsion of the Peisistratids.[3]

The importance of the socio-historical setting of the literati who produced the biblical and early Jewish texts investigated in this volume (Ben Zvi, Bos, Berge, and Bolin) and of those who interacted with them over time (Fitzpatrick-McKinley, Ego, and Edelman) has been duly noted and explored in various ways. Recognizing that the literati primarily would have served the royal administration during the monarchy and probably served the imperial neo-Babylonian and Achaemenid administrations as well, the change in circumstance that prompted initial and secondary reflection was not likely the loss of jobs, though perhaps some of those deported in 598, 587, and 582 BCE as prisoners-of-war ended up as scribes in private employment or in situations where their skills were not put to use.[4]

---

1. "Memory and Political Thought in the Late Persian/early Hellenistic Yehud/Judah: Some Observations," 9–26.
2. "Memory and Political Thought," 9–11.
3. "The Three Constitutions in Greek Political Thought," 201–18.
4. The appropriateness of describing the literati as elites is debated. In this collection, both J. M. Bos and T. M. Bolin apply this label to them, but they are not necessarily meaning to imply thereby that they belonged to a landed aristocracy, if such had existed. Bos calls them "a semi-elite scribal-priestly class," signaling their elite status was prestige-related, but not necessarily based on the traditional ownership of land and affiliation by birth to a small number of recognized families with such status ("Memories of Judah's Past Leaders Utilized as Propaganda in Yehud," 28). Bolin refers to them as elites, but specifically

Introduction

Those authoring the biblical and early Jewish texts, however, probably continued primary employment in some sort of official imperial capacity, including administration of the temple, after it was rebuilt. The change that occurred involved one from a local monarchy to an imperial regime.

But the change to an imperial political regime seems to have prompted a crisis in identity among the literati, some of whom now were based in Babylonia, due to forced emigration as prisoners-of-war. The gentilic label "Judean" still designated a geographical region in the southern Levant that applied to those living there as well to those who had once lived there, and their descendants. This included, in addition to those forcefully removed to Babylonia, refugees who had fled to Egypt, who augmented existing groups there who had originated in Judah, like the mercenaries who served at Elephantine, for example. It also included groups that had fled to Transjordan.

The hill-country of Judah overlapped with what was known in Achaemenid administration as a unit called Yehud.[5] This unit probably had been established by the Neo-Babylonian administration, perhaps alongside a separate unit called Benjamin.[6] In light of recent evidence that indicates how some areas conquered by the neo-Babylonians were assigned to Neo-Babylonian temples to administer rather than directly administered by the crown,[7] it may be that there was a more significant change in administrative policy in the region between the Neo-Babylonian and Persian regimes than previously thought.

As is evident from a reading of the Hebrew Bible, the literary repertoire the literati produced indicates their ideological focus on the temple in Jerusalem. Both Ben Zvi and K. Berge note the role the temple played as a social institution that, on the one hand, did not compete for political power with the appointed Persian governor, but which, on the other hand, "played an important role alongside the literati in constructing and enabling the social reproduction of the 'Israel' they envisaged and remembered."[8] The temple

---

elites who created, preserved, and read texts, which in the historical context of the southern Levant, is not identical to the landed aristocracy but to professional scribes who can be deemed elite by virtue of their rare reading and writing abilities ("At the Hands of Foreign Kings: Divine Endorsement of Foreign Rulers in the Hebrew Bible in the Memory of Persian and Hellenistic Yehud, " 128). In sociological terms, the scribes would have belonged to the "retainer class," although this term is also problematic when applied to the ancient southern Levant. It is not clear that ancient Israel, Judah, or the Assyrian, Babylonian, or Persian Empires were or included societies that were organized according to formal class hierarchy.

5. For differing reconstructions of the boundaries of Yehud, see, for example, D. V. Edelman, *The Origins of the 'Second' Temple: Persian Imperial Policy and the Rebuilding of Jerusalem*, BibleWorld (London: Equinox, 2005), 209–80; O. Lipschits, *The Fall and Rise of Jerusalem: Judah Under Babylonian Rule* (Winona Lake, IN: Eisenbrauns, 2005), 134–84.

6. The book of Jeremiah refers repeatedly to Benjamin and Judah as separate units. The import of the distinction remains debated. For a discussion, see for example, P. R. Davies, *The Origins of Biblical Israel*, LHBOTS 485 (London: T&T Clark, 2007), 105–26; idem, "Reading Jeremiah," in *The One Who Reads May Run: Essays in Honour of Edgar W. Conrad*, ed. R. Boer, M. Carden, and J. Kelso, LHBOTS 553 (London: T&T Clark, 2012), 3–9.

7. Y. Levavi and M. Jursa, "The Neo-Babylonian Empire: The Imperial Periphery as Seen from the Center" (paper presented at the Annual Meeting of the SBL, San Diego, CA, 23 November 2014). This paper was presented at an invited session on the theme Neo-Babylonian Imperial Provincial Policy in Assyria and the West, sponsored by the section Current Historiography and Ancient Israel and Judah.

8. Ben Zvi, "Memory and Political Thought," 11–12. It perhaps is relevant also to note that in Babylonia, the Achaemenids reassigned the *ashipu* and *baru*, scribal professionals who had formerly been palace

had imperial endorsement, and undoubtedly, its revenues were taxed by the local Persian administrators as a steady source of income. At the same time, however, it became the base from which an alternative, unofficial power structure could be conceptualized for the religious community called Israel. The literati who produced the majority of the biblical books were Judean by descent,[9] but the community they envisioned and created in their literature was called Israel, not Judah.

In this society-within-a society, YHWH served as king and set the laws, not the imperial ruling monarch in Persepolis, who, at most, could serve as a chosen human agent (Isa 44:28; 45:1–7) but need not do so on a regular basis, generation after generation. In this envisioned world, the guardians and teachers of Torah, i.e., the literati, became the most important human agents, even though they were not necessarily among the elders[10] or judges who administered justice within the imperial province. They created unofficial authority and status for themselves within the religious community of Israel through the mystification of Torah, particularly as expressed in the book of Deuteronomy, but which was meant to be assumed as valid more generally. Mystification has been documented in anthropological studies as a fairly widespread strategy for gaining unofficial power within a society.[11]

Bearing in mind the historical setting and circumstances of the authors of the various biblical books, it should not be surprising that theocracy was envisioned as the preferred or ideal political system for YHWH's chosen community, Israel. The temple was the earthly

---

staff, to serve as temple personnel, as part of a move to concentrate all cuneiform knowledge and writing among temple personnel. For details, see W. Sallaberger and F. Huber Villiet, "Priester.A.1," in *Reallexicon der Assyriologie und vorderasiatischen Archäologie*, vol. 10, ed. M. P. Streck (Berlin: de Gruyter, 2005), 617–40, esp. 620, 632. In Egypt, according to the inscription on the statue of Udjahorresnet, they made the temple of Neith the location of a "House of Life," which contained a library with holdings that went well beyond religious and theological compositions. According to K. Nordh, however, this would have been a continuation of earlier pharaonic practice and not an innovation (*Aspects of Ancient Egyptian Curses and Blessings: Conceptual Background and Transmission,* Boreas: Uppsala Studies in Ancient Mediterranean and Near Eastern Civilizations 26 [Uppsala: Acta Universitatis Upsaliensis, 1996], 107). Even so, it would reflect a consistent policy, regardless of from where that policy derived it inspiration. This raises the possibility that even in backwater Yehud, once the temple was rebuilt, it housed scribes who formerly would have worked in the palace and that the temple library would have included examples of works that might have originated in former royal circles. There was time to remove such documents to Mizpah, the new Neo-Babylonian regional administrative seat, before Jerusalem was destroyed. A secondary emphasis on the former native Davidic dynasty in the biblical texts that otherwise emphasize the Jerusalemite temple and its ideology might have arisen from the concentration of local knowledge and wisdom, secular and religious, under the custodianship of the temple and its personnel in the Persian period.

9. The first five books were accepted as authoritative by the Samarian Israelite community was well, and more work needs to be done to establish if any of these might have been written by literati based in the province of Samaria. For the argument that Deuteronomy might constitute one such book, see P. R. Davies, "The Authority of Deuteronomy," in *Deuteronomy–Kings as Emerging Authoritative Books: A Conversation*, ed. D. V. Edelman, ANEM 6 (Atlanta, GA: SBL, 2014), 27–47, esp. 33–34.

10. For a detailed discussion of the role of elders in the administration of justice at the village and town level, whether under a monarchic or imperial administration, see the contribution by T. Stordalen ("Imagining the Memory of an Elder: Job 29–30").

11. For a fuller discussion of both mystification in anthropology and the role of the Levitical priests in Deuteronomy, see the contribution in this volume by K. Berge, "Mystified Authority: Legitimating Leadership Through 'Lost Books'," 41–56.

palace where the deity YHWH could become manifest in various ways: via 'glory' (כבוד) and via 'name/reputation' (שׁם),[12] the latter perhaps conceived of as recorded in Torah[13] and possibly equated with the scroll beside the Ark that the King was to have a copy made of and spend his days studying (Deut 17:18–20). However, in books outside of Deuteronomy, the deity's reputation may have been conceived of as encapsulated in the wider collection of writings that came to comprise the Hebrew Bible. All the stories of what this deity had done for its special people would contribute to remembering and transmitting its reputation on earth. As the deity's seat of worldly power, the temple became a logical focal point to represent the deity's political rule over its chosen people, Israel, which was scattered geographically within the Empire of the day.[14]

The concept that the ruling monarch, whether of an Empire, a territorial kingdom, or a more limited city and its immediate hinterland, was the earthly representative and vice-regent of a particular deity who was deemed king of heaven was widespread in the ancient Near East. The literati worked with this familiar concept but emphasized the divine dimension over the human one. They seem to have recognized, however, that pure theocracy, without one or more divine designated human agents, was a utopian ideal. Thus, they explored the pros and cons of different types of official agents: native Davidic kings,[15] foreign imperial kings,[16] "judges,"[17] governors,[18] priests,[19] elders,[20] and unofficial agents, like the Levitical priests in charge of Torah,[21] the prophet like Moses,[22] and temporary,

---

12. For these differing theological conceptions, see T. Mettinger, *Dethronement of Sebaot: Studies in the Shem and Kabod Theologies* (Lund: CWK Gleerup, 1982).

13. See D. Edelman, "God Rhetoric: Reconceptualizing Yahweh Sebaot as Yahweh Elohim in the Hebrew Bible," in *A Palimpsest: Rhetoric, Ideology, Stylistics and Language Relating to Persian Israel*, ed. E. Ben Zvi, D. Edelman, and F. Polak (Piscataway, NJ: Gorgias, 2009), 81–107, esp. 88–91.

14. The inclusion of Samarians within the religious community of Israel and the existence of two main temple sites for YHWH, one on Mt. Gerizim and one in Jerusalem, each claiming to be the site intended in the book of Deuteronomy, should not be overlooked. Israel is envisioned as comprised of descendants of the twelve tribes, wherever they resided in the Empire.

15. For fuller discussion, see especially the essay by R. Müller ("Israel's King as Primus Inter Pares: The 'Democratic' Re-conceptualization of Monarchy in Deut 17:14–20").

16. For a fuller discussion, see the essay by Bolin ("At the Hands").

17. For more detailed discussions, see in particular the essays of G. P. Miller ("The Kingdom of God in Samuel") and D. V. Edelman ("Remembering Samson in a Hellenized Jewish Context [Judges 13–16]").

18. For a discussion of the role of the governors Sanballat and Nehemiah in memory in the Nehemiah Memoir, see the essay by A. Fitzpatrick-McKinley ("Models of Local Political Leadership in the Nehemiah Memoir"). The main thrust of her essay centers on unofficial leadership via patron-client relationships in the southern Levant in the first half of the fifth century BCE, but such leadership was implemented by Persian-appointed officials, who were able to build a stronger power base because of their official connections.

19. For detailed discussions, see, for example, the essays by Miller ("Kingdom of God"), A.-M. Schol-Wetter ("Judith Maccabee? On Leadership, Resistance, and the Great Deeds of Little People").

20. While the primary examples of the endorsement of leadership by the elders is found in Exod 24:1, 9–11; Num 11:16–17, 24–30, Stordalen ("Imagining an Elder") has discussed their likely role in society in this volume, using Job 29–30 as his primary biblical evidence.

21. For a detailed discussion, see the essay by Berge ("Mystified Authority").

22. For a detailed discussion, see the essay of Ben Zvi ("Memory and Political Thought").

grass-roots leaders during a crisis, like Esther[23] and Judith.[24] Yet, they reconceptualized the role of any future Davidic monarch so that he effectively became an example of a pious individual who did not lead the people in war but lived his life by Torah and dispensed justice according to its precepts (Deut 17:18–20). In the book of Ezekiel,[25] he assumes a new title, נגיד ('leader', 'the one set beside'), instead of מלך, ('king'), which helps signal that this envisioned form of monarch differs dramatically from the kings "who govern ... other nations" (1 Sam 8:5).[26]

The present volume should be of interest to biblical scholars, ancient historians of ideas, classicists, students of political science, and anyone interested in discussions of the pros and cons of various forms of political leadership in the Hebrew Bible. All are welcome to expand their horizons through its individual and collective offerings.

Diana V. Edelman
Oslo, 26 July, 2015

Bibliography

Davies, P. R. 2014. "The Authority of Deuteronomy." In *Deuteronomy–Kings as Emerging Authoritative Books: A Conversation*, edited by D. V. Edelman, 27–47. ANEM 6. Atlanta, GA: SBL.

———. 2012. "Reading Jeremiah." In *The One Who Reads May Run: Essays in Honour of Edgar W. Conrad*, edited by R. Boer, M. Carden, and J. Kelso, 3–9. LHBOTS 553. London: T&T Clark.

———. 2007. *The Origins of Biblical Israel*. LHBOTS 485. London: T&T Clark.

Edelman, D. 2009. "God Rhetoric: Reconceptualizing Yahweh Sebaot as Yahweh Elohim in the Hebrew Bible." In *A Palimpsest: Rhetoric, Ideology, Stylistics and Language Relating to Persian Israel*, edited by E. Ben Zvi, D. Edelman and F. Polak, 81–107. Piscataway, NJ: Gorgias.

———. 2005. *The Origins of the 'Second' Temple: Persian Imperial Policy and the Rebuilding of Jerusalem*. BibleWorld. London: Equinox.

Levavi, Y and Jursa, M. 2014. "The Neo-Babylonian Empire: The Imperial Periphery as Seen from the Center." Paper presented at the Annual Meeting of the SBL. San Diego, CA, 23 November.

Lipschits, O. 2005. *The Fall and Rise of Jerusalem: Judah Under Babylonian Rule*. Winona Lake, IN: Eisenbrauns.

Mettinger, T. 1982. *Dethronement of Sebaot: Studies in the Shem and Kabod Theologies*. Lund: CWK Gleerup.

Nordh, K. 1996. *Aspects of Ancient Egyptian Curses and Blessings: Conceptual Background and Transmission*. Boreas: Uppsala Studies in Ancient Mediterranean and Near Eastern Civilizations 26. Uppsala: Acta Universitatis Upsaliensis.

Sallaberger, W. and F. Huber Villiet. 2005. "Priester.A.1." In *Reallexicon der Assyriologie und vorderasiatischen Archäologie*, Vol. 10, edited by M. P. Streck, 617–40. Berlin: de Gruyter.

---

23. For a detailed discussion, see the essay by B. Ego ("At the Crossroads of Persian and Hellenistic Ideology: The Book of Esther as 'Political Theology'").
24. For a detailed discussion, see the essay by Schol-Wetter ("Judith Maccabee?").
25. For a detailed discussion, see the essay by C. Nihan ("Reconsidering Davidic Kingship in Ezekiel").
26. For the import of this phrase in 1 Sam 8, see the essay by W. Oswald ("Monarchy, Oligarchy, and Democracy in the Constitutional Debate in Herodotus and in 1 Samuel 8").

— 2 —

Memory and Political Thought in the Late Persian/Early Hellenistic Yehud/Judah: Some Observations

Ehud Ben Zvi

Explorations concerning what we would call political thought, in the narrow sense of the term "political,"[1] and particularly involving negotiating arguments for the strengths and weaknesses of various political regimes, were alive and well in the early Second Temple period, at least among the literati.[2] These explorations existed in spite of the lack of an "independent" polity.[3]

---

1. One may maintain that almost anything in the Hebrew Bible is "political" or relates to the "political sphere," in one way or another. Even more narrowly, pentateuchal "laws"—be they prescriptive, descriptive of a real or a perceived utopian society, or instructive examples of what the ideal law of the ideal king (i.e., YHWH) is or should be, or any combination of the above—and any laws and regulations anywhere in the Hebrew Bible or for that matter in any other written or non-written corpus of a social group involve and exemplify "political" thought. This said, and to keep the discussion manageable within the parameters of a chapter in a volume, the present contribution deals only with "political" thought in a very narrow sense, namely the discourse about political regimes, their potential strengths and weaknesses, and potential appropriate responses to both.

2. While the argument mentioned in the previous note suggests a wide-opening of "political thought," some would argue that proper political thought in the sense of political philosophy, namely a rational discourse about "the political sphere," including regime types, was either precluded, or at least severely hindered, by widespread social acceptance of the principle of divine selection of both political regimes and rulers. It suffices for the present purposes to note that such claims fail to take into full account the social roles and the human, socially construed and fluid character of what is agreed among members of a particular society or group as divinely ordained and, if taken to their logical consequences, would be tantamount to maintaining that proper political thought in the sense of political philosophy did not exist in most historical societies over time and space. Certainly, in all ancient Near East political regimes, rulers were thought of as shaped and legitimized by the divine sphere, but the ancient Near East is surely not unique in this respect. (Our contemporary Canadian coins still bear marks of such an understanding and even if one may correctly argue that the relevant expression is just a "fossilized remainder" of a bygone era, the same could not be said of many Canadians or Brits only 100 years ago.) On the Sumerian King List in general, see, e.g., N. Yoffee, *Myths of the Archaic State: Evolution of the Earliest Cities, States, and Civilizations* (Cambridge: Cambridge University Press, 2005), 55 and passim and the cited bibliography; cf. on similar matters though from a very different perspective, see Y. Hazony, *The Philosophy of Hebrew Scripture* (Cambridge: Cambridge University Press, 2012).

3. The idea that a group should have an experience of "independent polity" (or at least aim to establish one in its own time) to engage in "political philosophy" has contributed to a tendency to claim that there was no "political philosophy" among Medieval Jewish thinkers (e.g., Maimonides). In the last

In fact, they were facilitated and partially shaped by this lack.[4] In a similar manner, such explorations of political thought were not pre-empted but actually facilitated, in particular ways, by the socially agreed assumption in ancient Israel and the ancient Near East in general that political regimes and rulers were grounded in the divine realm.[5]

To be sure, the literati did not carry out these explorations by writing or through readings and rereadings of works comparable in any way or form to Plato's *Republic* or Aristotle's

---

decades, such a trend has been under increasing attack, for good reasons. See, for instance, R. Lerner, "Moses Maimonides," in *History of Political Philosophy*, ed. L. Strauss and J. Cropsey, 3rd ed. (Chicago, IL: University of Chicago Press, 1987), 228–47; A. Melamed, "Is There a Jewish Political Thought? The Medieval Case Reconsidered," *Hebraic Political Studies* 1 (2005): 24–56.

4. It is not by chance that one does not find the motif of kingship as a divine civilizing gift in the repertoire of the literati of the early second Temple period. On the whole, it is reasonable to assume that the lack of a local king may have opened up thought possibilities and that social conditions were more conducive to an expansion of the boundaries of political thought on matters of potential regimes within a community that exists without a local, functioning monarchy and especially without the usually associated, pervading cultural/ideological discourses that socialize local groups to accept the office of the king as a "normal," "natural" phenomenon when the latter are not present. Similarly, a group that does not have to engage in the daily negotiations involved in making of the type of political decisions that a local king and his court has to make regularly and implement is likely to be "freer" to imagine utopian or dystopian polities and the roles allocated to various offices in them. Explorations in political thought do not have to be restricted to the doable, nor must they be conducted by those actually involved in managing practical political affairs.

5. For instance, this is the case when the association with the divine shapes and communicates claims of a "natural polity" and "natural" state of affairs. To illustrate with the widely-known case of the Sumerian King List (SKL), the well-known Mesopotamian motif that kingship descended from heaven as stated there not only is an endorsement of a monarchical regime but of (a) particular monarchic system in which kings/dynasties from a variety of cities since "the beginning" circulated hegemonic power over an area among themselves—since the situation held from the "beginning" and the vicissitudes of time, this state of affairs is construed as "natural," (b) an (imagined, socially construed) shared space over which these rulers and dynasties governed, i.e., a "natural" political territory, with some more or less clear boundaries, and (c) the since "the beginning" and thus "natural" internal organization of this "natural" realm, namely around a selected number of urban centres (and, of course, including prominent instances of mnemonic "forgetfulness," see the case of Lagash). To be sure, none of above were "natural," but the fact that they were shaped and communicated as such sheds light on the political thought of at least a particular group (originally, probably the royal court in Ur III). One may notice also that the implied narrative about the circulation of kingship among cities served not only to shape a sense of territory but also provided an explanation for political discontinuities. It even turned them into central pieces of a mnemonic narrative communicating a sense of overall continuity and a kind of "naturality" in which "seemingly" chaotic tendencies and events are necessarily subsumed under a larger, "objectively" presented and remembered, permanent political order set according to a divine and divinely enforced plan. In sum, the SKL explores, imagines, construes, and communicates a sense of "state," of shared territory and its main features, of a collective memory, and reaffirms the power of a particular dynasty in the present (and near future, one would assume) while explaining why other divinely ordained dynasties ceased to exist. It does so without entering into mnemonically common denigrations of previous rulers and the potential implications of such denigrations for the very concept of monarchy. In addition, the SKL explores the potential concept of female *kingship* (Kubaba of Kish) by safely putting it in the past as a unique occurrence. Pragmatically, then, it is constructed as a possible, but extremely rare case in the "natural order." Some memories of Kubaba's rule span a very long time. She and her rule are attested in much later omen literature; see U. S. Koch, *Babylonian Liver Omens: The Chapters Manzāzu, Padānu and Pān tākalti of the Babylonian Extispicy Series Mainly From Aššurbanipal's Library* (Copenhagen: The Carsten Niebuhr Institute of Near Eastern Studies, University of Copenhagen, 2000), 401–2. In other words, the SKL addresses multiple issues related to political thought, and the reference to the divine realm only facilitates such explorations.

Politics. But why would they? As is widely known, the spectrum of well-attested literary genres in "classical" Athens does not necessarily overlap with that of Jerusalem or that of other ancient Near Eastern societies and polities (e.g., Babylon, Assyria). Nothing comparable to works such as Plato's *Republic* or Aristotle's *Politics* is present in the core literary repertoires of any of these societies and thus, not surprisingly, not in ancient Israel.

But none of this indicates that political thought was not explored in ancient Israel or the ancient Near East in general.[6] The exploration of ancient political thought in the form of works such as Plato's *Republic* or Aristotle's *Politics* was characteristic of a particular social, political and cultural system. In other environments, explorations of matters of political thought took other forms, more akin to the cultural norms, expectations, and concept-exploring tools that existed in these societies. Within the world of the literati of the late Persian period, the exploration of political regimes was carried out, like many other "thorny" issues, through narratives about the past and the associated memories.[7] Here, too, social memory provided the playground for such explorations.

These explorations were not carried out in a vacuum. Although an "independent" polity is not a pre-condition for political thought, the latter is never disassociated from the political "realities" of those involved in political thinking. For instance, unlike some classical Greek/Athenian political thinkers, Yehudite literati did not live in a relatively large, independent polity often sharply divided, and in which there tended to exist strong social/political tensions such that keeping internal peace and stability was a serious challenge that had to be addressed in political theory.

Instead, the Yehudite literati lived in a poor, lightly populated and marginal province, within one of the many satrapies of the Persian Empire. They were governed by a Persian-appointed governor. As in most if not all empires, one should assume the continuous existence of asymmetric negotiations of power between imperial appointees and local elites; the literati were not in charge of the political affairs in Yehud, which, in any case, were of limited and local scope. Thus, the challenges encountered by the local elite in Yehud were far different from those met by the political, intellectual, and administrative elites in Athens or any other central capital city. But again, this does not mean that the Jerusalemite literati were devoid of political thought, only that theirs would have to be substantially different from what was discussed in Greek cities.

As their literary repertoire clearly indicates, the ideological perspective of the literati of Yehud was centered on the Jerusalemite temple. Moreover, they were likely associated in one way or another with the temple as a social institution. The latter was not directly competing for political power with the governor but, nevertheless, played an important role alongside the literati in constructing and enabling the social reproduction of the "Israel"

---

6. To be sure, political thought and the history of political thought as usually studied within Political Science has always been far more focused on the issues raised in Greek polities (and esp. Athens) than to those of late Persian Jerusalem or, for that matter, those of any number of other polities. This propensity is due to a number of reasons that include, but are not restricted to, the importance of the "Classics" in political thought, the focus on "Western political thought," and traditional preferences for political thought as it relates to the "independent state" vs. matters of inner and intra-state, partially autonomous or local communities. It is worth noting that some of these tendencies are becoming less pronounced in recent decades.

7. One may say, for instance, that Xenophon's "historiographic" works do the same. Narrative exploration of ideological and theological matters are certainly nothing new or unique to the literati discussed here but were a widely attested transcultural trend. The emphasis on differences between ancient Near Eastern or ancient Israelites modes of addressing these matters and "Greek" models must be rebalanced, but the matter requires a separate discussion.

they envisaged and remembered.[8]

Since this "Israel" (hereafter, Israel) of glorious but tragic past and of an eventual utopian future was at the center of their literary and ideological work, it is not surprising that as the literati explored political thought through texts and the memories of past and future "Israel" that these texts reflected, shaped, and evoked, the latter were mainly not about their present minor Persian administrative unit, the province of Yehud governed by a Persian-appointed governor. In fact, the presence of Persian governors was widely ignored in the world of *core* texts of the community, indicating they were construed as not worth remembering.[9] Instead, they explored political thought as it related to their core interest: their ideological Israel; that is, the one that populated their memories of the past and the future and with whom they identified as a text-centered/memory-centred community.

Focusing on that Israel and bracketing the Persian governor of Yehud and even Yehud as a dependent polity did not mean and could not have meant the literati were uninfluenced by Persian imperial discourse. To the contrary, as is transculturally common, the literati engaged in processes of appropriation and resignification of imperial ideas.

Since they lived within a "world" empire,[10] when they imagined the future, they did so also in terms of a "world empire." But, unsurprisingly, they imagined a proper world in which the nations and their presents would flow to Jerusalem rather than to Persepolis.

---

8. For other discussions in this volume of the social setting, role, and motivations of the literati, see the essays by J. M. Bos ("Memories of Judah's Past Leaders Utilized as Propaganda in Yehud"), K. Berge ("Mystified Authority: Legitimating Leadership Through 'Lost Books'"), and T. M. Bolin ("At the Hands of Foreign Kings: Divine Endorsement of Foreign Rulers in the Hebrew Bible in the Memory of Persian and Hellenistic Yehud").

9. The substantial problems in reconstructing the historical list of governors of Yehud during the Persian period, despite Josephus and some numismatic evidence, attest to this lack of reference to them in the texts that eventually ended up in the Hebrew Bible. This is not surprising. The literati did not consider their own period as worth remembering and focused their imagination and mnemonic landscape on past and future Israel, rather than their present Israel. Since they were not worthy of being remembered, Persian governors were construed as having no significant impact on the main mnemonic narrative of Israel as understood and shaped by these literati. There are two exceptions to this tendency to consider individual Persian governors as unworthy of inclusion among the figures that Israel is supposed to remember. The first exception reflects the "gravitational pull" of the Jerusalemite temple within the mnemonic universe of the literati: Zerubbabel. Given his role in the re-establishment of the temple, his figure had to be remembered, both as a Persian governor and a Davidide. See E. Ben Zvi, "The Yehudite Collection of Prophetic Books and Imperial Contexts: Some Observations," in *Divination, Politics and Ancient Near Eastern Empires*, ed. A. Lenzi and J. Stökl, ANEM 7 (Atlanta, GA: SBL, 2014), 145–69. Significantly, Zerubbabel is not a Moses-like figure, even though he stands—as he had to—close to the renewed Aaron, i.e., Joshua, the high priest. The study of Zerubbabel as a site of memory in Yehud requires a separate discussion, which I plan to address elsewhere. The second exception concerns another Persian governor who was Judean: Nehemiah. Even if some form of the so-called Nehemiah memoir is from the Persian period, the text cannot be considered part of the main core of texts reflecting the central discourse of the period. See E. Ben Zvi, "Re-negotiating a Putative Utopia, Social Memory and the Stories of the Rejection of Foreign Wives and Children in Ezra-Nehemiah: A Case for Re-negotiating the Historical Gaze," in *About Worlds that Could Not Be—Constructing Utopia in Chronicles, Ezra and Nehemiah*, ed. F. Uhlenbruch and S. J. Schweitzer, LHBOTS (London: Bloomsbury, 2016), 105–28.

10. The concept of "empire" is in itself open for discussion. For one possible and often cited definition of the term "empire" and a discussion of the large degree of variation among empires, see C. M. Sinopoli, "The Archaeology of Empires," *Annual Review of Anthropology* 23 (1994): 159–80. (For the definition see p. 160). Cf. M. Chavalas, "The Age of Empires: 3100–900 BCE," in *A Companion to the Ancient Near East*, ed. D. C. Snell (Malden, MA; Oxford: Blackwell, 2005), 34–47.

They constructed a world in which YHWH, their own deity, stood in the role assigned in imperial ideology to the Wise Lord (Ahura Mazda) and, to some extent, the Persian king. They thought of local divine laws and temple rituals, not Persian dāta and rituals, as upholding cosmic order.[11]

Not surprisingly again, they also thought that the permanent well-being of all humankind or, to use Achaemenid terminology, its 'happiness' (šiyāti), was impossible in the present world (see references to utopian futures). Thus, what can be achieved in the present is, at most, a durative state of well-being/blessing or, to use Achaemenid terminology, a "long-happiness" or "the state of an individual whose ritual and moral comportment (obedience to God's law and perfect performance of sacrifice) succeeds in making him 'happy while living'."[12] From an imperial perspective, long-happiness in this world is potentially global and open to "all kinds of (good) men." The Yehudite parallel to the concept of the blessed state of "happy while living" in *this world*[13] is clearly attested in Ps 1. One can easily see that the focus in these cases is and cannot be but local; see v. 2.

Significantly, in both cases, proper human leadership is needed. In the imperial context, it is the role of the Persian king to provide that leadership and to guard and protect people from all countries. In the Yehudite context, the human leader could not be a Persian king, but far more important for present purposes is the fact that the ideological role of the Persian king was *not* taken up by any local leader of the polity in Yehud as such.

Within this discursive, ideological context, the role of the necessary, proper, human leadership in Yehud was, in essence, to protect the community from the chaos, destruction, terror, and unhappiness that result from disregarding YHWH's instructions, as construed by the group. The main role of the necessary leadership in the present world, then, was to defeat, as much as possible, an entropic tendency to abandon YHWH and YHWH's *tôrâ* within the community, which was the local functional equivalent to the imperial "Lie." This leadership did not have to be "heroic" in the common sense of the world but had to be *tôrâ* knowledgeable, *tôrâ* abiding, YHWH fearing, and able to convince the community to fear YHWH and follow YHWH's instructions.[14] Not surprisingly, such a role is that of "the righteous (ones)" who socialize people to find their delight in YHWH's *tôrâ* and to want to meditate on it day and night (see Ps 1:2).

---

11. See E. Ben Zvi, "The Yehudite Collection of Prophetic Books and Imperial Contexts."

12. B. Lincoln, *'Happiness for Mankind': Achaemenian Religion and the Imperial Project*, Acta Iranica 53 (Leuven: Peeters, 2012), 418–19.

13. That is, when they community construed and imagined worlds that, from their perspective, existed, could exist or could have existed within "history" as they knew it. These worlds stand in contradistinction to futures that are located beyond the "end of history," i.e., permanent future, ideal worlds essentially different from the one in which the community lived, even if these futures were construed in the present and out of the present.

14. Cf. XPh (i.e., Xerxes's so-called daiva-inscription), § 4b, 4d if one understands the text to state "worship Ahuramazda and Arta reverent(ly)" (so, for instance, P. Briant, *From Cyrus to Alexander: A History of the Persian Empire*, trans. P. D. Daniels [Winona Lake, IN: Eisenbrauns, 2002], 550–51; a reading that goes back to Kent). This, however, is only one of the possible readings. See esp. P. O. Skjærvø, "Old Persian Arta," *Encyclopedia Iranica* II/ 7:696, available also open-access at http://www.iranicaonline.org/articles/asa-means-truth-in-avestan#pt2; see also A. Kuhrt, *The Persian Empire: A Corpus of Sources from the Achaemenid Empire* (London: Routledge, 2007), 305–6. The question of a potential, partial conceptual overlap between some of the features attributes of *tôrâ*/wisdom in Israel during the early Second Temple period and *arta* is beyond the scope of this contribution.

On the surface, it might seem surprising to find that some roles usually attributed to the Great King (i.e., the Persian king) were comparable to those associated in Yehud's discourse, or at least or more precisely, in the Yehudite literati's discourse that centered ideologically on Jerusalem, with those of the proper teachers of *tôrâ*, the literati themselves. But this is merely a particular extension and resignification of a very common viewpoint in the ancient Near East. The role of the Great King was widely understood as being that of the delegate of the gods on earth whose task is to bring divine order, well-being, and happiness to humankind and to stem tendencies towards chaos and the eventual but sure suffering it brings upon people. Within the discourse of the Yehudite literati and given the strong association of YHWH and *tôrâ*, that royal role could have been fulfilled only by teachers of *tôrâ*, who serve as delegates/servants of YHWH. The resources they had in their hands are different than those of the Great Kings. They do not have armies, large bureaucracies, and plenty of material and human resources at their disposal, but none of these were necessary for socializing the community in Yehud into following YHWH, accepting him as the actual ruler of the world, even though hidden from most humanity, and achieving happiness.[15] Moreover, as the literati are partially "royalized," the possibility opens for Israel as the (construed) community that follows YHWH and YHWH's *tôrâ* to be partially "kingicized." Significantly, images of a "kingicized" or "priesticized" Israel, or both, appear in multiple places in the repertoire of core books held by the literati[16] and are part and parcel of their discourse about themselves and Israel. This construction of Israel played also an important role in facilitating the imagination and the construction of memories about the great, future empire ruled by YHWH, in which Jerusalem (rather than to Persepolis) will serve as the central imperial city to which non-Israelite nations and their resources will flow. The city and its temple will pour out wisdom, well-being, and the like to all nations.[17] Within that world YHWH is the king of kings, but, (a "priesticized", "kingized" and one may say, "literaticized" [e.g., Deut 4:6]) Israel is YHWH's delegate on earth, and in such a function, such Israel (in the form of its representatives/symbolic embodiments, such as priests and literati) is in charge, *inter alia*, of teaching *tôrâ* to the nations and running the proper cult necessary for the well-being of the world.

Given the common attribution of sun-like features to kings in the ancient Near East,[18] it is not surprising that, in this future world evoked time and again and remembered socially

---

15. Cf. with some aspects of Stoic and Epicurean political theory.

16. See, e.g., the image of the covenant between YHWH and Israel, rather than YHWH and the king—both in the past and in the future (for the latter, see Jer 50:5). See also Exod 19:6; Isa 55:3–11 and multiple expressions in Chronicles, e.g. the conclusion to the account of Zedekiah. On the latter, see E. Ben Zvi, "Reshaping the Memory of Zedekiah and His Period in Chronicles," in *Congress Volume Munich 2013*, ed. C. M. Maier, VTSup 163 (Leiden: Brill, 2014), 370–95, esp. 393–94. These images of a royal Israel were balanced with others that also existed in the repertoire of the community. On these matters, see E. Ben Zvi "A Balancing Act: Settling and Unsettling Issues Concerning Past Divine Promises in Historiographical Texts Shaping Social Memory in the Late Persian Period," in *Covenant in the Persian Period: From Genesis to Chronicles*, ed. R. J. Bautch and G. N. Knoppers (Winona Lake, IN: Eisenbrauns, 2015), 109–130.

17. I discussed the future empire of YHWH and its importance within the social memory of the literati in my article, "Yehudite Collection," esp. 158–65.

18. The sun-like image of the king as a permanent source of light is well-known in the ancient Near East. See, e.g., E. Frahm, "Rising Suns and Falling Stars: Assyrian Kings and the Cosmos," in *Experiencing Power, Generating Authority: Cosmos, Politics, and the Ideology of Kingship in Ancient Egypt and Mesopotamia*, ed. J. A. Hill *et al.* (Philadelphia: University of Pennsylvania Museum of Archaeology and Anthropology, 2013), 97–120, esp. 99–101.

through the reading and rereading of core texts, YHWH's (/Israel's) city (i.e., Jerusalem) becomes a worldly source of "light" (cf. Isa 60, esp. vv. 1–3) and Israel becomes "a light to the nations" (see Isa 42:6).

But, as indicated above, the main focus of this contribution is on memories of the past—not the future—that existed among the literati in the late Persian/early Hellenistic period. Besides the obvious practicalities and limitations of the genre of a chapter in a volume, the reason behind this choice is that, although memories of utopian futures served as important playgrounds to imagine political regimes and to address and comment indirectly on present political regimes, their main gist was to explore various forms of social and political organization considered pertinent to and particularly characteristic of imagined worlds *essentially different* from the one in which the community lived. The focus here is far more on political thought as related to worlds like the one in which the community lived, not on political thought as applied to and/or explored via imaginary societies not fully governed by the rules of societies in the "world as is."[19]

Thus, in what follows I will focus on social memories of the past that served as a kind of playground in which different political structures and forms of government could be explored and their strengths and weakness shown and remembered. But the mentioned "attribution" of some royal roles to Israel—but not others, e.g., military leader—especially to the Yehudite literati in a "world" that is still not utopian must be kept in mind. It is part and parcel of an encompassing social mindscape that could not but influence and constrain, in some ways, the shaping of social memories, because they played a significant role in shaping the literati's grammar of mnemonic preferences and dis-preferences.

There were a large number of other types of social, ideological, and mnemonic constraints governing the grammars involved in the adoption and social reproduction of memories of the past, and they also had an impact on the way memories of the past could and did play as the ground in which and through which to explore matters of political thought. For instance, (a) Moses's leadership had to be lionized, because it was associated in social memory with the mythical founding of the community; (b) the Davidic/Solomonic time had to be (at least partially) lionized, because it was associated with the building of the Jerusalemite temple, a place of unique and cosmic importance within the discourse of the literati; (c) the centrality of the divine instruction/*tôrâ*—as understood by the literati—had to be maintained since, this was a community that construed itself as a text-centred group and following *tôrâ* was associated with blessing and happiness; (d) the centrality of Jerusalem had to maintained; (e) the monarchic period as a whole had to be vilified to explain the catastrophe of 586 BCE; and (f) necessary mechanisms to *contain* what was seen as a normal tendency for society and the people in it to go astray over time (i.e., "social entropy") had to be imagined as existing in the past and as having failed, given that the community knew well of the calamity that befell Judah at the time of the fall of the monarchic polity.[20]

---

19. The study of political thought as applied and explored in such utopian (or for that matter, also dystopian) worlds requires significant use of additional methodological approaches (e.g., utopian studies and particularly its areas of overlap with political thought). All these matters require a separate discussion that goes well beyond the boundaries of the present chapter. For some preliminary explorations in these matters see, e.g., my "The Yehudite Collection of Prophetic Books and Imperial Contexts," and, from a very different standpoint, "Re-negotiating a Putative Utopia, Social Memory and the Stories of the Rejection of Foreign Wives and Children." Much more work on these issues is needed.

20. I explored the concept of "social entropy" in my "Analogical Thinking and Ancient Israel Intellectual History: The Case for an 'Entropy Model' in the Study of Israelite Thought," in *Relating to the Text*.

In addition, memories of founding periods were necessarily memories of unique and incomparable situations and personages, and thus they are unlikely to provide the best communal "playground" in which to explore the strengths and weaknesses of political regimes in non-founding, "normal" times. Since no human could be imagined as taking the place of the first and primary Moses or the first and primary David, then the political regimes of their times were not necessarily the best illustrations of the possibilities and limitations of, for instance, monarchy as such, or the ad hoc regime construed mnemonically around Moses.

This said, a few noteworthy observations about these memories of founding periods still can be advanced. To begin with, Moses was remembered not only as the best leader but also as the head of a "regime" that faced much opposition during his life and at times had to be maintained by the use of divine, destructive force. Moses, and alongside him, Aaron were remembered as leaders who were neither chosen by nor served at the pleasure of the people, the heads of the community as a whole, or chiefs of tribal or other subgroups within Israel (see, e.g., Num 16). Proper leaders are appointed and maintained by YHWH and serve at YHWH's pleasure. This is to be expected within the context of royal ideology in the ancient Near East, except that Moses, the founding lawgiver, is saliently not called a king and is not the founding figure of the local dynasty, even if he clearly bears some royal attributes.[21] Instead, he is designated a prophet. As for Aaron, the priest, he is appointed by YHWH and not Moses. Significantly, the kind of "legitimacy" test that was remembered as used to decide the identity and character of the proper priesthood to balance tendencies towards a "democratization" of the priesthood in Num 16 is not necessarily applicable to decide cases of political leadership, be they judges, kings, or the like).

A second observation is that the regime that existed during Moses's time, lionized as it was, was remembered as often unable to socialize Israel to follow YHWH's *tôrâ* in its time and so was unable to avoid the consequences of such behavior on the community in his own time. In addition, he was remembered as unable to keep future generations well socialized into the *tôrâ* of the proper, divine YHWH.[22]

Turning to the second main founding period within this context, David was remembered as the founding king and the temple of Jerusalem was associated with him (Solomon will be discussed below). David is, as one would expect, lionized in Kings, Chronicles, and Psalms. But not only was his regime remembered (see Samuel and Psalms) as one that, at times, faced strong opposition and led to civil war, but, above all, he himself through his actions became an agent of chaos and disaster for Israel. Chronicles "normalizes" the memory of the founding figure, David, but the book of Samuel was also read and evoked memories. Since Solomon is the actual founder of the temple, one may have anticipated that his reign was imagined as a unique period of peace and prosperity. This expectation is fulfilled, but again the book of Kings asked the community to remember this founding figure of YHWH's cho-

---

Interdisciplinary and Form-Critical Insights on the Bible, ed. T. J. Sandoval and C. Mandolfo, JSOTSup 384; London: T&T Clark International, 2003), 321–32.

21. On Moses as a quasi-royal figure, see, e.g., T. C. Römer, "Moses, the Royal Lawgiver," in *Remembering Biblical Figures in the Late Persian and Early Hellenistic Periods: Social Memory and Imagination*, ed. D. V. Edelman and E. Ben Zvi (Oxford: Oxford University Press, 2013), 81–94 (82–85); J. Lierman, *The New Testament Moses*, WUNT 2 (Tübingen: Mohr Siebeck, 2004), 66–70, and recently, I. D. Wilson, *Kingship and Memory in Ancient Judah* (Oxford: Oxford University Press, forthcoming) and bibliography cited in these works.

22. E.g., Deut 31:20; and cf. Deut 30:1–5; 32:19–25 and, among others, the pragmatic message in late Persian Yehud of Deut 28:15–68; 29:13–27; 30:17–19.

sen dynasty and the very archetype of the wise king/man as also an agent of chaos in his old age. Moreover, by doing so, it also raised a memory touching on a substantial potential pitfall of monarchies as political systems. In addition, both Chronicles and Kings evoke strong memories of a troubled political transition after his death, whose lasting consequences were still present for all to see in the days of the remembering community.

I will return to these observations, but in what follows I want briefly to address a few additional memories that have a direct bearing on constructions of monarchy as an institution and which are not directly associated with the central Mosaic and Davidic/Solomonic sites of memory. First Samuel 8 reminded the community not only that instituting the monarchy was tantamount to rejecting YHWH as king but also hinted that a polity run by a pious prophet (/ priest) was more consonant with accepting YHWH as king (see explicitly v. 7). The same text in vv. 5, 20 evokes Deut 17:14 and vice versa. Kingship is allowed, but the community was supposed to evaluate the expressed desire to behave like "all the nations" negatively, which, within the discourse of the period, was construed as a partial self-othering of Israel and undesirable. Whereas Deut 17:14–20 balanced matters by construing a *tolerated* monarchy unlike that of "all the nations" in which the king read *tôrâ* as his main positive duty (cf. Josh 1:8), texts such as Sam 12 called the attention of the community to the fact that the kings of Israel were, indeed, like those of the "other nations," as did the story evoked by Kings as a whole.

Such negative images are balanced by some positive ones, but the social memory reflected, shaped and conveyed by Kings as whole was and *could not but be* that monarchy, be it Davidic or not, not only did not pre-empt the catastrophe of the fall of the monarchic polities but actually led to it,[23] despite the presence of some pious kings. Significantly, Josiah, the most pious, restoring king in Kings, is remembered as reconnecting Israel to an ideal period before the monarchy (2 Kgs 23:22); namely that of the Judges.[24]

Memories that problematize kingship as an institution are encoded in and communicated by not only Samuel-Kings or the core narrative about the fall of monarchic Israel but are encoded in and communicated in a variety of other books. For instance, in Judges, besides the well-known parable of Jotham (Judg 9:7–15), there is the clear implication in Abimelech's speech to the "lords" of Shechem:

מַה־טּוֹב לָכֶם הַמְשֹׁל בָּכֶם שִׁבְעִים אִישׁ כֹּל בְּנֵי יְרֻבַּעַל אִם־מְשֹׁל בָּכֶם אִישׁ אֶחָד

"Which is better for you, to be ruled by seventy men, by all the sons of Jerubbaal, or to be ruled by one man?" (Judg 9:2).

---

23. To be sure, this type of understanding of the office of the king reappears in later communities. See Deut. R. 5.11 "the Rabbis say: The Holy One, blessed be He, said: 'In this world you asked for kings, and kings arose in Israel and caused you to fall by the sword.' Saul caused them to fall on Mount Gilboa. Whence this? And the men of Israel fled from before the Philistines (I Sam. 31:1). David brought about a plague, as it is said, So the Lord sent a pestilence upon Israel (II Sam. 24:15). Ahab was the cause of the withholding of rain from them [Israel], as it is said, There shall not be dew nor rain these years, etc. (I Kings XVII, 1). Zedekiah was the cause of the destruction of the Temple. When Israel saw what befell them on account of their kings they all began to cry out: 'We do not desire a king, we desire our first king,' [as it is said], For the Lord is our Judge, the Lord is our Lawgiver, the Lord is our King; He will save us (Isa 23:22). Whereupon God replied: 'By your life, I will do so.' Whence this? For it is said, "And the Lord shall be king over all the earth, etc. (Zech 14:9)," Soncino Translation.

24. Cf. 2 Chr 35:18. The restorative action of Hezekiah, in Chronicles, however, is anchored in the ideal period of Solomon (2 Chr 30:26). Solomon and David are the founding figures associated with the Temple in Jerusalem in Chronicles. Hezekiah is a kind of second Solomon, and the intended readership of the book cannot but notice that he "reopens" the temple.

In what is a very rare, directly expressed deliberation about alternative political regimes,[25] Abimelech and his addressees in the world portrayed in the book were imagined to believe that rule by one man is better; that is, monarchy is better than kin-based aristocracy. The readers of the book, however, can only think that בעלי שכם, usually translated 'the lords of Shechem' and meant to refer most likely to the "(landowning) 'citizens' of Shechem," would have been much better off picking the rule of the seventy over the rule of the one.[26] Remembering the story was also recounting and communicating that the city assembly of "citizens" is not the proper institution to select a king.[27] Although such an approach is widespread in the ancient Near East (and not only there), it is worth noting that these city assemblies of "citizens" (X-בעלי, in which X stands for the name of a city/town) tended to be associated with negative contexts (see Jos 24:11; Judg 9:2; 20:5; 1 Sam 23:11; 2 Sam 21:12).

This tendency is consistent with general political discourse and accompanying memoryscape in which city authorities and their "sub-level polities" were construed as being essentially of secondary (and often problematic) importance and in need of checking by the central government of the central polity, however, it is conceived to be, rather than the opposite. Even in Deuteronomy, in which the "elders of the city" figure prominently, their power was understood as necessarily under check by the central powers of the polity/community, including, from an ideological perspective, the central *tôrâ* but also those imagined/remembered as enforcing its power over "rebel" cities (e.g., Deut 13:13–19; cf. Deut 17:1–13).

---

25. Cf. and contrast with Herodotus, *Hist.* 3.80–82.
26. The critique of monarchy here does not have to be restricted to that of the Northern Kingdom, at least not from the perspective of readers of the book of Judges in the late Persian/early Hellenistic period. For a different position, see B. P. Irwin, "Not Just Any King: Abimelech, the Northern Monarchy, and the Final Form of Judges," *JBL* 131 (2012): 443–54, who maintains, inter alia, that the speech of Jotham was read as a text providing support for the Davidic line. Some scholars have stressed that the text in Judg 9 evokes an image of a "dynastic house" established by Gideon and overthrown by Abimelech (e.g., T. J. Schneider, *Judges* [Collegeville, MN: Liturgical Press, 2000], 136–37), but even if this is the case, the reference to a government by seventy removes any doubt that the text is not talking about a monarchy. While Abimelech represents monarchy, the rule of the seventy may represent a kind of kinship/dynastic based aristocracy or oligarchy, but certainly not a monarchy. On the concept of seventy, see also Exod 24:1, 9; Num 11:16, 24–25. The difference here is, of course, that there is not a higher office above them and that the seventy belong to one family.
27. The same is true of the meeting of "the assembly of Israel" in Shechem reported in 1 Kgs 12, given tendencies toward temporal helicality in social memory. The case of Jeroboam, however, is far more complex, since he, unlike Abimelech, was selected and appointed by YHWH through a prophet (1 Kgs 11:29–32), but to be sure, this is not the main point to which the social mindshare of the literati in Yehud is drawn in the story of 1 Kgs 12 or that of 2 Chr 10. The idea of selecting a "ruler" within and by a group of seemingly "equals" occurs in the ancient Near East in a variety of ways, though it is not dominant. One may mention, for instance, the gods' selection of Marduk in Enuma Elish or, and substantially different, the election of Darius as king as narrated in Herodotus's *Hist.* 3.83. But nothing similar is positively seen in the corpus of literature of ancient Israel. Approval by Israel of the proper king and even more importantly, of the dynasty appointed by YHWH is commended and remembered positively, but this is not the same as having the right to select a king from among a group of aristocrats. In fact, the approval of such a proper king is just a variant of the basic concept of accepting YHWH's path. The same holds true, significantly, for accepting the rule of a legitimate Davidic king appointed by a foreign hegemonic king whose power was imagined to reflect YHWH's will (e.g., 2 Kgs 23:33–34; 24:17; 2 Chr 36:3–4, 10. The actions of עַם־הָאָרֶץ in e.g., 2 Kgs 21:24; 23:30; 2 Chr 33:25; 36:1 are of a different kind than the selection of kings by the "citizens" of Shechem or the "assembly" of Israel in that city and were understood as actions meant to appoint the divinely chosen, proper Davidide. Neither Josiah or Jehoahaz were "elected" to office by the "people of the land.")

The main polity/community was again Israel, in whatever conceived form, and sub-Israelite communities/polities primarily were construed as secondary and fully dominated by the center. Thus, Israel was construed and remembered as essentially either a "unitarian polity" or as a polity that should have been and eventually would be unitarian. From the perspective of the Yehudite literati, it would be governed according to a unitarian, divinely given *tôrâ*, as they understood it. Despite all the references to the "tribes" and the like, the imagined "state" of the Yehudite literati and their imagined Israel were essentially envisaged as unitarian, and one may say, even monocultural. Again, this may not be surprising,[28] but it has implications concerning perceived preferences for political systems that centralize power in general, be they, e.g., ad hoc leaders such as Moses, "judges" who, despite their often very local endeavors, were remembered as Israel's judges (e.g., Jud 3:7–31 and passim), a judge/priest/prophet like Samuel, or properly selected hereditary kings like the Davidides, and, as importantly, for its centralization in Jerusalem, since the time of David.

Although, as indicated above, multiple political regimes could have been imagined as coherent with centralization and even centralization in Jerusalem—a point to which I will return, within the mnemonic landscape of the Yehudite literati, thinking of such centralization via memories of the past would have evoked images of a (Davidic) monarchic system. In fact, the anti-monarchic memories associated with Abimelech, the Shechemite king, were balanced and informed within the book of Judges itself by readings of and memories evoked by the concluding narratives in the book that, on the surface, seem to suggest a period without kings is a chaotic era. This is emphasized by the common expression, "in those days there was no king" (Judg 17:6; 19:1; 21:5). The main role of the final chapters was to lead in a tortuous way towards the establishment of the proper (Davidic) monarchy based in Jerusalem.

But the same readers of the text read it within a context. No text was ever read in a vacuum, and no particular memory ever existed in a vacuum. These Jerusalemite-centered literati were all well aware of the catastrophe brought about by the monarchy, and they would not fail to note that the common coda to "in those days there was no king," namely אִישׁ הַיָּשָׁר בְּעֵינָיו יַעֲשֶׂה, 'people would do what is good in their own eyes' (see Judg 17:6; 21:25), does not really call for a monarchy as the solution to the situation, because people are not supposed to do what is right in the sight of another human but in the sight of YHWH. Even if a king were to be a teacher of *tôrâ* to the people, he would be, at best, an ad hoc prophet (see 2 Chronicles, 2 Kgs 17:13) or a kind of literati (cf. Josh 1:8), and if he just enforces the teachings of the prophets and their texts (i.e., the literati), then it is not the institution of monarchy that solves the situation.

In addition, memories problematizing the institution of monarchy as such, even Davidic monarchy, are conveyed by books that are not historiographical in character and which do not have to encode and communicate the core narrative of the fall of the monarchy.[29] The most obvious of these is Qohelet,[30] but Ruth also construes and communicates a memory

---

28. This tendency is far more typical or stronger in local, relatively small polities than large empires, which by necessity must include engagement with a multiplicity of cultures. It is not by chance that when these literati envisaged their future world empire ruled by YHWH and centered in Jerusalem, they were far more open to diversity (e.g., Mic 4:1–5).

29. For a recent, detailed discussion of many of these texts, as well as of texts lionizing the concept within the "historical" and "prophetic" books, see Wilson, "Kingship Remembered."

30. See J. Barbour, *The Story of Israel in the Book of Qohelet: Ecclesiastes as Cultural Memory* (Oxford: Oxford University Press, 2012).

of a good Israelite society in which there were no kings (cf. 2 Kgs 23:22), Davidic or otherwise, even if the story leads to David, the founder (along with Solomon) of the temple.

A community that problematizes monarchy as an institution, while still lionizing the founders of the temple; a community whose social memory stressed that the founding and most lionized kings selected by YHWH failed to provide consistent peace and well-being for the community (see 1 and 2 Kings); a community that saliently associated the primary transitions of power at the founding of a/the dynasty with severe upheaval; such a community is not necessarily one that considers or imagines monarchy as a *necessarily* good political regime.

Problematizing monarchy as an institution to such a degree and in multiple ways represents somewhat of an anomaly within the common political thought that characterized the area for millennia.[31] It is not only that "all the nations" had kings (as texts such as Deut 17:14; 1 Sam 8:5, 20 explicitly communicate) but that monarchy was usually considered a necessity and a gift from the gods. Divinely appointed or legitimized kings were seen as crucial to maintain order and well-being. Everyone knew that kings could go astray and enable the emergence of chaos, but within the general ideological discourse of the area, such kings or dynasties were eventually deposed and replaced by new divinely selected kings who restored order. At times, the change took place within the same dynasty. Kings, good and bad, could come and go, but the *institution* was seen as essential to guard against chaos re-emerging and to allow order, prosperity and well-being to exist.

The same worldview was at work in the construction of the Persian Great King and his crucial role in bringing happiness to people. This worldview was certainly well-known to the community in Yehud, but most significantly, it could not but be considered ideologically problematic for a Jerusalem-centered community, and not just becasue the community in Yehud and its neighbors had no king. Rather, the problem arose in part becasue they had a king—the king of Persia. Certainly, the community, which saw itself as a temporal manifestation of Israel, thought that order, well-being, and peace could only be maintained by observing YHWH's instructions and faithful worship in Jerusalem. But, within their world, the Persian Great King was never imagined as aware of either. The most he could be imagined and remembered as doing was enabling a local leadership, knowledgeable of *tôrâ* and proper worship, to socialize the community in appropriate ways and to conduct the ritual of the temple (see discussion above).

Such a local leadership did not and could not include a local king, as they well knew. In a sense, within this ideological and very historically contingent perspective, not having a "real," (/mythical) human king was associated with acknowledging YHWH as king; whereas acknowledging the *ideology* of an existing human king and thus transforming him into a "real" (/mythical) king, could only be construed in this discourse as rejecting YHWH's kingship.

---

31. As usual, some exceptions can be found. It has been proposed, for instance, that the institution of monarchy was a late-comer to Emar associated with Hittite control, but for a more recent assessment, see A. Otto, "The Organization of Residential Space in the Mittani Kingdom as a Mirror of Different Models of Governance," in *Constituent, Confederate, and Conquered Space: The Emergence of the Mittani State*, ed. E. Cancik-Kirschbaum, N. Brisch, and J. Eidem (Berlin: de Gruyter, 2014), 33–60 (39–41) and bibliography. Most importantly, however, monarchy as an *institution* is *not* tantamount to a palace-based local society. In addition, it is obvious that kings could and did exist in antiquity along with powerful collective, local leaderships, be they local kings (e.g., Old Assyrian kings, before Šamši-Adad) or "imperial"/"hegemonic" kings (e.g., Seleucid kings). The existence of sub-monarch levels and local, non-royal political institutions is a given in the area. None of this, however, raised questions about the very existence or appropriateness of kingship as an institution.

But if so, and leaving aside political regimes that will take hold when the "presently-existing" world known to the community will come to an end and utopia becomes a reality, which alternatives did they have in terms of local political organization and how did memory contribute to such a debate?

Certainly, they accepted the present reality of the Great King as the overarching monarch of their *oecumene* and most likely did not even conceive of an alternative. They certainly did not reject completely the very *concept* of monarchy, as is obvious from the fact that they thought of YHWH, inter alia, through the language of king. Thinking and imagining YHWH was, among other things, thinking and imagining a king. But the Great King on earth was not the king of Israel and was unable, from the perspective of the community, to perform the roles that would maintain the cosmic order set by YHWH, which were associated with the Jerusalemite temple and *tôrâ*, This being the case, what political regime would be ideal for the community in Yehud, which served as an embodiment of "Israel"? Which one would provide the key component for furthering order and well-being to "Israel" in the pre-utopian world? Clearly, this is a question of political thought, and to some extent, one of theoretical political thought, given the circumstances in Yehud.

Memories of the past played an important role in negotiating potential answers. Memories of the past strongly reminded the literati that monarchy as an institution, even if instituted by YHWH, was not necessary or even likely to be able to fulfil these roles in the long term. But the same holds true for a revised form of polity in which the monarch reigns but is strongly advised by members of the elite (i.e., a "consultative" monarchy, or one may say a kind of hybrid between monarchy and aristocracy), as memories of Zedekiah conveyed by the book of Jeremiah indicate.[32] The same holds true as well for priestly dynastic regimes, in which the head priest bears some royal attributes (e.g., the case of Eli and Samuel). Although there were very positive memories of the period of Judges, this type of leadership was remembered as necessarily raising substantial transitional difficulties and thought of as unstable. Counter-memories showing it did not provide stable peace and well-being were also in abundance. Ad hoc, unique political regimes (e.g., Moses) were remembered but provided no practical example for the community, because they were unique.

The so-called "democratization" tendency actually involved an ideological kingicization/Davidization of Israel or its priesticization, as attested in diverse texts (e.g., Isa 55:3; Exod 19:6—see above). This tendency, encoded in and communicated through various memories, could not present a model for an inner political regime in Yehud—though it plays a role in processes of imagining and vicariously experiencing YHWH's future empire.[33]

Finally, memories of local aristocratic groups (e.g., government by the chiefs, elders, heads of Israel and the like) remembered by the community made clear that aristocratic regimes or even potentially broader regimes of that kind (e.g., the "rebels" associated with Korah) may fail and often failed to bring Israel to follow YHWH/*tôrâ* and eventuate a relatively long, even if temporary, period of well-being.[34] The *vox populi* could also be wrong

---

32. I have discussed these matters elsewhere; see E. Ben Zvi, "Reshaping the Memory of Zedekiah," esp. 383–86 and bibliography cited there.

33. See above.

34. Stable well-being belongs to the future utopian period. From the perspective of the community, even the positive references to a form of elders' local government in Deuteronomy would fail to reflect the centrality of the temple the literati so much wished to advance, and would not necessarily provide a better local regime than royal appointees (cf. memories of Moses and Solomon as rulers who appointed a secondary level of regime administrators).

and lead astray Israel (e.g., the "murmuring" generation, the people's support for Absalom against David).

One needs to keep in mind that just as the community remembered that all the mentioned regimes could and did fail, they also remembered that they could and at times did succeed, *for a while*. A judge like Ehud led to 80 years of peace, a prophet/ruler like Moses was certainly a success, a prophet/priest like Samuel was a pious and successful ruler, Joshua's polity was successful in his time, and a significant number of kings were remembered as pious and successful, probably more so in Chronicles than Samuel-Kings. Similarly, at times, the elders provided good local government.[35] But from the perspective of the ideological discourse and social memory of the Yehudite literati, the periods of relatively long term peace and well-being were not dependent on the institutional type of political leadership but to a very substantial extent, to whether or not Israel followed YHWH. From the perspective of the group, this was tantamount to following YHWH's *tôrâ*, as they construed it to be.[36]

In fact, one may say that the social memory shared by the literati of the early Second Temple period included numerous sites of memory that hammered home the point time and again that the ability to lead Israel to willing obedience of YHWH was not dependent on *any* particular political office. It is a truism to say that negative images make the point. But positive images make it as well.

Moses, Joshua, some judges, some priests, and some prophets could all perform the task of leading Israel to willing obedience of YHWH. As Chronicles's integrative mnemonic landscape makes explicit, anyone who can perform that task is a prophetic character.[37] Although some of these prophetic characters were remembered as carrying direct political power (e.g., Joshua, Samuel, David, and some kings who proclaimed godly messages and actually led Israel/Judah to willing obedience of YHWH for a while), the two roles did not have to be carried out by the same person. Moreover, when this actually occurred, often either the political role or the role of the successful conveyor of godly messages were construed as temporary. Examples include the Samuel of memory in terms of political leader-

---

35. Ezra-Nehemiah constructs and communicates memories of something that might resemble a "citizens' assembly" (Ezra 10) and of an ad hoc, representative committee of Yehud, including "our officials, our Levites, and our priests" (see Neh 9–10), along with elements of an assembly. From the perspective of the implied author of the book (Ezra-Nehemiah), these "political" bodies acted in a praiseworthy way, but their perceived success was not due to any intrinsic quality of the assemblies or the representative committee that such institutions may have had but to the actions of Ezra and Nehemiah, both of whom were characterized as leaders who brought Israel back to YHWH and YHWH's *tôrâ*. Without these guardians of *tôrâ* (see below), these ad hoc institutions would have not worked. It is not the institution, but the presence of a proper guardian that makes "success"—as understood by the readership that identifies with these two characters and the implied author of the book of Ezra-Nehemiah—possible. See below. Whether the readers read Ezra-Nehemiah or Ezra and Nehemiah makes no difference in this regard.

36. It is worth noting that comparable approaches existed in other societies and polities of the ancient Near East and in the Greek world. From Xenophon's perspective, "it is for want of things like faithfulness and obedience that Greece lacked a stable political order both within states and between them" (R. J. Kroeker, "Politics and Personality: Characterization in Xenophon's Hellenica" [Unpublished PhD thesis, University of Alberta, 2002], 25). A longing for a stable political order is a major factor in Xenophon.

37. I have discussed this issue elsewhere; see E. Ben Zvi "Chronicles and its Reshaping of Memories of Monarchic Period Prophets: Some Observations," in *Prophets, Prophecy, and Ancient Israelite Historiography*, ed. M. J. Boda and L. M. Wray Beal (Winona Lake, IN: Eisenbrauns, 2013), 167–88 and bibliography cited there. For another discussion in this volume of the role of prophets as conceived in the Hebrew Bible, see J. M. Bos, "Memories of Judah's Past Leaders Utilized as Propaganda in Yehud."

ship, memories of David evoked in Samuel, or of Asa in Chronicles, all of whom remained political leaders but eventually led Israel astray. Furthermore, there were many important memories of periods in which the prophetic voice and the ruler were clearly two different individuals, such as Samuel and Saul, Isaiah and Hezekiah, and Shemaiah and Rehoboam. Reading Chronicles involved also remembering the existence of the community of northern Israelites that was non-Davidic, non-monarchic, and without a clear and long-term political structure but which still was pious because they followed the advice of a prophetic voice: that of Oded (see 2 Chr 28:8–15).

Finally, given the importance of the temple in the Jerusalem-centered discourse of Yehud and the lack of a local king at the time, it is not difficult to understand the emergence of a character such as Jehoiada, the priest. Jehoiada served as a successful prophetic character but was remembered also as embodying as many royal attributes as was possible, given the constraints of imagining a priest in the monarchic period in 2 Chr 23–24. There is even a note about his burial among the kings of Judah (see in particular 2 Chr 23:16, 18–19; 24:3, 12, 14–16). Not only was Jehoiada's role (not the king's) construed as necessary for the well-being of Israel in his time, but he was remembered as living even longer than Moses and Joshua within an ideological context that construed length of days with divine blessing. This construction of Jehoiada was likely a projection of an ideal priestly, Jerusalemite ruler like the one the community would like to have, retrojected within a narrative and mnemonic world of a past, monarchic/Davidic Judah. and yet there was only one Jehoida in the entire set of memories of the community.

Although we may imagine that the community around the temple would have liked to have had such an ideal priestly leader, memories of other prophetic guardians of Israel, who were by no means imagined as the head priest of the Jerusalemite temple and YHWH, were prominent, too, and more than balanced the picture. Significantly, the implied author of Chronicles, an historian or shaper and communicator of memories of the past, was likely construed at the time as a prophetic voice guarding Israel. The literati who identified with voiced implied authors and characters in authoritative books, who also were the only ones who could directly access and produce these books, saw themselves as potentially performing a socializing role similar to that of these guardians.

What can be learned from all these considerations? Memories of the past served as a useful playground to explore concepts related to political thought in the early Second Temple period. These explorations clearly led the community to conclude that none of the usual political regimes provided social institutions required for the well-being of Israel. This said, beyond the variety of vignettes and particular memorable events and characters, an integrative concept emerged, brought together, and provided particular significance to the multiplicity of variegated images and memories. This concept is the necessity of prophetic guardianship—"prophetic" here in the sense of the understanding of the concept communicated by Chronicles.

Diversity remains, because there is no formal office of a guardian to be held. There may be one or many prophetic guardians at one time, and he/they may or may not yield direct political power, be active directly or fulfill the role through surrogates or as a governing influence on those in power, and may or may not carry additional social roles. But without a prophetic guardian or guardians, no stable political system could exist within the discourse and world of knowledge of the literati; without godly prophetic guardians, no one would able to lead Israel to willing obedience of YHWH's will and *tôrâ* and, thus, to well-being. As expressed in Hos 12:14, "by a prophet YHWH brought Israel up from Egypt, and by a (Mosaic) prophet it was guarded/guarded itself."[38]

To some extent, the literati themselves took, within their own discourse, the role of the prophetic guardians of their community and generation, and by doing so, they further appropriated some features or expectations associated with kings and priests, while not removing them from the potential system. Until the time that *tôrâ* would become "biologically" embedded among the members of the community (e.g., Jer 31:33–34), their absolutely necessary role, at least in their own mind, remained.[39]

Whereas types of leadership and political regimes were remembered, and remembering them meant remembering that they could come and go and that none possessed an intrinsic salvific value of their own for Israel in the world as is,[40] whether Yehud/Judah/Israel was part of an earthly large empire (e.g., the Achaemenid empire) or not (e.g., monarchic Judah), the crucial importance of the divine instruction and the associated prophetic guardianship remained the most crucial institution for Israel's well-being within that discourse.

Of course, the literati in Yehud were not the only ones in antiquity to doubt that any political organization provides the key for a successful, stable polity that brings happiness to its people. For instance, according to Polybius, one of the most important political thinkers of the Hellenistic period, monarchy, aristocracy, and democracy carry the seeds of their own failure and downfall. For this reason, he argues in favor of systems in which one or two individuals with substantial power who occupy the structural slot of the "monarch," the "people" and the aristocrats keep each other in balance, as in the case of his Lycurgus's Sparta and above all, Republican Rome. He stressed the importance of a system of checks and balances, in which different political institutions carry their own powers and may support or oppose other institutions or "parts" of the state. For him, the best political organization was one in which there is a self-balancing distribution of powers.[41] The Yehudite literati would have agreed with him on the need for checks and balances to the power of

---

38. On the reflexive meaning of the *niphal* see, for instance, Jouon-Muraoka (P. Joüon, *A Grammar of Biblical Hebrew*, trans. and rev. by T. Muraoka, 2nd ed., Subsidia biblica 27 [Rome: Pontifical Biblical Institute, 2006]) 51a,c; WOC (B. K. Waltke and M. O'Connor, *An Introduction to Biblical Hebrew Syntax* [Winona Lake, IN: Eisenbrauns, 1990]) 23.4b. The *niphal* form of the root שמר carries a reflexive meaning in most of its occurrences in the Hebrew Bible.

    Given that Chronicles constructs the second half of the Manasseh's reign as one that embodies in the situation of an Israel/Manasseh who has been in Babylon for its/his sins and has repented and is allowed to come back to the land, it is worth noting that this period is imagined as one in which *multiple* prophets continuously advised the king (see the reference to הַחֹזִים הַמְדַבְּרִים אֵלָיו בְּשֵׁם יהוה אֱלֹהֵי יִשְׂרָאֵל in 2 Chr 33:18). Moreover, Chronicles informs its readers that the words of these prophets were worthy of being recorded for posterity and referred to:

    וְיֶתֶר דִּבְרֵי מְנַשֶּׁה ... וְדִבְרֵי הַחֹזִים הַמְדַבְּרִים אֵלָיו בְּשֵׁם יהוה אֱלֹהֵי יִשְׂרָאֵל הִנָּם עַל־דִּבְרֵי מַלְכֵי יִשְׂרָאֵל
    "Now the rest of the acts of Manasseh, ... and the words of the seers who spoke to him ... these are in the Annals of the Kings of Israel," (2 Chr 33:18). This is particularly significant, since Manasseh is remembered to have come to the land to rule it, unlike Israel, who came back but is not ruling it.

39. Compare with the polity shaped in the imagination of the sages during periods in which the Mishnah and the Talmuds emerged in late antiquity Palestine and "Babylonia." For a somewhat similar understanding of the unofficial role of the Levitical priests as "guardians" and how they attempt to assign themselves authority in this capacity, see the essay in this volume by K. Berge, entitled "Mystified Authority: Legitimating Leadership Through 'Lost Books'."

40. That is before the materialization of YHWH's empire or the anticipated appearance of people with "biologically" implanted *tôrâ*.

41. See esp. Polybius, *Histories*, 6.

any known leader, be it a king, judge, priest, or unique ad hoc, divinely appointed individuals. But their solution was different. They did not advocate distributing "sovereign" or "independent" powers among several political institutions within the polity, so they may balance each other, but instead, they imagined what I have called here "guardianship," namely an unofficial, but fully necessary through history and in the present of the community, institution fulfilled by either an individual or a group and whose role was to socialize Israel, ruler and community, to follow YHWH and YHWH's *tôrâ*.

The historically contingent circumstances of Yehud, a small province within a large satrapy, within a large empire, the social mindscape of the literati, their ideological world and their social roles contributed to the shaping of this important aspect of their political thought, just as they contributed to their understanding that neither the Great King nor a vassal king is actually necessary for the stable, happiness and well-being of their community (see the sentiment expressed in Ps 1, among other places). Their memories about the past served as a kind a language in which they could express their (implied?) thoughts on the matter.

Bibliography

Barbour, J. 2012. *The Story of Israel in the Book of Qohelet: Ecclesiastes as Cultural Memory*. Oxford: Oxford University Press.

Ben Zvi, E. 2016 "Re-negotiating a Putative Utopia, Social Memory and the Stories of the Rejection of Foreign Wives and Children in Ezra-Nehemiah: A Case for Re-negotiating the Historical Gaze." In *Worlds that Could Not Be—Constructing Utopia in Chronicles, Ezra and Nehemiah*, edited by F. Uhlenbruch and S. J. Schweitzer, 105–128. LHBOTS. London: Bloomsbury.

———. 2015. "A Balancing Act: Settling and Unsettling Issues Concerning Past Divine Promises in Historiographical Texts Shaping Social Memory in the Late Persian Period." In *Covenant in the Persian Period: From Genesis to Chronicles,* edited by R. J. Bautch and G. N. Knoppers, 109–130. Winona Lake, IN: Eisenbrauns.

———. 2014. "Reshaping the Memory of Zedekiah and His Period in Chronicles." In *Congress Volume Munich 2013*, edited by C. M. Maier, 370–95. VTSup 163. Leiden: Brill.

———. 2014. "The Yehudite Collection of Prophetic Books and Imperial Contexts: Some Observations." In *Divination, Politics and Ancient Near Eastern Empires*, edited by A. Lenzi and J. Stökl, 145–69. ANEM 7. Atlanta, GA: SBL.

———. 2013. "Chronicles and its Reshaping of Memories of Monarchic Period Prophets: Some Observations." In *Prophets, Prophecy, and Ancient Israelite Historiography*, edited by M. J. Boda and L. M. Wray Beal, 167–88. Winona Lake, IN: Eisenbrauns.

Briant, P. 2002. *From Cyrus to Alexander: A History of the Persian Empire*. Translated by P. D. Daniels. Winona Lake, IN: Eisenbrauns.

Chavalas, M. 2005. "The Age of Empires: 3100–900 BCE." In *A Companion to the Ancient Near East*, edited by D. C. Snell, 34–47. Malden, MA; Oxford: Blackwell.

Frahm, E. 2013. "Rising Suns and Falling Stars: Assyrian Kings and the Cosmos." In *Experiencing Power, Generating Authority: Cosmos, Politics, and the Ideology of Kingship in Ancient Egypt and Mesopotamia*, edited by J. A. Hill, P. Jones, and A. J. Morales, 97–120. Philadelphia, PA: University of Pennsylvania Museum of Archaeology and Anthropology.

Hazony, Y. 2012. *The Philosophy of Hebrew Scripture*. Cambridge: Cambridge University Press.

Irwin, B. P. 2012. "Not Just Any King: Abimelech, the Northern Monarchy, and the Final Form of Judges." *JBL* 131: 443–54.

Joüon, P. 2006. *A Grammar of Biblical Hebrew.* Translated and revised by T. Muraoka. 2nd ed. Subsidia biblica 27. Rome: Pontifical Biblical Institute.

Koch, U. S. 2000. *Babylonian Liver Omens: the Chapters Manzāzu, Padānu and Pān tākalti of the Babylonian Extispicy Series Mainly From Aššurbanipal's Library.* Copenhagen: The Carsten Niebuhr Institute of Near Eastern Studies, University of Copenhagen.

Kroeker, R. J. 2002. "Politics and Personality: Characterization in Xenophon's Hellenica." Unpublished PhD thesis, University of Alberta.

Kuhrt, A. 2007. *The Persian Empire: A Corpus of Sources from the Achaemenid Empire.* London: Routledge.

Lerner, R. 1987. "Moses Maimonides." In *History of Political Philosophy*, edited by L. Strauss and J. Cropsey, 228–47. 3rd ed. Chicago, IL: University of Chicago Press.

Lierman, J. 2004. *The New Testament Moses.* WUNT 2. Tübingen: Mohr Siebeck.

Lincoln, B. 2012. *'Happiness for Mankind': Achaemenian Religion and the Imperial Project.* Acta Iranica 53. Leuven: Peeters.

Melamed, A. 2005. "Is There a Jewish Political Thought? The Medieval Case Reconsidered." *Hebraic Political Studies* 1: 24–56.

Otto, A. 2014. "The Organization of Residential Space in the Mittani Kingdom as a Mirror of Different Models of Governance." In *Constituent, Confederate, and Conquered Space: The Emergence of the Mittani State*, edited by E. Cancik-Kirschbaum, N. Brisch and J. Eidem, 33–60. Berlin: de Gruyter.

Römer, T. C. 2013. "Moses, the Royal Lawgiver." In *Remembering Biblical Figures in the Late Persian and Early Hellenistic Periods: Social Memory and Imagination,* edited by D. V. Edelman and E. Ben Zvi, 81–94. Oxford: Oxford University Press.

Schneider, T. J. 2000. *Judges*. Collegeville, MN: Liturgical Press.

Sinopoli, C. M. 1994. "The Archaeology of Empires." *Annual Review of Anthropology* 23: 159–80.

Skjærvø, P. O. "Old Persian Arta." *Encyclopedia Iranica* II/ 7:696. Available also open-access at http://www.iranicaonline.org/articles/asa-means-truth-in-avestan#pt2.

Waltke, B. K. and M. O'Connor. 1990. *An Introduction to Biblical Hebrew Syntax*. Winona Lake, IN: Eisenbrauns.

Wilson, I. D. *Kingship and Memory in Ancient Judah*. Oxford: Oxford University Press. Forthcoming Jan 2017).

Yoffee, N. 2005. *Myths of the Archaic State: Evolution of the Earliest Cities, States, and Civilizations*. Cambridge: Cambridge University Press.

— 3 —

Memories of Judah's Past Leaders Utilized as Propaganda in Yehud

James M. Bos

Introduction

Memory is both fragile and malleable, subject to fragmentation, consolidation, conflation, revision, and forgetting. This is true for both the memories held by individuals as well for the memories shared by social groups (from small families to large nations).[1] Social groups, especially, strive to retain memories about their past (via museums, archives, commemorations [a word which of course literally denotes remembering together], educational curricula that involve history, etc.).[2] This is because memories appear to be an essential aspect of both personal and social identity. One feature that delimits one social group from another is the contours of the memories shared within each.[3] Memories, though, are not just about the past. In fact, memories are always recalled, remembered, in the present.[4] Memories to a large degree shape the present and provide a trajectory for the anticipated future.[5]

---

1. I am not going to provide an extensive overview of social memory theory. For a very helpful concise yet thorough introduction, see A. Kirk, "Social and Cultural Memory," in *Memory, Tradition, and Text: Uses of the Past in Early Christianity*, ed. A. Kirk and T. Thatcher (Atlanta, GA: SBL, 2005), 1–24. For a more comprehensive discussion, see E. Zerubavel, *Social Mindscapes: An Invitation to Cognitive Sociology* (Cambridge, MA: Harvard University Press, 1997). For social or cultural memory theory applied to the Hebrew Bible, in addition to the other essays in this volume, one should consult the essays in *Remembering Biblical Figures in the Late Persian and Early Hellenistic Periods: Social Memory and Imagination*, ed. D. V. Edelman and E. Ben Zvi (Oxford: Oxford University Press, 2013).

2. Individuals and smaller social groups like families remember things like birthdays and anniversaries (and other notable events from their shared past). In fact, our families even help us remember ourselves when they tell stories of our youth that we individually do not recall. See Zerubavel, *Social Mindscapes*, 83.

3. Yankees fans' memories of the last century of baseball differ from those of Cubs fans, even when the site(s) of memory is/are shared. The American Civil War is remembered differently in the northeastern United States than in the American South. Examples could be multiplied. See Zerubavel, *Social Mindscapes*, 90–91.

4. One can, however, have memories of having had memories in the past, but the memory is still being recalled in the present. I have unfortunately not read enough of the scientific (neurological studies, etc.) or philosophical literature to say much more on this point.

5. On the level of the individual, something so simple as brushing one's teeth is learned early in a child's

Thus, at the national level, contemporary politicians frequently resort to recalling aspects of their nation's shared past to articulate their vision for guiding the nation in the years to follow. They assume correctly that most individuals whom they are addressing share very similar memories about these events or historical figures that they are recalling to remembrance. However, the number of historical figures and events to which they can allude and have it be meaningful is often somewhat limited. Most Americans, for example, have some shared memories about George Washington and Abraham Lincoln but virtually none about Millard Fillmore (the last Whig president). In this instance, Americans (particularly those most responsible for shaping the educational curricula, but with the implicit concession of those receiving the education) have not found Fillmore's presidency to be worth remembering and thus it has essentially been forgotten. There are other reasons to forget than simply an apparent lack of significance. Republican politicians heartily recall Ronald Reagan but not Richard Nixon (due to the Watergate scandal), and Democratic politicians hesitate to recall Jimmy Carter or compare themselves to him.[6] In other words, some memories are prioritized, valued, retained, and granted continued relevance over others. Very often the memories selected for recall by contemporary politicians are politically expedient (but not uncontested;[7] their opponents will recall the memories in a way more favorable to them, and each side will shape the memories recalled from the "reservoir" of cultural memory to their liking; no memory is ever recalled in exactly the same way each time). The shared memories, in these instances, are recalled in order to legitimize a particular policy, or to convince the public to support one politician over another. In other words, shared cultural memories are frequently utilized in political propaganda (from the national to local level; and in both the present and the past). To push this idea a bit further, politicians' (or their public relation team's) ability to select, shape (manipulate), and even invent shared memories that serve to garner public support for their leadership and their favored policies makes them ripe for use in political propaganda.

Constructing an analogy between contemporary methods of propaganda employed by American or European politicians and that of the leaders of Persian-period Yehud is not fully appropriate.[8] The many differences between a small province whose leadership consisted of a Persian-appointed governor and a semi-elite scribal-priestly class, on the

---

life through parental reminding and may include the transmission of stories about what happens to individuals who do not brush their teeth regularly. For adults, one could mention the necessity of remembering to pay the monthly bills or the annual income tax along with hundreds of other activities that (perhaps subconsciously) require memory. In the distant past, there can be no doubt that memory, the ability to communicate memories, and the ability to use memories of the past to construct plans for the future, all aided early hominem survival.

6. Anecdotally, in a recent class on the New Testament, I was discussing social memory and how it might help us understand the development of the traditions about Jesus. As an example of how difficult it is for a social group to remember events from the prior generation without constant recall, I asked the students (most of whom were born in the early 1990s) what they remembered about Carter. No one remembered anything. In contrast, most knew a few basic "facts" about Reagan, significantly, the "same" basic "facts."

7. See Zerubavel, *Social Mindscapes*, 12. He discusses the cognitive battlefields that often exist between social "camps."

8. See the frequently cited objections to such a comparison in Enenkel and Pfeijffer ("Introduction," in *The Manipulative Mode: Political Propaganda in Antiquity: A Collection of Case Studies*, ed. K. A. E. Enenkel and I. L. Pfeijffer [Leiden: Brill, 2005], 2–3). They include the lack of a centrally organized "propaganda machine" in the distant past; the aggressive dissemination of information in modern nations; and the much more massive audience targeted by modern propaganda.

one hand, and massive nation-states with democratically elected leaders, on the other, do not need to be spelled out. That being said, the literature produced in Yehud (and later, Judea) bears witness to the utilization of shared memories about "Israel" that were shaped and re-shaped in the hands of the scribal-priestly class in ways that benefited them, that legitimized their continued leadership role in the province (at the expense of other potential leaders), and that funneled resources into the Jerusalem temple with which they were associated.[9] This kind of control over shared memories (via selection, manipulation, and distribution), even if conducted on a much smaller scale, is not completely dissimilar to the manner in which contemporary propaganda makes use of shared memories.

Some scholars of propaganda have been hesitant to speak of propaganda as a phenomenon that existed prior to World War I.[10] This is in part because before this time period, propaganda was not a phenomenon that most human beings appear to have recognized or studied.[11] Furthermore, the variety of media and the variety of techniques used to disseminate information has multiplied in the last century. Thus, any theory evaluating contemporary or near contemporary forms of propaganda can only be used with great caution for earlier time periods. One risks anachronism, especially because "propaganda" is an English word with cognates in some related languages, but it has no equivalent in Hebrew. That said, I think that it is quite clear that human beings in the distant past used available media to disseminate information in ways that were advantageous to them. For example, it might be difficult to argue that the Neo-Assyrian wall reliefs were not propaganda.[12] So although one can easily demonstrate that the intensity or consistency of ancient propaganda comes nowhere close to the phenomenon today, aspects of the strategic dissemination of information still obtain, even if the ancients themselves did not recognize it as a distinct category of human behavior.

Defining Propaganda

Providing a concise definition of the word "propaganda" that applies to all times and places is perhaps impossible, as indicated by the wide variety of proposals put forward by theorists.[13] This is in part due to the fact that the specific configuration and implementation of

---

9. For other discussions in this volume of the social setting, role, and motivations of the literati, see the essays by E. Ben Zvi ("Memory and Political Thought in the Late Persian/early Hellenistic Yehud/Judah: Some Observations"), K. Berge ("Mystified Authority: Legitimating Leadership Through 'Lost Books'"), and T. M. Bolin ("At the Hands of Foreign Kings: Divine Endorsement of Foreign Rulers in the Hebrew Bible in the Memory of Persian and Hellenistic Yehud").

10. See J. Ellul, *Propaganda: The Formation of Men's Attitudes*, trans. K. Kellen and J. Lerner (New York: Knopf, 1965), 74; and S. Cunningham, *The Idea of Propaganda: A Reconstruction* (Westport, CT: Praeger, 2002), 18–19.

11. This may be due to the very characteristic feature of propaganda to induce targeted audiences to overlook, misrecognize, or take for granted the power imbalances that the elite seek to maintain and expand (see below).

12. P. M. Taylor (*Munitions of the Mind: A History of Propaganda from the Ancient World to the Present Day*, 3rd ed. [Manchester: Manchester University Press, 2003]) begins his study of propaganda with ancient Mesopotamia. One should note that his focus is primarily on warfare and how the elite managed to get others to fight and die for them. The anthology *Propaganda and Communication in World History Volume 1: The Symbolic Instrument in Early Times*, ed. H. D. Lasswell, *et al.* (Honolulu: University Press of Hawaii, 1979) also has two chapters devoted to ancient Mesopotamia and one to ancient Egypt.

13. See the comprehensive discussions in the following: Ellul, *Propaganda*; Cunningham, *The Idea of Propaganda* (especially his summary list on pages 176–78); and G. S. Jowett and V. O'Donnell, *Propaganda*

propaganda differs in each cultural context in which it appears. For example, during and after World War I and throughout World War II, in the United States the term "propaganda" often connoted something false and deceptive, something evil, especially when carried out by the other side. For Americans, it was something the Nazis engaged in. There was much less awareness of how the U.S. media and leadership were shaping Americans' views of the other side in ways that contemporary scholars would consider propagandistic. Propaganda is subtle, secretive, pervasive, difficult to recognize or quantify, and this is what makes a definition of the term so elusive.[14] The theoretical study of propaganda, which has historically been carried out primarily by sociologists and psychologists, also has significant overlap with other disciplines. This would include especially communication theory, mass media studies, language theory, persuasion theory, and epistemology. Space and time prohibit a discussion of each, so I will limit myself to putting forward a rather broad definition of propaganda that I find suitable for the ancient Near East and then progress to discussing some of the characteristics of propaganda that cannot be captured in a one-sentence definition.

I define ancient propaganda as the production and subsequent dissemination of information by elite factions through available media, the intent of which is to alter or expand the worldview of the audience or audiences in ways that result in, whether realized consciously or not, increased power, prestige, legitimacy, and access to resources for the producers (and to a lesser extent, the distributers) of the information.[15] In the ancient world, these media would of course include, among other things, monumental structures and everything they connoted to subject populations, monumental displays (victory stela, etc.), festivals of various kinds (e.g., royal coronations), coinage (when it had developed), and most importantly for this essay, the production and distribution of literature.

Characteristics of Propaganda

Of all the theories about propaganda published to date that have attempted to capture and explain the essence of this concept, Stanley Cunningham's effort is in my view the most successful.[16] He emphasizes throughout his book that most intuitive notions about propaganda are often too simplistic. Calling it "thought control," "spin-doctoring," "dis-

---

and Persuasion, 3rd ed. (London: Sage Publications, 1999). For the Near East in particular, see the overview in J. L. Cooley, "Propaganda, Prognostication, and Planets," in *Divination, Politics, and Ancient Near Eastern Empires*, ed. A. Lenzi and J. Stökl, ANEM 7 (Atlanta, GA: SBL, 2014), 7–13. He provides samples of definitions of propaganda; unfortunately, his bibliography does not include the seminal monograph by Stanley Cunningham.

14. C. Carey humorously suggests that "defining propaganda is a bit like trying to catch a greased pig: slippery" ("Propaganda and Competition in Athenian Oratory," in *The Manipulative Mode: Political Propaganda in Antiquity: A Collection of Case Studies*, ed. K. A. E. Enenkel and I. L. Pfeijffer [Leiden: Brill, 2005], 65).

15. Or, to use the terminology of Pierre Bourdieu, propaganda results in increased economic, cultural, and symbolic capital (cf. D. Swartz, *Culture and Power: The Sociology of Pierre Bourdieu* [Chicago, IL: University of Chicago Press, 1997], 65–94), where economic capital includes liquid currency, property, etc., while cultural capita involves education (especially at the highest levels), social networks (including those yielding "appropriate" sexual partners), a recognized sense of aestheticism in the arts, etc., and finally, symbolic capital involves the control of the ideological machinery generating, maintaining, and justifying the social disparity in these spheres of capital.

16. Cunningham, *Idea of Propaganda*. Significantly, he does not consider propaganda proper to have existed prior to the early 20th century. Obviously, I disagree with him on this point. Another weakness in this otherwise very valuable discussion is that he rarely discusses the material effect of propaganda, that is, its impact on the flow of resources.

information," or "psychological manipulation," which at times may be partially accurate descriptors of propaganda, does not really do justice to the complexity of the phenomenon. He argues for situating the theoretical study of propaganda within the field of philosophy, and he concludes that the essential feature of propaganda is that it is a form of pseudo-communication, or in his words, "a complex array of epistemic deficits."[17] In other words, propaganda is the transmission and reception of defective information *and* an attitude of indifference to (in his view) superior epistemic categories like truth, reason, and evidence by both the propagandist and the often unwitting consumers of propaganda. As such, and in contrast to most other theorists, Cunningham considers propaganda to be inherently unethical.[18] The epistemic deficit of propaganda, however, does not mean that propaganda consists of falsehoods. On the contrary, propaganda often involves real data, so-called facts, and thus can be said to employ the truth, but it does so selectively. And it also employs the perceived or actual truth not because it is true but because it provides the best means to the desired end. This misuse or abuse of truth is thus part of what makes it defective information. Propagandistic information is also epistemically defective in the sense that it is often presented in such a way as to discourage reason and analysis of data, and in contrast, tends to exploit human emotions, insecurities, and prejudices.[19] Such defective information is often conveniently distributed through slogans or catch phrases that are easily remembered but which fall significantly short of a reasoned argument.

Building on the work of Jacques Ellul,[20] Cunningham also discusses how propaganda is used to construct an ideological environment.[21] In the modern world it is not the single pamphlet or commercial that produces an effect on the masses as a whole. It is the barrage of information through a variety of media over a long period of time that has a cumulative effect. Importantly, in most instances the propaganda is so subtle it is not perceived by those it affects most, even though most individuals are, or claim to be, aware that politicians and corporations are attempting to mold their opinions (confer the effectiveness of so-called "negative ads"). In the ancient world the information load was significantly lower, but the elite were just as successful in creating hegemonic ideologies that benefitted them (e.g., the notion of divine kingship in Egypt). In ancient Yehud, one such successful ideology was the notion that Yahweh had just one legitimate house, the one in Jerusalem (unless one was a Samarian, in which case, Mt. Gerizim was thought to be the place of Yahweh's choosing; note the competing claims of rival elite). It was not just one text read one time by which this ideology gained prominence. Rather, it was the repeated readings, the re-remembering via reading, of numerous texts (Deuteronomy, the Priestly layers of the Torah, Chronicles, Ezra-Nehemiah, Ezek 40–48, the Zion motif in Isaiah and the Psalms, Haggai, etc.) that so saturated the thinking of the elite and sub-elite in Yehud that there was a thorough adoption and implementation of this ideology.[22] Competing ideologies, not to mention competing

---

17. Cunningham, *Idea of Propaganda*, 176.
18. Cunningham, *Idea of Propaganda*, 127–53. The remainder of this paragraph is a summary of his chapter on the ethics of propaganda.
19. Consider here the political advertisements that question whether the opposing candidate is really capable of answering the 3 am phone call, or worse, those that stoop to using racist tropes.
20. Ellul, *Propaganda*, esp. pp. 193–202.
21. Cunningham, *Idea of Propaganda*, 38–47.
22. One can compare and contrast the discussion of intentionality in the concept of agency by K. Berge in this volume ("Mystified Authority: Legitimating Leadership Through 'Lost Books'.")

temples, were dismissed and polemicized with great success. The effect of the ideology was the increased power and prestige of the Jerusalem temple and the priesthood working there and, not to be overlooked, a substantial increase in the resources that were funneled to this temple and its priests; that is, the propagandistically-created-and-promoted ideology surrounding the Jerusalem temple resulted in increased economic and cultural capital for a sector of Judean society (to the disadvantage of their competitors).[23]

Next, for propaganda to be effective, it must be distributed efficiently. Furthermore, it is not usually the highest elite who are the active propagandists (i.e., the king himself is not composing the monumental inscription and chiseling it into the stone). They receive help from allied persons and institutions (and in some cases, potentially neutral figures or even opponents). In this regard, Cunningham notes the important role that is played in the propagation of the dominant ideology by what he designates as "para-epistemic institutions."[24] In our contemporary world, these institutions would include the various forms of mass media, like TV, radio, newspapers, and the internet, as well as things like think tanks, lobbyists, corporations of various kinds, religious institutions, and even potentially schools and universities (although for Cunningham, the latter ideally should privilege "truth" and evidence, thus allowing them to remain separate from the propaganda "machine"; I am less optimistic about the "objectivity" of the educational process, and for the ancient world in particular, education involved a socialization process that might be termed indoctrination). These are the institutions that shape the flow of information to the masses, and because of their role in disseminating information (essential to the administration's messaging strategies), they also benefit, although somewhat indirectly, from the propaganda distributed (and often not nearly to the extent that the primary elite benefit; this would be especially so in the ancient world).

As the media controlling the flow of information, the para-epistemic institutions necessarily have some capability of selecting, shaping, and emphasizing what information they deem important (especially in modern democratic societies). Without them, the overarching worldview promoted by the elite would be substantially more difficult to construct and maintain, or in some cases, to de-construct with counter-propaganda. In ancient Yehud, the scribal class working within the administration (whether temple or governor's office, or both) I think can be classified as a para-epistemic institution, since their role involved shaping and distributing elite propagandistic information. Unfortunately, there is much that we do not know about the mechanisms of the distribution of the information they produced. I assume the literature composed was read aloud periodically to the "public." These readings would likely have occurred during the annual festivals at the very least. Whether or not the literature was readily available or widely known in the most distant villages is perhaps impossible to ascertain.[25] In any case, the small literate portion of Yehud's population no

---

23. Significantly, the flexibility of cultural memory allowed for this ideology to be promoted over a very long time period in many different socio-historical contexts. In other words, in the early Persian period it effectively served to legitimize the newly rebuilt temple in Jerusalem over against the temple in Bethel, while in the next few centuries it became the focal point of the contest between Samaria and Jerusalem (and probably also the temples in Elephantine, Leontopolis, an unknown location in Idumea, and likely temples elsewhere). In more recent times, the propagandistic ideology of the Jerusalem temple has been in a memory contest with Islam and its adherents' (no less propagandistic) claims to the temple mount.

24. Cunningham, *Idea of Propaganda*, 117–24.

25. If the narrative in 2 Chr 17:7–9, where Jerusalem officials go to "all the cities of Judah" to teach the "book of the Torah of Yahweh," reflects the actual practice of the administration of Yehud/Judea, then

doubt played an essential role in constructing and disseminating the elite's perspective on a variety of issues, and in this role, they contributed to the formation and cultivation of the dominant ideologies present in Yehud.

Propaganda also often has as its purpose ideological conformity and social or ideological integration;[26] for example, during the Cold War, Americans were propagandized to think of Communism as a great threat to humanity,[27] or in the not so distant past, that Iran was part of the axis of evil. Herman and Chomsky, very appropriately I think, designate this process of ideological persuasion in democratic societies "the manufacturing of consent" (cf. the title of their book).[28] This manufacturing of consent often involves the provision of a quasi-canonical view of historical events (i.e., a preferred way of remembering the past), such as the necessity or the justness of a certain war.[29] It tends to oversimplify matters, casting opponents as wholly bad, eliminating gray areas ("you are for us or against us"). Highly relevant to this paper, it also often tends to construct mythologies surrounding figures of the past whose deeds are then commemorated (e.g., Ellul mentions Joseph Stalin in Russia and Davy Crockett in the U.S.;[30] many others can be identified). However, the "consensus" is rarely unquestioned (hence the necessity of manufacturing the consent). Opposing factions may have alternative ways of remembering the past (consider how Democrats and Republicans remember Franklin Delano Roosevelt's policies during the Great Depression, or how the North and South remember the Civil War).[31] The flexibility of memory enables the contest. Despite ancient Yehud not being a modern society like those being discussed by the theorists above, numerous aspects of the ideological and cultural conformity resulting from propaganda are clearly visible in the literature produced in this small province.[32] This will become clear in the discussion to follow.

Propaganda and Collective Memory

In my view, much of the literature now contained in the Hebrew Bible can be viewed, read, and analyzed as a form of ancient propaganda. These texts contain information (often in the form of memory, in the sense that few, if any, of the texts were composed contemporary with the events they describe) that was transmitted through one of the media available to the elite in ancient Yehud, namely, written texts. The production of literature in the ancient world was not a leisure activity, and I find it unlikely that significant time and resources would

---

the distribution of information that provided material and ideological advantage to the Jerusalem temple might have been quite widespread. Neh 8 reflects a more centralized reading of the Torah. I would like to thank Ehud Ben Zvi for reminding me (how a propos!) of these two passages.

26. Ellul, *Propaganda*, has much to say about the role of propaganda in facilitating social integration (see especially pages 70–79).

27. The effects of this propaganda still lingers strongly in the United States. For example, not so long ago a Republican politician claimed that many Democrats were in fact Communists. This was not a compliment!

28. E. S. Herman and N. Chomsky, *Manufacturing Consent: The Political Economy of the Mass Media* (New York: Pantheon Books, 1998).

29. See Herman and Chomsky's discussion of the Vietnam War (*Manufacturing Consent*, 169–252).

30. Ellul, *Propaganda*, 172.

31. As a native northerner who now lives in Mississippi, I have quickly become acutely aware of the different ways this war is remembered.

32. On the role of literature as a medium of propaganda in the classical world, see Enenkel and Pfeiffer, "Introduction," 9.

have been expended producing and preserving these texts if they were not thought to produce some benefit to the elite who produced them, whoever they might have been. While most members of the community/communities in Yehud probably could not read the texts themselves, as mentioned above, I find it likely that they were read aloud to a broader audience. Both the location of the reading, perhaps in or near the temple compound in Jerusalem, and the person reading the text, such as a priest or another elite individual, would have had an impact on the perceived authority and importance of the text being read (this would also be true if the texts were carried to peripheral towns to be read aloud; the dress, deportment, and other identifying features of the delegation arranging and carrying out the public reading would have signaled to the audience their claim to authority).

The temple in Jerusalem, as a para-epistemic institution, functioned similarly to the way that "respected" institutions today handle the flow of information. Secondly, and most importantly, the scribal tradents of these books were involved in the construction of a rather particular set of ideologies (one of which was briefly discussed above) regarding Judah and Israel's past as well as their future. These ideologies were propagandistic in nature (such as the legitimacy of David's lineage or the centrality of the temple in Jerusalem), providing material advantage and legitimate power to some individuals while disadvantaging others. Significantly, as the tradents constructed these ideologies, they often utilized and re-configured memories about Israel and Judah's past leadership—kings and prophets especially—to do so.

Some of these memories of past leadership are so obviously propagandistic that little might need to be said about them, but in order to demonstrate the characteristics of propaganda contained in them, I will examine a couple of obvious examples before turning to some less obvious examples. Let me begin with the stories about David contained in the Hebrew Bible. David's role as the first "legitimate" king of Israel ("Israel"?) granted him a large position in the memory of later Judahites.[33] However, his legitimacy was not a given; it had to be promoted, probably from the time he first took power and throughout the monarchic period, a span of time I am not considering in this essay, and then into the Persian period and beyond. In the early Persian period, it appears that some individuals in Yehud favored a return to Davidic rule (cf. the presentation of Zerubbabel in Haggai and Chronicles) while others were content with other leaders (such as the governor in Mizpah; perhaps a "Saulide"). During this time, the memories about David now contained in Samuel underwent significant re-shaping in order to combat the claims to legitimacy of any non-Davidide.[34] Of all the oracles the historical David (assuming he did exist and that he did rule some of the territory associated with Israel and Judah) must have received from his court prophets, it is the oracle of Yahweh's promise to him of an eternal dynasty that is highlighted, selected for repeated recall. (It is immaterial whether such an oracle was every given to the historical David; it was remembered as an historical oracle). This oracle, in conjunction with the stories remembered about Saul being de-legitimized, thus served to bolster the legitimacy of later Davidides.[35] How many of such Davidides actually

---

33. This should not be unexpected: George Washington, Bismark, Ataturk, etc. also occupy similar space in the memories of the nations they are associated with.

34. See my discussion about the polemic against Benjamin and Saul in the book of Hosea in J. M. Bos, *Reconsidering the Date and Provenance of the Book of Hosea: The Case for Persian-Period Yehud*, LHBOTS 580 (New York: Bloomsbury, 2013), 70–87.

35. Significantly, it is highly probable that the elite in northern Yehud (that is, in the region of Benjamin when the provincial capital was still at Mizpah) remembered Saul and his exploits quite differently than

held power and received the benefit of this propaganda during the later Persian and Hellenistic period is difficult to determine. But the ideology once entrenched did not die off. In the late first century CE, many Christians considered Jesus of Nazareth to have been descended from King David, and the rabbinic literature from a few centuries later would also view the (future) Messiah as the "Son of David." Additionally, the rabbinic Patriarchs would claim Davidic descent as well. So successfully had the ideology of the legitimacy of David's dynasty been propagated that these heirs of Second Temple Judaism could conceive of no other legitimate ruler of Israel than one who could trace his ancestry back to David.[36]

Turning then to how Josiah was remembered in the narrative now found in 1 Kgs 22–23 and its slightly different parallel in 2 Chr 34–35, the narrator informs his audience that Josiah reigned for 31 years. Much must have happened during that time both in Judah and internationally (the waning of Assyrian power, the reemergence of Egypt, the rise of Babylonia), yet the only memory that dominates is the one associated with Josiah's so-called reform.[37] With the exception of his death, which is rather brief and muted in the Kings account, all other memories are essentially forgotten, not having been worth remembering. So why remember his "reform"? Well, clearly the narrator holds to the view that the temple in Jerusalem is the only legitimate place to bring regular offerings to Yahweh (and the only place to celebrate the annual holidays like Passover). Furthermore, the priests working at other shrines are considered illegitimate. Thus, the narrator recalling the "good"[38] Josiah's efforts to rid the land of the "illegitimate" shrines and the paraphernalia within them along with their officiants thus cultivated in the earliest audiences exposed to this story a desire to be on the side that did "right" in Yahweh's eyes, like Josiah. Although one might think it rather benign that the narrator and those individuals in following centuries who read aloud and disseminated the story via other means were promoting an ideology of the legitimacy of the temple in Jerusalem, its acceptance, as the history of Judaism confirms, means the material and social benefits to the elite in Jerusalem, particularly the priesthood located there, would have been significant. This would have included, among other things, eating a diet of the best meats and grains available, which likely resulted in better general health, physical attractiveness, and longevity in comparison with other less privileged individuals in Yehud. This would have consequences for the acquisition of sexual partners and the number of offspring that could be cared for and raised to maturity—with all the additional cultural and economic capital at their disposal for the next generation to follow. The negative consequences for competing sacred sites would also have been measurable.

---

the southern, pro-Davidic Jerusalemites, making the figure of Saul in the memoryscape a site of intense conflict.

36. Notably, the legitimacy of David's lineage was not uncontested in Yehud. Jeremiah is remembered to have uttered an oracle in which the dynasty was to come to an end (cf. Jer 22:27–30). In my view, such an oracle represents the Benjaminite perspective that the Samuel tradents were contesting in the early Persian period.

37. The word "reform" is of course tendentious and reflects the narrator's stance on his actions against the perceived illicit cults outside of Jerusalem. An attempt at an unbiased evaluation of the memory of Josiah's actions might suggest a rather more negative portrayal of his deeds, one that highlights his murderous rampage.

38. The grouping of all remembered Judahite and Israelite kings into one of two categories, good or bad, is another feature of the text in Kings that is propagandistic. It provides an easily remembered evaluation of each of the kings, some that are to be revered and imitated, others to be denigrated. There is no middle ground.

Now, the memories of Josiah[39] are not the only ones utilized to construct and promote an ideology favoring the Jerusalem temple. Consider the figure of Haggai.[40] The book of Haggai records a selection of oracles that the prophet ostensibly uttered before the temple in Jerusalem was rebuilt in the early Persian period. Unfortunately, we do not know much about this figure, how long he was active as a prophet, or what other oracles he might have delivered. What is significant is that the oracles the Judahite elite remembered (whether consciously or not) are primarily focused on this temple and on Zerubabbel, as noted above.[41]

The first oracle in the text contains a memory of the people in Yehud being not particularly concerned with rebuilding the temple—a temple in which the elite priests would work, receive payment, and be granted their social prestige for their valued occupation. The prophet Haggai is remembered as providing Yahweh's corrective. Such disregard for the temple in Jerusalem was not acceptable. The next oracles in 1:3–6 continue shaping how the audience should regard this temple. The first question—"Is it a time for you to live in your paneled houses while this house lies in ruins"—serves to draw attention to the untenable situation that existed at that time, at least as viewed by Haggai and those promoting his message. More significantly, the question identifies a potential site of anxiety for people in the ancient world. Temples housed the gods who ensured the well being of the land and its population. And in this oracle, the god himself brings attention to his non-functional house. A non-functional temple, it is implied, would yield a non-cooperative god. The question posed to the audience may also imply that the people ought to have felt some guilt over this still unbuilt temple, a guilt that could be resolved rather simply by rectifying the situation. For later readers who were remembering Haggai's message after the temple had been rebuilt, the text promoted a concern for continuing to maintain the temple's upkeep lest their economic security deteriorate. Thus, the remembered oracles target the vulnerable emotions of their audience, particularly their concern for economic well-being, which is highly characteristic of much propaganda.

The next part of the oracle builds on the people's potential anxiety by asking them to focus on their less than prosperous economic situation. The NRSV translates "Consider how you have fared." More literally it reads, "Set your heart on your matters." The same statement reappears in v. 7 and a variant of it shows up again in 2:16. This repetition marks it as a slogan of sorts. It is reminiscent of contemporary campaign commercials that ask the audience: "are you better off now than you were four years ago?" Such commercials inevitably suggest voting for a candidate that will improve one's economic security. Similarly, here in Haggai, it is suggested that the people's poor harvests will improve in the future if only they adopt Haggai's point of view and expend their energy and funds rebuilding (or, for later readers, maintaining, supplying) the temple. From a modern perspective, this appears a rather naïve argument, but it probably was not perceived as such in the ancient world.

---

39. It should be noted that some memories of Josiah retained in the Hebrew Bible are not so overwhelmingly positive (e.g., Jer 3:6–10).

40. The figure of Solomon in Kings and David in Chronicles could be examined here, but the memories of their role in building and configuring the temple are so obviously propagandistic that I do not find it necessary to discuss them.

41. For a discussion of how the ideology of the temple present in Haggai contrasts with that found in other portions of the Hebrew Bible, see E. Assis, "The Temple in the Book of Haggai," *JHebS* 8 (2008): 1–10. For another discussion in this volume of the role of prophets as conceived in the Hebrew Bible, see E. Ben Zvi, "Memory and Political Thought in the Late Persian/early Hellenistic Yehud/Judah: Some Observations."

That said, I think we can still consider the rather one-sided "argument" to be deficient epistemically, which is one of the key features of propaganda. The information is deficient at the very least because restoring Yahweh's temple in Jerusalem is given as the *only* solution to what might have been a real problem, even though other potential solutions might have been thought possible at that time in that place, including making offerings to Baal and Asherah or other fertility deities, which potentially might have required less labor and fewer resources, but which would have benefited a different elite. Instead, the only solution put forward is one that benefitted primarily if not exclusively the Yahweh-worshipping leadership in Jerusalem during the Persian period and beyond.

Other memories about the leaders of Judah and Israel in the monarchic period can also be considered propaganda. For example, a good number of texts contain memories about prophetic oracles or royal activity that served to provide a "canonical" explanation for past historical events, most notably, the severe military losses to Assyria and subsequently, Babylonia. The tradents explained these military disasters as punishment by Yahweh, whose anger had driven him to abandon or even attack his own people. For Israel, the memory of Jeroboam I installing the calves in non-Jerusalemite temples figures prominently. Subsequent Israelite kings were not remembered to have corrected this "error," leading to Yahweh's exiling all of Israel to Assyria[42] (cf. 1 Kgs 12 and 2 Kgs 17). For Judah, Manasseh's excessive evil is singled out (cf. 2 Kgs 21), but numerous other kings are judged to have been guilty as well. Judah's punishment was only delayed because of the few "good" kings.

Now, explaining military defeat as being due to a god's anger was not uncommon in the ancient Near East (cf. as one example, the Mesha Inscription), but the Judahite tradents added a twist to the more common worldview. Yahweh was angry not because he was improperly provisioned nor because his temple was unkempt, but rather because the people were worshipping other gods like Baal or the Queen of Heaven in addition to him. In the view of these tradents, Yahweh required exclusive devotion, and he had repeatedly informed his people of this requirement in the past through his messengers the prophets (the true prophets, anyway). But the prophets had not been heeded, or so the tradents remembered, and the military defeats that figured so prominently in their memoryscape functioned as confirmation of this "fact." Moreover, the kings of the past, with a few exceptions, are remembered as being the most adverse to the prophets' messages. The memory of Jehoiakim slowly cutting apart and burning the scroll with Jeremiah's words in Jer 36 is a particularly vivid example of this. The remembered opposition between the prophets of old and the kings of the past is also evident in Hosea (cf. chs.10 and 13 especially). The priests of the past, though, are also sometimes remembered as opposing the "true" prophets. In the memory of Jeremiah's life being threatened due to his pronouncement of doom against Jerusalem (Jer 26), the priests figure prominently as his accusers. The tradents also remembered an oracle by Zephaniah that made all leaders of Judah's past culpable—officials, judges, prophets, and priests (3:1–5).

The implications of such a view of the leaders of the past were not insignificant for the tradents' present in the later Persian period and beyond. I think we have an excellent example of a contemporary leadership attempting to legitimize itself by disassociating from ineffectual past leadership, something that almost always takes place after a significant disaster befalls a nation or group of people. In essence, the transmitters of these texts promoting the worship of Yahweh alone, often with Jerusalem as the sole legitimate place for bringing him

---

42. This statement in 2 Kgs 17:23 is not historically accurate, but that is immaterial.

offerings, were implying that they were not like the past leadership who messed up. They recognize what had been done wrong and they will not repeat the mistakes of prior leaders. They acknowledged that the true prophets of the past had obviously been right, and as the bearers of the prophetic message, the tradents' view of things, and the elite whom they represented, must then necessarily also be right. Their posture as transmitters of Yahweh's words and as the provisioners of the "correct" view of the past would have almost certainly bolstered their prestige.

Moreover, the texts leave little room for debate on the matter. I think that Cunningham's point about the epistemic deficit of propagandistic information is particularly appropriate to the texts collected in the Hebrew Bible on this point—because other explanations for these past calamities are not explored, other opinions could not be right. Furthermore, because history had proven the prophets of the past correct, their message was just as important in the present. Exclusive devotion to Yahweh was the only correct option for contemporary Judahite religious praxis, according to these tradents. And it was important to them that all of Yahweh's people hold this view, because not doing so put the larger community at risk for further calamity. In this respect, propaganda's role in fostering ideological conformity and social integration is clearly evident. The tradents very clearly desire that all of their co-religionists adopt their way of looking at the past.

The idea that propaganda exploits emotions and insecurity is clearly in play here as well. In the decades following the destruction of Jerusalem and during the years of it being rebuilt, there must have been significant anxiety about how to prevent such a thing from happening again. In offering an explanation for why the destruction had occurred in the first place, the tradents also provided an answer for how to prevent future disasters—serve Yahweh alone and do so in the proper way. Although modern readers might find this answer rather dissatisfying, for ancient Judahites it would have seemed quite logical. And it is not like there were other, more realistic options readily available to them. So the prophetic books, along with the narratives in Kings and Chronicles, likely served to reduce anxiety about the future, not just by explaining the past and by explaining how to avoid a repeat, but also by plotting out a path towards restoration and even providing a vision of a utopian future for those who heeded the tradents' messages. It seems that the perceived correctness of the prophets' predictions about judgment would have given the audience confidence that their predictions about the future were just as correct.

Additionally, the adoption of the worldview propagated by the texts now collected in the Hebrew Bible would have had further implications for leadership in Yehud. Any individual, but particularly individuals among the leadership, who did not espouse the "correct" worldview would have been equated with the leadership of the past who had opposed the prophets' worldview. This means that any priest or other religious functionary serving a deity other than Yahweh would have been delegitimized. Every temple devoted to Baal or another god was delegitimized from the perspective of the tradents of these books. This obviously could have had economic implications as well. The number of devotees bringing offerings to Yahweh would have presumably risen, perhaps only marginally, or gradually over a long period of time, but it would have risen nonetheless. Thus, priests serving Yahweh, particularly in Jerusalem, would have been receiving more grain and meat, and not just any grain or meat, but that of the highest quality (cf. the oracles remembered in Mal 1 about the quality of the offerings being brought to Yahweh/the priests of Yahweh). As mentioned above, this likely had implications for the size and health of their families and even impacted on successive generations within these priestly families.

Now, I do not want to be too cynical here. I do not think the scribal tradents in Yehud are thinking consciously that by promoting the worldview of the prophets of old they will bring in more resources for the temple for which they likely worked. They were probably pious individuals who genuinely believed that what they wrote was true. But the net effect of their message placed some groups of individuals at a significant material and social advantage over others in the community and did so in a way that ensured a continued imbalance in legitimacy and access to economic and cultural capital for many generations.

In sum, then, I think it might be fruitful to pursue a continued analysis of the shaping and re-shaping of memories contained in the Hebrew Bible as a form of ancient propaganda, as texts containing information that appears to have been rather effective in constructing and perpetuating a hegemonic worldview insisting on exclusive devotion to Yahweh, a worldview that then had a significant impact on the distribution of power and resources in Yehud (Judea).

Acknowledgement

I would like to thank Professors Ehud Ben Zvi and Diana Edelman for the invitation to contribute to this volume as well as for their helpful comments and suggestions to improve the quality of the essay during the revision process.

Bibliography

Assis, E. 2008. "The Temple in the Book of Haggai." *JHebS* 8: 1–10.

Bos, J. M. 2013. *Reconsidering the Date and Provenance of the Book of Hosea: The Case for Persian-Period Yehud*. LHBOTS 580. New York: Bloomsbury.

Carey, C. 2005. "Propaganda and Competition in Athenian Oratory." In *The Manipulative Mode: Political Propaganda in Antiquity: A Collection of Case Studies*, edited by K. A. E. Enenkel and I. L. Pfeijffer, 65–100. Leiden: Brill.

Cooley, J. L. 2014. "Propaganda, Prognostication, and Planets." In *Divination, Politics, and Ancient Near Eastern Empires*, edited by A. Lenzi and J. Stökl, 7–31. ANEM 7. Atlanta, GA: SBL.

Cunningham, S. *The Idea of Propaganda: A Reconstruction*. Westport, CT: Praeger, 2002.

Edelman, D. V. and E. Ben Zvi, eds. 2013. *Remembering Biblical Figures in the Late Persian and Early Hellenistic Periods: Social Memory and Imagination*. Oxford: Oxford.

Ellul, J. 1965. *Propaganda: The Formation of Men's Attitudes*. Translated by K. Kellen and J. Lerner. New York: Knopf.

Enenkel, K. A. E. and I. L. Pfeijffer. 2005. "Introduction." In *The Manipulative Mode: Political Propaganda in Antiquity: A Collection of Case Studies*, edited by K. A. E. Enenkel and I. L. Pfeijffer, 1–12. Leiden: Brill.

Herman, E. S. and N. Chomsky. 1998. *Manufacturing Consent: The Political Economy of the Mass Media*. New York: Pantheon Books.

Jowett, G. S. and V. O'Donnell. 1999. *Propaganda and Persuasion*. 3rd ed. London: Sage Publications.

Kirk, A. 2005. "Social and Cultural Memory." In *Memory, Tradition, and Text: Uses of the Past in Early Christianity*, edited by A. Kirk and T. Thatcher, 1–24. Atlanta, GA: SBL.

Lasswell, H. D., D. Lerner, and H. Speier, eds. 1979. *Propaganda and Communication in World History: Volume 1: The Symbolic Instrument in Early Times*. Honolulu: University Press of Hawaii.

Swartz, D. 1997. *Culture and Power: The Sociology of Pierre Bourdieu*. Chicago, IL: University of Chicago Press.

Taylor, P. M. 2003. *Munitions of the Mind: A History of Propaganda from the Ancient World to the Present Day*. 3rd ed. Manchester: Manchester.

Zerubavel, E. 1997. *Social Mindscapes: An Invitation to Cognitive Sociology*. Cambridge, MA: Harvard University Press.

— 4 —

Mystified Authority:
Legitimating Leadership Through "Lost Books"

Kåre Berge

Biblical scholars agree that the Persian and early Hellenistic periods were pivotal in the production of biblical books.[1] A much more disputed question is how the books relate to Judahite, post-exilic leadership.[2] It seems clear that the authors belonged to a rather small group of literati that appeared as cultural elites. Were these literati themselves part of the religious-political leadership in Yehud? Do they represent other, possibly illiterate leaders, not being leaders themselves? We cannot presume that the scribes were all in the service of (religious and political) leadership.[3] We do not even know if the authority system that we possibly may read out of the books represents established facts in Yehud, counter-factual ideas of leadership, or marginal and contested leadership. Do the books represent people outside the present leadership system, who intended to make a case for their position?[4]

Biblical books, especially Deuteronomy, vest authority in the text rather than in social groups. On this point, T. Eskenazi is correct.[5] This, however, does not invalidate the idea

---

1. This article was first presented at the EABS meeting in 2013, then again in a revised form at a workshop at the Centre for Advanced Study (CAS) in Oslo, organized by the group "Local Dynamics of Globalization." It is here reworked for the present topic. I thank the participants and especially Birgit Meyer, Utrecht University, for useful comments, and Diana Edelman, University of Oslo and CAS, for multiple conversations on this and related topics.

2. Needless to say, there are a number of works dedicated to studies of biblical books as ideological legitimations of social / religious institutions and leadership, see for instance the recent M. Lynch, *Monotheism and Institutions in the Book of Chronicles*, FAT 2/64 (Tübingen: Mohr Siebeck, 2014). See his conclusions about the stable priesthood and its authority in pp. 205–6.

3. This is argued, with reference to literature, by M. A. Christian, "Priestly Power that Empowers: Michel Foucault, Middle-tier Levites, and the Sociology of 'Popular Religious Groups' in Israel," *JHebS* 9 (2009): 1–81 n. 49.

4. For other discussions in this volume of the social setting, role, and motivations of the literati, see the essays by E. Ben Zvi ("Memory and Political Thought in the Late Persian/early Hellenistic Yehud/Judah: Some Observations"), J. M. Bos ("Memories of Judah's Past Leaders Utilized as Propaganda in Yehud"), and T. M. Bolin ("At the Hands of Foreign Kings: Divine Endorsement of Foreign Rulers in the Hebrew Bible in the Memory of Persian and Hellenistic Yehud").

5. T. C. Eskenazi, "The Missions of Ezra and Nehemiah," in *Judah and the Judeans in the Persian Period*, ed.

that biblical books legitimate (claims to) leadership authority. Eskenazi's claim that the Torah demystifies the priests' role and broadens religious and political authority at the expense of priests and other elites should be qualified if not questioned, as should the idea of an egalitarian community.[6] The connection between a claimed egalitarian or "democratic" idea in Deuteronomy and the pre-exilic *'am ha'areṣ*, argued by F. Crüsemann, presupposes the pre-exilic dating, which lacks convincing arguments.[7] Even when it is clear that texts like Deuteronomy ground the law in some kind of metaphysical reality,[8] this serves as a legitimizing device for some social agents. Scholars commonly agree that Deuteronomy engages in discussion about leadership. It is reasonable to presume that this book, at the very least, legitimates a leadership group ("the Priestly Levites") as responsible for and in charge of the literary Torah.[9] As M. Christian points out, data in Deuteronomy

---

M. Oeming and O. Lipschitz (Winona Lake, IN: Eisenbrauns, 2006), 509–29 (512).

6. See also M. G. Brett, "National Identity as Commentary and as Metacommentary," in *Historiography and Identity (Re)formulation in Second Temple Historiographical Literature*, ed. L. Jonker, LHBOTS 534 (New York: T&T Clark, 2010), 29–40 (32).

7. F. Crüsemann, *Die Tora: Theologie und Sozialgeschichte des alttestamentlichen Gesetzes* (Munich: Kaiser, 1992), 248–51 and the succeeding chapters. His idea is that the deuteronomic law and the "actual folk-sovereignty" which he claims to be articulated in Deuteronomy, should reflect the political initiative of "the Judean country-folk" in the century after the military reduction of Judah in 701. His major argument is the law of the tithes in Deuteronomy, which "protects the Israelite farmers from being indebted to anyone except the liberating God itself ..." (258; author's own translations of all thee quotations). For a similar conclusion about the date of the tithing laws, see also J. R. Lundbom, *Deuteronomy: A Commentary* (Grand Rapids, MI: Eerdmans, 2013), 502. See also P. Altmann, *Festive Meals in Ancient Israel: Deuteronomy's Identity Politics in Their Ancient Near Eastern Context*, BZAW 424 (Berlin: de Gruyter, 2011), chapters 5 and 6. This is a possible, but to my mind unwarranted claim. It seems clear that the tithing law goes against what could be accepted by a royal (imperial) government (the king is absent from the tithe, the Israelites are to eat their taxes, Altmann p. 226). These scholars do not explain convincingly how a practice of missing payment to the imperial king would be tolerated during Assyrian vassalship. Furthermore, their conclusion presupposes that there is a direct relationship between the book and social reality, which is an unwarranted presumption. Deuteronomy may be a visionary or utopian description of an ideal society, see P. R. Davies, "The Authority of Deuteronomy," in *Deuteronomy–Kings as Emerging Authoritative Books: A Conversation*, ed. D. V. Edelman, ANEM 5 (Atlanta, GA: SBL, 2014), 27–48. See also my article, "Literacy, Utopia and memory: Is There a Public Teaching in Deuteronomy?" *JHebS* 12 (2012): 1–19. The visionary or utopian interpretation explains much better the possibility of the missing payment to the imperial king. C. L. Crouch has offered valid, fundamental criticism of the proposed relationship between Deuteronomy and the Assyrian vassal treaties, which undercuts previous arguments that have located the Deuteronomic laws in the Assyrian period (*Israel and the Assyrians: Deuteronomy, the Succession Treaty of Esarhaddon, and the Nature of Subversion*, ANEM 8 (Atlanta, GA: SBL, 2014). We do not know if the Persians really used the Second Temple for tax collection purposes (contra J. Schaper, "The Jerusalem Temple as an Instrument of the Achaemenid Fiscal Administration," *VT* 45 [1995]: 528–39). If not, it would have been easier for the authors of Deuteronomy to imagine the tithes as elements of "Israelite" festival meals.

8. So Brett, "National Identity as Commentary and as Metacommentary," 39.

9. See M. Leuchter, "Coming to Terms with Ezra's Many Identities in Ezra-Nehemiah," in *Historiography and Identity (Re)formulation in Second Temple Historiographical Literature*, ed. L. Jonker, LHBOTS 534 (London: T&T Clark, 2010), 41–64 (55). At least in their treatment of Ezra-Nehemiah, scholars believe that there was some kind of cooperation between the dissemination and interpretation of the literary tradition by the Levites and the central political and religious power; see Christian, "Priestly Power that Empowers: Michel Foucault, Middle-tier Levites, and the Sociology of 'Popular Religious Groups' in Israel," footnote 74 and Leuchter (right above). This has to be the group of Levites that L. Jonker calls the "the technical Levites," see L. Jonker, "David's Officials According to the Chronicler (1 Chronicles 23–27): A Reflection of Second Temple Self-Categorization?" in *Historiography and Identity (Re)formula-*

"points to Levites playing a significant role in promoting a new concept of leadership."[10] So, regardless of whether this refers to factually established social structures or to "utopian" or visionary, ideological ideas, Deuteronomy legitimates leadership by the leaders' relation to the biblical book. This is the reason why I select this text as my primary object of study.

There are discussions of how Deuteronomy actually envisions the leadership position of the Levites. Some think that the book relegates them from temple service to subordinated positions. The negative remarks about the Levites in Deut 31:24–27 also point in this direction. This paper offers no historiographical proposition about post-exilic Judahite leaders. Also, it offers no new exegesis of biblical texts. It attempts to present one way in which some biblical books, first and foremost Deuteronomy, could possibly legitimate leadership authority. What mechanisms are at work when "books" legitimate social power? As A. Cohen has demonstrated in his studies of the formation of informal authority systems, one important factor is some kind of mystification.[11] In this paper, I will combine this idea with the anthropological theory of mimesis and alterity. I apply this to my material in order to understand how representations of lost books can make these very representations an embodied encounter with the biblical divinity for those confronted with them; that is, how mimesis and alterity legitimize and authorize these writings as "divine" books. In turn, this legitimizes leadership.

The Idea of Lost Books

Among the lost scrolls in the Hebrew Bible, there are three or four that attract my interest. The first is the scroll that was eaten by a prophet (Ezek 2–3); the second is the one that

---

tion in Second Temple Historiographical Literature, ed. L. Jonker, LHBOTS 534 (New York and London: T&T Clark, 2010), 65–92 (86–87). See also Christian, "Priestly Power that Empowers," 53. At least in Deuteronomy, the ideology places the Levitical scribes in a social position that takes over functions normally attributed to the king. Hence, it is clear that at this point, the reference to the book legitimates (claimed, at least) leadership. J. Berquist postulates that the Dtr History was first produced by Persian imperial scribes for archival means, not meant to be read. At some point (Berquist does not speculate on the date, but logically after the rebuilding of the Temple), the archival copy stored in the Second Temple was read by the scribes, this time as a narrative instead of (an archived) object, see J. L. Berquist, "Identities and Empire: Historiographic Questions for the Deuteronomistic History in the Persian Period," in Historiography and Identity (Re)formulation in Second Temple Historiographical Literature, ed. L. Jonker, LHBOTS 534 (New York: T&T Clark, 2010), 3–14 (9–10). I find this hypothesis strange in addition to being unsupported. The reference to Polaski's article on stone inscriptions is irrelevant, as inscriptions like this and other wall inscriptions may have served a specific purpose in coffins and burial chambers, but such functions are difficult to find in archives of the empire. In addition, the length of the narrative(s) in the Dtr History exceeds by far those inscriptions (e.g., the Deir Allah inscriptions).

10. Christian, "Priestly Power that Empowers," 55. For reasons that I cannot go into here, I do not agree with his dating of the relevant texts to the monarchic (Josianic) time. I see it as more plausible to date the relevant texts to post-exilic, possibly Persian time. See also p. 57: the biblical text "authorizes Levites to try cases in lieu of the monarch," and p. 61: Deuteronomy proposes the Levitical priests as the future leaders of Israel's official religion.

11. A. Cohen, Custom and Politics in Urban Africa: A Study of Hausa Migrants in Yoruba Towns (London: Routledge, 2004); idem, The Politics of Elite Culture: Explorations in the Dramaturgy of Power in a Modern African Society (Berkeley: University of California Press, 1981); idem, Two-Dimensional Man: An Essay on the Anthropology of Power and Symbolism in Complex Societies (London: Routledge & Kegan Paul, 1974). For two other studies in this volume that deal with different kinds of informal or non-official leadership, see Anne Fitzpatrick-McKinley, "Models of Local Political Leadership in the Nehemiah Memoir," and Anne-Mareike Schol-Wetter, "Judith Maccabee? On Leadership, Resistance, and the Great Deeds of Little People."

was burnt by an obstinate king (Jer 36); the third scroll was found during the renovation of the temple (2 Kgs 22–23) and stemmed from remote time; and finally is the scroll put beside the Ark of the Covenant (Deut 31), which may be the same as the third one, which triggered the renovation of the cult. The point is, the first two are lost, but we know their contents from a copy, from a replica, or otherwise from the presentations of it by the biblical books of Ezekiel or Jeremiah. In the case of Deuteronomy and 2 Kgs 22–23, it is slightly different, but the result is the same: Second Kings does not say anything about the removal of the Ark and the scroll at the capture of Jerusalem. There is no mention of the Ark or the scroll in the biblical story of the rebuilding of the Temple. We do not know if there was any Ark at the time of the Second Temple.[12] In the *fiction*, it belongs to the pre-exilic Temple. In any case, again according to the *fiction*, the original Scroll, placed beside the Ark, is invisible to the public, and if it still was there in the Persian–period Temple, it was accessible only to the High Priest once a year.

So, there is something about the physicality of scrolls that were there, got lost, and are replicated in the new physicality of the biblical texts. It is this aspect of biblical texts as "things" on which I want to reflect, that is, how these physical objects create an embodied encounter with "divine alterity"—an expression I will return to—and how they make the sacred present. It is inspired by recent studies on how "things" mediate belief. How do we interpret these ideas of lost and represented scrolls in light of the "new materiality?"

The so-called "thingly turn" is a subset of "the material turn" in humanities and social sciences since the mid-1980s (e.g., B. Meyer and D. Morgan). In studies of antiquity, it is represented by studies of the "agency" of archaeological artifacts and art; and it has been introduced into the anthropology of religion by a number of scholars, for instance, as phenomenology of embodiment.[13] So far, its benefit for exegetical studies of the Bible has been less explored. There are two sets of questions in "the thingly turn."

The first relates to the catchwords of agency and index. We may choose to regard biblical texts as agents or rather, as material indexes. This means that they appear as material (visible, physical) entities that motivate inferences, responses, or interpretations by their recipients, or as an entity from which the observer can make a casual inference.[14] This aspect of inference-making is particularly important in regard to biblical texts. In other words, as "things," biblical texts appear as persons—that is, in a social-relational sense. Following another expression by A. Gell, a "thingly reading" of biblical texts is an analysis of *apparently irrational* behavior in relation to these texts. By irrational, I mean, e.g., social acts like veneration or other acts of piety. Such behavior is, of course, basically inacces-

---

12. It is difficult to judge about the *historical reality* of the post-exilic description of the Solomonic temple in the Priestly source. Does it reflect a post-exilic existence of the Ark in the temple? Does Deut 31 indicate a similar existence of the Ark of the Covenant, the tablets, and the Scroll, in post-exilic time? Josephus (in *Contra Apionem* Book I) states that there was no picture in the temple, only two altars and a candle; see M. Köckert, "Vom Kultbild Jahwes zum Bilderverbot," *Zeitschrift für Theologie und Kirche* 106 (2009): 371–406. Does the fierce argument against pictures in Deut 4, which possibly is post-exilic, indicate the factual presence of a picture of Yahweh in the temple? See idem, "Die Entstehung der Bilderverbot," in *Die Welt der Götterbilder*, ed. H. Spieckermann and B. Groneberg, BZAW 376 (Berlin: de Gruyter, 2007), 272–90 (288–90).

13. S. R. Steadman and J. Ross, eds., *Agency and Identity in the Ancient Near East* (London: Equinox, 2010); A. Gell, *Art and Agency: An Anthropological Theory* (Oxford: Oxford University Press, 1998); M. A. Vásquez, *More Than Belief: A Materialist Theory of Religion* (Oxford: Oxford University Press, 2011).

14. Gell, *Art and Agency*, ix, 9, 13, especially pp. 17–19.

sible in biblical study because we do not know how intended or actual ancient audiences reacted, but we can, to a certain extent, look at how later biblical editors and authors have reacted to a text. Gell, picking up the term from U. Eco, uses the word "abduction" for this inference-drawing: as an index, the biblical text is not "language" in the sense that one reads it according to linguistic models; its semiotic value lies more in the area of "social others." That means the inferences we draw are more logical than linguistic: the texts are treated as if they had "physiognomies" like people.[15]

There is intentionality in the concept of agency. Agency is primarily a notion applied to the human capacity for motivated, reflexive action (e.g., what goal did an individual intend to achieve by this building or that text?), and only secondarily and metaphorically attributed to things. "Intention" as a mental act is connected with biblical texts only as something attributed to them by so-called "primary agents," that is, reading or listening persons. On the other hand, studies of ancient Mesopotamia show that they held rather a strong view regarding the capacity for objects to exert agency.[16] So, at least one should define agency as something taking place in the interaction between humans and texts. People may be "patients" in relation to texts as things; they may "suffer" from the texts. Or to put it in the words of P. Pels, to be responsive to a biblical text's agency is to suffer from it.[17] Pels also states that as material agents, biblical texts are underdetermined with regard to meaning.

The second question or aspect of "the thingly turn" in relation to biblical texts relates to representation, or rather resembling, supposing that the texts are depictions of an imaginary thing, God, or rather, God's appearance.[18] Of course, the texts are aniconic representations that require special interpretation. Following D. Houtman and B. Meyer, the question is how "the 'beyond' to which religious texts refer (call it the transcendental, spiritual, or invisible) is rendered tangible and becomes present in the world," that is, how the biblical texts as material objects make the sacred present.[19] In this connection, Houtman and Meyer also state that "what features as material or immaterial depends on socially shared, authorized discourses or [...] 'semiotic ideologies'." So, what kind of semiotic ideology do we face in the biblical texts of this paper? The fact that the Law of Moses and the words of God are rendered in material form indicates that the semiotic ideology does not simply code the material stuff as basically immaterial.[20]

Our first step is to ask: how are literacy, writing, and book scrolls regarded and esteemed in the culture of the Hebrew Scriptures? It is reasonable to think that in general, at some stage of the religion-history behind the Hebrew bible, the Torah scroll replaced the origi-

---

15. Gell, *Art and Agency*, 15.
16. M. H. Feldman, "Object Agency? Spatial Perspective, Social Relations, and the Stele of Hammurabi," in *Agency and Identity in the Ancient Near East*, ed. S. R. Steadman and J. Ross, Approaches to Anthropological Archaeology (London: Equinox, 2010), 148–65 (150) with references.
17. P. Pels, "The Modern Fear of Matter: Reflections on the Protestantism of Victorian Science," in *Things: Religion and the Question of Materiality*, ed. D. Houtman and B. Meyer (New York: Fordham University Press, 2012), 27–39 (29–30). One can compare and contrast here the understanding of texts as propaganda discussed in the essay in this volume by J. M. Bos, "Memories of Judah's Past Leaders Utilized as Propaganda in Yehud."
18. Gell, *Art and Agency*, 25.
19. B. Meyer and D. Houtman, "Introduction: Material Religion - How Things Matter," in *Things: Religion and the Question of Materiality*, ed. D. Houtman and B. Meyer (New York: Fordham University Press, 2012), 1–26 (7).
20. For the terminology, see Meyer and Houtman, "Introduction," 18.

nal image of Yahweh in the ark.[21] On the other hand, one should consider the possibility that the utopian vision of Deuteronomy and the Prophets downplays the material aspect by reducing material evidence to signs of an immaterial future.[22] I am focusing on the materiality of biblical texts, that is, adhering to the physicality of the texts, in the double meaning of scroll and their visual appearance. My issue is with the Bible as an elite product: How did the literati work so as to create an embodied encounter with the biblical divinity for those confronted with the book, to make their theology or religious positions a lived "structuration?"[23] How are we to understand biblical texts as world-making practice?[24]

What is the Meaning of Lost Books?

In the book of Ezekiel, the eaten book may or may not be a book within the book. In the Jeremiah story and in Deuteronomy and 2 Kgs 22–23, there is a book within the book, to borrow an expression from J. P. Sonnet.[25] Obviously, there is something about lost books that are witnessed only through the present books of the Bible. What is the semiotic meaning of these lost books? This is a pragmatic question, which looks at how religion, in this case a biblical scroll, *works*. From one point of view, these lost books legitimize the written ones, giving them a "canonical" authority. The original scrolls were from God (Ezek 2–3), from Moses and God (Deut 31), from the remote past (2 Kgs 22–23), or from the mouth of Jeremiah the prophet communicated to his messenger Baruch (Jer 36).

---

21. K. van der Toorn, *The Image and the Book: Ionic Cults, Aniconism, and the Rise of Book Religion in Israel and the Ancient Near East* (Leuven: Peeters, 1997).

22. See Pels, "Modern Fear of Matter," 39.

23. J. C. Ross and S. R. Steadman, "Agency and Identity in the Ancient Near East: New Paths Forward," in *Agency and Identity in the Ancient Near East*, ed. S. R. Steadman and J. C. Ross, Approaches to Anthropological Archaeology (London: Equinox, 2010), 1–10 (1).

24. There is no reason to think that literacy was spread beyond small elite groups, see I. M. Young, "Israelite Literacy: Interpreting the Evidence," *VT* 48 (1998): 239–53, 408–22. Also, there are reasons to think that the "book religion" of Deuteronomy was not widespread before the Hellenistic period; see K. L. Noll, "Was There Doctrinal Dissemination in Early Yahweh Religion?" *BibInt* 16 (2008): 395–427. In another article ("Literacy, Utopia and Memory: Is there a Public Teaching in Deuteronomy?"), I have argued that the picture of a reading community (6:7–9) is a late addition; see also J. van Seters, "The Origin of the Hebrew Bible: Some New Answers to Old Questions," *Journal of Ancient Near Eastern Religions* 7 (2007): 87–108, 219–37. In my same article, I argue the idea of a public teaching in Deuteronomy is a utopia of a society of scribes. Remarks about the oral presentation of Deuteronomy, 4:1; 5:1; 31:11–12 (van Seters, "Origin of the Hebrew Bible," 99) do not contradict this, as it attests to the fact that speaking and hearing was the normal communicative form in the society at the time of the text's origin. Cognitive research on religion indicates that the kind of monotheism or "doctrinal religion" presented in Deuteronomy is not part of what P. Boyer calls the "cognitive optimum" and will need special action for survival; see Noll, "Was There Doctrinal Dissemination?," 410, 15; I. Pyysiäinen, *How Religion Works: Towards a New Cognitive Science of Religion* (Leiden: Brill, 2003). There are many studies of how the elite were being educated in the written texts of the Bible. D. M. Carr has focused on how the biblical texts "were part of a cultural project of incising key cultural-religious traditions—word for word—on people's mind," see D. M. Carr, *Writing on the Tablet of the Heart: Origins of Scripture and Literature* (Oxford: Oxford University Press, 2005), 8, 10. This is what he calls "enculturation" of the elite scribal class, and the aspect he focuses on is the education of "long-duration texts" of the bible. However, his focus, as is that of many others, is the technical side of the transmission and production of literary texts. My focus is somewhat different, as they do not aim at understanding the feelings, senses, and belief that the texts "intend" to inculcate in the addressees.

25. J.-P. Sonnet, *The Book within the Book: Writing in Deuteronomy*, BibInt 14 (Leiden: Brill, 1997).

The prophet Ezekiel *eats* the scroll in 2:9–10 and 3:1–3: "Cause your belly to eat, and your bowels, fill (it) with this scroll." He is physically mixing it with bodily fluid and transforming it into digested matter. There is a similar case in Jer 15:16. I doubt that the "eaten" words are literally the words being communicated in the now available biblical books. There is nothing about the digested book being "spit" out again, as some scholars think. The eaten words authorize the prophets. They have been informed by God, but the words they "ate" are not substantially the same as they proclaim through the books. There is distance and maybe approximation, but no direct similarity, not to say identity. It is this approximation that is my first issue. It has been claimed that this "eating" is a sign of the prophet's obedience.[26] This only partially explains the case. The "eating of words" corresponds to what the anthropologist P. Stoller has described from the Songhay people of the Republic of Niger. To be eaten by words, or to eat the words, means to learn.[27] Similarly, one "eats power," meaning that words both empower and overpower one's body. Stoller writes:

> In many North and West African societies learning is understood not in terms of "reading" and "writing," but in the gustatory terms of bodily consumption. This means that body and being are fused in consumptive or gustatory metaphors. Human beings eat and are eaten. People are transformed through their internal digestive processes.[28]

The griots in Sahelian West Sahara "eat history" and thus are "owned" by the words they have ingested. They have been mastered by words, he says, or by history, that is, the story about the past.[29]

We may gain support for this interpretation from the cognitive study of tradition and authoritative specialists in divination by P. Boyer. He argues that truth in traditional, formalized speech (ritual and divination) is linked to its surface properties, its iconic aspect, its property as phonic event, its material occurrence.[30] According to Boyer, the criteria of traditional truth is not that some people have acquired an accurate representation of a certain domain of reality; rather, there is "a link between the realities described and the utterance." The setting for this, in Boyer's presentation, is divination and initiation; "the crucial element in the ritual is […] the fact that the candidates have been 'exposed' to the power or influence of the ancestors."[31] This is "the causal criteria." Boyer states: "Divination in itself is not a guarantee of veracity, no more than initiation rites in themselves make people truthful. The point is that such elements can become criteria of truth only if the listeners have specific assumptions about the way the utterances are produced."[32]

If this is relevant also in regard to the biblical texts, I would conclude that the textual authority of the books I am studying is a statement about the way the book is produced: it is regarded as authoritative by those who accept the book because it links the reality

---

26. M. Greenberg, *Ezechiel 1–20*, HThKAT (Freiburg: Herder, 2001), 79.
27. P. Stoller, *Sensuous Scholarship* (Philadelphia: University of Philadelphia Press, 1997), 47.
28. Stoller, *Sensuous Scholarship*, 6.
29. Stoller's view of the preservation (or actually re-creation) of oral tradition is similar to the Parry and Lord model, which sees every new performance as a re-creation, keeping the structure invariable but altering the content (*Sensuous Scholarship*, 32, 63).
30. P. Boyer, *Tradition as Truth and Communication* (Cambridge: Cambridge University Press, 1994), 88. For the succeeding presentation, see pp. 97–100.
31. Boyer, *Tradition as Truth*, 98.
32. Boyer, *Tradition as Truth*, 100.

described in the book with the utterances of the book. Those accepting the authority of the books have certain assumptions about the way the utterances are produced.

In the books of Ezekiel and Jeremiah, the prophets are "owned" by the word of God, but what they "spit out" is not identical with the words they have been eating. The eaten book is not similar to the message spoken by the prophet and written down; it is the device that makes the prophet "another person," giving him authority, making him a person taught by God, a God-learned man. On the other hand, the prophets imitate God. Seen from the opposite perspective and regarding prophetic activity as some sort of mimicry of God, the prophet's activity has a spiritual "God-copy" out there.[33] This idea of something similar but not identical corresponds to the play on likeness and appearance in Ezekiel, e.g., in 1:26: "and upon the shape of a throne there was the shape like the appearance of a man." In this regard, there is an idea of approximation in Ezekiel that later in this paper I will interpret in terms of a theory of mimesis and alterity.

The materiality or bodily aspect of the prophet Ezekiel's eating becomes clear in the succeeding text, which describes the prophet's fate very physically: it causes the prophet's forehead to be harder than flint. The spirit will "set him on his feet," they will "put ropes upon him and bind him," and God will make his tongue cling to his palate, but he will also open the prophet's mouth. All this stands in the same line as what Stoller described about the African society he studied.

And still there is something similar about the physicality of all these lost but re-presented books. I am not posing the theological question of authority but the anthropological one, or maybe one should call it a question of the hermeneutics of authority: What is it about this relation between the lost original and the copies that gives the copies—just that, I think—their "authoritative" function? What kind of authority is this? What is it that creates the *sense* of a sacred authority in the audience? There is something about the mysterious, but how to access it? There is something about mimesis, but how to make sense of it? My focus is not on the formal authority of the re-created books but on their sacral functionality, the way they work as religious texts.

The idea of these lost books seems to be different from "The books of the kings of Israel and Judah" that we meet in Chronicles (e.g., 1 Chr 9:1; 2 Chr 16:11, 27:7), and even the דברי שלמה in 2 Chr 9:29, which was written, כתובים על דברי נתן הנביא, giving the text an authoritative aura.[34] The text-centered community behind these late books needed to legitimize their understanding as "exegetes of Scriptures,"[35] but there is no focus here on the physicality of those pre-existing books. In Neh 8, the physicality is an issue, but there is no idea of a lost book.[36] So, what interests me is this combined idea of the lost book as a physical object. This is explicit in Ezekiel and Jer 36 but implicit also in Deuteronomy and 2 Kings, because one would know that the originals had disappeared with the Ark when the temple was destroyed or were hidden from the public behind the walls of the Second Temple.

---

33. M. Taussig, *Mimesis and Alterity: A Particular History of the Senses* (London: Routledge, 1993), 100 speaks of a mimetic world where things have spirit-copies.

34. See J. Blenkinsopp, "Ideology and Utopia in 1–2 Chronicles," in *What Was Authoritative for Chronicles?* ed. E. Ben Zvi and D. V. Edelman (Winona Lake, IN: Eisenbrauns, 2011), 99.

35. E. Ben Zvi, "One Size Does Not Fit All: Observations on the Different Ways That Chronicles Dealt with the Authoritative Literature of Its Times," in *What Was Authoritative for Chronicles?* ed. E. Ben Zvi and D. V. Edelman (Winona Lake, IN: Eisenbrauns, 2011), 13–35 (31).

36. J. C. Vanderkam, *From Revelation to Canon: Studies in the Hebrew Bible and Second Temple Literature* (Leiden: Brill, 2000), 5.

In order to understand the representation of lost books, I will focus on the issue of copies of the original, which brings me to the theory of mimesis and copy, and then, at the end, with memory, in fact, mimetic memory. It is evident that the idea of a pattern and its copy, or its *Vorbild* and its *Abbild*, is a religious essential in the Hebrew Bible. Thus, Moses sees a תבנית ('pattern',) in heaven, which is the model for the earthly sanctuary, the Tabernacle or Tent of Meeting in the desert, Exod 25:9, 40. And similarly, David, as a new Moses so to speak,[37] draws up a תבנית for the Solomonic temple, 1 Chr 28:11–19, see also 2 Chr 35:4, 15. In a similar vein, the idols are just this in Deut 4:16–18 and Isa 44:13. In Ezek 8:3, 10 and 10:8, the religious items ("things") are images or copies or better, representations (obviously two-dimensional, so they are not quite like or identical with) of animals and other things. I have also mentioned the idea of "likeness of similarity" in Ezekiel. To my mind, the idea of original and copy in my four texts must be interpreted within this field of original and copy, which seems to be an important characteristic of religious matters ("things"). What does that mean to our understanding of the religious "semiotic ideology?"

The theoretical line goes from J. Frazer through W. Benjamin, T. Adorno, and M. Taussig. This leads me to what they call the mimetic faculty.[38] One is able to grasp that which is strange, other, through resemblances, through copies of it. Benjamin calls the mimetic faculty the original compulsion of persons to become and behave like something else. In other words, the ability to imitate gives access to the world. T. Adorno states that the anthropological grounding of human nature is indissolubly linked to imitation.[39] The ability to mime is the capacity to Other. Walter Benjamin refers to mimicry in dance, cosmologies, and in divinations revealed by the entrails of animals and constellations of stars. I think we could add also the mimetic act of writing down "copies" of originally received but lost or "eaten" divine books! Copying and the mimesis processing of lost books creates a sense of getting hold of it, and at the same time it avoids the delusion of a presence of that which is being remembered and reproduced. To put it simply, it is there, but it is not really there!

Admittedly, a first look at the book of Deuteronomy seems to contradict this sense of distance and estrangement. Deuteronomy stresses "today" and the formula, "not with your fathers but with you, who are here today." It also lacks any story of how the generation of the Deuteronomic story submits to the covenant expressed in Deut 28, which many scholars interpret as a challenge to the readers to submit themselves to the same covenant. However, the basic framework of Deuteronomy is a story about past events. Those directly addressed in the story world belong to a lost time and listened to the text of a scroll now lost. So, the problem is to find the right balance between this historical memory and the deictic "today." Too often, commentators have taken the "today" at face value, applying the admonitions directly to the readers of the book of Deuteronomy. Also, one could argue that the "canon formula" in, e.g., Josh 1:7, indicates direct identity. However, this is related to the person (in the fiction) reading the "book within the book," not to the book as read by the (post-exilic) readers.

How, then, should we describe the relationship between the readers of Deuteronomy and its "today," and what is its effect? One should relate this to the sensorial mode of thinking. Listening to the texts or reading them, which means looking at the biblical texts, is

---

37. Ben Zvi, "One Size Does Not Fit All," 31.
38. Stoller, *Sensuous Scholarship*, 66.
39. A. Huyssen, *Present Pasts: Urban Palimpsests and the Politics of Memory* (Stanford, CA: Stanford University Press, 2003), 123.

to impute agency to them; that is, if not intention and will, then at least, to put it in the words of B. Latour, to make the biblical texts talk; that is, to produce scripts of what they are making people do.[40] Seeing or hearing the biblical texts is to see (or hear) another seeing us. This is clear in the notion of witnesses in Deuteronomy, who are watching us, that is, behaving as agents. In Deut 31:26, Moses commands that "this book of the law" be put by the side of the Ark of the Covenant. This book will be a witness against the people, and after having spoken "these words" in the ears of the people, then "I (Yahweh) will call to witness against them heaven and earth" (v. 28). There are three witnesses: the scroll of the book, heaven and earth, and the written song that always will be on their mouth.

"Heaven and earth" as witnesses correlate to the divine witnesses in the ancient Near Eastern covenant tradition. They are not without spiritual power. As witnesses, they watch over the doings of the people. The scroll of the book, by its presence beside the Ark of the Covenant, also watches over the people. It is clear that there is a spiritual presence in it. So, it is a "thing" in the sense of Houtman and Meyer.[41] In this regard, the texts are agents; or rather, they are indexes of divine agency in the world, but the original book of Moses, which was beside the Ark, is lost to the reading community of the book of Deuteronomy and only known through its presentation in the book of Deuteronomy itself, which, I assume they would know, is the work of human agency. So, God's presence in the world is enmeshed in human agency, that is, by the makers of the biblical book. God's appearance or agency is bound to human-made indexes "from which we abduct God's agency over the world."[42] To repeat a point made above, the mimicry of God's words, e.g., in Deuteronomy, implies that God is "trapped" inside the likeness of his words, which makes him a "passive agent." The readers or listeners suffer his words but at the same time he is powerful only through these human representations.

We are dealing with the sensory mode of mimetic approximation. When looking at biblical texts as agents, we apply the sensorial, participatory mode of thinking, not the non-sensorial one of literate thinking that normally characterizes exegetical, literary work. This we do by looking at the texts as "things," in this case books that have been lost and are represented or replicated. In his chapter on Spiegelman's *Maus: A [Holocaust] Survivor's Tale*, A. Huyssen, from whom I have already borrowed, shows how the work creates a mimetic relationship between the traumatic events in the past and those hearing the story, first by the survivor's son and then by the audience of his story; but it is a mimetic *approximation*. The important thing is what he says about the dimensions of mimesis that lie outside linguistic communication:

> [m]imesis in its physiological, somatic dimension is Angleichung, a becoming or making similar, a movement toward, never a reaching of, a goal. It is not identity […] It rather requires us to think identity and nonidentity together as nonidentical similitude and in unresolvable tension with each other.[43]

There is an effect of estrangement in the mimetic approximation that we also can see in the biblical texts above. The picture of eating the scroll, making it taste like honey, and the picture of the old man Moses jogging up and down the mountain make the scenes strange.

---

40. B. Latour, *Reassembling the Social: An Introduction to Actor-Network-Theory*, Clarendon Lectures in Management Studies (Oxford: Oxford University Press, 2005), 80.
41. Meyer and Houtman, "Introduction," 17.
42. Gell, *Art and Agency*, 114.
43. Huyssen, *Present Pasts*, 127.

The Benjamin-Adorno-Taussig-Gell line of thought on mimesis that I have applied here unfolds from Frazer's idea of the magic of similarity and contact in *The Golden Bough*. Applied to the four texts discussed here, this means that the "magic" of the divine word, or the word of the prophet, lies in the similarity between the present written text and the lost "original," the one that emanated from God (either "authored" by God, belonging to ancient time, or the original). Again, as representations of the original books, the biblical books affect "the original to such a degree that the representation shares in or acquires the properties of the represented."[44] It is from the intangible inner aspect that the power comes. But it is the capacity to mime that engenders mastery. The authors of the present books get hold of "the word of God" by means of their likeness without, though, giving up on the Alterity of the divine.

By referring to the eaten book, which affected the senses (taste), there is the strongest appeal to the Otherness of cultural memory. In Jer 36:2, the prophet is told to take a scroll of a book (מגלת ספר) and write on it. The picture is very much related to the book as a physical substance. It (*ha=sefer*) was written in ink. The scroll was read aloud for the king as he was sitting by the fire; and after Yehudi had read "in the ears of the king" three and four columns of the scroll, the king took a scribe's knife, cut it, and threw the whole scroll on the fire (v. 23).

Seeing biblical texts as mimetic products, a mimesis of, for instance, the original, lost, burnt, or eaten book, is to grasp the strange. It corresponds to the strange vision appearing before the eyes of Ezekiel of something that is likened to the image of God's glory. Ezekiel's eating of the book certainly emphasizes the strange, but at the same time, copying the original book also engenders a sense of comprehension, mastery. There is some sensorial aspect here, something connected to sensation.

Finding an old book of divine instruction in the temple is not unknown in ancient literature, as an Egyptian case about Ramsesses IV shows.[45] We know from Mesopotamia and Egypt that the scribes guarded secret knowledge, which, for instance, may have emanated from the mouth of the god Ea. Once deposited in the temple, the tablets there seem to have become the sacred property of the deity of the temple.[46] This idea of secretness, of the hiddenness of the book, is exactly what we meet in Deuteronomy.

If we look at the presentation of the scroll in Deut 31, it is clear that it represents the word of Yahweh and thus, partakes in some kind of sacredness. As such, it also has the fundamentally ambiguous or ambivalent character that characterizes the sacred according to E. Durkheim, R. Otto, and M. Eliade.[47] It is the means by which one can learn to do right and thus receive blessing, but it is also the threatening witness against the people if they do wrong. Jeremy Biles talks about "paramediation." In his presentation, this term "refers to those modes of materiality through which believers take themselves to be in the presence of something heterogeneous, paranormal, or deriving from the beyond."[48] This, he says, refers to "the religious uncanny," also signaling how material mediums

---

44. Taussig, *Mimesis and Alterity*, 47–48, cited also by Gell, *Art and Agency*, 100.

45. D. B. Redford, "Ancient Egyptian Literature: An Overview," in *Civilizations of the Ancient Near East*, ed. J. M. Sasson (Peabody, MA: Hendrickson, 2000), 2223–41 (2225).

46. K. van der Toorn, *Scribal Culture and the Making of the Hebrew Bible* (Cambridge, MA: Harvard University Press, 2007), 64.

47. J. Biles, "Out of This World: The Materiality of the Beyond," in *Religion and Material Culture: The Matter of Belief*, ed. D. Morgan (London: Routledge, 2010), 129–45 (139).

48. Biles, "Out of This World," 139.

"[provoke] intellectual uncertainty" and "recall the dual, ambivalent, or uncertain nature of the religious uncanny."[49] Even more, what he calls the everyday medium saliently embodies "attributes classically associated with the sacred: contradiction, ambivalence, undecidability, or otherness."[50] He thus links the paramediation of the medium with the "inexplicable residue, that surplus of felt meaning, which purely rational accounts of the heterogeneous and paranormal struggle to explain."[51] He talks about the interpenetration of the material with the otherworldly in the lived experiences of the believers.

It is clear that the idea of the scroll of the Law that once existed beside the Ark but is now lost, the Song that has to be in the mouth of the people, and their function as witnesses (together with heaven and earth) contributes to the feeling of the uncanny linked to the book of Deuteronomy itself. In this connection, with M. Vásquez, I am not talking about theological essence but the existential, phenomenological, experiential, and relational; an encounter within a relation.[52]

Biblical Texts as Memories of Lost Books

The special thing about "the book of the Torah of Moses" that he put by the side of the Ark is that, in the exilic and post-exilic era, it did not exist. It was not only hidden, it was not there. It existed only as the book of Deuteronomy itself, which somehow testifies to or represents the "Book of the Torah of Moses" (because Deuteronomy also narrates the writing down of this book, so it contains more than that specific book). Let me proceed along this track by applying another set of theories.

The small book by A. Forty and S. Küchler, *The Art of Forgetting*, has called into question the Aristotelian view of objects and memory, that is, that memories can be transferred to solid material objects that by virtue of their durability can preserve the memories beyond their purely mental existence.[53] The most viable argument is the memory of Holocaust survivors, which shows that the hard thing is not to forget but exactly the opposite. The difficulty is also, they maintain, to make memorials without sanitizing the horror by making it tolerable to remember. Even more generally interesting in my regard is their reference to the French philosopher M. de Certeau.

---

49. Biles, "Out of This World," 139.
50. Biles, "Out of This World," 139.
51. Biles, "Out of This World," 139.
52. Vásquez, *More than Belief*, 114. G. Lynch, "Object Theory: Toward an Intersubjective, Mediated, and Dynamic Theory of Religion," in *Religion and Material Culture: The Matter of Belief*, ed. D. Morgan (London: Routledge, 2010), 36–51 (40) develops his own theory of relations with sacred others: The sacred object is, he says, on one hand an object in a material sense. But the sacred object is also an object in a psychological sense, he says, it is "a dynamic focus for subjective associations and feelings in the mental world of the religious adherent," and he states further "that the relationship with the sacred object can affect the psychological structures and feeling-states of the adherent" (43). This is also developed by Vásquez, who refers to and develops Thomas Csordas's cultural phenomenology of embodiment: in an attempt to liberate the "intimate, spontaneous, and embodied encounter with divine alterity (*More than Belief*, 114) from the subject-object divide, he holds that this is an existential phenomenon; alterity is "the inescapability of our embodied nature" and "what is pre-objective, and thus 'foundational,' is not the sacred as an autonomous reality, as noumena, but the embodied, biological-cultural experience of finitude, of simultaneous intercorporality and estrangement from others and from 'nature,' including our own bodies" (115).
53. A. Forty and S. Küchler, eds., *The Art of Forgetting* (Oxford: Berg, 1999), 2–7.

> For de Certeau, the principal feature of memory is 'that it comes from somewhere else, it is outside of itself, it moves things about,' and that when it ceases to be capable of this alteration, when it becomes fixed to particular objects, then it is in decay. Seen in these terms, objects are the enemy of memory, they are what tie it down and lead to forgetfulness.[54]

If I read de Certeau correctly, he claims that mobilizing memory is inseparable from its being altered; as he says, "memory derives its interventionary force from its very capacity to be altered—unmoored, mobile, lacking any fixed position."[55] De Certeau's point of reference is an event or a circumstance that, in speaking about memory, is something that is lost ("it is only a memory"). The object of memory is remembered only when it has disappeared. What is more interesting here, however, is that memory, as he says, develops a natural ability or "aptitude for always being in the other's place without possessing it, and for profiting from this alteration without destroying it."[56] In regarding memory as coming from somewhere else, outside of itself, of being a sense of the other, memory is something that cannot really be inscribed. In my reading, this is exactly the paradox expressed by the idea that the texts the audience should remember were written down (by Jeremiah and Moses in Deut 31, and probably by God in the case of Ezekiel) and then were to be eaten and digested, lost in the temple's destruction, or burned in the fire. The point is, even when the texts of the lost imprints are recalled or reconstructed and now accessible to the audience of the new texts, there is room not only for estrangement but also for distance, change, creativity—in fact, otherness—when the present texts are read as memories of the divine revelations to Moses, Jeremiah, Ezekiel.

Conclusion

My point here is pragmatic: one aspect of the functionality of the biblical texts is as a legitimating device for leadership in post-exilic Yehud. My point of departure by reading the texts discussed here is that they are all presented as sites of memory: they are discussing the past. This is explicit in Deuteronomy and in the Prophets as well, e.g., "These are the words that came to the prophet in the days of ..." etc. My issue is to understand the hermeneutics of authority in these texts about the past for the reading audience of the biblical texts as they were known in post-exilic time. And for this purpose, I have picked out those three or four texts about the physicality of lost books and their representations by the present biblical books.

Returning now to the "today" formula in Deuteronomy, the biblical text is a site of memory, remembering the first and now lost imprints of God's commandments and Moses's explications and remembering that Moses challenged the Exodus generation to submit to the covenant. But just by reading the present text as a site of memory, the people cannot simply assume the role of the Exodus generation. Because this memory lives as a "responsive alteration" to the presence of the biblical readings, the post-exilic audience cannot simply mechanically adapt the statements in the books but have to work with the tension between the Otherness of the memories in the textual "sites of memory" and the challenges of the readers' present situation.

I will definitely not claim that the texts discussed here are similar to those in Chronicles. But I do think that, in general terms, what this issue of lost and re-presented books does

---

54. Forty and Küchler, *Art of Forgetting*, 2–7.
55. M. de Certeau, *The Practice of Everyday Life* (Berkely: University of California Press, 1984), 86.
56. De Certeau, *Practice of Everyday Life*, 87.

is something similar to what E. Ben Zvi describes in his studies of the Chronicler's use of authoritative books. If I understand Ben Zvi correctly, he holds that the literati who formed Chronicles, at least in some cases, regarded the authoritative books as instantiations or objectifications of "the truly authoritative meaning." He writes:

> This approach [i.e., the Chronicles' approach] to sources involved rejecting readings of books as literary units that bear their respective meanings in and by themselves. The main content and meaning of the transmitted and operative tradition is thus dissociated from the text itself as presented to the originally intended readership of each of these authoritative books.[57]

Our conclusions converge, I think, at the point that "divine authority" is not in the texts themselves but in some kind of meeting with the divine alterity that resides somewhere behind the present biblical texts. In terms of leadership, this strategy of mystification emphasizes Yahweh as the ultimate leader and source of authority for Israel defined as a religious community living within the confines of imperial provinces. Of course, this is not the only way of mystifying religious leadership in the bible, but there are few instances in which mystification happens through ideas of lost books.

Bibliography

Altmann, P. 2011. *Festive Meals in Ancient Israel: Deuteronomy's Identity Politics in Their Ancient Near Eastern Context*. BZAW 424. Berlin: de Gruyter.

Ben Zvi, E. 2011. "One Size Does Not Fit All: Observations on the Different Ways That Chronicles Dealt with the Authoritative Literature of Its Times." In *What Was Authoritative for Chronicles?*, edited by E. Ben Zvi and D. V. Edelman, 13–35. Winona Lake, IN: Eisenbrauns.

Ben Zvi, E., and D. V. Edelman, eds. 2011. *What Was Authoritative for Chronicles?* Winona Lake, IN: Eisenbrauns.

Berge, K. 2012. "Literacy, Utopia and Memory: Is there a Public Teaching in Deuteronomy?" *JHebS* 12(3): 1–19.

Berquist, J. L. 2010. "Identities and Empire: Historiographic Questions for the Deuteronomistic History in the Persian Period." In *Historiography and Identity (Re)formulation in Second Temple Historiographical Literature*, edited by L. Jonker, 3–14. New York: T&T Clark.

Biles, J. 2010. "Out of This World: The Materiality of the Beyond." In *Religion and Material Culture: The Matter of Belief*, edited by D. Morgan, 129–45. London: Routledge.

Blenkinsopp, J. 2011. "Ideology and Utopia in 1–2 Chronicles." In *What Was Authoritative for Chronicles?*, edited by E. Ben Zvi and D. V. Edelman, 89–103. Winona Lake, IN: Eisenbrauns.

Boyer, P. 1994. *Tradition as Truth and Communication*. Cambridge: Cambridge University Press. Repr. 2004.

Brett, M. G. 2010. "National Identity as Commentary and as Metacommentary." In *Historiography and Identity (Re)formulation in Second Temple Historiographical Literature*, edited by L. Jonker, 29–40. New York: T&T Clark.

Carr, D. M. 2005. *Writing on the Tablet of the Heart: Origins of Scripture and Literature*. Oxford: Oxford University Press.

Certeau, M. de. 1984. *The Practice of Everyday Life*. Translated by Steven Rendall. Berkely: University of California Press. Repr., 1988.

---

57. Ben Zvi, "One Size," 28.

Christian, M. A. 2009. "Priestly Power that Empowers: Michel Foucault, Middle-tier Levites, and the Sociology of 'Popular Religious Groups' in Israel." *JHebS* 9(1): 1–81.

Cohen, A. 2004. *Custom and Politics in Urban Africa: A Study of Hausa Migrants in Yoruba Towns*. London and London: Routledge.

———. 1981. *The Politics of Elite Culture: Explorations in the Dramaturgy of Power in a Modern African Society*. Berkeley: University of California Press.

———. 1974. *Two-Dimensional Man: An Essay on the Anthropology of Power and Symbolism in Complex Societies*. London: Routledge & Kegan Paul.

Crouch, C. L. 2014. *Israel and the Assyrians: Deuteronomy, the Succession Treaty of Esarhaddon, and the Nature of Subversion*. ANEM 8. Atlanta, GA: SBL.

Crüsemann, F. 1992. *Die Tora: Theologie und Sozialgeschichte des alttestamentlichen Gesetzes*. Munich: Kaiser.

Davies, P. R. 2014. "The Authority of Deuteronomy." In *Deuteronomy–Kings as Emerging Authoritative Books: A Conversation*, edited by D. V. Edelman, 27–48. Atlanta, GA: SBL.

Eskenazi, T. C. 2006. "The Missions of Ezra and Nehemiah." In *Judah and the Judeans in the Persian Period*, edited by M. Oeming and O. Lipschitz, 509–29. Winona Lake, IN: Eisenbrauns, .

Feldman, M. H. 2010. "Object Agency? Spatial Perspective, Social Relations, and the Stele of Hammurabi." In *Agency and Identity in the Ancient Near East*, edited by S. R. Steadman and J. Ross, 148–65. London: Equinox.

Forty, A., and S. Küchler, eds. 1999. *The Art of Forgetting*. Oxford: Berg.

Gell, A. 1998. *Art and Agency: An Anthropological Theory*. Oxford: Oxford University Press.

Greenberg, M. 2001. *Ezechiel 1–20*. HThKAT. Freiburg: Herder.

Huyssen, A. 2003. *Present Pasts: Urban Palimpsests and the Politics of Memory*. Stanford, CA: Stanford University Press.

Jonker, L. 2010. "David's Officials According to the Chronicler (1 Chronlicles 23-27): A Reflection of Second Temple Self-Categorization?" In *Historiography and Identity (Re)formulation in Second Temple Historiographical Literature*, edited by L. Jonker, 65–92. New York: T&T Clark.

Köckert, M. 2009. "Vom Kultbild Jahwes zum Bilderverbot." *Zeitschrift für Theologie und Kirche* 106: 371–406.

———. 2007. "Die Entstehung der Bilderverbot." In *Die Welt der Götterbilder*, edited by H. Spieckermann and B. Groneberg, 272–90. BZAW 376. Berlin: de Gruyter.

Latour, B. 2005. *Reassembling the Social: An Introduction to Actor-Network-Theory*. Clarendon Lectures in Management Studies. Oxford: Oxford University Press.

Leuchter, M. 2010. "Coming to Terms with Ezra's Many Identities in Ezra-Nehemiah." In *Historiography and Identity (Re)formulation in Second Temple Historiographical Literature*, edited by L. Jonker, 41–64. New York: T&T Clark.

Lundbom, J. R. 2013. *Deuteronomy: A Commentary*. Grand Rapids, MI: Eerdmans.

Lynch, G. 2010. "Object Theory: Toward an Intersubjective, Mediated, and Dynamic Theory of Religion." In *Religion and Material Culture: The Matter of Belief*, edited by D. Morgan, 36–51. London: Routledge.

Lynch, M. 2014. *Monotheism and Institutions in the Book of Chronicles*. FAT 2/64. Tübingen: Mohr Siebeck.

Meyer, B. and D. Houtman. 2012. "Introduction: Material Religion—How Things Matter." In *Things: Religion and the Question of Materiality*, edited by D. Houtman and B. Meyer, 1–26. New York: Fordham University Press.

Noll, K. L. 2008. "Was There Doctrinal Dissemination in Early Yahweh Religion?" *BibInt* 16: 395–427.

Pels, P. 2012. "The Modern Fear of Matter: Reflecdtions on the Protestantism of Victorian Science." In *Things: Religion and the Question of Materiality*, edited by D. Houtman and B. Meyer, 27–39. New York: Fordham University Press.

Pyysiäinen, I. 2003. *How Religion Works: Towards a New Cognitive Science of Religion*. Leiden: Brill.

Redford, D. B. 2000. "Ancient Egyptian Literature: An Overview." In *Civilizations of the Ancient Near East*, edited by J. M. Sasson, 2223–41. Peabody, MA: Hendrickson.

Ross, J. C., and S. R. Steadman. 2010. "Agency and Identity in the Ancient Near East: New Paths Forward." In *Agency and Identity in the Ancient Near East*, edited by S. R. Steadman and J. C. Ross, 1–10. London: Equinox.

Schaper, J. 1995. "The Jerusalem Temple as an Instrument of the Achaemenid Fiscal Administration." *VT* 45: 528–39.

Sonnet, J.-P. 1997. *The Book within the Book: Writing in Deuteronomy*. BibInt 14. Leiden: Brill.

Steadman, S. R., and J. Ross, eds. 2010. *Agency and Identity in the Ancient Near East*. Approaches to Anthropological Archaeology. London: Equinox.

Stoller, P. 1997. *Sensuous Scholarship*. Philadelphia: University of Philadelphia Press.

Taussig, M. 1993. *Mimesis and Alterity: A Particular History of the Senses*. London: Routledge.

Toorn, K. van der. 2007. *Scribal Culture and the Making of the Hebrew Bible*. Cambridge, MA: Harvard University Press.

———. 1997. *The Image and the Book: Ionic Cults, Aniconism, and the Rise of Book Religion in Israel and the Ancient Near East*. Leuven: Peeters.

Van Seters, J. 2007. "The Origin of the Hebrew Bible: Some New Answers to Old Questions." *Journal of Ancient Near Eastern Religions* 7: 87–108, 219–37.

Vanderkam, J. C. 2000. *From Revelation to Canon: Studies in the Hebrew Bible and Second Temple Literature*. Leiden: Brill.

Vásquez, M. A. 2011. *More Than Belief: A Materialist Theory of Religion*. Oxford: Oxford University Press.

Young, I. M. 1998. "Israelite Literacy: Interpreting the Evidence." *VT* 48: 239–53, 408–22.

— 5 —

Israel's King as *Primus Inter Pares*: The "Democratic" Re-conceptualization of Monarchy in Deut 17:14–20

Reinhard Müller

The book of Deuteronomy drafts a constitution for the biblical Israel that is based on a set of distinct theological ideas revolving around the concept of YHWH's covenant with his people (see esp. Deut 26:16–19).[1] This concept and the related ideas are the foundation for Israel's incomparable identity among the nations (see Deut 4:7–8, 32–34; 33:29).[2] All political institutions and processes mentioned in Deuteronomy are closely related to this concept. Kingship forms a part of the Deuteronomic constitution but is adjusted to Israel's singular identity. In the perspective of Deuteronomy, it is a political institution also found in all the nations that surround Israel (Deut 17:15). Deuteronomy's concept of kingship, however, plays no discernible role in the history of Israelite kingship found in the Former Prophets. We read in the books of Samuel and Kings about an Israelite monarchy that deviated substantially from the outset from the Deuteronomic idea of this political institution.

The Deuteronomic concept of YHWH's people has been recently reconstructed by D. Markl as a "constitutional theocracy."[3] According to Markl, in this theocracy, Mosaic Torah mediates (see, e.g., Deut 4:8) the rule of the divine king YHWH (see Deut 33:5), and the knowledge of the Torah is "democratized" by an egalitarian culture of learning that embraces all members of the Israelite society.[4] Markl's interpretation of Deuteronomy

---

1. On Deuteronomy's covenant theology, see esp. C. Levin, *Die Verheißung des neuen Bundes: in ihrem theologiegeschichtlichen Zusammenhang ausgelegt*, FRLANT 137 (Göttingen: Vandenhoeck & Ruprecht, 1985), 95–114; T. Veijola, *Das fünfte Buch Mose: Deuteronomium, Kapitel 1,1–16,17*, ATD 8/1 (Göttingen: Vandenhoeck & Ruprecht, 2004), 4–5.

2. The motif of Israel's incomparability among the peoples corresponds to the old idea of YHWH's incomparability among the gods, and is probably deduced from that idea, see R. Müller, "Der unvergleichliche Gott: Zur Umformung einer polytheistischen Redeweise im Alten Testament," in *Gott – Götter – Götzen: XIV. Europäischer Kongress für Theologie (11.-15. September 2011 in Zürich)*, ed. C. Schwöbel, Veröffentlichungen der Wissenschaftlichen Gesellschaft für Theologie 38 (Leipzig: Evangelische Verlagsanstalt, 2013), 304–19, here 314–18.

3. D. Markl, *Gottes Volk im Deuteronomium*, BZAR 18 (Wiesbaden: Harrassowitz, 2012), 307.

4. Markl, *Gottes Volk*, 301: "Die Kenntnis und kompetente Anwendung der Tora soll durch eine allgemein gesellschaftlich verbreitete Lernkultur 'demokratisiert' werden."

can be exemplified in the so-called constitutional proposal (Deut 16:18–18:22) that lies at the center of the Deuteronomic constitution. This passage regulates the main administrative and religious bodies of Israel: the judiciary, the king, the priests, and the prophet. N. Lohfink compared the constitutional proposal with the modern concept of the separation of powers, since it balances these bodies by separating their authority.[5] At the same time, Lohfink stressed a crucial difference from the modern political concept: the constitutional proposal brings Israel's administrative bodies into line with an instruction of divine origin as it is contained in the written Mosaic Torah.[6]

This twofold limitation of political power is realized most impressively in the law or statute[7] on kingship in Deut 17:14–20. According to this statute, the king's possessions have to be strictly limited, and he is obliged to study the Torah permanently. More precisely, studying the Torah is the only royal task that is explicitly mentioned in Deut 17, and it seems that an Israelite king who rules in accordance to Deut 17 has no further obligations at all. This peculiar concept of kingship, accurately designated a "'constitutional' monarchy" by B. M. Levinson,[8] markedly deviates from the perception and self-presentation of kingship in the ancient Near East, including monarchic Israel and Judah.[9] All these cultures ascribed two basic tasks to the king: to defend his realm against enemies and to enforce justice within his realm. By doing so, the king was imagined to act piously on behalf of the god(s) of the state, and the king's wealth was regarded as a representation of his pious relationship to the god(s). Early royal Psalms and other early texts of the Hebrew Bible show that this concept was basically shared in monarchic Judah,[10] and these texts seem to have no knowledge of Deut 17.[11] Why does Deuteronomy's law on kingship differ so clearly from the traditional concepts of kingship in the ancient Near East and monarchic Israel and Judah? What is the precise meaning of this statute, and what can be said about its literary and historical contexts?

1. The Literary Horizon of Deuteronomy 17

The law on kingship in Deut 17:14–20 is found after the laws concerning the central court (17:8–13) and before the section that defines the rights of the Levitical priests (18:1–8). It shares some expressions and motifs with the surrounding passages, particularly the men-

---

5. N. Lohfink, "Die Sicherung der Wirksamkeit des Gotteswortes durch das Prinzip der Schriftlichkeit der Tora und durch das Prinzip der Gewaltenteilung nach den Ämtergesetzen des Buches Deuteronomium," in *Studien zum Deuteronomium und zur deuteronomistischen Literatur I*, SBAB 8 (Stuttgart: Katholisches Bibelwerk, 1990), 305–23, esp. 315–17; see also Markl, *Gottes Volk*, 301.

6. Lohfink, "Die Sicherung," 317–22.

7. C. Bultmann, *Der Fremde im antiken Juda: Eine Untersuchung zum sozialen Typenbegriff 'ger' und seinem Bedeutungswandel in der alttestamentlichen Gesetzgebung*, FRLANT 153 (Göttingen: Vandenhoeck & Ruprecht, 1992), 147, correctly notes that the law on kingship should be better called a "Monarchiestatut" (statute on kingship), since it revolves around the legitimacy of monarchic government in Israel.

8. B. M. Levinson, "The Reconceptualization of Kingship in Deuteronomy and the Deuteronomistic History's Transformation of the Torah," *VT* 51 (2001): 511–34, here 531.

9. See esp. G. N. Knoppers, "The Deuteronomist and the Deuteronomic Law of the King: A Reexamination of a Relationship," *ZAW* 108 (1996): 329–46, here 329–30.

10. See Levinson, "Reconceptualization," 512–18.

11. Theocratic or nomistic perspectives that are more or less in accordance with Deut 17:14–20 have been introduced only secondarily into the royal Psalms, see the additions in Ps 18:22–23 and Ps 21:8 as well as the younger Ps 89 (vv. 31–33) and 132 (v. 12).

tion of the Levitical priests (17:9, 18; 18:1). However, in marked contrast to the surrounding laws, the law on kingship opens with a distinct outlook on the ensuing history of biblical Israel (17:14): "When you have come into the land that YHWH your God is giving you, and have taken possession of it and settled in it, and you say: 'I want to set a king over me …'."

The opening looks ahead to the conquest of the land and envisages a certain moment after the conquest and the occupation when the people express their wish for a king. Similar openings can be found in the law on the prophet in Deut 18:9 and in the commandment about the presentation of the first fruits in 26:1; the latter is particularly similar to 17:14. The "historicizing" opening of the law on kingship differs significantly from the surrounding paragraphs. To be sure, references to the conquest or the divine gift of the land can also be found in the preceding laws concerning the judiciary (16:18aβ, 20; 17:2), and the formula about the divine choosing of the place of worship (in 17:9, 10; 18:7) seems to refer implicitly to a future point of time in Israel's history.[12] However, the passages before and after the law on kingship *do not open with this perspective*. There are good arguments that the references to the divine gift of the land did not belong to the oldest stratum of the Deuteronomic law code,[13] and this leads to the assumption that Deut 17:14–20 was not an original part of this code.[14] This theory cannot be fully substantiated here—we would need a comprehensive redaction critical analysis of the constitutional proposal—but it is indirectly corroborated by the scarcity with which Deuteronomy refers to an Israelite kingship. Apart from Deut 17:14–20, an Israelite king is mentioned only once more in Deuteronomy,[15] in Deut 28:36, in a curse that announces the exile.[16] The Israelite monarchy is not a prominent theme in Deuteronomy, and this fits well with the theory that the law on kingship in Deut 17 is only loosely connected with the core of the Deuteronomic code.

---

12. R. G. Kratz, *The Composition of the Narrative Books of the Old Testament* (London: T&T Clark, 2005), 123–24. It is, however, possible that the Masoretic reading יבחר "he will choose" is secondary, compared to some witnesses of the LXX that seem to attest בחר "he chose," in accordance with the reading of the Samaritan Pentateuch, see A. Schenker, "Le Seigneur choisira-til le lieu de son nom ou l'a-t-il choisi? L'apport de la Bible grecque ancienne à l'histoire du texte samaritain et massorétique," in *Scripture in Transition*, ed. A. Voitila and J. Jokiranta (Leiden: Brill, 2008), 339–51.

13. See J. C. Gertz, *Die Gerichtsorganisation Israels im deuteronomischen Gesetz*, FRLANT 165 (Göttingen: Vandenhoeck & Ruprecht, 1994), 33–41 and 45–52, on Deut 16:18, 20; 17:2.

14. Thus esp. L. Perlitt, "Der Staatsgedanke im Deuteronomium," in *Language, Theology, and the Bible*, ed. S. E. Balentine and J. Barton (Oxford: Clarendon, 1994), 182–98, here 187–89; Gertz, *Die Gerichtsorganisation Israels*, 29–32; R. Müller, *Königtum und Gottesherrschaft: Untersuchungen zur alttestamentlichen Monarchiekritik*, FAT 2/3 (Tübingen: Mohr Siebeck, 2004), 202–6; pace U. Rüterswörden, *Von der politischen Gemeinschaft zur Gemeinde: Studien zu Dt 16,18–18,22*, BBB 65 (Frankfurt am Main: Athenäum, 1987), 54–58.

15. Deut 33:5 refers not to the human king but to the divine king YHWH, see, e.g., Müller, *Königtum und Gottesherrschaft*, 227; Markl, *Gottes Volk*, 286–87.

16. Deut 28:36 clearly resumes Deut 17:14–15, see e.g., G. Seitz, *Redaktionsgeschichtliche Studien zum Deuteronomium*, BWANT 93 (Stuttgart: Kohlhammer, 1971), 280; the verse formed possibly no original part of the curse section, see, e.g., H. U. Steymans, *Deuteronomium 28 und die adê zur Thronfolgeregelung Asarhaddons: Segen und Fluch im Alten Orient und in Israel*, OBO 145 (Freiburg: Universitätsverlag; Göttingen: Vandenhoeck & Ruprecht, 1995), 259f; differently C. Koch, *Vertrag, Treueid und Bund: Studien zur Rezeption des altorientalischen Vertragsrechts im Deuteronomium und zur Ausbildung der Bundestheologie im Alten Testament*, BZAW 383 (Berlin: de Gruyter, 2008), 190–91, who takes only v. 36b as an addition.

2. The Literary Growth of Deut 17:14–20

There are indications that the law on kingship was written by more than one hand.[17] Several models of its literary history have been proposed that differ in details but usually share the assumption that vv. 18–19, according to which the king is commissioned to write the Torah in a book and to read it every day, were not original elements of the law.[18]

The strongest argument for this theory is based on the relationship between v. 17 and v. 20. The infinitive clause in v. 20aα לבלתי רום לבבו מאחיו ('that his heart be not exalted above his brothers') formulates no logical consequence to the themes mentioned in the immediately preceding text. According to v. 19, the king is obliged to study the Torah in order to learn the fear of YHWH and to obey the divine statutes. The humility referred to in the ensuing v. 20 is not usually mentioned as an effect of Torah obedience in Deuteronomy. What is often mentioned instead as an effect of obedience is the prolongation of life,[19] a motif found in v. 20b. The reference to the humility of the king in v. 20aα fits much more as an immediate continuation of v. 17. "Verse 20 follows naturally after v. 17 and explains why the king is warned not to increase his wealth, referred to in v. 17"[20]:

17 ולא ירבה לו נשים
ולא יסור לבבו
וכסף וזהב לא ירבה לו מאד
20 לבלתי רום לבבו מאחיו

17 And he shall not acquire numerous wives for himself,
lest his heart turn aside.
Nor shall he acquire much silver and gold for himself,
20 that his heart be not exalted above his brothers.

A strikingly similar combination of expressions and motifs can be found in the context of a broad parenetic passage in Deut 8:12 "Lest when you have eaten and are full ... 13 and when your herds and your flocks multiply (ירבין), and silver and gold multiply for you (וכסף וזהב ירבה לך), and all that you have multiplies (ירבה), 14 your heart then be exalted (ורם לבבך) and you forget YHWH your God ..." If there is a literary historical connection between both texts, which is quite probable, given the singular combination of expressions and motifs in both passages (cf. esp. וכסף וזהב לא ירבה לו מאד "nor shall he acquire much silver and gold for himself" in Deut 17:17b with וכסף וזהב ירבה לך ('and silver and gold multiply for you'), this would corroborate the theory that vv. 18–19 did

---

17. Differently, e.g., C. Schäfer-Lichtenberger, *Josua und Salomo: Eine Studie zu Autorität und Legitimität des Nachfolgers im Alten Testament*, VTSup 55 (Leiden: Brill, 1995), 80–81, and R. Achenbach, "Das sogenannte Königsgesetz in Deuteronomium 17,14–20," *ZABR* 15 (2009): 216–33, here 218–19, who assume that Deut 17:14–20 is a coherent composition.

18. Thus, already C. Steuernagel, *Das Deuteronomium*, 2nd ed. (Göttingen: Vandenhoeck & Ruprecht, 1923), 118–19, and see, e.g., Rüterswörden, *Von der politischen Gemeinschaft*, 63–64, 66; M. Rose, *5. Mose*, 2 vols., ZBK 5 (Zürich: Theologischer Verlag, 1994), 1:75–77; F. García López, "Le roi d'Israël: Dt 17,14-20," in *Das Deuteronomium: Entstehung, Gestalt und Botschaft*, ed. N. Lohfink, BETL 68 (Leuven: University Press, 1985), 277–97, here 285–87; R. D. Nelson, *Deuteronomy: A Commentary*, OTL (Louisville, KY: Westminster John Knox, 2002), 216; C. Nihan, "Rewriting Kingship in Samuel: 1 Samuel 8 and 12 and the Law of the King (Deuteronomy 17)," *HeBAI* 2 (2013): 315–50, here 328–29, with n. 41.

19. Cf. Deut 4:26, 40; 5:16, 33; 6:2; 11:9; 22:7; 25:15; 30:18, 20; 32:47.

20. M. Weinfeld, *Deuteronomy and the Deuteronomic School* (Oxford: Clarendon, 1972), 5 n. 1.

not form an original part of Deut 17:14–20. Deuteronomy 8 does not refer to the written Torah, and Deut 17:17, 20 coincide with Deut 8:12–14 in the idea that wealth has the potential to cause condemnable pride.[21]

An additional argument for the secondary nature of vv. 18–19 lies in the fact that the opening of v. 18 looks ahead to the king's accession to the throne:

והיה כשבתו על כסא ממלכתו ...

And after he has taken seat upon the throne of his kingdom ...

This does not completely fit in after the instructions of vv. 16–17, since they refer to a period when the king already sits on his throne; in a coherent composition, one would expect the temporal clause that opens v. 18 to be found at the beginning of v. 16.

Apart from that, one can surmise that the latter parts of v. 20 are part of the same literary unit as vv. 18–19, as first proposed by C. Steuernagel,[22] although it is difficult to find cogent inner-textual arguments for this assumption; at least, the slightly awkward repetition of [ו]לבלתי ('[and] so that not') may indicate that v. 20aβb has been added by another hand.[23] We will see that the formulaic phrases in v. 20aβb are in the context of the Deuteronomistic phraseology of Deuteronomy's framework closely related to the phrases of v. 19.

Smaller additions can probably be found in vv. 15 and 16. Verse 15b, which strictly forbids[24] making a foreigner king, stands in marked contrast to v. 15a that announces the divine election of the king.[25] Similar additions that aim at separating Israel from foreigners (נכרי) can be found in 14:21, 15:3 and 23:21.[26] With regard to the Israelite kingship, this prohibition may particularly refer to Abimelech, the first king in Israel who was the offspring of a mixed marriage between the Israelite Gideon and a Shechemite concubine (Judg 8:31; 9:1)[27] and whose kingdom was founded on a massacre and ended in catastrophe.[28]

---

21. *Pace* Schäfer-Lichtenberger, *Josua und Salomo*, 80, who tries to refute this conclusion by arguing that the king's copy of the Torah serves to remind him of YHWH, as an analogy to the commandment in Deut 8:18 "you shall remember YHWH your God" that is addressed to the people; however, Deut 8:12–14 does not refer to the written Torah, but stresses that pride may be the direct consequence of wealth.

22. Steuernagel, *Deuteronomium*, 119.

23. García López, "Le roi d'Israël," 286–87; Nihan, "Rewriting Kingship in Samuel," 329 n. 42.

24. By use of לא תוכל "do not dare" (cf. Deut 12:17; 16:5; 22:3), see Nelson, *Deuteronomy*, 22:3.

25. Steuernagel, *Deuteronomium*, 118, and see, e.g., Müller, *Königtum und Gottesherrschaft*, 199; Nihan, "Rewriting Kingship in Samuel," 327.

26. On Deut 15:3 cf. C. Levin, "Rereading Deuteronomy in the Persian and Hellenistic Periods: The Ethics of Brotherhood and the Care of the Poor," in *Deuteronomy to Kings as Emerging Authoritative Books: A Conversation*, ed. D. V. Edelman, ANEM 6 (Atlanta, GA: SBL, 2014), 49–71, here 53, 56.

27. Suggested by D. Daube, "One from among your Brethren Shall You Set King over You," *JBL* 90 (1971): 480–81. In addition to that, Nelson, *Deuteronomy*, 223, suggests that the passage may refer also to "historical experiences such as the potential imposition of Tabeel (Isa 7:6)." According to T. Römer, *The So-Called Deuteronomistic History: A Sociological, Historical and Literary Introduction* (London: T&T Clark International, 2005), 139, Deut 17:15b "alludes to the foreign (Phoenician) influences in the Northern kingdom, which, according to the Deuteronomists, hastened the fall of Samaria." As an alternative to such possible references to the monarchic period or its literary description in the former prophets, Deut 17:15b may be understood as a rejection of the idea that Kyros or the Achaemenide kings could be seen in light of Isa 45 as legitimate Israelite kings, as proposed by Achenbach, "Das sogenannte Königsgesetz," 228.

28. On the literary history and theological impact of these motifs see Müller, *Königtum und Gottesherrschaft*, 96–117.

Verse 16b stands out from the context by use of the second person plural[29]—a grammatical feature not often found in Deut 12–26. The half-verse refers to a divine ban on the return to Egypt that is nowhere explicitly formulated in the extant Pentateuch; this reference possibly draws on a short word of God quoted in Exod 13:17 ("for God said, 'Lest the people repent, when they see war, and they return to Egypt'") and is related to the idea that a return to Egypt would abrogate Israel's identity and existence as YHWH's people (see esp. Deut 28:68).[30]

3. Deuteronomy 17 and 1 Samuel 8

A main problem concerning Deut 17 is the relationship between this law and the request by Israel's elders for a king in 1 Sam 8.[31] It is highly improbable that both texts have been written independently from each other, since according to 1 Sam 8:5, the elders express their desire for a king by using almost the same words as found in Deut 17:14. Most notable is the use of the verb שׂים ('to set') with the object מלך ('king') this expression is exclusively found in these two passages.[32] This phrase is used in both Deut 17:14 and 1 Sam 8:5 in the context of a request by the people (in 1 Sam 8 represented by the elders):

Deut 17:14	1 Sam 8:5
אשימה עלי מלך ככל הגוים אשר סביבתי	שימה לנו מלך לשפטנו ככל הגוים ...
"I want to set a king over me, like all the nations that are around me!"	"... set for us a king to judge us like all the nations!"

It is disputed how both passages are related to each other in the literary history. In light of the conceptual differences between Deut 17 and 1 Sam 8, there are basically two options.[33] Either 1 Sam 8:5 is literarily dependent on the law on kingship,[34] or Deut 17 was formu-

---

29. Steuernagel, *Deuteronomium*, 118.

30. Similarly Rose, *5. Mose*, 1:81–82, who draws attention to the motif of the return to Egypt in Hos 8:13 and 9:3 as a possible background of Deut 17:16b.

31. For another discussion of different aspects of 1 Sam 8 in this volume, see the essay by W. Oswald ("Monarchy, Oligarchy, and Democracy in the Constitutional Debate in Herodotus and in 1 Samuel 8").

32. This peculiar expression is best explained as created in analogy to Samuel's act of making his sons judges for Israel (1 Sam 8:1: וישם את בניו שפטים לישראל), which does not refer to the founding of a new political institution but to the appointment of individuals to an already existing office (cf. Exod 2:14; 2 Sam 15:4). This explanation gives an additional argument for the priority of 1 Sam 8 in relation to Deut 17; see Müller, *Königtum und Gottesherrschaft*, 127.

33. A third option would be the theory that both texts were written by the same Deuteronomistic author, thus P. Särkiö, *Die Weisheit und Macht Salomos in der israelitischen Historiographie: Eine traditions- und redaktionskritische Untersuchung über 1 Kön 3–5 und 9–11*, Schriften der Finnischen Exegetischen Gesellschaft 60 (Helsinki: Finnische Exegetische Gesellschaft, 1994), 224–36; Römer, *So-Called Deuteronomistic History*, 139–43; J. Vermeylen, "The Book of Samuel within the Deuteronomistic History," in *Is Samuel among the Deuteronomists? Current Views on the Place of Samuel in a Deuteronomistic History*, ed. C. Edenburg and J. Pakkala, SBLAIL 16 (Atlanta, GA: SBL, 2013), 67–91, here 75–76, 81–83. However, since Deut 17 and 1 Sam 8 differ considerably in their view of the monarchy (see below), this theory seems much less probable than the two options mentioned above.

34. Thus esp. M. Noth, *The Deuteronomistic History*, JSOTSup 15, (Sheffield: JSOT Press, 1981), 88; trans. of *Überlieferungsgeschichtliche Studien: Die sammelnden und bearbeitenden Geschichtswerke im Alten Testament*, (Königsberg: Königsberger Gelehrte Gesellschaft, 1943), 100; Levin, *Die Verheißung des neuen Bundes*, 86; T. Veijola, *Das Königtum in der Beurteilung der deuteronomistischen Historiographie: Eine redaktionsgeschichtliche Untersuchung*, Annales Academiae scientiarum fennicae B 193 (Helsinki: Suomalainen Tiedeakatemia, 1977), 68–69, and recently C. Nihan, "1 Samuel 8 and 12 and the Deuteronomistic Edition of Samuel," in *Is Samuel among the Deuteronomists? Current Views on the Place of Samuel*

lated in light of 1 Sam 8.³⁵ In my opinion, the second option is more probable. There are three main arguments in favor of Deut 17 being formulated on the basis of 1 Sam 8.

First, while according to 1 Sam 8:5 the elders use almost the same words as in Deut 17:14, the entire chapter does not contain unambiguous references to the peculiar concept of kingship that is unfolded in the Mosaic law. The elders do not mention that such a law concerning kingship exists³⁶; nor do Samuel and YHWH, when criticizing the request (1 Sam 8:6–18), refer to this law or allude to its content.³⁷ This lack of clear reference is all the more important since the antimonarchic tendency of 1 Sam 8:6–18 is not entirely in line with Deut 17. Although the elders do not use the same, precise words found in Deut 17:14, they do nothing that is fundamentally in conflict with the Mosaic law, since according to Deut 17:14–15*³⁸ the request for an Israelite kingship is not prohibited *per se*. It is a remarkable contrast to Deut 17 that the request by the elders is qualified as having been "evil in the eyes of Samuel" (1 Sam 8:6) and that YHWH even states that the elders, by requesting a king, "rejected" him "from being king over them" (1 Sam 8:7).³⁹ If 1 Sam 8 would have been written in light of Deut 17, we could expect to find in this chapter some explanation as to why the request for a king is suddenly regarded as such an evil act.

To be sure, Deut 17 does not ascribe to the king programmatically the task of 'judging' Israel (שפט). The elders deviate in this regard from the Deuteronomic law since they request a king "to judge us," although this aspect of their request is comprehensibly motivated by their complaint about the corruption of Samuel's sons (1 Sam 8:5a: "And they said to him, 'Behold, you yourself have grown old, and your sons do not walk in your ways ...'"; cf. vv. 1–3).⁴⁰ In addition, the elders refer to the military leadership of the king when they reject Samuel's warning against kingship (1 Sam 8:20). One could argue that the elders *deliberately* avoid referring to the Mosaic commandment, since they are aware they are deviating from the Deuteronomic idea of monarchy; they want a king who fulfills the main traditional tasks of kingship, doing justice and waging war, and this may be understood as

---

    in a Deuteronomistic History, ed. C. Edenburg and J. Pakkala, SBLAIL 16 (Atlanta, GA: SBL, 2013), 225–73, here 229–40; idem, "Rewriting Kingship in Deuteronomy," 322–39.

35. Thus esp. W. Dietrich, "History and Law: Deuteronomistic Historiography and Deuteronomic Law Exemplified in the Passage from the Period of the Judges to the Monarchical Period," in *Israel Constructs its History: Deuteronomistic Historiography in Recent Research*, ed. A. de Pury, T. Römer, and J.-D. Macchi, JSOTSup 306 (Sheffield: Sheffield Academic, 2000), 315–42, here 322–24; Müller, *Königtum und Gottesherrschaft*, 125–130; Achenbach, "Das sogenannte Königsgesetz," 219–30.

36. *Pace* Nihan, "1 Samuel 8 and 12," 233, who argues that "the combination of the phrases שימו לנו מלך and ככל הגוים [in 1 Sam 8:5] sufficed to mark the citation of Deut 17:14; the reference to the nations surrounding Israel did not need to be quoted in full, because it no longer played a central role in the narrative." However, the fact remains that 1 Sam 8:5 is not explicitly marked as a quotation of Deut 17:14.

37. Achenbach, "Das sogenannte Königsgesetz," 223.

38. The asterisk refers to the reconstructed original version that comprises only parts of these verses.

39. 1 Sam 8:7b–9a probably forms a later interpolation, as indicated by the resumptive repetition (*Wiederaufnahme*) of v. 7a in v. 9a, see, among others, Dietrich, "History and Law," 325; Müller, *Königtum und Gottesherrschaft*, 130–31; Nihan, "Rewriting Kingship," 340. It is nevertheless difficult to imagine that this addition was written with knowledge of Deut 17, as Nihan presupposes, since it is in sharp contrast to the permission to appoint a king given in Deut 17:14–15*.

40. Cf. Dietrich, "History and Law," 323–24: "If we read the account in 1 Sam 8.1-22 for its own sake, we get the impression that the Elders have good reasons to desire the establishment of a king: they formulate this desire relatively innocently and in all good conscience."

an implicit rejection of the commandment of Deut 17:14–20*. Therefore, it could seem that YHWH instructs Samuel to utter a sharp warning against *such* a kingdom, because a kingdom that corresponds to the request by the elders cannot be in line with Deuteronomy's idea of an Israelite monarchy. However, the problem remains in this perspective that 1 Sam 8 does not refer explicitly to the concept of kingship contained in the Mosaic commandment[41]; neither Samuel nor YHWH, when criticizing the request by the elders, refer or allude to the fact that Moses once gave Israel a different idea of kingship.[42]

It is therefore easier to assume that Deut 17:14–20* was written after 1 Sam 8 had been completed[43] than the other way around. This theory explains the peculiar phenomenon that 1 Sam 8, on the one hand, seems to imply that the elders deliberately transgressed the Mosaic commandment, while, on the other, the entire chapter does not contain any distinct reference to the Deuteronomic concept of kingship.

Second, a particular argument is related to the so-called משפט המלך ('justice of the king') in 1 Sam 8:11–18, the polemical speech with which Samuel warns the elders against the installation of an Israelite monarchy. Samuel's warning against the excessive abuse of power by the king is in marked contrast to the limitations of military power and material wealth that are imposed on the king in Deut 17. Samuel predicts that the king will dispossess the Israelites of their most precious properties, thus perverting justice.[44] Deuteronomy 17, by contrast, conceives of a humble king who has neither a powerful army nor a large harem and great treasures, whose heart is not exalted above his brothers. Samuel therefore polemicizes against a kingship that deviates substantially from the Deuteronomic idea of an Israelite monarchy—a polemic that is certainly related to the factual course of Israelite history as recorded in Samuel and Kings. But what is most remarkable is the fact that the Deuteronomic idea of kingship *is not within the horizon of this polemic*. It is therefore difficult to explain the antimonarchic polemic of 1 Sam 8:11–18 as a commentary on Deut 17[45]; this would imply that the author(s) of 1 Sam 8 regarded the Deuteronomic ideal of a

---

41. Nihan, "Rewriting Kingship," 337 n. 67, correctly stresses that the "scribal practice of explicitly quoting pentateuchal laws is actually rare in the Hebrew Bible and mostly concerns ritual laws specifically." The problem here, however, is that the reactions of Samuel and YHWH to the people's request *are in peculiar conflict with Deut 17*; 1 Sam 8 does not indicate—neither explicitly nor implicitly—how the antimonarchic polemic of vv. 6–18 is related to the concept of an ideal Israelite monarchy as it is unfolded in Deut 17.

42. Thus, it is questionable that "the reception of Deut 17 in Samuel aptly introduces the history of Israelite and Judean kings with a commentary on the law of the king," as Nihan states: "By aligning its account of the origins of kingship with the corresponding prescription in Deut 17:14–15, the Samuel narrative does acknowledge the law's authority to a certain extent. Yet, it also simultaneously points out that this law largely remained an ideal that was never implemented at the time when Israel and Judah were effectively ruled by native kings." ("Rewriting Kingship," 338–39). It is particularly difficult to explain the polemic against kingship in 1 Sam 8:11–18 as a commentary on the law of Deut 17:14–20 that acknowledges this law's "authority to a certain extent," see the following point 2.

43. The question to which extent 1 Sam 8 is the result of literary growth (see particularly Veijola, *Das Königtum*, 53–72; Müller, *Königtum und Gottesherrschaft*, 119–47) should be separated from this problem, since all verses of 1 Sam 8 need to be investigated concerning their relationship to Deut 17.

44. See Müller, *Königtum und Gottesherrschaft*, 137–46.

45. *Pace* Nihan, "Rewriting Kingship," 338, who states: "Contrary to Deuteronomy 17, ... the Samuel account does not seek to restrain the king's prerogatives but on the contrary insists on the many potential abuses to which these prerogatives will lead ..." I find it difficult to imagine that this view of kingship that is in such sharp contrast to Deut 17 would have been formulated without any implicit or explicit reference to the ideal of Deut 17.

humble king as simply irrelevant—which is difficult to imagine.

In addition, it has to be noted that the single motifs of Samuel's polemic differ considerably from the three prohibitions of Deut 17:16–17. For example, 1 Sam 8:11–18 does not refer to the king's possessions of silver and gold (Deut 17:17b); instead of a reference to the king's harem (Deut 17:17a), 1 Sam 8:13 mentions that the king will force the daughters of the Israelites to serve in his palace. The antimonarchic polemic in 1 Sam 8:11–18 has a logic of its own,[46] and it is not clear that this logic is deduced from Deut 17. Nothing indicates that Samuel's polemic against the excessive abuse of royal power was written with knowledge of the limitations of royal power expressed in Deut 17. We will see later that it is more probable that the prescriptions in Deut 17:16–17* refer, among other things, to the opening of Samuel's speech in 1 Sam 8:11.[47]

Third, the broad *protasis* of Deut 17:14 envisages a certain situation in Israel's future when the people will ask for a king, and the ensuing *apodosis* in v. 15a gives permission to install a king, under the condition that the king shall be the one whom YHWH will choose. This peculiar combination of motifs is difficult to explain without reference to the request by the elders in 1 Sam 8:5 and to Samuel's announcement in 1 Sam 10:24 that Saul is 'the one whom YHWH has chosen' (אשר בחר בו יהוה). Why does the law on kingship refer to a request by the people at all, if not with knowledge of this request in 1 Sam 8:5?[48] A similar request by the people is not mentioned elsewhere in Deuteronomy. And why does Deut 17:15* transfer the formula of divine election from the chosen place to the chosen king, if not with reference to 1 Sam 10:24, where the election of Saul among the people is the result of the casting of lots (1 Sam 10:20–23)?[49]

This argument is corroborated by a syntactical detail. In Deut 17:15a, the grammatical mode of the *figura etymologica* שום תשים is ambivalent; it can be understood permissively,[50] since it answers the preceding request by the people: "You *may certainly* set over yourself a king." Yet, it also figures as a strict commandment, since it refers to the divine election of the king: "You *shall surely* set over yourself as king whom YHWH your God will choose."[51] This peculiar syntactical ambivalence can best be explained with the assumption that Deut 17:15* refers at the same time to both the request by the elders in 1 Sam 8:5 and the divine election of Israel's first king in 1 Sam 10:20–24; the implicit reference to the request by the elders explains the permissive aspect of שום תשים, and the reference to the divine election justifies the possibility of reading this phrase as a jussive.

---

46. See F. Crüsemann, *Der Widerstand gegen das Königtum: Die antiköniglichen Texte des Alten Testaments und der Kampf um den frühen israelitischen Staat*, WMANT 49 (Neukirchen-Vluyn: Neukirchener Verlag, 1978), 66–70; Müller, *Königtum und Gottesherrschaft*, 139–45.

47. See below section 4.

48. *Pace* Nihan, "Rewriting Kingship," 326, who explains the reference to a request by the people for a king (Deut 17:14) with the fact that Deut 17 "construes kingship as an essentially exogenous institution, ... whereas all other offices are [in Deuteronomy] initiated by YHWH himself." However, the exogenous nature of kingship according to Deut 17:14 is not a sufficient reason as to why the motif of a request by the people has been created in the context of Deuteronomy; Deut 17:14 is still more easily explained as a reference to the narrative logic of 1 Sam 8:1–5.

49. Thus esp. Achenbach, "Das sogenannte Königsgesetz," 220.

50. Thus, e.g., P. C. Craigie, *The Book of Deuteronomy*, NICOT (Grand Rapids, MI: Eerdmans, 1976), 253.

51. Cf. Nelson, *Deuteronomy*, 223, who correctly notes this ambivalence, although he does not separate v. 15b from 15a: "The grammar of v. 15 is permissive (cf. 12:20; 18:6–8). However, this permission is limited by the requirements of divine choice and ethnic kinship ..."

To be sure, one can argue for the opposite development in the literary history. Christophe Nihan, who defends the priority of Deut 17 with detailed observations, particularly draws attention to the phrase ככל הגוים אשר סביבתי ('like all the nations that are around me') (Deut 17:14) that is in part repeated in the request by the elders in 1 Sam 8:5 (ככל הגוים 'like all the nations') and 20 (והיינו גם אנחנו ככל הגוים 'and we want to be like all the nations'). He argues that this phrase "appears to be at home in Deut 17," while its "function ... within the narrative context of 1 Sam 8 is not entirely clear."[52] According to Nihan, "the construction of kingship as a 'foreign' institution [in Deut 17] serves to introduce the following requirement in v. 15a that the king has to be elected by YHWH in order to compensate for the exogenous origin ascribed to royalty."[53]

It is, however, not convincing that the reference to the peoples plays no role in the context of 1 Sam 8 and so must be quoted from Deut 17:14, as Nihan claims. The elders, who complain about the corruption of Samuel's sons (compare 1 Sam 8:5a with 1 Sam 8:3), imply that the absence of a king in Israel is a political disadvantage so that they want to assimilate to the nations in this regard[54]; it has to be kept in mind that, up to this point of the narrative, Israel suffered in the period of the judges for decades from foreign nations.[55] A reference to the nations and their political constitution (cf. the mention of foreign kings in Judg 3:8, 12; 4:2; 11:12) can therefore appear as a rather natural and logical theme in the context of 1 Sam 8; this motif does not have to be explained as a quotation from Deut 17.[56]

In addition, Nihan stresses that in 1 Sam 8 "the key issue" in the people's request "is the שפט-role associated with the royal office"[57]; this is particularly highlighted by the fact that the "further reference to the people's speech [in 1 Sam 8:6] entirely leaves out the reference to other nations, but keeps the phrase לשפטנו."[58] "This sophisticated construction, in which the audience's attention is gradually focused on the phrase לשפטנו as the central descriptor of the king's activity, would make little sense if the author of 1 Sam 8 were freely composing his account of the origins of kingship in Israel. It is much easier to explain if one assumes that this scribe was trying to reinterpret some received material, in this case the beginning of the Deuteronomic law of the king (Deut 17:14)."[59]

This detailed argument is, however, not compelling. It is not entirely clear why the sequence of 1 Sam 8:5–6, "in which the audience's attention is gradually focused on the phrase לשפטנו as the central descriptor of the king's activity" has to be explained as a reinterpretation of Deut 17. It is correct that 1 Sam 8:6aγ תנה לנו מלך לשפטנו 'Give us a king

---

52. Nihan, "1 Samuel 8 and 12," 232; cf. idem, "Rewriting Kingship," 331–33.
53. Nihan, "Rewriting Kingship," 332.
54. See also Müller, *Königtum und Gottesherrschaft*, 128.
55. On the context of this motif in redaction history, see R. Müller, "Images of Exile in the Book of Judges," in *The Concept of Exile in Ancient Israel and its Historical Contexts*, ed. E. Ben Zvi and C. Levin, BZAW 404 (Berlin: de Gruyter, 2010), 229–40.
56. Deut 17:14 adds אשר סביבתי ('that are around me') in order to differentiate between the nations in the land, as referred to in Deut 4:38; 7:1, 17, 22; 8:20; 9:1, 4–5; 11:23; 12:2, 29–30; 18:9, 14; 19:1; 20:15; 31:3, and the surrounding nations; the expression כל הגוים אשר סביבתי 'all the nations that are around me' is in Deuteronomy exceptional, since surrounding nations are elsewhere mentioned as עמים 'peoples' (Deut 6:14; 13:8) or איבים 'enemies' (Deut 12:10; 25:19). This observation may imply an additional argument for the priority of 1 Sam 8.
57. Nihan, "Rewriting Kingship," 334.
58. Nihan, "Rewriting Kingship," 333.
59. Nihan, "Rewriting Kingship," 334.

to judge us'!) is a shortened and slightly modified repetition of 1 Sam 8:5b (שימה לנו ... מלך לשפטנו ככל הגוים '... set for us a king to judge us like all the nations'!), but this can be easily explained within the narrative logic of 1 Sam 8:1–6[60]; the focus on the שפט-role of the king is a rather natural motif here, since it is related to the elders' complaint about the misbehavior of Samuel's sons *as judges* (v. 5a; and see v. 3). Nihan's model would imply that, due to the elders' request (v. 6a: וירע הדבר בעיני שמואל כאשר אמרו תנה לנו מלך לשפטנו 'And the thing was evil in the eyes of Samuel, when they said, "Give us a king to judge us!"' Samuel's anger has something to do with Deut 17, but this is in no way clear. First Samuel 8:6 does not suggest that Samuel is angry because the elders transgress the Deuteronomic law on kingship; rather, it seems that Samuel is angry about the elders' intention to abandon Israel's foundational non-monarchic constitution. At the same time, the motif of Samuel's anger implies that the installation of an Israelite kingship will bring evil upon the people (see particularly v. 18, which implies that the king will oppress the Israelites like the foreign rulers in the period of the judges)[61]; the phrase "the thing was evil in the eyes of Samuel" is conspicuously similar to the recurrent formula in the book of Kings 'he did what was evil in the eyes of YHWH' (ויעש הרע בעיני יהוה),[62] and this similarity may even imply that an Israelite kingship as such will be something evil. All this is in peculiar conflict with Deut 17, since, as stressed above, Deut 17 does not forbid a request for a king *per se*. In my opinion, it is easier to explain Deut 17:14 as a reinterpretation of 1 Sam 8 that already reacts to the strong critique of the monarchy in 1 Sam 8 by developing the idea of an Israelite kingship that would make such a critique unnecessary.

Nihan's third main argument is related to the continuation of 1 Sam 8 in 1 Sam 10:17–27, the account about Saul's divine election by lot. According to Nihan, "the narrative sequence uniting 1 Sam 8 and 10:17–27 was apparently modeled on the sequence formed by Deut 17:14 + 15a. While the people's request in 8:5 hints at the situation already projected in Deut 17:14, it leaves open the related issue of the king's election by YHWH in 17:15a. That issue is then taken up in the account of Saul's designation."[63] In addition, Nihan points to the narrative of David's divine election in 1 Sam 16:1–13, which explicitly continues the narrative of Saul's rejection in 1 Sam 15 (see 1 Sam 16:1). Because certain parallels between 1 Sam 16:1–13 and 1 Sam 10:17–27 indicate that David's election has to be seen in contrast to Saul's election,[64] Nihan assumes that both accounts belong to the same redactional layer[65]; he claims that "in the context of the Samuel narratives, the account of 16:1–13 explains why, even though both Saul and David were divinely designated, it was nonetheless the dynasty of the Judahite David and not of the Benjaminite Saul that was eventually selected to rule over 'Israel'."

---

60. This problem is not necessarily linked to the question whether 1 Sam 8 forms a coherent composition or consists of more than one layer, *pace* Nihan, "Rewriting Kingship," 333–34, and see Müller, *Königtum und Gottesherrschaft*, 120–30.
61. See Müller, *Königtum und Gottesherrschaft*, 135–35.
62. 1 Kgs 11:6; 15:26, etc.
63. Nihan, "Rewriting Kingship," 335.
64. Cf. Nihan, "Rewriting Kingship," 336: "While the account of ch. 16 avoids expressly contradicting the notion that Saul was divinely appointed as king, the parallel between Eliab and Saul's fate nonetheless suggests some degree of ambiguity in Saul's designation; by contrast, David's choice by YHWH is expressed quite unambiguously (16:12b)."
65. Similarly K.-P. Adam, *Saul und David in der judäischen Geschichtsschreibung: Studien zu 1 Samuel 16–2 Samuel 5*, FAT 51 (Tübingen: Mohr Siebeck, 2007), 158–61.

These arguments carry different weight. First, although 1 Sam 16:1–13 contains some remarkable parallels to 1 Sam 10:17–27,[66] the account of David's divine election cannot decide whether 1 Sam 10:17–27 depends on the law on kingship or not.[67] Second, it is certainly possible that the sequence of 1 Sam 8 and 10 has been composed in light of Deut 17:14–15*, but the opposite remains possible as well; as shown above, the combination of motifs in Deut 17:14–15* is in the Deuteronomic context highly exceptional, which is most easily explained by the assumption that Deut 17:14–15* was written in view of the narrative sequence of 1 Sam 8 and 10:17–27. Third, it is certainly correct that in 1 Sam 10:24 (הראיתם אשר בחר בו יהוה 'Do you see the one whom YHWH has chosen'?) the Deuteronomic formula of the divine election of the sanctuary (e.g., Deut 17:9) seems to have been transferred to king Saul,[68] but it is not necessary to assume that 1 Sam 10:24 has been deduced from Deut 17:15a. According to Nihan, the transfer of the election formula to the king originated in the Deuteronomic context, but it is impossible to find compelling reasons that would exclude the opposite. First Samuel 9:1–10:16 relates how Saul was secretly anointed by Samuel as Israel's first king, which implies that YHWH had chosen Saul among the people. The ensuing narrative in 1 Sam 10:17–27 about the people's gathering in Mizpah illustrates how the divine act of choosing Saul was made public among the Israelites,[69] before Saul led the people into war against the Ammonite aggression (1 Sam 11:1–11, see esp. v. 7); after the people had gathered in Mizpah (1 Sam 10:17), Saul was chosen by lot from all Israelite tribes (1 Sam 10:20–23), and Samuel proclaimed the result of this procedure with an expression that is self-evident in this context: "Do you *see* whom YHWH has chosen?" In contrast to Samuel, the people had not seen YHWH's chosen one before. The motifs of 1 Sam 10:17–27 can therefore be consistently explained within the narrative logic of 1 Sam 9–10 and do not need to have been deduced from Deut 17:15*.[70] The literary horizons of the prohibitions that are formulated in Deut 17:16–17*, 20* can further substantiate the proposed literary development from 1 Sam 8 to Deut 17.

4. Deuteronomy 17 and Israel's Experiences with Kingship

If Deut 17:14–20* has been composed in light of 1 Sam 8, it is probably no coincidence that the first of the three limitations of royal power in Deut 17:14–20* is related to the military (Deut 17:16): "Only he shall not acquire many horses for himself ..." The משפט המלך in 1 Sam 8:11 begins with the same theme: "Your sons he will take and assign to his cavalry ..." A king who has not many horses will not be able to build an army in which the sons of the Israelites can be forced to serve. The perspective of Deut 17:16, however, goes

---

66. See esp. P. K. McCarter, *I Samuel: A New Translation with Introduction, Notes and Commentary*, AB 8 (New York: Doubleday, 1980), 277–78.

67. 1 Sam 10:17–27 does not unambiguously aim at contrasting Saul's election with the election of David, and it is therefore not necessary to assume that both accounts lie on the same literary level. In my opinion, it is much more probable that 1 Sam 16:1–13, which clearly draws on 1 Sam 10:17–27, was composed considerably later than the account of Saul's election. In any case, 1 Sam 16:1–13 revolves around the contrast between Saul and David, but it is difficult to see how this topic is connected with the problem of the literary historical relationship between 1 Sam 10 and Deut 17.

68. See Müller, *Königtum und Gottesherrschaft*, 165–66.

69. See McCarter, *I Samuel*, 195.

70. For a more extensive explanation of 1 Sam 10:17–27, see Müller, *Königtum und Gottesherrschaft*, 158–175.

far beyond 1 Sam 8.⁷¹ The prohibition against having numerous horses brings Solomon to mind⁷²; 1 Kgs 5:6 (MT; see 3 Kgdms 10:26 LXX) refers to large numbers of horses in Solomon's possession. Also, the motif of horses bought in Egypt is mentioned in the Solomonic narrative (1 Kgs 10:28). In addition, one feels reminded of Isa 31:1: "Woe to them who go down to Egypt for help and rely on horses ...!" But Deut 17:16* goes even beyond that by interpreting the purchase of horses in Egypt as a reversal of the Exodus⁷³: "... lest he return the people to Egypt in order to acquire many horses," which probably means that the king shall not sell Israelites into Egyptian slavery to get horses in exchange.⁷⁴

The second restriction of royal power in Deut 17 also is evocative of Solomon (Deut 17:17): "And he shall not acquire numerous wives for himself, lest his heart turn aside." According to 1 Kgs 11, Solomon's thousand wives led him to turn apostate from YHWH (1 Kgs 11:3): "And he had seven hundred wives and three hundred concubines, and his wives turned away his heart."⁷⁵ It is therefore probable that the phrase in Deut 17:17aα ולא יסור לבבו 'lest his heart turn aside' refers to the theme of the First Commandment. The closest parallel of the phrase ולא יסור לבבו is found Jer 17:5, which clearly refers to apostasy from YHWH: 'Cursed is the man ... whose heart turns away from YHWH' (מן יהוה יסור לבבו).⁷⁶

Finally, the law on kingship also limits the king's wealth (v. 17b, 20aα): "nor shall he acquire much silver and gold for himself, that his heart be not exalted above his brothers." Again, it is probable that this refers to the fabulous treasures of Solomon mentioned in 1 Kgs 9 and 10. The law on kingship interprets such wealth as a source of arrogance. This brings Solomon's son and successor Rehoboam to mind who, according to 1 Kgs 12, acted toward the people with extreme arrogance, thus jeopardizing the unity of Israel's monarchy. Yet, there is also another passage in the book of Kings that probably lies within the horizon of Deut 17. According to 2 Kgs 20:13, king Hezekiah showed the messengers of the Babylonian king "all his treasure house, the silver, the gold, the spices, the precious oil, and the house of his armory." This act of royal hubris provoked an oracle of doom (v. 16–17): "And Isaiah said to Hezekiah: 'Listen to the word of YHWH: Behold, days are coming when all that is in your house, and that which your fathers have stored up until this day, shall be carried to Babylon ...'"

These probable literary references indicate that the law on kingship tries to sketch the consequences that arose from the failure of the Israelite monarchy.⁷⁷ The king is not allowed to possess a large cavalry, since this would lead at least some of the Israelites back into Egyptian slavery, causing a reversal of the exodus; the closeness of Deut 17:16* to the prophetic perspective of Isa 31:1 suggests that this limitation of royal power reacts to

---

71. Achenbach, "Das sogenannte Königsgesetz," 229.

72. Thus already S. R. Driver, *A Critical and Exegetical Commentary on Deuteronomy*, ICC (Edinburgh: T&T Clark, 1902), 211.

73. Cf. Achenbach, "Das sogenannte Königsgesetz," 229, who refers to the probable literary horizon of this motif in prophetic texts like Jer 42:10–22; Hos 9:3; 11:5 and in Num 14:3–4 etc.

74. Steuernagel, *Deuteronomium*, 118.

75. Cf. Driver, *Deuteronomy*, 212; Achenbach, "Das sogenannte Königsgesetz," 229–30, who points to the fact that the probably secondary passage 1 Kgs 11:2a seems to refer already to the prohibition of Deut 7:3–4.

76. Cf. also the similar phrase in Ezek 6:9.

77. Cf. already Driver, *Deuteronomy*, 210: "... though the nucleus of the law may be ancient (v. 15), in its present form it is doubtless designed as an attempt to check the moral and religious degeneracy which the monarchy, as a fact, too often displayed."

the devastating military experiences of Israel and Judah from the 8th to the 6th centuries. A harem that is too large would be a source of apostasy from YHWH—a motif that clearly refers to the book of Kings, in which it is made clear that apostasy was the crucial reason for the downfall of the monarchy. And royal wealth is the source of pride that comes before the fall (cf. Prov 16:18; 18:12), which again refers implicitly to the catastrophes of kingship. Positively said, the law on kingship commits the king to both strict loyalty to YHWH and humility among his brothers (cf. Ps 131:1).

The peculiar phrase in Deut 17:20aα לבלתי רום לבבו מאחיו ('so that his heart be not exalted among his brothers') refers to the Deuteronomic idea of a "single people of brothers," as L. Perlitt called it, quoting F. Schiller's *Wilhelm Tell*.[78] In this context, it becomes probable that Deut 17 programmatically echoes the warning of Deut 8:12–14, according to which the wealth that will be acquired by the people in the land could result in pride, and forgetting the God of the Exodus. "Giving way to pride, the king would repeat in himself, and in the midst of the people, the depravity that threatens the people itself."[79]

At the same time, the text is conspicuously silent regarding the governmental obligations of the king. Deuteronomy 17:14–20* (esp. v. 14b) may imply that an Israelite king who would be installed according to this law would act as a potential representative of the Israelite people among the nations, since the nations are usually governed by kings. However, the text also makes clear that such an Israelite kingship would have no further political obligations. A kingship that would be in accordance to Deut 17 would not function as a government of the people. The traditional royal obligations of defending the people and guaranteeing that justice is done are not mentioned at all. The Deuteronomic law on kingship permits only that Israel may install a monarchy without any monarchic functions. Such a monarchy can indeed be called "constitutional."[80]

5. The King and his Copy of the Torah

According to vv. 18–19, which probably are a late addition, immediately after his ascension to the throne, the king has "to write down for himself a copy of this Torah in a book." This act has to be done מלפני הכהנים הלוים 'from before the Levitical priests'. The peculiar preposition מלפני 'from before' refers in all likelihood to the idea that the original document of the Torah is in the hands of the Levitical priests: "And Moses wrote down this Torah and gave it to the priests, the sons of Levi ..." (Deut 31:9).[81] The opening of the law on kingship (Deut 17:14) envisages a certain time after the conquest when the people will intend to appoint a king, and from this perspective, Deut 17:18 refers to a book that will exist at that future point of time and will be kept by the priests.[82] Thus, מלפני 'from before' probably implies that the king takes the original document, written by Moses himself, from the priests and sits down in front of them in order to draw up his personal copy under their supervision.[83]

---

78. L. Perlitt, "'Ein einzig Volk von Brüdern': Zur deuteronomischen Herkunft der biblischen Bezeichnung 'Bruder,'" in *Deuteronomium-Studien*, FAT 8 (Tübingen: Mohr Siebeck, 1994), 50–73.
79. J.-P. Sonnet, *The Book within the Book: Writing in Deuteronomy*, BibInt 14 (Leiden: Brill, 1997), 81.
80. See n. 8.
81. Achenbach, "Das sogenannte Königsgesetz," 231.
82. Lohfink, "Die Sicherung," 318.
83. Sonnet, *Book within the Book*, 74.

The content of this document is defined by the term התורה הזאת 'this Torah'. Its use in Deut 17:18 indicates that it refers to the entire instruction that Moses is giving to Israel on the day of his death in the plains of Moab; in this sense the Mosaic instruction of Deut 5–28 is introduced with the term התורה in Deut 4:44, and it is probable that Deut 17:18–19 refers particularly to this superscription.[84] At the same time, the image of this Torah document is open to incorporate the entire book written by Moses according to Deut 31:24 (including Deut 1–32).[85]

After the king has finished writing down his copy of the Torah, he has another duty, as stated in v. 19. The Mosaic Torah 'shall accompany him' (והיתה עמו), thus becoming "the king's *vade mecum*,"[86] and he shall read "in" his copy of the Torah (בו)[87] every day. The purpose of this permanent study is described with typical Deuteronomistic phrases that are closely parallel to Deut 31:12–13, a passage that explains why the priests and elders have to read the Torah every seven years to all the people. Particularly notable is the phrase למד ליראה את יהוה 'learn to fear YHWH', which creates a close link between Deut 17:19 and Deut 31:1, since it is attested only once more in Deuteronomy[88]:

Deut 17:19	Deut 31:12–13
19 והיתה עמו וקרא בו כל ימי חייו למען ילמד ליראה את יהוה אלהיו לשמר את כל דברי התורה הזאת ואת החקים האלה לעשתם ...	12 הקהל את העם האנשים והנשים והטף וגרך אשר בשעריך למען ישמעו ולמען ילמדו ויראו את יהוה אלהיכם ושמרו לעשות את כל דברי התורה הזאת 13 ובניהם אשר לא ידעו ישמעו ולמדו ליראה את יהוה אלהיכם כל הימים אשר אתם חיים על האדמה אשר אתם עברים את הירדן שמה לרשתה
And it shall be with him and he shall read in it all the days of his life <u>so that he may learn to fear YHWH his God</u>, <u>by observing</u> all the words of this Torah and these statutes <u>to do them</u>, ...	12 Assemble the people—men, women, and children, as well as the aliens residing in your towns—so that they may hear and <u>learn to fear YHWH your God</u> and <u>be careful to do</u> all the words of this law, 13 and so that their children, who have not known it, may hear and <u>learn to fear YHWH your God</u>, as long as you live in the land that you are crossing over the Jordan to possess.

---

84. Prior to Deut 17:18, התורה is, apart from Deut 4:44 (cf. 1:5; 4:8), mentioned only in Deut 17:11; however, Deut 17:11 uses the term התורה for the priestly instruction, which clearly differs from the perspective of Deut 17:18.

85. Similarly G. Braulik, "Die Ausdrücke für 'Gesetz' im Buch Deuteronomium," in *Studien zur Theologie des Deuteronomiums*, SBAB 2 (Stuttgart: Katholisches Bibelwerk, 1988), 11–38, here 36–38, and cf. H. Knobloch, *Die nachexilische Prophetentheorie des Jeremiabuches*, BZAR 12 (Wiesbaden: Harrassowitz, 2009), 266, who correctly observes that the formulation וכתב לו את משנה התורה הזאת על ספר is particularly similar to Deut 31:24 (ויהי ככלות משה לכתב את דברי התורה הזאת על ספר עד תמם).

86. Craigie, *Book of Deuteronomy*, 257.

87. The masc. refers to the book, not to the Torah, which is the subject of והיתה.

88. Deut 14:23.

A comparison with Deut 5:32–6:2 corroborates that in Deut 17, the king is programmatically subjected to what is the obligation of the entire people.[89] In Deut 5:32–6:2, we find exactly the same phrases as in Deut 17:20aβb:

Deut 5:32–6:2	Deut 17:19–20
32 ושמרתם לעשות כאשר צוה יהוה אלהיכם אתכם <u>לא תסרו ימן ושמאל</u>	19 והיתה עמו וקרא בו <u>כל ימי חייו</u> למען ילמד ליראה את יהוה אלהיו לשמר את כל דברי התורה הזאת ואת <u>החקים</u> האלה לעשתם
33 בכל הדרך אשר צוה יהוה אלהיכם אתכם תלכו למען תחיון וטוב לכם והארכתם ימים בארץ אשר תירשון	20 לבלתי רום לבבו מאחיו <u>ולבלתי סור מן המצוה ימין ושמאול</u> <u>למען יאריך ימים</u> על ממלכתו <u>הוא ובניו</u> בקרב ישראל
1 וזאת <u>המצוה החקים</u> והמשפטים אשר צוה יהוה אלהיכם ללמד אתכם לעשות בארץ אשר אתם עברים שמה לרשתה	
2 למען תירא את יהוה אלהיך לשמר את כל חקתיו ומצותיו אשר אנכי מצוך <u>אתה ובנך ובן בנך כל ימי חייך ולמען יארכן ימיך</u>	

32 And observe to do just as YHWH your God has commanded you, <u>do not turn aside to the right or to the left</u>.	19 and it shall be with him and he shall read in it <u>all the days of his life</u> so that he may learn to fear YHWH his God, by observing all the words of this Torah and these <u>statutes</u> to do them,
33 You shall walk on the whole way that YHWH your God has commanded you, so that you may live, and that it may be well with you, and that you may prolong your days in the land that you will take over.	20 that his heart be not exalted above his brothers <u>nor he turn aside from the commandment, to the right or to the left</u>, <u>so that he may prolong his days</u> over his kingdom, <u>he and his sons</u> in the midst of Israel.
6:1 And this is <u>the commandment</u>—the statutes and the ordinances—that YHWH your God commanded to teach you in the land into which you are crossing to take it over,	
2 so that you may fear YHWH your God, by observing all his statutes and his commandments that I am commanding you, <u>you and your son</u> and your son's son <u>all the days of your life</u>, and <u>so that you may prolong your days</u>.	

In particular, it is probable that 'the commandment' (המצוה) mentioned in 17:20aβ refers to the commandment introduced in 6:1. According to 5:32 and 6:1, the king "shall not turn aside from the commandment to the right and to the left," and by doing so, he will "prolong his days over his kingdom, he and his sons in the midst of Israel." This allusion to the dynastic principle is probably inspired by Deut 6:2, which refers to the children and grandchildren of every Israelite. And, like every Israelite, the king will prolong his life by observing the commandment.

---

89. On the inner logic of Deut 6:1–2 in relation to Deut 5 cf. particularly E. Otto, *Deuteronomium 4,44–11,32*, HThKAT (Freiburg im Breisgau: Herder, 2012), 790–92; differently Veijola, *Das 5. Buch Mose*, 131–41.

Even the idea of the king reading every day in the written Torah is probably deduced from Deut 6:2, since this passage accordingly stresses that every Israelite is obliged to observe the commandments "all the days of his life." At the same time, the motif of the king reading in the book of the Torah forms a remarkable contrast between Deut 17:19 and both Deut 5:32–6:2 and Deut 31:12–13. The king is brought into a much more intimate relationship with the Torah than the common people, since he is obliged to study his own copy of the Torah that shall accompany him wherever he goes. This image of a piously reading king[90] may mirror the self-perception of the late Deuteronomistic scribes.[91]

6. A Late Deuteronomistic Reconceptualization of Kingship: The King as *Primus Inter Pares*

It is most striking that the entire law on kingship says nothing about the political dimensions of this institution. The traditional tasks of kingship, leading warfare and enforcing justice, seem deliberately ignored.[92] The lack of reference to the king's military leadership corresponds to Deuteronomy's laws on warfare that do not mention the king (Deut 20; 21:10–14; 24:5). The lack of reference to the king as the highest judge[93] corresponds to the preceding law in Deut 17:8–13, according to which the central judicial authority lies in the hands of the Levitical priests and "the judge that shall be in those days" (v. 9; cf. v. 12); it is unclear who is imagined to officiate as this judge, but the judge is not called king. Deuteronomy, therefore, separates the king from all judicial and military power. One could ask why such a kingship is necessary at all. The authors of Deut 17 would have answered that kingship is indeed not a necessary institution for Israel, as the opening of this law shows. But they also would have stressed that, since the Israelites once wanted to have a king like the surrounding nations—in the background lies the memory of Israel's long monarchic history—this kingship would have been better founded as an institution with no essential political power. Since such an apolitical kingship had not been established in Israel's history, the historical Israelite kingship necessarily failed.[94] Deuteronomy 17 can therefore be read as an implicit etiology for the downfall of the Israelite and Judahite monarchies. At the same time, the text may also imply that for Israel's future beyond the exile the inauguration of such an institution remains a possibility, at least theoretically, although Deut 17 makes clear that kingship is far from being an institution that is necessary for Israel's identity.

More important is that the Mosaic law depicts an "ideal citizen king," as R. Nelson aptly formulated.[95] This king is a member of an egalitarian society, and it is his duty not to elevate himself above the others. Like all the people, he is obliged to remain loyal to

---

90. It has often been observed that the image of the reading king stands already close of the idea of a permanent pious meditation on the Torah, as in Josh 1:8, which probably alludes to Ps 1. However, Deut 17:19 does not yet talk explicitly about a meditation at day and night, and therefore it might be slightly older than Josh 1:8 and Ps 1, see, e.g., Weinfeld, *Deuteronomy and the Deuteronomic School*, 5 n. 1.

91. Cf. the important study of T. Veijola, "Die Deuteronomisten als Vorgänger der Schriftgelehrten: Ein Beitrag zur Entstehung des Judentums," in *Moses Erben: Studien zum Dekalog, zum Deuteronomismus und zum Schriftgelehrtentum*, BWANT 149 (Stuttgart: Kohlhammer, 2000), 192–240.

92. Achenbach, "Das sogenannte Königsgesetz," 219–20.

93. Cf. 2 Sam 14; 15:4; 1 Kgs 3; 7:7; Ps 72.

94. On the description of the failures of the monarchic history in Samuel and Kings cf. particularly E. Ben Zvi, "Looking at the Primary (Hi)Story and the Prophetic Books as Literary / Theological Units within the Frame of the Early Second Temple: Some Considerations," *SJOT* 12 (1998): 26-43.

95. Nelson, *Deuteronomy*, 225.

YHWH, the god of the Exodus, and to learn and practice total observance of the divine commandment contained in the Mosaic Torah. Yet, the egalitarianism is not complete. The king has one privilege, based on his ownership of a copy of the Torah. It is his duty and, at the same time, his privilege to study this document every day of his life. This is more than the average Israelite can do. It is no coincidence that the Deuteronomic image of the Israelite king brings to mind a learned scribe who is able to copy the Torah by himself and to read and re-read his own exemplar of it permanently. In this regard, the king gets the role of a *primus inter pares*, and it can be assumed that the scribes of the Persian period who transmitted the written Torah perceived themselves correspondingly.

To be sure, this has nothing to do with democracy in a strict sense, if democracy is defined as the process in which political decisions are deduced from the will of the people's majority. The "democratic"—or egalitarian—element that can be found in Deuteronomy instead is the obligation to abide with the Mosaic commandment. No one is exempt from this obligation, and everybody is bound to follow the Torah. Deut 17 constructs a kind of constitutional monarchy by portraying the king as a representative of the people's fear of YHWH. At the same time, this concept indicates indirectly that such an egalitarian society under Mosaic Torah needs those who are experts in this Torah, since they are the ones who are able to study it every day.

Bibliography

Achenbach, R. 2009. "Das sogenannte Königsgesetz in Deuteronomium 17,14–20." *ZABR* 15: 216–33.

Adam, K.-P. 2007. *Saul und David in der judäischen Geschichtsschreibung: Studien zu 1 Samuel 16–2 Samuel 5*. FAT 51. Tübingen: Mohr Siebeck.

Ben Zvi, E. 1998. "Looking at the Primary (Hi)Story and the Prophetic Books as Literary / Theological Units within the Frame of the Early Second Temple: Some Considerations." *SJOT* 12: 26-43.

Braulik, G. 1988. "Die Ausdrücke für 'Gesetz' im Buch Deuteronomium." In *Studien zur Theologie des Deuteronomiums*, 11–38. SBAB 2. Stuttgart: Katholisches Bibelwerk.

Bultmann, C. 1992. *Der Fremde im antiken Juda: Eine Untersuchung zum sozialen Typenbegriff 'ger' und seinem Bedeutungswandel in der alttestamentlichen Gesetzgebung*. FRLANT 153. Göttingen: Vandenhoeck & Ruprecht.

Craigie, P. C. 1976. *The Book of Deuteronomy*. NICOT. Grand Rapids, MI: Eerdmans.

Crüsemann, F. 1978. *Der Widerstand gegen das Königtum: Die antiköniglichen Texte des Alten Testaments und der Kampf um den frühen israelitischen Staat*. WMANT 49. Neukirchen-Vluyn: Neukirchener Verlag.

Daube, D. 1971. "One from among your Brethren Shall You Set King over You." *JBL* 90: 480–81.

Dietrich, W. 2000. "History and Law: Deuteronomistic Historiography and Deuteronomic Law Exemplified in the Passage from the Period of the Judges to the Monarchical Period." In *Israel Constructs its History: Deuteronomistic Historiography in Recent Research*, edited by A. de Pury, T. Römer, and J.-D. Macchi, 315–42. JSOTSup 306. Sheffield: Sheffield Academic Press.

Driver, S. R. 1902. *A Critical and Exegetical Commentary on Deuteronomy*. ICC. Edinburgh: T&T Clark.

García López, F. 1985. "Le roi d'Israël: Dt 17,14–20." In *Das Deuteronomium: Entstehung, Gestalt und Botschaft*. Edited by N. Lohfink, 277–97. BETL 68. Leuven: University Press.

Gertz, J. C. 1994. *Die Gerichtsorganisation Israels im deuteronomischen Gesetz*. FRLANT 165. Göttingen: Vandenhoeck & Ruprecht.

Knobloch, H. 2009. *Die nachexilische Prophetentheorie des Jeremiabuches*. BZAR 12. Wiesbaden: Harrassowitz.

Knoppers, G. N. 1996. "The Deuteronomist and the Deuteronomic Law of the King: A Reexamination of a Relationship." *ZAW* 108: 329–46.

Koch, C. 2008. *Vertrag, Treueid und Bund: Studien zur Rezeption des altorientalischen Vertragsrechts im Deuteronomium und zur Ausbildung der Bundestheologie im Alten Testament*. BZAW 383. Berlin: de Gruyter.

Kratz, R. G. 2005. *The Composition of the Narrative Books of the Old Testament*. London: T&T Clark.

Levin, C. 2014. "Rereading Deuteronomy in the Persian and Hellenistic Periods: The Ethics of Brotherhood and the Care of the Poor." In *Deuteronomy to Kings as Emerging Authoritative Books: A Conversation*, edited by D. V. Edelman, 43–71. ANEM 6. Atlanta, GA: SBL.

———. 1985. *Die Verheißung des neuen Bundes: in ihrem theologiegeschichtlichen Zusammenhang ausgelegt*. FRLANT 137. Göttingen: Vandenhoeck & Ruprecht.

Levinson, B. M. 2001. "The Reconceptualization of Kingship in Deuteronomy and the Deuteronomistic History's Transformation of the Torah." *VT* 51: 511–34.

Lohfink, N. 1990. "Die Sicherung der Wirksamkeit des Gotteswortes durch das Prinzip der Schriftlichkeit der Tora und durch das Prinzip der Gewaltenteilung nach den Ämtergesetzen des Buches Deuteronomium." In *Studien zum Deuteronomium und zur deuteronomistischen Literatur I*, 305–23. SBAB 8. Stuttgart: Katholisches Bibelwerk.

Markl, D. 2012. *Gottes Volk im Deuteronomium*. BZAR 18. Wiesbaden: Harrassowitz.

McCarter, P. K. 1980. *I Samuel: A New Translation with Introduction, Notes and Commentary*. AB 8. New York: Doubleday.

Müller, R. 2013. "Der unvergleichliche Gott: Zur Umformung einer polytheistischen Redeweise im Alten Testament." In *Gott – Götter – Götzen: XIV: Europäischer Kongress für Theologie (11.-15. September 2011 in Zürich)*, edited by C. Schwöbel, 304–19. Veröffentlichungen der Wissenschaftlichen Gesellschaft für Theologie 38. Leipzig: Evangelische Verlagsanstalt.

———. 2010. "Images of Exile in the Book of Judges." In *The Concept of Exile in Ancient Israel and its Historical Contexts*, edited by E. Ben Zvi and C. Levin, 229–40. BZAW 404. Berlin: de Gruyter.

———. 2004. *Königtum und Gottesherrschaft: Untersuchungen zur alttestamentlichen Monarchiekritik*. FAT 2/3 Tübingen: Mohr Siebeck.

Nelson, R. D. 2002. *Deuteronomy: A Commentary*. OTL. Louisville, KY: Westminster John Knox.

Nihan, C. 2013. "1 Samuel 8 and 12 and the Deuteronomistic Edition of Samuel." In *Is Samuel among the Deuteronomists? Current Views on the Place of Samuel in a Deuteronomistic History*, edited by C. Edenburg and J. Pakkala, 225–73. SBLAIL 16. Atlanta, GA: SBL.

———. 2013. "Rewriting Kingship in Samuel: 1 Samuel 8 and 12 and the Law of the King (Deuteronomy 17)." *HeBAI* 2: 315–50.

Noth, M. 1981. *The Deuteronomistic History*. JSOTSup 15. Sheffield: JSOT Press. Translation of *Überlieferungsgeschichtliche Studien: Die sammelnden und bearbeitenden Geschichtswerke im Alten Testament*. Königsberg: Königsberger Gelehrte Gesellschaft, 1943.

Otto, E. 2012. *Deuteronomium 4,44–11,32*. HThKAT. Freiburg im Breisgau: Herder.

Perlitt, L. 1994. "'Ein einzig Volk von Brüdern': Zur deuteronomischen Herkunft der biblischen Bezeichnung 'Bruder.'" In *Deuteronomium-Studien*, 50–73. FAT 8. Tübingen: Mohr Siebeck.

---. 1994. "Der Staatsgedanke im Deuteronomium." In *Language, Theology, and the Bible: Essays in Honour of James Barr,* edited by S. E. Balentine and J. Barton, 182–98. Oxford: Clarendon.

Römer, T. 2005. *The So-Called Deuteronomistic History: A Sociological, Historical and Literary Introduction.* London: T&T Clark International.

Rose, M. 1994. *5. Mose.* 2 vols. ZBK 5. Zürich: Theologischer Verlag.

Rüterswörden, U. 1987. *Von der politischen Gemeinschaft zur Gemeinde: Studien zu Dt 16,18–18,22.* BBB 65. Frankfurt am Main: Athenäum.

Särkiö, P. 1994. *Die Weisheit und Macht Salomos in der israelitischen Historiographie: Eine traditions- und redaktionskritische Untersuchung über 1 Kön 3–5 und 9–11.* Schriften der Finnischen Exegetischen Gesellschaft 60. Helsinki: Finnische Exegetische Gesellschaft.

Schäfer-Lichtenberger, C. 1995. *Josua und Salomo: Eine Studie zu Autorität und Legitimität des Nachfolgers im Alten Testament.* VTSup 55. Leiden: Brill.

Schenker, A. 2008. "Le Seigneur choisira-til le lieu de son nom ou l'a-t-il choisi? L'apport de la Bible grecque ancienne à l'histoire du texte samaritain et massorétique." In *Scripture in Transition,* edited by A. Voitila and J. Jokiranta, 339–51. Leiden: Brill.

Seitz, G. 1971. *Redaktionsgeschichtliche Studien zum Deuteronomium.* BWANT 93. Stuttgart: Kohlhammer.

Sonnet, J.-P. 1997. *The Book within the Book: Writing in Deuteronomy.* BibInt 14. Leiden: Brill.

Steuernagel, C. 1923. *Das Deuteronomium.* 2nd ed. Göttingen: Vandenhoeck & Ruprecht.

Steymans, H. U. 1995. *Deuteronomium 28 und die adê zur Thronfolgeregelung Asarhaddons: Segen und Fluch im Alten Orient und in Israel.* OBO 145. Freiburg: Universitätsverlag; Göttingen: Vandenhoeck & Ruprecht.

Veijola, T. 2004. *Das fünfte Buch Mose: Deuteronomium, Kapitel 1,1–16,17.* ATD 8/1. Göttingen: Vandenhoeck & Ruprecht.

---. 2000. "Die Deuteronomisten als Vorgänger der Schriftgelehrten: Ein Beitrag zur Entstehung des Judentums." In *Moses Erben: Studien zum Dekalog, zum Deuteronomismus und zum Schriftgelehrtentum,* 192–240. BWANT 149. Stuttgart: Kohlhammer.

---. 1977. *Das Königtum in der Beurteilung der deuteronomistischen Historiographie: Eine redaktionsgeschichtliche Untersuchung.* Annales Academiae scientiarum fennicae B 193. Helsinki: Suomalainen Tiedeakatemia.

Vermeylen, J. 2013. "The Book of Samuel within the Deuteronomistic History." In *Is Samuel among the Deuteronomists? Current Views on the Place of Samuel in a Deuteronomistic History,* edited by C. Edenburg and J. Pakkala, 67–91. SBLAIL 16. Atlanta, GA: SBL.

Weinfeld, M. 1972. *Deuteronomy and the Deuteronomic School.* Oxford: Clarendon.

— 6 —

The Kingdom of God in Samuel

Geoffrey P. Miller

This paper discusses certain texts in the Hebrew Bible that address the idea of theocracy, the political system in which authority is exercised by God's representative on earth. The treatment of this topic in the Hebrw Bible is subtle and nuanced, recognizing virtues in theocratic rule but concluding, overall, that it does not deliver sustainable and effective governance in the real world.

1. Methodology

The story of the Israelite people, extending from Genesis to 2 Kings,[1] contains within it an extended analysis of political obligation and governmental design—a political philosophy that rivals in sophistication the theories put forward by Plato and Aristotle in ancient Greece.[2] The key to unlocking the Bible's political theory is to understand that the narratives are employed for expository and analytical purposes.[3] They set up and investigate basic questions about government that have also occupied later thinkers: What is the

---

1. The material from Genesis through 2 Kings is sometimes referred to in biblical scholarship as the "primary history." See D. N. Freedman, "The Earliest Bible," in *Backgrounds for the Bible*, ed. M. P. O'Connor and D. N. Freedman (Winona Lake, IN: Eisenbrauns, 1987), 29–38.

2. See generally G. P. Miller, *Ways of a King: Legal and Political Ideas in the Bible* (Göttingen: Vandenhoeck & Ruprecht, 2011). For other works identifying political-theoretical themes in biblical texts, see J. G. McConville, *God and Earthly Power: An Old Testament Political Theology, Genesis-Kings* (London: T&T Clark International, 2006); M. Walzer, *Exodus and Revolution* (New York: Basic Books, 1985); J. Rosenberg, *King and Kin: Political Allegory in the Hebrew Bible* (Bloomington: Indiana University Press, 1986); S. D. Sperling, *The Original Torah: The Political Intent of the Bible's Writers* (New York: New York University Press, 1998); J. Berman, *Created Equal: How the Bible Broke with Ancient Political Thought* (Oxford: Oxford University Press, 2008); B. M. Levinson, *Deuteronomy and the Hermeneutics of Legal Innovation* (Oxford: Oxford University Press, 1977); M. Morgenstern, *Conceiving a Nation: The Development of Political Discourse in the Hebrew Bible* (University Park: Pennsylvania State University Press, 2009).

3. This paper deals with the biblical text in its present form and argues that the people responsible for the contents of that text were concerned, in part, with political ideas. The history of composition of these texts, a central theme of much biblical scholarship, is not within the scope of the present analysis.

justification for the compulsory power that political leaders exercise over their subjects? Can human beings achieve a good and decent life in the absence of government and law? What is the basis for authority exercised within families and kinship groups? What is leadership and how is it achieved? What is law and how are legal obligations created? What criteria validate claims to political authority? What is a nation and how is it created? What is sovereignty? What principles of justice govern the distribution of resources within a society? What are the advantages and disadvantages of monarchy compared with other forms of national government? What limits, if any, constrain a monarch's power? These and other questions are framed for analysis and insightfully discussed through the medium of the narratives of Israel's leaders and their relationship with Israel's God.

Narrative may not seem like a useful approach to political theory, given that the task of interpretation is complicated by the need to supply a reliable means of associating the actors and elements of setting with political ideas and problems. However, narratives can serve as the basis of effective analysis—so effective that narrative analysis it is widely used today and is even a dominant approach in ostensibly scientific fields such as economic theory.[4] Using narrative, the analyst can frame issues for discussion by specifying elements of the setting—when, where, and how events take place—and also the cast of characters—the figures to whom action is attributed within the narrative. The plot, the events that transpire in the narrative, is then a form of experiment: the analyst explores how events play out and, based on these results, can make normative assessments about the strengths or weaknesses of different arrangements.

As compared with discursive analysis, narratives and their analysis offered certain advantages that could have been particularly salient in the social setting of ancient Israel. They offer mnemonic benefits in that vibrant stories are easier to remember and pass on in the culture than dry analytical tomes.[5] The artistic quality of narratives enhances their communicative effect: people enjoy and remember works with entertainment value. Even if every member of the audience did not fully grasp the matters under consideration, some would nevertheless understand them.[6] Further, narratives offered means for authenticating the validity and reliability of the message being conveyed by associating the text with materials already familiar in the culture. Rhetorical devices such as etiology and etymology perform this function, as do techniques such as associating the narratives with ancestral figures already endowed by the culture with charismatic authority.

---

4. As Nobel Laureate R. E. Lucas, Jr. puts it, economists are "storytellers, operating much of the time in worlds of make believe. We [economists] do not find that the realm of imagination and ideas is an alternative to, or a retreat from, practical reality. On the contrary, it is the only way we have found to think seriously about reality" ("What Economists Do," 9 December, 1988, http://homepage.ntu.edu.tw/~mjlin/lucas.pdf).

5. On orality in ancient Israel, see, e.g., S. Niditch, *Ancient Israelite Religion* (Oxford: Oxford University Press, 1997); E. A. Seibert, *Subversive Scribes and the Solomonic Narrative: A Rereading of 1 Kings 1-11* (New York: T&T Clark, 2006), 46–49.

6. The Bible's political theory is similar to what T. Hobbes said of Thucydides that "the narration itself doth secretly instruct the reader, and more effectually than can possibly be done by precept." T. Hobbes, *On the Life and History of Thucydides*; online: https://archive.org/details/grecianwarhobb00thucuoft. On Hobbes's Tucydides see I. D. Evrigenis, "Hobbes's Thucydides," *Journal of Military Ethics* 5 [Special Issue: "Thucydides and Civil War"] (2006), 303-316.

2. The Garden of Eden

In the Hebrew Bible, the treatment of theocracy as a form of government begins at the beginning, in the Garden of Eden story.[7] The elements of setting in this narrative provide a clue to the political question being evaluated. Unlike the rest of the world, the garden is civilized: carefully designed, well watered, and scrupulously maintained. It has borders that separate the wild from the tame.[8] It is protected against incursion: Adam and Eve fear no threat from outside. It is governed by a rule of law clearly announced and vigorously enforced. It is home to human beings and animals living in harmony with one another. It is also a venue for productive activity: Adam and Eve tend the garden on God's behalf. Symbolically, the garden represents a defined territory of land over which governance can be exercised.

The cast of characters provides further information. God creates the garden and all its creatures. He treats the territory as his property, walking there in the afternoon to enjoy its cooling breeze (Gen 3:8).[9] He cares for the inhabitants and seeks to enhance their welfare. He provides them with food, a reasonable degree of freedom, and an opportunity for satisfying work. He understands their needs even better than they do themselves: it is God, not Adam, who realizes that man needs a companion if he is to enjoy a satisfying life. From the standpoint of political theory, God is the benevolent monarch of this small domain.[10]

Adam is a productive worker and leading figure within Eden. God trusts Adam and gives him important responsibilities. Eve is Adam's helpmate. She feeds her husband and influences him from behind the scenes. The garden is also home to animals who apparently have the ability to speak and reason. Symbolically, Adam, Eve, and the animals are the population of this territory—citizens, sorted according to a hierarchy of status, who are subject to God's rule.

What about God's commands for the garden? God decrees that Adam and Eve may eat any fruit except for the fruit from the tree of knowledge. This dietary rule is both general

---

7. The literature on the provenance of this text is vast and contentious. Among scholars advocating for a relatively early dating, see E. W. Nicholas, *The Pentateuch in the Twentieth Century* (Oxford: Oxford University Press 1998); R. E. Friedman, *Who Wrote the Bible?* (New York: Harper & Row, 1987). Scholars advocating for a later dating of the narrative include J. Van Seters, *A Prologue to History: The Yahwist as Historian in Genesis* (Louisville, KY: Westminster John Knox, 1994); N. P. Lemche, *The Israelites in History and Tradition* (Louisville, KY: Westminster John Knox, 1998); P. R. Davies, *In Search of "Ancient Israel,"* JSOTSup 148 (Sheffield: JSOT Press, 1992); and T. L. Thompson, *Early History of the Israelite People* (Leiden: Brill, 1992).

8. That the garden was bounded is obvious from the detail that God places cherubim to guard against Adam and Eve's return after their expulsion; the cherubim would not have known what to guard if there were no borders. Later images of the garden often depict the area as surrounded by a wall, even though no wall is referenced in the text itself. See, e.g., F. Motta, "'Geographica Sacra': The Placing of Paradise in Late Seventeenth-Century French Theology," in *The Earthly Paradise: The Garden of Eden from Antiquity to Modernity*, ed. R. F. Psaki and C. Hindley (Binghamton, NY: Academic Studies in the History of Judaism, Global Publications, State University of New York at Binghamton, 2002), 283–311.

9. The image of the garden would have evoked associations with kingship; gardens in the biblical times were important privileges of monarchs. See 2 Kgs 21:18, 25:4. On the general association of God with the concept of kingship, see for example, J. J. Niehaus, *God at Sinai: Covenant and Theophany in the Bible and Ancient Near East* (Grand Rapids, MI: Zondervan, 1995), 84–93.

10. The association of God with a king is consistent with other biblical texts as well as ancient Near Eastern practices. See Exod 15:18; Num 23:21; 1 Sam 8:7; Pss 24, 93, 96, 97, 99; J. W. Watts, *Reading Law: The Rhetorical Shaping of the Pentateuch* (Sheffield: Sheffield Academic, 1999), 100–101.

and comprehensive. Because everyone must eat, the rule pertains to everyone. Moreover, the scheme covers the entire field of what fruits may and may not be eaten. This rule is thus an excellent symbol for the laws that a ruler imposes on the subjects within his or her territory.

In combination, the elements of the Eden story present a simple model of political organization: a small society established within a well-defined territory containing citizens and a household, as well as a government, organized according to law, and offering its inhabitants the benefits of civilization and the opportunity to engage in productive labor. The narrative setting thus presents a simplified model of a political entity—a mini-state that provides governance under law and prosperity for those who live within its borders.

Governance in the garden is theocratic: God is the monarch of this domain. There is, however, an important difference between the theocracy of the Garden of Eden and theocracies in the real world. In ordinary life, theocratic rule is enforced by someone who is—or who purports to be—God's chosen representative. In the Garden of Eden, theocratic rule is carried out by *God himself* with no human intermediary. The direct nature of theocratic rule in the garden provides a clue to the Bible's evaluation of the advantages and disadvantages of theocratic rule. The message is that in an ideal world—in a utopia where God rules directly rather than through human agency—theocracy is the best form of government. Those who would challenge theocratic rule in this circumstance, like the serpent, deserve to be cursed and reviled because they foment treason against the sole and legitimate ruler of such an idealized realm.

The biblical authors do not, however, draw the conclusion that theocratic rule is best for actual human societies. Adam and Eve are expelled from God's presence and can never return. God will no longer rule over them directly. Practical governance in the real world, if it is to exist at all, must be administered by flesh-and-blood human beings. The question posed is whether theocracy, an excellent form of government in a society directly ruled by God, is also the most desirable system in a society ruled by human beings.

3. Moses

The latter question is first investigated in the Moses narratives. Moses is not one of the elders and is not from a leading family. He is not even distinctively Israelite since he is raised by Egyptians, lives abroad, and marries a foreign woman. His claim to leadership is based on his connection with God: he is called by divine command; governs Israel as God's faithful and loyal agent; receives frequent revelations; channels God's words to the people; exercises delegated supernatural powers; visits God's own habitation; and enjoys a license to parlay with the deity.[11] Moses, in short, is portrayed in the Bible as a theocratic leader—indeed, as a paragon of theocratic rule.

Yet even Moses, as worthy as he is, does not succeed in being God's perfect agent.[12] Numbers 20 tells the story of how God gives Moses a staff and tells him to command a rock to produce water. Moses does as God commands, but instead of speaking to the rock,

---

11. Moses is nearly a paradigm of the charismatic figure described in the work of M. Weber: one of those natural leaders, "neither officeholders nor incumbents of an 'occupation' ... [who arise in times of] psychic, physical, economic, ethical, religious, political distress." These leaders, in Weber's view, are "holders of specific gifts of the body and spirit; and these gifts have been believed to be supernatural, not accessible to everybody." M. Weber, *From Max Weber: Essays in Sociology*, ed. and trans. H. H. Gerth and C. W. Mills (Oxford: Oxford University Press, 1946), 245.

12. See W. H. Propp, "The Rod of Aaron and the Sin of Moses," *JBL* 107 (1988): 19–26; M. Margaliot, "The Transgression of Moses and Aaron: Num. 20:1–13," *JQR* (New Series) 74 (1983): 196–228.

he strikes it with his staff. When God learns of Moses's action, he becomes angry. Because Moses "did not trust in me enough to honor me as holy in the sight of the Israelites," God announces, "he will not be allowed to lead his followers into the Promised Land" (Num 20:12). God's response to what might seem like a slight transgression carries a message from the standpoint of political theory. If a representative as divinely favored as Moses is unable to carry out God's wishes in full, then how will any other human being be capable enough to be faithful to God's will?

4. The Golden Calf

The story of Moses's transgression is a step in the analysis of theocratic rule within the Hebrew Bible. But the Moses narratives demonstrate only that in the real world, unlike the ideal setting of the Garden of Eden, even the best of theocratic rulers can never perfectly represent God's will. More analysis remains to be done by way of investigating whether theocratic rule can, nevertheless, offer a desirable form of government for actual human societies. The latter question is addressed in the story of the golden calf.[13]

While Moses is away on Sinai, the people entreat Aaron to "make us gods that will go before us. As for this fellow Moses who brought us up out of Egypt, we do not know what has happened to him" (Exod 32:1). Aaron asks people to hand over their golden earrings, forges an idol in the form of a calf, builds an altar, and organizes a "festival to the Lord" (Exod 32:5). The next morning the people participate in burnt offerings and sacrifices, enjoy a communal feast, and revel before the idol (Exod 32:6). When Moses observes the festivities, he angrily destroys the idol (Exod 32:20) and, with the help of the Levites, kills three thousand idolaters (Exod 32:28).

The story of the golden calf sets up the question of what happens when a theocratic ruler is less worthy than Moses. The story depicts Aaron as stepping into a leadership role. The people have lost faith in Moses. They demand that Aaron provide new leadership not as Moses's agent, but rather as his replacement. Aaron, it appears, is willing to oblige. He performs classic leadership tasks: he collects resources for public purposes (the earrings), builds public facilities (the calf), organizes collective action (the sacrifice and revel), and exercises control over a symbol of national identity (the calf).

Aaron's leadership in Israel, although brief, is theocratic in nature. The people's demand is couched in theocratic terms: they ask Aaron to "make us gods who will go before us." Aaron's acts of leadership are explicitly theocratic: he builds a religious symbol (the calf) and organizes a celebration of worship (the sacrifice and revel). Aaron's actions as theocratic leader, moreover, are consistent with his general role in the biblical narratives: although he never again seeks to supplant Moses's authority, he is associated with a priestly office throughout the Hebrew Bible (Exod 28, 29, 30:7–10, 17–21, 30–32, 39; Lev 2:1–3, 8, 9; Num 3:1–10, 16:36–50, 17, 18; Josh 21:19; Ps 99:6).

Aaron's abortive attempt at theocratic rule is condemned. When God discovers what Aaron and the Israelites are doing, he accuses the people of corruption and disloyalty (Exod

---

13. Among notable contributions to the vast literature on the golden calf episode, see, for example, D. Frankel, "The Destruction of the Golden Calf: A New Solution," *VT* 44 (1994): 330–39; S. E. Loewenstamm, "The Making and Destruction of the Golden Calf," *Biblica* 48 (1967): 481–90; J. W. Watts, "Aaron and the Golden Calf in the Rhetoric of the Pentateuch," *JBL* 130 (2011): 417–30; M. Aberbach and L. Smolar, "Aaron, Jeroboam, and the Golden Calves," *JBL* 86 (1967): 129–40; J. M. Sasson, "The Worship of the Golden Calf," in *Orient and Occident: Essays Presented to Cyrus H. Gordon on the Occasion of his Sixty-fifth Birthday*, ed. H. A. Hoffner, Alter Orient und Altes Testament 22 (Neukirchen-Vluyn, 1973), 151–59.

32:7–8). So significant is this sin that God vows to destroy the Israelites and eliminate their legacy (Exod 32:10); only deft and diplomatic intercession by Moses is able to turn aside God's wrath (Exod 32:11–14). The story thus conveys the message that even a leader as god-favored as Aaron—a figure who in other respects enjoys a status subordinate only to Moses—can fall into disaster when he establishes himself as a theocratic leader.

In addition to this global judgment, the golden calf narrative provides more specific information about the risks associated with theocratic government. Three problems are highlighted. First, the narrative explains that the selection of the theocratic ruler is fraught with danger. Consider the people's demand to Aaron: even though their request has the gravest implications for their nation's future, they do not deliberate or debate the pros and cons. They capriciously abandon the leader who has led them out of Egypt with miraculous effect, guided them through the desert, and delivered them to the mountain of God. They are experiencing no crisis nor urgent need to change their fundamental system of authority. Their demand appears whimsical, poorly considered, and motivated by the excitement of the moment rather than a sober assessment of their situation. From the standpoint of political theory, the message is that the selection process for theocratic rules is not controlled and may result in the elevation to high office of someone who is not suited for the position.

Aaron also faces criticism for his role in the transition to theocratic rule. He is obligated to Moses on numerous grounds. Moses is Aaron's brother, his comrade in arms, his leader, and his guide. More than anyone else, Aaron could be expected to maintain confidence in Moses and to counsel the people to await his return. Yet when the people approach Aaron with the request that he supplant his brother and revolutionize Israel's governance, he hardly thinks twice. Even though he has not received any word from God endorsing his acceptance of the new position, Aaron listens to the people and takes the lead in organizing a fundamental challenge to Moses's rule. If a figure such as Aaron, admirable in so many respects, can fall for the lure of theocratic rule, others less worthy will find the temptation even more enticing. The narrative of the golden calf incident thus suggests that potential leaders will find it all too easy to use the claim to theocratic rule as a path to power.

A second critique, also found in the golden calf episode, is that theocratic rule does not encourage sober and effective behavior by the public. The Israelites become so excited about the golden calf that they nearly lose their senses. They "indulge in revelry" around the idol (Exod 32:6), "running wild" and "out of control" (Exod 32:25). The noise of their celebrations is so chaotic that Joshua, a seasoned fighter, interprets it as evidence of warfare (Exod 32:17). God's judgment on this behavior is harsh; the revelry weakens the Israelites and makes them reviled and traduced by other nations (Exod 32:25). The message is that the ecstatic quality sometimes associated with theocratic rule is poorly suited for developing a stable nation which can command respect from enemies and demand a place of honor among other nations.

The third and deepest critique of theocratic rule in the episode of the golden calf is that it frequently diverts rather than directs fidelity to God. Of all the Israelites other than Moses, Aaron is most expected to resist idolatry. Yet Moses is away for only a short time before Aaron falls into these evil practices. The message is that the inherently personal nature of theocratic rule imposes few checks on the ruler's authority. If the purported theocratic ruler falls into sinful practices, the people will follow. Beyond this, a theocratic ruler faces a perverse incentive to change religious practices when doing so will undermine potential rivals (consider how, from Aaron's point of view, the golden calf would have undermined the people's lingering loyalty to Moses).

5. Gideon

The story of the golden calf advances the critique of theocratic rule in several respects: it demonstrates that the process of selecting a theocratic ruler is dangerous and unreliable; it argues that theocratic rule is poorly suited for motivating desirable public behavior; and it claims that theocratic rule may result in apostasy rather than in enhanced fidelity to God. These arguments, however, are developed in the abstract context of the wilderness wanderings. While they suggest that theocracy is likely to be problematic for Israelites in the Promised Land, they do not demonstrate that proposition. The story of Gideon begins the analysis of theocracy in this more specific context.[14]

After Gideon saves the Israelites from the Midianites, the people ask him to rule as a dynastic king (Judg 8:22). Gideon rebuffs them, saying "I will not rule over you, nor will my son rule over you. The Lord will rule over you" (Judg 8:23). Gideon asks the people to give him golden earrings from their share of the plunder. The people contribute eight hundred shekels of gold and jewels, ornaments, and dyed fabric (Judg 8:26). Gideon makes an ephod—a priestly garment fabricated out of gold threads and dyed cloth (Exod 29:3)—and sets this object up in his home town of Ophrah.[15] The experiment ends poorly: "all Israel prostituted themselves by worshiping it there, and it became a snare to Gideon and his family" (Judg 8:27).[16]

What happens after Gideon's death is even worse. Israel continues to engage in unsanctioned worship, only now they turn to the Canaanite Baal as their god and abandon Israel's God entirely (Judg 8:33–34). They also fail to respect the claims of Gideon's family, in spite of all the services he has provided (Judg 8:35). Gideon's death is followed by a bloody war of succession in which Abimelek, one of his sons and a follower of the Canaanite Baal, murders seventy of his brothers. Abimelek's treachery earns him a leadership position, but he soon faces a revolt by the city of Shechem (Judg 9:22–49). He brutally suppresses the uprising but dies in ignominious fashion with a stone having been dropped on him by a woman from another city (Judg 9:51–55).

The story of Gideon and his sons continues the critique of theocratic government. Gideon's brusque rejection of the people's invitation to rule over them might be seen as commendable, given that he turns down what many ambitious people most desire—the chance to be the king—for the ostensibly pious reason that Israel should be ruled by God.[17] It quickly becomes clear, however, that in declining the kingship, Gideon is not rejecting the call to rule, rather he is rejecting the position of dynastic monarch in favor of a different leadership role. Gideon sets himself up as a theocratic ruler—not a king, but rather one who claims the right to rule as God's representative on earth.

The Bible's judgment of Gideon's theocratic rule is harsh. The narrative illustrates two principal critiques that echo those found in the golden calf narrative. First, theocratic rule,

---

14. On the Gideon narratives, see, e.g., C. F. Whitley, "The Sources of the Gideon Stories," *VT* 7 (1957): 157–64; V. Endris, "Yahweh versus Baal: A Narrative-Critical Reading of the Gideon/Abimelech Narrative," *JSOT* 33 (2008): 173–95; G. A. Auld, "Gideon: Hacking at the Heart of the Old Testament," *VT* (1989): 257–67; L. K. Klein, *The Triumph of Irony in the Book of Judges*, JSOTSup 68, Bible and Literature 14 (Sheffield: Almond Press, 1988), 68–80.

15. See G. H. Davies, "Judges VIII 22–23," *VT* 13 (1963): 151–57.

16. On the creation of the ephod as a precursor to idolatry, see D. M. Sharon, "Echoes of Gideon's Ephod: An Intertextual Reading," *JNES* 30 (2006): 89–102.

17. See B. Lindars, "Gideon and Kingship," *JTS* 16 (1965): 315–26; I. de Castelbajac, "Le cycle Gédéon ou la condamnation du refus de la royauté," *VT* 57 (2007): 145–61.

even if instituted by one who enjoys God's favor, is all too easily twisted into idolatry and sinful practices. The germ of this critique is found in the narrative of Gideon's ephod, which, like the golden calf, is fabricated out of golden earrings contributed by the Israelites. The reference to the sin of the golden calf carries with it an implicit criticism of Gideon's conduct. Gideon is barely exempted from the charge of idolatry, but the allusion to the golden calf episode implies that his creation of the ephod is unwise and dangerous. The suggestion is that even though Gideon may have established the shrine in Ophrah out of pious motivations, the unchecked power that he and his family acquire due to his role as theocratic ruler leads them into dangerous practices. The situation deteriorates further once the theocratic ruler has left the scene, because his (or her) successor may lack a bona fide connection with the deity. This happens in Gideon's case: immediately after his death, all pretense of fidelity to Israel's God is abandoned.

The second critique of theocracy found in the Gideon narrative concerns the issue of succession. Because the theocratic ruler claims to act as God's personal representative on earth, the norms of succession associated with other sorts of political authority—for example, patriarchal or monarchal power—are not available to manage the transition from one ruler to the next. Consequently, the issue of succession may be determined by violence and disorder rather than by the operation of legally recognized procedures. Moreover, there is no assurance that the successor who does assume power will govern with the same wisdom as his predecessor. These dangers come to pass in the Gideon narrative when Abimelek massacres his brothers and subjects the land to a violent tyranny.

6. Samuel

The story of Gideon presents theocratic rule in Israel under inauspicious conditions. Gideon is not commissioned by God to take over leadership of Israel. Like Aaron before him, he responds to the petition of the people without obtaining evidence of divine commission. It is hardly surprising, therefore, that the theocratic rule instituted by Gideon ends badly. The experiment set up by the Gideon narrative, while it illustrates things that can go wrong in theocratic rule, does not demonstrate that a similarly bad outcome will occur in all plausible conditions of Israel's life in the Promised Land.

The latter task is undertaken in the narratives of Samuel.[18] Although the Bible refers to Samuel as "judging" Israel, his conduct contrasts with that of prior leaders of the Israelite confederacy. He has been devoted to the priesthood from early childhood and is inspired by nothing other than religious fervor. He is the recipient of genuine revelation, and he speaks with God frequently and regularly consults him on matters of public importance. Samuel's call to leadership is different from that of other judges. In his case, the people do not cry out to God to rescue them from worldly oppression. Rather, they experience a spiritual revival: they "mourned and sought after the Lord" (1 Sam 7:2). Samuel acts only after receiving assurances that they are indeed returning to God with all their hearts (1 Sam 7:3). When the people gather in Mizpah to anoint Samuel as their leader, they do not arm themselves for battle. Instead, they participate in a ritual of confession (1 Sam 7:6). Samuel's defense of the people is religious rather than military in nature. He does not defeat the Philistines through valor in battle but rather by devoting a burnt offering to the Lord (1 Sam 7:9–10). Samuel, in short, is a true theocratic leader—the first after the set-

---

18. See L. M. Eslinger, *Kingship of God in Crisis: A Close Reading of 1 Samuel 1–12* (Sheffield: Sheffield Academic, 1985).

tlement of the Promised Land who enjoys a legitimate commission to act in this capacity.[19] In the figure of Samuel, therefore, the Bible can explore whether theocratic rule provides effective governance for Israel under the best of conditions.

The assessment of theocracy under Samuel is subtle and complex. On the one hand, theocratic rule seems to have delivered significant benefits, since Israel displays loyalty to God during this period. The people put away offending images and rituals. Samuel also achieves a modicum of national security. The Philistines withdraw from captured towns, and the Amorites do not threaten Israel (1 Sam 7:13–14). In some ways it is a halcyon period.

On the other hand, none of the texts in the Hebrew Bible view theocracy as a viable system of government in the long term, even under a ruler as worthy as Samuel. Although Samuel ousts the Philistines from Israelite territory, these enemies do not disappear. When Saul comes on the scene, God tells Samuel that the new king will "rescue [Israel] from the Philistines" (1 Sam 9:16)—a remark that would not be needed if Samuel had eliminated the risk from that quarter. It turns out that a Philistine garrison is occupying Gibeah in Benjamin at the time of Saul's anointment (1 Sam 10:5). Samuel, moreover, does not establish a viable governance apparatus for Israel. His only administrative appointments are to commission his sons as judges—and they turn out to be disasters (1 Sam 8:1–3). He does nothing to create institutions capable of governing a substantial nation. Even after he has led Israel for a long time, he makes a living providing oracles for pocket change (1 Sam 9:8–13). In spite of the decision at Mizpah, Samuel never really consolidates national leadership. While Samuel's integrity is unimpeachable, moreover, the same cannot be said for those around him. His sons pervert the administration of justice and Samuel does nothing to control them. Nor is it clear that others who are less objectionable would be available if Samuel's sons were removed from office. Lacking genuine revelation, Samuel's successors are likely to resort to divination or pretense.

Theocratic rule in Israel is very brief, amounting to only part of Samuel's lifespan. Even then, it comes to be rejected by nearly everyone. The people convene another assembly and demand a king (1 Sam 8:4–5). Even after Samuel warns them about all the hardships that the kings will impose, they remain adamant (1 Sam 8:19–20). God is not a strong supporter of theocratic rule either. He does not institute this form of government and never indicates that it is the only appropriate system for Israel. He tells Samuel to accede to the people's demand for a king, even though he knows that Samuel detests the idea (1 Sam 8:7–9). God would not do this if he were fundamentally committed to theocracy as a form of government for Israel.

An adverse judgment of theocratic rule in Israel is coded through the story of Samuel's sons. Samuel, like his predecessor Eli, has two bad sons who corrupt their offices (1 Sam 8:1–3). By providing unworthy sons for Samuel, the author of the narrative establishes that theocratic rule is at an end: one bad son could be an accident, but two show that the entire line is defective. Unlike the sons of Eli, Samuel's sons are not killed. But their role in Israel's government ends just as effectively. In Samuel's farewell address to the people, he says "and now, behold, *the king* walks before you; and I am old and grey, *and behold, my sons are with you*" (1 Sam 12:2; emphasis added). This mention of Samuel's sons is more than a touching sign of parental devotion; it establishes that Samuel's line—and theocracy as a form of government—has come to an end. Samuel's sons are no longer leaders in Israel; they are simply members of the public who, like everyone else, are subject to the authority of the king.

---

19. His predecessor, Eli, is a transitional figure who cannot be considered a true theocratic leader.

Conclusion

Overall, we can understand the assessment of theocracy in a range of biblical texts as follows: in a perfect world, theocracy would be an ideal system of government. The kingship of God is, after all, the form of government that operated in the utopia of the Garden of Eden. But an ideal world does not exist in ordinary experience. In the real world, where flesh-and-blood human beings exercise rule, theocratic government is subject to shortcomings. Its institutions do not deliver the benefits of government over the long term. It is subject to abuse, because theocratic leadership is intrinsically autocratic. The person chosen as the theocratic ruler may not receive genuine revelations from God and may not rule according to God's wishes. Theocratic rule all too easily degenerates into apostasy. And it performs poorly as a guarantor of national security. Overall, it is not optimal as a model for governing a substantial nation.

Yet, the author's conclusion that theocracy is not feasible in the real world does not obviate the importance of the idea. Theocratic rule remains an inspirational benchmark against which other forms of government can be assessed. And although theocracy disappears from Israel during the time of the kings, the power of religious authorities does not. The fact that a figure like the prophet and judge Samuel in 1 Samuel 8–12 once ruled Israel gives religious officials and prophets of later times a claim to authority—one which is used rarely, and which may in practice be more theoretical than real, but also one which remains an element of constitutional organization through the entire history of ancient Israel.

Bibliography

Aberbach, M. and L. Smolar. 1967. "Aaron, Jeroboam, and the Golden Calves." *JBL* 86: 129–40.

Auld, G. A. 1989. "Gideon: Hacking at the Heart of the Old Testament." *VT*: 257–67.

Berman, J. 2008. *Created Equal: How the Bible Broke with Ancient Political Thought*. Oxford: Oxford University Press.

Davies, G. H. 1963. "Judges VIII 22-23." *VT* 13: 151–57.

Davies, P. R. 1992. *In Search of "Ancient Israel"*. JSOTSup 148. Sheffield: JSOT Press.

De Castelbajac, I. 2007. "Le cycle Gédéon ou la condamnation du refus de la royauté." *VT* 57: 145–61.

Endris, V. 2008. "Yahweh versus Baal: A Narrative-Critical Reading of the Gideon/Abimelech Narrative." *JSOT* 33: 173–95.

Eslinger, L. M. 1985. *Kingship of God in crisis: a close reading of 1 Samuel 1–12*. Sheffield: Sheffield Academic.

Evrigenis, I. D. 2006. "Hobbes's Thucydides," Journal of Military Ethics 5 [Special Issue: "Thucydides and Civil War"] (2006): 303–16.

Frankel, D. 1994. "The Destruction of the Golden Calf: A New Solution." *VT* 44: 330–39.

Freedman, D. N. 1987. "The Earliest Bible." In *Backgrounds for the Bible,* edited by M. P. O'Connor and D. N. Freedman, 29–38. Winona Lake, IN: Eisenbrauns.

Friedman, R. E. 1987. *Who Wrote the Bible?* New York: Harper & Row.

Hobbes, T. *On the Life and History of Thucydides*. online: https://archive.org/details/grecianwarhobb00thucuoft (orig. publ. 1628).

Klein, L. R. 1988. *The Triumph of Irony in the Book of Judges*. JSOTSup 68. Bible and Literature Series 14. Sheffield: Almond Press.

Lemche, N. P. 1998. *The Israelites in History and Tradition*. Louisville, KY: Westminster John Knox.

Levinson, B. M. 1977. *Deuteronomy and the Hermeneutics of Legal Innovation*. Oxford: Oxford University Press.

Lindars, B. 1965. "Gideon and Kingship." *JTS* 16: 315–26.

Loewenstamm, S. E. 1967. "The Making and Destruction of the Golden Calf." *Biblica* 48: 481–90.

Lucas, R. E. Jr., "What Economists Do." 9 December, 1988. http://homepage.ntu.edu.tw/~mjlin/lucas.pdf.

Margaliot, M. 1983. "The Transgression of Moses and Aaron: Num. 20:1–13." *JQR New Series* 74: 196–228.

McConville, J. G. 2006. *God and Earthly Power: An Old Testament Political Theology, Genesis-Kings*. London: T&T Clark International.

Miller, G. P. 2011. *Ways of a King: Legal and Political Ideas in the Bible*. Göttingen: Vandenhoeck & Ruprecht.

Morgenstern, M. 2009. *Conceiving a Nation: The Development of Political Discourse in the Hebrew Bible*. University Park, PA: The Pennsylvania State University Press.

Motta, F. 2002. "'Geographica Sacra': The Placing of Paradise in Late Seventeenth-Century French Theology." In *The Earthly Paradise: The Garden of Eden from Antiquity to Modernity*, edited by R. F. Psaki and C. Hindley, 283–311. Binghamton, NY: Academic Studies in the History of Judaism, Global Publications, State University of New York at Binghamton.

Nicholas, E. W. 1998. *The Pentateuch in the Twentieth Century*. Oxford: Oxford University Press.

Niditch, S. 1997. *Ancient Israelite Religion*. Oxford: Oxford University Press.

Niehaus, J. J. 1995. *God at Sinai: Covenant and Theophany in the Bible and Ancient Near East*. Grand Rapids, MI: Zondervan.

Propp, W. H. 1988. "The Rod of Aaron and the Sin of Moses." *JBL* 107: 19–26.

Rosenberg, J. 1986. *King and Kin: Political Allegory in the Hebrew Bible*. Bloomington: Indiana University Press.

Sasson, J. M. 1973. "The Worship of the Golden Calf." In *Orient and Occident: Essays Presented to Cyrus H. Gordon on the Occasion of his Sixty-fifth Birthday*, edited by H. A. Hoffner, 151–59. Alter Orient und Altes Testament 22. Neukirchen-Vluyn: Neukirchener Verlag.

Seibert, E. A. 2006. *Subversive Scribes and the Solomonic Narrative: A Rereading of 1 Kings 1–11*. New York: T&T Clark.

Sharon, D. M. 2006. "Echoes of Gideon's Ephod: An Intertextual Reading." *JNES* 30: 89–102.

Sperling, S. D. 1998. *The Original Torah: The Political Intent of the Bible's Writers*. New York: New York University Press.

Thompson, T. 1992. *Early History of the Israelite People*. Leiden: Brill.

Van Seters, J. 1994. *A Prologue to History: The Yahwist as Historian in Genesis*. Louisville, KY: Westminster John Knox.

Walzer, M. 1985. *Exodus and Revolution*. New York: Basic Books.

Watts, J. W. 2011. "Aaron and the Golden Calf in the Rhetoric of the Pentateuch." *JBL* 130: 417–30.

Watts, J. W. 1999. *Reading Law: The Rhetorical Shaping of the Pentateuch*. Sheffield: Sheffield Academic.

Weber, M. 1946. *From Max Weber: Essays in Sociology*. Edited and translated by H. H. Gerth and C. W. Mills. Oxford: Oxford University Press.

Whitley, C. F. 1957. "The Sources of the Gideon Stories." *VT* 7: 157–64.

— 7 —

Reconsidering Davidic Kingship in Ezekiel

Christophe Nihan

1. Introduction

While limited in number, references to the Davidic rulers comprise a consistent thread in the book of Ezekiel.[1] Despite numerous studies devoted to this topic, the significance of these references is disputed, and the question of how central, precisely, Davidic kingship is in Ezekiel remains a controversial issue.[2] The reason for this, in particular, is that the discourse on Davidic rulers in Ezekiel is often complex and ambiguous, and takes place at several levels simultaneously. In the first part of the book, centered on the fall of Jerusalem (chs. 4–24), references to the last kings of Judah are predominantly critical (see Ezek 19), although one text, in particular, appears to envision some sort of continuation for the Davidic line after the exile (Ezek 17, especially vv. 22–24). The same notion is taken over

---

1. The present essay is a thoroughly revised and expanded version of a paper given at a seminar organized by Ehud Ben Zvi and Diana Edelman at the 2013 conference of the *European Association of Biblical Studies* (EABS) in Leipzig. I want to thank the participants of the seminar for several helpful comments during the discussion. I also want to thank Julia Rhyder and Hervé Gonzalez for their kind assistance in the preparation and editing of this essay, as well as for their remarks and suggestions. All remaining errors and infelicities are exclusively mine. While the literature on this topic is abundant, bibliographical references have deliberately been kept to a minimum for the sake of readability. Unless otherwise specified, all translation of the biblical text are my own.

2. See, among others, K. Seybold, *Das davidische Königtum im Zeugnis der Propheten* (Göttingen: Vandenhoeck & Ruprecht, 1972), 145–52; I. Duguid, *Ezekiel and the Leaders of Israel*, VTSup 56 (Leiden: Brill, 1994), 10–57; A. Laato, *A Star Is Rising: The Historical Development of the Old Testament Royal Ideology and the Rise of the Jewish Messianic Expectations* (Atlanta, GA: Scholars Press, 1997), esp. 167–73 and 219–20; P. Joyce, "King and Messiah in Ezekiel," in *King and Messiah in Israel and the Ancient Near East: Proceedings of the Oxford Old Testament Seminar*, ed. J. Day, JSOTSup 270 (Sheffield: Sheffield Academic, 1998), 323–37; D. Bodi, "Le prophète critique la monarchie: le terme *nasi* chez Ézechiel," in *Prophètes et rois: Bible et Proche-Orient*, ed. A. Lemaire (Paris: Editions du Cerf, 2001), 249–57; D. I. Block, "Bringing Back David: Ezekiel's Messianic Hope," in *The Lord's Anointed: Interpretation of Old Testament Messianic Texts*, ed. P. E. Satterthwaite, R. E. Hess, and G. J. Wenham (Grand Rapids: Baker, 1995), 167–88; idem, "Transformation of Royal Ideology in Ezekiel," in *Transforming Visions: Transformations of Text, Tradition, and Theology in Ezekiel*, ed. W. A. Tooman and M. Lyons (Eugene, OR: Pickwick), 208–46.

in two key oracles later in the book, Ezek 34 and 37, both of which refer to "David" as the leadership figure of the post-restoration era. Yet the role assigned to that figure remains unclear: for some, he is presented as a "messianic" king of sorts,[3] whereas for others this postmonarchic ruler has lost, in effect, many of his traditional prerogatives.[4]

Adding further complexity to this issue, the discourse on the post-monarchic ruler is continued in the last section of the book, the visions of chs. 40–48 that describe this ruler with the same term already used in Ezek 34 and 37—נשיא, 'prince'. However, the roles assigned to this ruler in chs. 40–48 differ in significant ways from what we find in Ezek 34 and 37. The discontinuity in this respect between chs. 40–48 and the rest of the book is already signaled by two general observations: first, in these chapters, the *nāśîʾ* is no longer explicitly identified with a *Davidic* ruler; and second, chs. 40–48 never use the term מלך, except in the context of a critique against the past kings of Judah (43:7–9). While several commentators assume that the description of the נשיא in Ezek 40–48 involves a negative view of kingship, others have argued for a more balanced approach.[5] In any event, the relationship between the נשיא in Ezek 40–48 and the discourse on Davidic kingship has not been satisfactorily clarified.

This brief essay will seek to shed some light on the concept of Davidic leadership in Ezekiel, examining what image of Davidic rulers—past, present and future—is construed, how consistent that image is throughout the book, and what primary functions it serves. The approach will be largely synchronic, leaving aside most issues related to the identification of literary strata in order to focus on the overall image of Davidic rulers in Ezekiel.[6] While there are several reasons to privilege a synchronic approach over a more redaction-critically oriented one, especially from a social-historical perspective,[7] that approach nonetheless calls for some brief methodological comments. First, we need to be clear that when we talk about "Ezekiel" we are talking about a *literary work* consisting of various oracles and visions associated with the authority of a distinct prophetic figure, which needs to be read and interpreted

---

3. Thus, e.g., Laato, *Star is Rising*, 167–73; Block, "Bringing Back David," esp. 77–89.

4. Compare, e.g., Joyce, "King and Messiah." Overall, Joyce concludes that that "there is no ultimately significant role for royal mediators" in Ezekiel and that "the function of king has melted away" to the profit of an exclusive emphasis on YHWH's sanctity (337).

5. For a typical representative of the view that chs. 40–48 entail a largely critical view of kingship, see, e.g., J. Z. Smith, *To Take Place: Toward Theory in Ritual* (Chicago, IL: University of Chicago Press, 1987), 61 and passim. For additional references, see below the discussion on the נשיא in chs. 40–48.

6. Elsewhere, I have addressed in more details the relationship between the composition of Ezekiel, especially the second part of the book—chs. 33–39 and 40–48—and the development/transformation of ruler ideology: see C. Nihan, "De la fin du jugement sur Jérusalem au jugement final des nations en Ézéchiel: Ézéchiel 33–39 et l'eschatologie du recueil," in *Les prophètes de la Bible et la fin des temps*, ed. J. Vermeylen (Paris: Editions du Cerf), 99–146.

7. As E. Ben Zvi has argued in a number of essays, a proper social-historical approach to ancient Israelite scriptures should focus on the effects produced by reading and re-reading these scriptures rather than on the various stages through which they reached their final form, independently of how confident one may be in reconstructing these stages. See, for instance, "Towards an Integrative Study of the Production of Authoritative Books in Ancient Israel," in *The Production of Prophecy: Constructing Prophecy and Prophets in Yehud*, ed. D. V. Edelman and E. Ben Zvi, BibleWorld (London: Equinox, 2009), 15–28. One may note, in addition, that there is no consensus at the moment regarding the compositional history of Ezekiel, even though internal as well as external evidence—such as the existence of at least two variant editions preserved in MT and the Old Greek—suggests that the book has undergone a fairly complex process of development. See below.

as such. Whether, and to what extent, these oracles and visions may or may not go back to a historical figure is ultimately impossible to prove in the absence of any external evidence and—from a social-historical perspective—is largely irrelevant.[8] Second, we also need to take into account that it is misleading, in a number of ways, to talk about "*the* book" of Ezekiel as if it were a single, monolithic entity. The comparison between MT and other ancient versions—especially the main witnesses to the Old Greek of Ezekiel (LXX^A, LXX^B, and p967)—indicate that there was, in effect, significant fluidity in the composition and transmission of the Ezekiel traditions during the Neo-Babylonian, Persian and even Hellenistic (or at least early Hellenistic) periods; furthermore, it indicates that these traditions were circulated in at least two variant editions, since p967 preserves not only a generally shorter text than MT but also a distinct arrangement for chs. 36–40.[9] The extent to which this fluidity impacts the portrayal of Davidic kingship in Ezekiel is an issue to which we will have to return,[10] but in any event, even a predominantly synchronic approach cannot ignore the basic fact that the establishment of a single, more or less unified edition of the text of Ezekiel is *not* the starting point but a late development in the transmission of these traditions.

2. Davidic Rulers between Past and Future

One aspect of the book's discourse regarding Davidic leadership, with which we may begin, concerns the references to the Judahite rulers of the past. While some allusions to these rulers can occasionally be found later in the book (Ezek 34:2–10; 43:7–9),[11] most references occur within chs. 4–24, a section of the book that focuses on the history of Jerusalem and Judah/Israel up to the second capture of the city by Nebuchadnezzar's army in 587 BCE. Significantly enough, the treatment of Davidic rulers in these chapters exclusively focuses on the last kings of Judah: there is no mention of—or even allusion to—the founding figures of the Judahite royalty (i.e., David or Solomon) in this section of the book. Likewise, Davidic kings are consistently absent from the main historical retrospectives found in Ezek 16 and 23 (compare also Ezek 20:5–31).[12] These observations already point to the com-

---

8. To be clear, I am not denying that at least a portion of the materials found in Ezekiel is best contextualized in an early Neo-Babylonian setting, which is also the setting ascribed to the prophet himself. However, this only tends to support the assumption that these materials were composed in the historical context of the early sixth century BCE, *not* that they were uttered by the prophet himself.

9. For a recent and comprehensive reassessment of this issue, see I. E. Lilly, *Two Books of Ezekiel: Papyrus 967 and the Masoretic Text as Variant Literary Editions*, VTSup 150 (Leiden: Brill, 2012). In the case of chs. 36–40, the shorter version of p967, with its different order for chs. 38–39, is corroborated by one codex of the Old Latin, L^W. As Lilly and others have argued, the combined evidence provided by p967 and L^W suggests that the version of chs. 36–40 preserved in these manuscripts may well correspond to the Old Greek of Ezekiel.

10. Especially because some scholars have argued that the edition of Ezek 36–40 in MT would point to an improved role for the Davidic king/messiah in the eschatological battle against Gog. See below.

11. As is assumed by several commentators, the critique against the "bad shepherds" in Ezek 34:2–10 is arguably aimed against Judahite kings primarily, although it could also comprise other, foreign monarchs who ruled over Israel. D. I. Block, *The Book of Ezekiel: Chapters 25–48*, NICOT (Grand Rapids, MI: Eerdmans, 1998), 282, suggests that the bad shepherds in Ezek 34 would refer to "the noblemen around Zedekiah, including the elders of Jerusalem," yet this may be too specific in my opinion.

12. As noted, e.g., by Block, "Transformation of Royal Ideology," 11–12; see also my comments in C. Nihan, "The Memory of Ezekiel in Postmonarchic Yehud," in *Remembering Biblical Figures in the Late Persian and Early Hellenistic Periods: Social Memory and Imagination*, ed. D. V. Edelman and E. Ben Zvi (Oxford: Oxford University Press, 2013), 415–48, here 439–40.

plexities of Ezekiel's discourse on kingship, suggesting in particular that it is problematic to interpret that discourse as being simply on a par with other traditions, like 2 Sam 7 or Ps 89, which highlight David's role as the founder of an "everlasting" dynasty.[13]

Furthermore, the image of the last kings of Judah that is developed in chs. 4–24 is predominantly a negative one. In Ezek 19, the prophet is commanded to utter a funerary lament, or 'dirge' (קינה), on the "princes" of Israel, which consistently emphasizes the ruthlessness and the violence associated with the last Judahite kings (see 19:1–9). The dirge refers to a 'lioness' (לביא) that raised two cubs that learned to capture prey and devour humans (19:3, 6) before being captured and taken into exile. The second lion, in particular, is presented as a bearer of ruin and destruction, destroying cities and devastating the land (19:7). There is an obvious, albeit sophisticated, reversal of royal imagery at work here. The association of lion imagery with kings is well attested in the iconographic and literary traditions of the ancient Near East. In particular, the lion typically figures in iconographic contexts depicting royal hunts, where it signifies the wild animals and other chaotic forces over which the monarch is victorious.[14] In addition, in both royal inscriptions and reliefs the monarch himself can also be represented as a lion, and we find several examples of this representation in Egypt, in Mesopotamia, and in Hatti; in such contexts, the king-as-lion similarly expresses royal might and dominance, especially (albeit not exclusively) in militaristic contexts.[15] As aptly observed by B. A. Strawn in a recent study, the two aspects are closely connected: because he is victorious over the lion, the monarch can also appropriate its strength for himself.[16] The depiction of Judahite kings as lions in Ezek 19 fits, therefore, within a broad ancient Near Eastern tradition. Furthermore, the reference to the "lioness" in v. 2, if it is taken as a reference to the royal house of Judah (or Jerusalem as a royal city?), and not to a specific individual,[17] may also be related to the tradition of Judahite administrative seals bearing the image of a lion in the Iron Age II, which will be continued in the Persian period.[18] In the lament of Ezek 19, however, the Davidic king, as

---

13. As argued, e.g., by D. I. Block, "The Tender Cedar Sprig: Ezekiel on Jehoiachin," *HeBAI* 1 (2012), 173–202; in the case of Ezek 17. According to Block, the reference to the continuation of Jehoiachin's line after the exile in 17:22–24 would ultimately indicate that "YHWH will not forget his ancient word to David" (73). However, this reading is already problematic in light of the fact that there is no clear reference to the traditions about an everlasting Davidic dynasty in this chapter. On Ezek 17, see further below.

14. For the Assyrian reliefs, see P. Albenda, "Lions on Assyrian Wall Reliefs," *ANES* 6 (1974): 1–27; for the Egyptian reliefs, see J. Śliwa, "Some Remarks Concerning Victorious Ruler Representations in Egyptian Art," *Forschungen und Berichte, Archäologische Beiträge* 16 (1974): 97–117. For a comprehensive treatment of this topic in the context of ancient Near Eastern depictions of rulers, see now B. A. Strawn, *What Is Stronger than a Lion? Leonine Image and Metaphor in the Hebrew Bible and the Ancient Near East*, OBO 212 (Fribourg: Academic Press / Göttingen: Vandenhoeck & Ruprecht, 2005), 153–74, esp. 161–74 ("The Lion Hunt").

15. For a survey of the materials, see now Strawn, *What Is Stronger?*, 174–81.

16. See Strawn, *What Is Stronger?*, 181: "The lion is not only, therefore, a *threat* that must be overcome by the great monarch in his role as defender; the lion is equally an *ally* insofar as the monarch can appropriate the lion as an image for the royal self. There is an obvious connection between these two aspects: it is the conquerer [sic] of the lion who can then claim to have equal, but even greater, strength" (emphasis original).

17. For a critique of the possibility that the lioness would refer to Hamutal, mother of Jehoachaz and Zedekiah (2 Kgs 23:31; 24:18), see W. Zimmerli, *Ezekiel 1: A Commentary on the Book of the Prophet Ezekiel, Chapters 1–24*, Hermeneia (Minneapolis, MN: Fortress, 1979), 394.

18. For a discussion of these seals, see O. Keel and C. Uehlinger, *Dieux, déesses et figures divines* (Paris: Cerf, 2001), 188–93. Whether, and to what extent, the description of YHWH as a "lion" roaring from Zion

a lion, does not protect his territory but turns it into a wasteland instead (cf. חרב Hiphil, v. 7), to the point that his capture by neighboring nations appears as an act of deliverance from tyranny and oppression (v. 8).[19] The representation of the king as a lion here has been thoroughly deprived of the positive aspects that this representation usually conveys in royal contexts, to be replaced instead with the more common image of the lion as the threat *par excellence*, the enemy of humans, domestic animals, and society in general.[20] While it is agreed that the first lion, which is taken captive to Egypt, must refer to Jehoahaz (see 2 Kgs 23:31–34), the identity of the second lion is more disputed; arguably, it is best identified with Zedekiah, although other references cannot be entirely excluded.[21] This is consistent with the observation that other allusions to Zedekiah, as Judah's last ruler, are likewise entirely negative.[22]

A more complex picture, however, is presented by the oracle preserved in Ezek 17, which this time uses plant imagery to contrast the fate of the last two rulers of Judah, Jehoiachin and Zedekiah.[23] While Zedekiah, referenced as the vine stock mentioned in vv. 5–10, is condemned for breaking his treaty with the king of Babylon (vv. 15, 16, 19), Jehohiachin, who is designated as the "topmost shoot" of a cedar, is taken away to be replanted in a "land of merchants and a city of traders" (vv. 3–4)—a clear allusion to the king's fate as a royal hostage in the Babylonian court, which is attested by the mention of Jehoiachin and five of his sons among the residents of the royal palace receiving food rations in two Babylonian tablets dating from the 13th year of king Nebuchadnezzar (= 592 BCE).[24] Furthermore, the finale of the oracle—at least in its present form—announces in vv. 22–24 that at some

---

(Amos 1:2; 3:8; Jer 25:30; Joel 4:16; and cf. also Hos 11:10) is related to this tradition remains a disputed matter, which cannot be further discussed in the context of this essay.

19. As aptly noted, e.g., by Block, "Transformation of Royal Ideology," 218. See also the recent discussion by Strawn, *What Is Stronger?*, 56–57.

20. On the depiction of the lion as the threat par excellence, see Strawn, *What Is Stronger?*, 134–52, esp. 145–50, with several examples.

21. For the identification of the second lion with Zedekiah, see, e.g., W. H. Brownlee, *Ezekiel 1–19*, WBC 28 (Waco, TX: Word, 1986), 297. Alternatively, a reference to Jehoiachim has sometimes been proposed (e.g., Block, "Transformation of Royal Ideology," 19), but this solution seems unlikely since that king was never deported to Babylon. Another possibility would be to identify the second lion with Jehoiachin, who was deported to Babylon; see, e.g., Zimmerli, *Ezekiel 1*, 393–94 and 395–96. Yet this reading is not consistent with the generally high view of this monarch in Ezekiel; see further below. C. Begg, "The Identity of the Princes in Ezekiel 19: Some Reflections," *Ephemerides Theologicae Lovanienses* 65 (1989): 358–69, here 364, proposes interpreting the second lion as combining a reference to Jehoiachim and Zedekiah, a solution that is certainly possible.

22. See Ezek 12:10, 12; 21:30, and compare also Ezek 17, on which see below. The mention in 19:14 to the fire consuming the shoot vine is presumably a reference to Zedakiah's rebellion against the king of Babylon, as most commentators understand (e.g., Zimmerli, *Ezekiel 1*, 398). In this case, Zedekiah's reign is identified here with the termination of the royal Davidic house.

23. The identification of these two rulers is clear from the interpretation of the 'parable' (משל) of vv. 2–10 that is subsequently given in vv. 9–21, and is generally accepted by commentators; see, e.g., Zimmerli, *Ezekiel 1*, 361–64.

24. For the original edition of these tablets, see E. F. Weidner, "Jojachin, König von Juda, in babylonischen Keilschrifttexten," in *Mélanges syriens offerts à Monsieur René Dussaud*, 2 vols., Bibliothèque archéologique et historique 30 (Paris: Geuthner, 1939), 923–35; for the mention of Jehoiachin and his sons, see tablet C, II, l. 17–18, and compare also with tablet B, reverse, l. 38–39. The date is preserved only in tablet C and corresponds to 592 BCE.

point in the future, YHWH himself will pluck off a "tender (sprig)" (רך) from 'the very top of the cedar' (מצמרת הארז הרמה) to plant it back in the "land of Israel" upon a mountain "high and lofty," where it will become a "noble" or a 'majestic' cedar (ארז אדיר, v. 23).[25] Here, therefore, some form of reestablishment of the Davidic line through Jehoiachin's offspring is already considered in the context of the section of the book focusing on Jerusalem's fall (chs. 4–24).[26] The positive view of Jehoiachin that is apparent here is consistent with a general trend that can observed within Ezek 4–24. Of the last rulers of Judah, Jehoiachin is the only one to be designated by the title מלך (see Ezek 1:2; 17:12).[27] Likewise, the fact that the oracles and the visions contained in the book are consistently dated after the year of Jehoiachin's exile clearly suggests Jehoiachin, and not Zedekiah, is presented as the last legitimate ruler of Judah; this observation also suggests, in addition, that Jehoiachin's significance as a royal figure does not merely end with his captivity in Babylon but somehow extends beyond the events of 597 BCE.

While the description of the Davidic ruler's role in the future is fairly brief and allusive in Ezek 17:22–24, a number of points can nonetheless be made; this is all the more clear when this passage is read in contrast with the oracle of Ezek 19 and its depiction of Judah's last kings, as the connections between ch. 17 and the last part of ch. 19, vv. 10–14, invite us to do.[28] As rightly pointed out by some commentators, the reference in v. 23 to the majestic cedar is reminiscent of the well-known motif of the "cosmic tree" in the ancient Near East.[29] In both iconographic and literary sources, the cosmic tree is typically associ-

---

25. This unit (vv. 22–24) is often considered to be a later addition to the oracle, which is indeed plausible; see, e.g., Zimmerli, *Ezekiel 1*, 366–67; further K.-F. Pohlmann, *Das Buch des Propheten Hesekiel (Ezechiel). Kapitel 1–19*, ATD 22/1 (Göttingen: Vandenhoeck & Ruprecht, 1996), 254–56. At the same time, it needs to be observed that this unit rounds off nicely the whole oracle by returning to the fate of the "tender cedar sprig" that was replanted in Babylon at the very beginning of the chapter (17:3–4). As such, the relationship of vv. 22–24 to the rest of the oracle is much less artificial than it has sometimes been assumed by commentators (compare, e.g., Zimmerli).

26. Block, "Tender Cedar Sprig," 63–64, following others, sees a possible reference to a Josiah-like figure. However, the lexical connections that he identifies in support of this interpretation are not very strong in my opinion. The reference to the 'tender (sprig)' (רך) can be explained in the context of the plant imagery used in this oracle, and it seems unnecessary to connect it with traditions outside of Ezekiel, such as Huldah's oracle about the "tenderness" of Josiah's heart (2 Kgs 22:19 = 2 Chr 34:27), especially in the absence of other significant terminological links between these texts.

27. For this observation and its implications, see my comments in C. Nihan, "The *nāśîʾ* and the Future of Royalty in Ezekiel," in *History, Memory, Hebrew Scriptures: A Festschrift for Ehud Ben Zvi*, ed. I. D. Wilson and D. Edelman (Winona Lake, IN: Eisenbrauns, 2015), 229–46, here 231.

28. As several commentators have observed, there are several connections between Ezek 17 and the second part of ch. 19, vv. 10–14, which similarly resorts to the plant/vine imagery to describe the fate of the last kings of Judah. See, e.g., Zimmerli, *Ezekiel 1*, 397–98, who argues that vv. 10–14 would have been added to ch. 19 as a way of presenting this oracle as the conclusion to ch. 17. For a detailed treatment of these parallels, see further, e.g., Pohlmann, *Buch des Propheten Hesekiel*, 242–44; as well as the recent discussion by Block, "Tender Cedar Sprig," who also points to the differences between the vine imagery in Ezek 17 and 19:10–14.

29. For this motif in Ezek 17, see especially M. Metzger, "Zeder, Weinstock und Weltenbaum," in *Ernten, was man sät. Festschrift für Klaus Koch zu seinem 65. Geburtstag*, ed. D. R. Daniels, U. Glessmer, and M. Rösel (Neukirchen-Vluyn: Neukirchener Verlag, 1991), 197–229, here 212–18. Compare also the brief comments on this point in the recent treatment by Block, "Tender Cedar Sprig," 65. I want to thank M. Rotem Avery Meir, a student at Tel Aviv University, who first drew my attention to the significance of this motif in Ezek 17 in a paper he gave in one of my Ezekiel classes during a stay at the University of Lausanne.

ated with the divine ordering of the world and the reassertion of divine power over the threat of chaos.[30] In the context of royal iconography, specifically, it is a symbol of the royal order maintained by the king, as the god's agent on earth, as is well attested in the case of Assyrian iconography in particular.[31] A similar association between the royal cedar, as a symbol or an image of Davidic leadership, and cosmic order is attested in Ezek 17, which describes in v. 23b how the cedar will shelter all sorts of birds and other winged creatures among its branches; a similar description of the cosmic tree is also found in a further passage, Ezek 31:6, which mentions in addition to "the birds of the sky" the "wild animals" and even the "great nations," all of which benefit from the protection provided by the tree.[32]

Like Ezek 19, therefore, the finale of the oracle of Ezek 17 makes use of traditional ancient Near Eastern (royal) imagery to describe the Davidic ruler, but the way in which this imagery is put to use in both texts goes in separate ways. Whereas in Ezek 19 the lion metaphor was used to criticize the violence of the last rulers of Judah, turning against their own people instead of protecting them, in Ezek 17 the cosmic tree imagery is now used to describe the role of the future Davidic ruler, Jehoiachin's offspring, in a world that has been restored to order and harmony after the exile. There is no indication in these verses that the Davidic ruler would play an active part in the restoration itself, and it is incorrect, in my opinion, to speak of a "messianic" conception expressed in the last verses of ch. 17.[33] Instead, the last verse (v. 24), which concludes the oracle by highlighting the notion of divine sovereignty and imperialism by means of a gnomic statement ("I, YHWH, bring low the high tree and make high the low tree, I dry up the green tree and make the dry tree flourish"), strongly suggests that YHWH, here, is represented as the sole agent in the reestablishment of an ordered world.[34] The Davidic ruler, for his part, is cast in a subordinated

---

30. For the iconographic record, see especially the detailed study of this motif by U. Winter, "Der Lebensbaum im Alten Testament und die Ikonographie des stilisierten Baumes in Kanaan/Israel," in *Das Kleid der Erde, Pflanzen in der Lebenswelt des alten Israel*, ed. H. Schweizer (Stuttgart: Calwer Verlag / Neukirchen-Vluyn: Neukirchener Verlag, 2002), 138–62, esp. pp. 147–54. As noted by Winter, the typical association of the tree with a divinely ordered world also accounts for the fact that iconographic representations of this tree often highlight its symmetry. Compare, e.g., Winter's comments in the case of the representation of the cosmic tree on a Syrian seal of the Middle Bronze (ca. 1750 BCE): "Die Stilisierung des Baumes und die Symmetrie der Darstellung unterstreichen die Funktion des Baumes, heilvolle Ordnung zu repräsentieren" (147–48).

31. See on this S. Parpola, "The Assyrian Tree of Life: Tracing the Origins of Jewish Monotheism and Greek Philosophy," *JNES* 52 (1993): 161–208, here 165–69; and compare also the comments by Winter, "Lebensbaum," 147–54. Parpola concludes that the tree "symbolizes the divine world order maintained by the Assyrian king" (168). He also highlights the fact that in some reliefs the king himself can take the place of the tree, between the winged genies surrounding the latter, which he relates to the representation of the Assyrian king as the "Perfect Man," the embodiment himself of the world order established by the gods.

32. For this parallel, see Block, "Tender Cedar Sprig," 66. However, it seems unnecessary to read the mention of the birds in 17:23 as a reference to the nations.

33. Thus, e.g., Metzger, "Zeder, Weinstock und Weltenbaum," 217–18 ("Der Weltenbaum wird zur Metapher für den Messias").

34. Here, I fully agree with Block, "Tender Cedar Sprig," 67, when he states that "this oracle is not about Davidic imperialism; it is about YHWH's cosmic sovereignty and fidelity." He also helpfully notes several parallels with gnomic statements similar to Ezek 17:24 elsewhere in the Hebrew Bible (ibid., 67 n. 93). However, it is dubious, in my opinion, whether Block is right to identify the "tree brought low" with Zedekiah and the "tree made high" with Jehoiachin. These references are best understood, it seems to me, as a general statement about divine imperialism, as the gnomic formulation of v. 24 already suggests. It may not be necessary to look for a more specific reference.

role: he is the deity's administrator, presiding over a newly pacified and stabilized world. As we will see, this utopian conception of the post-monarchic era, and the role assigned to the Davidic ruler in that era, is largely consistent with the view further developed in the second part of the book, even though the language is different.

3. David as Utopian Ruler in Ezek 34 and 37

As already mentioned, a reference to "David" as a future ruler figures in two key oracles, Ezek 34 and 37, that belong to the second part of the book (chs. 33–48) focusing on the restoration of Israel after the exile. While the passages mentioning David are brief, the language used deserves closer attention.

> Ezek 34:23–24
> 23 I will establish over them one shepherd (רעה אחד), who will tend them, my servant David (את עבדי דויד): it is he who will tend them, and it is he who will be a shepherd for them. 24 Whereas I, YHWH, will be their god, my servant David (את עבדי דוד) will be a prince (נשיא) among them (בתוכם). It is I, YHWH, who have spoken.
>
> Ezek 37:24–25
> 24 My servant David (עבדי דוד) will be king (מלך; OG: ἄρχων, 'prince') over them, so that there will be one shepherd (רעה אחד) for them all. They will follow my customs, observe my statutes, and practice them. 25 They will reside in the land that I gave to my servant Jacob, where your ancestors previously resided—they will reside upon it, they, their children, and the children of their children, forever (עד עולם);[35] and David my servant (ודוד עבדי) will be their prince (נשיא), forever (לעולם).

It is immediately apparent that the two passages present several significant parallels. There are reasons to believe that this observation points the fact that they are not from the same hand, and that one is rewriting the other, with Ezek 34:23–24 being arguably a revision of 37:24–25.[36] In the final form of the book, however, the two passages are clearly complementary, describing together the role assigned to the future ruler in the post-restoration era. While the identification of this ruler with "David" is somehow unique in the prophetic traditions, this is most likely a reference to a member of the Davidic dynasty, as commentators usually understand it.[37] As long noted, the designation of this Davidic ruler in Ezek 34 and 37 significantly differs in one regard. In Ezek 34 David is described as a נשיא, 'prince', a title that is typically reserved in Ezekiel for vassal rulers.[38] In the MT

---

35. This comment is missing from the Old Greek of Ezekiel and could be a later gloss.

36. See for this my discussion in Nihan, "De la fin du jugement," 114–18. In general, this is the position advocated by the majority of commentators who acknowledge that the comparison between Ezek 34 and 37 points to some form of revisional activity; compare, e.g., K.-F. Pohlmann, *Das Buch des Propheten Hesekiel (Ezechiel). Kapitel 20–48*, ATD 22/2 (Göttingen: Vandenhoeck & Ruprecht, 2001), 468. For the contrary, see, however, A. Klein, *Schriftauslegung im Ezechielbuch: Redaktionsgeschichtliche Untersuchungen zu Ez 34–39*, BZAW 391 (Berlin and New York: de Gruyter, 2008), 175–79. However, this solution seems less compelling to me, especially because Ezek 34:23–24 consistently tends to emphasize the subordinated role of the Davidic ruler vis-à-vis Ezek 37, which is easier to explain if Ezek 34 is revising ch. 37 rather than the other way round. See below.

37. The alternative view proposed by a few commentators, who read here a reference to David's resurrection, seems especially unlikely. Compare, e.g., P. Beauchamp, "Pourquoi parler de David comme d'un vivant?," in *Figures de David à travers la Bible*, ed. L. Desrousseaux, Lectio divina 177 (Paris: Cerf, 1999), 225–41.

38. On this aspect of the term נשיא in Ezekiel, see the detailed discussion by Duguid, *Ezekiel and the Leaders*

of Ezek 37, this future ruler is simultaneously presented both as a king, מֶלֶךְ (v. 24), and a prince, נשׂיא (v. 25); the reference to David as a king is consistent with the previous description in 37:15–23, which already announces the reunion of Judah and Ephraim under the aegis of 'one king' (מלך אחד, v. 22), who is now identified in v. 24 with "David." The matter is further complicated, however, by the fact that in vv. 22 and 24 all the main witnesses to the Old Greek (p967, LXX^A, and LXX^B) read ἄρχων, 'prince', which normally renders the Hebrew נשׂיא in the Greek text of Ezek 1–39, instead of βασιλεύς, 'king'. As I have argued in detail elsewhere, it is unnecessary to assume that the Greek translators of Ezekiel had before them a Hebrew text that read נשׂיא in 37:22 and 24, whereas the reading מלך in MT would reflect a change introduced by a later edition.[39] The use of the term מלך in MT is entirely consistent with a dominant theme in the oracle of 37:15–28, which refers to the recreation of a Davidic kingdom including Judah and Samaria (Ephraim).[40] Furthermore, the combined use of the terms מלך and נשׂיא in Ezek 37:24–25 creates a sophisticated but nonetheless coherent picture of the future Davidic ruler, in which the term מלך highlights his role in continuing the Davidic monarchy of the past, whereas the term נשׂיא emphasizes this ruler's subordination to the deity; in addition, the designation of the Davidic ruler as נשׂיא builds a connection with the description of the utopian ruler in chs. 40–48 (more on this below).[41] The subordinated role of the future Davidic ruler is further accentuated in the oracle of Ezek 34:23–24: there, David is no longer described as a king ruling 'over' (על) the people but as a 'prince among them' (נשׂיא בתוכם). Arguably, the rendering of מלך with ἄρχων in 37:24 (and 37:22) in the Greek tradition represents an attempt to align the oracle of 37:24–25 with the conception laid out in 34:23–24.[42]

These preliminary remarks lead to a more general issue, which concerns the role assigned to the Davidic ruler in Ezek 34 and 37. While it has occasionally been argued that these chapters would refer to a Davidic "messiah" of sorts, this category is actually misleading in a number of ways.[43] In particular, as in Ezek 17:22–24 already, there is no indication in

---

of Israel, 10–57, as well as my recent discussion in Nihan, "*Nāśîʾ* and the Future of Royalty," 230–31, with additional references.

39. Nihan, "*Nāśîʾ* and the Future of Royalty," 232–34. For the view that the occurrence of the term מלך in Ezek 37:24 MT represents a later revision, possibly from the Hasmonean period, see especially J. Lust, "Messianism in LXX-Ezekiel: Toward a Synthesis," in *The Septuagint and Messianism*, ed. M. Knibb, BETL 195 (Leuven: Peeters, 2006), 417–30; idem, "Ezéchiel dans la Septante," in *Les recueils prophétiques de la Bible. Origines, milieux, et contexte proche-oriental*, ed. J.-D. Macchi et al. (Genève: Labor et Fides, 2012), 337–58; as well as A. S. Crane, *Israel's Restoration: A Textual-Comparative Exploration of Ezekiel 36–39*, VTSup 122 (Leiden: Brill, 2008), 119–26 and 250–63.

40. While this political unit is not expressly designated as a "kingdom," the notion is nevertheless implied by the statement at the end of v. 22 that Judah and Ephraim will "no longer be two nations (גוים) and will no longer be divided into two *kingdoms* (ממלכות).”

41. There is no need, therefore, to assume that the term נשׂיא in Ezek 37:25 would correspond to a later revision of the oracle, seeking to downplay the role of the Davidic king, as proposed by some commentators; see, e.g., L. C. Allen, *Ezekiel 20–48*, WBC 29 (Dallas: Word, 1990), 195. The combined use of the terms מלך and נשׂיא in Ezek 37:24–25 MT is, in effect, perfectly deliberate and coherent.

42. Note, in particular, how the Old Greek renders the first clause of 37:24 with "my servant David will be ἄρχων *in their midst* (ἐν μέσῳ αὐτῶν)," which is the exact equivalent of the statement found in 34:24a: ועבדי דוד נשׂיא בתוכם. There is no need, therefore, to assume that the rendering of מלך with ἄρχων in 37:24 should necessarily imply a polemical statement against kingship. See further on this my discussion in Nihan, "*Nāśîʾ* and the Future of Royalty," 233–34.

43. See, e.g., Block, "Bringing Back David," esp. 77–89; cf. also Laato, *Star is Rising*, 167–73. The identifica-

these texts that the Davidic ruler will take an active part in the deliverance of the people—a trait that generally is regarded as a basic defining feature of the category of "messiah" in most studies devoted to this topic in ancient Jewish and Christian traditions.[44] While both Ezek 34 and 37 situate the reestablishment of the Davidic ruler in the context of a complex scenario that includes the gathering of the Diaspora in the Land of Israel (34:11–15; 37:21) as well as, in Ezek 37, the recreation of the Davidic kingdom (37:22) and the eventual purification of the people (37:23), *all* these acts of deliverance are consistently assigned to YHWH alone, as the formulation of 34:15, e.g., makes clear ("It is I who will tend to my flock, and it is I who will make them lie down—oracle of the Lord YHWH"). In similar fashion, the ending of ch. 34, vv. 25–30, describes the situation of the Israelite community within the Land post-restoration in a language that consistently highlights the sole agency of the deity in protecting the community from the wild beasts (v. 25) and the enemies (v. 28) as well as in ensuring abundant harvests and general prosperity (v. 26, 27, 29).[45]

A similar picture emerges when we take into account the oracle of Ezek 38–39, which describes the battle against Gog and his coalition that will take place 'at the end of days' (באחרית הימים, 38:16). The defeat of Gog's army in the Land of Israel is represented here as the definitive manifestation of YHWH's sovereignty over the nations,[46] as well as the eventual vindication of Israel against their oppressors.[47] As such, it marks the beginning of a new era in which war has disappeared (as is signified by the destruction of the weapons of Gog's army [39:9]) and a stable order is definitely established.[48] Here also, YHWH is presented as the sole agent responsible for the defeat of Gog's army (38:18–22; 39:1–6) and the consequent reestablishment of an ordered world. By contrast, the Davidic ruler is

---

tion of the Davidic ruler with a "messianic" figure has already been criticized by other scholars; compare, e.g., Joyce, "King and Messiah," 336–37.

44. Compare, e.g., F. García Martínez, "Messianische Erwartungen in den Qumranschriften," *Jahrbuch für biblische Theologie* 8 (1993): 171–208, here 172, who describes "messianic figures" ("messianische Gestalten") as "agents of deliverance at the end of times" ("Agenten endzeitlicher Errettung"). Similarly, W. Rose, *Zemah and Zerubbabel: Messianic Expectations in the Early Postexilic Period*, JSOTSup 304 (Sheffield: Sheffield Academic, 2000), 23 defines the "messiah" as "a future royal figure sent by God who will bring salvation to God's people and the world and establish a kingdom characterized by features like peace and justice." J. Fitzmyer, *The One Who Is to Come* (Grand Rapids, MI: Eerdmans, 2007), 1, refers to "an anointed human agent of God, who was sent by Him as a deliverer and was awaited in the end time." For a similar approach, see already, e.g., A. S. Van der Woude, *Die messianischen Vorstellungen der Gemeinde von Qumran*, Studia semitica neerlandica 3 (Assen: van Gorcum, 1957), 5 ("eine eschatologische Erlösergestalt").

45. The formulation of this unit, which shares several significant parallels with Lev 26:4–13, is particularly complex and would require an extended discussion. For the purpose of the present essay, however, these issues may be left aside.

46. This notion is repeated at several key places in the oracle, see 38:23; 39:7; further 39:21–22.

47. As is expressed in particular, in the statement of 39:10: "They (the Israelites) will plunder those who plundered them, they will pillage those who pillaged them—oracle of the Lord YHWH."

48. As noted by some commentators, the description of the burning of the weapons of war by the Israelites in 39:9–10 can be connected with the general theme of the destruction of the weapons of war in several (late) texts from the Prophets and the Psalms; compare Hos 2:20; Zech 9:10; Ps 46:10; 76:4. See, e.g., W. Zimmerli, *Ezekiel 2: A Commentary on the Book of the Prophet Ezekiel, Chapters 25–48*, Hermeneia (Philadelphia: Fortress, 1983), 300. More recently, see especially the treatment of this topic by S. Boe, *Gog and Magog. Ezekiel 38–39 as Pre-text for Revelation 19,17–21 and 2,7–10*, WUNT 2/135 (Tübingen: Mohr Siebeck, 2001), 125–26 (but note, however, that some of the biblical references he indicates are incorrect); compare also the comments by Klein, *Schriftauslegung*, 136.

never mentioned, and there is no intimation whatsoever that he would have a role to play in this utopian scenario. In effect, the alternative—and presumably older—arrangement preserved for Ezek 36–40 in the Old Greek (p967 and L^W), where the battle against Gog is placed immediately before Ezek 37, even suggests that the reestablishment of the Davidic ruler will take place only *after* Gog's defeat and the eventual pacification of the world by the deity.[49] Here, as it appears, the Davidic ruler has been definitely deprived of one of the most basic prerogatives of kings in the ancient Near East: warfare and military leadership.[50]

This conclusion does not mean, however, that the Davidic ruler described in Ezek 34 and 37 has merely become a minor figure, a leader of diminished significance. In other ways, the Davidic ruler depicted in these chapters retains much of his former importance. Two points, in particular, may be mentioned here. First, the conception laid out in Ezek 34 and 37 maintains a unique role for the Davidic ruler as the deity's representative and agent. This unique mediating role is highlighted through the two additional titles that are conferred on this ruler, since David is described in both oracles as the '(only) one servant', עבד אחד, as well as the '(only) one shepherd', רעה אחד; in effect, this emphasis on the exclusive role of the Davidic ruler is consistent with the observation that *no other divine agent* is mentioned alongside David within chs. 33–39. Like the terms מלך and נשיא discussed already, both titles carry significant royal overtones: "servant of YHWH" is a typical designation for David elsewhere in the Hebrew Bible,[51] whereas "shepherd" is a common title for kings in the ancient Near East, which is also used in some biblical texts for the Davidic kings (compare, e.g., Jer 23:1–6).[52] Furthermore, the description of David as the "one shepherd" takes particular significance in the context of Ezek 34, since YHWH himself is already compared to a "shepherd" earlier in the oracle (vv. 11–16) when he brings back into the Land the Israelites who had been "dispersed" by the previous "bad shepherds" (vv. 2–10)—presumably a reference to the Israelite kings of the past, although it may also include foreign rulers who dominated over Israel.[53] While the Davidic ruler, as noted above, has no part in the gathering of the Israelite community and the re-creation of an ordered world, the reapplication

---

49. Contrary to J. Lust and A. S. Crane (see above, n. 39), I see no indication that the arrangement of the MT, in which ch. 37 comes *before* the description of YHWH's battle against Gog, would imply an increased role for the Davidic ruler in that battle. See my discussion in Nihan, "*Nāśî'* and the Future of Royalty," 232–33.

50. For the relationship between kings and military power/leadership in the ancient Near East, see, e.g., in the case of the Assyrian kings, S. Maul, "Der assyrische König – Hüter der Weltordnung," in *Gerechtigkeit. Richten und Retten in abendländischen Tradition und ihren altorientalischen Ursprüngen*, ed. J. Assmann, B. Janowski, and M. Welker (Munich: Wilhelm Fink Verlag, 1998), 65–77. In the case of ancient Israel, this notion is still preserved in a number of traditions like, e.g., Ps 2:8–9 or Ps 45:4–6. For the parallels between Ps 2:8–9 and the military dimension of kingship in the Neo-Assyrian world, see, e.g., E. Otto, "Politische Theologie in den Königspsalmen zwischen Ägypten und Assyrien. Die Herrscherlegitimation in den Psalmen 2 und 18 in ihren altorientalischen Kontexten," in *"Mein Sohn bist du" (Ps 2,7). Studien zu den Königspsalmen*, ed. E. Otto and E. Zenger, Stuttgarter Bibelstudien 192 (Stuttgart: Verlag Katholisches Bibelwerk, 2002), 33–65.

51. This designation for David is especially prominent in the books of Samuel, Kings, Psalms and Chronicles. For a discussion of this term, see, e.g., Block, *Ezekiel 25–48*, 299, who notes that עבדי is used no less than 31 times in total for David in the Hebrew Bible, and that it is also applied to postexilic royal figures such as Zerubbabel (Hag 2:23) of Zemah ("Branch") in Zech 3:8 and 6:12.

52. For a brief but nevertheless helpful discussion of the ancient Near Eastern record with regard to the designation of kings as "shepherds," see Block, *Ezekiel 25–48*, 280–81.

53. See above, n. 11.

of the term רעה to David in 34:23–24 nonetheless emphasizes that it is he, and he alone, who is tasked with maintaining this ordered world once the Israelites have been reunited within the land of their ancestors, and that in doing so he acts as the deity's representative.

Second, and closely related to this, the Davidic ruler is consistently presented in these chapters as a figure of national unity. While this notion is already apparent in Ezek 34, it is especially developed in the oracle of ch. 37. The reestablishment of a Davidic ruler takes place in the context of the reunion of Judah and Ephraim/Israel into a single kingdom (37:16–19), governed by 'one king', מלך אחד (v. 22). Furthermore, the reign of this king is characterized as an era in which the Israelite community, after being brought back into its land, will eventually be reconciled with their god: the people will observe the divine laws (חקת and משפטים, v. 24b), whereas YHWH will conclude a 'covenant of peace' (שלום ברית) with them and reestablish his presence among them via the (central) sanctuary (v. 26–27).[54] While the role of the Davidic ruler in this utopian scenario remains somewhat undefined, the construction of v. 24–27 nevertheless identifies him as the central figure that binds together the Israelite community, the land of the ancestors and the cult of the national deity, as per the traditional ancient Near Eastern conception.

Taking these observations together, we are now in a position to appreciate the transformation of the figure of the Davidic ruler that takes place in Ezek 34 and 37, as well as its implications. Overall, the image of the Davidic ruler that we find in Ezek 34 and 37 is inseparable from what could be called a utopia of "divine imperialism" that runs through all the section comprising Ezek 33–39. Within this utopia, the traditional role of the Davidic ruler has been considerably re-signified: in particular, he is no longer associated with any sort of military leadership and takes no part in the deliverance of the community or in the final battle against Gog and his army. Instead, his role is exclusively associated with the administration of a world that has been previously pacified and reordered by the deity alone. While this conception necessarily implies a restricted role for the Davidic ruler, he nevertheless remains at the same time the *exclusive* agent of the deity in the new order defined in and by Ezek 33–39, as well as the central figure for both political and cultic unity. As such, the construction of the Davidic ruler in these chapters reaffirms the centrality of the institution of Davidic kingship, while at the same time highlighting the need for its redefinition in a post-monarchic context.[55]

4. Furthering Utopian Kingship: The נשיא in Ezekiel 40–48

The issue is further complicated, however, by the fact that additional references to a post-monarchic ruler can also be found in the final section of the book, consisting of the various 'visions' (מראות) of a new temple and of the land of Israel. While a comprehensive discussion of the various references to the נשיא in Ezek 40–48 is beyond the limits of this short essay, some basic observations can nevertheless be made here.

Because this section of the book specifically insists on the role of the נשיא in the cult, a number of scholars have assumed that the נשיא has been transformed in Ezek 40–48 into

---

54. While the term מקדש in 37:26b clearly refers to the (central) temple itself, the statement והיה משכני עליהם that follows in v. 27a seems to refer to more than just the physical sanctuary, and may be understood to describe the mode of divine presence that will characterize the new utopian era. Accordingly, the statement in v. 27a is perhaps best rendered as 'my dwelling-presence will be over/with them'.

55. For other considerations of utopian views in the Hebrew Bible in this volume, see the essay by E. Ben Zvi ("Memory and Political Thought in the Late Persian/early Hellenistic Yehud/Judah: Some Observations"), 9–26.

a mere patron of the cult, a figure somehow comparable to the ἄρχων βασιλεὺς in Athens or the *rex sacrorum* in Rome and with little or no political power.[56] In addition, for some scholars this transformation would decisively indicate a critical view of the monarchy as well as a general concern for significantly restricting the royal office in these chapters.[57] However, it is questionable whether this approach does justice to the evidence. As other scholars have rightly noted, a general feature of the visionary scenario described in Ezek 40–48 is precisely that power and status are defined predominantly, if not exclusively, in terms of ritual roles and access to the sanctuary.[58] To conclude that the emphasis placed on the cultic role of the נשיא in these chapters would necessarily signal a de-politization of this figure is, therefore, erroneous. Instead, this phenomenon needs to be contextualized within the general logic of the visions. Furthermore, a number of passages suggest, in effect, that the נשיא remains a figure of prestige and influence. He is assigned a special portion of land, distinct from the tribal allotments (Ezek 45:7–8a; 48:21–22), upon which he may own servants (46:17); and while he cannot dispose of other estates, the exhortation of 45:9–12 nonetheless implies that he retains some degree of political and judicial authority over the territory of Israel as a whole. The way in which the 'princes of Israel' (נשיאי ישראל) are exhorted in this passage to do משפט וצדקה (45:9) is particularly interesting, since the construct משפט וצדקה is often used in the Hebrew Bible to describe the rule of righteous kings; obviously, the נשיא, here, is expected to take over a key attribute of royal power in ancient Israel.[59]

Moreover, the description of the cultic roles of the נשיא indicates, in effect, that he retains a unique mediatory function within the community. In particular, he is closely associated with the various sacrifices offered in the context of the communal feasts enumerated in 45:17, which are designated as the 'appointed times of the House of Israel' (מועדי בית ישראל) and include the new moon, the sabbaths, as well as all the annual festivals.[60] The נשיא is responsible for presenting the animals, the cereals, and the oil for

---

56. For this view, see already O. Procksch, "Fürst und Priester bei Hesekiel," *ZAW* 58 (1940/41): 99–133, here 117.

57. See, e.g., Smith, *To Take Place*, 61; K. R. Stevenson, *Vision of Transformation: The Territorial Rhetoric of Ezekiel 40–48*, SBLDS 154 (Atlanta, GA: Scholars Press, 1996), 109–23 and 151–54; and in a somewhat more balanced way, Joyce, "King and Messiah," esp. 336–37, where he speaks of a "dialectical critique of monarchy" in chs. 40–48. Compare also J. D. Levenson, *Theology of the Program of Restoration of Ezekiel 40–48* (Sheffield: Sheffield Academic PrHSM 10 (Missoula, MT: Scholars Press, 1976), 113, who describes the נשיא in Ezek 40–48 as an "apolitical messiah," "a figure of great honour, but impotent."

58. For this observation, see already S. Niditch, "Ezekiel 40–48 in a Visionary Context," *CBQ* 48 (1986): 208–24, here 219; further, e.g., Duguid, *Ezekiel*, 53. A similar argument is developed by Block, "Bringing Back David," 93.

59. In Jeremiah, in particular, it is used once to characterize king Josiah (22:15) and twice to characterize Zemah, the "sprout" who will renew the Davidic line in the future (23:5 and 33:15 MT, and see Duguid, *Ezekiel*, 54. On the collocation משפט וצדקה and its relation to royal power in the Hebrew Bible, see, e.g., H. Niehr, "The Constitutive Principles for Establishing Justice and Order in Northwest Semitic Societies with Special Reference to Ancient Israel and Judah," *ZABR* 3 (1997): 112–30, and most recently O. Artus, "Mise en oeuvre du droit et de la justice par les figures exemplaires de l'Ancien Testament: Abraham, David, Salomon, Josias," in *Loi et Justice dans la Littérature du Proche-Orient ancien*, ed. O. Artus, BZAR 20 (Wiesbaden: Harrassowitz Verlag, 2013), 225–33, here 227–29.

60. Presumably, the mention of the חגים, 'festivals', at the beginning of the verse (45:17) works as a general descriptor for the enumeration that follows: new moon festivities, Sabbaths, as well as 'all the other appointed times of the House of Israel' (בכל מועדי בית ישראל). For a similar interpretation, see, e.g.,

the sacrifices, which are collected from the Israelites in the form of a תרומה, a sacred contribution (45:13–16).⁶¹ Moreover, Ezek 45:17 insists that it is the נשיא who somehow "accomplishes" the various sacrifices offered during the communal feasts: "It is he who shall accomplish (הוא יעשה) the sin offering, the cereal offerings, the whole burnt offerings and the peace offerings, to make atonement on behalf of the house of Israel." The same notion is repeated a little further, in the description of the two festivals taking place in the first and seventh months of the year (Ezek 45:21–24, 25), which are similarly 'accomplished' (also with עשה) by the נשיא. Clearly, this cannot refer to the actual performance of the sacrifices, since only the Zadokide priests are allowed to enter the court and approach the sacrificial altar (see Ezek 44:15–16, and further 40:46; 42:13–14; 45:4). More likely, it seems to indicate that the נשיא, while not performing the ritual himself, is nonetheless responsible for supervising its accomplishment. Significantly enough, in the Old Greek of Ezek 40–48, this responsibility is apparently further extended to include the daily burnt offering that, in the MT, is placed under the supervision of the Zadokide priests (Ezek 46:13–15).⁶² As we can see here, the נשיא is not a mere "sponsor" of the cult—as is frequently assumed—but, rather, its patron and guardian.⁶³

The distinct status of the נשיא within the cult is further highlighted in a number of ways. Only he is allowed to sit before the eastern gateway to eat his sacrificial meals there "before YHWH" (Ezek 44:3)—a privilege that sets him apart from both the priestly functionaries and the rest of the lay community and which suggests that he enjoys a unique relationship with the deity.⁶⁴ Yet the distinct status of the נשיא and his demarcation from the rest of the community is also signified in other, more subtle ways. For instance, during the festivals only the נשיא is allowed to turn around in the court and exit via the gate through which he entered the sacred precincts (46:8), whereas the other lay Israelites must exit via the gate opposite the one through which they entered (46:9). This distinct status of the נשיא is all the more remarkable and significant since, as observed by some commentators, there is no reference whatsoever to other lay representatives of the community.⁶⁵ This is no coincidence but, rather, a logical consequence of the egalitarian conception that permeates the tribal conception of Israel in Ezek 40–48. There is simply no upper class, no nobility, no magistrates, no reference to terms such as שרים or סגנים; above all, since the tribal estates

---

Block, *Ezekiel 25–48*, 659.

61. The wording of 45:16, in addition, implies that the collection of this sacred contribution is placed under the responsibility of the נשיא. The תרומה described here is clearly distinct from the contribution already mentioned in 44:30, which concerns the first products of the harvest.

62. Whereas the MT of 46:13–15 apparently ascribes the responsibility of the daily burnt offering to the priests (referred to with the second person plural pronoun in v. 15), in the LXX the use of the third person singular pronoun—which, in the previous verses, is used to refer to the ἀφηγούμενος (= נשיא)—suggests that this responsibility is now transferred from the priests to the ruler himself.

63. As aptly observed, in particular, by Block, *Ezekiel 25–48*, 660: "Under this constitution, the *nāśîʾ* plays a critical part: he is guardian and patron of the cult."

64. That this ritual act is a privilege that "indexes" the distinct status of the נשיא within the community is emphasized by the formulation of the beginning of this verse in MT: את הנשיא נשיא הוא 'only the prince, (since) he is the prince...' As noted by various commentators, the particle *ʾet* before the subject has a clear emphatic function in this context (e.g., Allen, *Ezekiel 20–48*, 244). LXX and Syr omit the second occurrence of נשיא, which could suggest that MT reflects a dittograph (Zimmerli, *Ezekiel 2*, 438); in any case, they do retain the 3rd person singular pronoun.

65. See, in particular, Levenson, *Theology*, 113; Duguid, *Ezekiel*, 130.

are equally divided and cannot be alienated, there is no social mobility and, therefore, no possibility for the emergence of such an upper class that could dispute the prerogatives of the נשיא. The only distant echo of landed nobility that remains is the expression עם הארץ; but this notion has been drastically re-signified in Ezek 40–48 and appears now to refer to the cultic community as a whole rather than to a distinct elite group within Israel.[66] As such, while the tribal concept developed in Ezek 40–48 serves to protect the people from the potential abuses of its ruler, it also simultaneously secures that ruler's privileged position as the *sole* community leader.

These remarks can help us reevaluate the broader issue of the view of royalty expressed in Ezek 40–48, as well as its relationship to the views expressed in other parts of the book. Overall, it seems that the description of the נשיא in Ezek 40–48 *seeks not so much to de-emphasize or criticize royalty*—as it has often been assumed—*but to reinterpret it significantly from a distinctive, utopian perspective*, which is defined throughout the last section of the book (chs. 40–48) and which consistently emphasizes the primacy of the deity and its temple. In keeping with this distinct utopian conception, the role of the נשיא is now predominantly defined in relationship to the temple and its rituals; there are only hints of other, non-cultic roles and functions for this ruler (see 45:9–12). Furthermore, the נשיא is now subjected to new constraints that are consistent with the utopia defined in Ezek 40–48. In particular, his access to the temple is restricted—he is allowed to stand at the gate of the inner court where the Zadokide priests offer the sacrifices to the deity but cannot enter that court (see 46:2–3);[67] and he cannot reallocate the land, apart from his own estates, because that land has been assigned by YHWH to the Israelites tribes as their נחלה ('inheritance) and אחזה ('property') and, therefore, cannot be taken back from them (46:16–18). Within these constraints, however, the נשיא nonetheless retains a unique mediatory function: he is the sole leader of the lay community, the patron as well as the guardian of the cult, and he enjoys as such a privileged relationship to the deity. The royal function, as we can see here, has not so much been abandoned or "downgraded" as radically transformed and re-signified in a new (utopian) context.

This transformation is further expressed by the fact that the נשיא not only is contrasted once with the Judahite kings of the past (Ezek 43:7–9) but is never expressly identified as a member of the Davidic dynasty; in a sense, this phenomenon is even more obvious in the Old Greek of Ezek 40–48, which no longer renders the Hebrew נשיא with ἄρχων, as in chs. 1–39 but with ἀφηγούμενος (a nominal form of the verb ἀφηγέομαι 'to lead').[68] Arguably, there are reasons to presume that the identification of the נשיא in Ezek 40–48 with a Davidic ruler would have been apparent to the ancient audiences of the book, as most commentators tend to assume. In particular, this identification is prepared by the ending of ch. 37, which associates the reestablishment of the sanctuary with the reestablishment

---

66. See Ezek 45:16, 22; 46:3, 9, and contrast the use of this term in other parts of the book, like Ezek 7:27; 22:29, where it retains its traditional meaning of landed nobility. For this observation and its implication regarding the status of the נשיא in Ezek 40–48, see Duguid, *Ezekiel*, 131, as well as my comments in Nihan, "*Nāśîʾ* and the Future of Royalty," 238–39.

67. See on this, e.g., Block, *Ezekiel 25–48*, 671.

68. Alternatively, the synonymous form ἡγούμενος is also used on two occasions, Ezek 44:3; 45:7. For this phenomenon, see the study by F. Raurell, "The Polemical Role of the ΑΡΧΟΝΤΕΣ and ΑΦΗΓΟΥΜΕΝΟΙ in Ez LXX," in *Ezekiel and his Book: Textual and Literary Criticism and their Interrelation*, ed. J. Lust, BETL 74 (Leuven: Presses Universitaires, 1986), 85–89, although I would dispute his idea that the phenomenon itself would be indicative of the fact that ἄρχων is a largely negative term in Ezek LXX.

of David as a נשׂיא (v. 24–28); the connection is even more obvious in the arrangement preserved by p967 and L^W, where 37:24–28 comes immediately before chs. 40–48 and serves as a general introduction to the last part of the book.[69] Other indications, albeit less direct, similarly support the identification of the נשׂיא in chs. 40–48 with a member of the Davidic dynasty.[70]

Even so, however, the fact that this identification is no longer explicit within the last part of the book cannot be ignored. Rather, it already signals that the representation of the utopian ruler is *not* simply continuous with the references to a future Davidic ruler in earlier parts of the book (namely, Ezek 17, 34, and 37). It also implies, at the same time, a significant degree of discontinuity. This observation, in turn, raises a more general issue regarding the coexistence of multiple royal utopias in Ezekiel, which I will now briefly address by way of a conclusion.

5. Royal Utopias in Ezekiel: Coherence and Complexity

Contrary to other prophetic books, especially Isaiah, the book of Ezekiel does not consider alternative forms of leadership after the Exile. There is no notion, for instance, that the roles of the Davidic kings could be taken over in postmonarchic times by a foreign ruler—like, e.g., Cyrus (Isa 42:1–7; 44:24–28; 45:1–7, 9–13)—or by the Judean community as a whole, or a portion thereof (see especially Isa 55:3–5). There is also no indication that the Davidic rulers of the future will need to share their power with other leading groups or families, as per the view expressed, for instance, in Jer 33:14–26 MT, where the Davidic house will rule again over Judah and Israel alongside the Levitical priests. Instead, the book of Ezekiel is characterized by its reassertion that Davidic kingship remains, after the exile, the principal form of human leadership; and this conception is developed in a number of passages of the book that contain utopian scenarios referring—in more or less detail—to a postmonarchic royal mediator.[71] At the same time, however, the discourse on the future of Davidic kingship in Ezekiel is by no means simple or straightforward but, on the contrary, remarkably complex and sophisticated in a number of ways. Three observations, in particular, can be made based on the previous discussion.

First, the reassertion of the centrality of Davidic kingship in Ezekiel is by no means simply apologetic. On the contrary, it is embedded within a memory of the Davidic kings of the past that is predominantly negative. This conclusion applies, in particular, to the last kings of Judah referenced in the first part of the book—see, especially, Ezek 19—although in other parts of the book this negative memory is extended to the Davidic kings in general (Ezek 34:2–10; 43:7–9). At the same time, however, this negative view is somehow balanced in the first part of the book by the references to some form of continuation of the Davidic dynasty through Jehoiachin. The fact that the oracles of Ezekiel are consistently dated according to the year of Jehoiachin's deportation already indicates that Jehoiachin's significance as a royal figure does not merely end with his captivity in Babylon but some-

---

69. For a detailed discussion of this phenomenon, see T. A. Rudnig, *Heilig und Profan: Redaktionskritische Studien zu Ez 40–48*, BZAW 287 (Berlin: de Gruyter, 2000), 65–77.

70. See my discussion of the evidence in Nihan, "*Nāśî'* and the Future of Royalty," 234–35, with further references to the relevant scholarly literature.

71. For the concept of "utopia" applied to prophetic texts, see, e.g., S. J. Schweitzer, "Utopia and Utopian Literary Theory: Some Preliminary Observations," in *Utopia and Dystopia in Prophetic Literature*, ed. E. Ben Zvi, Publications of the Finnish Exegetical Society 92 (Helsinki: Finnish Exegetical Society; Göttingen: Vandenhoeck & Ruprecht, 2006), 13–26.

how extends beyond the events of 597 BCE. This notion finds further expression in the finale to Ezek 17:22–24, which announces the reestablishment in the future of a Davidic king over Israel who will issue from Jehoiachin.

Second, the way in which the first part of the book describes the fall of Jerusalem (chs. 4–24) and holds together a significantly critical view of the Davidic kings with the hope for some sort of continuation of the Davidic monarchy after the Exile is consistent with the references to the reestablishment of a Davidic king in the second part of the book, especially in chs. 34 and 37. On the one hand, the continuity between this Davidic ruler and the Davidic kings of the past is affirmed in a way that is more straightforward and explicit than in other prophetic traditions, which often refer to the Davidic ascendency of the utopian ruler in an oblique way (compare, e.g., Isa 11:1–5, Mic 5:1–5, or Zech 9:9–10).[72] In Ezek 34 and 37, to the contrary, this ruler is repeatedly identified as "my servant David" (four times overall in 34:23–24 and 37:24–25); furthermore, his rule is uniquely associated in Ezek 37 with the reestablishment of a united kingdom comprising both Judah and Ephraim/Israel (37:19, 22)—a notion unparalleled in other prophetic traditions.

On the other hand, however, the description of the Davidic ruler in Ezek 34 and 37 also indicates that the traditional roles and prerogatives associated with the Davidic king will be significantly re-defined and transformed. In particular, the Davidic ruler is no longer ascribed a military function, and he has no apparent role whatsoever to play in the people's deliverance; as such, and contrary to a widespread belief, there is no expectation of a "messianic" king in Ezekiel. While the Davidic ruler remains the deity's exclusive agent and representative, his task is solely defined as presiding over and administering a world that has been definitely re-ordered by YHWH himself. This conception is consistent with the utopian view of the Davidic ruler that is already briefly mentioned at the end of Ezek 17 (vv. 22–24), although the tree imagery developed there emphasizes the cosmic significance of this ruler in maintaining the ordered world recreated by the deity. In addition, his characterization not only as מלך, 'king' (37:24 MT) but also, simultaneously, as נשיא, 'prince' (37:25) highlights his subordinated role vis-à-vis the deity, and this trend is pursued in the description of 34:23–24 as well as in the Greek version of 37:24–25, which exclusively refer to him as נשיא and no longer as מלך.

Third, overall, the references to "David" as a utopian ruler in Ezek 34 and 37 point to a sophisticated *renegotiation* of royal power in a postmonarchic context: the centrality of the Davidic king and its privileged relationship to the deity is maintained, while his roles are simultaneously reinterpreted and even transformed. This renegotiation of royal power in Ezekiel reaches its climax in the last section of the book, chs. 40–48. The representation of the נשיא that we find here is consistent with the general utopian conception developed in these chapters. The roles of the נשיא are almost exclusively defined in relationship to the temple and its rituals, and new constraints are placed upon him, especially with regard

---

72. Isaiah 11:1–5 alludes to the Davidic origins of the utopian ruler through the mention in v. 1 of a "shoot" from the "root of Jesse," the father of David; compare 1 Sam 16:1–13, further 1 Sam 17:12–31 MT, etc. Mic 5:1–5, for its part, merely mentions that this ruler will come from to "Bethlehem Ephrata" (Mic 5:1), Bethlehem being identified in other traditions as the town of David's family (1 Sam 16:4; 17:12 MT; 17:15 MT; 20:6, 28, etc.). In Zech 9:9–10, finally, the Davidic origins of the utopian king is no longer stated, and can only be inferred from the language of this passage; in particular, the description of the ruler's territory in v. 10b is reminiscent of the extent of the Davidic kingdom, and takes up verbatim the language of Ps 72:8, a royal psalm ascribed to Solomon. See further on this, e.g., C. L. Meyers and E. M. Meyers, *Zechariah 9–14*, AnBib 25C (New York: Doubleday, 1993), 172–73.

to the acquisition and distribution of land. Even so, however, the נשיא somehow retains a unique mediatory function: he is not only a figure of prestige but, above all, the guardian and patron of the cult. Royal power has not merely "melted away";[73] rather, it has been thoroughly redefined and resignified in an even more extensive way than was already the case in other parts of the book. While the use of the term נשיא in Ezek 40–48 creates a link with the oracles of chs. 34 and 37, the relationship is not straightforward: there are also clear elements of discontinuity, such as the fact that the Davidic origins of the נשיא are no longer expressly stated and that this ruler is now clearly contrasted with, and demarcated from, the Davidic kings of the past (Ezek 43:7–9). In effect, the increased utopian dimension of the description for the נשיא in Ezek 40–48 corresponds to the distinct *genre* of these chapters: they are no longer formulated as mere oracles referring to a future reality—as per Ezek 34 and 37:15–28—but comprise a collection of 'divine visions' (מראות אלהים) describing an *alternative* reality in which an imagined society is organized around a visionary sanctuary.[74]

In the end, this survey of the evidence points to the existence, or rather the *co*-existence, of multiple utopian views of Davidic kingship and its afterlife in post-monarchic times within the book of Ezekiel. As we have seen, these utopian views share some general features. In particular, they concur in asserting the necessity of a royal mediator who enjoys a privileged relationship to the deity and who is consistently represented as ruling over an ideal world that has been re-ordered and pacified by YHWH. In addition, they also concur in the notion that this royal mediator will be different from, and superior to, the Davidic kings of the past, whose rule will no longer be characterized by the oppression of the Israelite community—as per the last kings of Judah referenced in Ezek 19:2–10—but will be associated now with righteousness and prosperity within the land, as expressed by the images used in different passages of the book (see, e.g., Ezek 17:23; 37:24b–25a; 45:9–12).

The *roles* (and to some extent even the status) ascribed to this ideal ruler, however, differ significantly from one text to the other. In Ezek 17, he is identified with the cosmic tree, the very symbol of a divinely reordered world; in Ezek 34 and 37 he is identified with the "good shepherd" watching over the Israelites who have been gathered back into the land of their ancestors; whereas in Ezek 40–48 he is recast as the patron and guardian of the cult

---

73. Thus Joyce, "King and Messiah," 337.
74. The notion that Ezek 40–48 does not describe a future sanctuary, but a visionary one, has been highlighted in a number of studies: see, in particular, Niditch, "Ezekiel 40–48," as well as an insightful study by H. Liss, " 'Describe the Temple to the House of Israel': Preliminary Remarks on the Temple Vision in the Book of Ezekiel and the Question of Fictionality in Priestly Literatures," in *Utopia and Dystopia in Prophetic Literature*, ed. E. Ben Zvi, Publications of the Finnish Exegetical Society 92 (Helsinki: Finnish Exegetical Society; Göttingen: Vandenhoeck & Ruprecht, 2006), 122–43. As aptly remarked by Liss, the temple of Ezekiel is consistently presented as a temple that has *already* been built (Ezek 40–42); furthermore, there is no indication that its structure is meant to be reproduced by the Israelite community. Instead, the command to build the sanctuary has been replaced in 43:11 by a command to write down the whole vision of the temple so that the community of Israel may keep/observe (שמר) its entire 'design' (צורתו כל את) and perform its "ordinances" (according to MT; the Greek tradition preserves here a somewhat different reading). See Liss, " 'Describe the Temple'," 141–43. Other features in these chapters, such as, e.g., the description of the allocation of land among the twelve tribes in Ezek 47–48—where Judah is placed north of Benjamin! (48:7, 23)—would have signaled to the ancient audience of Ezekiel that they were not faced with a realistic description but an alternative re-imagination of their society. For a different view, compare, e.g., J. T. Strong, "Grounding Ezekiel's Heavenly Ascent: A Defense of Ezek 40–48 as a Program for Restoration," *SJOT* 26 (2012): 192–211.

within an imagined society centered around a visionary temple. As such, the image of the Davidic royal ruler that is created by the book is neither inconsistent nor simply straightforward or homogeneous: it is both coherent and complex, involving various representations that simultaneously complement and correct each other.

This conclusion is consistent with the observation already made by E. Ben Zvi in a seminal essay, where he remarks that the phenomenon of multiple utopias within the same prophetic book is a general feature of prophetic writings.[75] In particular, notes Ben Zvi, this phenomenon reflects the need in these writings to articulate a general picture of the ideal order imagined, while simultaneously accommodating a number of viewpoints and allowing for a degree of flexibility in the actualization of that ideal. The same point can be made with regard to the representation of the Davidic kingship in Ezekiel. For the postmonarchic audiences of the book, the different utopian views that coexist within the book define something like a "grammar" for thinking about the afterlife of Davidic kingship, outlining not only the continuities and discontinuities of future royal rulers with the Davidic kings of the past but also the various roles that these rulers will be able to take in the imagined ideal society.

Bibliography

Albenda, P. 1974. "Lions on Assyrian Wall Reliefs." *ANES* 6: 1–27
Allen, L. C. 1990. *Ezekiel 20–48*. WBC 29. Dallas: Word.
Artus, O. 2013. "Mise en oeuvre du droit et de la justice par les figures exemplaires de l'Ancien Testament: Abraham, David, Salomon, Josias." In *Loi et Justice dans la Littérature du Proche-Orient ancien*, edited by O. Artus, 225–33. BZAR 20. Wiesbaden: Harassowitz.
Beauchamp, P. 1999. "Pourquoi parler de David comme d'un vivant?" In *Figures de David à travers la Bible,* edited by L. Desrousseaux, 225–41. Lectio divina 177. Paris: Cerf.
Begg, C. 1989. "The Identity of the Princes in Ezekiel 19: Some Reflections." *Ephemerides Theologicae Lovaniensis* 65: 358–69.
Ben Zvi, E. 2009. "Towards an Integrative Study of the Production of Authoritative Books in Ancient Israel." In *The Production of Prophecy: Constructing Prophecy and Prophets in Yehud*, edited by D. V. Edelman and E. Ben Zvi, 15–28. BibleWorld. London: Equinox.
———. 2006. "Utopias, Multiple Utopias, and Why Utopias at All? The Social Roles of Utopian Visions in Prophetic Books within Their Historical Context." In *Utopia and Dystopia in Prophetic Literature*, edited by E. Ben Zvi, 55–85. Publications of the Finnish Exegetical Society 92. Helsinki: Finnish Exegetical Society; Göttingen: Vandenhoeck & Ruprecht.
Block, D. I. 2012. "The Tender Cedar Sprig: Ezekiel on Jehoiachin." *HeBAI* 1: 173–202.
———. 2010. "Transformation of Royal Ideology in Ezekiel." In *Transforming Visions: Transformations of Text, Tradition, and Theology in Ezekiel*, edited by W. A. Tooman and M. Lyons, 208–46. Eugene, OR: Pickwick.
———. 1998. *The Book of Ezekiel: Chapters 25–48*. NICOT. Grand Rapids, MI: Eerdmans.
———. 1995. "Bringing Back David: Ezekiel's Messianic Hope." In *The Lord's Anointed: Interpretation of Old Testament Messianic Texts*, edited by P. E. Satterthwaite, R. E. Hess, and G. J. Wenham, 167–88. Grand Rapids, MI: Baker.
Bodi, D. 2001. "Le prophète critique la monarchie: le terme *nasi* chez Ézechiel." In *Prophètes et rois:*

---

75. See E. Ben Zvi, "Utopias, Multiple Utopias, and Why Utopias at All? The Social Roles of Utopian Visions in Prophetic Books within Their Historical Context," in *Utopia and Dystopia in Prophetic Literature*, ed. E. Ben Zvi, Publications of the Finnish Exegetical Society 92 (Helsinki: Finnish Exegetical Society; Göttingen: Vandenhoeck & Ruprecht, 2006), 55–85.

Bible et Proche-Orient, edited by A. Lemaire, 249–57. Paris: Editions du Cerf.

Boe, S. 2001. *Gog and Magog. Ezekiel 38–39 as Pre-text for Revelation 19,17–21 and 2,7–10*. WUNT Series 2, 135. Tübingen: Mohr Siebeck.

Brownlee, W. H. 1986. *Ezekiel 1–19*. WBC 28. Waco, TX: Word.

Crane, A. S. 2008. *Israel's Restoration: A Textual-Comparative Exploration of Ezekiel 36–39*. VTSup 122. Leiden: Brill.

Duguid, I. 1994. *Ezekiel and the Leaders of Israel*. VTSup 56. Leiden: Brill.

Fitzmyer, J. 2007. *The One Who Is to Come*. Grand Rapids, MI: Eerdmans.

García Martínez, F. 1993. "Messianische Erwartungen in den Qumranschriften." *Jahrbuch für biblische Theologie* 8: 171–208.

Joyce, P. 1998. "King and Messiah in Ezekiel." In *King and Messiah in Israel and the Ancient Near East: Proceedings of the Oxford Old Testament Seminar*, edited by J. Day, 323–37. JSOTSup 270. Sheffield: Sheffield Academic.

Keel, O. and C. Uehlinger. 2001. *Dieux, déesses et figures divines*. Paris: Cerf.

Klein, A. 2008. *Schriftauslegung im Ezechielbuch: Redaktionsgeschichtliche Untersuchungen zu Ez 34–39*. BZAW 391. Berlin: de Gruyter.

Laato, A. 1997. *A Star Is Rising: The Historical Development of the Old Testament Royal Ideology and the Rise of the Jewish Messianic Expectations*. Atlanta, GA: Scholars Press.

Levenson, J. D. 1976. *Theology of the Program of Restoration of Ezekiel 40–48*. HSM 10. Missoula, MT: Scholars Press.

Lilly, I. E. 2012. *Two Books of Ezekiel: Papyrus 967 and the Masoretic Text as Variant Literary Editions*. VTSup 150. Leiden: Brill.

Liss, H. 2006. "'Describe the Temple to the House of Israel': Preliminary Remarks on the Temple Vision in the Book of Ezekiel and the Question of Fictionality in Priestly Literatures." In *Utopia and Dystopia in Prophetic Literature*, edited by E. Ben Zvi, 122–43. Publications of the Finnish Exegetical Society 92. Helsinki: Finnish Exegetical Society; Göttingen: Vandenhoeck & Ruprecht.

Lust J. 2012. "Ezéchiel dans la Septante." In *Les recueils prophétiques de la Bible. Origines, milieux, et contexte proche-oriental*, edited by J.-D. Macchi, C. Nihan, T. Römer, and J. Rückl, 337–58. Genève: Labor et Fides.

———. 2006. "Messianism in LXX-Ezekiel: Toward a Synthesis." In *The Septuagint and Messianism*, edited by M. Knibb, 417–30. BETL 195. Leuven: Peeters.

Maul, S. 1998. "Der assyrische König – Hüter der Weltordnung." In *Gerechtigkeit. Richten und Retten in abendländischen Tradition und ihren altorientalischen Ursprüngen*, edited by J. Assmann, B. Janowski, and M. Welker, 65–77. Munich: Wilhelm Fink Verlag.

Metzger, M. 1991. "Zeder, Weinstock und Weltenbaum." In *Ernten, was man sät. Festschrift für Klaus Koch zu seinem 65. Geburtstag*, edited by D. R. Daniels, U. Glessmer, and M. Rösel, 197–229. Neukirchen-Vluyn: Neukirchener Verlag.

Meyers, C. L. and E. M. Meyers. 1993. *Zechariah 9–14*. AnBib 25C. New York: Doubleday.

Niditch, S. 1986. "Ezekiel 40–48 in a Visionary Context." *CBQ* 48: 208–24.

Niehr, H. 1997. "The Constitutive Principles for Establishing Justice and Order in Northwest Semitic Societies with Special Reference to Ancient Israel and Judah." *ZABR* 3: 112–30.

Nihan, C. 2015. "The *nāśīʾ* and the Future of Royalty in Ezekiel." In *History, Memory, Hebrew Scriptures: A Festschrift for Ehud Ben Zvi*, edited by I. D. Wilson and D. Edelman, 229–46. Winona Lake, IN: Eisenbrauns.

———. 2013. "The Memory of Ezekiel in Postmonarchic Yehud." In *Remembering Biblical Figures in the Late Persian and Early Hellenistic Periods: Social Memory and Imagination*, edited by

D. V. Edelman and E. Ben Zvi, 415–48. Oxford: Oxford University Press.

———. 2010. "De la fin du jugement sur Jérusalem au jugement final des nations en Ézéchiel: Ézéchiel 33–39 et l'eschatologie du recueil." In *Les prophètes de la Bible et la fin des temps*, edited by J. Vermeylen, 99–146. Paris: Editions du Cerf.

Otto, E. 2002. "Politische Theologie in den Königspsalmen zwischen Ägypten und Assyrien. Die Herrscherlegitimation in den Psalmen 2 und 18 in ihren altorientalischen Kontexten." In *"Mein Sohn bist du" (Ps 2,7). Studien zu den Königspsalmen*, edited by E. Otto and E. Zenger, 33–65. Stuttgarter Bibelstudien 192. Stuttgart: Verlag Katholisches Bibelwerk.

Parpola, S. 1993. "The Assyrian Tree of Life: Tracing the Origins of Jewish Monotheism and Greek Philosophy." *JNES* 52: 161–208.

Pohlmann, K.-F. 2001. *Das Buch des Propheten Hesekiel (Ezechiel). Kapitel 20–48*. ATD 22/2. Göttingen: Vandenhoeck & Ruprecht.

———. 1996. *Das Buch des Propheten Hesekiel (Ezechiel). Kapitel 1–19*. ATD 22/1. Göttingen: Vandenhoeck & Ruprecht.

Procksch, O. 1940/41. "Fürst und Priester bei Hesekiel." *ZAW* 58: 99–133.

Raurell, F. 1986. "The Polemical Role of the ΑΡΧΟΝΤΕΣ and ΑΦΗΓΟΥΜΕΝΟΙ in Ez LXX." In *Ezekiel and his Book: Textual and Literary Criticism and their Interrelation*, edited by J. Lust, 85–89. BETL 74. Leuven: Presses Universitaires.

Rose, W. 2000. *Zemah and Zerubbabel: Messianic Expectations in the Early Postexilic Period*. JSOTSup 304. Sheffield: Sheffield Academic.

Rudnig, T. A. 2000 *Heilig und Profan: Redaktionskritische Studien zu Ez 40–48*. BZAW 287. Berlin: de Gruyter.

Schweitzer, S. J. 2006. "Utopia and Utopian Literary Theory: Some Preliminary Observations." In *Utopia and Dystopia in Prophetic Literature*, edited by E. Ben Zvi, 13–26. Publications of the Finnish Exegetical Society 92. Helsinki: Finnish Exegetical Society; Göttingen: Vandenhoeck & Ruprecht.

Seybold, K. 1972. *Das davidische Königtum im Zeugnis der Propheten*. Göttingen: Vandenhoeck & Ruprecht.

Śliwa, J. 1974. "Some Remarks Concerning Victorious Ruler Representations in Egyptian Art." *Forschungen und Berichte, Archäologische Beiträge* 16: 97–117.

Smith, J. Z. 1987. *To Take Place: Toward Theory in Ritual*. Chicago, IL: University of Chicago Press.

Stevenson, K. R. 1996. *Vision of Transformation: The Territorial Rhetoric of Ezekiel 40–48*. SBLDS 154. Atlanta, GA: Scholars Press.

Strawn, B. A. 2005. *What Is Stronger than a Lion? Leonine Image and Metaphor in the Hebrew Bible and the Ancient Near East*. OBO 212. Fribourg: Academic Press; Göttingen: Vandenhoeck & Ruprecht.

Strong, J. T. 2012. "Grounding Ezekiel's Heavenly Ascent: A Defense of Ezek 40–48 as a Program for Restoration." *SJOT* 26: 192–211.

Van der Woude, A. S. 1957. *Die messianischen Vorstellungen der Gemeinde von Qumran*. Studia semitica neerlandica 3. Assen: van Gorcum.

Weidner, E. F. 1939. "Jojachin, König von Juda, in babylonischen Keilschrifttexten." In *Mélanges syriens offerts à Monsieur René Dussaud*, 923–35. 2 vols. Bibliothèque archéologique et historique 30. Paris: Geuthner.

Winter, U. 2002. "Der Lebensbaum im Alten Testament und die Ikonographie des stilisierten Baumes in Kanaan/Israel." In *Das Kleid der Erde, Pflanzen in der Lebenswelt des alten Israel*, edited by H. Schweizer, 138–62. Stuttgart and Neukirchen-Vluyn: Calwer Verlag and Neukirchener Verlag.

Zimmerli, W. 1983. *Ezekiel 2: A Commentary on the Book of the Prophet Ezekiel, Chapters 25–48*. Hermeneia. Philadelphia, PA: Fortress.
———. 1979. *Ezekiel 1: A Commentary on the Book of the Prophet Ezekiel, Chapters 1–24*. Hermeneia. Minneapolis, MN: Fortress.

— 8 —

Imagining the Memory of an Elder: Job 29–30

Terje Stordalen

It is commonly accepted that local leadership in the Iron Age Southern Levant typically consisted of local family heads making up a group of elders.[1] Biblical literature does not give much information on such institutions, but one instance is reflected—in a decidedly stylized fashion—in Ruth 4. In the book of Deuteronomy, groups of elders seem to be integrated into a larger legal system, subordinated under local and central judges or priests, princes, and other rulers.[2] To a reader familiar with modern social organization, this might suggest that elders took part in the same kind of social power and exchange as other levels in the hierarchy—only in smaller measure. There is, however, reason to think that the leadership and power exerted by elders would have been of a different nature than that of judges, priests, or political rulers associated with the state. One challenge in researching this issue is that the social formations headed by elders were oral, and it is not easy to document historically the precise social discourse that went on in these settings. Modes of leadership reflected in biblical literature seem mainly to reflect social discourse in other types of social formations. Incidentally, however, two chapters in the book of Job provide a glimpse into the social discourse of local elder leadership. As I have argued elsewhere, the intensely scribal and intellectual book of Job richly reflects imagery and practices that must have originated in oral settings.[3] In this essay I argue that Job 29–30 reflects a kind of rhetoric that was traditional in local formations of the Southern Levant. Interpreted in a comparative perspective, this rhetoric provides hints as to the nature of social discourse in local social formations—and hence to the kind of leadership the readers of these chapters would have expected local elders to exert.

---

1. For biblical scholars confirming this view, see for instance, T. M. Willis, *The Elders of the City: A Study of the Elders-Laws in Deuteronomy*, SBL Monograph Series 55 (Atlanta, GA: SBL, 2001); P. McNutt, *Reconstructing the Society of Ancient Israel*, Library of Ancient Israel (Louisville, KY: Westminster John Knox, 1999), 91, 100f, etc.
2. See Deut 19:1–13; 21:1–9, 18–21; 22:13–21; 25:5–10.
3. T. Stordalen, "'His place does not recognise him' (Job 7:10): Reflections of Non-Inscribed Memory in the Book of Job," in *Cultural Memory in Biblical Exegesis*, ed. P. Carstens, T. B. Hasselbalch, and N. P. Lemche (Piscataway, NJ: Gorgias, 2012), 47–68.

1. Chapters 29–30 in the Composition of the Book

The section of Job 29–31 that contains what could perhaps be classified as an autobiographical complaint (chs. 29–30)[4] and an oath of innocence (ch. 31) seems to be situated at a very salient point in the composition of the book: I take it as the opening of the second unit of speeches in the book. This view may need further comment since the compositional order of this book is anything but obvious.[5] Without entering into the debate about secondary additions and levels of compositional intention, let me suggest that a key to reading the text, as is well known, lies in the narrative rubrics.[6] These are the thin layers of narrative voice that keep the speeches together between the end of chapter 2 and the closing narrative in 42:7–17. A second key lies in the propensity for numerical symbolism in the book, evident, for instance, in 1:2 and manifest at several points throughout the book.

a) Job 3–28

Combining these keys seems to throw new light on the structural anatomy of chs. 3–28. Unlike scholars focusing upon the "disorder" in the sequence in the third cycle of speeches (chs. 22–27/28),[7] chs. 3–28 could, in fact, be perceived as a carefully constructed totality. The propensity for numeric symbolism dominates the compositional anatomy of this part of the book. After an opening curse and lament by Job (ch. 3), each friend makes a speech. Every single one of them provokes an immediate response by Job. Every speech is introduced by narrative rubrics, using the verbs ענה and אמר, resulting in six marked speeches in the first cycle.[8] The same pattern with the same sequence is repeated in the second cycle, again holding six marked entries.[9] The only compositional development from the first to the second cycle seems to be that the speeches of the friends become shorter, which may perhaps indicate that they are running out of arguments. This strict regularity of the two first cycles prepares reading expectations for the third round while also priming the reader's sensitivity to changes in the pattern.

At first, the third cycle looks confusing. For one thing, the speeches of the friends now become very short, but that could be consistent with the shortening trend in cycle two. More confusing is the fact that the content of some of these speeches seem to deviate in profile from what was said by these speakers before. Really confusing is the fact that Zophar, the third friend, does not even get a say. And most disturbingly, the last speech of Job contains a chapter that has every mark of being a separate, traditional piece (ch. 28).

---

4. The genre of chs. 29–30 is debated. C. Westermann, *Der Aufbau des Buches Hiob*, Calwer theologische Monographien 6 (Stuttgart: Calwer, 1977), 59–65 identifies ch. 30 as complaint (*Klage*), and ch. 29 as retrospect (*Rückblick*). D. J. A. Clines, *Job 21–37*, WBC 18A (Nashville: Nelson, 2006), 978 calls ch. 29 (and, apparently, 30) a "description of an experience," which seems to me to under-communicate the performative aspect of the passage.

5. An illustration of the complexity of this discussion is given in A. de Wilde, *Das Buch Hiob: eingeleitet, übersetzt und erläutert*, Oudtestamentische studiën 22 (Leiden: Brill, 1981), for instance 1–18 (and commentary). One reconstruction, still widely reflecting a majority view, is that of Westermann, *Aufbau* (cf. further below).

6. A similar approach was taken already in É. Dhorme, *A Commentary on the Book of Job*, 2nd ed. (Nashville: Nelson, 1984), esp. xxxvi–lii, but with a different end result.

7. See classically Westermann, *Aufbau*, 128–30; N. C. Habel, *The Book of Job*, OTL (Philadelphia: Westminster, 1985), 37f, and recently Clines, *Job 21–37*, 628–30, etc., all with earlier literature.

8. Job 4:1, 6:1, 8:1, 9:1, 11:1, 12:1.

9. Job 15:1, 16:1, 18:1, 19:1, 20:1, 21:1.

Could there, nevertheless, be a method in this apparent madness?

The silencing of Zophar could be seen as consistent with the gradual silencing of the friends. Having Job's speech take the place that Zophar's would have occupied is, in a strange way, consistent with the apparent flux of perspectives between Job and the friends in this last cycle. Admittedly, Job disagrees with his own earlier propositions, but, in a strange fashion, he says approximately what was to be expected at this location in the composition! The compositionally most difficult issue, however, is the loss of one marked speech: as opposed to the previous two cycles, there are only five marked speeches in the third cycle of the first part of the book.[10]

The solution may lie in ch. 28, which occurs as a sort of coda cast in a different voice. Formally, of course, ch. 28 is marked as spoken in the voice of Job (cf. 27:2). That, however, is evidently strange.[11] It does not fit the "requirement" of this compositional slot (cf. above), and it does not follow the voice of Job. If he were the speaker, and if Wisdom were indeed to be inaccessible to humans (as is the point in Job 28), Job should have been inclined to dismiss Wisdom and its deity altogether; either as ethically ignorant (cf. 23:13–17, 24:1–25, etc.), or as unreliably erratic (cf. 16:7–22, etc.). The praise of Wisdom in ch. 28 gives the impression of being a traditional piece, much like the frame tale of the book.[12] My point is not that the chapter actually *was* a piece of tradition,[13] but that it is *staged* as such in the book. Job 28 meets the reader's eye as something that, within the fiction of the book, existed prior to and independent of the story about Job. If so, in the world narrated in the book, this chapter makes up a separate speech in the voice of *tradition*—an entity whose voice has, in fact, appeared in several sideward glances earlier in the book.[14]

I suggest taking ch. 28 as a separate speech, marked as such not by narrative rubrics but by the above literary indications. The special marking identifies this speech as pivotal in the dialogue: it occupies a compositional space that would normally have contained the voice of Job, but it says things contrary to some of his earlier utterances that also are contrary to some of what the friends have maintained. In this way, the struggle between different characters and positions becomes less clear-cut.[15] Chapter 28 transforms the stalemate argument and hints at positions that could perhaps even be shared among the characters. So, on the one hand, the discourse of the friends seems to be coming to a halt, but, on the other hand, the problems identified by Job are beginning to be transformed. Reading Job 28 in this way, the final cycle of the first part has six speeches, like the first two cycles, although one is marked differently.

b) Job 29:1–42:6

The preceding arguments provide a lens for finding order in the second half of the dialogue as well (29:1–42:6). Following the narrative rubrics, this part contains four speeches by

---

10. Job 22:1, 23:1, 25:1, 26:1, 27:1.

11. The almost universal view that the chapter is a separate piece has recently been acknowledged again by J. Crenshaw, *Reading Job: A Literary and Theological Commentary*, Reading the Old Testament (Macon, GA: Smyth & Helwys, 2011), 122.

12. A presentation of scholarship to this view: A. Lo, *Job 28 as Rhetoric: An Analysis of Job 28 in the Context of Job 21–31*, VTSup 97 (Leiden: Brill, 2003), 2–15.

13. See further on Newsom below.

14. T. Stordalen, "Dialogue and Dialogism in the Book of Job," *SJOT* 20 (2006): 18–37, 18, 30–31.

15. This would be my way of re-phrasing the position taken by Lo, *Job 28*, cf. 15–16, 233–36.

Elihu,[16] three by YHWH,[17] and two by Job.[18] Taken in their order of appearance, the numbers descrease, leaving the reader on alert as to what in the book might fill the expected position of number one in that sequence. Moreover, four + three + two speeches add up to the number nine, which can be seen as three times three—perhaps alluding to the three cycles and the three friends in the first half of the book. In any event, nine speeches in the second part is precisely half as many as the eighteen speeches of the first part—when leaving the two opening pieces (ch. 3 and chs. 29–31) out of the equation. For that very reason, nine is also the number of speeches narrated to have been given by Job in the first part. A schematic representation of this compositional pattern of the book could be as follows:

1–2 Narrative frame
3 Opening first part of dialogue
4–28 Three cycles of dialogues (18 speeches)
29–31 Opening second part of dialogue
32–42:6 Four + three + two speeches (9 speeches)
42:7–17 Narrative frame

c) Job 29–30 in the book

For present purposes, the important point in the above reflection is that the compositional order suggests that chapters 29–31 fill a role in the second part of the dialogue that is somehow comparable to the role played by Job's curse and lament (ch. 3) in the first part. Both units initiate a set of speeches and both serve as starting points for the ensuing exchange. Chapters 29–31 are divided into two parts: one complaint (chs. 29–30) and one oath of innocence (ch. 31). While the latter may have no correspondence in chapter 3, the complaint is parallel in many ways to the curse and lament in chapter 3. The two, however, do not have the same profile, and this difference will prove important for the present investigation. While the curse and lament in chapter 3 seems to focus more upon cosmological issues, the complaint in Job 29–30 is more concerned with social aspects of suffering. N. Habel observed that Job 28 echoes passages where wisdom delivers self-praise (Prov 8, Sir 24, etc.).[19] If curse (and implicitly blessing) lies at the heart of the opening of the first half of the dialogue (Job 3), then the opening of the second half (Job 29–31) is more oriented towards praise and disdain. Without being able to argue this observation in full in the present discussion, I would say these two openings establish two poles around which the book revolves in elliptical patterns. For instance, the cosmological orientation of the curse and lament (ch. 3) is clearly echoed in the divine speeches in chs. 38–41, whereas the focus on honor and praise (chs. 29–30) is foreshadowed, for instance, in the first speech of Eliphaz (Job 4) and in other parts of Job's debate with his friends. It seems that as the book develops it attempts to strike a balance between these two dimensions of suffering. If so, one must readily admit that modern readings of the book primarily have been preoccupied with cosmological questions, in practice ignoring (or forgetting?) that there are also powerful social dimensions to the existential dilemma.

---

16. Job 32:12, 34:1, 35:1, 36:1.
17. Job 38:1; 40:1, 6.
18. Job 40:3; 42:1.
19. Habel, *Job*, 405–6.

2. The Rhetorical Profile of the Complaint

a) Social Orientation

This essay focuses only on the complaint in Job 29–30. Contrary to common opinion, this section should not be called a soliloquy: the address is made to an audience and aims at some sort of public effect.[20] This is confirmed by its classification in 29:1 as a משל, that is, a text or a byword that is publicly known because of its striking formulation or story. At the heart of this משל lies the proponent's remembering his happy past (mostly portrayed in ch. 29) in contrast to his miserable present (mostly reflected in ch. 30). His memories of happy 'months of the past' (29:2 ירחי־קדם) are now haunting Job in his misfortune: 'My belly boils and is never still; days of affliction now lie before me' (30:27, מעי רתחו ולא־דמו קדמני ימי עני).

What, precisely, is remembered, though? It is not so much past blessings as the public recognition of these blessings: "The ear that heard [me], declared me to be happy (אשרי), and the eye that saw approved of me." (29:11). Emphasis upon public recognition occurs also in 29:7–10, 13, 21–25; 30:25). Conversely, public disdain dominates Job's present as described in ch. 30 (see vv. 1, 9–14). The main axis of this discourse clearly seems to be honor and shame and the social exchange around this dynamic.[21]

b) Rhetorical Configuration

Before exploring the social aspects of this reported memory, we must recognize that the literary configuration of these two chapters—and of the book—makes it very complicated to use this complaint as a simple reflection of social realities. Clearly, the book of Job is fiction, and the fictional world of the hero seems occasionally to differ from that of the expected audience. For instance, Job lives in a world located in the indistinct and distant east (1:3). As an archetypically rich member of society, he lives in tents and is surrounded by large herds,[22] much like the distant patriarchs of Genesis, but he also has a seat in the city gate (29:7). In Job's world, it seems to be possible that a prominent man could be blessed with a symbolic number of sons, daughters, sheep, camels, oxen, and donkeys (1:2–3) and then get slammed by an equally symbolic number of maladies in a truly iconic configuration of evils (1:14–19).

C. Newsom has identified the frame tale of the book as conspicuously conventional, indeed as a "pseudonaive" "hyper example" of the genre of a traditional story.[23] She is evidently right: the opening tale overstates traditional elements in a parodic (or near parodic) voice. And life in this (near) parody has the potential for characteristically strange experience: it is a world that must be geographically, temporally, and socially distant from the book's intended audience.

---

20. With Habel, *Job*, 404. For the conventional position, see for instance H. H. Rowley, *Job*, New Century Bible (London: Nelson, 1970), 185; R. E. Murphy, *Wisdom Literature: Job, Proverbs, Ruth, Canticles, Ecclesiastes, and Esther*, Forms of the Old Testament Literature 13 (Grand Rapids, MI: Eerdmans, 1981), 38–39.
21. Excellently argued by C. A. Newsom, *The Book of Job: A Contest of Moral Imaginations* (Oxford: Oxford University Press, 2003), 187–94.
22. Job 5:24; 8:22; 11:14; 12:6; 15:34; 18:6, 14–15; 19:12; 20:26; 21:28; 22:23; 29:4; 31:31.
23. Newsom, *Book of Job*, 36–41, etc. Similarly questioning the "traditional" nature of the frame tale, see in particular Y. Hoffman, *A Blemished Perfection: The Book of Job in Context*, JSOTSup 213 (Sheffield: Sheffield Academic, 1996), 267–76, with history of research and comments on the nature of the tale as "anti-mimetic" (271–74).

This distance has implications for calculating the communicative production of Job 29–30. The author sets a stage where the narrator reports on Job's (somewhat strange) world, and it remains up to the audience to calculate the significance of Job's memory by way of conferring or comparing the narrated world to circumstances in the audience's everyday world. When imagining the performative effect of professing such a memory in that narrative world, the audience would engage categories and perceptions from their own, everyday realities. And it would only be in the reader's categories and perceptions that a historically oriented scholar could hope to find reflections of past social realities, not in the fantasy of the text. The following is an attempt to take this literary and rhetorical complication seriously while asking how categories in the text may have been "derived in some fashion from [concepts] recognizable to the [...] audience."[24]

3. Staging Job as an Extraordinary Elder

What are the roles that Job remembers from his happy past? Posting that question rapidly makes us attentive to the creative nature of Job's professed memory. First, there may be a trajectory of archaism in these chapters. The view of Job as a dweller in a tent (29:4) seems to be part of such a strategy. The less common term ירח (month) in 29:2 is elsewhere used in stories narrating pre-monarchic and early monarchic times.[25] Another possible archaizing strategy involves examples of imagery that are unknown in other biblical literature: perhaps it was rare and advanced, or perhaps it was created for the occasion by the author.[26] All this serves to place Job in a world different from the one known by the audience.

Perhaps as an invitation to the reader's imagination of that archaic world, or as a rhetorical device, Job appears to be remembering himself as occupying a number of roles that would presumably be incompatible in the reader's everyday world. In some passages he appears like a ruler.[27] Other passages seem to recall him as a judge or a legal officer of sorts.[28] In yet other instances, he occurs as something like a communal advisor,[29] perhaps

---

24. Newsom, *Book of Job*, 281 n. 18.

25. Exod 2:2; Deut 21:13; 33:14; 1 Kgs 6:37–38; 8:2; 2 Kgs 15:13. (And apart from that only Zech 11:8 and Job 3:6; 7:3; 29:2; 39:2). The more common term is חדש, which has 224 occurrences across the Tanakh.

26. One example is 29:4 בימי חרפי (lit.: 'the days of my winter'; NRSV: "when I was in my prime"). On interpreting this creative metaphor, see E. Good, *In Turns of Tempest: A Reading of Job* (Stanford, CA: Stanford University Press, 1990), 296.

27. See the simile in 29:25 and compare the eulogy in 29:12–17 with Ps 72. Among scholars seeing Job as king, see B. V. Malchow, "A Royal Prototype in Job 29," in *The Psalms and Other Studies on the Old Testament Presented to Joseph I. Hunt*, ed. J. C. Knight and L. A. Sinclair (Nashotah, WI: Nashotah House Seminary, 1990), 178–84; Clines, *Job 21–37*, 995.

28. Notably 29:16, cf. 'in the council of Eloah' (29:4, בסוד אלוה). Seeing Job mainly as a judge: K. Budde, *Das Buch Hiob*, Handkommentar zum Alten Testament 2/1 (Göttingen: Vandenhoeck & Ruprecht, 1896), 163f, 165f; G. Hölscher, *Das Buch Hiob*, Handbuch zum Alten Testament 17 (Tübingen: Mohr Siebeck, 1937), 69; cf. D. Wolfers, *Deep Things out of Darkness: The Book of Job. Essays and a New English Translation* (Kampen: Kok Pharos, 1994), 96: "legislative, executive, and spiritual leader." J. E. Hartley, "From Lament to Oath: A Study of Progression in the Speeches of Job," in *The Book of Job*, ed. W. A. M. Beuken, BETL 114 (Leuven: Peeters, 1994), 79–100, 95–96, connects the emphasis on justice to the oath of innocence in ch. 31.

29. Job 29:1 (cf. Num 21:27; Ezek 16:44, etc.) and 29:21–24. This is the profile of Job emphasized in G. Fohrer, *Das Buch Hiob*, KAT 16 (Gütersloh: Gütersloher Verlagshaus Gerd Mohn, 1963), 407–8.

aspiring toward the priestly[30] or even prophetic.[31] Also, one might perceive him as a landowner, a local nobleman of first rank.[32] Adding to the impression of the strong rhetoric of the passage, these chapters engage conventional spiritual poetry as well as conventional imagery for individual happiness.[33] Both may denote experiences in a wide variety of social registers, which helps one to gloss over possible tensions in Job's memory.

For purposes of historical reflection, this literary and rhetorical configuration poses a challenge. The excess of roles and the rich imagery may belong to the narrative fiction of an archaic world, or it could reflect excessive rhetoric applied by the proponent. In either case, the text does not offer a straightforward basis for reconstructing social realities in the world of the audience.

Whenever social context is *explicitly* reflected in these chapters (i.e., in apparent non-symbolical language), it seems to be that of traditional life in a local town or village.[34] Job's encounter with chiefs and rulers and his king-like appearance occur in the frame of the city gate (29:7, cf. vv. 7–25), as does the administration of justice, with its deliberations (Job 29:9–10 and 29:21–23) and legal negotiations (Job 29:14–16, and cf. vv. 12–17). A local setting seems to be presumed for Job's crying (in a ritual of grief?) for the poor in society as well (30:25). Job seems to be depicted as an outstanding elder who is capable of integrating the other roles listed in these chapters: as an elder, he is vocal like a bard (29:21–23), insightful like a prophet (29:23), gracious like a priest (29:24), and as confident and imposing as a ruler (29:25). As an elder, he passes judgment and maintains social standards (29:12–17). And as a prominent member of a leading local family—which is what would have brought him to the elder group in the first place—he may be responsible for hiring and dismissing workers (30:2). Also, Job expects to die with his family; implicitly, his name is to be remembered locally (29:18–20).[35] The additional roles, then, appear as rhetorical or symbolical devices that enhance the view of Job as an Elder. In short, a competent reader of these chapters would see Job as a prominent elder,[36] a local hero recognized by his peers as a match for any judge, bard, chief, or prince.

4. Imagining the Memory of an Elder

Elder institutions are generally recognized to have been based on kinship structures. While the relevant biblical Hebrew words could hardly be taken as technical social terminology, the language is fairly consistent: בית אב 'father's house' denotes the household

---

30. Thus Good, *In Turns of Tempest*, 299, focusing the priestly "robe and turban" (29:14).

31. Cf. 29:23. Most scholars see prophecy in Job mainly in ch. 4, but see Clines, *Job 21–37*, 993.

32. Thus S. R. Driver and G. B. Gray, *A Critical and Exegetical Commentary on the Book of Job*, ICC (Edinburgh: T&T Clark, 1921), 247: "Job's great estate lay near a large town […]." Similarly F. Hesse, *Hiob*, ZBK 14 (Zürich: Theologischer Verlag, 1978), 162f; R. L. Alden, *Job*, New American Commentary 11 (Nashville: Broadman & Holman, 1993), 282, 286; cf. Dhorme, *Job*, 419–20, 422; and with extensive argumentation M. Hamilton, "Elite Lives: Job 29–31 and Traditional Authority," *JSOT* 32 (2007): 69–89.

33. Cf. respectively Job 30:16–23, 26–31 and Job 29:2–6, 18–20.

34. Newsom, *Book of Job*, 187 coins the striking characterization "village patriarchy" for the social scene in which this chapter is set.

35. Contrary to Good, *In Turns of Tempest*, 300. For the figure of family and (loss of) name, see 30:8; 18:17. Further on name / memory and topography / locality cf. T. Stordalen, "'His place does not recognise him,'" esp. 32–41.

36. Similarly already for instance A. Weiser, *Das Buch Hiob*, 5th ed., ATD 13 (Göttingen: Vandenhoech & Ruprecht, 1968), 205–6.

family, משפחות, 'clan' often names the extended family, and שבט or מטה usually denote the larger 'tribe'. Elders in a given council would likely emerge from any of these levels (household, clan, or tribe) that were relevant in each case. The social and symbolic basis for such elder groups seems, however, to have been the household family, which remained politically and ideologically dominant across the Levant in the Bronze and Iron Ages.[37]

Town and city elders, like the ones appearing in Deuteronomy,[38] must have headed what could be seen as social fields of traditional social discourse.[39] Based on knowledge of local history, ecology, and tradition, they would have served as interpreters and negotiators of local versions of forms of social life that were widely shared in the ancient Levant. The body of elders also served to symbolize the specific, local version of this ethos that they were to champion. Actual social discourse must likely have varied from one locality to another, but it is difficult to retrieve data on such variation. If Job 29–30 reflects imagined traditional leadership by an elder (cf. above), this text may provide unique insight into an actual exchange of power and authority in a traditional local setting.[40] In the following I attempt to recover parts of the social discourse reflected in these two chapters.

4.1 Comparative Perspectives

As seen above, D. Schloen argued that patrimonial family units occurred in small variations throughout the Eastern Mediterranean in the Bronze and Iron Ages. Similar kinds of formations existed in classical Hebrew society,[41] but none of the textual, archaeological, or historical comparative records provide much detail about specific discourses or local variations. We need a broader basis for reflection. In the following I attempt to combine material and insights from three distinct domains: biblical passages, comparative historical records, and critical social analysis.

For empirical and critical reflection on societies potentially similar to that imagined in Job 29–30, I turn to two very different classics in social science, namely P. Bourdieu's description of the Algerian tribe of Kabyle[42] and Fei Xiatong's analysis of social discourse in late pre-modern China.[43] Bourdieu described the social ecology symbolized by local family heads as "a self-regulating device": a social organism where tradition had been so internalized in individual members (through the phenomenon he called *habitus*) that there

---

37. J. D. Schloen, *The House of the Father as Fact and Symbol: Patrimonialism in Ugarit and the Ancient Near East*, Studies in the Archaeology and History of the Levant 2 (Winona Lake, IN: Eisenbrauns 2001), esp. 255–316.

38. Deut 19:1–13; 21:1–9, 18–21; 22:13–21; 25:5–10, see again Willis, *Elders of the City*.

39. T. Stordalen, "Horse Statues in Seventh Century Jerusalem: How to Assess Religious Diversity and Similarity in Late Iron II?" *HeBAI* 4(1): 106–132.

40. Similarly Newsom, *Book of Job*, 187.

41. See Willis, *Elders of the City*, 19–27; McNutt, *Reconstructing Society*, 101, 110–11, et passim; C. L. Meyers, "The Family in Early Israel," in *Families in Ancient Israel*, ed. L. G. Perdue, J. Blenkinsopp, *et al.* (Louisville, KY: Westminster John Knox, 1997), 1–47.

42. P. Bourdieu, *Outline of a Theory of Practice* (Cambridge: Cambridge University Press, 1977). See also for instance P. Bourdieu, *The Logic of Practice* (Cambridge: Polity, 1990). For evaluation of how best to assess this work, cf. several entries in J. E. Goodman and P. A. Silverstein, eds., *Bourdieu in Algeria: Colonial Politics, Ethnographic Practices, Theoretical Developments* (Lincoln: University of Nebraska Press, 2009).

43. Fei Xiaotong, *From the Soil: The Foundations of Chinese Society: A Translation of Fei Xiaotong's Xiangtu Zhongguo*, trans. G. G. Hamilton and Wang Zheng (Berkeley: University of California Press, 1992).

were only a manageable number of contestable areas left in the social discourse.[44] Social exchange was regulated by a sense of honor, which was "nothing other than the cultivated disposition, inscribed in the body schema and in the schemes of thought, which enables each agent to engender all the practices consistent with the logic [of the relevant case]."[45] In view of such tradition and *habitus*, there is an absence of genuine law, but this "must not lead us to forget that any socially recognized formulation contains within it an intrinsic power to reinforce dispositions symbolically."[46] An individual who meticulously follows traditional "rules" would "win the group over to his side by ostentatiously honouring the values the group honours."[47] In Bourdieu's interpretation, this is the "logic" that underlies and regulates traditional practice, a setup where rules and values are generally internalized in all members of society. Bourdieu does not comment on the issue, but it is evident that elders would be shaped by the same *habitus* and be obliged to respect it.

The Chinese social anthropologist Fei described a strikingly parallel situation for late traditional Chinese society.[48] In two of his deceptively simple chapters Fei described the "rule by elders"[49] in a "society without litigation."[50] A core point in his discussion is this:

> In a relatively static society, culture is stable. There are very few new problems. Living consists primarily of following a set of traditional recipes. In a society completely regulated by tradition, there would be no politics, just education. Although such a society does not actually exist, rural society comes close. [...] The simplicity of political action in [traditional Chinese] society is described in the [traditional Chinese] sayings "To govern is to say little" [...] and "To rule is to do nothing" [...].[51]

In traditional China, Fei insists, the village is the unit—whether it consists of a handful of families or several hundred. Villages are fairly isolated from each other and sometimes in dispute or feuding, but internally in the village there is very strong social integration. "Every child grows up in everyone else's eyes, and in the child's eyes everyone and everything seem ordinary and habitual."[52] As with the Kabyle, late traditional Chinese honor systems (which, in many respects, of course, were not identical to those in Algeria) were dominated by collective morals and convention. Social doxa was reproduced through practicing specific relations and patterns of behavior among families and individuals in a local society, the patterns of which had been negotiated over past generations. Trust in such a society derives from familiarity and depends on "people who are so enmeshed in customary norms that they cannot behave in any other way."[53]

---

44. Bourdieu, *Outline*, 11, cf. 10–15 and wider 1–58. See similarly Bourdieu, *Logic of Practice*, 100f, 110, cf. 98–121.
45. Bourdieu, *Outline*, 15.
46. Bourdieu, *Outline*, 21.
47. Bourdieu, *Outline*, 22.
48. Fei, *From the Soil*, 132. Fei, who had studied with Malinowski in London, first published the chapters in this book as popularizing articles for upcoming state officials in the newly established People's Republic of China in 1947.
49. Fei, *From the Soil*, 114–19.
50. Fei, *From the Soil*, 101–7.
51. Fei, *From the Soil*, 117.
52. Fei, *From the Soil*, 41, cf. the context.
53. Fei, *From the Soil*, 43.

Fei gave a striking illustration of the complexity of social discourse in such a society, based on the metaphor of seeing the most important social relationship—kinship—as concentric circles formed when a stone is thrown into a lake:

> Everyone has this kind of kinship network, but the people covered by one network are not the same as those covered by any other. [...] Therefore the web of social relations linked with kinship is specific to each person. Each web has a self as its center, and every web has a different center. [...] Like the ripples formed from a stone thrown into a lake, each circle spreading out from the center becomes more distant and at the same time more insignificant. [...] In these elastic networks that make up Chinese society, there is always a self at the center of each web. But this notion of the self amounts to egocentrism, not individualism. [...] [T]he Chinese system of organization [is] that of a pattern of discrete circles, the differential mode of association.[54]

Obviously, those who serve as heads of such traditional social formations are nothing like the executive leaders of postmodern markets or new public managements. They also did not have room for the navigation practiced (or commonly fantasized?) by noblemen in European feudal societies. Their space for exerting leadership would be limited and deeply pre-formatted. Basically, an elder would have to provide an interpretation of shared tradition and practice that sits well with the already dominant *habitus*. This *habitus* was formed, in the first place, through the very practice the leader is expected to administrate. There is, therefore, a sense of reciprocity and double dependency between heads and members of such traditional social formations. The elder depends on the community for recognition, while members in society depend on the interpretation of tradition provided by elders.[55]

In these kinds of formations, individuals would have been born and cultured into families and clans (and perhaps tribes) that had specific patterns of exchange with other families and clans (and tribes). Individuals at various points in this social texture would be (or become) aware of these negotiated relations and they would have to respect them and internalize them (as *habitus*). This would limit and restrain the action of individuals, households, clans, and tribes. But it would also support them, in the sense that everyone had a commonly recognized place in the social web, and the social discourse would respect that. All these insights are relevant for interpreting the social discourse being imagined in Job 29–30—a challenge to which we now turn.

4.2. A Comparative Social Reading of Sections in Job 29–30

There are good reasons to think that the depictions of social discourse in traditional societies described by Bourdieu and Fei might be helpful for interpreting reflections of social exchange and alignment in biblical passages involving elders. First, as a detailed example, portrayals of parents bringing their rebellious children to the elders (as in Deut 21:18–21 and 22:13–21) resonate with Bourdieu's note that "the defeated man who has done his duty [for instance by bringing his kin to the elders] incurs no blame."[56] Similar patterns of shaming and honoring were observed by J. K. Campbell.[57] Second, on a larger scale, the

---

54. This metaphor goes through an entire chapter on "The Differential Mode of Association," 61–70. Citations taken from pp. 63, 65, 67, 67–68.
55. As one of few biblical scholars who comments on this, see Newsom, *Book of Job*, 188–89.
56. Bourdieu, *Outline*, 13.
57. J. K. Campbell, *Honour, Family and Patronage: A Study of Institutions and Moral Values in a Greek Mountain Community* (Oxford: Oxford University Press, 1964), 112–13, describes how a man saves his name

legislation involving decisions rendered by elders in Deuteronomy reflects a perception of the village as the social unit, as was also described for China by Fei. Household families are expected to honor the ethos symbolized by the elders on behalf of the local group. In passages like Deut 19:12 and 21:1–9, local elder groups interact with neighboring elder councils from other towns or villages. This indicates that family units were segments in a social and symbolic economy that was bounded off by the local area and symbolized by the town's group of elders.[58]

4.2.1. Job 30:2–8: Echo of Traditional Rhetoric

Job 29–30 gives every impression of evoking the reader's perceptions of local social discourse. And yet, one can only proceed from text to social reality with the utmost caution.[59] As discussed above, these chapters invite the reader to *imagine* a social discourse of a foreign world: the society portrayed there might have seemed untypical, even archaic, to the intended audience. Elements such as the encounter with chiefs (שׂרים) and nobles (נגידים) in 29:10–11 or the royal appearance (29:24–25) seem like rhetorical devices or artistic imaginations. Yet it is less clear whether the image of Job presiding in court (29:12–17) is creative or (partly) realistic.[60] Given all these challenges in assessing the text, a better entry point for our purpose seems to be the passage where Job describes his *current* situation—namely Job 30, and esp. vv. 2–8 and 9–15 respectively: these are a little less fraught with difficulties.

In his experience described in 30:2–8 (with v. 1 as an introduction and simultaneously a prelude to 30:9–15), Job is heading a network of families (30:1) and carries some kind of responsibility for employing or organizing people in his own generation (30:2–8). In this capacity he has passed negative, indeed shocking, evaluations concerning certain "useless" (30:2) individuals who were allegedly "driven out of the midst [of society? of the camp?]."[61] People (presumably in the local community) are said to have treated these individuals "like thieves" (30:5). According to 30:8, these people were 'fools' (בני־נבל) 'without names/reputations' (בני בלי־שׁם) who 'were driven from the land' (נכאו מן־הארץ).

Some scholars read Job 30:2–8 as an implicit moral critique of Job, having him reveal that he has, in fact, been dealing with fellow humans in ways that are inconsistent with his claims of integrity in ch. 29.[62] In such a reading, it is not entirely clear whether the descriptions of the outcast are realistic, rhetorical, or both. An earlier approach,[63] now re-gaining momentum in politically sensitive scholarship, takes Job 30:2–8 as a more or less realistic portrayal of people who were marginalized in society. Scholars have referred to these people

---

by shaming a close kinsman who had dishonored himself and his family.

58. Thus also Meyers, "Family in Early Israel," 36, 40, cf. 32–41, taking this unit as a "residential kinship group" (13).

59. Cf. above, and note how Newsom, *Book of Job*, 191, 281 n. 18 avoids making claims about society and instead, limits herself to an analysis of rhetorical strategies. Even so, her use of empirical social models makes her argument balance on a very sharp edge here.

60. Habel, *Job*, 410, aptly notes the similarities between this section and the legendary passages in Aqhat II.v.5–7.

61. 30:5, מן־גו יגרשׁו.

62. Thus for instance J. G. Janzen, *Job*, Interpretation: A Bible Commentary for Teaching and Preaching (Atlanta, GA: John Knox, 1985), 205f; Good, *In Turns of Tempest*, 303–5; and Clines, *Job 21–37*, 997–99, etc.

63. The classical reading may be illustrated by Habel, *Job*, 419: "[…] a class of outcasts who lived like wild beasts in the desert scrub and wilderness caves."

as "nobodies," as "desperately poor people [...] excluded from the towns and villages," as "characterized by abject poverty [and ...] social exclusion,"[64] and even as people "outside the set of relationships of obedience and subservience described in ch. 29."[65] If, however, the society reflected in Job 30 were even remotely akin to those observed by Bourdieu or Fei, it is difficult to imagine there could have existed village families that were excluded and living outside the web of local relations.[66] In traditional village life, everyone knows the place of everyone else. And while social discipline may be harsh for those at the bottom, nobody is really outside the social web. The fictional biblical text itself implicitly confirms this when referring to the children of those "having been chased away."[67] If such children were still around in the fictive world, their forefathers could hardly have been literally driven away from that scene.

It seems to me, therefore, that the audience called upon to calculate the effect of the text would not have taken these verses to describe that fictional world literally. It seems more likely that they would have heard Job's harsh words in 30:2–8 as a specimen of rhetorical shaming. As Campbell says, "anything which leads to, or is the basis of, low prestige is the matter for shame"—and such shaming may occur as open ridiculing, especially if the one being ridiculed is of low prestige.[68] In biblical literature there is a trajectory of irony that is uncomfortably explicit for modern (academic) taste, irony that would be very suitable for such shaming.[69] Taking Job 30:2–8 to reflect such rhetorical practice, it depicts Job, the prominent elder, to be voicing a commonly recognized social order. From the description of Fei, we learn that "[t]he neighbourhood of a powerful family may expand to the whole village, while a poor family's neighbourhood is composed only of two or three nearby families."[70]

Job, the prominent elder, talking from within his own well-connected epicentre of concentric relations, seems to be playing on such disparity. He is saying something like: "these people are not part of *my* neighborhood (although I do not deny that they live in this village). And as the symbolic head of this village, I express my disgust on behalf of the majority." This could very well reflect the discipline occurring in a traditional ethos that had been internalized to the extent of becoming "natural" for those exposed to it—i.e., becoming their *habitus*. If there is a layer of arrogance in Job's speech in 30:2–9, it would be the arrogance generated by such a traditionalist ethos and its self-sufficient majority. And if there is a stint of critique in the author letting Job remember his speech in this way, then it is a critique of such traditionalist arrogance and of the moral imaginations on which it would have been based.[71]

In conclusion, what we have in Job 30:2–8 is not a historically realistic description of social situations but more like a recording of a kind of ridiculing habitually applied by

---

64. Citations from Crenshaw, *Reading Job*, 129; Clines, *Job 21–37*, 997, 998; Newsom, *Book of Job*, 190.
65. Hamilton, "Elite Lives," 82. This work goes a long way towards taking Job 29–30 as realistic reflections of an estate owner and nobleman—using M. Weber's view of economy and social power as a basis for charting Job's former social status.
66. Compare rich people's responsibility for the poor as described in Bourdieu, *Outline*, 180, 194 et passim.
67. See discussion on text and on social implications in Clines, *Job 21–37*, 996–97.
68. Campbell, *Honour, Family and Patronage*, quotation p. 310, 313, cf. 310–15.
69. For a discussion of this irony, see E. M. Good, *Irony in the Old Testament* (Philadelphia: Westminster, 1965); I. J. J. Spangenberg, "Irony in the Book of Qohelet," *JSOT* 72 (1996): 57–69.
70. Fei, *From the Soil*, 64.
71. This, of course, is the main argument in Newsom, *Book of Job*, and needs not be repeated here.

top members in local-level society and directed downwards. And precisely as such, the passage testifies very clearly to the presence in classical Hebrew society of the kind of social discourse described by Bourdieu and Fei: this "recorded" ridiculing makes evident the presence of a traditionalist, local discourse of the kind dominated by a shared *habitus* and conventionally headed by elders. This would have been a social paradigm, indeed an experience, which the reader activated in processing this text. Through this lens, we are beginning to get a glimpse of the dynamics of local social discourse in the society behind the book of Job, and there is more.

4.2.2. Job 30:9–15: The Reversal of an Elder

As announced in 30:1, roles are reversed in the section 30:9–15. Job is now on the receiving end of the social whip, as the children of those "useless" forebears now 'don't mind spitting in [his] face' (30:10, מפני לא־חשכו רק)—a body language with strong derogatory implications. They ridicule him publicly (30:11–14) so that his honor is "chasing (around) like wind."[72] Job has been shamed, in the first place, by his iconic misfortune and has become a 'mocking song' (נגינה).[73] The descriptions of the attacks seem to be metaphorical: most scholars agree that the section portrays public mocking or ridiculing rather than specific action.[74] Contributing to this view is a stock of conventional imagery in Job 29:3–6 and 30:16–23; 27–31. The contents of practically all these verses are paralleled in psalms and other kind of religious utterances.[75] They are utterly conventional and cannot be read as specific descriptions of Job's experience.

Still, these conventional expressions help make a vital point in the social discourse in which this section is set: an outstanding elder is expected to be successful in 'matters of religion. Indeed, the elder Job appears to have been as great a success in religion as he was in economy (cf. Job 1:2–3). And the afflicted Job is every bit as miserable in religion as he is in personal and family life (cf. 30:26–31). Religion, of course, codifies and symbolizes traditional values in a society. Leadership in such a society demands more than simply respecting tradition: that is expected from everyone.

The recognition and authority of a leader, on the other hand, depends on his ability to *excel* in traditional ways and values. And the verification of such excellence is success in economy, religion, and also rhetoric (as in 30:2–8).[76] Job's iconic misfortune, therefore, created the opportunity for his adversaries to put him to public shame. The misfortune, and apparently only that, was what reversed the social hierarchy from that presented in 30:2–8 to that in 30:9–15. Job has lost his family as well as his good fortune. The loss made his social rank fall below those families that earlier he could easily scorn in public. This is again a very strong indication of the presence of some traditionalist discourse like those described by Fei and Bourdieu.

---

72. 30:15, תרדף כרוח נדבתי. There are textual and philological problems in this verse. My rendition tries to make sense of the MT, taking 'a chasing honour' to be a figure for the restlessness of a dishonored life.

73. Cf. similar sense in Ps 69:13; Lam 3:14.

74. Elaborate exposition in Clines, *Job 21–37*, 1002–5. See also for instance Dhorme, *Job*, 436; Fohrer, *Hiob*, 419.

75. This is generally recognized since Westermann, *Aufbau*, 59–60, 61–65.

76. For a slightly different understandig of the characterstics of an elder, see the artle in this volume by W. Oswald, "Monarchy, Oligarchy, and Democracy in the Constitutional Debate in Herodotus and in 1 Samuel 8."

5. Imagining the Memory of an Elder

It is time to pull the different threads of this essay together toward the theme of leadership by elders. First, I have argued that in chs. 29–30, Job should be seen as an iconically prominent elder in the environment of a local town or village. These chapters make up one of the few passages in the book that provide a sustained indication of specific social background. The impression they make nevertheless agrees well with the picture of Job in the so-called framing narrative of the book (chs. 1–2 and 47:7–17). And, as I shall argue shortly, this view of the proponent is compatible with his portrayal throughout the dialogues.

Secondly, the comparative studies of Bourdieu and Fei have suggested that the kind of social formation of villages and towns imagined by the book of Job would have been dominated by local lore defined by topographical and historical specifics and negotiated locally in kinship and family relations. The body set to oversee the practicing of such values would be a group of family heads, basing their authority on kinship ideology and an ethos that was nominally shared by all.

Serving as symbolic representations for the social discourse in the group and between that group and neighboring groups, elders and councils of elders would have had limited space for exerting leadership. Basically, they would be expected to reinforce such practice and morale as was already generally recognized. Their leadership would have been limited also by a marked reciprocity between leaders and society and a double dependence between them. Granted, every now and then there would likely occur a case where the solution was not obvious. But one may suspect that even in such instances, an elder would do best if he were able to find a solution that resonated with commonly accepted wisdom and shared tradition.

Thirdly, and most strikingly, the recognition and authority of an elder as imagined in Job 29–30 seems to have had little to do with the way this elder performed his actual office. Rather, criteria for being recognized as an elder—in addition to the likely criterion of kinship and family background—seem to have been the ability to employ traditional ways successfully to ensure personal and familial success. This implication becomes clearer when including the narrative of chs. 1–2 into the equation, an inclusion that Job himself offers when recoding his misfortune. If Job, the prominent elder, stops being an elder because he encounters misfortune, then fortune was a basis for elder leadership.

Finally, in late pre-Modern China as chronicled by Fei, "To govern is to say little."[77] At this point, the society shining through in the book of Job may seem to have been rather different. In this book, excellence in traditional ways seems to be particularly well illustrated by rhetorical skills. Chapter 29 focuses more on the public recognition of Job's work and less on such aspects of his work that a Western reader might refer to as "inner" or "moral" qualities. Job's ability to conjure public recognition and awe through apt and acceptable action is what this chapter is about. The same orientation is unpleasantly clear in 30:2–8, as seen above: Job, the outstanding elder, puts sharp and shocking words to commonly shared sentiments. Taking chs. 3 and 29–31 as opening statements for the two parts of the dialogue in the book (cf. section one, above), this emphasis upon rhetorical skill is greatly enhanced. Each of the two parts trigger a veritable storm of affective rhetoric (at least in the eye of the speakers). The composition of the book takes a form that vaguely echoes modern speech contests—or better: it compares to the institution of public challenge among the

---

77. Fei, *From the Soil*, 132.

Algerian Kabyle as described by Bourdieu.[78] Job is portrayed as a master of rhetoric. If rhetorical superiority is a hallmark of traditional leadership, then the book wants its audience to see Job as an extraordinary elder.

In sum, what should be imagined to have been the basis of the leadership exerted by Job the elder? Apparently, it would be his extraordinary family situation, his iconic fortune, his reputable religious and moral integrity, and his indisputable rhetorical excellence. And do note: of these, the only virtue that Job does not lose is the rhetorical excellence. I might argue that the entire book could be read as a discourse probing and problematizing the validity of each of these virtues—in Job, in society, and in God—but that will have to be left for another occasion.

Bibliography

Alden, R. L. 1993. *Job*. New American Commentary 11. Nashville: Broadman & Holman.
Bourdieu, P. 1990. *The Logic of Practice*. Cambridge: Polity.
———. 1977. *Outline of a Theory of Practice*. Cambridge: Cambridge University Press.
Budde, K. 1896. *Das Buch Hiob*. Handkommentar zum Alten Testament 2/1. Göttingen: Vandenhoeck & Ruprecht.
Campbell, J. K. 1964. *Honour, Family and Patronage: A Study of Institutions and Moral Values in a Greek Mountain Community*. Oxford: Oxford University Press.
Clines, D. J. A. 2006. *Job 21–37*. WBC 18A. Nashville: Nelson.
Crenshaw, J. 2011. *Reading Job: A Literary and Theological Commentary*. Reading the Old Testament. Macon, GA: Smyth & Helwys.
Dhorme, É. 1984. *A Commentary on the Book of Job*. 2nd ed. Nashville: Nelson.
Driver, S. R. and G. B. Gray. 1921. *A Critical and Exegetical Commentary on the Book of Job*. ICC. Edinburgh: T&T Clark.
Fei, X. 1992. *From the Soil: The Foundations of Chinese Society. The Foundations of Chinese Society: A Translation of Fei Xiaotong's Xiangtu Zhongguo*. Translated by G. G. Hamilton and Wang Zheng. Berkeley: University of California Press.
Fohrer, G. 1963. *Das Buch Hiob*. KAT 16. Gütersloh: Gütersloher Verlagshaus Gerd Mohn.
Good, E. M. 1990. *In Turns of Tempest: A Reading of Job*. Stanford, CA: Stanford University Press.
———. 1965. *Irony in the Old Testament*. Philadelphia: Westminster.
Goodman, J. E. and P. A. Silverstein, eds. 2009. *Bourdieu in Algeria: Colonial Politics, Ethnographic Practices, Theoretical Developments*. Lincoln: University of Nebraska Press.
Habel, N. C. 1985. *The Book of Job*. OTL. Philadelphia, PA: Westminster.
Hamilton, M. 2007. "Elite Lives: Job 29–31 and Traditional Authority." *JSOT* 32: 69–89.
Hartley, J. E. 1994. "From Lament to Oath: A Study of Progression in the Speeches of Job." In *The Book of Job*, edited by W. A. M. Beuken, 79–100. BETL 114. Leuven: Peeters.
Hesse, F. 1978. *Hiob*. ZBK 14. Zürich: Theologischer Verlag.
Hoffman, Y. A. 1996. *A Blemished Perfection: The Book of Job in Context*. JSOTSup 213. Sheffield: Sheffield Academic Press.
Hölscher, G. 1937. *Das Buch Hiob*. Handbuch zum Alten Testament 17. Tübingen: Mohr Siebeck.
Janzen, J. G. 1985. *Job*. Interpretation: A Bible Commentary for Teaching and Preaching. Atlanta, GA: John Knox.

---

78. Bourdieu, *Outline*, 11: "To make someone a challenge is to credit him with the dignity of a man of honour, since the challenge, as such, requires a riposte and therefore is addressed to a man deemed capable of playing the game of honour, and of playing it well. […] 'The man who has no enemies,' say the Kabyles, 'is a donkey' (the symbol of passivity)."

Lo, A. 2003. *Job 28 as Rhetoric: An Analysis of Job 28 in the Context of Job 21–31*. VTSup 97. Leiden: Brill.

Malchow, B. V. 1990. "A Royal Prototype in Job 29." In *The Psalms and Other Studies on the Old Testament Presented to Joseph I. Hunt*, edited by J. C. Knight and L. A. Sinclair, 178–84. Nashotah, WI: Nashotah House Seminary.

McNutt, P. 1999. *Reconstructing the Society of Ancient Israel*. Library of Ancient Israel. Louisville, KY: Westminster John Knox.

Meyers, C. L. 1997. "The Family in Early Israel." In *Families in Ancient Israel*, edited by L. G. Perdue, J. Blenkinsopp, J. J. Collins, and C. L. Meyers, 1–47. Louisville, KY: Westminster John Knox.

Murphy, R. E. 1981. *Wisdom Literature: Job, Proverbs, Ruth, Canticles, Ecclesiastes, and Esther*. Forms of the Old Testament Literature 13. Grand Rapids, MI: Eerdmans.

Newsom, C. A. 2003. *The Book of Job: A Contest of Moral Imaginations*. Oxford: Oxford University Press.

Rowley, H. H. 1970. *Job*. New Century Bible. Nelson.

Schloen, J. D. 2001. *The House of the Father as Fact and Symbol: Patrimonialism in Ugarit and the Ancient Near East*. Studies in the Archaeology and History of the Levant 2. Winona Lake, IN: Eisenbrauns.

Spangenberg, I. J. J. 1996. "Irony in the Book of Qohelet." *JSOT* 72: 57–69.

Stordalen, T. 2015. "Horse Statues in Seventh Century Jerusalem: How to Assess Religious Diversity and Similarity in Late Iron II?" *HeBAI* 4(1): 106–132.

———. 2012. "'His place does not recognise him' (Job 7:10): Reflections of Non-Inscribed Memory in the Book of Job." In *Cultural Memory in Biblical Exegesis*, edited by P. Carstens, T. B. Hasselbalch and N. P. Lemche, 47–68. Piscataway, NJ: Gorgias.

———. 2006. "Dialogue and Dialogism in the Book of Job." *SJOT* 20: 18–37.

Weiser, A. 1968. *Das Buch Hiob*. 5th ed. ATD 13. Göttingen: Vandenhoech & Ruprecht.

Westermann, C. 1977. *Der Aufbau des Buches Hiob*. Calwer theologische Monographien 6. Stuttgart: Calwer.

Wilde, A. de. 1981. *Das Buch Hiob: eingeleitet, übersetzt und erläutert*. Oudtestamentische studiën 22. Leiden: Brill.

Willis, T. M. 2001. *The Elders of the City: A Study of the Elders-Laws in Deuteronomy*. SBL Monograph Series 55. Atlanta, GA: SBL.

Wolfers, D. 1994. *Deep Things out of Darkness: The Book of Job. Essays and a New English Translation*. Kampen: Kok Pharos.

— 9 —

At the Hands of Foreign Kings:
Divine Endorsement of Foreign Rulers in the Hebrew Bible in the Memory of Persian and Hellenistic Yehud

Thomas M. Bolin

The study of social memory is a burgeoning field in biblical studies but presents scholars with distinctive challenges.[1] In the case of well-documented cultures, this approach offers

---

1. Among descriptions of memory studies are H. Barstad, "History and Memory: Some Reflections on the 'Memory Debate' in Relation to the Hebrew Bible," in *The Historian and the Bible: Essays in Honour of Lester L. Grabbe*, ed. P. Davies and D. V. Edelman (New York: T&T Clark, 2010), 1–10; and the detailed discussion of D. V. Edelman's introduction in *Remembering Biblical Figures in the Late Persian & Early Hellenistic Periods: Social Memory and Imagination*, ed. D. V. Edelman and E. Ben Zvi (Oxford: Oxford University Press, 2013), xi–xxiv. For a use of social memory in studying ancient Israel, see P. Davies, *Memories of Ancient Israel: An Introduction to Biblical History—Ancient and Modern* (Louisville, KY: Westminster John Knox, 2008), 105–23. One of the more prolific scholars in this area is E. Ben Zvi: "A Contribution to the Intellectual History of Yehud: The Story of Micaiah and its Function within the Discourse of Persian-Period Literati," in *The Historian and the Bible: Essays in Honour of Lester L. Grabbe*, ed. P. Davies and D. V. Edelman (New York: T&T Clark, 2010), 89–102; "On Social Memory and Identity Formation in Late Persian Yehud: A Historian's Viewpoint with a Focus on Prophetic Literature, Chronicles and the Dtr. Historical Collection," in *Texts, Contexts and Readings in Postexilic Literature Explorations into Historiography and Identity Negotiation in Hebrew Bible and Related Texts*, ed. L. Jonker (Tübingen: Mohr Siebeck, 2011), 95–148; "Remembering the Prophets through the Reading and Rereading of a Collection of Prophetic Books in Yehud: Methodological Considerations and Explorations," in *Remembering and Forgetting in Early Second Temple Judah*, ed. E. Ben Zvi and C. Levin (Tübingen: Mohr Siebeck, 2012), 17–44; "The Study of Forgetting and the Forgotten in Ancient Israelite Discourse/s: Observations and Test Cases," in *Cultural Memory in Biblical Exegesis*, ed. P. Carstens, T. Hasselbach, and N. P. Lemche (Piscataway, NJ: Gorgias, 2012), 155–74; "Toward a Sense of Balance: Remembering the Catastrophe of Monarchic Judah/(Ideological) Israel and Exile through Reading Chronicles in Late Yehud," in *Chronicling the Chronicler: The Book of Chronicles and Early Second Temple Historiography*, ed. P. Evans and T. Williams (Winona Lake, IN: Eisenbrauns, 2013), 247–65; "Prophetic Memories in the Deuteronomistic Historical and the Prophetic Collections of Books," in *Israelite Prophecy and the Deuteronomistic History: Portrait, Reality and the Formation of a History*, ed. M. Jacobs and R. E. Person (Atlanta, GA: SBL, 2013), 75–102; "Reading and Constructing Utopias: Utopia/s and/in the Collection of Authoritative Texts/Textual Readings of Late Persian Period Yehud," *Studies in Religion/Sciences Religieuses* 42 (2013): 463–76; "The Memory of Abraham in Late Persian/Early Hellenistic Yehud/Judah," in *Remembering Biblical Figures in the Late Persian & Early Hellenistic Periods: Social Memory and Imagination*, ed. D. V. Edelman and E. Ben Zvi (Oxford: Oxford University Press, 2013),

a detailed look into the construction and maintenance of group identity. Analysis of how Mussolini selected and shaped Italy's Roman past to tell a story about Fascist Italy as Rome redivivus or of the selective and synthetic picture of Martin Luther King Jr. in U.S. social memory—which pays lip service to King's life while at the same time muting his more uncomfortable challenges to American society—offers insights hitherto under-appreciated in traditional historical research.[2] As is ever the case, rich data yield rich results. But what are we to do when asking questions of social memory about a culture like ancient Yehud, for which data are scarce and, where present, often enigmatic? Any attempt at analysis of social memory in ancient Israel will, of necessity, be provisional and run the risk of slipping into a history of interpretation,[3] given that the artifacts of social memory for study are the biblical texts. The architects of these ancient textual memories can only be the very small percentage of elites who created, preserved, and read those texts.

One of the first scholars of antiquity to write on social memory, J. Assmann, makes the advent of writing the foundation and center of social memory. Because writing is a form of preservation, it "creates" memory.[4] Canonical writing fixes that memory, leaving room only for later interpretation, but not the addition of written texts to the body of cultural memories. Writing, therefore, is used as a means of social control by elites in a society.[5] While Assmann is certainly correct to link writing in earlier ancient Levantine cultures with elites, he seems to make too much of the oral-written divide, specifically in the claim that writing "fixes" memory. Recent research shows that oral–written interaction in antiq-

---

3–37; "Monogynistic and Monogamous Tendencies, Memories and Imagination in Late Persian/Early Hellenistic Yehud," *ZAW* 125 (2013): 263–77; "Chronicles and its Reshaping of Memories of Monarchic Period Prophets: Some Observations," in *Prophets, Prophecy, and Ancient Israelite Historiography*, ed. M. Boda and L. M. Wray Beal (Winona Lake, IN: Eisenbrauns, 2013), 167–88; "The Yehudite Collection of Prophetic Books and Imperial Contexts: Some Observations," in *Divination, Politics and Ancient Near Eastern Texts*, ed. A. Lenzi and J. Stökl (Atlanta, GA: SBL Press, 2014), 145–69; cf. bibliography at Ehud Ben Zvi "Publications," http://www.ualberta.ca/~ebenzvi/ebz-publications.html.

2. Among other examples are H. Schuman, B. Schwartz, and H. D'Arcy, "Elite Revisionists and Popular Beliefs: Christopher Columbus, Hero Or Villain?" *Public Opinion Quarterly* 69 (2005): 2–29; B. Schwartz, "Collective Memory and History: How Abraham Lincoln Became a Symbol of Racial Equality," *The Sociological Quarterly* 38 (1997): 469–96. See also Davies, *Memories of Ancient Israel*, 112–13.

3. Indeed, the subtitle of a recent study of Ecclesiastes refers to social memory, with the project described by the author as "a search for traces of older texts within Ecclesiastes" (J. Barbour, *The Story of Israel in the Book of Qohelet: Ecclesiastes as Cultural Memory* [Oxford: Oxford University Press, 2012], 4 cf. 81–82 for discussion of cultural memory).

4. J. Assmann, *Cultural Memory and Early Civilization: Writing, Remembrance, and Political Imagination* (Cambridge; Cambridge: Cambridge University Press, 2011), 4–8; ET of *Das kulturelle Gedächtnis: Schrift, Erinnerung und politische Identität in frühen Hochkulturen*, 6th ed. (Munich: Beck, 2007).

5. Assmann, *Cultural Memory*, 47–49, 79, 108. Here Assmann is following M. Halbwachs's discussion of the rise of Christianity in his 1925 volume, *Les Cadres sociaux de la mémoire* (Paris: F. Alcan, 1925), reprint: *On Collective Memory* (trans. L. A. Coser; 1925; repr., [Chicago, IL: University of Chicago Press, 1992). Of course, not all ancient societies leave behind only texts for scholars to examine for evidence of cultural memory. Nor are all texts from antiquity the product of elites. Here one can think of graffiti, which is plentiful in the Greco-Roman period but also the use of texts and the plastic arts by non-elites from that same era. For example, the numerous examples of bylaws and other texts from the various associations, which are clearly not the products of elites (cf. R. Ascough, P. Harland, and J. S. Kloppenborg, *Associations in the Greco-Roman World: A Sourcebook* [Waco, TX: Baylor University Press; Berlin: de Gruyter, 2012]). Also appropriate are the hundreds of epitaphs left by non-elites in Rome and elsewhere throughout the imperial period.

uity was dynamic and ran both ways, thereby making texts a fluid medium of preservation and transmission.[6]

This essay explores the social memory in Yehud of foreign kings in the Persian and Hellenistic periods, specifically the ways in which Yahweh was thought to regard these non-Jewish monarchs. My approach uses archaeology, relevant classical and ancient Near Eastern texts, and Persian/Hellenistic era Jewish texts to construct as full a *Weltanschauung* as possible of Jewish readers. This will establish a social location for readers and reveal the kinds of thinking about foreign kings at the time, which then may be used with some confidence to consider how these readers remembered such figures in the biblical texts they composed and preserved.[7]

A Brief Observation on the Community in Yehud During the Persian and Hellenistic Periods

Archaeological evidence about Yehud in the Persian period shows that Jerusalem was a small site, although not too small to contain an administrative bureaucracy, as was also the case with nearby Ramat Rahel. In a recent analysis of survey data in Yehud from the Persian and Hellenistic periods, O. Lipschits and O. Tal note three types of settlements in Yehud during this time: administrative centers, military strongholds, and rural estates.[8] Analysis of seals in Yehud spanning the entire Persian period shows that the Persians exercised significant administrative control in the region because it was a buffer zone with Egypt, which revolted several times under Achaemenid rule.[9] The Jerusalem temple would have been under Persian oversight,[10] and the understanding of foreign rulers by scribes who read and preserved texts there would have been influenced by the fact that they owed their livelihoods to the patronage of a non-Jewish king. In the Hellenistic period, the

---

6. E.g., D. M. Carr, *The Formation of the Hebrew Bible: A New Reconstruction* (Oxford: Oxford University Press, 2011), 13–101. Of interest, at least to me, is that the title of Assmann's volume in the German original makes clear that he is talking about elites (*Hochkulturen*). This is omitted in the title of the English translation. See also the critique of Assman's overemphasis on writing in N. P. Lemche, "Solomon as Cultural Memory," in *Remembering Biblical Figures in the Late Persian & Early Hellenistic Periods: Social Memory and Imagination*, ed. D. V. Edelman and E. Ben Zvi (Oxford: Oxford University Press, 2013), 158–81 (167).

7. The careful reader of this essay will have already noted how the discussion has moved from social memory to the interpretation of texts. This is part of the inherent risk mentioned above in engaging in the study of social memory in antiquity. Regarding this method for the study of ancient Israel, Lemche refers to it as a "mission impossible," because "the people supposed to have this memory are themselves part of the memory of the people who wrote the literature" ("Solomon," 162).

8. O. Lipschits and O. Tal, "The Settlement Archaeology of the Province of Judah: A Case Study," in *Judah and the Judeans in the Fourth Century B.C.E.*, ed. O. Lipschits, G. Knoppers, and R. Albertz (Winona Lake, IN: Eisenbrauns, 2007), 33–52 (34–35).

9. O. Lipschits and D. Vanderhooft, "Yehud Stamp Impressions in the Fourth Century B.C.E.: A Time of Administrative Consolidation?" in *Judah and the Judeans in the Fourth Century B.C.E.*, ed. O. Lipschits, G. Knoppers, and R. Albertz (Winona Lake, IN: Eisenbrauns, 2007), 75–94.

10. J. Schaper, "The Jerusalem Temple as an Instrument of the Achaemenid Fiscal Administration," *VT* 45 (1995): 528–39; L. Fried, *The Priest and the Great King: Temple-Palace Relations in the Persian Empire* (Winona Lake, IN: Eisenbrauns, 2004); and M. Knowles, *Centrality Practiced: Jerusalem in the Religious Practice of Yehud and the Diaspora during the Persian Period* (Atlanta, GA: SBL, 2006), 105–20. See also the observation of Lipschits and Tal, "Jerusalem — as the temple city of Judah — was thus flanked by villages and agricultural estates that formed the predominant type of settlement" ("Settlement Archaeology," 34).

region continued in strategic importance, placed as it was between the rival Seleucid and Ptolemaic kingdoms. Jerusalem grew, and large-scale construction was undertaken there.

Evidence also supports the existence of an elite class with access to luxury items and an openness to Greek culture beginning in the Persian period.[11] Such a group of elites in a Hellenized world would have had recourse to texts and a need for literary competence. Their influence will be seen on social memory in Hellenistic Jerusalem and its environs, and it is important to note that these readers are of a different social location from the administrative scribes in the Persian period. The latter group continued into the Hellenistic period, keeping records and preserving texts in the Jerusalem temple. Memories were constructed differently by these two groups, because they had different priorities and, in some cases, different value systems. The temple administrative personnel would be greatly concerned for the sanctity of their god's dwelling, the preservation of texts and records, and the proper maintenance of rituals and other functions on site. A figure like Ezra would have been most resonant with these men.

The Hellenistic elites would also see themselves as faithful to the Jewish religious faith and practice, but as elites they would also be sensitive to norms and practices that would enhance their standing among peers and social superiors. To many in this group, these two goals would not be in conflict with each other. The commands of the Law were to seen to be compatible with the life of a cultured elite male in the Mediterranean oikoumene. Ben Sira, with his clear devotion to the Tora but a location among the wealthy of Jerusalem, would be an example of this kind of person.[12]

Both groups would have contained priests, and both were reading many of the same texts. N. P. Lemche argues that "the literati of the ancient Near East thus belonged to a middle class...most helpful to the members of the elite."[13] While this is true perhaps of pre-Hellenistic cultures, it would be different in a world where proficiency in culturally canonical texts marked a person as an elite.[14] Both of these identifiable groups of readers and creators of texts need to be accounted for in any discussion of Jewish social memory from the fifth-first centuries.[15]

---

11. I have a more detailed discussion of this in T. Bolin, "1–2 Samuel and Its Role in the Cultivation of Jewish Paideia in the Persian and Hellenistic Periods," in *Deuteronomy-Kings as Emerging Authoritative Books: A Conversation*, ed. D. V. Edelman (Atlanta, GA: SBL, 2014), 133–58 (135–38).

12. For other discussions in this volume of the social setting, role, and motivations of the literati, see the essays by E. Ben Zvi, ("Memory and Political Thought in the Late Persian/early Hellenistic Yehud/Judah: Some Observations"), J. M. Bos ("Memories of Judah's Past Leaders Utilized as Propaganda in Yehud"), and K. Berge ("Mystified Authority: Legitimating Leadership Through 'Lost Books'").

13. Lemche, "Solomon," 169.

14. D. M. Carr, *Writing on the Tablet of the Heart: Origins of Scripture and Literature* (Oxford: Oxford University Press, 2005), 201–14. However, not all elites would be as docile toward Jewish religious tradition. Whoever preserved the book of Qohelet would have seen in its author a voice conversant with larger intellectual currents, while at the same time being both knowledgeable and highly critical of the religious status quo.

15. Any speculation about groups, parties, or sects that may lie behind the biblical text must be approached with caution. I have already pointed out the tendency among scholars to posit groups behind every biblical text (T. Bolin, *Freedom Beyond Forgiveness: The Book of Jonah Re-Examined* [Sheffield: JSOT Press, 1997], 40). Social memory, however, is not about the composition of texts, but about how those texts play a role in a group's construction, shaping, and preservation of shared memories. Here is where the study of cultural memory in the biblical area encompasses, and runs the risk of falling into, composition history, redaction history, and history of interpretation.

Of Kings and Gods

Social memory is shaped by a society's values and conventions. Among the latter are ways of telling stories about significant people, events, or practices. A culture's plotlines for certain explanatory narratives can remain stable for a long period of time, and some plotlines transcend cultures.[16] Because these plotlines reinforce cultural norms, stories about kings will reveal cultural attitudes toward them—or at least the attitudes of those who remembered and handed on the stories. Throughout the ancient Near Eastern and Mediterranean worlds, kings claimed a special relationship to the gods or to a specific patron deity. They often portrayed themselves as intermediaries between the divine and human worlds. Hand in hand with this relationship was the assertion that the king was not like other people; he was higher, greater. For example, the Sumerian term for "king," LÚ.GAL, literally means, 'big man'. Stories about the kings emphasized this and were told in part to reinforce the king's exalted status.[17] Among these plotlines, the most well known might be the tale type of the hero endangered at birth, with extant examples from Assyria (Sargon),[18] Israel (Moses), Greece (Cyrus in Herodotus), and Rome (Romulus and Remus). The purpose of this tale is to show how the future king was set aside from birth for greatness and protected by higher powers, even as a vulnerable infant. There is a shadowy side to the privilege of divine care enjoyed by kings. The gods' favor could be lost, sometimes without apparent cause or explanation.[19] The king in the story thus became a moral exemplar—either positive or negative—either of kingship in particular or of humankind in general. This is easily seen in longer tales about kings. In the two different extant recensions of the Gilgamesh epic, the earlier shows how Gilgamesh progresses from being a bad king to a good one. This version is expanded to make Gilgamesh a figure representing humanity, whose journey from ignorance to existential wisdom is intended to teach the reader to undertake the same intellectual growth.[20] In the Iliad two kings are contrasted. Agamemnon is the bad king, whose pride leads him

---

16. In cultural memory studies, scholars refer to "templates," universal mental structures that create "ontological categories/concepts with associated expectations" (Edelman, "Introduction," xvi). W. Burkert has argued that certain tale-types prevalent in ancient Mediterranean religions rely on universal mental categories (*Creation of the Sacred: Tracks of Biology in Early Religions* [Cambridge, MA: Harvard University Press, 1996], 56–79).

17. Thus, the claim of the Sumerian King List that the earliest kings were descended from the gods and lived for tens of thousands of years or the earliest stories of Gilgamesh in the underworld. Royal inscriptions also made this emphasis, with the king referring to the gods marching before him in battle or using the epithet, "beloved of D.N." for himself.

18. I designate the Sargon birth legend as Assyrian on the basis of the dating of the extant copies of the text, which demonstrate the time period that the stories were still in circulation, rather than when they originated.

19. In one of the more famous historical examples, in 705 BCE, Sargon II of Assyria was killed in battle and left unburied and his body never recovered. His son, Sennacherib, is portrayed in a text as concerned about how his father's end both expressed divine displeasure and how to make things right with the gods again. Sennacherib states, "While thus [reverently] pondering [in my heart] over the deeds of the gods, the death of Sargon, [my father, who was killed in the enemy country] and who was not interred in his house…" (text, translation, and discussion in H. Tadmor, B. Landsberger, and S. Parpola, "The Sin of Sargon and Sennacherib's Last Will," *State Archives of Assyria Bulletin* 3 (1989): 3–51 (3–15); cf. E. Frahm, "Nabû-zuqup-kēnu, das Gilgameš-Epos und der Tod Sargons II," *Journal of Cuneiform Studies* 51 (1999): 73–90.

20. A. George, *The Babylonian Gilgamesh Epic: Introduction, Critical Edition, and Cuneiform Texts*, 2 vols. (Oxford: Oxford University Press, 2003), 1:17–39. The so-called Cuthean Legend of Naram Sin recounts how the king is punished by Enlil for desecrating a temple (J. G. Westenholz, *The Legends of the Kings of Akkade: The Texts* [Winona Lake, IN: Eisenbrauns, 1997], 267–332).

to enrage Achilles and imperil the Greek siege of Troy. Priam is Agamemnon's foil, the good king whose act of self-abasement assuages Achilles's wrath. The two kings are placed, respectively, in the opening and final books of the epics as bookends and contrasts.[21] In the Hebrew Bible, the long narrative of David presents a multidimensional figure of great moral complexity. The attribution of some psalms to David and the superscriptions to some of those psalms demonstrate a process of appropriating some of the events of David's tumultuous biography and applying them to the trials of those who read these psalms.[22]

In the classical Greek tradition, stories of kings and their treatment by the gods become standard in the writing of tragedies. The main characters in many Greek tragedies are kings, showing that they are seen to be appropriate, if not ideal, figures to be placed at divine whim. Aristotle notes this when he discusses in the Poetics the need for a tragic hero to be both honored and fortunate (ἐν μεγάλῃ δόξῃ ὄντων καὶ εὐτυχίᾳ, 1453a). The treatment of kings by the gods figures prominently also in historiography, beginning with Herodotus. The opening sections of Histories details the generations-long curse on the family of the Lydian king Croesus, beginning with Croesus's ancestor, Gyges, who killed the legitimate Lydian king and usurped the throne (Histories 1.7–46). This delayed divine punishment is exacted five generations later when Croesus is defeated by Cyrus. In this narrative Herodotus has included another story, in which the king's beloved son is killed in fulfillment of a prophecy the king does everything in his power to thwart. That prophecy is also divine punishment, this time for Croesus's belief that he is the most blessed of all human beings.[23] After the death of his son and his defeat by Cyrus, Croesus—like Gilgamesh centuries before—becomes the wise king who has learned from suffering. As he is about to be burned to death, Croesus muses on a great lesson taught to him years ago about blessedness. He had disregarded the lesson at the time but now sees its wisdom.[24]

In the biblical text, the closest thing to a tragic king apart from David is Josiah. A king faithful to the covenant, he is blindsided by the finding of a forgotten book of Mosaic law in the Temple.[25] Despite his fervent attempt to right all of the cultic wrongs in the kingdom,

---

21. There are numerous parallels between books 1 and 24: There are eleven days of Achilles's anger before the divine council in book 1 and eleven days of the pro-Greek gods' anger in book 24 before the divine council. There are nine days of plague in book 1 and nine days set aside for Hector's funeral in book 24. In book 1 Zeus accepts a request of Thetis to give Achilles glory and in book 24 Zeus orders Thetis so that Achilles will gain glory. Chryses coming to ask Agamemnon to return his daughter in Book 1 parallels Priam's coming to ask Achilles for his son in book 24. Agamemnon comes to Achilles's lodging in Book 1 to take Briseis away, and Priam comes to Achilles's lodging in book 24 to take Hector. Surviving copies of relief panels known as tabula Iliaca that use pictures and text to narrate the Homeric epics have books 1 and 24 paired, with similar iconography. For discussion of the tabula, see M. Squire, *The Iliad in a Nutshell: Visualizing Epic on the Tabulae Iliacae* (Oxford: Oxford University Press, 2011).

22. See J. Blenkinsopp, *David Remembered: Kingship and National Identity in Ancient Israel* (Grand Rapids, MI: Eerdmans, 2013) and J. Wright, *David, King of Israel, and Caleb in Biblical Memory* (Cambridge; Cambridge: Cambridge University Press, 2014).

23. ἔλαβέ ἐκ θεοῦ νέμεσις μεγάλη Κροῖσον, ὡς εἰκάσαι, ὅτι ἐνόμισε ἑωυτὸν εἶναι ἀνθρώπων ἀπάντων ὀλβιώτατον (*Histories* 1.34).

24. *Histories* 1.86. Croesus's words save his life, but Herodotus may be implying that the king's wisdom would have made him unafraid of death.

25. For a detailed discussion of the literary and ideological background to 2 Kgs 22, see K. M. Stott, *Why Did They Write This Way? Reflections on References to Written Documents in the Hebrew Bible and Ancient Literature* (New York: T&T Clark, 2008). J. Assmann, himself sums up the motif of the discovered book succinctly: "What is new legitimates itself as the old that has been forgotten" (J. Assmann, *Religion and*

Yahweh pronounces the doom of Jerusalem, but with a consolation prize for his faithful king: Josiah will die "in peace" (2 Kgs 22:20) and be long in his tomb when the end comes. This might seem harsh to modern theological sensibilities, but the announcement to a king of an inevitable doom—and the ensuing narration of said king's futile efforts to avert his fate—is the stuff of Greek tragedy. In this regard, note how the long description of Josiah's purging of any non-Yahwistic cult in 2 Kgs 23:4–25 is concluded by the terse notice that Yahweh 'nevertheless' (אך) did not relent from his wrath against Jerusalem. What gives this story a particularly poignant twist is that only half of Yahweh's promise is fulfilled. Rather than dying in peace, Josiah is killed in battle with Pharaoh Necho, his death occupying only twenty words in the Hebrew text.[26] The text does not say why Josiah went out to meet Necho in battle, nor does it tell us that the king fought valiantly or died bravely.[27] The text also says nothing about Yahweh's reaction to Josiah's violent death. Was Necho acting as Yahweh's agent?[28] After all, Yahweh's "gift" to Josiah is that the king will not live to see the downfall of Jerusalem. Did the pharaoh and Josiah somehow manage to thwart fate? The reader is left to wonder in this instance, as in the case of some other foreign rulers in the Tanakh.[29]

Yahweh's Attitude Toward Foreign Kings in Earlier Biblical Texts[30]

In the biblical literature that may have been edited rather than composed in the post-exilic period, there is a fairly consistent view of Yahweh's attitude toward foreign kings.[31] As commanders of their armies, they are his tools used to punish the wayward Israelites for their sins. This is the repeated pattern in Judges of course, but it is also used in describing the rulers of the major political powers. So, Shalmanessar destroys Samaria and deports its citizens because they did not follow the Mosaic covenant (2 Kgs 18:9–12). What is important to note is that Yahweh's approval of these rulers is temporary, based on their usefulness to his plans, and it can be revoked. This is explicitly stated in Jeremiah regarding Nebuchadnezzar, as discussed below.

A variant on this theme is the proud foreign ruler who does not know that his military success is due to Yahweh's favor. This ignorance brings down divine wrath. The most

---

Cultural Memory: Ten Studies [trans. R. Livingstone; Stanford, CA: Stanford University Press 2006], 100).

26. At least one writer refers to Josiah's death as "one of the most tragic events in Israel's history" (T. Mann, "Theological Reflections on the Denial of Moses" *JBL* 98 [1979]: 481).

27. 2 Kgs 23:29: בימיו עלה פרעה נכה מלך מצרים על מלך אשור על נהר פרת וילך המלך יאשיהו לקראתו וימיתו במגדו כראתו אתו.

28. The version of this story in 2 Chronicles—with a significant difference from that in 2 Kings—is discussed below.

29. What does Yahweh think of Hiram of Tyre, who supplied the artisans and material for the construction of the deity's own temple? Or of the Pharaoh who married his daughter to Solomon? Or to the Queen of Sheba? For other considerations of the depiction of Josiah in biblical memory in this volume, see comments made by W. Oswald in his contribution, "Monarchy, Oligarchy, and Democracy in the Constitutional Debate in Herodotus and in 1 Samuel 8."

30. The Tanakh does not state Yahweh's opinion of every foreign king mentioned in the Bible. Among those who fall into this group are Tiglath-Pileser/Pul of Assyria, So (Osorkon), Taharqa of Egypt, and Evil-Merodach (Amel-Marduk) of Babylon.

31. I am well aware of the numerous issues surrounding the dating of the biblical texts and the extraordinary amount of print matter they have generated. At the risk of working with a blunt edge, for the sake of making this essay manageable, I am designating as "post-exilic" those texts that may with reasonable certainty be said to have been *composed* in the Persian or Hellenistic eras.

elaborate example deals with Sennacherib's siege of Jerusalem (Isaiah 36–37 // 2 Kings 18–19).³² The account appears to be a conflation of two separate memories of the siege. One has Hezekiah's officials taking the Rabshakeh's message to Isaiah directly. Another has a different message from the Rabshakeh brought to Hezekiah, who opens it before the Ark for Yahweh to "read."³³ The oracle from Isaiah is originally a response to Hekekiah's officials but in the extant account is made to do double duty in responding also to Hezekiah's direct appeal to Yahweh. In both of the messages, Sennacherib boasts about defeating other nations and claims that Yahweh will not be able to save Jerusalem, just as the gods of other nations could not save their peoples (2 Kgs 18:35 // Isa 36:20). While this statement is consonant with royal self-aggrandizement common in Assyrian inscriptions,³⁴ the sin here is in equating Yahweh with the other impotent gods. Yahweh delivers an oracle through Isaiah asserting his own agency in Sennacherib's success and promising punishment.³⁵ Yahweh makes clear it is 'because' (יען, Isa 37:29 // 2 Kgs 19:28) Sennacherib has boasted of his deeds without justification that the deity will drag him away like a disobedient pack animal. The resulting death of Sennacherib's entire army overnight leaves no room for doubt about the source of this calamity.

Sennacherib's foil in the biblical text is Cyrus, whose victories are also claimed by Yahweh. However, whereas Sennacherib is blamed for not knowing that Yahweh is the cause of his success, Cyrus is blessed with victory and plunder by Yahweh, despite the same fact, which Yahweh openly acknowledges (ולא ידעתני, Isa 45:4–5). The obvious explanation for this contrast is that Cyrus is allowing the Jerusalemite temple to be rebuilt and Judah's exiles to return, but that is not explicit in the text. To the contrary, Sennacherib appears to be fulfilling Yahweh's will in threatening Jerusalem just as much as is Cyrus in restoring it. The difference lies in Sennacherib's boast.

Both of these texts themselves make interesting use of memory by using imagery from the Exodus to describe Yahweh's actions with both kings. With Sennacherib, it is the death of his entire army overnight at the hands of an angel, which combines the nocturnal destroyer of the tenth plague (Exod 12) with the destruction of pharaoh's army in the Red Sea (Exod 14), complete with parallel phrases about the site of all the corpses (Isa 37:36: והנה כלם פגרים מתים; Exod 14:30: וירא ישראל את מצרים מת על שפת הים). Regarding Cyrus, the use of Exodus imagery in Second Isaiah has long been known,³⁶ but I want to emphasize the interesting contrast in the use of the motif of "knowing Yahweh." In Exodus, pharaoh makes

---

32. Cf. the discussion of this text in R. Hobson, "The Memory of Sennacherib in Late Persian Yehud," in *Remembering Biblical Figures in the Late Persian & Early Hellenistic Periods: Social Memory and Imagination*, ed. D. V. Edelman and E. Ben Zvi (Oxford: Oxford University Press, 2013), 199–220.

33. For recent discussion of the source critical questions in this text, see P. S. Evans, *The Invasion of Sennacherib in the Book of Kings: A Source-Critical and Rhetorical Study of 2 Kings 18–19* (Leiden: Brill, 2009), and the essays in L. L. Grabbe, ed., *Like a Bird in a Cage: The Invasion of Sennacherib in 701 BCE* (London: Sheffield Academic, 2003).

34. Isaiah's oracle, quoting Sennacherib, closely resembles Assyrian texts extolling the king's military prowess, specifically in the felling of trees in Lebanon. See the discussion in W. R. Gallagher, *Sennacherib's Campaign to Judah: New Studies* (Leiden: Brill, 1999).

35. Compare this with the oracle against Assyria in Isa 10 and the metaphor there of the axe boasting over the one who wields it.

36. There is here an interesting analogue with Cyrus's Babylonian foundation cylinder, which parallels the actions of Marduk in *Enuma Elish* in such a way as to be a deliberate echo of that text by the Babylonian priests of Marduk, who were supported by Cyrus and who doubtless composed the text of the cylinder.

clear to Moses during their first meeting that he does not know Yahweh (לא ידעתי את יהוה, Exod 5:2) while in Isaiah, Yawheh repeats the statement that Cyrus does not know him (ולא ידעתני, Isa 45:4–5). As in the contrast with Sennacherib discussed above, so here too, Cyrus is "guilty" of the same oversight as the pharaoh, but reaps reward instead of punishment.

Given the large numbers of references to the Exodus throughout the Tanakh, Egypt deserves separate treatment in this discussion. The pharaoh of the Exodus is unnamed, as are the Egyptian kings who deal with Abraham, Joseph, and Solomon. Yahweh's attitude toward the Pharaoh of the Exodus is clear: he is an unworthy rival who foolishly dares to challenge the power of the god of the Hebrews. The two unnamed Pharaohs in Genesis fulfill narrative roles more akin to storytelling or folklore, which will be explored further below.

Of the named pharaohs in the Tanakh—Shishak, So (Osorkon) Taharqa, Hophra, and Necho—only Shishak, Hophra, and Necho reveal any information about how Yahweh regards them. He views each of them differently. Shishak is mentioned twice. In 1 Kgs 11 he shelters Jeroboam from Solomon's wrath and in 1 Kgs 14 he raids Jerusalem and removes the wealth of the temple and the palace (1 Kgs 14:26: ויקח את אצרות בית יהוה ואת אוצרות בית המלך ואת הכל לקח). The narrative in 1 Kgs 14:22–25 makes clear immediately prior to recounting Shishak's raid that Rehoboam committed numerous cultic crimes against the covenant with Yahweh. What the text does not say is that Shishak's plundering of the temple was in response to or a result of these sins. Verse 26 begins without any transition from the preceding verse and thus reads like the introduction of a new portion of the narrative. This is anomalous in the Deuteronomistic History, where the narrator is ordinarily at pains to make clear that foreign destruction is the justified divine response to forsaking of the covenant (2 Kgs 17:7–18; 24:2–4).

Jeremiah and Ezekiel both have oracles against Egypt for going to war against the Babylonians, whom both prophets see as Yahweh's instrument to punish Judah. Jeremiah 44:30 is an oracle against the Pharaoh Hophra (Apries), where Yahweh equates the fate of Hophra with that of Judah's last king, Zedekiah. Jeremiah 46 is a taunt against Necho, who was defeated by Nebuchadnezzar at Carchemish in 603 BCE. In v. 17, Yahweh gives Necho a new name, שאון העביר המועד which means something along the lines of 'the noisemaker who lets the hour pass', clearly an insult to Necho's loss at Carchemish, his pre-engagement boasting, and the subsequent squandered opportunity to be the power in the Levant. Chapters 30–32 in Ezekiel are a series of laments and taunts over Egypt's defeat by Babylon.

The most prominent foreign king in the Tanakh is the Babylonian Nebuchadnezzar, whose name occurs more than 120 times, with over a quarter of these occurrences in Jeremiah.[37] Three times, Yahweh refers to Nebuchadnezzar as 'my servant' (עבדי, Jer 25:9, 27:6, 43:10).[38] Yahweh states that he fights on the side of Nebuchadnezzar against Jerusalem (Jer 21:5) and has given the command to the Babylonians to attack Jerusalem (Jer 34:22).[39] The exiles are commanded by Yahweh to pray to him for the welfare of

---

37. The term "pharaoh" occurs more than 280 times, but this is a title, and not a name.

38. "Nebuchadnezzar is a central, reviled character who was, nonetheless, instrumental in divine action and salvation... Indeed, he was as much a servant as Cyrus" (J. Stökl, "Nebuchadnezzar: History, Memory, and Myth-Making in the Persian Period," in *Remembering Biblical Figures in the Late Persian & Early Hellenistic Periods: Social Memory and Imagination*, ed. D. V. Edelman and E. Ben Zvi [Oxford: Oxford University Press, 2013], 259).

39. Similarly in Ezekiel, Yahweh refers to Nebuchadnezzar as 'king of kings' (מלך מלכים, Ezek 26:7) and describes the Babylonian victory over Egypt as the wage Yahweh has paid Nebuchadnezzar for his work in Jerusalem.

Babylon (Jer 29:7), with the assumption that those prayers will be heard. Abruptly, however, Yahweh's attitude changes. He calls for Babylon's doom, saying that he will punish Nebuchadnezzar for his crimes and use another nation as his instrument (Jer 25:12–14). Nebuchadnezzar is compared to Assyria, which Yahweh used to punish Samaria but which was subsequently destroyed (Jer 50:17–19). Yahweh brags that he has tricked Babylon and entrapped it (Jer 50:23–24). For Yahweh, Nebuchadnezzar is but an implement, a cup now shattered (Jer 51:7–8), a club now set aside (Jer 51:20–23).

Yahweh's new geopolitical instrument to achieve his will are the Medians, whom he has stirred to punish Nebuchadnezzar for his crime of sacking the Jerusalem temple (Jer 51:11). Given that elsewhere in the Tanakh, including the book of Jeremiah, Nebuchadnezzar is said to have taken the city at Yahweh's command, if this seems arbitrary or even unjust on Yahweh's part, perhaps that is because it is. It is reminiscent of Yahweh's surprising condemnation in Job 42 of the three friends who have defended him against Job.[40]

This all too brief overview shows that the default portrayal of Yahweh's attitude toward foreign rulers in these earlier biblical texts is that he views them as instruments of his will regarding Israel. Any agency on the part of these kings is understood as insubordination to their true master, Yahweh. Implicit in this view is both the supremacy of Yahweh among all the other gods and the primacy of Israel in the eyes of that god. But this primacy is unlike that ordinarily found in other ancient Near Eastern royal ideologies. There the god's support for the nation is paired with support for its king, and the foreign king is the quintessential Other. In the Tanakh, the foreign king is the instrument of the defeated king's own god, who punishes the ruler and his people for wrongdoing. This is not to say that ancient Near Eastern cultures never interpreted political disaster as divine punishment. They did, as is seen in the example discussed above of Sennacherib's consultation of religious personnel to explain the death of his father, Sargon II, in battle. The determination of causality and blame in the light of a disaster both preserves a culture's religious worldview and provides an element of control for the future.[41] With the consistent portrayal of foreign kings as agents of Yahweh, the biblical material engages in a careful articulation of paradoxical claims, i.e., that Yahweh is the god of Israel but also that the god of Israel gives victory to Israel's enemies.[42] This portrayal exerted a strong pull in ancient Israelite/Jewish memories, but during the Persian and Hellenistic periods, other ways were created of remembering foreign kings and Yahweh's attitude toward them.

Yahweh's Attitude Toward Foreign Kings in Persian and Hellenistic Era Biblical Texts

After many words, we arrive at the putative subject of this essay. In the biblical texts that mention foreign kings by name, there is continuity with the portrayal of them as both tools of Yahweh and the nemesis of Yahweh's people found in earlier texts. There are also new articulations of memory that point to the social location of the different groups of scribes and elite males in Yehud discussed above. The discussion below arranges these texts according to these different groups and how they would have constructed these memories.

The successors to the scribal retainer class that existed in Jerusalem before the Exile were those priests and scribes connected with the second temple. As mentioned above, they

---

40. For discussion see D. J. A. Clines, *Job 38–42* (Nashville: Nelson, 2011).
41. P. L. Berger, *The Sacred Canopy: Elements of A Sociological Theory of Religion* (New York: Doubleday, 1967), 3–101 and Burkert, *Creation of the Sacred*, 102–28.
42. "In the strictly binary terms of the Deuteronomistic History, faithless Israel was destroyed by the very enemy who proved impotent against YHWH's faithful" (Hobson, "Memory of Sennacherib," 212).

would have viewed the Persian administration favorably, given that imperial support for the temple was an essential part of its ongoing viability. First and Second Chronicles give witness to the memories of this group. Not surprisingly, the role of the temple and its personnel are prominent throughout.[43] To be sure, there is also continuity in the belief that foreign rulers are the instruments of Yahweh used to punish a disobedient Israel/Judah (2 Chr 36:17). But the portrayal of foreign kings and Yawheh's attitude toward them is also different from that in the earlier biblical texts discussed above.[44] Memories are shaped over time, both unintentionally and by design. A potential unintentional shaping in 2 Chronicles is the spelling of the name of the Assyrian king known by Bible readers as Tiglath-Pileser. This is the Hebrew rendering in 2 Kgs 15:29 (תִּגְלַת פִּלְאֶסֶר) of the Akkadian, Tukultī-apil-Ešarra. 1–2 Chronicles consistently spells it, תִּלְגַת פִּלְנְאֶסֶר.[45] Foreign names in cultural memory can often change, as they are either not well understood, or the system of transliteration is not standardized.[46] In the case of Tiglath-Pileser, the biblical authors also knew him by his shortened name, Pulu (written as פּוּל).[47]

Memory simplifies stories over time, erasing contradictions, and the shortening of stories is an editing of memory. The account of Sennacherib's siege of Jerusalem in 2 Chr 32 shows no evidence of the awkward joining of two different accounts found in 2 Kings discussed above. The version in 2 Chronicles focuses on the speech of the Rabshakeh before Jerusalem and omits the text of the letter that Sennacherib sends to Hezekiah in 2 Kgs 19:10–13.[48] After the Rabshakeh's speech, the narrator mentions in passing (vv. 16–17) that Sennacherib's messengers spoke additional insults to both Hezekiah and Yahweh and that the Assyrian king also sent letters (note the plural, ספרים) to taunt (לחרף) Yahweh. As a compressed narrative, the letter of Sennacherib that was in the older account of 2 Kings is "summarized" by the narrator in 2 Chronicles, who uses the summary to offer an interpretation of the letter. By contrast, the account in 2 Kings contains no evaluative statement of the narrator to Sennacherib's letter, and it is only with Yahweh's oracle to Isaiah that the reader comes to know Yahweh's reaction towards Sennacherib's boasts. Yahweh's attitude toward Sennacherib in 1 Kings has been adopted by the narrator in 2 Chronicles as his own.

---

43. See P. S. Evans, "The Function of the Chronicler's Temple Despoliation Notices in Light of Imperial Realities in Yehud," *JBL* 129 (2010): 31–47.

44. While it has long been held that Chronicles is a revision of Kings, R. Klein has argued that Chronicles is drawing upon a different source than Kings (*2 Chronicles* [Minneapolis, MN: Fortress, 2012]). R. Person makes a strong case for the independence of Deuteronomy and Chronicles (*The Deuteronomic History and the Book of Chronicles: Scribal Works in an Oral World* [Atlanta, GA: SBL Press, 2010]). A definitive answer to this question is not essential for the study of Chronicles as a locus of cultural memory (Edelman, "Introduction," xxii–xxiii).

45. 1 Chr 5:6, 26; 2 Chr 28:20. The Syriac and some LXX manuscripts of 1–2 Chronicles use the spelling found in 1 Kings.

46. A modern example of the latter is the variety of spellings in Western news outlets of the name of the late Libyan dictator, Muammar el-Qaddafi: E. O'Carroll, "Gaddafi? Kadafi? Qaddafi? What's the correct spelling?" *The Christian Science Monitor*, February 22, 2011. Online: http://www.csmonitor.com/World/2011/0222/Gaddafi-Kadafi-Qaddafi-What-s-the-correct-spelling. Names from other cultures are also misunderstood due to different naming conventions. In modern times, the Roman dictator Gaius Julius Caesar is remembered as "Julius Caesar," as if Julius was his given name. In fact, Julius is the *nomen*, the name of the family and more equivalent to the modern surname and Gaius is the *praenomen*, or given name.

47. A. K. Grayson, "Tiglath-Pileser," *ABD* 6:552.

48. What S. Japhet describes as "comprehensive epitomization" (*I & 2 Chronicles* [Louisville, KY: Westminster John Knox, 1993], 977).

Paradoxically, memory can also amplify a story, because filling in gaps is another way to resolve ambiguity. This is the case with the account in Chronicles of Josiah's death at the hands of Necho. As discussed above, the account in 2 Kgs 23 is tantalizingly brief and ambiguous, leaving the reader to wonder about Yahweh's attitude toward Necho. This is not the case in 2 Chr 35, where Necho sends envoys to Josiah to dissuade the Judean king to fight, pointing out that he is not attacking Jerusalem and that Yawheh (whom Necho refers to as אלהים) has commanded Necho to undertake his attack at Carchemish. Necho goes so far as to claim in v. 21 that Yahweh is with him and that Josiah is opposing God by opposing Necho (חדל לך מאלהים אשר עמי ואל ישחיתך). This is really quite a stunning narrative compared to the earlier version in 2 Kings. While the Egyptian king claiming to speak for Yahweh and declaring himself to be acting on the command of Yahweh is something already seen in the account of Sennacherib's siege of Jerusalem, Necho's claim here is neither propaganda nor blasphemy. Necho speaks for Yahweh and speaks the truth.[49]

What this expansion on the memory of Josiah's death at the hands of Necho has done is erased the ambiguity of the memory that is preserved in 2 Kings. There is no longer any doubt as to Yahweh's role in the death of Josiah. But this clarity comes at the cost of Josiah's character, for in disobeying Necho's advice that he stand down, Josiah also disobeyed God.[50] This cost him his life, as the end of Necho's message makes clear when he warned Josiah that Yahweh might destroy him.[51]

This memory of Necho as being sent by God to fight at Carchemish recontextualizes and problematizes Jeremiah's oracles against Necho and his engagement with the Babylonians. This expanded memory takes a different track from the one of Sennacherib's siege discussed above. There, the narrator of Chronicles expresses what had once been the view of Yahweh: Sennacherib had blasphemed. In this way, the narrative itself takes a stand on the foreign king's actions by aligning with Yahweh's view of them.

What has happened to the memories of Yawheh's attitudes toward these foreign kings (now understood as the distant past for the Persian and Hellenistic era readers) is at both a continuation of the belief that these rulers are unwitting servants of Yahweh and an intensification of this attitude, given that the memories have been shaped to emphasize this fact, either through abridgement or expansion. A source-critical approach might view these changes as conscious redaction by the Chronicler of the account in 2 Kings. Such deliberate intentionality is not necessary when looking at these differences from the standpoint of memory studies, because memories are shaped over long periods of time and change can often be seen as organic. This is not to say that such changes are innocent of ideological concerns. Precisely because social memories are constitutive of group identity, they are continually adapted to support that identity through time. The temple personnel of the Persian period would have naturally agreed with the view that foreign rulers do the will

---

49. "[F]or the author and his religious environment, pagans could also channel genuine revelations" (J. Blenkinsopp, "Remembering Josiah," in *Remembering Biblical Figures in the Late Persian & Early Hellenistic Periods: Social Memory and Imagination*, ed. D. V. Edelman and E. Ben Zvi (Oxford: Oxford University Press, 2013), 236–56 [246]). "This, then, is a position from which there is no escape…Josiah's battle, fought in spite of an explicit divine warning, is a transgression" (Japhet, *1 & 2 Chronicles*, 1057).

50. This creates a second ambiguity, perhaps inadvertently, in that Josiah's early death is understood as a favor from Yahweh to the faithful king (2 Chr 34:28). Josiah's going into battle in disguise (2 Chr 35:22) creates an interesting parallel with the story of Patroclus going to fight wearing Achilles's armor *Iliad* 15–16. There too, the ruse is part of a larger divine plan that ends in the death of the disguised warrior.

51. By use of the Hiphil of שחת in v. 21.

of Yahweh and indeed, given that these priests and scribes were in part reliant upon the support of a foreign ruler, a continued view of foreign rulers under the guidance Yahweh makes good sense.

The second social group in the Persian and Hellenistic periods that would have preserved and shaped cultural memories are the male elites of Jerusalem and Yehud, some of whom would also have been priests. While these elites would have shared the concern for the prestige and importance of the Jerusalem temple that the priests and scribes had, they would also have looked to their normative texts for confirmation of their social values as male elites in a Mediterranean world. Texts for elites would have functioned in a variety of settings, ranging from cultic to educational to entertainment,[52] with a good deal of overlap among them. The majority of these texts would have been narratives that drew upon common themes, motifs, and stock characters, the building blocks of storytelling (and collective memory) in antiquity. Among these stock characters is the great king of the world, who appears in a number of Persian and Hellenistic Jewish narratives.[53] Sometimes the great king is given the name of a historical monarch. This is the case of Cyrus in Greek literature, whose historical deeds are recontextualized or simply forgotten by Greek writers, who portray the Persian monarch instead as a negative moral exemplar of luxury and decadence.[54]

A more complex fate befalls the Babylonian Nebuchadnezzar in Jewish memory. As J. Stökl details, the madness of Nebuchadnezzar in Dan 4 is dependent upon earlier stories of Nabonidus that circulated in multiple cultural contexts and which have here been transferred to Nebuchadnezzar.[55] The transference of stories from one king to another, whether by accident or design, fits with the overall lack of historical accuracy in these Persian and Hellenistic Jewish narratives. In Dan 5–6 Nebuchadnezzar is succeeded by Belshazzar, whose death brings into power the Persian Darius, who in turn is succeeded by Cyrus. This arrangement bears very little resemblance to the actual succession order from Nebuchadnezzar onward into Persian rule.[56] Both of these phenomena, i.e., transference of stories from one figure to another and the shortening and reordering of dynasts, are both examples of how cultural memory is shaped in a process of addition by subtraction, as was seen above in the streamlining of memories in 2 Chronicles.

The portrayal of Nebuchadnezzar in Daniel is ambiguous. While the Babylonian king is still remembered as the destroyer of Yahweh's temple (1:1–2) the language of God's handing over the rule of the whole world to him is almost identical to that used of Cyrus in 2 Chr 36

---

52. What P. R. Davies refers to as "serious entertainment": "[I]f one is serving not scribes but merchants or landowners less didactic and more entertaining forms of literature may be offered for their patronage" (*Scribes and Schools: The Canonization of the Hebrew Scriptures* [Louisville, KY: Westminster John Knox, 1998], 143).

53. L. K. Handy, *Entertaining Faith: Reading Short Stories in the Bible* (St. Louis, MO: Chalice, 2000), 26–27.

54. L. Mitchell, "Remembering Cyrus the Persian," in *Remembering Biblical Figures in the Late Persian & Early Hellenistic Periods: Social Memory and Imagination*, ed. D. V. Edelman and E. Ben Zvi (Oxford: Oxford University Press, 2013), 283–94 [290–92]).

55. Stökl, "Nebuchadnezzar," 261 and the detailed discussion in P.-A. Beaulieu, "Nabonidus the Mad King: A Reconsideration of His Steles from Harran and Babylon," in *Representations of Political Power: Case Histories from Times of Change and Dissolving Order in the Ancient Near East*, ed. M. Heinz and M. Feldman (Winona Lake, IN: Eisenbrauns, 2007), 137–66.

56. I.e., Nebuchadnezzar, Amel-Marduk, Neriglissar, Labaši-Marduk, Nabonidus, Belshazzar, Cyrus, Cambyses, Bardiya, Darius I.

and Ezra 1.[57] Daniel 1–4 can hardly be called a narrative, being a collection of three variant stories in which Nebuchadnezzar plays a role in challenging or threatening Jewish males but then has a conversion experience and acknowledges the power of the Jewish god (2:46, 3:29, 4:1–3).[58] The story of Nebuchadnezzar's dream in Dan 2 is itself a variant of Pharaoh's dreams in Gen 41, with Daniel playing the role of Joseph, the interpreter of dreams and follower of God. Nebuchadnezzar's dream, like those of Pharaoh in Genesis, is sent by God and apparently for the king's benefit.[59] The king's reaction, like Pharaoh's, is to exalt the messenger, and as Pharaoh makes Joseph second in the kingdom, Nebuchadnezzar worships Daniel, has incense offered to him, and acclaims Daniel's god as supreme in 2:46–47.

In this episode, Nebuchadnezzar is seen to be favored by God in his having been given dominion over the world and insight into the world's end by him. By contrast, the story of Nebuchadnezzar's madness in Daniel 4 is a story of divine punishment of the king on account of his pride. Walking through his city, Nebuchadnezzar attributes its glory to his own efforts (4:27 [30 ET] referring to Babylon as the city די אנה בניתה לבית מלכו בתקף חסני). The story repeats the motif of the king having an enigmatic dream that Daniel interprets for him, as in Dan 2. But the purpose of this dream is to announce divine punishment on Nebuchadnezzar to teach him the lesson that the God of heaven is the true kingmaker and ruler of the earth (4:23 [26 ET]:שליט שמיא; cf. 4:29: שליט עליא במלכות אנשא ולמן די יצבא יתננה).

This is the same sin as that of Sennacherib in 2 Kings discussed above, with the significant difference that Nebuchadnezzar is temporarily punished, whereas Sennacherib dies.[60] Nebuchadnezzar not only survives but recounts what befell him in a first-person account that begins and ends with praise of the one true God (3:32–33, 4:34). As in the case with his dream in Dan 2, Nebuchadnezzar here is viewed favorably by God, who punishes him temporarily for the same sin that merited death for Sennacherib. And this is Nebuchadnezzar's last appearance in Daniel. In Dan 5, his son Belshazzar is king and the assumption is that Nebuchadnezzar lived out the rest of his life with proper respect for God. The ambiguity with these two stories is created by the placement of the third story of Nebuchadnezzar between them.

In Dan 3, Nebuchadnezzar is both an idolater and a tyrant who succumbs to rage at the refusal of the three young Jewish men to worship his statue. Even his "conversion" is rather skin-deep, as he commands brutal punishments for any who blaspheme against the Jewish god (3:29). This story about Nebuchadnezzar is also different from the two others in Daniel in that the king has no dreams sent from God in need of interpretation. His contact with the divine is seeing the angel in the fiery furnace. But even taking this ambiguity into

---

57. מלכא מלך מלכיא די אלה שמיא מלכותא חסנא ותקפא ויקרא יהב לך (Dan 2:37). Note the parallel use of the phrase "God of heaven," in 2 Chr 36:23.

58. Cf. J. J. Collins, *Daniel* (Minneapolis, MN: Fortress, 1993), 27–29, 45. These stories also draw upon the motif of the wise courtier endangered by the king, which is at least as old as Ahiqar.

59. This is clear in Gen 41, where the dreams warn Pharaoh of the impending famine. Nebuchadnezzar's dream has no direct benefit to him but rather, is a vision of the end of days sent by God, who is described as a "revealer of mysteries" (גלא רזין Dan 2:28). Daniel reiterates this at the conclusion of his interpretation in 2:45: רב הודע למלכא מה די להוא אחרי דנה.

60. 2 Kings 19:35–36 recounts in rapid succession how the angel of Yahweh destroyed the entire Assyrian army followed by Sennacherib's returning home and being murdered by his sons while praying in a temple. This gives the impression that the king's death followed quickly after the failed siege of Jerusalem—and is thus part of Yahweh's punishment—when in fact he did not die until almost twenty years later, in 681.

account, the overall impression of the memories of Nebuchadnezzar articulated in Dan 1–4—which certainly predate the Maccabean context for the entire book[61]—show no trace of Nebuchadnezzar's condemnation in Jeremiah as a temporary tool of Yahweh set aside at the end of its use. Rather, the Babylonian king has been recast as the great king in a series of court tales adapted for a Jewish milieu. In this regard, his relationship with God has been reimagined. Nebuchadnezzar is now favored by God and, when he does sin, is given fair warning of punishment and a chance to repent.

The overall positive memory of God's attitude toward Nebuchadnezzar in Daniel is emphasized by the equally negative treatment his son, Belshazzar, receives from God. Belshazzar's crimes are twofold: he worships idols and uses the temple's sacred vessels for a feast (5:2, 23). However, Nebuchadnezzar is also an idolater, who mandates worship of a giant golden statue in Dan 3. What precipitates the disembodied hand/invisible scribe sent from God to Belshazzar (as the text makes clear in 5:24), is the use of the temple vessels at the banquet. To this is added Daniel's condemnation of the king's own pride when he had the clear lesson of his father's humiliation by God to learn from (5:22).

Unlike the dreams sent to his father, which were meant either as a blessing or a call to repent, the theophany to Belshazzar is the announcement of condemnation. Even though Belshazzar honors Daniel, as did Nebuchadnezzar before him, he is killed that very night. The contrast between God's forbearance with Nebuchadnezzar and one-strike only approach to Belshazzar is stark, and their combined effect is to offer a positive and negative example, respectively, not simply of kingship, but of the nature of wisdom and repentance. Nebuchadnezzar was favored by God, and when he forgot that he owed his power to divine beneficence, he was punished and given a chance to repent. Belshazzar had his father's experience as an example, and that was his minatory lesson. His sin, therefore, is greater because it was committed with knowledge. Daniel 1–5 then presents the divine treatment of these kings in ways common in describing monarchs in Hellenistic storytelling.[62]

Understanding the influence of Hellenistic narrative plotlines is essential to seeing how memories of foreign kings continued to be shaped from the fourth century BCE onward, both in texts that would become canonical and those that would not. The portrayal of the king of Nineveh in Jon 3, for example, has nothing to do with the Assyrians remembered in the Hebrew Bible but rather, is a complete expression of the Hellenistic great king of the world and possibly dependent upon a heavily orientalized, legendary Greek tradition of Nineveh's last king, Sardanapallus.[63] On the other hand, a late text such as Tobit, which shows knowledge of the Ahiqar story, demonstrates how persistent older narratives were in the cultural memory of educated Jewish elites. Memories continued to be both created and shaped in a fertile intellectual atmosphere that used traditional materials in highly imaginative ways. The identities of numerous groups in the Second Temple period were not only sustained by these memories but used as weapons in oftentimes acrimonious polemic.

---

61. So Collins, *Daniel*, 35–38.

62. Upon Belshazzars's death, Darius succeeds him and institutes Persian hegemony. While the narrative of the Lion's Den in Dan 6 is yet another example of a court tale, Darius is portrayed as devoted to Daniel and his god from the outset. This squares with the fairly consistent, positive portrayal of Persian kings in later biblical texts, which is due to the persistent memory of Cyrus as the rebuilder of Jerusalem and the Persian monarchy as supporter of the temple.

63. T. Bolin, "'Should I Not Also Pity Nineveh?' Divine Freedom in the Book of Jonah," *JSOT* 67 (1995): 109–21.

Bibliography

Ascough, R. S., P. A. Harland, and J. S. Kloppenborg. 2012. *Associations in the Greco-Roman World: A Sourcebook*. Waco, TX: Baylor University Press; Berlin: de Gruyter.

Assmann, J. 2011. *Cultural Memory and Early Civilization: Writing, Remembrance, and Political Imagination*. Cambridge: Cambridge University Press.

———. 2006. *Religion and Cultural Memory: Ten Studies*. Translated by Rodney Livingstone. Stanford, CA: Stanford University Press.

———. 1992. *Das kulturelle Gedächtnis: Schrift, Erinnerung und politische Identität in frühen Hochkulturen*. Munich: Beck.

Barbour, J. 2012. *The Story of Israel in the Book of Qohelet: Ecclesiastes as Cultural Memory*. Oxford: Oxford University Press.

Barstad, H. 2010. "History and Memory: Some Reflections on the 'Memory Debate' in Relation to the Hebrew Bible." In *The Historian and the Bible: Essays in Honour of Lester L. Grabbe*, edited by P. R. Davies and D. V. Edelman, 1–10. LHBOTS 530. London: T&T Clark.

Beaulieu, P.-A. 2007. "Nabonidus the Mad King: A Reconsideration of His Steles from Harran and Babylon." In *Representations of Political Power: Case Histories from Times of Change and Dissolving Order in the Ancient Near East*, edited by M. Heinz and M. H. Feldman, 137–66. Winona Lake, IN: Eisenbrauns.

Ben Zvi, E. 2014. "The Yehudite Collection of Prophetic Books and Imperial Contexts: Some Observations." In *Divination, Politics and Ancient Near Eastern Texts*, edited by A. Lenzi and J. Stökl, 145–69. Atlanta, GA: SBL.

———. 2013. "Chronicles and its Reshaping of Memories of Monarchic Period Prophets: Some Observations." In *Prophets, Prophecy, and Ancient Israelite Historiography*, edited by M. Boda and L. M. Wray Beal, 167–88. Winona Lake, IN: Eisenbrauns.

———. 2013. "The Memory of Abraham in Late Persian/Early Hellenistic Yehud/Judah." In *Remembering Biblical Figures in the Late Persian and Early Hellenistic Periods: Social Memory and Imagination*. Edited by D. V. Edelman and E. Ben Zvi, 3–37. Oxford: Oxford University Press.

———. 2013. "Monogynistic and Monogamous Tendencies, Memories and Imagination in Late Persian/Early Hellenistic Yehud." *ZAW* 125: 263–77.

———. 2013. "Toward a Sense of Balance: Remembering the Catastrophe of Monarchic Judah/ (Ideological) Israel and Exile through Reading Chronicles in Late Yehud." In *Chronicling the Chronicler: The Book of Chronicles and Early Second Temple Historiography*, edited by P. Evans and T. Williams, 247–65. Winona Lake, IN: Eisenbrauns, .

———. 2013 "Prophetic Memories in the Deuteronomistic Historical and the Prophetic Collections of Books." In *Israelite Prophecy and the Deuteronomistic History: Portrait, Reality and the Formation of a History*, edited by M. Jacobs and R. E. Person, 75–102. Atlanta, GA: SBL.

———. 2013. "Reading and Constructing Utopias Utopia/s And/in the Collection of Authoritative Texts/Textual Readings of Late Persian Period Yehud." *Studies in Religion/Sciences Religieuses* 42: 463–76.

———. 2012. "Remembering the Prophets through the Reading and Rereading of a Collection of Prophetic Books in Yehud: Methodological Considerations and Explorations." In *Remembering and Forgetting in Early Second Temple Judah*, edited by E. Ben Zvi and C. Levin, 17–44. FAT 85. Tübingen: Mohr Siebeck, .

———. 2012. "The Study of Forgetting and the Forgotten in Ancient Israelite Discourse/s: Observations and Test Cases." In *Cultural Memory in Biblical Exegesis*, edited by P. Carstens,

T. Hasselbach, and N. P. Lemche, 137–57. Perspectives on Hebrew Scriptures and its Contexts 17. Piscataway, NJ: Gorgias.

———. 2011. "On Social Memory and Identity Formation in Late Persian Yehud: A Historian's Viewpoint with a Focus on Prophetic Literature, Chronicles and the Dtr. Historical Collection." In *Texts, Contexts and Readings in Postexilic Literature: Explorations into Historiography and Identity Negotiation in Hebrew Bible and Related Texts,* edited by L. C. Jonker, 95–148. Tübingen: Mohr Siebeck, .

———. 2010. "A Contribution to the Intellectual History of Yehud: The Story of Micaiah and Its Function within the Discourse of Persian-Period Literati." In *The Historian and the Bible: Essays in Honour of Lester L. Grabbe,* edited by P. R. Davies and D. V. Edelman, 89–102. LHBOTS 530. London: T&T Clark.

———. 2009. "Towards an Integrative Study of the Production of Authoritative Books in Ancient Israel." In *The Production of Prophecy: Constructing Prophecy and Prophets in Yehud*, edited by D. V. Edelman and E. Ben Zvi, 15–28. London: Equinox.

———. "Publications," http://www.ualberta.ca/~ebenzvi/ebz-publications.html

Ben Zvi, E. and D. V. Edelman, eds. 2013. *Remembering Biblical Figures in the Late Persian and Early Hellenistic Periods: Social Memory and Imagination.* Oxford: Oxford University Press.

Ben Zvi, E. and C. Levin, eds. 2012. *Remembering and Forgetting in Early Second Temple Judah.* FAT 85. Tübingen: Mohr Siebeck.

Berger, P. L. 1967. *The Sacred Canopy: Elements of a Sociological Theory of Religion.* Garden City, NY: Doubleday.

Blenkinsopp, J. 2013. *David Remembered: Kingship and National Identity in Ancient Israel.* Grand Rapids, MI: Eerdmans.

———. 2013. "Remembering Josiah." In *Remembering Biblical Figures in the Late Persian and Early Hellenistic Periods: Social Memory and Imagination,* edited by Ehud Ben Zvi and Diana V. Edelman, 236–56. Oxford: Oxford University Press.

Bolin, T. 2014. "1–2 Samuel and Its Role in the Cultivation of Jewish Paideia in the Persian and Hellenistic Periods." In *Deuteronomy-Kings as Emerging Authoritative Books: A Conversation,* 133–58. Atlanta, GA: SBL.

———. 1997. *Freedom Beyond Forgiveness: The Book of Jonah Re-Examined.* Sheffield: JSOT Press.

———. 1995. "'Should I Not Also Pity Nineveh?' Divine Freedom in the Book of Jonah." *JSOT* 67: 109–21.

Burkert, W. 1996. *Creation of the Sacred: Tracks of Biology in Early Religions.* Cambridge, MA: Harvard University Press.

Carr, D. M. 2011. *The Formation of the Hebrew Bible: A New Reconstruction.* Oxford: Oxford University Press.

———. 2005. *Writing on the Tablet of the Heart: Origins of Scripture and Literature.* Oxford: Oxford University Press.

Carstens, P., T. Hasselbalch, and N. P. Lemche, eds. 2012. *Cultural Memory in Biblical Exegesis.* Perspectives on Hebrew Scriptures and its Contexts 17. Piscataway, NJ: Gorgias.

Clines, D. J. A. 2011. *Job 38–42.* Nashville: Nelson.

Collins, J. J. 1993. *Daniel: A Commentary on the Book of Daniel.* Hermeneia 27. Minneapolis, MN: Fortress.

Davies, P. R. 2008. *Memories of Ancient Israel: An Introduction to Biblical History – Ancient and Modern.* Louisville, KY: Westminster John Knox.

———. 1998. *Scribes and Schools: The Canonization of the Hebrew Scriptures.* Louisville, KY: Westminster John Knox.

Edelman, D. V. 2013. "Introduction." In *Remembering Biblical Figures in the Late Persian and Early Hellenistic Periods: Social Memory and Imagination,* edited by D. V. Edelman and E. Ben Zvi, xi–xxiv. Oxford: Oxford University Press.

Evans, P. S. 2010. "The Function of the Chronicler's Temple Despoliation Notices in Light of Imperial Realities in Yehud." *JBL* 129: 31–47.

———. 2009. *The Invasion of Sennacherib in the Book of Kings: A Source-Critical and Rhetorical Study of 2 Kings 18–19*. Leiden: Brill.

Evans, P. S. and T. F. Williams, eds. 2013. *Chronicling the Chronicler: The Book of Chronicles and Early Second Temple Historiography*. Winona Lake, IN: Eisenbrauns.

Frahm, E. 1999. "Nabû-zuqup-kēnu, das Gilgameš-Epos und der Tod Sargons II." *Journal of Cuneiform Studies* 51: 73–90

Freedman, D. N., ed. 1992. *Anchor Bible Dictionary*. 6 vols. New York: Doubleday.

Fried, L. S. 2004. *The Priest and the Great King: Temple-Palace Relations in the Persian Empire*. Biblical and Judaic studies from the University of California, San Diego 10. Winona Lake, IN: Eisenbrauns.

Gallagher, W. R. 1999. *Sennacherib's Campaign to Judah: New Studies*. Ledien: Brill.

George, A. R., ed. 2003. *The Babylonian Gilgamesh Epic: Introduction, Critical Edition and Cuneiform Texts*. 2 vols. Oxford: Oxford University Press.

Grabbe, L. L., ed. 2003. *Like a Bird in a Cage: The Invasion of Sennacherib in 701 BCE*. 2 Volumes. Sheffield: Sheffield Academic.

Halbwachs, M. 1925. *Les Cadres sociaux de la mémoire*. Paris: F. Alcan.

Handy, L. K. 2000. *Entertaining Faith: Reading Short Stories in the Bible*. St. Louis: Chalice.

Hobson, R. 2013. "The Memory of Sennacherib in Late Persian Yehud." In *Remembering Biblical Figures in the Late Persian and Early Hellenistic Periods: Social Memory and Imagination,* edited by D. V. Edelman and E. Ben Zvi, 199–220. Oxford: Oxford University Press.

Jacobs, M. R., and R. F. Person, eds. 2013. *Israelite Prophecy and the Deuteronomistic History: Portrait, Reality, and the Formation of a History*. Atlanta, GA: SBL.

Japhet, S. 1993. *I & II Chronicles: A Commentary*. Louisville, KY: Westminster John Knox.

Klein, R. W. 2012. *2 Chronicles: A Commentary*. Minneapolis, MN: Fortress.

Knowles, M. D. 2006. *Centrality Practiced: Jerusalem in the Religious Practice of Yehud and the Diaspora in the Persian Period*. Atlanta, GA: SBL.

Lemche, N. P. 2013. "Solomon as Cultural Memory." In *Remembering Biblical Figures in the Late Persian and Early Hellenistic Periods: Social Memory and Imagination,* edited by D. V. Edelman and E. Ben Zvi, 158–81. Oxford: Oxford University Press.

Lipschits, O. and O. Tal. 2007. "The Settlement Archaeology of the Province of Judah: A Case Study." In *Judah and the Judeans in the Fourth Century B.C.E.,* edited by O. Lipschits, G. N. Knoppers, and R. Albertz, 33–52. Winona Lake, IN: Eisenbrauns.

Lipschits, O. and D. Vanderhooft. 2007 "Yehud Stamp Impressions in the Fourth Century B.C.E.: A Time of Administrative Consolidation?" In *Judah and the Judeans in the Fourth Century B.C.E.,* edited by O. Lipschits, G. N. Knoppers, and R. Albertz, 75–94. Winona Lake, IN: Eisenbrauns.

Mann, T. W. 1979. "Theological Reflections on the Denial of Moses." *JBL* 98: 481–94.

Mitchell, L. 2013. "Remembering Cyrus the Persian." In *Remembering Biblical Figures in the Late Persian and Early Hellenistic Periods: Social Memory and Imagination,* edited by D. V. Edelman and E. Ben Zvi, 283–94. Oxford: Oxford University Press.

O'Carroll, E. "Gaddafi? Kadafi? Qaddafi? What's the correct spelling?" *The Christian Science Monitor*. February 22, 2011. Online: http://www.csmonitor.com/World/2011/0222/Gaddafi-Kadafi-Qaddafi-What-s-the-correct-spelling.

Person, R. F. 2010. *The Deuteronomic History and the Book of Chronicles: Scribal Works in an Oral World*. Atlanta, GA: SBL.

Schaper, J. 1995. "The Jerusalem Temple as an Instrument of the Achaemenid Fiscal Administration." *Vetus Testamentum* 45: 528–39

Schuman, H., B. Schwartz, and H. D'arcy. 2005. "Elite Revisionists and Popular Beliefs: Christopher Columbus, Hero Or Villain?" *Public Opinion Quarterly* 69: 2–29.

Schwartz, B. 1997. "Collective Memory and History: How Abraham Lincoln Became a Symbol of Racial Equality." *The Sociological Quarterly* 38: 469–96.

Squire, M. 2011. *The Iliad in a Nutshell: Visualizing Epic on the Tabulae Iliacae*. Oxford: Oxford University Press.

Stökl, J. 2013. "Nebuchadnezzar: History, Memory, and Myth-Making in the Persian Period." In *Remembering Biblical Figures in the Late Persian and Early Hellenistic Periods: Social Memory and Imagination*, edited by D. V. Edelman and E. Ben Zvi, 257–69. Oxford: Oxford University Press.

Stott, K. M. 2008. *Why Did They Write This Way? Reflections on References to Written Documents in the Hebrew Bible and Ancient Literature*. New York: T&T Clark.

Tadmor, H., B. Landsberger, and S. Parpola, 1989. "The Sin of Sargon and Sennacherib's Last Will." *State Archives of Assyria Bulletin* 3: 3–51.

Westenholz, J. G. 1997. *Legends of the Kings of Akkade: The Texts*. Winona Lake, IN: Eisenbrauns.

— 10 —

At the Crossroads of Persian and Hellenistic Ideology: The Book of Esther as "Political Theology"

Beate Ego

The Esther narrative in the Hebrew Bible describes the ways in which the Jewish people were threatened and saved throughout the Persian Empire during the reign of the Persian King Ahasuerus (Xerxes) (485–465 BCE).[1] Thus, as is clear from the outset, the narrative explicitly involves the political dimension of the Persian Empire. An analysis that considers the structure, intertextuality, and narrative components relating to history of traditions shows that the Persian Empire is not only the location for this action; rather, on a variety of levels, a deliberate examination of the ideology of the Persian Empire and its concept of leadership takes place in the tale. After a short description of the content of the narrative, I will first note various elements of the political discourse on leadership found in this story. I will then explain to what extent this is also connected to theological ideas, illuminating the historico-theological dimension of the narrative. The discussion will conclude with reflections on the dating of the account and its function in the context of the Festival of Purim.

1. Summary of the Narrative

King Ahasuerus's display of his power and glory in the presence of the important leaders of his Empire and of his people ends in disaster: the beautiful Vashti refuses to be presented at the festivities and in so doing, disavows the authority of the powerful despot. She is cast out and in her place, Esther is chosen to be queen (Esth 1:1–2:18). She is the niece of Mordecai, a Jew who himself or whose forefathers entered Babylonian exile under Nebuchadnezzar (Esth 2:5–7), and who, without the king's knowledge, managed to discover a conspiracy made by two eunuchs and saved the king's life (Esth 2:19–23). When Mordecai refuses to bow down to Haman, the second most powerful person in the realm (Esth 3:1–5), Haman becomes so enraged he resolves to kill Mordecai and annihilate his entire people. Against this backdrop, he elicits an edict from the king, which hands over all the Jews in the realm to be plundered and murdered. The time of the punishment by lot (Hebr. *pur*) is set for the thirteenth of Adar in the month of Nisan in the twelfth year

---

1. This chapter is a summary of the findings of my commentary on the book of Esther, which will appear in the series *Biblischer Kommentar*. I would like to thank Ulrike Guthrie of Bangor, Maine, USA, for translating the chapter from the German.

of King Ahasuerus's reign; in short, almost a year lies between the actual decision and the planned deadline for the implementation of the edict (Esth 3:6–15).

Mordecai, who is deeply troubled by these events, manages to convince his niece Esther to go and intercede with the king (Esth 4:1–17). Although Esther is queen, she does not have unrestricted access to her spouse; rather, she goes and has an audience before Ahasuerus without being called and with complete disregard for her own life. At her request, that same day he grants her the favor of appearing together with Haman at a banquet with her. On this occasion, Esther responds to her spouse's challenge to make a wish by issuing a further invitation to him and Haman that is to take place the very next day (Esth 5:1–8). Haman, who is absolutely delighted with this development, on the advice of his wife and his friends, has a gallows erected for Mordecai (Esth 5:9–14). Yet the following morning during the reading of the Chronicle, after the king learns it was Mordecai who discovered a conspiracy directed against him, Mordecai gains the king's respect. Ironically Haman, who actually wanted to appeal to the king regarding Mordecai's hanging, must now execute the royally ordered honoring of Mordecai. As a result, Haman's wife can predict her husband's utter downfall (Esth 6:1–13).

At the meal that takes place later that day, Esther reveals to the king that Haman had planned the annihilation of her own people (Esth 7:1–8). Now the tables are turned: the king orders the execution of Haman and at the same time allows Mordecai and Esther to declare a counter-edict that allows Jews to defend themselves against their enemies. When this becomes known, there is great rejoicing throughout the kingdom (Esth 8:1–17). The day that was actually set aside for the decimation of the enemies of the Jewish people now becomes a day in which the enemies of Israel are brought low and decimated. While the Jews gather in the provinces on the thirteenth day of the month of Adar, in the capital city of Susa the battles between the Jews and their enemies take place on the thirteenth and fourteenth days of the month of Adar. In Susa itself, five hundred people are killed (as well as the ten sons of Haman), but in the provinces the toll is 75,000 (Esth 9:1–18). As a result of the differing dates on which the battles took place, there are different holy days for the Jews of Susa and the Jews of the provinces (Esth 9:19). Following the events, Mordecai orders that all the Jews of the kingdom of Persia are to celebrate the victory annually (Esth 9:20–28); the book of Esther confirms the regulations for this festival in a second writing (Esth 9:29–32). The narrative closes by mentioning that Mordecai is installed in a high office that makes him second- in-rank to the king and that the events are described in the Chronicles of the Kings of the Medes and Persians (Esth 10:1–3).

The narrative elements developed in the story are organized within a *reversal structure*. The connections can be shown as follows with reference to an outline that A. Schmitt presents in his work, *Wende des Lebens*:[2]

---

2. A. Schmitt, *Wende des Lebens: Untersuchungen zu einem Situations-Motiv der Bibel*, BZAW 237 (Berlin: de Gruyter, 1996), 100; see also F. W. Bush, *Ruth, Esther*, WBC 9 (Dallas: Word, 1996), 324; M. V. Fox, *Character and Ideology in the Book of Esther*, 2nd ed., Studies on the Personalities of the Old Testament (Grand Rapids, MI: Eerdmans, 2001), 159–62; one can also find a similar compilation in E. Zenger, "Das Buch Ester," in *Einleitung in das Alte Testament*, 5th ed., ed. E. Zenger et al., Kohlhammer Studienbücher Theologie, 1.1; Stuttgart: W. Kohlhammer, 2004), 302–11 (305). For connections to older literature, see J. Steinberg, *Die Ketuvim: Ihr Aufbau und ihre Botschaft*, BBB 152 (Hamburg: Philo, 2006), 399–400; S. B. Berg, *The Book of Esther: Motifs, Themes and Structure*, SBLDS 44 (Missoula, MT: Scholars Press, 1979), 106–13.

Haman's ascendance to the most highly ranked ruler (3:1)	↔	Mordecai's ascendance to the position of vice-regent (10:2f.)
Servants' obeisance before Haman (3:2–6)	↔	Haman's obeisance before Esther (7:7f.)
Planned confiscation of Jewish wealth (3:9)	↔	Esther and her people take possession of Haman's wealth (8:1f.11b)
Ahasuerus hands over his signet ring to Haman (3:10)	↔	Ahasuerus hands over his signet ring to Mordecai (8:2a)
The king's first reprieve of the Jews (3:12)	↔	The king's second reprieve of the Jews (8:9–12)
The planned extermination of the Jews (3:13)	↔	Jews' vengeance toward their enemies (9:1–16)
Promulgation of the first reprieve (3:14)	↔	Promulgation of the second reprieve (8:13)
The messengers depart on horseback, and the reaction in the city of Susa (3:15)	↔	The messengers depart on horseback, and the reaction in the city of Susa (8:14f.)
Mordecai tears his clothes as a gesture of grief (4:1)	↔	Mordecai's investiture by the king (8:15a)
Consternation and grief among the Jewish population (4:3)	↔	Joy and jubilation among the Jewish population (8:17a)
The mighty Haman's discussion with his wife and friends (5:10–14a)	↔	The dejected Haman's discussion with his wife and friends (6:12f.)
The gallows erected by Haman for Mordecai (5:14b)	↔	Haman's demise on the gallows erected for Mordecai (7:10)

2. Various Elements of Political Discourse in Esther

We must not overlook the political concerns of this narrative and their implications for our understanding of leadership. The opening of the book already depicts in an impressive way the pomp and circumstance of the Persian king who rules over an Empire that stretches from India to Ethiopia (Esth 1:1–9). The king is depicted as the sovereign ruler of a multicultural state, a leader who shows his command through power and luxury but also through the harshness of his command and its professional enforcement with the help of a well-functioning bureaucratic apparatus as well as a perfectly-functioning mail and road system (Esth 1:22).[3] This depiction corresponds to the Persian ideology of rule, with its conception of a harmony between king, throne, and peoples, a harmony that conveys its underlying notion of knowledge about the world through its comprehensive system of order.[4] The harmony between all the peoples of the provinces and the king's *dat*, which is so

---

3. On the road and postal system in general, see P. Briant, *From Cyrus to Alexander: A History of the Persian Empire*, trans. P. D. Daniels (Winona Lake, IN: Eisenbrauns, 2002), 357–59; H. Koch, "Die achämenidische Poststrasse von Persepolis nach Susa," *Archaeologische Mitteilungen aus Iran* 19 (1986): 133–47; J. Wiesehöfer, *Das antike Persien: Von 550 v. Chr. bis 650 n. Chr.* (Düsseldorf: Albatros, 2005), 116–17.

4. T. Willi, "Der Weltreichsgedanke im Frühjudentum: Israel, Menschheit und Weltherrschaft in den bib-

impressively made clear through the command in the first chapter of the book, is disrupted by Vashti's obstinacy and her refusal to obey the king's command but is restored by her expulsion and the king's marriage to Queen Esther (Esth 1:9–2:18).

The episode of the eunuchs' plot to assassinate Ahasuerus, which is prevented by Mordecai, can also be understood as a disruption and restitution of kingly rule and its leadership (Esth 2:19–23). What ensues after the encounter between Mordecai and Haman is a focusing on the Jewish people, who likewise are under the control of the king of Persia. This exposes two arenas of conflict at once in Esth 3:1–5: the one arising from Mordecai's refusal to prostrate himself before Haman, and a second involving the incompatability of the Jewish worldview with the foreign ruler's ideology. Intertextual references point to the historical and political concerns of this little episode, which has such far-reaching consequences for the entire narrative: The genealogical references to "Mordecai, son of Jair, son of Shimei, son of Kish, a Benjaminite" (Esth 2:5) and "Haman, the son of Hammedatha, the Agagite" (Esth 3:1) connect this story to the earlier history of Israel. Because Mordecai is assigned to the Saulide line of Benjamin, and because the Gentile term 'Agagite' (האגגי) identifies Haman as a descendent of the Amalekite King Agag, these few words awaken associations with the conflict between Israel and its archenemy Amalek, which appears in 1 Sam 15:1–35.[5] Thus, the old conflict between Amalek and Israel that has ebbed and flowed from generation to generation is once again brought to the fore in the encounter between Haman and Mordecai: The symbolic name depicts Haman as a descendent of old enemies of Israel and also gives a historical basis to his appearance as a foe of the Jews.[6]

The importance of the motif of the refusal to prostrate likewise can only be deciphered through intertextual references, because the narrative is extremely cautious about expressing motives for Mordecai's behavior.[7] If Esth 3:4 suggests that Mordecai is a Jew, one could imagine that prostrating himself before Haman could not be reconciled with his national pride and thus, in the final analysis, was motivated by politics and nationalism.[8]

---

lischen Chronikbüchern," in *Exegese vor Ort Festschrift P. Welten*, ed. Chr. Maier *et al.* (Leipzig: Evangelische Verlagsanstalt, 2001), 389–409 (393).

5. Numerous studies on the book of Esther point to the narrative's connection to the Amalek tradition; see, among others, L. B. Paton, *A Critical and Exegetical Commentary on the Book of Esther*, ICC 20 (1908, repr., Edinburgh: T&T Clark, 1964), 194; H. Bardtke, *Das Buch Esther*, KAT 17/4–5 (Gütersloh: Gerd Mohn, 1963), 316; W. Dommershausen, *Die Estherrolle: Stil und Ziel einer alttestamentlichen Schrift*, Stuttgarter biblische Monographien 6 (Stuttgart: Katholisches Bibelwerk, 1968), 59; C. A. Moore, *Esther: Introduction, Translation and Notes*, AB 7B (Garden City, NY: Doubleday, 1971), 35; A. Meinhold, *Das Buch Esther*, ZBK 13 (Zürich: Theologischer Verlag Zürich, 1983), 43; G. Gerleman, *Esther*, 2nd ed., Biblischer Kommentar, Altes Testament 21 (Neukirchen-Vluyn: Neukirchener Verlag, 1982), 91; A. LaCocque, "Haman in the book of Esther," *Hebrew Annual Review* 11 (1987): 207–22; J. A. Loader, "Das Buch Ester," in *Das Hohelied, Klagelied, Das Buch Ester*, ed. H.-P. Müller, O. Kaiser and J. A. Loader, trans. I. v. Loewenclau, ATD 16/2 (Göttingen: Vandenhoeck & Ruprecht, 1992), 199–280 (240); A. Berlin, *Esther: Traditional Hebrew Text with the JPS Translation*, JPS Bible Commentary (Philadelphia, PA: Jewish Publication Society of America, 2001), 34. The connection between Haman und Amalek plays a significant role especially in the Haggadah; on this, see especially B. Ego, *Targum Scheni zu Ester: Übersetzung, Kommentar und theologische Deutung*, TSAJ 54 (Tübingen: Mohr Siebeck, 1996), 40–46.

6. Bardtke, *Esther*, 316.

7. H. M. Wahl, *Das Buch Esther: Übersetzung und Kommentar* (Berlin: de Gruyter, 2009), 91.

8. Thus, for example, Bardtke, *Esther*; Berlin, *Esther*; Bush, *Esther*; Clines, *Esther*; Dommershausen, *Estherrolle*; J. D. Levenson, *Esther: A Commentary*, OTL (Louisville, KY: Westminster John Knox, 1997) and Moore, *Esther*.

A further possible explanation could lie in Mordecai's arrogance.⁹ But one could also imagine that Mordecai was simply hurt that Haman was promoted, not him (who had, after all, shortly before saved the king's life).

Certainly, the intertextual dimension of the refusal to prostrate suggests that we are to assume a religious reason for Mordecai's behavior. In this context, the Hebrew narrative uses the turn of phrase לא יכרע ולא ישתחוה, literally: 'he did not kneel down and did not prostrate himself', so that presumably we are to assume a deliberate plot sequence here. The terms כרע and השתחוה can also be used separately in a secular context (see for example 2 Kgs 1:13 or 1 Sam 24:9; 2 Sam 1:2; 9:6; Ps 72:11); however, elsewhere in the biblical tradition the direct linking of the two verbs כרע and השתחוה, as found here in Esth 3:2 and Esth 3:5, always appears in connection with obeisance before God. To point to only one example: in Ps 22:28–29 it says,

> For the kingdom belongs to Yahweh,
> He is the ruler of all the peoples.
> Before him alone are all the powerful of the earth to prostrate themselves
> all those who will become dust bow down before him
>
> (וישתחוו כל דשני ארץ לפניו יכרעו כל יורדי עפר)

Further examples, such as Ps 95:6, 2 Chr 7:3, or 2 Chr 29:29, can easily be added. Given the fact that there are plenty of implicit theological references in the book of Esther and that Esth 3:2 and Esth 3:5 show the direct linking of the two verbs כרע and השתחוה, there is much to be said for the idea that by demanding obeisance, Haman claimed a quasi-divine status for himself and that for this reason, Mordecai denied him it.¹⁰ In any case, Mordecai's behavior toward Haman shows that there are limits to loyalty when Jews are living under foreign rule. One can almost read this event as a counterpart to the story of the conspiracy in Esth 2:21–23. Whereas in the one instance Mordecai chooses to act loyally toward a political leader, in the other instance this option is no longer possible.

A glance at the relevant extra-biblical sources shows that the motif of prostrating was at the center of a discussion that was of great importance for the ancient world. Among the Greek writers, for instance, we find unambiguous evidence that the Persians' choice not to prostrate oneself was a significant gesture as regards expressing honor, humility, and respect toward a person. Herodotus shows that prostrating oneself before a more highly ranked person¹¹ was an aspect of Persian convention in which the hierarchy between the different participatory persons was clearly expressed (1.134).

---

9. Thus, for example, E. J. Bickerman, "Esther," in *Four Strange Books of the Bible: Jonah, Daniel, Koheleth, Esther*, ed. E. J. Bickerman (New York: Schocken Books, 1967), 171–240 (43); Paton, *Esther*, ad loc.

10. Levenson, *Esther*, 67 also points to this connotation of these verbs or verbal connections, and then continues: "But if idolatry is the cause of Mordecai's noncompliance, the text is largely silent about this. In addition, it is difficult to see why the king commands that an underling be treated as god when he himself is not." R. Achenbach, "Vertilgen – Töten – Vernichten (Est 3,13): Die Genozid-Thematik im Esterbuch," *ZABR* 15 (2009): 282–315 (293) also draws attention to these connections.

11. At this point we need not pursue further the discussion of whether paying obeisance to someone consisted of kissing another's hand and a slight inclination of the upper body (thus Briant, *Cyrus*) or in actually prostrating oneself before someone (thus G. Ahn, *Religiöse Herrscherlegitimation im achämenidischen Iran: Die Voraussetzungen und die Struktur ihrer Argumentation*, Acta Iranica 3 and Textes et mémoires, 17 [Leiden: Brill, 1992]). On this matter, see J. Wiesehöfer, "Proskynesis," *Der Neue Pauly* 10 (2001): 443–44.

Yet in this connection, there seem to have been quite concrete problems between Persians and Greeks. For the Greeks, prostrating oneself before another could not be reconciled with the ideal of human freedom. Herodotus tells in book 7.136 of his *Histories* how Hydarnes, the Persian commander of all coastal inhabitants of Asia Minor, receives a delegation of Lacedaemonians who are en route to Greece on a diplomatic mission to the King of Persia. He encourages them to become "friends of the king" and to submit themselves to him. To this the Greeks respond that only a person who knows freedom can give such advice. Thereupon, Herodotus continues with his story:

> Thence having come to Susa and into the king's presence, when the guards commanded and would have compelled them to fall down and do obeisance to the king, they said they would never do that, not even if they were thrust down headlong; for it was not their custom (said they) to do obeisance to mortal men, nor was that the purpose of their coming.[12]

A corresponding argument can also be taken over from one of Plutarch's writings. Themistocles will only be allowed an audience with the king if he keeps to certain "rules of the game." Against this background, the chiliarch Artabanos directs the following words to Themistocles:

> O Stranger, men's customs differ; different people honour different practices; but all honour the exaltation and maintenance of their own peculiar ways. Now you Hellenes are said to admire liberty and equality above all things; but in our eyes, among many fair customs, this is the fairest of all, to honour the King, and to pay obeisance to him as the image of that god who is the preserver of all things. If, then, thou approvest our practice and wilt pay obeisance, it is in thy power to behold and address the King; but if thou art otherwise minded, it will be needful for thee to employ messengers to him in thy stead, for it is not a custom of this country that the King give ear to a man who has not paid him obeisance (Themistocles § 27).[13]

What is particularly noteworthy in this excerpt is the characterization of the king as the "image of [...] god." What becomes clear from this is that according to the Greek understanding, prostrating had theological overtones. It was suspected of meaning that the Persian king was claiming divinity for himself. As G. Ahn has shown, such a conception of royal ideology cannot be gleaned from the Persian sources themselves. Rather, these pieces of evidence show a clear distance between divinity and the king; nevertheless, at the same time, the king's superior position among other people is emphasized by his closer interaction with the deity than other individuals. The Greek assumption that the Persian king claimed divine status for himself on account of his subjects' proskynesis seems to have arisen as a result of an intercultural misunderstanding.[14]

The Callisthenes incident in the Alexander tradition makes clear the potential for conflict this gesture had in the context of Persian-Greek cultural contact. Plutarch hands down a relatively short reference to this episode in his *Life of Alexander* 54, in which he references a report by Chares of Mytilene. He reports that, after drinking from a bowl, Alexander had passed it to one of the friends at a banquet in spring of the year 327 BCE in Baktra. This friend took it, got up, went to the altar, took a drink, fell down, and then kissed

---

12. Herodotus, *Histories* 3.439, (Godley LCL). This usage is also quite clearly expressed in Herodotus's *Hist.* 3.86, when they narrate that Darius's lordship is recognized by the obeisance of his entourage.
13. Plutarch, Lives 2.73 (Perrin, LCL).
14. On this, see Ahn's explanations in *Herrscherlegitimation*, 180–227.

Alexander and reclined again. Now, after all the others had done the same thing in turn, Callisthenes took the bowl, and—while the king was engrossed in a conversation with some others—took a drink and immediately approached Alexander in order to kiss him. But when a certain Demetrius called out that Callisthenes ought not kiss Alexander because he had been the only one not to prostrate before him, Alexander allegedly avoided the kiss.[15]

The reason for Callisthenes's refusal to pay homage and obeisance to Alexander is not explained in the text. H. U. Wiemer suggests that the prostration before the king was an act of homage that Callisthenes refused because it seemed to him to be humiliating.[16] By contrast, Arrian's portrayal of the events points to the religious implications of the incident. According to Arrian (*Anab.* 4.10–12) the Greek Sophist Anaxarchus declared himself in favor of revering Alexander as God. At first this speech was taken up positively and people wanted to begin prostrating before him. But the Macedonians were angered by the speech and Callisthenes spoke against this custom. According to Arrian, Callisthenes argued that falling down was owed only to gods; only barbarians and not Greeks showed people this type of reverence:

> Anaxarchus, I declare Alexander unworthy of no honour appropriate for a man; but men have used numerous ways of distinguishing all the honours which are appropriate for men and for gods; thus we build temples and erect images and set aside precincts for gods, and we offer them sacrifices and libations and compose hymns to them, while eulogies are for men; but the most important distinction concerns the matter of obeisance. At greeting men receive a kiss, but what is divine, I suppose because it is seated above us and we are forbidden even to touch it, is for that very reason honoured by obeisance; dances, too, are held for the gods, and paeans sung in their praise. In this distinction there is nothing surprising, since among the gods themselves all are not honoured in the same way; and what is more, there are different honours for the heroes, distinct again from those paid to gods. It is not, therefore, proper to confuse all this, by raising mortals to extravagant proportions by excesses of honour, while bringing gods, as far as men can, down to a demeaning and unfitting level by honouring them in the same way as men. (Anab., 1.357, [Brunt and Robson, LCL])

Callisthenes issues an urgent warning against mixing customs intended, on the one hand, for God with customs meant, on the other hand, for heroes, because the gods would rage against all those who appropriated divine honors. Alexander, he says, should remind himself that even when he is overseas he should think about Greece and Greek customs. On his return to Greece, Callisthenes suggests, he would certainly not be able to force Greeks, as the most freedom loving of all people, to prostrate. After this fiery speech Alexander—according to our historian—apparently distanced himself from the attempt to let the Macedonians also bow before him. Only some of the Persians continued to prostrate. Callisthenes, who so vehemently opposed Alexander's wish that people fall down before him, soon had to pay for this courage with his life. After the banquet in Baktra, a conspiracy against the king was discovered. Because Callisthenes was closely connected with Hermolaus, the lead conspirator, he was alleged to have been involved in the plot so that Alexander had a good excuse to get rid of him.[17]

---

15. Quoted following H.-U. Wiemer, *Alexander der Große* (München: Beck, 2005), 138.

16. Wiemer, *Alexander*, 138.

17. On this, see Wiemer, *Alexander*, 138–40; cf. also the version of this story in Curtius Rufus 8.5. There, Kallisthenes argues that God should only allow himself to be honored as God after his death.

In any case, what becomes clear from this is that the Greek texts unanimously prove that prostrating could have had great significance in Persian courtly ceremonies. The custom was alien to the Greeks to the extent that it seemed to them to be the expression of the deepest despotism, which was deeply antithetical to their own freedom-loving way of life. In addition, the sources show that for them, falling down also had a religious connotation, since it was actually reserved for divinity alone. Against this backdrop the thought could conceivably arise on the part of the Greeks that the Persian king was being honored as God—a thought that, however, is not substantiated in any of our sources as being common among the Persians.

This tradition-historical background has multiple implications for the tradition of the book of Esther. What becomes clear in any case is that the narrator of the book of Esther understood the prostration before Haman in the Greek sense, as an expression of religious deference. In an intercultural and interreligious context, however, the motif has two immediate implications. On the one hand, this is a rejection of the Persian custom of proskynesis or doing obeisance before the king (even if on the basis of an intercultural misunderstanding). On the other hand, however, the prominence of the theme in the context of the reign of Alexander the Great certainly makes it probable that this moment in the narrative about Esther can be understood as a response to the tale of the proskynesis denied to Alexander the Great, and thus obviously assumes Greek supremacy.[18]

What is less interesting here is whether or not the event with Alexander really happened this way; it is far more important that already in Alexander's time there were traditions in circulation that addressed this leader's claim to be divine. Surely an important factor in the development of this tradition was Alexander's visit to the Siwa oasis, where he questioned the Oracle of Amun-Re that was identified with the god Zeus. On the basis of Egyptian conceptions, because of his visit to Siwa, the ruler was considered to be the son of the most high god. The fact that this conception was also adopted for Alexander can be seen in the numerous images on coins that depict the Macedonians as having bulls' horns, that is, the symbol that characterized Zeus-Ammon.[19] Thus, Mordecai's refusal to do obeisance also implies a rejection of the Hellenistic ruler cult.

A further aspect of the conflict over kingly rule is expressed in Haman's complaint before the king in Esth 3:8. Mordecai's refusal to do obeisance has so filled Haman with rage that he now wants to annihilate the entire Jewish people. The term *dat*, which already appears at the beginning of the narrative (1:8, 13), is used frequently in the discourse about Persian imperial ideology. The harmony between all the peoples of the provinces and the king's *dat*, which was made so visible in the first chapter of the book through the banquet context,

---

18. For another discussion in this volume of biblical texts that might interact with this tale, see the contribution by D. V. Edelman, "Remembering Samson in a Hellenized Jewish Context (Judges 13–16)."

19. The literature on this subject is immense; in this context I can point only to a small selection of it. See, *inter alia*, Chr. Habicht, *Gottmenschentum und griechische Städte*, 2nd ed., Zetemata 14 (München: Beck, 1970); H.-J. Klauck, *Die religiöse Umwelt des Urchristentums, II: Herrscher- und Kaiserkult, Philosophie, Gnosis*, Kohlhammer Studienbücher Theologie 9 (Stuttgart: Kohlhammer, 1996), 17–44; H. H. Schmitt, "Herrscherkult," *Kleines Lexikon des Hellenismus*, 2nd ed., ed. H. H. Schmitt and E. Vogt (Harrassowitz: Wiesbaden, 1993), 243–53; W. C. Schneider, "Herrscherverehrung und Kaiserkult," in *Neues Testament und Antike Kultur, III*, ed. K. Erlemann *et al.* (Neukirchen-Vluyn: Neukirchener Verlag, 2005), 210–17 (212–15); F. W. Walbank, "Könige als Götter: Überlegung zum Herrscherkult von Alexander bis Augustus," *Chiron* 17 (1987): 364–82, esp. 376–77; D. Zeller, *Menschwerdung Gottes—Vergöttlichung von Menschen*, Novum Testamentum et Orbis Antiquus 7 (Freiburg: Universitäts-Verlag, 1995), 166–70.

is now disrupted by the alleged disobedience of the Jewish people toward the royal law. Haman's complaint in Esth 3:8 accuses the Jewish people of separatism, which is based on the fact that they have their own *dat* and therefore refused to submit to the king's *dat*. If one were to consider this accusation in more general terms, Haman's declaration could be said to postulate a differentiation between the universal law of the realm and the particular law of a subject people, although here one can assume that the Torah is being referenced in the mention of the *dat* of the Jewish people.

The differentiation between the particular *dat* of the people of Israel and the universal law of the king mentioned in the book of Esther draws our attention to the problem inherent in the ideology of Persian kingship: the possibility that the particular law of a people becomes incongruent with the universal law of the Persian king, making a conflict almost unavoidable.[20] Thus, in the present context of the narrative, the refusal to do obeisance becomes a precedent *par excellence* by which the difference between the royal *dat* and the laws of Judaism is expressed.

The conflict is resolved by the annihilation of Haman and other Jewish enemies, after which the Jewish people are once again assimilated into the imperial structure. We see this aspect when Mordecai receives permission from the king to articulate the counter-edict and also is entrusted with the power of the royal seal (Esth 8:8–12). This aspect is then boldly underlined at the end of the narrative, when Mordecai's deeds are considered to be so significant that they are recorded in the "annals of the kings of Media and Persia." In addition, he gains the position of next-in-rank to the king, and in so doing, becomes a powerful leader (Esth 10:2–3). The ending of the narrative, with its reference to political notions, makes quite clear that the option of an independent state and a definitive overcoming of foreign rule is not at all the goal of the story. Only the lives of Haman and his family, who were intimately connected to this specific conflict, are extinguished; there is no second-guessing of the Persian king's authority. The recording of the name of Mordecai together with that of the king in the annals shows quite clearly that Mordecai is now integrated into the realm of power and the state's apparatus.

Thus, although the conclusion shows that an Israelite or a Jew who is far from the land of Israel can succeed in attaining a high position at a foreign royal court;[21] in the context of the Esther narrative, another aspect comes into play. The tension between the Persian kingdom and the Jewish people, as Haman formulates it in Esth 3:8 and as he reminds us in the context of the life-threatening edict of annihilation against the Jewish people, here finds its definitive resolution.

The notion of a distinction between the law of the realm and the specific law in the book of Esther differs fundamentally from the problematic depicted in the book of the Maccabees (cf. 1 Macc 1:41–64, esp. v. 49), in that what is sought in the books of the Maccabees is a loosening from foreign rule. Such a liberation of the Jews from foreign rule is beyond the imaginative scope of the book of Esther. Instead, after weathering the crisis, the Jews become harmoniously integrated into the Persian multinational state. Thus, in the final analysis, what is being confirmed in the book of Esther is the notion of the Persian kings' world rule.

---

20. Such a possibility is quite alien to Chronicles. On this matter, see Willi's instructive examination in "Weltreichsgedanke," 408.

21. Most fundamentally on this see, A. Meinhold, "Die Gattung der Josephsgeschichte und des Estherbuches: Diasporanovelle II," *ZAW* 88 (1976): 72–93.

3. Illuminating the Historico-Theological Dimension of the Narrative

Although it becomes clear that the Esther narrative examines Persian and Hellenistic concepts of leadership, it is much more difficult to figure out its theological dimensions. As is well known, the Esther narrative nowhere makes the theological side of the story explicit. In fact, it is numerous, intertextual connections that implicitly illuminate the theological dimensions of the events. Besides the refusal to do obeisance (Esth 3:2), whose importance has already been indicated above, one can also identify the motif of fasting (Esth 4:3, 16), Mordecai's call to Esther to intercede (Esth 4:14), and Seresh's claim of the unconquerability of the Jewish people (Esth 6:13). References to holy war motifs, which are clearly grasped by the end of the narrative, are of special significance.[22] The notion of horror that disables the enemy to such an extent that they cannot stop their attackers is the central motif. As in the case of the narrative about Rahab in Josh 2, news of the overwhelming force of the Israelites can so impress their enemies that they are prepared to support them. A further motif from this imaginative field is the calm that God brings about, according to the traditional versions. And yet the notion of calm points not only to holy war tradition but also—thus, inter alia, Isa 32:18—to salvation prophecies and thus has eschatological connotations. In this context, statements such as Esth 8:16, "For the Jews there was light and gladness (שמחה), joy (ששן) and honor," are also interesting. The combination of שמחה and ששן here reminds one of prophetic proofs found in salvation prophecies, such as Isa 51:11, although here the reference to Jerusalem is quite obvious. Behind the much discussed phrase in Esth 8:17, according to which the peoples of the world converted to Judaism or professed to be Jews (ורבים מעמי הארץ מתיהדים—an exact translation of the hapax legomenon is difficult), a religious motif like the pilgrimage to Zion could be concealed.[23] Through such subtle intertextual references to salvation prophecies, the traditions of holy war achieve an almost eschatological patina that places the historical events in a wider context, to the extent that Israel's future redemption is illuminated through victory over the enemies of Israel.

Finally, in addition to the *reversal structure*, which is so significant for the structure of the story, another important pivot on which events have 'turned' (הפך *niphal* – Esth 9:2), the *Spiegelprinzip*, points to the narrative's implicit theological meaning. By using this device, the narrator indicates that the interior happening is determined by a functional, cause-and-effect connection that, in the final analysis, is grounded in God's actions. The literary references to the more ancient biblical traditions show the continuity of divine action in history, making it apparent that, even in the Diaspora and even when under imperial rule, Israel nonetheless remains under God's protection.

Although it is difficult to nail down the content of intertextual references, nonetheless, the cumulative force of such references that might have theological implications raises the

---

22. Bardtke, *Esther*, 384; Gerleman, *Esther*, 132; Levenson, *Esther*, 271; Loader, "Ester," 271–72; A. M. Wetter, "Judging by Her: Reconfiguring Israel in Ruth, Esther, and Judith" (Unpublished PhD thesis, Utrecht University, 2014), 133–37, point to the link to the YHWH war. This perception of the YHWH-war in the biblical tradition is, in the first instance, connected with the narratives about the early days of Israel and the occupation of the land; in more recent traditions, such as in Chronicles or in both the Books of Maccabees, it enjoys a sort of revival.

23. On the connections between the text of the Hebrew book of Esther and the documentation from the prophetic tradition, see also B. Ego, "Die biblische Prophetie und das Esterbuch," in *Die unwiderstehliche Wahrheit: Studien zur alttestamentlichen Prophetie Festschrift A. Meinhold*, ed. R. Lux and E.-J. Waschke (Leipzig: Evangelische Verlagsanstalt, 2006), 513–30.

possibility that we should be assuming a theological point of departure. Against the background of contemporary literature of ancient Judaism and of the reception of the Esther and material in ancient sources like the Septuagint or the Targum, a theological implication of the narrative finally comes into focus. Even the Daniel legends and the books of the Maccabees can be enlisted as evidence for euphemistic speeches of God; already in the Septuagint, one can see plainly a process of the theologization of material that is then continued in the Rabbinic literature and in the Targum. Since it is unlikely that the fundamental intention of the Esther tradition is completely isolated in the literary tradition of ancient Judaism, and because it is unlikely that later exegesis brought an entirely new understanding to the narrative, one can assume it is probable that the Esther narrative could be pointing to the hidden action of God, who comes to the aid of his threatened people.[24] The fact that God's help and support is nowhere made explicit[25] can—apart from tradition-critical references—be interpreted through a reception orientation that suggests this narrative style awakens theological associations and encourages the reader to make his or her own theological interpretation of the story.[26]

4. Reflections on Dating the Book of Esther

Against this background, we have to ask about a historical reference point for this tradition. One can first establish that the Esther narrative, even if it appears in the guise of history, actually presents a fictional story. Therefore, one cannot *a priori* assume that this story sets down the memory of an actual, concrete instance of the persecution of and threat to the Jewish people. The persecution motif is rather to be understood as a literary topos, which, as such, can reach far beyond the factual and, at the same time, can "seismographically" articulate and narratively depict possible future problems.

If, with these methodological premises in mind, one searches for a plausible framework for the origin of this narrative, the answer appears from various different angles. Based on the numerous Persian words that appear in the text, the original location of the material is certainly plausible in the Eastern Diaspora.[27] Despite the supposed tolerance of the Per-

---

24. Besides individual commentaries, here I want to point to the following contributions: J. R. Kriel, "Esther: The Story of a Girl or the Story of Her God?," *Theologia Evangelica* 19 (1986): 2–14; J. A. Loader, "Esther as a Novel with Different Levels of Meaning," *ZAW* 90 (1978): 417–21; F. C. Rossow, "Literary Artistry in the Book of Esther and its Theological Significance," *Concordia Journal* 13 (1987): 220–28; H. M. Wahl, "'Glaube ohne Gott?': Zur Rede vom Gott Israels im hebräischen Buch Esther," *Biblische Zeitschrift* 45 (2001): 37–53. By contrast, see M. V. Fox, "The Religion of the Book of Esther," *Judaism* 39 (1990): 135–47 (146), who tries to see the hiddenness of God in the book of Esther as a sign that the author of the book wants to express his lack of confidence about God's role in the event.

25. The fact that the book of Esther draws to such a great extent upon the stylistic device of the hidden speech of God cannot be definitively explained in the final analysis. No doubt it corresponds to the general trend of the times, but as a stylistic device it also could be connected to the fact that the action takes place in the Diaspora. In this way, the narrator points to God's hidden action and shows that God also wants to allow his people to be divinely blessed outside of its own borders and far away from the Temple.

26. Cf. Wetter, *Judging*, 138–39; P. Nagel, "LXX Esther: 'More' God 'less' Theology," *Journal for Semitics* 17 (2008): 129–55 (150).

27. On this, compare Esth 9:19, where the narrator identifies his location. The terms פרוזים or פרוזות are often conveyed using the Talmudic understanding of the term: 'inhabitants of an unwalled settlement' or 'an unwalled settlement'. (For a similar interpretation see, among others, Fox, 113; Moore, 85). As Bush makes clear in *Esther*, 477, this corresponds more closely to a later understanding of the term.

sian rulers, there were events that hint at direct and in part even violent limitations on the autonomous exercise of religion.[28] In this regard, see Xerxes I's destruction of the Marduk sanctuary of Esangila in Babylon; in the so-called Daiva inscription, he says he destroyed the cities of the Daivas according to the will of Ahura Mazda and prohibited their continued worship (XPh 4–6).[29]

With reference to the Jewish people, the motif of threat is already sounded concretely in the context of the Daniel legends, for example, in Dan 6. In this tradition, which can be dated to the Persian era, it is individuals who must fear for their lives because of their faithfulness to the Torah.[30] The conflict over the temple of Elephantine, which was the first well-known event in Jewish history that can be understood as an outbreak of anti-Jewish sentiment, also falls into this period of Persian rule.[31] In the year 410 BCE, in the time of the rule of Darius II (424–405 BCE), the already hundred-year-long peaceful co-existence of Egyptians and Jews came to end when the Egyptians destroyed the Jewish Temple on the island in the Nile. As P. Schäfer has shown, this was a case both of a political and a religious conflict, in which Egyptian nationalism played a significant role. One took advantage of the absence of the Persian satraps, but in so doing, the Persian military governor supported the Egyptian Chnum priests. Granted, the administration of the Persian Empire, which was represented by the satrap Arsames, strongly supported the Jewish minority, punished the local governor, and permitted the reconstruction of the temple, albeit with a restriction on the offering of animal sacrifices.[32] Josephus (*Ant.* 9.297–310) also reports on the actions of the satrap Bagohi/Bagoas against the temple and the priesthood of Jerusalem between 404 and 398 BCE.[33]

A further important piece of evidence that reports rather concretely the mishandling of Jews loyal to the Law at the time of Alexander the Great can be found in Josephus's writing,

---

Even its translation as city Jews and country Jews (thus Bardtke, *Esther*) is unsatisfying, as this likewise does not fit the context. H. M. Niemann's explanations in "Das Ende des Volkes der Perizziter," *ZAW* 105 (1993): 233–57 are discursive; according to him, the root פזר implies the contrast between "here" and "there" or "inside" and "outside." Hence, the phrase היהודים הפרוזים refers to the Jews who live outside the region that falls within the jurisdiction of the town of Susa, whereas the phrase ערי הפרזות refers to those cities that are outside of the region. Thus, the same contrast that is expressed in vv. 16–18 with the "Jews, who were in Susa" (v.18) and the "remaining Jews, who were in the King's provinces" (v.16) is implied here.

28. R. G. Kratz, *Translatio imperii: Untersuchungen zu den aramäischen Danielerzählungen und ihrem theologiegeschichtlichen Umfeld*, WMANT 63 (Neukirchen-Vluyn: Neukirchener Verlag, 1991) reached similar conclusions with regard to the background of Dan 3 and Dan 6.

29. On this matter, see M. A. Dandamaev and V. G. Lukonin, *The Culture and Social Institutions of Ancient Iran*, trans. P. L. Kohl (Cambridge: Cambridge University Press, 1989), 352–53, for an expansive paper on the possible contextualizations of this inscription, in which Dandamaev, referencing E. Herzfeld, argues the case that this is about sanctuaries of local tribes or deities. On the Daiva inscription, see also Kratz, *Translatio*, 141. On Persian Realpolitik as a whole, see Dandamaev and Lukonin, *Culture*, 347–60.

30. On this matter, see I. Will-Plein, "Daniel 6 und die persische Diaspora," *Judaica* 47 (1991): 12–21.

31. P. Schäfer, *Judeophobia: Attitudes toward the Jews in the Ancient World* (Cambridge, MA: Harvard University Press, 1997), 177.

32. For more, see Schäfer, *Judeophobia*, 177–97; Kratz, *Translatio*, 141; W. D. Davies and L. Finkelstein, eds., *Cambridge History of Judaism I: Introduction; The Persian Period* (Cambridge: Cambridge University Press, 1984), 388–89.

33. Achenbach, "Vertilgen," 285.

Contra Apionem:

> 190 In another passage Hecataeus mentions our regard for our laws, and how we deliberately choose and hold it a point of honour to endure anything rather than transgress them. 191 "And so (he says), neither the slander of their neighbours and of foreign visitors, to which as a nation they are exposed, nor the frequent outrages of Persian kings and satraps can shake their determination; for these laws, naked and defenseless, they face tortures and death in its most terrible form, rather than repudaite the faith of their forefathers." 192 Of this obstinacy in defense of their laws he furnishes several instances. He tells how on the occasion Alexander, when he was in Babylon and had undertaken to restore the ruined temple of Bel, gave orders to all his soldiers, without distinction, to bring materials for the earth works; and how the Jews alone refused to obey, and even submitted to serve chastisement and heavy fines, until the king pardoned them and exempted them from this task. 193 Again, when temples and altars were errected in the county by its invaders, the Jews razed them all to the ground, paying in some cases a fine to the satraps, and in others obtaining pardon. (*C. Ap.* l.190–193 [Thackeray LCL])[34]

These individual pieces of evidence could also suggest that such a scenario was conceivable even for the Jews in the Persian Diaspora, and that, even if it was temporally and geographically limited, certain conflicts with the ideology of the Persian Empire could at least have been possible.

A further important clue for the dating of this narrative arises from the motif of the denied prostration. If one assumes that the original Esther narrative already contained this element and that this was a response to the reign of Alexander the Great, then dating the material to the early Hellenistic era seems plausible. Such a dating of the material, however, does not speak against the assumption that what we find in the Esther narrative is a conflict with the ideology of Persian imperialism. Rather, one must remember that a dichotomy between a Persian and a Greek origin for the material establishes a false duality. In towns like Susa, in which the influence of Hellenism is clearly evident, the Persian culture and imagination continued even after the advent of Hellenistic rule, and so Susa is practically an ideal place for a Persian-Greek cultural symbiosis.[35] In addition, in the Persian region one must reckon with a high degree of conservatism as regards how they handled their

---

34. I heartily thank my colleague Prof. Dr. A. Lange of the University of Vienna for this reference. On this, see also B. Schröder, *Die "väterlichen Gesetze": Flavius Josephus als Vermittler von Halachah an Griechen und Römer*, TSAJ 53 (Tübingen: Mohr Siebeck, 1996), 196 n. 99, who prefers to date this section to the time of Alexander the Great; see also, M. Stern, *Greek and Latin Authors on Jews and Judaism I: From Herodotus to Plutarch* (Jerusalem: Israel Academy of Sciences and Humanities, 1974), 35–44, who likewise does not preclude dating this tradition to the time of Alexander.

35. On this, see S. Hansen, A. Wieczorek, and M. Tellenbach, eds., Alexander der Grosse und die Öffnung der Welt: Asiens Kulturen im Wandel; Begleitband zur Sonderausstellung "Alexander der Große und die Öffnung der Welt – Asiens Kulturen im Wandel" in *den Reiss-Engelhorn Museen Mannheim*, Publikation der Reiss-Engelhorn-Museen 36 (Regensburg: Schell & Steiner, 2009). Alexander the Great stationed a garrison in Susa; under Antiochus III the Greek presence there intensified at the end of the third century BCE. The town became a Greek polis, which bore the name Seleukia on the Eulaios; for further information, see L. Martinez-Sève, "La ville de Suse à l'époque Hellénistique," *RAr* 33 (2002): 31–54 (31–32). For archaeological evidence for Persian-Hellenistic cultural contact, see M. A. R. Colledge, "Greek and non-Greek interactions in the art and architecture of the Hellenistic east," in *Hellenism in the East: The interaction of Greek and non-Greek Civilizations from Syria to Central Asia after Alexander*, ed. A. Kuhrt and S. Sherwin-White (London: Duckworth, 1987), 134–62.

own traditions about Persian royal ideology.³⁶ Thus, it also is conceivable that there was an educated author who had knowledge both of the authoritative Jewish traditions of his time and also of the Persian milieu and of Greek culture. The problem of a possible differentiation in the Persian ideology of kingship between Israel's particular law and the general law of the Empire in no way lost its relevance after the onset of Hellenistic rule; rather, Alexander's campaign exerted entirely new pressures on it, since now the balance between actual history and Israel's theological self-understanding had to be formulated anew.³⁷ Over the course of history, the significance of the material and its relevance became more and more clear, particularly when, in the third century BCE, anti-Semitic voices and then in the middle of the second century BCE religious persecution under Antiochus IV, made the particularity of Judaism and its threatened existence among the people of the world painfully obvious. Against this backdrop, it is also not surprising that the narrative became topical in the time of the Hasmoneans. One can assume that individual "Mordecai passages" like Esth 8:15 or Esth 9:3b–4 were first introduced to the text in the Hasmonean era. The statements in Esth 8:17 and Esth 9:27 that mention proselytism also belong to this era. Furthermore, one should mention at this point the concluding writings about Purim, which fit superbly well with the Hasmoneans' politics around feast days, which they wanted to inscribe into the collective consciousness of the people through the military might of the Jewish people.³⁸

5. The Function of the Esther Narrative in the Context of the Festival of Purim

On balance, we can conclude from this background that the festival of Purim, with its reading aloud of the Esther narrative, can be understood as an attempt to undertake a kind of mental positioning through the remembrance of this tradition in order to counter real or potential enemy threats. On the one hand, the Esther narrative aims to convey courage for behavior that is loyal both to its own tradition and to its political and social environs. On the other hand, the narrative creates a counterbalance to the threat and persecution of the Jewish people. If, in the end, the conflict between Mordecai and Haman is put into a complex salvation history framework through recourse to the Amalek tradition and the joy of the Jews at being allowed to resist is conveyed through complaints against traditions from the salvation story, then one can also understand the festival as an anticipation of future expectations of salvation. In this way, the Festival of Purim functions as a medium of collective consciousness, with whose help appropriate Jewish behavior in the encounter with different leadership concepts is demonstrated and the memory of overcoming the crisis and of being saved is made topical for all time and is newly inscribed in the consciousness.

6. Conclusion

In conclusion, we can establish that the Hebrew book of Esther tackles the ideology of Persian imperialism as well as the Hellenistic worship of rulers, and that in this context it

---

36. Cf. S. Sherwin-White and A. Kuhrt, *From Samarkand to Sardis: A New Approach to the Seleucid Empire* (Berkeley: University of California Press, 1993), 76.
37. On this, see also Kratz, *Translatio*, 284–85.
38. On this, see J. C. H. Lebram, "Purimfest und Estherbuch," in *Studies in the Book of Esther: Selected with a Prolegomenon* (New York: Ktav, 1982), 205–29 (228) along with the plausible explanations of J.-D. Macchi, "Instituting Through Writing: The Letters of Mordecai in Esther 9:20-28," in *Writing the Bible: Scribes, Scribalism and Script*, ed. P. R. Davies and T. Römer, Bible World (Durham: Acumen, 2013), 97–107 (104–5).

surveys the possibilities and limits of Israel's existence in the middle of the global population and under the reign of foreign peoples. It becomes clear that while Israel can come to terms with the leadership concept of a human king, because of its commandments and customs through which it differentiates itself from other people, it will always be in tension with its surroundings. The precedent par excellence in which this difference is supposed to be expressed is the concept of divine kingship, which Alexander the Great and various representatives of the Diadochi from the house of the Seleucids and Ptolemies would represent. By means of countless intertextual references and the reversal structure, the author of the book of Esther clarifies that even in the Diaspora, it is none other than the God of Israel who is behind all events and who holds the individual threads of events in his hands. When the narrator makes the so-called Spiegelprinzip an integral part of his story, he is clearly expressing his conviction that events are determined by a strong connection of cause-and-effect, a connection that, in the final analysis, is based on God's actions. The literary references to earlier biblical traditions show the continuity of God's action in history, a continuity that remains true in the Diaspora. In its totality, the Esther narrative can therefore be described as a narrative in which, in subtle ways, a conflict occurs between the Jewish people as both the people of the Torah and the people of the one God and a universal ideology of empire, a conflict that is heightened through the literary trope of the divinization of the ruler.

Bibliography

Achenbach, R. 2009. "Vertilgen – Töten – Vernichten (Est 3,13): Die Genozid-Thematik im Esterbuch." *ZABR* 15: 282–315.

Ahn, G. 1992. *Religiöse Herrscherlegitimation im achämenidischen Iran: Die Voraussetzungen und die Struktur ihrer Argumentation*. Acta Iranica 3 and Textes et mémoires 17. Leiden: Brill.

Arrian. 1976. Translated by P. A. Brunt and E. I. Robson. 2 vols. LCL. London: Heinemann.

Bardtke, H. 1963. *Das Buch Esther*. KAT 17/4–5. Gütersloh: Gerd Mohn.

Berg, S. B. 1979. *The Book of Esther: Motifs, Themes and Structure*. SBLDS 44. Missoula, MT: Scholars Press.

Berlin, A. 2001. *Esther: The Traditional Hebrew Text with the JPS Translation*. JPS Bible Commentary. Philadelphia: Jewish Publication Society of America.

Bickerman, E. J. 1967. "Esther." In *Four Strange Books of the Bible: Jonah, Daniel, Koheleth, Esther*, edited by E. J. Bickerman, 171–240. New York: Schocken Books, .

Briant, P. 2002. *From Cyrus to Alexander: A History of the Persian Empire*. Translated by P. D. Daniels. Winona Lake, IN: Eisenbrauns.

Bush, F. W. 1996. *Ruth, Esther*. WBC 9. Dallas: Word.

Clines, D. J. A. 1984. *The Esther Scroll: The Story of the Story*. JSOTSup 30. Sheffield: JSOT Press.

Colledge, M. A. R. 1987. "Greek and non-Greek Interactions in the Art and Architecture of the Hellenistic East." In *Hellenism in the East: The Interaction of Greek and non-Greek civilizations from Syria to Central Asia after Alexander,* edited by A. Kuhrt and S. Sherwin-White, 134–62. London: Duckworth.

Dandamaev, M. A. and V. G. Lukonin. 1989. *The Culture and Social Institutions of Ancient Iran*. Translated by P. L. Kohl. Cambridge: Cambridge University Press.

Davies, W. D. and L. Finkelstein, eds. 1984. *The Cambridge History of Judaism I: Introduction; The Persian Period*. Cambridge: Cambridge University Press.

Dommershausen, W. 1968. *Die Estherrolle: Stil und Ziel einer alttestamentlichen Schrift*. Stuttgarter biblische Monographien 6. Stuttgart: Katholisches Bibelwerk.

Ego, B. 2006. "Die biblische Prophetie und das Esterbuch." In *Die unwiderstehliche Wahrheit: Studien zur alttestamentlichen Prophetie Festschrift A. Meinhold,* edited by R. Lux and E.-J. Waschke, 513–30. Leipzig: Evangelische Verlagsanstalt.

———. 1996. *Targum Scheni zu Ester: Übersetzung, Kommentar und theologische Deutung.* TSAJ 54. Tübingen: Mohr Siebeck.

Fox, M. V. 2001. *Character and Ideology in the Book of Esther.* 2nd ed. Studies on the personalities of the Old Testament. Grand Rapids, MI: Eerdmans.

———. 1990. "The Religion of the Book of Esther." *Judaism* 39: 135–47.

Gerleman, G. 1982. *Esther.* 2nd ed. Biblischer Kommentar, Altes Testament 21. Neukirchen-Vluyn: Neukirchener Verlag.

Habicht, C. 1970. *Gottmenschentum und griechische Städte.* 2nd ed. Zetemata 14. München: Beck.

Hansen, S., A. Wieczorek, and M. Tellenbach, eds. 2009. *Alexander der Große und die Öffnung der Welt: Asiens Kulturen im Wandel; Begleitband zur Sonderausstellung "Alexander der Große und die Öffnung der Welt – Asiens Kulturen im Wandel" in den Reiss-Engelhorn Museen Mannheim.* Publikationen der Reiss-Engelhorn-Museen 36. Regensburg: Schell & Steiner.

Herodotus. 1975. Translated by A. D. Godley. 4 vols. LCL. London: Heinemann.

Josephus I: The Life, Against Apion. 1961. Translated by H. St. J. Thackeray. LCL. London: Heinemann.

Klauck, H.-J. 1996. *Die religiöse Umwelt des Urchristentums, II: Herrscher- und Kaiserkult, Philosophie, Gnosis.* Kohlhammer Studienbücher Theologie 9. Stuttgart: W. Kohlhammer.

Koch, H. 1986. "Die achämenidische Poststrasse von Persepolis nach Susa." *Archaeologische Mitteilungen aus Iran* 19: 133–47.

Kratz, R. G. 1991. *Translatio imperii: Untersuchungen zu den aramäischen Danielerzählungen und ihrem theologiegeschichtlichen Umfeld.* WMANT 63. Neukirchen-Vluyn: Neukirchener Verlag.

Kriel, J. R. 1986. "Esther: The Story of a Girl or the Story of Her God?" *Theologia Evangelica* 19: 2–14.

LaCocque, A. 1987. "Haman in the book of Esther." *Hebrew Annual Review* 11: 207–22.

Lebram, J. C. H. 1982. "Purimfest und Estherbuch." In *Studies in the Book of Esther: Selected with a Prolegomenon,* edited by C. A. Moore, 205–19. New York: Ktav.

Levenson, J. D. 1997. *Esther: A Commentary.* OTL. Louisville, KY: Westminster John Knox.

Loader, J. A. 1992. "Das Buch Ester." In *Das Hohelied, Klagelieder, Das Buch Ester,* edited by H.-P. Müller, O. Kaiser, and J. A. Loader, 199–280. Translated by Ilse v. Loewenclau. ATD 16/2. Göttingen: Vandenhoeck & Ruprecht.

———. 1978. "Esther as a Novel with Different Levels of Meaning." *ZAW* 90: 417–21.

Macchi, J.-D. 2013. "Instituting through writing: The letters of Mordecai in Esther 9:20–28." In *Writing the Bible: Scribes, Scribalism and Script,* edited by P. R. Davies and T. Römer, 97–107. Bible World. Durham: Acumen.

Martinez-Sève, L. 2002. "La ville de Suse à l'époque Hellénistique." *RAr* 33: 31–54.

Meinhold, A. 1983. *Das Buch Esther.* ZBK 13. Zürich: Theologischer Verlag Zürich.

———. 1982. "Die Gattung der Josephsgeschichte und des Estherbuches: Diasporanovelle II." In *Studies in the Book of Esther: Selected with a Prolegomenon,* edited by Carey A. Moore, 284–305. New York: Ktav. Previously published in *ZAW* 88 (1976): 72–93.

Moore, C. A. 1971. *Esther: Introduction, Translation and Notes.* AB 7B. Garden City, NY: Doubleday.

Nagel, P. 2008. "LXX Esther: 'More' God 'less' Theology." *Journal for Semitics* 17: 129–55.

Niemann, H. M. 1993. "Das Ende des Volkes der Perizziter." *ZAW* 105: 233–57.

Paton, L. B. 1964. *A Critical and Exegetical Commentary on the Book of Esther*. ICC. Repr., 1908, Edinburgh: T&T Clark.

Plutarch's *Lives*. 1968. Translated by B. Perrin. 11 vols. LCL. London: Heinemann.

Rossow, F. C. 1987. "Literary Artistry in the Book of Esther and its Theological Significance." *Concordia Journal* 13: 220–28.

Schäfer, P. 1997. *Judeophobia: Attitudes toward the Jews in the Ancient World*. Cambridge, MA: Harvard University Press.

Schneider, W. C. 2005. "Herrscherverehrung und Kaiserkult." In *Neues Testament und Antike Kultur*, III, edited by K. Erlemann, K. L. Noethlichs, K. Scherberich, and J. Zangenberg, 210–17. Neukirchen-Vluyn: Neukirchener Verlag.

Schmitt, A. 1996. *Wende des Lebens: Untersuchungen zu einem Situations-Motiv der Bibel*. BZAW 237. Berlin: de Gruyter.

Schmitt, H. H. 1993. "Herrscherkult." In *Kleines Lexikon des Hellenismus*. 2nd ed., edited by H. H. Schmitt and E. Vogt, 243–53. Wiesbaden: Harrassowitz Verlag.

Schröder, B. 1996. *Die "väterlichen Gesetze": Flavius Josephus als Vermittler von Halachah an Griechen und Römer*. TSAJ 53. Tübingen: Mohr Siebeck.

Sherwin-White, S. and A. Kuhrt. 1993. *From Samarkhand to Sardis: A New Approach to the Seleucid Empire*. Berkeley: University of California Press.

Steinberg, J. 2006. *Die Ketuvim: Ihr Aufbau und ihre Botschaft*. BBB 152. Hamburg: Philo.

Stern, M. 1974. *Greek and Latin Authors on Jews and Judaism I: From Herodotus to Plutarch*. Jerusalem: Israel Academy of Sciences and Humanities.

Wahl, H. M. 2009. *Das Buch Esther: Übersetzung und Kommentar*. Berlin: de Gruyter.

———. 2001. "'Glaube ohne Gott?': Zur Rede vom Gott Israels im hebräischen Buch Esther." *Biblische Zeitschrift* 45: 37–53.

Walbank, F. W. 1987. "Könige als Götter: Überlegung zum Herrscherkult von Alexander bis Augustus." *Chiron* 17: 364–82.

Wetter, A. M. 2014. "Judging By Her: Reconfiguring Israel in Ruth, Esther, and Judith." Unpublished PhD thesis, Utrecht University.

Wiemer, H.-U. 2005. *Alexander der Große*. München: Beck.

Wiesehöfer, J. 2005. *Das antike Persien: Von 550 v. Chr. bis 650 n. Chr*. Düsseldorf: Albatros.

———. 2001. "Prosyknesis." *Der Neue Pauly* 10: 443–44.

Willi, T. 2001. "Der Weltreichsgedanke im Frühjudentum: Israel, Menschheit und Weltherrschaft in den biblischen Chronikbüchern." In *Exegese vor Ort Festschrift P. Welten,* edited by C. Maier, R. Liwak, and K.-P. Jörns, 389–409. Leipzig: Evangelische Verlagsanstalt.

Willi-Plein, I. 1991. "Daniel 6 und die persische Diaspora." *Judaica* 47: 12–21.

Zeller, D. 1988. *Menschwerdung Gottes – Vergöttlichung von Menschen*. Novum Testamentum et Orbis Antiquus 7. Freiburg: Universitäts-Verlag.

Zenger, E. 2004. "Das Buch Ester." In *Einleitung in das Alte Testament,* 5th ed., edited by E. Zenger *et al.*, 302–11. Kohlhammer Studienbücher Theologie 1/1. Stuttgart: Kohlhammer.

— 11 —

Models of Local Political Leadership in the Nehemiah Memoir

Anne Fitzpatrick-McKinley

Leadership Structures in Yehud, Samaria, and Their Environs: The Upper Tier

The biblical traditions about the Persian period have been extensively interrogated to an extent that many would now disregard them as a reliable source for reconstructing anything of a historical Yehud, not least about its leadership. The Nehemiah Memoir, however, has been taken by many scholars to provide a more reliable account, and in this paper I will restrict myself to a discussion of the types of leadership reflected in this text in the period before Nehemiah finally succeeded in restructuring Jerusalem's leadership by his appointment of Hananiah and others (Neh 7:2). The Nehemiah Memoir (hereafter NM) is identified by some as most of Neh 1:1–7:5; 11:1–2; 12:31–43;[1] while other scholars include Neh 1:1–7:5, parts of 12:27–43 and 13:4–31.[2] Whatever it might have originally included, the Memoir is widely regarded as the record of the achievements of Nehemiah in the middle of the fifth century BCE and is taken to reflect something of historical events, with some arguing that the NM is the only historically reliable account of the Persian period.[3]

---

1. For example, J. Blenkinsopp, *Ezra–Nehemiah* (London: SCM, 1988), 46–48.
2. These include L. L. Grabbe, *Ezra–Nehemiah* (London: Routledge, 1998), 154–55. Ackroyd, on the other hand does not include Neh 13:4–31 as part of the original memoir (P. Ackroyd, *The Chronicler in His Age*, JSOTSup 101 [Sheffield: Sheffield Academic, 1991], 28).
3. Such scholars include C. C. Torrey, *Ezra Studies*, ed. with a Prolegomenon by W. F. Stinespring ([1910]; repr., New York: Ktav, 1970). A number of scholars, including U. Kellermann (Nehemia Quellen, Überlieferung und Geschichte, BZAW 102 [Berlin: Töpelmann, 1967], 32–36) and J. Wright (*Rebuilding Identity: The Nehemiah Memoir and its Earliest Readers* [Berlin: de Gruyter, 2004], 323) have assumed that for the most part, Neh 9–13 represents later additional material to the memoir. On the other hand, Blenkinsopp (*Ezra–Nehemiah*, 351–64) and H. G. M. Williamson (*Ezra and Nehemiah*. Old Testament Guides [Sheffield: Society of Old Testament Study, 1987], 382–84) believe that there are parts of Neh 11:1–13:31 that contain material original to the NM. While these chapters have been regarded by most as the work of a historical figure Nehemiah, Torrey regarded only Neh 1–6 as historical (*Ezra Studies*, 238–41), and recently, a number of scholars have built on Torrey's idea of a shorter account. V. Hurowitz, for example, regards the original memoir as a building report analogous to other ancient Near Eastern building reports, comprising only Neh 1–6 and Neh 12 (*He Has Built Me an Exalted House: Temple Building in the Bible in Light of Mesopotamian and Northwest Semitic Writings*, JSOTSup 115

Models of Local Political Leadership in the Nehemiah Memoir

I have argued elsewhere that one way of reading the evidence of the NM leads to the conclusion that Nehemiah may be understood as a leader of a *birta* who was sent to Jerusalem from Susa in order to curtail the power of local elites in the region, including the leaders named in the NM who come from Samaria, Ammon, Ashdod, and Geshem the Arab, whose provenance is not stated in the text.[4] These indigenous rulers (by which I mean native to Syria-Palestine and not just to Yehud) appear to have exercised a strong influence in the region with Sanballat perhaps appearing as the highest ranking of patron-type leaders. Sanballat is nowhere named in the text of the NM as *pehah*, a fact that is not surprising when we take into account the ideological purpose of the Memoir, which is to credit Nehemiah with the re-establishment of Jerusalem while discrediting other leaders in the region who opposed his mission. In spite of the absence of the title *pehah* for Sanballat, it seems likely that he held a position that would have been something equivalent to the position of *pehahs* elsewhere. That Sanballat was *pehah* in Samaria is also made likely by the fact that Samaria had been an important administrative center in the region since Assyrian hegemony was established over Samaria in the eighth century. The Assyrians had first appointed an administrator there as early as the eighth century BCE. A Sanballat is named as governor in the Elephantine papyri (*TAD* A.4.7, 8/ 9) and in the Wadi Daliyeh papyri as well as in Josephus (*Ant.* 11),[5] but it is clear that there were a number of Sanballats, and F. M. Cross distinguishes between a late fifth century Sanballat of the NM and the Elephantine papyri, an early fourth century Sanballat from the Wadi Daliyeh texts, and a Sanballat of Josephus from the late fourth century BCE.[6] In my view, it is impos-

---

[Sheffield: Sheffield Academic, 1992]; 121–24; 226–40). Following Hurowitz, Wright identifies the basic form of the NM as a building narrative, but he identifies the original report as including less verses: Neh 1:1a,11b; 2:1–6, 11, 15–18; 3:28 and 6:15 (Rebuilding Identity, 124–25).

4. A. Fitzpatrick-McKinley, *Empire, Power and Indigenous Elites: A Case Study of the Nehemiah Memoir* (Leiden: Brill, 2015). K. Hoglund thinks that a citadel was built in response to Greek movements in the Mediterranean (*Achaemenid Imperial Administration in Syria Palestine and the Missions of Ezra and Nehemiah*, SBLDS 125 [Atlanta, GA: Scholars Press, 1992] and D. V. Edelman thinks that imperial motivation is to be seen primarily in the desire of the Persians to establish a fort which would serve as the new provincial seat in the region (*The Origins of the 'Second' Temple': Persian Imperial Policy and the Rebuilding of Jerusalem*, [London: Equinox, 2005], 344–45). Undoubtedly, both of these explanations offer an important part of the explanation for Nehemiah's imperial mission. In addition, in my view, an important aspect of imperial motivation for sending Nehemiah to Jerusalem to establish a *birta* is to be sought at a far more localized level: the curbing of power of local leaders who were extending their rule beyond their authorized remit. Wright, on the other hand, regards the wall building as a communal project with no imperial motivation (*Rebuilding Identity*, 85). Wright's understanding is based on his argument that the accounts of opposition to wall building—even those that concern Judahites—do not belong to the original story of Nehemiah's wall building. In my view, however, the accounts of opposition both from within and from outside of Yehud form an integral part of the original account of Nehemiah. G. W. Ahlström suggests that Nehemiah forced the walling of Jerusalem in an attempt to override Mizpah's authority without imperial authorization (*The History of Palestine from the Paleolithic Period to Alexander's Conquests*, JSOTSup 146 [Sheffield: Sheffield Academic, 1993], 146). M. Smith is also of the view that no imperial strategy lies behind Nehemiah's wall building project but that Nehemiah, made a request which was granted by the Persian king (*Palestinian Parties and Politics that Shaped the Old Testament* [New York: Columbia University Press, 1971], 126–27).

5. The relationship between these Sanballats is difficult to determine. R. G. Kratz thinks that the Sanballat of the Elephantine papyri can be identified with the Sanballat from the bulla of Wadi Daliyeh (*Das Judentum im Zeitalter des Zweiten Tempels* [Tübingen: Mohr Siebeck, 2004], 96).

6. F. M. Cross, "Aspects of Samaritan and Jewish History in Late Persian and Hellenistic Times," *HTR* 59 (1966): 201–11.

sible to determine whether the Sanballat of the NM might be the same as the figure in the Elephantine papyri, and all that can be concluded is that a *pehah* appears to have functioned in Samaria for much of the Persian period.[7] Just because Samaria may have consistently had *pehahs* does not mean that its relationship with the imperial government was stagnant, and in some periods, *pehahs* ruling from Samaria may have been more loyal to the Persian government than those in other regions.

Seals and coins from the period indicate that individuals bearing the title *pehah* also operated from within Yehud for much of the Persian period, although it is possible that some of them were not *pehahs* over Yehud but only of various towns and the districts around them and, therefore, of lower rank than the term *pehah* in other contexts indicates.[8] Seals demonstrate that local rulers operated in Tell en-Nasbeh and Ramet Rahel in the Neo-Babylonian and early Persian periods, and from Jerusalem only in the later period (perhaps relatively late in the fifth century, given the evidence of the Elephantine papyri).[9] No evidence exists to confirm that these *pehahs* operated from Jerusalem (or indeed in most cases that they were governors over a *medinah* known as Yehud), and while the size of Jerusalem has been greatly exaggerated, Finkelstein has recently argued for a settlement with a population of only a few hundred.[10] The figures on these seals are clearly referred to as *pehah*, but we do well to bear in mind that the titulature used by the Persians could often be ambiguous and the term *pehah* was used not just of governors but also of sub-governors,[11] and it is also possible that local dynasts adopted the title and applied it to themselves even when they had not been appointed by the Persians. We need to be cautious in relation to what we read into the *pehah* seals from Yehud, since in some sources a leader could be referred to as a *pehah* but did not seem to fulfil the role of *pehah* as elsewhere defined.[12]

The term *satrap* could be equally ambiguous, and while Pharnazabus holds the title *satrap*, a local family in his employ also uses the title of themselves, at least according to Xenophon's account (*Hell.* 3.1.10–15). While Alt argued that in the early Persian period

---

7. For discussion of evidence of seals and coins see Y. Meshorer and S. Qedar, Samarian Coinage (Jerusalem: The Israel Numismatic Society, 1999); C. Uehlinger, "Powerful Persianisms in Glyptic Iconography of Persian Palestine," in *The Crisis of Israelite Religion: The Transformation of Religious Tradition in Exilic and Post Exilic Times*, ed. B. Becking and M. C. A. Korpel (Leiden: Brill, 1999), 134–82 (142).

8. To suggest that pehah had a wider meaning is not necessarily to arrive at Alt's conclusion that these minor figures must have fallen under Samarian rule (A. Alt, "Die Rolle Samarias bei der Entstehung des Judentums," in *Kleine Schriften zur Geschichtes des Volkes Israel* [Munich: Beck, 1953], 5–28). See F. M. Cross, "The Discovery of the Samaria Papyri," *Biblical Archaeologist* 26 (1963): 110–21 and M. J. W. Leith, *Wadi Daliyeh I: The Wadi Daliyeh Seal Impressions, Discoveries in the Judaean Desert* 24 (Oxford: Clarendon, 1997), 10–11. For discussion of Yehud seals, see Fitzpatrick-McKinley, *Empire, Power and Indigenous Elites*, 157–64.

9. J. R. Zorn, "Tell en-Nasbeh and the Material Culture of the Sixth Century," in *Judah and the Judeans in the Neo-Babylonian Period*, ed. O. Lipschits and J. Blenkinsopp (Winona Lake, IN: Eisenbrauns, 2003), 413–47.

10. I. Finkelstein, "Jerusalem in the Persian (and early Hellenistic) Period and the Wall of Nehemiah," *JSOT* 32 (2008): 501–20.

11. S. E. McEvenue points out that the term *pehah* could have more than one meaning ("The Political Structure in Judah from Cyrus to Nehemiah," *CBQ* 43 [1981]: 353–64). Although the reading *phw* is now accepted by most scholars, F. M. Cross had argued for the reading *phr* (potter) ("Judean Stamps," *Eretz-Israel* 9 [1969]: 20–27).

12. For discussion, see Fitzpatrick-McKinley, *Empire, Power and Indigenous Elites*, 150–51.

Yehud fell under direct Samarian control,[13] no Yehud seals with Samarian provenance have been found, and a number of scholars have argued for a high degree of administrative independence in Yehud for at least the latter part of Persian rule.[14] Thus, what I think we see reflected in the NM is Samarian dominance over Jerusalem exercised through the patron-client type relationship between Tobiah and Sanballat.[15] This dominance may not have been part of Persian policy in the region.

In Neh 4:3, the armies of Samaria assemble before Sanballat, prompted to assemble we can assume to deal with the threat to Sanballat's rule introduced by Nehemiah's mission to repair the walls of Jerusalem and to install a troop there. Of all the local leaders affected by Nehemiah's imperial mission, Sanballat's client Tobiah probably stood to lose the most; he had, after all, enjoyed extensive influence in Jerusalem and its environs (Neh 6:17–18). The assembly of the army appears to have included Tobiah the Ammonite, and in Neh 4:7–8, the Arabs and Ashdodites are also present, preparing to fight against Nehemiah and the builders of the wall. The presence of these local indigenous leaders before Sanballat may well indicate that they are functioning as his clients, a type of relationship likely to have been regulated by the swearing of oaths, mutual gift exchange, mutual exchange of services (for example, loyalty on the part of the client will be rewarded by the patrons' protection of the client's position and the granting to him of access to important individuals contributing to the sustaining of an elite network, giving the client an advantage over his peers),[16] and marriage. In Neh 6:17–18, it becomes clear that the rulers of Jerusalem have sworn oaths to Tobiah and that he is related to the Jerusalemite rulers through marriage.[17] In this

---

13. Alt, "Die Rolle Samarias," 5–28. Alt has been followed by E. Stern, who used the evidence of seals to support Alt's thesis (*The Material Culture of the Land of the Bible in the Persian Period* [Warminster: Aris & Phillips, 1982], 209–13) and by McEvenue ("Political Structure in Judah").

14. C. Carter, *The Emergence of Yehud in the Persian Period: A Social and Demographic Study*, JSOTSup 294 (Sheffield: Sheffield Academic, 1999), 300–301. Scholars arguing for a high degree of independence for Yehud include Carter, *Emergence of Yehud*, 280; Hoglund, *Achaemenid Imperial Administration*, 69–84; and P. Briant, *From Cyrus to Alexander: A History of the Persian Empire*, trans. P. T. Daniels (Winona Lake, IN: Eisenbrauns, 2002), 503–4; 913; 976. P. Ackroyd thinks that since the letters from Elephantine are addressed to leaders from both Samaria and Jerusalem, at least early in the Persian period, there was a link between the settlements ("Archaeology, Politics and Religion: The Persian Period," *The Iliff Review* 39 [1982]: 5–24).

15. I have previously argued that relations between Sanballat, Tobiah, Geshem and the leading men of Jerusalem should be understood on the basis of patron-client relations (A. Fitzpatrick-McKinley, "Ezra, Nehemiah and Some Early Greek Lawgivers," in *Rabbinic Law in its Roman and Near Eastern Setting*, ed. C. Hetzer [Berlin: Mohr Siebeck 2003], 17-48 [28; 31–33]). D. Edelman also regards patron-client relations as key to exploring the background to the dispute between Nehemiah and local leaders (D. Edelman, "Nehemiah's Adversary, Tobiah the Patron," in *Historie og Konstruktion*, eds. M. Müller and T.L. Thompson [Københaven: Museum Tusculanums Forlag, 2005], 106–14).

16. R. Westbrook, "Patronage in the Ancient Near East," *JESHO* 42 (2005): 210–33 (215). Here Westbrook is adopting the views of J. Waterbury, "An Attempt to Put Patrons and Clients in Their Place," in *Patrons and Clients in Mediterranean Societies*, ed. E. Gellner and J. Waterbury (London: Duckworth, 1977), 329–42 (332) and A. Wallace-Hadrill, "Patronage in Roman Society: From Republic to Empire," in *Patronage in Ancient Society*, ed. A. Wallace-Hadrill (London: Routledge, 1989), 63–97 (72–73).

17. Patronage is a type of relationship found in the Roman context, and it must be admitted that the language of patronage that is so evident in the Roman sources is not found in sources from the ancient Near East. Nonetheless, as Westbrook points out, there are strong indicators that many types of political relations found in the Near Eastern environment show characteristics of client-patron type relationships, even if the explicit language of the Roman context is not present ("Patronage," 213). N. P. Lemche also

relationship, Sanballat is clearly the socially and politically dominant partner, with Tobiah in a subservient role, but with the expectation that Sanballat will come to his assistance to stop the interference of this newly arrived Persian appointee in Jerusalem, who sought to sever his relationship with his clients Eliashiv and the leading men of Jerusalem. Patronage may be too precise a term, and it should be noted that it can co-exist with and use the terminology of legal and especially kinship relations (see further below).[18]

These relationships of patronage (as well as those that were legal, commercial, or based in kinship and which can co-exist with patron-client relationships)[19] may in some cases have enjoyed Persian approval while in others they were largely ignored as long as problems did not arise, but they tended to develop under their own momentum and were very much rooted in local relationships, contexts, and conditions. These local magnates ensured order in the regions and they did this primarily because of the prestige they held among the local populations; held sometimes because they occupied traditional roles, other times because they had inherited leadership and yet other times through a combination of force and persuasion. In the exercise of their leadership, the local knowledge they held of traditional practices, legal, social, commercial and cultic, for example, would have informed the way in which they structured their own rule and the rule of their clients.[20]

In spite of this high degree of autonomy, they could use their status of Persian appointees to ensure that the population towed the line. There may have been periods when the Persian government, including its local Iranian representatives, were too occupied with other problems, both local and central and internal and external, to have taken much notice of the shifting in relations of local power that probably went on all around them. Such conditions, as well as the geographical and political diversity of Yehud and its environs, facilitated movement up and down the political and social ladders throughout the period of Persian rule. By the same token, a competitive climate among the local Iranian officials in Palestine and other regions of Ebar Nahara, intermittently complicated by events at the royal court (that often accompanied dynastic changes), probably ensured that movement up and down the ladder of power was a condition there, too.

But if Sanballat were a *pehah* operating on behalf of the Persians, what explains his opposition to Nehemiah's attempt to carry out the king's orders? Sanballat was a Persian-approved appointee who, like many other local rulers appointed by the Persians, enjoyed a good deal of influence in the region over which they were assigned, which was an aspect of rule by indigenous rulers that seems to have been tolerated by the Persians (see further below). From the NM we see this ruler from Samaria stepping beyond the authority the Persians are likely to have granted him. The leaders from Ammon, Ashdod, and Arabia who assembled before Sanballat (Neh 4) appear to have operated in a patron–client type relationship with

---

argues for the importance of patron-client relations and concludes that in the period between 1300 and 800 BCE, many political relationships may be characterized as based on the patronage system (*Early Israel: Anthropological and Historical Studies on Israelite Society before the Monarchy*, VTSup 37 [Leiden: Brill, 1985], 223–25; 245–74).

18. Westbrook, "Patronage," 212.
19. Westbrook, "Patronage," 212.
20. For three additional discussions in this volume of non-official forms of leadership, which sometimes could involve governmental appointees, as here, see E. Ben Zvi ("Memory and Political Thought in the Late Persian/early Hellenistic Yehud/Judah: Some Observations"), K. Berge ("Mystified Authority: Legitimating Leadership Through 'Lost Books'"), and A.-M. Schol-Wetter ("Judith Maccabee? On Leadership, Resistance, and the Great Deeds of Little People").

him, indicating that Sanballat's influence and power extended outside the boundaries of Samaria and its environs. The presence of Arab traders in the region is now confirmed by a sixth century inscription.[21] Did Sanballat extend himself too far into regions that were not supposed to come under his rule (other than perhaps when assembling troops from these regions on behalf of the Persians), and did he stand to have his sphere of influence reduced once Jerusalem's walls had been finished and the troop installed?[22]

Prior to Nehemiah's efforts to repair the walls and gates of Jerusalem, other attempts may have been made by the Persians to fortify the settlement, but they had failed (Neh 1:3),[23] and Nehemiah's reference to previous *pehahs* of Jerusalem could be taken to imply that they had been overthrown, perhaps by Tobiah with the support of Sanballat, for no *pehah* is present when Nehemiah arrives in Jerusalem with a troop (Neh 2:9). In Neh 1:3, Nehemiah reported to the king what may be a reference to an earlier abandonment of the wall-building project, an abandonment likely to have been rooted in the peoples' reluctance: the project was expensive (as Neh 5 implies), it took workers off farmland, and there was an alternative—they could continue to rely on the protection and patronage of Tobiah, who was a high-ranking client of Sanballat of Samaria. Moreover, it is clear that the priest Eliashiv and the leading men of Jerusalem were far more satisfied with their relationship with Tobiah than they were with Nehemiah's new regime. Tobiah had enjoyed the loyalty of the "men of Jerusalem," who were "bound to him by oath" prior to Nehemiah's arrival (Neh 6:17–18).[24] Significantly, it would appear that the Jerusalem elites (חרים) wished to continue this relationship with Tobiah, speaking of "his good deeds behind Nehemiah's back" (Neh 6:19), and while Nehemiah was attempting to establish himself and his troop in Jerusalem, they continued to inform Tobiah of affairs in Jerusalem. While Nehemiah was away in Susa, they took the opportunity to reinstate Tobiah, who was given a chamber in the temple by the high priest (Neh 13:7). This must surely have been intended to re-establish his status as patron over Jerusalem's leaders once and for all.[25]

From the perspective of the residents of Jerusalem, their nobles and leaders, and the highest ranking of them, Tobiah and the priest Eliashiv, Nehemiah's absence had provided them with the opportunity to restore things to normal and to re-confirm their allegiance to their patron Tobiah (Neh 13:4–8), who may have been of Judean extraction.[26] Tobiah and his

---

21. A. Lemaire, "New Perspectives on the Trade between Judah and South Arabia," in *New Inscriptions and Seals Relating to the Biblical World*, ed. M. Lubetski and E. Lubetski (Atlanta, GA: SBL, 2012), 93–110.

22. Xenophon reports that it was the duty of the satrap to assemble troops (*Cyr.* 8.6; *Oec.* 4.5).

23. This reference is Neh 1:3 could refer to damage to the settlement that took place in the Persian period and not to the earlier Babylonian destruction.

24. Fitzpatrick-McKinley, "Ezra, Nehemiah and Some Greek Lawgivers," 28; 31–33; Edelman, "Nehemiah's Adversary, Tobiah the Patron," 106–114.

25. The term translated as 'chamber' is לשכה (Neh 13:5). In Neh 13:7, it is נשכה. It is difficult to see precisely the significance of Tobiah's installation here, but it probably indicates his centrality in some economic activities. In Neh 13:5, 9, there is a list of commodities stored in a chamber in the temple, including tithes and frankincense, which may have been traded by Geshem the Arab. Various Arabian peoples controlled the spice trade from at least the ninth century BCE to the Roman period, and Minaen dominance of the trade seems likely in this period (Lemaire, "New Perspectives," 93–110).

26. His names and the names he gave his sons are Yahwistic. Also, Jer 40:11 and 2 Kgs 25:25 record how Judeans fleeing the Babylonians had gone to Ammon to seek safety there, and early in the Neo-Babylonian period, it seems that some Judeans were living within the sphere of influence of Baalis, king of Ammon. Ezekiel 27 could very well indicate the Ammonites had a long history of trade with Yehud. . D. Edel-

clients in Jerusalem were persistent, reluctant to end what must have been a mutually beneficial relationship that probably enabled Jerusalem elites to become part of a wider elite network in the region dominated by Sanballat. Nehemiah 6:17–18 reports that Tobiah had married into an influential Jerusalem family, and Nehemiah suggests that it was because of this marriage between a member of a leading Ammonite family of YHWH-worshippers and the leading priestly family of Jerusalem that the "men of Judah" owed him loyalty: "… in those days the nobles of Yehud sent many letters to Tobiah, and Tobiah's letters came to them. For many in Yehud were sworn to him by oath because he was the son in law of Shecaniah, the son of Arah" (Neh 6:17–18).

Marriage played an important role in the formation and sustaining of elite networks in the ancient world and in the formation of trading networks, and it is no wonder that upon his return from Susa, when he discovered Tobiah had been given a chamber in the temple, Nehemiah set about addressing the question of intermarriage. In Neh 13:23, he bans marriage with Ammonites, Ashdodites, and Moabites, thus rendering the marriage of Tobiah to the daughter of Shecaniah illegitimate and also rendering Judean-Ashdodite relations illegitimate.[27]

Having failed in their earlier attempts to attack the workers on the project, Sanballat and his clients try a new tactic. In Neh 6:2, Sanballat and Geshem attempt to persuade Nehemiah to leave Jerusalem and meet them in one of the villages in the plain of Ono, but suspicious of their intentions, Nehemiah refuses. His refusal is followed by Sanballat's sending of a letter accusing him of planning rebellion against the king, an accusation that may have been commonly made toward those who were perceived by other local leaders as too aggressive.[28] In attempting to check Nehemiah's activities in Jerusalem, Sanballat probably presented himself as the loyal *pehah* of the Persian governor (cf. Neh 2, where Sanballat also says he suspects Nehemiah of rebellion). But it is more likely to have been Sanballat who was taking matters into his own hands in attempting to prevent the establishment of a *birta* in Jerusalem. Nehemiah 6 seems to imply that Sanballat is open to negotiation: if Nehemiah is to become king over the Yehudîm, an ambition he denies, Sanballat seems to be suggesting that perhaps they can come to some agreement (Neh 6:7). Nehemiah's refusal

---

man identifies two Tobiahs in the Nehemiah Memoir; a Tobiah of an early edition of the Memoir that was composed during the life-time of Tobiah and who is likely to have been a returnee, and a Tobiah of a later edition of the Memoir, Toubias the Ammonite, the commander of the third century BCE *birâ* (Edelman, "Nehemiah's Adversary," 112).

27. The Ashdodites had assembled before Sanballat at Samaria to respond to Nehemiah's project in Jerusalem (Neh 4:7). Marriage with Ashdodites is nowhere else banned in the Hebrew Bible. For a full discussion, see Fitzpatrick-McKinley, Empire, Power and Indigenous Elites, 230–42. The ban on intermarriage does not appear to have had any lasting effect: Isa 56:6–8 and 66:21 envision a covenant community that includes converts, some of whom would even become priests and leaders. Discussion of intermarriage, with the exception of Ezra 7–10, which is later than the NM, first appears in the literature of the Maccabean period. In Jub 16 and 17, all Israelites and not just priests must observe the ban (C. Hayes, "Intermarriage and Impurity in Ancient Jewish Sources," *HTR* 91 [1999]: 3–36 [6]), but we cannot be certain whether this reflects a commonly held view or a sectarian view.

28. On the other hand, we should not dismiss the possibility that there was some ambition to restore kingship, particularly if consideration is given to D. Edelman's suggestion that Zerubbabel and Nehemiah may have been the same historical person, a Davidic governor of Yehud from the time of Artaxerxes I (D. Edelman, "Were Zerubbabel and Nehemiah the Same Person?" in *Far From Minimal: Celebrating the Work and Influence of P. R. Davies*, ed. D. Burns and J. W. Rogerson [London: T. & T. Clark, 2012], 112–31).

to engage with Sanballat is followed by plots against Nehemiah by the Jerusalemite supporters and clients of Tobiah, who try to induce Nehemiah to go into the temple, 6:9–12) presumably because he will be unguarded there and they can be rid of him once and for all. Resistance to Nehemiah is strong both from leaders within Jerusalem and its environs and from other regions that would have been affected (Samaria, Ammon Ashdod); indeed, the atmosphere is far from ideal for a restorer of the great city of Jerusalem, who will be remembered in Jewish tradition for his rebuilding of the city (see further below).

While Sanballat is clearly at the top of the local political hierarchy that existed between these indigenous elites in the region, it is not Sanballat but his client Tobiah who exercised some kind of direct control in Jerusalem, and at no point does Sanballat ever enter Jerusalem or negotiate directly with its leaders, Eliashiv the priest and the leading men of Jerusalem. Once his attempts to attack the builders of the wall have failed, and once Nehemiah seems to have won the day, we hear no more of Sanballat, who perhaps retreated, having done his duty to protect his client's interests in Jerusalem (thereby, of course, protecting his own interests) and in any case, perhaps not daring to go any further in interfering with the imperial appointee. Tobiah, however, continues to threaten Nehemiah's plans through the continuation of his relationship with his client Eliashiv and the leading men of Jerusalem. It is Tobiah who has the most to lose, having networked his way into the affairs of Jerusalem and its leaders by marrying the daughter of Shecaniah, having secured the oaths of the leaders of the city, and later, being granted a chamber in the temple.

Is there any justification for the argument that the NM reflects Sanballat as the *pehah* of a *birta*, extending his rule through the sealing of patron-client type relationships with local leaders and a consequent increase in his independence from the Persian authorities? The idea of the Persians permitting self-governance by subject peoples has been examined extensively, with a number of scholars, such as L. Fried, rejecting the characterization.[29] Nonetheless, if self-governance is indeed an exaggeration that has led to much idealism about Persian tolerance, it is clear that indigenous rulers were left in place in some districts, and some of these appear not to have declined in influence as a result of Persian rule but, in fact, to have extended their influence. G. Barjamovic suggests that in the ancient world, rule of powerful centers over outlying regions did not lead to the erosion of the influence of local rulers but rather, enhanced the ability of local rulers to maintain a high degree of independence;[30] ancient empires such as those of the Assyrians and the Babylonians allowed and frequently even supported the continuation of local elites and their rule.[31] In Barjamovic's view, large empires provided more scope for self-government and local autonomy than territorial monarchies because of the distance from the center of rule, which created the opportunity for local elite networks to impact their local environments. In the ancient world in any case, imperial rule was, in general, often indirect, exercised through local clients and local institutions.[32]

---

29. L. Fried, *The Priest and the Great King: Temple Palace Relations in the Persian Period*, Biblical and Judaic studies from the University of California, San Diego 10 (Winona Lake, IN: Eisenbrauns, 2004).

30. G. Barjamovic, "Civic Institutions and Self-Government in Southern Mesopotamia in the Mid-First Millennium B.C.," in *Assyria and Beyond: Studies Presented to Mogens Trolle Larsen*, ed. J. G. Dercksen (Nederlands: Instituut vor Het Nabije Oosten, 2004), 47–98.

31. See Fitzpatrick-McKinley, *Empire, Power and Indigenous Elites*, 8–38.

32. Fitzpatrick-McKinley, *Empire, Power and Indigenous Elites*, 8–38.

A. G. Keen argues that Persian rule was conducive to the continuation of rule by subject monarchs, at times even ensuring the preservation of various forms of native rule to varying degrees, depending on the conditions they encountered.[33] M. Liverani argues that the problems created by the vast distances over which ancient empires sometimes ruled was overcome by the use of an intricate system of governors and provincial administrators, but significantly, within this system, indigenous leaders often played a vital role.[34] Exaction of tribute formed the basis of these policies, and M. Given refers to the existence of the competing economic forces of imperial exaction, on the one hand, and a hidden economy operated by subject elites, on the other.[35]

Overall then, we have a context within which figures such as Sanballat ruled and could become increasingly competitive. Within such conditions, it was inevitable that these indigenous rulers would assert themselves as much as they could and even seek to expand.[36] This could create the problem of indigenous elites operating too much within their own sphere of interests, to the detriment of imperial interests (a condition I think may be reflected in the NM), and there are a number of examples of indigenous elites operating under Persian rule but exercising more autonomy than the Persians perhaps would have sanctioned.

Lycia under Persian rule, for example, was a region where indigenous elites demonstrated a good deal of independence from their Persian rulers, in some periods rejecting Persian rule and even entering into alliances with Athens, leading some scholars to conclude there were periods when Persia virtually lost all control of the region.[37] But forming alliances with Athens was not the only way in which the indigenous dynasts in Lycia asserted themselves,

---

33. A. G. Keen is not suggesting that such attempts to preserve these systems was due to an enlightened cultural tolerance on the part of the Persians but rather, due to political astuteness (*Dynastic Lycia: A Political History of the Lycians and their Relations with Foreign Powers, c. 545–362 BC* [Leiden: Brill 1998], 39). See also M. Dandamayev and V. Lukonin, who note that the Persians retained the traditional division of *nomes* in Egypt, generally not interfering with this system, and replacing only a portion of local civil servants with Persians, while the majority of civil servants were Egyptians (*The Culture and Social Institutions of Ancient Iran* [Cambridge: Cambridge University Press, 1989], 103–4). When the Neo-Assyrians expanded into the Zagros Mountains region, the Median city lords remained in power, ruling on a hereditary basis over an extensive area centered on a fortress. These centers continued to exist even after Assyria turned some areas of the region into provinces (K. Radner, "An Assyrian view on the Medes," in *Continuity of Empire (?) Assyria, Media, Persia: Proceedings of the International Meeting in Padua, 26th—28th April 2001*, ed. G. B. Lanfranchi, M. Rost, and R. Rollinger, HANEM 5 [Padova: S.A.R.G.O.N. Editrice e Libreria, 2003], 37–64).

34. M. Liverani, "Nelle pieghe del despotismo Organismi rappresentativi nell' antico Orienta," *Studi Storici* 34 (1993): 7–33 (23).

35. M. Given, *The Archaeology of the Colonized* (London: Routledge, 2004), 164. The operation of hidden economies was no doubt part of how the indigenous elites behind the NM functioned (see further below).

36. Barjamovic, "Civic institutions," 48. This can be witnessed even of the Assyrians in spite of their reputation for destruction of the nations they conquered. The governors appointed by the Assyrians to the Babylonian city states (not to the regional provinces) were virtually all selected from the local elite, although they did not share the same status as the bēl pāhutu ('governors of provinces'). These local elites served as the link between the city-state and the citizens of the empire, and dynasties of local elites functioning as governors were created (Barjamovic, "Civil Institutions," 54–55). In addition, heads of the city-states dealt with the "citizens of the city," or the "city elders and assembly," groups made up largely of the prominent families. According to Barjamovic, these bodies made decisions, defined city policy, and legislated for the city (Barjamovic, "Civil Institutions," 55–94).

37. T. R. Bryce, "Political Unity in Lycia during the 'Dynastic' Period," *JNES* 42 (1983): 31–42.

and in the case of Xanthus, we witness a ruling family exerting its influence over neighboring dynasts for generations.[38] Within the context of competing local dynasts, a pattern of territories being subdivided can be witnessed, as land is seized by an upstart neighbor or as a client of one of the more influential dynasts is awarded with land.[39] Such division of land can only have increased competitiveness between these native rulers. An inscription from Xanthus shows the rulers of the settlement (and other towns) being permitted to collect the taxes from a nearby harbor.[40] At one point, however, Xanthus was threatened by an upstart indigenous dynastic family, likely resulting in much instability. The Persian response may have been the establishment of the fort of the Kardakes in the region[41] and/or the inclusion of Lycia under the rule of the satrap of neighboring Caria, as Fried argues.[42]

In Phoenicia the Persians may have deliberately created conditions that would ensure the local ruling elite remained in competition with each other. J. D. Grainger suggests such a strategy of preventing too much collaboration between local elites ultimately could have resulted in revolt.[43] The subdivision of territories was an imperial measure also known from Phoenicia and Asia Minor and seems to have been used to ensure that no one city and its ruler became too powerful over too extensive a territory. So, for example, in Phoenicia, the loyal king of Sidon is given territories from neighboring Dor and Joppa, which had not shown loyalty to the Persians (Eshmunazar Inscription). Nehemiah was sent to complete the walls and to establish Jerusalem as a *birta*, a development that would essentially subdivide the region, much of which seems to have come under the influence of Sanballat and his clients. By the time of Nehemiah's arrival, they were sufficiently independent of Persian authority to resist this carrier of Persian orders.

Like the Lycian dynasts, the Mysian peoples and their rulers also demonstrated a significant degree of independence from Persian authorities, and Xenophon reports their regular rebellions (*Hell.* 3.1.13), although they also served in the army of Pharnabazus (*Hell.* 4.1.24). One of the Paphlygonian dynasts is said by Xenophon to have come to the assistance of the Spartan king Agesilaus, supplying him with soldiers and horses. Xenophon

---

38. Bryce, "Political Unity," 31–42.

39. The Poem of Arbinas outlines local disputes and wars between indigenous elites in and around the region of Xanthus and Briant thinks that such disputes continued much as they had done before the Persian period (Briant, *From Cyrus*, 608–9).

40. A bilingual inscription from Xanthus (Greek-Lycian) sees the satrap Pixadorus grant a tithe of the harbor to the town of Xanthus and the neighboring towns of Tlos, Pinana, and Kandaynda and they are permitted to collect it "however they wish." For this inscription see, J. Bousquet, "Une nouvelle inscription trilingue a Xanthos?" *RAr* (1986): 101–6.

41. The context for the establishment of this fortress may have been the development of an increasingly assertive elite (N. Sekunda, "Achaemenid Settlement in Caria, Lycia and Greater Phrygia," in *Achaemenid History IV, Asia Minor and Egypt: Old Cultures in a New Empire, Proceedings of the Gronigen 1998 Achaemenid History Workshop*, ed. H. Sancisi-Weerdenburg and A. Kuhrt (Leiden: Nederlands Instituut voor het Nabje Oosten, 1991), 83–143 [89–91]).

42. Fried, *Priest and the Great King*, 153–54.

43. J. D. Grainger, *Hellenistic Phoenicia* (Oxford: Clarendon, 1991),111–12. M. N. Weiskopf suggests that the Achaemenid administrators dealing with Paphlagonia often sought to "play tribes against each other," thereby exploiting intra-tribal conflict rather than trying to alleviate it. This was a means of ensuring that the tribes were never sufficiently united to threaten surrounding and more settled and productive regions. Overall, Weiskopf suggests that the most characteristic feature of Persian rule in Anatolia was an absence of rigid systems and policies ("Achaemenid Systems of Governing in Anatolia," [Unpublished PhD thesis, University of California, 1984], 201).

reports that even before this act of rebellion against Persian rule, the Paphlagonian dynast had already declined to continue allegiance and payment to Persia, having refused to attend when summoned by the king (*Hell.* 4.1.3). Diodorus reports that prior to this, like other subject dynasts and chiefs, the Paphlagonian chiefs were required to supply one troop to the local satrap (*Diodorus* 14.22.5). But it is important to note that Mysia and Paphlagonia were not ruled by one dynast but by many, and according to Briant, the region was divided into many chieftaincies (though Diodorus reports that both Mysia and Paphlygonia had a satrap, 14.11.3, 15.90.3) with the potential for subdivision of territory whenever a ruler broke away from a chief.[44] Such subdividing of territories can also be seen in Lycia as competition between indigenous rulers increased and rulers broke away from each other.

That the Mysian peoples were frequently troublesome to the king is reflected in two passages in Xenophon, who reports that their many tribes are troublesome (*Anab.* 2.513) and that they (and the Pisidians) occupy rugged country (meaning they were difficult to reach) and "contrive to overrun and damage the king's territory and to preserve their own freedom" (Xenophon, *Mem.* 3.5.26). Nonetheless, they are recorded to have provided the king with troops, and there were military communities under the command of the Persian king settled in Mysia (*Anab.* 7.8.15). Weiskopf suggests that the Achaemenid administrators dealing with Paphlagonia often sought to "play tribes against each other" (as they played the Phoenician cities against each other), thereby exploiting intra-tribal conflict rather than trying to alleviate it.[45] This may have been a means of ensuring that the tribes were never sufficiently united to threaten surrounding and more settled and productive regions. Overall, Weiskopf suggests that the most characteristic feature of Persian rule in Anatolia was an absence of rigid systems and policies,[46] and perhaps it is conditions like these that we glimpse through the NM where Sanballat, in spite of being a Persian appointee, extended his rule by acting as a patron of weaker local rulers such as Tobiah, whom he makes subordinate, the leaders of Ashdod, and Geshem the Arab. Tobiah, in turn, exercises his influence beyond his territory in Ammon to the settlement of Jerusalem, where he has cultivated a relation with Elishiv and the leading men of Jerusalem, a relationship that it would appear had been sanctioned by Sanballat as the most dominant of local leaders.

Inscriptions from Tayma appear to indicate that indigenous rulers who operated in that region with Persian approval sometimes became very ambitious, and rather than being content to restrict themselves to a region over which they had traditionally enjoyed sovereignty while paying tribute to the Persians, there is evidence that they extended their rule to nearby regions, such as Ruba and Hagm. Rule by chiefs and kings from Tayma had been exercised for centuries, and this was often expressed through the idea that Salm, the deity of the city, could include in his sacrifices for neighboring gods. Inscriptions dating to the fifth century indicate that two more local versions of the god *Salm* were drafted onto the pantheon of Tayma, *Salm of Hagm* (Tayma 1) (*Hagm* is a region north of Tayma) and *Salm of Ruba* (Tayma 20), and while Babylonian gods are named, there is no reference in the inscriptions to Persian gods or to Persian rulers, other than in the dating formula.

The inclusion of the gods Salm of Ruba and of Hagm would have symbolized the formalization of a new relationship between the ruler of Tayma and the rulers of Ruba and Hagm, who now became subordinate to him, owing him tribute and loyalty in return for protec-

---

44. Briant, *From Cyrus*, 642.
45. Weiskopf, "Achaemenid Systems," 201
46. Weiskopf, "Achaemenid Systems," 201.

tion and the guarantee of their continued rule in their districts. What is striking is that *TA* 1 indicates that, since Persian administrators resided in the towns of Tayma (and also Dedan and Elath), the incorporation of the god *Salm of Haym* might well have taken place with the approval of the local Persian administration. Hence, we see an example of a local ruler extending his rule with Persian approval,[47] just as the rulers of Xanthus and other local dynasts were given permission to collect the harbor taxes, indicating their sovereignty over these settlements; in the latter case a sovereignty permitted by the Persian authorities. For a time Sanballat may have functioned in a similar way to the king of Tayma, extending his rule to areas such as Ammon, and through his clients in Ammon (one of whom and perhaps the highest ranking of whom was Tobiah), his influence extended indirectly to Jerusalem; but while the extension of territory by the king of Tayma was approved by the Persians, there is no indication that Sanballat's extension into Ammon was approved, although it had probably been tolerated for a time, and Nehemiah's walling of Jerusalem and his establishment of a troop there under imperial orders may imply that Sanballat's extension of his influence through his client Tobiah was to be checked by this Persian appointee.

Two other incidents of indigenous rulers behaving with a good deal of autonomy and competing with other indigenous rulers are worth mentioning. At Elephantine, the indigenous Khnum priests seem to have disrupted the settlement by blocking access to a well that had, up until that point, been shared with the priests of the altar house to Yahô (according to Briant's interpretation).[48] What is reflected here is a struggle to control an important resource, and the Persian authorities do not seem to have stepped in to intervene with any force whatsoever. Rather, after some years passed, they seem to have permitted the Yahô priests to rebuild their place of sacrifice, but with various restrictions put in place (TAD A4.9). Furthermore, while the Egyptian Vidranga is punished (TAD A4.7) we hear nowhere that the priests of Khnum, who in TAD A4.7 are named as the instigators of the destruction of the temple used by soldiers in the employ of the Persian government, were called to account for disrupting things in this important garrison town, and the episode may reflect the type of problem Persian authorities frequently encountered; a local dispute between minor rulers and holders of office threatens stability in the region.

A final example comes from a story in Xenophon. He explains how a Babylonian widow named Mania petitions to be allowed to succeed her husband as satrap in Dardanus in Phyrgia. In this instance, it is clear that "satrap" is to be understood as a role fulfilled by an indigenous ruler in a specified region on behalf of the owner of the land, the Persian Pharnazabus. Xenophon reports the granting of her request by the Persian Pharnabazus and notes not only how Mania ruled the cities assigned to her by Pharnabazus but how she even conquered new cities on his behalf (*Hell.* 3.1.10–15). In *Hellenica* 3, Pharnazabus demonstrates his pleasure with Mania, and she succeeds in gaining new territories for him

---

47. Weiskopf, "Achaemenid Systems," 213–14; E. A. Knauf, "The Persian Administration in Arabia," *Transeuphratène* 2 (1990): 201-217 (206, 211). For the inscription, see I. Rabinowitz, "Aramaic Inscriptions of the fifth century from a North Arabian Shrine in Egypt," *JNES* 15 (1958): 1–9 (2).

48. P. Briant, "Inscriptions multilingues d'époque achéménide: le texte et l'image," 91–115 in *Le décret de Memphis: Actes du Colloque de la Fondation Singer-Polignac*, ed. D. Valbelle and J. Leclant (Paris: Fondation Singer-Polignac, 1999). A number of other explanations have been offered; see recently I. Kottsieper, "Religionspolitik der Achämeniden und die Juden von Elephantine," in *Religion und Religionskontakte im Zeitalter der Achämeniden*, ed. R. G. Kratz (Gütersloh: Gütersloher Verlagshaus, 2002), 150–78; A. Joisten-Pruschke, "Light from Aramaic Documents," in *The World of Achaemenid Persia: History, Art and Society in Iran and the Ancient Near East*, ed. J. Curtis and S. Simpson (London: I. B. Tauris, 2010), 41–50.

and managing the Greek mercenaries who fight with her. After a number of years, however, a rival to her position appears in the person of her son-in-law, who murders her and sends gifts to Pharnazabus, arguing that he should now be "satrap." His request, however, is denied and Pharnazabus vows to avenge the murder of his trusted appointee and to remove the upstart son-in-law. In this case, we see family rivalry within a ruling indigenous family. Would such events have been typical? It is difficult to say, but the system of empowering indigenous elites and subdividing territories between them must have led to increased competition, and in my view, such competition may lie at the heart of the NM.

Thus, throughout Persian ruled territories there are many examples of indigenous rulers extending their territories and competing with each other while, at the same time, not entering into open rebellion against the Persians but continuing to supply troops and tribute. In many cases we witness that the Persians respond to such extensions of territory and rule, although in different ways: in Lycia, by the establishment of a fort of the Kardakes, presumably to deal with upstart elites; in the case of the murder of the Persian appointed satrap, Mania, by avenging her death; and in the case of a Samarian ruler whose sphere of political influence was extending well outside of the territory of Samaria to Ammon and through the rulers of Ammon into Jerusalem, by the walling of the city of Jerusalem and the establishment of a *birta* there.

The persistence of local forms of leadership and styles of rule is also evident, with chiefs, kings, and dynasts appearing in various territories (Paphlagonia, Mysia, Lycia, Phoenicia), and leadership in Jerusalem and its environs was probably also rooted in traditional forms. There may be evidence for the survival of local forms of leadership in Persian ruled districts in some of Xenophon's account. Xenophon claims to have led a military unit of 10,000 mercenaries to Armenia and refers to their encounters with the *Komarchai*, "village heads." The term appears to refer to individuals who were heads of single villages but also of a number of villages.[49] The Borsippa archive, which dates to the reigns of Cambyses and Darius, refers to the "headman of the Egyptians," which Waerzeggers takes to refer to a community leader of Carian-Egyptians who were resident in Borsippa.[50] The Āl-Yahūdu archive records Judeans holding positions as tax collectors and foremen.[51]

As I shall later demonstrate, the heads or chiefs of households, villages, and towns also appear to have formed part of the structures through which Yehud and its environs were ruled in the time of Nehemiah (Neh 11:3). It is likely that while an official Persian inscription may refer to an individual native ruler as a *pehah*, locals may have related to him as a tribal chief or as king. In the Xanthus trilingual inscription, the native perception of the status of the town differs from the imperial perception, so the ruler of Xanthus is referred to as a *pehah* over a polis in the local Lycian version but as a *pehah* over a *birta* in the imperial version.[52] The discrepancy between the native and the imperial designations may

---

49. J. Wiesehöfer, *Ancient Persia* (London: I. B. Tauris, 2001), 62–64.

50. C. Waerzeggers, "The Carians of Borsippa," *Iraq* 68 (2006): 1–22. For fuller discussion of the Carians of Borsippa, see Fitzpatrick-McKinley, *Empire, Power and Indigenous Elites*, 89.

51. K. Abraham, "The Reconstruction of Jewish Communities in the Persian Empire: The Āl-Yahūdu Clay Tablets," in *Light and Shadows—The Catalog—The Story of Iran and the Jews*, ed. H. Segev. (Tel Aviv: Beit Hatfutsot, 2010), (http://www.bh.org.il/iran---article.aspx), 264–68. For general background and significance of tablets see Pearce, "New Evidence," 399–412.

52. The Aramaic text reads *birta*; for this translation see A. Dupont-Sommer, "La stèle trilingue récemment découverte au Létoon de Xanthos: le texte araméen," *CRAIBL*, 1974, 132–49. The Lycian version of the text refers to Xanthus as a "city"—polis, according to Laroche's translation (E. Laroche, "L'inscriptions lycienne," in *Fouilles de Xanthos VI, la stèle trilingue de létoon*, ed. H. Metzger, E. Laroche [Paris: Klinck-

indicate how the local ruler represented himself to the population over which he held sway, while from the imperial perspective he and his settlement (the *birta*) exist only with the permission of and in the service of the Persian king. It seems likely, then, that on a day-to-day basis, rulers like Sanballat and Geshem operated more or less as kings, chiefs, and dynasts but reported to the Persians as *pehahs*.

The suggestion that the NM reflects a situation where Sanballat had overstepped the mark in extending his influence into surrounding regions, including Jerusalem through his client Tobiah, is further supported by the fact that unlike the Persian officials in Ezra 4, although Sanballat accuses Nehemiah of rebellion against the king (Neh 2:19; 6:6), he does not in the end (as far as we can tell) petition the Persian satrap or king in relation to his attempts to stop Nehemiah completing the walls. Instead, he resorts to assembling his clients (in Neh 4 Arabs, Ashdodites, and Ammonites gather before him) to attack the builders (Neh 6:7), sending letters that threaten but also offer to negotiate, and finally plotting to assassinate the founder of the new *birta*. We can only assume that Sanballat did not send a petition to the Persian king because he realized that Nehemiah was carrying out an imperial order, the implementation of which would be the curtailment of his involvement in Jerusalem, which he had exercised through his client Tobiah, and likely other regions.

Further evidence that Nehemiah's wall-building is part of an imperial order to bring stability to a region where indigenous rulers were becoming too independent and not simply "a communal project," as J. Wright has recently argued it was[53] and as the story of Nehemiah is remembered in Jewish tradition, is found in Neh 2:8. This verse indicates that the Empire provided the wood, indicating it was an imperially authorized undertaking. More important, however, is the occurrence of the word *pelekîm* in Neh 3:9. A. Demsky has concluded that this term *pelek* is to be compared to the Akkadian term *pilku*, which designates tax levied from districts in the form of conscripted labor. In Assyrian texts, the cognate term *pilku* indicates workers employed in building walls or other structures on behalf of the Assyrians.[54] Thus, the Jerusalem and Judahite families who carried out Nehemiah's orders may well have been compelled to do so as part of the tribute their district owed to their imperial overlords.

Compulsory labor would account for their understanding of their participation in the project as a form of tribute that increased the hardship upon them as they struggled to pay "the king's tribute" and to pay back loans to the upper classes in Jerusalem (חרים and סגנים Neh 5:1–15). It also would account for their abandonment of the wall-building project prior to Nehemiah's renewed attempts. Moreover, their confinement to the city to complete the walls (Neh 4:22) kept the population from their normal livelihoods.

A further hardship on the people may have been provision for Nehemiah and his men. Xenophon describes one of the duties of the satrap to have been to provide troops with rations and wages, and where appropriate, with land usufruct, all of which must have been levied from the local populations (*Cyr.* 8.6; *Oec.* 4.5).[55] From the Borsippa Archive, it is clear that a form of tribute levied on the residents of Borsippa was the provision of food and probably also shelter for the newly arrived groups of Judean and Carian soldiers and

---

sieck, 1979], 49–127).

53. Wright, *Rebuilding Identity*, 157. He dismisses the conflict with Sanballat and Tobiah as the product of a later stage in the editing of the original Memoir.
54. A. Demsky, "Pelekh in Nehemiah 3," *IEJ* 33 (1983): 242–44.
55. C. Tuplin, "Xenophon and the Garrisons of the Achaemenid Empire," *Archäologische Mitteilungen aus Iran* 20 (1987): 167–245.

their families, who would reside in the town either permanently or while they awaited deployment.[56] The supply of rations and shelter for Nehemiah's soldiers (at least temporarily until their quarters were built) must have been a further cause of hardship and resentment. In Neh 5:10–15, Nehemiah persuades his men (אחי ונערי) to return what they have taken from the residents (fields, vineyards, houses, crops, and silver [Neh 5:11]) and vows not to take the governor's portion that previous governors had exacted (Neh 5:14–15).

Minor leaders in Yehud and Jerusalem

Under the heading of minor rulers, I want to examine those rulers who were already present in Jerusalem and its environs when Nehemiah arrived there and not those whom he later appointed (such as Hananiah and others bearing the title *paqid*; Neh 7:11). Lemche has described the conditions of Persian period Yehud as "anarchistic,"[57] but it is clear from the discussion so far that Nehemiah arrived into a highly structured agrarian society that, although under Persian rule, also operated with traditional forms of rule that resembled patron-client relationships. While it may have been Sanballat's duty to assemble an army to serve the Persians, he was also capable of assembling these soldiers to assist him against anyone who opposed his rule. To some extent, from a Persian perspective he had gone off mission and used his position as *pehah* to establish himself as a powerful ruler in the locale, just as dynasts and chiefs did in other regions like Xanthus and Paphlagonia.

Lemche suggests that a possible consequence of conditions from the Neo-Babylonian period and its aftermath was "retribalization," by which he means an intensification of the political role of families and lineages.[58] He even suggests that this may be reflected in the presence of genealogical lists in the priestly tradition. The general interest in the period to determine who was and who was not a Judean could be taken to indicate that a movement towards such "retribalization" was taking place.[59]

The term "retribalization" could be misleading, however, insofar as it seems to suggest a return to a pre-monarchic social organization and may seem to imply that for a period, relations of kinship had declined in importance, which they probably never did. Nevertheless, there may have been reorganization that divided regions into sub-districts, and this may be reflected in the references to *districts* and *half-districts* in Neh 3:9–18, which seem to indicate that a Jerusalem, much declined in status and size, had been divided into at least two districts: one ruled by Rafaya son of Cur and the other by Shallum the son of Hallochesh and his daughters. Both of these families must have exercised a good deal of influence in the region and must have dominated the districts over which they ruled, even if they are likely to have been subordinate to Tobiah.

---

56. Waerzeggers, "Carians," 1–22.

57. Lemche, *Early Israel*, 176.

58. Lemche, *Early Israel*, 176.

59. Lemche, Early Israel, 178. Here Lemche advises caution because of the stereotypical nature of tribal lists. J. Blenkinsopp also discusses the persistence of a tribal consciousness, and perhaps even an intensification of it after the Neo-Babylonian destruction and extending into the Persian period ("Benjamin Traditions Read in the Early Persian Period," in *Judah and the Judeans in the Persian Period*, ed. O. Lipschits and J. Blenkinsopp [Winona Lake, IN: Eisenbrauns, 2006], 629–45). Y. Levin stresses the importance of genealogies as literary devices in the Persian period in the context of an agrarian society based on the household and clan units and in this sees continuity with Israel and Judah of the Iron Age ("From Lists to History: Chronological Aspects of the Chronicler's Genealogies," *JBL* 123 [2004]: 601–36).

The term חצי, however, usually translated as 'half', can also mean 'middle', and hence the translation "ruler of the middle district of Jerusalem" is possible. At the same time, it is worth noting that while Neh 3:19 refers to work done by the ruler of Mizpah, 3:15 refers to work done by the ruler of the *pelek* of Mizpah. Were *pelekim* districts near a city but perhaps lay outside it or were considered separate from it for some reason? What precisely the role of the leaders (*sar*) over districts and half districts was is not clear, and it becomes even more puzzling when we take into account our uncertainty about what precisely *pelek* designates.

The term *sar* occurs more than 400 times in the Hebrew Bible, usually in association with royal or military matters.[60] At the same time, in the book of Ezra such a military association is not as evident (although the administrative function is evident in Ezra 8:25, where it refers to the *sarim* of the Persian king), and we find the terms "*sar* of the Abot—Israel" (Ezra 8:29) and "*sar* of the priests and Levites" (8:24; 8:29). In Jdgs 8:6, it seems to refer to local leaders (the *sarim* of Succoth). D. Edelman on the other hand, argues for a primarily military meaning for *sar* as it occurs in Nehemiah, and she notes the application of the title to Hananiah, who will be *sar* over the *birta* of Jerusalem (Neh 7:2) as well as the evidence of seals.[61] In Neh 2:9 there is reference to a *sar* of the army. In any case, if Jerusalem were primarily a *birta*, then administrative and military functions are likely to have overlapped.

In addition to these rulers, there is a long list of individuals who repaired various parts of the walls or gates; presumably, they supplied the labor and perhaps even some of the materials, and presumably in so doing they fulfilled their family's, household's, or district's duty to contribute. As in Lycia and Tayma, the environment may have given rise to the strengthening of some local families who established dynasties, a condition that, in itself, increased the importance of genealogies as a means by which such newly emerging elites could claim legitimacy. These ruling families of Jerusalem and its environs seem to operate under the patronage of Tobiah, although perhaps indirectly through Eliashiv and the ruling men who have sworn an oath to him. Nehemiah 7:70 refers to "heads (ראש) of fathers' houses," who contributed to the wall-building project, and in Neh 5:7 there is reference to חרים and סגנים, usually translated as nobles and prefects.[62] A nobleman, Meshullam ben Berechiah, who is named in Neh 3:4 as assisting in the building of the wall, had married his daughter to a son of Tobiah (Neh 6:18). R. Albertz has described Meshullam ben Berechiah as a high-ranking official who was close to Sanballat, a closeness that must have been enhanced by this marriage (Neh 3:30).[63]

M. Avi Yonah suggested that Yehud was sub-divided into six districts (adding one to Aharoni's five), which were further divided into two. His evidence is Neh 3, the list of those towns that contributed to the building of the walls. Each of these districts had a local "capital": Jerusalem, with Ramat Rahel as an important center, Keilah, with Adullam as

---

60. In Gen 21:22, *sar* is used of the commander of an army as it is in 2 Sam 23:19 where David's commanders are designated *sar*. In Jdgs 8:6, however, it may simply refer to local leaders—the *sarim* of Succoth.

61. Edelman, *Origins of the "Second" Temple*, 217–22.

62. The term סגן is unusual: BDB gives i) ruler, prefect, governor, a subordinate ruler; ii) prefects (of Assyria and Babylon); iii) petty rulers or officials. H. Zucker has argued that it refers to Persian commanders who were under Nehemiah's command (Studien zur Jüdischen Selbstverwaltung im Altertum [Berlin: Schocken Verlag, 1936], 24).

63. A. Albertz, "Purity Strategies and Political interests in the Policy of Nehemiah," in *Confronting the Past: Archaeological and Historical Essays on Ancient Israel*, ed. S. Gitin, J. P. Dessel, and E. Wright (Winona Lake, IN: Eisenbrauns, 2006), 199–206 (201–3).

a "capital," Mizpah, with Gibeon as a center, Bet Haccarem, with Zanoah as center, Bet-Zur, with Tekoah as center, and Jericho, with Sana'ah as a center.[64] However, Avi Yonah's reconstruction depends on the translation of the term *pelek* as "district," and this is by no means certain.

As already noted, Demsky has argued that the term should be translated as "corvee labor" rather than district.[65] Nonetheless, we should bear in mind that it is very likely that even if the term referred to "corvee labor," such labor was usually taken from regions ruled by an administrator, often a member of the local elite who perhaps held a traditional leadership role and title (for example, chief, head of a household, or village), so it could still reveal something about the breakdown of Yehud into administrative districts. We should also bear in mind, however, that boundaries could frequently change, so the districts referred to here, if district is, indeed, the correct translation, may reveal information only about Nehemiah's time. Edelman notes that five of the places referred to as *pelek* in Neh 3 were probably all sites of forts: so, for example, Jerusalem, Mizpah, Bet-Hakkerem (Ramat-Rahel), Khirbet-Keilah, and Bet-Zur housed forts in the Persian period.[66] In her view, labor provided by these *pelekim* may have been provided by soldiers of these forts operating under a military commander and is being distinguished from labor provided by others: goldsmiths, shepherds, and perfumers, for example.[67]

Similar to many other regions under Persian rule (Lycia, Paphlagonia, and Mysia for example), the boundaries of the small, rural district of Yehud were likely to have fluctuated constantly and were, in any case, ill-defined. This fluctuation would have resulted largely from two factors: of a lack of Persian presence in what was a relatively unimportant region and changing relations and shifting dominance among the local leaders such as Sanballat, Tobiah, and Eliashiv and their clients. At least until later in the Persian period, its inhabitants may never have understood themselves to have been part of a precisely defined geographical and political unit but rather, may have felt their allegiance to lie in more local units, such as clans and villages, as seems likely from the units out of which the labor is drawn in Neh 3,[68] or perhaps the regions referred to as "districts" and "half-districts" or

---

64. M. Avi Yonah, *The Holy Land: From the Persian to the Arab Conquests* (Grand Rapids: Baker Book House, 1966), 13–33. With regard to Beth-Zur, it has been argued that in the Persian period and even in the early Hellenistic period, the site shows barely any signs of occupation (R. W. Funk, "Beth-Zur," in *The New Encyclopedia of Archaeological Excavations in the Holy Land*, vol. 1, ed. E. Stern. [New York: Simon & Schuster, 1993], 260–61). E. Stern, however, believes that there is evidence of occupation and economic activities at the site (*Material Culture*, 432–43). R. Reich thinks that a Persian governor resided in Beth-Zur ("Assyrian Royal Buildings in the Land of Israel," in *The Architecture of Ancient Israel*, ed. H. Katzenstein, A. Kempenski, and R. Reich [Jerusalem: Jerusalem Exploration Society, 1992], 214–22). Another one of Avi-Yonah's centers, Gibeon, is thought by J. B. Pritchard to have been unoccupied in the Persian period ("Gibeon," in *The New Encyclopedia of Archaeological Excavations in the Holy Land*, vol. 2. ed. E. Stern [New York: Simon & Schuster, 1993], 513) and Stern thinks activity and occupation at Gibeon were restricted to the early Persian period (*Material Culture*, 432–33). Thus, the evidence is difficult to interpret.

65. Demsky, "Pelekh," 242–44, and see L. L. Grabbe, *A History of Jews and Judaism in the Second Temple Period, Volume I: The Persian Province of Judah* (London: T&T Clark, 2004), 139.

66. Edelman, *Origins of the 'Second' Temple*, 213–16.

67. Edelman, *Origins of the 'Second' Temple*, 216.

68. Lemche describes a period of retribalization (Early Israel) while D. Smith-Christopher argues for the renewed importance of the structure of the Beth-Av, which becomes a much larger unit in this period, resembling more the structure and size of the tribe (The Religion of the Landless: *The Social Context of*

perhaps middle districts in the NM, which were ruled by powerful families like that of Rephaiah son of Hur (Neh 3:9) and Shallum son of Hallohesh and his daughters (Neh 3:12).[69] Consequently, they are more likely to have regarded themselves as living under the protection (with the corresponding duties) of a powerful, local family, a condition already observed in Lycia and among the Mysian and Paphlagonian chiefdoms[70] and which I think may be reflected in the relationship enjoyed by the leading men of Jerusalem and the priest Eliashiv with Tobiah.

The diversity of forms of leadership shows the persistence of traditional forms of political leadership in Yehud and in neighboring regions and districts, just as we have seen the persistence of a variety of forms in other conquered regions such as Tayma, Paphlygonia, Mysia, and Lycia. The term סגן, used to describe some sort of officials or leaders in Yehud, may have an Assyrian or Babylonian origin.[71] Nonetheless, while such diversity can be observed, these rulers appear to have operated on the common basis of hereditary rule and kinship ties, including those cultivated by marriage, which remained important. These local powers could be classified as minor leaders in the region who were subject to local, higher-ranking noblemen; in Jerusalem, this nobleman was Tobiah the Ammonite. The participation of these leaders of districts and half-districts in Nehemiah's building project came only after much coercion from Nehemiah, and Nehemiah records that while Tekoa supplied workers, the rulers of Tekoa would not lower their necks (Neh 3:5). What is likely indicated by this is the reluctance of these local leaders to participate and their ongoing resistance to Nehemiah's leadership and to the leaders he would install in the *birta*.

While these minor rulers were all far lower down in the political pecking order than Sanballat, Tobiah, and even Eliashiv, they were nonetheless not to be ignored by Nehemiah, who, in the end, had to introduce some conciliatory measures in order to see his imperial wall building project completed. In response to the complaints of the people about the hardship the completion of the imperial building project was causing, Nehemiah promises

---

the Babylonian Exile [Bloomington, IN: Meyer-Stone, 1989], 5–11).

69. It should be noted that elsewhere in Achaemenid documents, *pilku* (equivalent to *pelek*) appears to refer to a district (Avi Yonah, *Holy Land*, 13–33).

70. Briant notes that Paphlagonia was split between several rival chiefdoms (*From Cyrus*, 642). Moreover, archaeology reveals that there was not much change in Paphlagonia under Achaemenid rule. Nonetheless, we should not think that these chiefdoms were in any way "cut off" from wider influences; L. Summerer and A. von Kienlin have shown that the architecture of tombs from Paphlagonia shows both Greek and Persian influence ("Achaemenid Impact in Paphlagonia: Rupestral Tombs in the Amnias Valley," http://www.pontos.dk/publications/books/bss-11-files/bss-11-summerer). Xenophon (*Hell.* 4.1.12–15) reports marriages between Paphlagonian and Achaemenid elites. Thus, it is not intended that the categorization "chiefdom" indicates a simpler political form that has not quite reached the sophistication of a state.

71. The persistence of such forms of traditional leadership ought not to be attributed to tolerance on the part of the Persians but is more likely to have been part of what was a practical response to on-the-ground conditions encountered in some regions. Such a response is likely to be attributable to different reasons in each location: for example, R. Thapar has argued that the continuation of the chieftaincy form among the Paphlagonians is to be accounted for by the fact that it was a region without "much economic potential" ("The State as Empire," in *The Study of the State*, ed. H. J. M. Claessen and P. Skalmik [The Hague: Mouton 1981], 409–26). We should note, however, that the appearance of tombs in Paphlagonia that display Achaemenid and Greek features (Summerer and von Kienlin, "Achaemenid Impact in Paphlagonia: Rupestral tombs in the Amnias Valley," 195–221) will not permit us to oversimplify the situation among the Paphlagonian peoples. A. Kuhrt maintains that the Paphlagonian tribes were fairly strictly administered by the Persians (*The Persian Empire: A Corpus of Sources of the Achaemenid Period* [London: Routledge, 2007], 826).

to return property that had been confiscated by the priests, thus disempowering the disloyal Eliashiv and his entourage (Neh 5:12). In Neh 5:7, the nobles and leaders of Jerusalem (חרים and סגנים) are rebuked for usury. The text clearly implies that both the חרים and סגנים are local elites who oppress their "brethren," not "foreigners" or Persians.[72] In Neh 5:10, Nehemiah turns to his own men ('my brethren' אחי and 'my servants' נערי); presumably, the text is referring to those soldiers who had travelled from Susa with Nehemiah. He bids them to restore the fields, vineyards, olive yards, houses, and one hundredth part of the money and grain that had been given by the residents of Jerusalem to Nehemiah's men. Again, our Borsippa texts may provide a parallel: the duty of the provision of rations and shelter for both Judean and Carian immigrants in Borsippa who were in the employ of the Persians fell to the citizens of Borsippa. Like the administrators in the Borsippean texts that relate to establishing a system for providing rations to immigrant Judean and Carian soldiers, it is Nehemiah's job to see that the new arrivals to Judah, there to fulfil an imperial mission, are provided for so as to ensure their successful settlement and the establishment of the troop in the *birta*. But the fierce and persistent resistance he encounters from already well-established leaders and their clients means that he is forced to compromise; it is more a case of Nehemiah's wresting the population of Jerusalem and its environs from the influence of local leaders than it is a case of his winning it.

A brief word on Neh 5, Nehemiah's so-called socio-economic reforms, is pertinent. Prior to widespread use of coinage, debt in the ancient world was a relationship of obligation that bound the debtor to the creditor rather than a financial matter. It is no wonder, then, that Nehemiah paid such attention to debts. His goal, after all, was to regulate the elites who opposed him and to curb their influence in Jerusalem, and as we have seen, the most appropriate way to describe the socio-political system in Nehemiah's day is as a system of multi-layered, patron-client type relations, at the heart of which were relationships between leaders of various standing and the local populations.

When Nehemiah cancelled debts, he may have been attempting to disempower the elites, the nobles, and leaders in Jerusalem and its environs and to wrest the local population from their influence so that they could make a new pledge to him and to his power base, the imperially recognized *birta* of Jerusalem. Thus, as in the aftermath of the reforms instituted by Solon, the allegiance of the small landholders (presumably most of the population) shifted. Although those in debt may have been somewhat relieved as a result of Nehemiah's reform, his primary goal was to complete the walls and to curtail the power of the elite in relation to the population he was trying to wrest from their grip.

The immediate target of his reform would have been the class of creditors, who formed an increasingly powerful subset of the elite. Creditors would only have been found among the better-off classes, and outside of Jerusalem, it seems likely that patrons like Ṭobiah and Geshem would have provided this service to their clients (some of whom resided in and outside of Jerusalem) as a normal part of services offered by patrons to clients. Tobiah and his family, as well as the wealthier influential class in Jerusalem who had demonstrated such loyalty to Tobiah, may have been the direct targets of his economic reform.

Understanding debt as a relationship of obligation that can last for generations (rather than as a simple financial matter) means that the debt cancellation of Nehemiah can be viewed as part of his attempt to limit the influence of local leaders who stood in the way of his imperial mission. Not only are the creditors deprived of what they are owed;

---

72. Although see above, n. 62.

more importantly, the debts are cancelled and with them, any obligation of loyalty to the creditor. The same observation applies to Solon's reforms. It is likely that all of Nehemiah's wealthy opponents were both creditors and debtors at some level in what was quite a complex and multi-layered system of socio-economic and political relationships.

For the poor, as Grabbe notes, this was a mixed blessing. While they had their legal relations of obligation to their creditors severed, they may now have found themselves without a creditor.[73] Without patronage and protection, they could perhaps do nothing more than adjust their allegiance, turning to Nehemiah and his appointees for support, and more specifically, to the new economy centered on the *birta* in Jerusalem. First, they would become obliged to complete the wall and eventually, after Nehemiah's easing of their economic plight, (in which he claims to have had the support of his men, Neh 5), their loyalty to the city's new leadership in the form of Hananiah the *sar* of the *birta* would follow (Neh 7:2).

If this presentation of the political context of Nehemiah's reforms is reasonable, then his reforms would have been met with severe opposition because they would have threatened long-standing relations between clients and patrons. Nonetheless, the leaders—or at least some of them—became part of the new set of political relationships established by Nehemiah; it was the Yehudîm and the סגנים who sat at his table after the reforms of Neh 5, as well as those who had come from among the nations (Neh 5:17).

Nehemiah's severing of relations between the wealthier leaders (who were in a position to offer credit) and the poor proved only temporary, and while Nehemiah was away from Jerusalem, older patron-client relationships were restored: Tobiah was reinstated, and the economy based around the temple chamber and the priesthood reverted to the old system (Neh 13:4). Jerusalemite and Yehudite nobles reversed Nehemiah's Sabbath regulations by permitting labor and trade on the Sabbath (Neh 13:15–16), and the Levites retreated to the countryside (Neh 13:10). The rulers of Jerusalem and Eliashiv the priest played a vital role in reinstating Tobiah's economic policies in Jerusalem and the social and political loyalties that accompanied them (client-patron relationships). These restored relations would have displaced those newly established by the imperial appointee, Nehemiah.

Nehemiah's attempt to establish limits and boundaries to trading practices on the Sabbath is likely also to fit into his overall mission to change the allegiance of the Yehudîm by eliminating some of their patrons. Here again, Nehemiah probably severed links within a trading network that had existed between Jerusalemite leaders and others like Geshem and merchants from Tyre, who now fell outside the boundaries of Jerusalem. Trade in the ancient Near East was conducted on the basis of personal relationships between individuals and trading families, and often such relationships lasted centuries.[74] They were governed by oaths of loyalty and systems of gift exchange and other diplomatic gestures (such as marriage between influential families; and perhaps the granting of a chamber in the temple to Tobiah by Elishiv should be understood as an aspect of such relationships) and were crucial to the ancient economy. Nehemiah could not have hoped to sever the relationships and bonds between the nobles in Jerusalem and Yehud who opposed him and individuals such as Tobiah, who supported them in this opposition, without directing his attention to trade relationships. There is no doubt that trade was conducted between the Jerusalemite nobles

---

73. Grabbe, *Ezra-Nehemiah*, 164.
74. For the importance of this aspect of trade in the ancient world, see P. Kohl, "The Ancient Economy, Transferable Technologies in the Bronze Age World System: A View from the Northeastern Frontier of the Ancient Near East," in *Centre and Periphery in the Ancient World*, ed. M. Rowlands, M. Larsen, and K. Kristiansen (Cambridge: Cambridge University Press, 1987), 13–24 (15–17).

and Yehudîm and "foreigners" living outside the city and that it was an important aspect of patron-client relationships (Neh 13:15–17).

Nehemiah 13:16 specifically identifies the "men of Zor" (Tyre) who dwelt within the city as interfering with the Sabbath by selling to "the men of Judah and Jerusalem" on the Sabbath, but they only could have conducted trade with the co-operation of the Yehudîm inside the city; hence, it is the "nobles" of Yehud with whom Nehemiah pleads (Neh 13:17).[75] In Neh 13:15, reference is made to Yehudîm "bringing in goods" to Jerusalem to sell on the Sabbath. Thus, the ban on Sabbath trade was directed not just at "foreigners" but more particularly, at the Yehudîm and the nobles of the Yehudîm who persisted in conducting relations with them, thereby inhibiting the implementation of Nehemiah's plan for Jerusalem. There is no indication, however, that these trading activities were to come to an end; rather, they were no longer to be conducted on the Sabbath, and the reason for this is likely to have been rooted in Nehemiah's personal motives (and not in imperial plans) to transform Jerusalem into a settlement in line with his own understanding of the ideal Jerusalem. At the same time, since Nehemiah had succeeded in enforcing his will in relation to trade on the Sabbath, he had also won the right to oversee trade activities and the relationships between Jerusalemites and traders from outside Jerusalem in matters going beyond Sabbath trade.

What could Nehemiah have hoped to achieve by this? While his motivation may have been simply (or partly) religious, (he simply did not want the Sabbath profaned [Neh 13:17]), his insistence that all should observe the Sabbath could be part of his effort to enforce the recognition of Jerusalem and its cultic laws not just on Yehudîm, but also on all those who traded with the Yehudîm over whom he now asserted his authority. Once achieved, such recognition would bring with it the recognition of the authority of Jerusalem, its *birta*, its governor, and its priesthood and would achieve new status in the region for this settlement. Trade with those living in Jerusalem was now controlled through Nehemiah and his men, and with the revival(?) of this trade law relating to the Sabbath, it would not be possible to conduct trade without his (or his appointee's) knowledge; no one could pass through the gate, which would now function as a mechanism through which trading relations could be monitored. Perhaps this had other implications; it is possible that some kind of toll was introduced that was payable by traders entering and leaving the city (Yehudîm and non-Yehudîm), and if that were the case, then the Persians would have been satisfied to increase revenue; it would have been of little consequence to them that their appointee revived an old Jerusalem cultic law to do so.[76] Perhaps something about the trade conducted between the men of Jerusalem, the Yehudîm, and foreigner elites who operated

---

75. For detailed discussion of the traders from Tyre, see D. Edelman, "Tyrian Trade in Yehud under Artaxerxes I: Real or Imagined?" in *Judah and Judeans in the Persian Period*, ed. O. Lipschits and M. Oeming (Winona Lake, IN: 2006), 207–46.

76. Assyrian administration controlled fairly inaccessible regions such as the Zagros region by establishing check-points through which the pastoralists would have to pass. This enabled the Assyrians to tax this group of subjects in spite of the instability of their lifestyle and their inaccessibility and to demand tolls for passage between seasonal pastures (A. Greco, "Zagros Pastoralism and Assyrian Imperial Expansion," in *Continuity of Empire (?) Assyria, Media, Persia, Proceedings of the International Meeting in Padua, 26th—28th April 2001*, ed. G. B. Lanfranchi, M. Roaf, and R. Rollinger, HANEM 5 [Padova: S.A.R.G.O.N. Editrice e Libreria, 2003], 65–78). The aforementioned inscription from Xanthus recounts how the leaders of Xanthus, Tlos, Pinara, and Kandaya, were permitted by the satrap to keep one tenth of the "harbor tax" for themselves, presumably in return for overseeing the trade and ensuring that all levies and taxes were exacted. For the text, see Kuhrt, *Persian Empire*, 703, n.12.

in a network led by the Samarian leader Sanballat may have included the monitoring of trade and traders who may have sought to evade imperial tolls and taxes. Were the men of Tyre managing to evade such tolls and taxes, which would have been illegal from an imperial perspective?

Remembering and Forgetting Leaders of the Persian Period

Reading between the lines of the NM, a highly charged and competitive environment between local leaders and their higher ranking patrons can be reconstructed, and Nehemiah had to contend with all of them, from the higher ranking Sanballat to the leading men of Jerusalem and its districts. Such an environment was far from ideal and significantly dissonant with what ideals of return would have envisaged; a far cry indeed from the imagining in the Second Isaiah of a new exodus from Babylonia back to the Promised Land (Isa 52:1–4) and a far cry from later Jewish idealization of the period, seen, for example, in the traditions in Ben Sira and 2 Maccabees.

While many models of leadership appear in the NM, only the leadership of Nehemiah would be remembered in later tradition.[77] In the Memoir, the leaders of districts are present only in order to form part of the background to Nehemiah's work, playing a minor role as obstacles to be overcome through Nehemiah's ultimate elimination of the more powerful leaders like Sanballat and his client, Tobiah. It could be argued that Nehemiah was more loyal to the Persian government than he was to the Yehudîm; at least that is certainly how the rulers and upper classes of Jerusalem must have seen it—how else could we account for their turning back to Tobiah? As I shall demonstrate, this competitive environment and the major and minor rulers who opposed Nehemiah will be virtually airbrushed out of later traditions about Nehemiah in favor of a leader who was of the people, so to speak, implementing their will and remaining mindful of their needs.

The virtual elimination of the voices of local rulers as genuinely representing the views of the Yehudîm in these later traditions about the Persian period is also accompanied by a representation of Nehemiah as a more pious figure. It is widely agreed that later editors have inserted an account about Ezra into the NM (Neh 8:1–8); Ezra appears quite suddenly to persuade the people, to move them to prayer, and to evoke from them a commitment to observe the Torah.[78] Up until this point in the account, everything Nehemiah has done would seem to have served his purpose of establishing a *birta* in Jerusalem and eliminating local rulers like Tobiah, Sanballat, and Geshem from its affairs, and it is clear that the nobles of Jerusalem stand on the side of Tobiah, not Nehemiah.

But this pragmatist (as Grabbe has described him)[79] failed to meet the expectations of later communities of interpreters as they searched through the past to find traces of themselves and of their religious practices, and it is possible that the traditions about Ezra were developed to fill this gap. As we shall see, for those who preserved the memory of Nehemiah, we frequently encounter embellishment that associates him with practices not

---

77. For a discussion and possible explanations of the "overlooking" of the canonical traditions about Jeshua and Zerubbabel (Ezra 1–6 and Haggai and Zech 1–8) in later traditions such as Sirach 49:11–16 and 1 Esdras 5:47–50, see Edelman, "Were Zerubbabel and Nehemiah," 124.

78. In many respects, Ezra fits into the Greek notion of the ideal lawgiver insofar as the importance of the ability of a good lawgiver to persuade rather than to force was a significant element in the embellishment of the primary traditions about Greek lawgivers; for discussion, see Fitzpatrick-McKinley, "Ezra Nehemiah," 17–49.

79. Grabbe, *Ezra-Nehemiah*, 189–92.

originally credited to him, and in some cases, he bears little resemblance to the figure in the NM. From this later perspective, and perhaps particularly during the period of Hasmonean rule, the re-walling of Jerusalem must have been viewed as a foundational moment in the history of Jerusalem and its temple, part of the narrative of the great return, but it lacked some fundamental components of later Judaism: the willingness of the people to observe Torah and the presence of a Torah scribe and priest such as Ezra.

In Neh 8:9, Nehemiah is introduced into the scene (we cannot assume his presence in Neh 8:1–8 where Ezra reads the law), thus bringing him into direct association with Ezra the pious Torah scholar, despite the chronological problems this creates.[80] At this point, the writer notes the differences between Nehemiah and Ezra: Nehemiah is a governor and Ezra is a scribe and a priest (Neh 8:9). Perhaps the author points to the differences to demonstrate here the appropriateness of dual leadership, a point of contention by the end of Hyrcanus's reign,[81] or perhaps he is simply trying to reconcile two conflicting accounts or traditions.

Now the Levites are also given a role as teachers (Neh 8:9), a role that is not ascribed to them in the original NM. There they were appointed as gatekeepers (Neh 13:22), a task first assigned to Nehemiah's own men (Neh 13:19). Through this clarification of roles, the writer has acknowledged that the reader might at this point become confused by the association of these two, once separate figures. By allowing the Torah-pious priest/scribe Ezra to take the stage, the author demonstrated first that Nehemiah, the Persian appointed, non-priestly, non-scribal ruler of Jerusalem, acknowledged the important role of priests, particularly in relation to teaching and ruling on Torah, and the importance of teaching it to the people.

We can compare this view to the lack of respect shown in the NM to the priest Eliashiv, the loyal client of Tobiah, which again from the perspective of later Judaism, might have been somewhat problematic.[82] Secondly, Nehemiah's work takes on a new tone with Nehemiah the pragmatist immediately becoming associated with Torah observance. Rather than having to cajole the people and persuade them through the cancellation of debts, he is shown to have their support: he is present with Ezra when Ezra reads the law (Neh 8:9).

While the insertion of these chapters into the NM establishes an association between Nehemiah the founder of the *birta* and the Torah, and between Nehemiah and the priest and scribe Ezra, other traditions do not make this association. Nehemiah is a crucial figure in the traditions of the restoration of Jerusalem in Sirach, where Ezra does not appear at all, but here Nehemiah is not associated with the Torah: he is the builder of the walls, gates, and houses (Sir 48:13), and it could be argued that this account is more faithful to the original NM, which was an expansive building report, particularly in so far as it attributes the restoration of the temple to Zerubbabel and Joshua (Sir 48:11–12). Ben Sira's concern appears to have been to show how the temple city was the fulfilment of the covenant, and

---

80. We again witness here a similar step to that taken by those who embellished the primary traditions about Greek lawgivers: the more pragmatic figure takes on a moral and philosophical role through his fictional meeting/association with a philosopher (Fitzpatrick-McKinley, "Ezra, Nehemiah and some Early Greek Lawgivers," 17–49).

81. Jubilees, too, takes the point of view that there should be a separation, so the author creates new historical roles for Levi (religious) and Judah (secular) (D. Mendels, *The Rise and Fall of Jewish Nationalism*, Anchor Bible Reference Library [New York: Doubleday, 1992], 44, 70; idem, "Hecataeus of Abdera and a Jewish 'patrios politeia,'" *ZAW* 95 (1983): 97–110.

82. In the Memoir, Eliashiv is a leader of secondary importance: he appears subservient to Tobiah.

for this, the basic building report of the heroic figure Nehemiah served his purposes very well. Nehemiah became a central node in the memory, standing alongside figures such as Abraham, David, Elijah, and Simon the high priest, to whom over twenty verses are dedicated, a fact which reflects the author's concerns with conditions in his own day.[83]

Nehemiah also appears in 2 Maccabees, the date and provenance of which is not agreed; proposed dates range from 164 BCE to the middle of the first century CE, with suggested provenances of Jerusalem or Alexandria.[84] T. A. Bergren has described the work as a "pro-Judas, Hasmonean propaganda."[85] In its current form, it represents an expansion of the tradition in NM or of some other memory of Nehemiah not known to us. As in Sirach, Nehemiah is remembered as a builder, but while Sirach credits the building of the temple to Zerubbabel and Joshua (Sir 49:11–12),[86] here it is credited to Nehemiah, who is also credited with the building of the altar; there is no mention of his building of walls and houses (Sir 48; 2 Macc 1:18). In the tradition in 2 Maccabees, as in Sirach, no reference is made to Nehemiah's ban on intermarriage. As I have argued elsewhere, his attention to the issue was based on his desire to eliminate his opponents through the dissolution of their marriages to Jerusalem families,[87] and since 2 Maccabees makes no reference to any opposition to Nehemiah, no potentially contentious reference is made to his ban on intermarriage. There is not much evidence that intermarriage was regarded as a problem until much later, in any case.[88] Nor do the authors who commit the story of Nehemiah to writing in 2 Maccabees make any reference to opposition to him from Sanballat and others, a theme that plays such a central role in the NM.

A further and quite dramatic departure from the original memoir is the association of Nehemiah with the preservation of the fire of the first temple (2 Macc 1:19–36), which is

---

83. B. L. Mack notes that for the authors of Ben Sira, the temple state was an appropriate climax to Israel's covenantal history (*Wisdom and the Hebrew Bible: Ben Sira's Hymn in Praise of the Fathers*, [Chicago, IL: University of Chicago Press, 1985], 84). If the author of Ben Sira knew of a figure Ezra, he must have been so minor that he is not even mentioned. If he did not know of a figure Ezra, we need not necessarily conclude that Ezra was not a historical figure or even that the sources about him post-date Ecclesiasticus; such sources may simply have been transmitted in other circles. For the rejection of Ezra as historical and the view that what is reflected here is anti-Hasmonean ideology dating to some time after 180 BCE see J.C.H. Lebram, "Die Traditionsgeschichte der Esragestalt und die Frage nach dem historischen Esra," in *Achaemenid History I: Sources, Structures and Synthesis*, ed. H. Sancisi-Weerdenburg (Leiden: Instituut voor het Nabije Oosten, 1987), 103–38.

84. D. de Silva, *Introducing the Apocrypha: Message, Context and Significance* (Grand Rapids, MI: Baker House, 2002), 269–70. J. J. Collins describes it as a summary of the history some time close to the Maccabean crisis and before 124 BCE (*Between Athens and Jerusalem, Jewish Identity in the Hellenistic Diaspora* [Grand Rapids, MI: Eerdmans, 2000], 77–78).

85. T. A. Bergren, "Ezra and Nehemiah Square Off in the Apocrypha and Pseudepigrapha," in *Biblical Figures Outside the Bible*, ed. M. E. Stone and T. A. Bergren (Harrisburg: Trinity, 1998), 340–66 (359).

86. Later, Nehemiah and Zerubbabel seem to have been regarded as one and the same person (b. Sanh 38a), as D. Schwartz notes (*2 Maccabees* [Berlin: de Gruyter, 2008], 152). Edelman explores the possibility in detail and has suggested that Zerubbabel and Nehemiah may indeed have been the same person, which would explain why Nehemiah is credited with work elsewhere associated with Zerubbabel. This would explain a number of problems associated with the traditions, including the royal overtones ascribed to Nehemiah in the Memoir (Edelman, "Were Zerubbabel and Nehemiah," 125–31).

87. Fitzpatrick-McKinley, *Empire, Power and Indigenous Elites*, 230–38.

88. See discussion in Hayes, "Intermarriage and Impurity," 3–36 and C. Hayes, *Gentile Impurities and Jewish Identities: Intermarriage and Conversion from the Bible to the Talmud* (Oxford: Oxford University Press, 2002), 53–55; 73–81.

not even hinted at in the NM.[89] The account of the rededication of the temple by Nehemiah and the miraculous finding of the oil that had been used in the sacrificial fire of the first temple is a high point of the entire narrative. It is followed by Jonathan the high priest leading the people in prayer, exercising a similar role to that of Ezra and the Levites in the later tradition of Neh 8–9. As he is portrayed in the NM, the figure of Eliashiv may have been more of a nuisance to Nehemiah than the serious threat his patron Tobiah represented and, by extension, Sanballat, who was subservient to Tobiah. Moreover, Eliashiv was untrustworthy, betraying Nehemiah when he was away at Susa (Neh 13). While there is no account of Eliashiv leading the people in prayer in the NM, here Nehemiah, who has officiated over the lighting of the sacrifice, instructing the priests (2 Macc 1:21), takes a step back (just as he appears to have done in Neh 8), allowing the high priest Jonathan to lead him (and the people) in prayer (2 Macc 1:23).

Leadership has been newly defined: Nehemiah is the builder of the temple and the altar, the non-priestly civic leader operating with the approval of the Persian king, even instructing the priests, but deferring to the priests when it comes to the point of carrying out the rituals.[90] Nehemiah instructs on sacrifices, but he does not perform them.[91] The community is given a passive but participatory role in so far as they are led in prayer by the high priest, and the writer notes of the priests officiating under Nehemiah's instructions that they are "pious priests of the time," (2 Macc 1:19), a statement the author may have found necessary since he lived after the time of Jason, Menelaus, and Alcimus.[92]

Thus, Nehemiah's leadership in 2 Maccabees represents some significant departures from the account in the NM: he was a leader who encountered no opposition from the priesthood, the people, or neighboring leaders but had their full support. He was leader who had restored not the walls, but the temple and the altar. In all of this he had the support of the Persians (2 Macc 1:33),[93] and there is no hint that his mission was to establish a *birta* in Jerusalem on behalf of the Persian government. One of the most intriguing aspects of this memory of Nehemiah is the account of his role in the preservation of the fire of the first temple. Nowhere else is he credited with this, and the idea of guarding, protecting, or hiding the fire is not found in any other place in the Bible, leading Blenkinsopp to suggest that it is likely the author invented his material, although he concedes that the author may have drawn on material that circulated during his own time.[94]

Bergren suggests that the author of 2 Maccabees needed to establish continuity between the first and the second temples (2 Macc 1:20–36; 2:13–15) in order to demonstrate the legitimacy of the institution and its rituals in his own day, and the memory of the figure of Nehemiah enabled him to do so, with the fire fulfilling precisely the function

---

89. See my earlier discussion of this tradition in A. Fitzpatrick-McKinley, "What did Nehemiah do for Judaism," in *A Wandering Galilean: Essays in Honour of Sean Freyne* (Leiden: Brill 2009), 112–15. See also discussion of tradition of fire and its association with Nehemiah in Edelman, "Were Zerubbabel and Nehemiah," 120–25.

90. For discussion of the importance of the authors' choice of Nehemiah precisely because he was a non-priestly, non-royal figure, Edelman, "Were Zerubbabel and Nehemiah," 125.

91. In 2 Macc 1:18, however, no mention of the priests is made, and it appears to be Nehemiah who offered sacrifice.

92. As Schwartz observes (*2 Maccabees*, 152).

93. He thus contrasts with the later Hasmonean ruler Aristobolus, as Edelman notes ("Were Zerubbabel and Nehemiah," 127).

94. Blenkinsopp, *Ezra-Nehemiah*, 56.

of establishing continuity: this was the fire that had been ignited by YHWH in the time of Moses.[95] Schwartz suggests an allusion to 1 Kgs 18:33–38, where before YHWH's fire lights the sacrifice, the offering is doused with water, as it is here (2 Macc 1:21),[96] creating a link between Nehemiah and the prophet Elijah. In Lev 9:24, fire from YHWH lights the sacrifice, and in Lev 10:1–2, the sons of Aaron are punished for lighting a sacrifice with "strange fire" viz. not the fire that came out from YHWH. The theme of YHWH's lighting of the fire does not occur very often in the Hebrew Bible, but in each case, it appears to counteract an attempt to light the sacrifice with fire from another source: in Leviticus the sons of Aaron use a strange fire, in 1 Kgs 18 the prophets of Baal fail to bring down a fire to light the sacrifice.

In 2 Maccabees the purpose may have been to respond to protests about the purity of the temple as it existed under the Hasmonean leaders, which amounted to the argument that the new temple was not as good as the first. Lest the reader be in doubt about the credentials of the sacred, sacrificial fire Nehemiah had used to light the sacrifice of the newly dedicated temple (2 Macc 1:18), 2 Macc 2 serves to reassure: "One finds in the records that Jeremiah the prophet ordered those who were being deported to take some of the fire," while he himself hid the tent, the ark, and the altar of incense in a cave on the Mountain of Moses until YHWH would gather his people together again (2 Macc 2:4–8). Thus, Nehemiah had used the fire Jeremiah had instructed to be hidden, and now Moses and Solomon are brought into the account; they, too, had witnessed YHWH's ignition of the sacrifices following their prayer to YHWH (2 Macc 2:8–10), and in v. 13 we are told that "the same things are reported in the records and in the memories of Nehemiah," viz. Nehemiah had prayed just as Moses and Solomon had done and fire had come down from heaven to consume the sacrifice. Nehemiah's credentials are thereby well established and his original imperial mission to establish a *birta* in Jerusalem has been completely airbrushed out of the account, as have all accounts of opposition to him from the leaders of Jerusalem, its neighborhoods, and its environs: instead, Nehemiah's leadership centers around the temple, and he is the guardian and preserver of the fire, who instructs the priests on how it should be ignited again by YHWH. He stands alongside Moses, Jeremiah, and Solomon. Gone are his pragmatic concerns and his egotistical interests so central to the NM;[97] his only concern is with the temple, its continuity, and the purity of the fire that will light the sacrifice.

Most importantly for the author, through this association with the founder of the second temple, Judas's credentials are established and compared with those of later Hasmonean rulers.[98] As Schwartz observes, the theme of the fire is taken up again in 2 Macc 10:3, where we find out why Nehemiah instructed the priests to pour the unused oil out onto the rocks: the oil will lie there until it will be rekindled by Judas during his re-dedication of the temple, when it will be used to light the sacrifice ("Having ignited rocks and extracted fire from

---

95. Bergren, "Ezra and Nehemiah Square Off," 340–66. Edelman also notes that the crucial aspect of the fire narrative is the establishment of continuity between the first and the second temple but is not convinced that Nehemiah is the model for Judas since Nehemiah is contrasted with him, as well as with Moses and Solomon, in so far as in this tradition he has neither priestly nor royal connections ("Were Zerubbabel and Nehemiah," 120, 127).
96. Schwartz, *2 Maccabees*, 153. The Greek term usually translated as "liquid" literally means "water" (Schwartz, *2 Maccabees*, 153).
97. Grabbe, *Ezra-Nehemiah*, 144–45.
98. Edelman, "Were Zerubbabel and Nehemiah," 127.

them").[99] Thus, not only did Nehemiah instruct the pious priests as to where the sacred fire had been hidden, but after he had ensured that the sacrifice was correctly ignited by the fire from the first temple, he made provision for the days of his successor (now also a successor standing in the line of Moses, Solomon, and Jeremiah) by once again guarding the fire by pouring it in the form of oil onto the rocks, where Judas and his men can recover it after their liberation of the temple. In a sense, then, the memory of Nehemiah's leadership in 2 Maccabees is really more about the creation of a memory of Judas Maccabaeus, and the themes are more pertinent to the early Hasmonean ruler than to the Nehemiah of the Memoir.

How has the theme of the preservation of the fire and the guardianship of the fire by the deported pious priests and their descendants (2 Macc 1:20) become so central to the account when it was not a major theme in the Hebrew Bible? In fact, it did not appear at all in the earlier traditions about Nehemiah's leadership, nor in the account of the rededication in 1 Macc 4:41–58. Perhaps part of an explanation is hinted at in the text, which notes how impressed the king of the Persians was with the miraculous preservation of the fire and its guardianship from the time of the destruction of the temple and the period of return and rebuilding (2 Macc 1:30–33).

It is possible that the theme of the eternal fire, and more particularly of its guardianship, has found its way into the account of Nehemiah through contact with Persian culture. In vv. 33–34, the authors record that when the king of Persia heard about the fire hidden since the days of the Babylonian deportation by the exiled priests and how it had been used by Nehemiah and the priests to ignite the sacrifice, he was so impressed he enclosed the site and made it sacred, honoring those who had guarded the fire and re-ignited it with the preserved liquid with gifts. Why was such attention given to the reaction of the Persian king?

Perhaps the authors are recognizing that the theme of the eternal fire would resonate with the Persians, viz. the Achaemenid rulers of the sixth to fourth centuries BCE, and their veneration of the eternal fire; hence, preserved in this strange story of Nehemiah is yet another memory that had undergone Persian influence and dates back before the writing of 2 Maccabees, although it was not preserved in the NM. However, since the authors of 2 Maccabees are clearly content to eliminate material as well as to introduce new material to their account, the question arises as to whether they were simply inventing a story about Nehemiah's role in preserving the fire for which they had no basis in either history or earlier memory.

But why would the authors attempt to impress the Persian rulers after their rule had ended in a time when the Seleucids were in power (if we give this part of the book an early date) or in a time when Jewish independence had been achieved (if we accept a later date for 2 Maccabees)? One could argue that they were claiming that foreign kings of the past had recognized the extraordinary nature of the eternal fire, believing themselves to be providing a useful lesson to the Seleucids: they needed to respect the temple cult as the Achaemenids had done. But I think there is a closer engagement here with Persian practices than sometimes assumed. Furthermore, the story of the guardianship of the fire of YHWH resonated with readers of the later Seleucid period and was written with that period in mind, not the Achaemenid era. While the theme of YHWH's fire as igniting the sacrifice appears in a number of places, the idea of guarding the sacred fire does not. Nowhere else was Nehemiah described in this way, and the only other hero of the past said to have preserved, kept, or guarded the sacred fire is Jeremiah, but that is also found in 2 Maccabees, directly after the

---

99. For this translation, see Schwartz, *2 Maccabees*, 528.

account of Nehemiah and the sacred fire, not in the book of Jeremiah itself (2 Macc 1:1).

While the fire of YHWH appears in the Hebrew Bible as the fire that lights the sacrifice (2 Chr 7:1–3 of the first temple built by Solomon; Lev 9:24 of the Tabernacle), there is no account of the lighting of the sacrifice by divine fire in any account dealing with the second temple, and Bergren suggests that this may have been the reason for the attribution of this act to Nehemiah in 2 Maccabees.[100] No notion of a keeper or guardian of the fire, however, is found in the Hebrew Bible. In Persian cultic tradition, on the other hand, figures known as guardians or keepers of the fire (*atarvakhsha*) appear in a number of accounts in connection with the *lan* ceremony, and the term appears frequently in the Persepolis fortification tablets;[101] Nehemiah and Jeremiah are the only two biblical figures to be credited with this.

Why should this idea of preserving and guarding the sacred fire appear in this memory of Nehemiah's leadership in 2 Maccabees rather than in earlier accounts of Nehemiah, which may have been influenced by Achaemenid tradition? It was in the Hasmonean period, when 2 Maccabees was likely composed, that Parthian and Jewish interests sometimes coincided,[102] and it is possible that this memory of Nehemiah was colored by contact not with Achaemenid Persia, but with Parthian ruled Persia, at a time when the Hasmonean kings were intermittently cultivating relations with the Parthian rulers, in whom they sometimes found willing allies.

The expansion of the Parthian Arsacid rulers into Mesopotamia took place at the same time as the Hasmonean state in Judea was emerging, and the Hasmoneans and Parthians would have found themselves with common interests, viz. the elimination of Seleucid control and interference in their affairs. There were times when Parthian efforts to defeat the Seleucids would have served the purposes of the Jews in Jerusalem well and times when rebellion in Palestine (in the 160s, for example,) indirectly would have helped advance Parthian interests.[103] At the same time, alliances constantly shifted: Hyrcanus I adopted an anti-Parthian stance when he went to war at the side of Antiochus VII Sidetes against Parthia in the 130s BCE (Josephus, *Ant.* 13.249–53).[104] Later on, the last of the Hasmonean kings, Mattathias Antigonus, became a Parthian ally within the context of the civil war.[105] Herod appealed to the Parthian ruler Phraates IV to release Hyrcanus, who had been well treated during his confinement in Parthia, being allowed to live among the Jewish community there (Josephus, *J.W.* 1.434; *Ant.*15.19–21). This indicates that good relations must have existed between Herod and Parthia,[106] even if the Parthians had shown a preference for the Hasmonean rulers.

A Tannaitic source (*Pal.* Talmud *Ber.* 7.2, *Naz.* 5.3) includes an account of a Parthian embassy to the court of Alexander Jannaeus, and while this is clearly a much later source reflecting a version of Pharisaic history, J. Neusner thinks that there may be a historical context for it in the time of Alexander Jannaeus, when the Armenian ruler Tigranes con-

---

100. Bergren, "Ezra and Nehemiah," 358.
101. J. Rose, *An Introduction to Zoroastrianism* (London: I. B. Tauris, 2011), 48.
102. T. Rajak, *The Jewish Dialogue with Greece and Rome* (Leiden: Brill, 2001), 266–67; J. Neusner, *A History of the Jews in Babylonia I: The Parthian Period* (Leiden: Brill, 1969), 33.
103. Neusner, *History of Jews*, 24.
104. Neusner thinks that Hasmonean involvement was forced (*History of Jews*, 25) but Rajak finds no evidence for this (*Jewish Dialogue*, 276).
105. Rajak, *Jewish Dialogue*, 276–77.
106. Rajak, *Jewish Dialogue*, 277–78.

quered territories in northern Syria and on the coast as well as advancing into Media.[107] This Armenian expansion led to Parthian recognition of a common interest with the Hasmoneans, prompting the embassy that Neusner suggests may even have been led by Jews.[108]

In the Roman period, at least for a time, Parthian engagement with Jerusalem was direct, and during the reign of the Parthian ruler Pacorus, Jerusalem was restored to the Hasmoneans, but not for long. After the death of Pacorus, Roman rule and Herod were restored (37 BCE).[109] That ideas of Persian cults, and in particular, of Persian sacred fire might have reached Palestinian Jews in this period is not an unreasonable suggestion, and it could have been a result either of Hasmonean-Parthian relations (which would explain why in 2 Macc 1:33, the author wants to show how impressed the Persian king was by the sacred fire preserved since the days of the first temple) or of the influence of Jews living in Parthian ruled regions of Mesopotamia, who by now were sending offerings to the temple in Jerusalem.

J. Rose has noted that the term *nephtar*, which occurs in 2 Maccabees, has a Persian form that itself derives from a Babylonian word for crude petroleum—*naphtha*—and further, that Strabo, the first-century geographer, refers to the existence of a fountain of *naphtha* next to the fires and the temple of Anea near Arbela in northern Babylonia (*Geogr.* 16.1.4). Moreover, the account in 2 Maccabees of how the Persian king ordered the enclosure of the fire finds a parallel in Parthian religion. Rose thinks the idea may have started in eastern Iran, from where we have the earliest evidence for fire temples, which date to the Parthian period.[110] Thus, Nehemiah's leadership is re-invented as a result of contact between Parthia and Judea, centuries after Nehemiah's Achaemenid imperial mission in Jerusalem and Nehemiah became a leader for the time.

Nehemiah is also associated with a memoir he himself had written and with the preservation of traditions in a library, including the writings of David, letters of the kings concerning sacrifice, and books about the kings and prophets (2 Macc 2:13–15). No other memory of Nehemiah's leadership preserves a tradition of his preserving books, but as Schwartz notes, the establishment of a library would typically have been attributed to Hellenistic kings.[111] Since the account is really more about establishing the credentials of Judas Maccabaeus, as Bergren and Edelman note,[112] there is a possible explanation for its inclusion here.

In 2 Maccabees, the figure of Nehemiah has been elevated to new heights, comparable to Solomon and to Jeremiah (2 Macc 2:1, 10),[113] and most importantly from the compiler's perspective, Nehemiah is said to have preserved the traditions, as Judas Maccabaeus would also do.[114] Thus, a Persian appointee who historically was sent to establish a *birta* in Jerusalem to control local leaders in the environment and sub-divide the region by depriving Samaria of influence has been radically transformed in this memorialization of him. While

---

107. Neusner, *History of Jews*, 26
108. Neusner, *History of Jews*, 26–27.
109. Neusner *History of Jews*, 30.
110. Rose, *Zoroastrianism*, 48.
111. Schwartz, *2 Maccabees*, 166
112. Bergren, "Ezra and Nehemiah," 259; Edelman, "Were Zerubbabel and Nehemiah," 123–31.
113. Although note Edelman's observation that Nehemiah is contrasted with Judas, Moses, and Solomon in having neither priestly nor royal credentials ("Were Zerubbabel and Nehemiah," 127).
114. Significantly, Bergren notes the schematization—Josiah—Zerubbabel–Ezra in the tradition of 1 Esdras (Bergren, "Ezra and Nehemiah," 353–54).

Eliasiv, the priest of the Jerusalemite temple, and Nehemiah were never on good terms in the NM, here in the account in 2 Maccabees, Nehemiah offers instructions to the priests for the renewal of sacrifice with the fire that had been hidden since the first temple, and he then stands back to allow the high priest Jonathan lead him and the people in prayer. That Nehemiah was neither a priest (as Ezra was) nor a royal figure (as Zerubbabel was) may have made him, as Edelman argues, an ideal choice. Unlike Zerubbabel, he was not a Davidide and, therefore, the Hasmonean's non-Davidide origins would not be highlighted.[115] That he was not a priest served to legitimate the Hasmonean's involvement in the cult.

This is a Nehemiah whose status has been elevated and, yet, who also knows his place and is respectful towards the priesthood. While the original Nehemiah of the NM needed supplementation with the account in Neh 8–9, which transformed him into a Torah-pious leader, the Nehemiah of 2 Maccabees has been far from negligent: he had preserved the traditions in Jerusalem for later generations, although there is no specific reference to Torah, but only to letters of the kings for sacrifices and the writings of the prophets (2 Macc 2:13–15).[116]

For other authors, the memory of Nehemiah in 2 Maccabees may not have met their criteria of ideal leadership, and aspects of the original account of stories of Nehemiah in the NM are played down or completely eliminated, with the invention of new achievements that do not appear in the NM. Josephus presents an account of the Persian period, presumably selecting from the traditions available to him (perhaps not necessarily Ezra-Nehemiah in their current form). Rather than expanding the account, he condenses the account of Nehemiah. I will not explore Josephus's treatment of Nehemiah in any depth here but refer to it only to demonstrate how traditions about the original leadership of Nehemiah remained open to fairly free expansion and reduction.[117]

In brief, it can also be noted that in spite of Nehemiah's relative prominence in early traditions about the return and the restoration of Jerusalem, it is largely around the figure of Ezra that a body of apocalyptic and rabbinic texts develop, a fact that should not surprise us, given the importance of Torah to these later writers, and we can conclude that the historic Nehemiah is most likely to have been a Persian appointee who attempted to curtail the expansion of local leaders, like Tobiah, into Jerusalem. For a time he dominated the memories of the Persian period, where he was remembered for having walled Jerusalem and having established its relative independence from surrounding political influences, an achievement that was important in the views of the authors of Ecclesiasticus and 2 Maccabees.

---

115. Edelman, "Were Zerubbabel and Nehemiah," 121–24.

116. Nehemiah is not the only figure to be credited with things with which he was not originally associated in what we regard as earlier accounts; so, for example, Ben Zvi observes how the patriarchs Abraham, Isaac, and Jacob were associated with a land they never entered (E. Ben Zvi, "The Memory of Abraham in Late Persian/Early Hellenistic Yehud/Judah," in *Remembering Biblical Figures in Late Persian and Early Hellenistic Judah*, ed. D. Edelman and E. Ben Zvi [Oxford: Oxford University Press, 2013], 3–37 [9]). Earlier traditions about Joshua clearly assign him a primarily military role, but later on, the figure is demilitarized to become a Torah scribe (E. A. Knauf, "Remembering Joshua," in *Remembering Biblical Figures*, 106–30 [113]).

117. For discussion, see L. H. Feldman, Studies in *Josephus' Rewritten Bible* (Atlanta, GA: SBL, 1998), 97–98. See also for brief discussion, Fitzpatrick-McKinley, "What did Nehemiah do for Judaism?," 93–120. For discussion of misanthropy as a charge against the Jews, see L. H. Feldman, *Jew and Gentile in the Ancient World* (Princeton, NJ: Princeton University Press, 1993), 125–84.

Bibliography

Abraham, K. 2010. "The Reconstruction of Jewish Communities in the Persian Empire: The Āl-Yahūdu Clay Tablets." In *Light and Shadows—The Catalog—The Story of Iran and the Jews,* edited by H. Segev, 264–68. Tel Aviv: Beit Hatfutsot.

Ackroyd, P. 1991. *The Chronicler in His Age.* JSOTSup 101. Sheffield: Sheffield Academic Press.

———. 1982. "Archaeology, Politics and Religion: The Persian Period." *The Iliff Re*view 39: 5–24.

Ahlström, G. 1993. *The History of Palestine from the Paleolithic Period to Alexander's Conquests.* JSOTSup 146. Sheffield: Sheffield Academic.

Albertz, A. 2006. "Purity Strategies and Political interests in the Policy of Nehemiah." In *Confronting the Past: Archaeological and Historical Essays on Ancient Israel,* edited by S. Gitin, J. P. Dessel, and E. Wright, 199–206. Winona Lake, IN: Eisenbrauns.

Alt, A. 1953. "Die Rolle Samarias bei der Entstehung des Judentums." In *Kleine Schriften zur Geschichtes des Volkes Israel,* 5–28. Munich: Beck.

Avi Yonah, M. 1966. *The Holy Land: From the Persian to the Arab Conquests.* Grand Rapids, MI: Baker Book House.

Barjamovic, G. 2004. "Civic Institutions and Self-Government in Southern Mesopotamia in the Mid-First Millenium BC." In *Assyria and Beyond: Studies presented to Mogens Trolle Larsen,* edited by J. G. Dercksen, 47–98. Leiden: Nederlands Instituut voor het Nabije Oosten.

Ben Zvi, E. 2013. "The Memory of Abraham in Late Persian/Early Hellenistic Yehud/Judah." In *Remembering Biblical Figures in the Late Persian & Early Hellenistic Periods: Social Memory and Imagination,* edited by D. V. Edelman and E. Ben Zvi, 3–37. Oxford: Oxford University Press.

Bergren, T. A. 1998. "Ezra and Nehemiah Square Off in the Apocrypha and Pseudipigrapha." In *Biblical Figures Outside the Bible,* edited by M. E. Stone and T. A. Bergren, 340–66. Harrisburg: Trinity International.

———. 1997. "Nehemiah in 2 Maccabees 1:10–2:18." *Journal for the Study of Judaism in the Persian, Hellenistic, and Roman Periods* 28: 249–70.

Blenkinsopp, J. 2006. "Benjamin Traditions Read in the Early Persian Period." In *Judah and the Judeans in the Persian Period,* edited by O. Lipschits and J. Blenkinsopp, 629–45. Winona Lake, IN: Eisenbrauns.

———. 1989. *Ezra-Nehemiah.* London: SCM.

Bousquet, J. 1986. "Une nouvelle inscription trilingue a Xanthos?" *RAr* 1986(1): 101–6.

Briant, P. 2002. *From Cyrus to Alexander: A History of the Persian Empire.* Translated by P. T. Daniels. Winona Lake, IN: Eisenbrauns.

———. 1999. "Inscriptions multilingues d'époque achéménide: le texte et l'image." In *Le décret de Memphis: Actes du Colloque de la Fondation Singer-Polignac,* edited by D. Valbelle and J. eclant, 91–115. Paris: Fondation Singer-Polignac.

Bryce, T. R. 1983. "Political Unity in Lycia during the 'Dynastic' Period." *JNES* 42: 31–42.

Carter, C. 1999. *The Emergence of Yehud in the Persian Period: A Social and Demographic Study.* JSOTSup 294. Sheffield: Sheffield Academic.

Collins, J. J. 2000. *Between Athens and Jerusalem: Jewish Identity in the Hellenistic Diaspora.* Grand Rapids, MI: Eerdmans.

Cross, F. M. 1969. "Judean Stamps." *Eretz-Israel* 9: 20–27.

———. 1966. "Aspects of Samaritan and Jewish History in Late Persian and Hellenistic Times." *HTR* 59: 201–11.

———. 1963. "The Discovery of the Samaria Papyri." *Biblical Archaeologist* 26: 110–21.

Dandamayev, M. and Lukonin, V. 1989. *The Culture and Social Institutions of Ancient Iran*. Cambridge: Cambridge University Press.

Demsky, A. 1983. "Pelekh in Nehemiah 3." *Israel Exploration Journal* 33: 242–44.

De Silva, D. 2002. *Introducing the Apocrypha: Message Context and Significance*. Grand Rapids, MI: Baker Book House.

Dupont-Sommer, A. 1974. "La stèle trilingue récemment découverte au Létoon de Xanthos: le texte araméen." *Comptes rendus de l'Académie des inscriptions et belles-lettres* 1974: 132–49.

Edelman, D. 2012. Were Zerubbabel and Nehemiah the Same Person?" In *Far From Minimal: Celebrating the Work and Influence of P. R. Davies*, edited by D. Burns and J. W. Rogerson, 112–31. LHBOTS 484. London: T. & T. Clark.

———. 2006. "Tyrian Trade in Yehud under Artaxerxes I." In *Judah and Judeans in the Persian Period*, edited by O. Lipschits and M. Oeming, 207–46. Winona Lake, IN: Eisenbrauns.

———. 2005. "Nehemiah's Adversary, Tobiah the Patron," In *Historie og Konstruktion*, edited by M. Müller and T. L. Thompson, 106–14. København: Museum Tusculanums Forlag.

———. 2005. *The Origins of the "Second Temple": Persian Imperial Policy and the Rebuilding of Jerusalem*. London: Equinox.

Feldman, L. H. 1993. *Jew and Gentile in the Ancient World*. Princeton, NJ: Princeton University Press.

———. 1998. *Studies in Josephus' Rewritten Bible*. Atlanta, GA: Scholars Press.

Finkelstein, I. 2008. "Jerusalem in the Persian (and early Hellenistic) Period and the wall of Nehemiah." *JSOT* 32: 501–20.

Fitzpatrick-McKinley, A. 2015. *Empire, Power and Indigenous Elites: a case study of the Nehemiah Memoir*. Leiden: Brill.

———. 2009. "What did Nehemiah do for Judaism?" In *A Wandering Galilean: Essays in Honor of Sean Freyne*, edited by Z. Rodgers with M. Daly-Denton, and A. Fitzpatrick-McKinley, 93–120. Leiden: Brill.

———. 2003. "Ezra, Nehemiah and Some Early Greek Lawgivers." In *Rabbinic Law in its Near Eastern and Roman Context*, edited by C. Hezser, 17–49. TSAJ 97. Tübingen: Mohr Siebeck.

Fried, L. S. 2004. *The Priest and the Great King: Temple Palace Relations in the Persian Period*. Biblical and Judaic studies from the University of California, San Diego 10. Winona Lake, IN: Eisenbrauns.

Funk, R. W. 1993. "Beth-Zur." In *The New Encyclopedia of Archaeological Excavations in the Holy Land*, Vol. 1, edited by E. Stern, 260–61. New York: Simon & Schuster.

Given, M. 2004. *The Archaeology of the Colonized*. London: Routledge.

Grabbe, L. L. 2004. *A History of the Jews and Judaism in the Second Temple Period, Volume 1. Yehud: A History of the Persian Province of Judah*. London: T&T Clark.

———. 1998. *Ezra-Nehemiah*. London: Routledge.

Grainger, J. D. 1991. *Hellenistic Phoenicia*. Oxford: Clarendon.

Greco, A. 2003. "Zagros Pastoralism and Assyrian imperial expansion." In *Continuity of Empire (?) Assyria, Media, Persia*, edited by G. B. Lanfranchi, M. Roaf, and R. Rollinger, 65–78. HANEM 5. Padova: S.A.R.G.O.N. Editrice e Libreria.

Hayes, C. 2002. *Gentile Impurities and Jewish Identities: Intermarriage and Conversion from the Bible to the Talmud*. Oxford: Oxford University Press.

———. 1999. "Intermarriage and Impurity in Ancient Jewish Sources." *HTR* 91: 3–36.

Hoglund, K. 1992. *Achaemenid Imperial Administration in Syria Palestine and the Missions of Ezra and Nehemiah*. SBLDS 125. Atlanta, GA: Scholars Press.

Hurowitz, V. 1992. *I Have Built Thee an Exalted House: Temple Building in the Light of Mesopotamian and North Semitic Writings*. JSOTSup 115. Sheffield: Sheffield Academic.

Joisten-Pruschke, A. 2010. "Light from Aramaic Documents." In *The World of Achaemenid Persia: History, Art and Society in Iran and the Ancient Near East,* edited by J. Curtis and S. Simpson, 41–50. London: I. B. Tauris.

Keen, A. G. 1998. *Dynastic Lycia: A Political History of the Lycians and Their Relations with Foreign Powers, c. 545–362 BC*. Leiden: Brill.

Kellermann, U. 1967. *Nehemia Quellen*, Überlieferung und Geschichte. BZAW 102. Berlin: Töpelmann.

Knauf, E. A. 2013. "Remembering Joshua." In *Remembering Biblical Figures in Late Persian and Early Hellenistic Judah*. Edited by D. Edelman and E. Ben Zvi, 106–30. Oxford: Oxford University Press.

———. 1990. "The Persian Administration in Arabia." *Transeuphratène* 2: 201–17.

Kohl, P. 1987. "The Ancient Economy, Transferable Technologies in the Bronze Age World System: A View from the Northeastern Frontier of the Ancient Near East." In *Centre and Periphery in the Ancient World,* edited by M. Rowlands, M. Larsen, and K. Kristiansen, 13–24. Cambridge: Cambridge University Press.

Kottsieper, I. 2002. "Religionspolitik der Achämeniden und die Juden von Elephantine." In *Religion und Religionskontakte im Zeitalter der Achämeniden*, edited by R. G. Kratz, 150–78. Gütersloh: Gütersloher Verlagshaus.

Kratz, R. G. 2004. *Das Judentum im Zeitalter des Zweiten Tempels*. Tübingen: Mohr Siebeck.

Kuhrt, A. 2007. *The Persian Empire: A Corpus of Sources of the Achaemenid Period*. London: Routledge.

Laroche, E. 1979. "L'inscriptions lycienne." In *Fouilles de Xanthos VI, la stèle trilingue de létoon,* edited by H. Metzger and E. Laroche, 49–127. Paris: Klincksieck.

Lebram, J. 1987. "Die Traditionsgeschichte der Esragestalt und die Frage nach dem historischen Esra." In *Achaemenid History I: Sources, Structures and Synthesis,* edited by H. Sancisi-Weerdenburg, 103–38. Leiden: Instituut voor het Nabije Oosten.

Leith, M. J. W. 1997. *Wadi Daliyeh I. The Wadi Daliyeh Seal Impressions*. Discoveries in the Judaean Desert. Oxford: Oxford University Press.

Lemaire, A. 2012. "New Perspectives on the Trade between Judah and South Arabia." In *New Inscriptions and Seals Relating to the Biblical World*, edited by M. Lubetski and E. Lubetski, 93–110. Atlanta, GA: SBL.

Lemche, N. P. 1985. *Early Israel: Anthropological and Historical Studies on Israelite Society before the Monarchy*. VTSup 37. Leiden: Brill.

Levin, Y. 2004. "From Lists to History: Chronological Aspects of the Chronicler's Genealogies." *JBL* 123: 601–36.

Liverani, M. 1993. "Nelle pieghe del despotismo Organismi rappresentativi nell' antico Orienta." *Studi Storici* 34: 7–33.

Mack, B. L. 1985. *Wisdom and the Hebrew Bible: Ben Sira's Hymn in Praise of the Fathers*. Chicago, IL: University of Chicago Press.

McEvenue, S. E. 1981. "The Political Structure in Judah." *CBQ* 43: 353–64.

Meshorer, Y. and S. Qedar. 1999. *Samarian Coinage*. Jerusalem: The Israel Numismatic Society.

Mendels, D. 1992. *The Rise and Fall of Jewish Nationalism*. Anchor Bible Reference Library. New York: Doubleday.

———. 1983. "Hecataeus of Abdera and a Jewish 'patrios politeia.'" *ZAW* 95: 97–110.

Neusner, J. 1969. *A History of the Jews in Babylonia. I. The Parthian Period*. Leiden: Brill.

Parpola, S. 2004. "National and Ethnic Identity in the Neo-Assyrian Empire and Assyrian Identity in post-Empire Times." *Journal of Assyrian Academic Studies* 18: 5–49.

Pearce, L. 2006. "New Evidence for Judeans in Babylonia." In *Judah and the Judeans in the Persian Period*, edited by O. Lipschits and M. Oeming, 300–411. Winona Lake, IN: Eisenbrauns, .

Pritchard, J. B. 1993. "Gibeon." In *The New Encyclopedia of Archaeological Excavations in the Holy Land*, Vol. 2, edited by E. Stern, 511–14. New York: Simon & Schuster.

Rabinowitz, I. 1958. "Aramaic Inscriptions of the fifth century from a North Arabian Shrine in Egypt." *JNES* 15: 1–9.

Radner, K. 2003. "An Assyrian view on the Medes." In *Continuity of Empire (?) Assyria, Media, Persia: Proceedings of the International Meeting in Padua, 26th—28th April 2001*, edited by G. B. Lanfranchi, M. Rost and R. Rollinger, 37–64. HANEM 5. Padova: S.A.R.G.O.N. Editrice & Libreria.

Rajak, T. 2002. *The Jewish Dialogue with Greece and Rome*. Leiden: Brill.

Reich, R. 1992. "Assyrian Royal Buildings in the Land of Israel." In *The Architecture of Ancient Israel*, edited by H. Katzenstein, A. Kempinski, and R. Reich, 214–22. Jerusalem: Jerusalem Exploration Society.

Rose, J. 2011. *Zoroastrianism: An Introduction*. London, I. B. Tauris.

Schwartz, D. 2008. *2 Maccabees*. Berlin: de Gruyter.

Sekunda, N. 1991. "Achaemenid Settlement in Caria, Lycia and greater Phyrgia." In *Achaemenid History VI: Asia Minor and Egypt: Old Cultures in a New Empire, Proceedings of the Groningen 1998 Achaemenid History Workshop*, edited by H. Sancisi-Weerdenburg and A. Kührt, 83–143. Leiden: Nederlands Instituut voor het Nabije Oosten.

Smith, M. 1971. *Palestinian Parties and Politics that Shaped the Old Testament*. New York: Columbia.

Smith-Christopher, D. L. 1989. *The Religion of the Landless: The Social Context of the Babylonian Exile*. Bloomington, IN: Meyer-Stone.

Stern, E. 1982. *The Material Culture of the Land of the Bible in the Persian Period*. Warminster: Aris & Phillips.

Summerer, L. and A. Von Kienlin, "Achaemenid Impact in Paphlagonia: Rupestral Tombs in the Amnias Valley." http://www.pontos.dk/publications/books/bss-11-files/bss-11-summerer.

Thapar, R. 1981. "The State as Empire." In *The Study of the State*, edited by H. J. M. Claessen and P. Skalmik, 409–26. The Hague: Mouton.

Torrey, C. C. 1970 [1910]. *Ezra Studies*. Edited with a Prolegomenon by W. F. Stinespring. New York: Ktav.

Tuplin, C. 1987. "Xenophon and the Garrisons of the Achaemenid Empire." *Archäologische Mitteilungen aus Iran* 20: 167–245.

Uehlinger, C. 1999. "Powerful Persianisms in Glyptic Iconography of Persian Palestine." In *The Crisis of Israelite Religion: The Transformation of Religious Tradition in Exilic and Post Exilic Times*, edited by B. Becking and M. C. A. Korpel, 134–82. Leiden: Brill.

Waerzeggers, C. 2006. "The Carians of Borsippa." *Iraq* 68: 1–22.

Wallace-Hadrill, A. 1989. "Patronage in Roman Society: From Republic to Empire." In *Patronage in Ancient Society*, edited by A. Wallace-Hadrill, 63–87. London: Routledge.

Waterbury, J. 1977. "An Attempt to Put Patrons and Clients in Their Place." In *Patrons and Clients in Mediterranean Societies,* edited by E. Gellner and J. Waterbury, 329–42. London: Duckworth.

Weiskopf, M. N. 1984. "Achaemenid Systems of Governing in Anatolia." Unpublished PhD thesis, University of California, Berkeley.

Westbrook, R. 2005. "Patronage in the Ancient Near East." *Journal of the Economic and Social History of the Orient* 42: 210–33.

Wiesehöfer, J. 2001. *Ancient Persia*. London: I. B. Tauris.

Williamson, H. G. M. 1987. *Ezra and Nehemiah*. Old Testament Guides. Sheffield: Society of Old Testament Study.

Wright, J. 2004. *Rebuilding Identity: The Nehemiah Memoir and its earliest Readers*. Berlin: de Gruyter.

Zorn, J. R. 2003. "Tell en-Nasbeh and the Material Culture of the Sixth Century." In *Judah and the Judeans in the Neo-Babylonian Period*, edited by O. Lipschits and J. Blenkinsopp, 413–47. Winona Lake, IN: Eisenbrauns.

Zucker, H. 1936. *Studien zur Jüdischen Selbstverwaltung im Altertum*. Berlin: Schocken Verlag.

— 12 —

The Three Constitutions in Greek Political Thought

Lynette Mitchell

In Greek political thought the idea of the three constitutions seems to have been formulated in terms of the rule of the one, the few, and the many by at least the first quarter of the fifth century BCE.[1] It is first referred to by Pindar in his encomiastic poem, the *Second Pythian*, which probably dates to 477/6[2] and which presents a tripartite division of constitutions: the rule of a τυραννίς, the wise (οἱ σοφοί), or the rowdy army (λάβρος στρατός) (lines 86–88). Pindar's formulation shows a significant shift had taken place in Greek political thought. Rather than political reflection centering in archaic terms on order and disorder or justice and injustice, as we find in Hesiod's *Works and Days* or the poetry of Solon of Athens from the early sixth century BCE,[3] it was now concerned with differentiating between constitutional forms. Nevertheless, Pindar could not have invented this formulation; he must be referring to ideas about constitutional rule that were current at the time.

This chapter will have five parts. It will begin by considering the origins of constitutional theory. It will then turn to a consideration of how the idea of the three constitutions was developed in the fifth century BCE, before looking in section 3 at how three constitutions became the framework for investigating a plurality of constitutional forms. In section 4, on the other hand, it will consider how the three constitutions were used, especially by Plato and Aristotle, to explore the idea of the "mixed" constitution and constitutional stability, before finally, in section 5, asking some key questions about why the model of the three constitutions was important in Greek political thought and why it has had an enduring legacy through the centuries.

---

1. I would like to thank the editors for inviting me to contribute to this volume and their very helpful comments on an earlier version.
2. C. M. Bowra thinks the poem dates to 468 (*Pindar* [Oxford: Oxford University Press, 1964], 410), though C. Carey considers this impossible since the poem cannot celebrate a victory in any of the major games (*A Commentary on Five Odes of Pindar: Pythian 2, Pythian 9, Nemean 1, Nemean 7, Isthmian 8*, [New York: Arno, 1981], 21).
3. See R. Balot, *Greek Political Thought* (Malden, MA: Blackwell, 2006), 16–47.

1. The Origins of the Three Constitutions

Constitutional theorizing must have had archaic origins. From the eighth century BCE, "Founders" and "Lawgivers" became important in the so-called colonization movement in their role of giving the new communities their νόμιμα, which encapsulated ritual but also constitutional forms and the political organization of the community.[4] For example, Thucydides names the founders and lawgivers of the cities of Sicily, whose role must have been like that of the Homeric Nausithous who, in founding the city of Scheria, divided up the land and defined the public and religious spaces (*Od.* 6.1–10). Certainly, in some of the earliest foundations, there seems to have been a recognition, even if this was not theorized, that stable government could be achieved through a combination of political forms: the mythic king of Phaeacia, Alcinous, was subject to a council of "kings" (*Od.* 8.390–391, cf. 6.53–55), and the real-life city of Cyrene, founded in the seventh century BCE by the Therans, had a king who seems to have acted in conjunction with some kind of council (principally Herodotus *Hist.* 4.150–67, 200–205).[5] This council, however, became strong enough by the sixth century to limit the king's hereditary powers by bringing into the city a specialist "lawgiver," Demonax of Mantineia. Appointed (or at least authorized) by the oracle of Apollo at Delphi, Demonax was given the task of restructuring the constitution, probably giving more power to the Theran nobility and a political role (in an assembly?) for colonists who had joined the foundation at the invitation of the Cyrenean Therans. Not all early law-reformers, however, were constitutionalists: Solon at Athens made laws at the beginning of the sixth century BCE, but strikingly, did not reform the constitution in any deep way[6] although he had been given the power to be more radical; likewise, as Aristotle notes, Pittacus, ruler and lawgiver in Mytilene in the seventh-century BCE, seems to have been concerned with issues of stability and public order rather than constitutional change (Aristotle, *Pol.* 1274b18–23). However, that Demonax and other lawgivers were given such powers of political reform suggests that by the sixth century BCE at least, reflection on constitutional forms was a well-established, if specialist, part of Greek political thought.

In fact, in Sparta in the mid-seventh century BCE, it is likely Lycurgus put in place a constitution that was to become the cornerstone of Spartan political stability and success through to the third century BCE. Although not all the reforms attributed to him can belong to the seventh century BCE,[7] Lycurgus's constitution, known as the Great Rhetra (Plutarch, *Lyc.* 6), was based on three different kinds constitutional forms: a form of autocracy (although in this case a dyarchy), a council of elders (γερουσία), and an assembly of citizens, each element of which was to work together. At some stage (possibly around

---

4. See principally I. Malkin, "Foundations," in *A Companion to Archaic Greece*, ed. K. A. Raaflaub and H. van Wees (Malden, MA: Wiley-Blackwell, 2008), 373–94.

5. On Cyrene, see E. Chamoux, *Cyrène sous la monarchie des Battiades* (Paris: de Boccard, 1953); B. Mitchell, "Cyrene: Typical or Atypical," in *Alternatives to Athens: Varieties of Political Organisation and Community in Ancient Greece*, ed. R. Brock and S. Hodkinson (Oxford: Oxford University Press, 2000), 82–102.

6. E.g., L. Mitchell, "New Wine in Old Wineskins: Solon, *Aretē* and the *Agathos*," in *The Development of the Polis in Archaic Greece*, ed. L. Mitchell and P. J. Rhodes (London: Routledge, 1997), 137–47.

7. S. Hodkinson, "The Development of Spartan Society and Institutions in the Archaic Period," in *The Development of the Polis in Archaic Greece*, ed. L. Mitchell and P. J. Rhodes (London: Routledge, 1997), 83–102; M. A. Flower, "The Invention of Tradition in Classical and Hellenistic Sparta," in *Sparta: Beyond the Mirage*, ed. A. Powell and S. Hodkinson (London: Routledge, 2002), 191–217.

700 BCE?) the ephorate was added,[8] comprising five men chosen from the people with full executive power for a year, to whom the kings had to swear annually that they would obey the law (Xenophon, *Constitution of the Lacedaemonians*, 15.7). Aristotle regarded the ephorate as the democratic element in the constitution, because they were drawn from the whole citizen body (e.g., *Pol.* 1265b38–40), and certainly in the fifth century BCE, the assembly of Spartan citizens, the Spartiates,[9] had only the power to ratify decisions made by the γερουσία and the ephors (see, for example, Thucydides 5.85–87).[10] Nevertheless, while the original Lycurgan formulation probably was not consciously an instantiation of the theorized "mixed constitution" (on which see further below), it represents some level of early reflection on constitutional forms and differentiation of different kinds of rule.

2. The Three Constitutions in the Fifth Century BCE

Nevertheless, as we have seen, by the beginning of the fifth century BCE, Pindar was able to produce a typology of constitutions that differentiated three forms we could recognize as the rule of the one, the few, and the many. The τυραννίς, interestingly, is not used negatively but simply as a reference to one who ruled alone. The rule of "the wise," on the other hand, is probably the equivalent of the council of elders found in most early Greek cities, such as the γερουσία at Sparta or the Areopagus at Athens. It is also interesting that there was an acceptance that even in the first quarter of the fifth century BCE, "the rowdy army" was consistent with, and perhaps even equivalent to, rule by the δῆμος.[11] Furthermore, it is even more significant that this formulation was known outside Athens, so that forms of political sovereignty were being differentiated in a context that was not necessarily trying to define democracy, even though, as we shall see, this was the very period in which a self-consciously democratic ideology was taking shape at Athens. It should not surprise us that there was a more general interest in constitutional forms, as this period was a time of political experimentation across Greece. In the early 440s, for example, the Boeotians established the first federal state based on a representative assembly, although there was probably a property restriction on citizenship (*Hellenica Oxyrhynchia* 16.2–4).[12] It is also significant that the ability to own arms (rather than land) could form the basis at an early stage of the conceptualization of citizenship, although the two would not be unconnected.

Yet it was at Athens that constitutional theorizing seems to have become a preoccupation of political thinkers, and the theorizing of democracy as the rule of the many was intimately concerned with its relationship to the rule of the one and the rule of the few. In part this was because of the concerns of the Athenians themselves with the theorizing of democracy. Although it is often argued that the systematic theorization of democracy arose against the attempt to theorize oligarchy as the rule of the few, which first began to take

---

8. See P. Cartledge, *Agesilaos and the Crisis of Sparta* (London: Routledge, 1987), 125–26.

9. In order to attain Spartan citizenship, Spartan youths had to complete the ἀγωγή, a state-run educational program, and to make a contribution from the produce of their land-holdings to the common mess. By the fourth century BCE, the number of Spartans able to conform to both criteria was limited, and the number of Spartiates had seriously declined: see P. Cartledge, *Sparta and Lakonia: A Regional History 1300 to 362 BC*, 2nd ed. (London: Routledge, 2002), 263–72.

10. See L. Mitchell, "Greek Government," in *A Companion to the Classical Greek World*, ed. K. Kinzl (Malden, MA: Blackwell, 2006), 367–86 (375–76).

11. K. A. Raaflaub, *The Discovery of Freedom in Ancient Greece* (Chicago, IL: University of Chicago Press, 2004), 206, 210, 345 n. 41.

12. Mitchell, "Greek Government," 372.

shape in the second half of the fifth century,¹³ democracy as it was first conceptualized was rule of the δῆμος, which seems in this case to have referred to the rule of the assembly,¹⁴ and was opposed to the rule of one man. In Aeschylus's *Persians*, written in 472 BCE, Queen Atossa asks who the leader of the army is and the Chorus reply: "They are called neither slaves (δοῦλοι) nor subjects (ὑπήκοοι) of any man" (241–42). Likewise in Aeschylus's *Suppliants*, possibly produced in the 460s, where we first see the formulation δήμου κρατοῦσα χείρ ('the hand of the δῆμος ruling') (604),¹⁵ King Pelasgus defers to decisions made by the assembly (398–401). On the other hand, the real-life reforms of Ephialtes of the same period were probably concerned with taking power from the council of elders, the Areopagus, and removing them to the assembly and the popular courts (*Athenaion Politeia* 25).¹⁶ Membership of the Areopagus was reserved for those who had held the archonship (*Athenaion Politeia* 3.6), although by this period, archons were appointed by lot (*Athenaion Politeia* 22.5). Against this background, it is of some interest that the primary means of defining democracy in theoretical terms was against rule of the one, not rule of the few.

This concern about the rule of one man ran deep in Athenian political culture. In particular, it seems it was in the aftermath of the Persian Wars and the attack by the Persians directed specifically at Athenian soil at Marathon in 490 BCE that a self-conscious theorizing of the Athenian constitution started to take shape, although whether it could be conceptualized and formulated as "democratic" this early is another matter.¹⁷ At its heart was a rejection of monarchy and what was imagined as absolutist Persian autocracy. This narrative of a constitution that rejected autocracy was given added importance by the fact that Hippias, the son of Pisistratus, who had been expelled in 510, accompanied the Persian fleet and brought it to Marathon in 490 BCE (Herodotus, *Hist.* 6.102, 107). The Athenian victory over the Persians was remembered and celebrated, as we can see from Herodotus, as a victory of freedom over slavery, and slavery specifically to the Persian king, whose agent was Hippias "the tyrant" (*Hist.* 6.109).

It is probably because of this association between Persian monarchy and the rule of the Peisistratids that ostracism¹⁸ was enacted (if not established) for the first time in 488/7

---

13. K. A. Raaflaub, "Contemporary Perceptions of Democracy in Fifth-century Athens," *Classica et Mediaevalia* 40 (1989): 33–70 (repr. *Aspects of Athenian Democracy* [*Classica et Mediaevalia; Dissertationes XI*], ed. W. R. Connor, *et al.* (Copenhagen: Museum Tusculanum, 1990], 33–70).

14. The word δῆμος, however, could cover a range of meanings: in the early sixth century BCE, Solon uses it to mean the whole people and sometimes the ordinary people as opposed to the ruling class; see P. J. Rhodes, "Oligarchs in Athens," in *Alternatives to Athens: Varieties of Political Organisation and Community in Ancient Greece*, ed. R. Brock and S. Hodkinson (Oxford: Oxford University Press, 2000), 119–36 (119–20).

15. δάμῳ ... κράτος ('power for the people') had already appeared in the Great Rhetra in the mid- seventh century BCE (Plutarch, *Lyc.* 6.1), although as we have seen, the power of the Spartan assembly was, in fact, severely limited. For the articulation of δημοκρατία in the 460s, see M. H. Hansen, "The Origin of the Term *demokratia*," *Liverpool Classical Monthly* 11 (1986): 35–36.

16. P. J. Rhodes, "The Athenian Revolution," in *Cambridge Ancient History: Volume 5, The Fifth Century*, 2nd ed., ed. D. M. Lewis *et al.* (Cambridge: Cambridge University Press, 1992), 62–95 (esp. 67–77); K. A. Raaflaub, "The Breakthrough of *Dēmokratia* in Mid-fifth-century Athens," in *Origins of Democracy in Ancient Greece*, ed. K. A. Raaflaub, J. Ober, and R. W. Wallace (Berkeley: University of California Press, 2007), 105–54.

17. See n. 15 above.

18. Ostracism was the exile for ten years by decree of the assembly of a man thought to be aspiring at autocracy. A quorum of 6000 was needed for a vote. The last ostracism was the that of Hyperbolus, probably

BCE, two years after Marathon, which was aimed at preventing individuals aspiring to autocracy (*Athenaion Politeia* 22.3). In fact, it was Hipparchus, son of Charmon, an associate of the Peisistratids (possibly a grandson of Hippias),[19] who was the first to be ostracized (*Athenaion Politeia* 22.4). This is probably also the context within which the story of the so-called "tyrannicides" was invented, in which it became part of a foundational "memory" of democracy that the assassination of Hipparchus in 514/13 BCE brought an end to the rule of the Peisistratids, although in reality it had not (as Thucydides at the end of the fifth century BCE is keen to point out: 6.53–59; cf. *Hist.* 5.55–65). It also may have been at this time that the original statue-group was set up in the market-pace at Athens and a cult of the tyrannicides was established,[20] and possibly also the drinking songs that celebrate the achievement of ἰσονομία ('equality under the law') by the tyrannicides were created.[21] Thucydides says that in 415 BCE, the Athenians, "remembering as much as they knew about them by hearsay" were quick to interpret any suspicious events as undemocratic and aimed at oligarchy or tyranny (6.60.1). Certainly, laws against tyrants were established at the end of the fifth century and beginning of the fourth century BCE.[22]

Further, by the end of the Persian Wars in 479 BCE, "freedom from slavery" had been adopted as a panhellenic (not just Athenian) slogan. The victory altar at Plataea was inscribed as a dedication by all Hellenes to Zeus Eleutherius, Zeus of freedom (Plutarch, *De Her. mal.* 873b = [Simonides] XV Page *FGE*),[23] while the gold tripod dedicated at Delphi referred to victory as rescue from slavery (Diodorus 11.33.2 = [Simonides] XVII (b) Page *FGE*).[24] For Herodotus, too, this was a general Greek phenomenon (see, for example, 7.104.4–5—here it is *Spartan* freedom that is opposed to Persian slavery).

However, democratic ideologues in particular seem to have appropriated freedom (and its opposition to slavery) as a particularly democratic value at a relatively early stage. The idea was also a very powerful one; it was not just political but also had ethical overtones because the rejection of tyranny was the rejection of slavery and also probably the celebration of the positive virtue of ἰσονομία. Again, one can see the power of social memory in forming political thought and defining political forms, especially through the definition of an Athenian political identity that is being created in contrast to an explicitly Persian "Other." M. Miller, for example, has made the case for a change in the iconography of

---

in 415 BCE (Plutarch, *Arist.* 7; cf. Aristotle, *Pol.*1284a3–22). On the ostracism of Hyperbolus, see P. J. Rhodes, "The Ostracism of Hyperbolus," in *Ritual, Finance, Politics: Athenian Democratic Accounts Presented to David Lewis*, ed. R. Osborne and S. Hornblower (Oxford: Oxford University Press, 1994), 85–98.

19. P. J. Rhodes, *A Commentary on the Aristotelian Athenaion Politeia*, rev. ed. (Oxford: Oxford University Press, 1993), 271–72.

20. This statue group was removed by Xerxes to Susa, and was returned to Athens by Alexander the Great.

21. It is possibly also from sometime around this point that proclamations and prayers were said in the assembly and the βουλή against tyrants (Aristophanes, *Av.* 1072–1074, *Thesm.* 338–339), though 479 is equally likely as a date for anti-Persian sentiment to be institutionalized.

22. Andocides 1.96–98; P. J. Rhodes and R. Osborne, eds., *Greek Historical Inscriptions 404–323 BC* (Oxford: Oxford University Press, 2003) no. 79. The first of the Athenian anti-tyranny laws may belong among Solon's reforms of the early sixth century BCE: *Athenaion Politeia* 8.4.

23. *This altar, by the might of Nike, by the work of Ares, trusting the courageous spirit of the soul, having driven out the Persians, common to free Hellas, the Hellenes built as the altar of Zeus Eleutherius (Zeus of Freedom).*

24. *The saviors of spacious Hellas dedicated this, having delivered their cities from hateful slavery* (δουλοσύνας στυγερᾶς ῥυσάμενοι πόλιας).

Athenian vase painting in the 460s BCE reflecting a heightened sense of the Persians as the "Other," against which a self-aware democracy, reflected in Ephialtes's reforms (above), defined itself.[25]

Nevertheless, democracy, wherever it was established and whatever form it took in the Greek world, seems to have adopted "Freedom" as its slogan.[26] Freedom as a positive value, however, may have had expression elsewhere in the ancient Near East prior to its deployment in Greek political thought.[27] Cyrus the Great was associated in Greek political thought with ideas of freedom,[28] and this may have been a political value that genuinely attached to his memory. It was certainly also the case that civic structures in which ideas about freedom from the rule of one man could develop had existed in the Near East long before the advent of the Greek city,[29] and it is by no means clear that the Greek city, with its assembly and council (even where there was also a ruling autocrat), grew up in a political vacuum.[30]

Despite the importance of the idea of democracy as freedom from slavery, that is not to say that there was not also in Athens in the mid-fifth century BCE a theoretical opposition between oligarchy and democracy, or at least between the supporters of democracy and their political opponents. There was opposition to the reforms of Ephialtes in the late 460s, and Ephialtes himself was assassinated; importantly, opposition to his explicitly democratic program is associated with Cimon's pro-Spartan stance.[31] With Ephialtes and his associates we clearly have political ideologues pursuing a political agenda. On the other hand, whether Cimon and his political supporters saw themselves as ὀλίγοι, as such, or could articulate an oligarchic program, is unlikely.

---

25. M. C. Miller, "Persians: the Oriental Other," *Source: Notes in the History of Art* 15.1 (1995) (*Special Issue: Representations of the "Other" in Athenian Art, c. 510–400 BC*): 39–44. However, for the complexity in representations of "orientalism" in this period, see also L. Mitchell, *Panhellenism and the Barbarian in Archaic and Classical Greece* (Swansea: Classical Press of Wales, 2007), esp. 124–49.

26. Democracy at Syracuse was established in the mid 460s BCE and was marked by the establishment of a cult of Zeus Eleutherius, but the democracy was extremely limited and, as a result, was very unstable (Diodorus 11.72.2–73.3). Herodotus also tells the story of Maeandrius at Samos (3.142–43), who wanted to secede from his autocratic rule (because he did not want to rule over men like himself [ἄνδρες ὅμοιοι]) and wanted to establish ἰσονομία, which Herodotus uses elsewhere as a synonym for δημοκρατία. The Samians were suspicious and refused his offer, so he imprisoned the most outspoken of them. Herodotus concludes: "For they [the Samians] did not, as it would seem, desire to be free (ἐλεύθεροι)."

27. See M. Martin III and D. C. Snell, "Democracy and Freedom," in *A Companion to the Ancient Near East*, ed. D. C. Snell (Malden, MA: Blackwell, 2005), 419–29.

28. L. Mitchell, "Remembering Cyrus the Persian: Exploring Monarchy and Freedom in Classical Greece," in *Bringing the Past to the Present in the Late Persian and Early Hellenistic Period: Images of Central Figures*, ed. E. Ben Zvi and D. V. Edelman (Oxford: Oxford University Press, 2013), 283–92.

29. See, for example, A. Kuhrt, "'Even a Dog in Babylonia is Free,'" in *Legacy of Momigliano*, ed. T. Cornell and O. Murray (London: The Warburg Institute; Turin: Nino Aragno Editore, 2014), 77–87; note also essays in M. H. Hansen, ed., *A Comparative Study of Thirty City-State Cultures* (Copenhagen: Royal Danish Academy, 2000).

30. On assemblies and councils, even with autocrats, in Greek cities: see Mitchell, *Heroic Rulers*, 126–43. For the idea of "peer-polity interaction," see A. Snodgrass, "Interaction by Design: The Greek City-State," in *Peer Polity Interaction and Sociopolitical Change*, ed. A. C. Renfrew and J. F. Cherry (Cambridge: Cambridge University Press, 1986), 47–58.

31. Rhodes, "Oligarchs in Athens," 126–28.

It was not until the late fifth century BCE that oligarchy itself appeared as a defined constitutional form.³² Writing in the 420s, Herodotus knew about ὀλιγαρχία as a constitutional form (e.g., 3.81.1), which he describes as rule of "the best people" (3.81.3). Another text dating to the 420s, written by the so-called Old Oligarch,³³ also opposes the wealthy, whom it also calls "the best people," with the "poor" and "worthless," whom it argues preserve δημοκρατία in their own interests (see, for example, 1.2–5).³⁴ In his description of the Peloponnesian War, Thucydides describes the revolution on Corcrya as a battle between the δῆμος or the πλῆθος ('the multitude') and the ὀλίγοι, 'the few' (3.74.2–3), but he also presents the whole Greek world as divided between those who supported Athens and democracy on the one hand, and Sparta and oligarchy on the other (3.82.1–2). Nevertheless, in the fourth century, after the oligarchic coups at Athens in 411 and 404/3 BCE were demonized for their atrocities, oligarchy was assimilated to tyranny: the oligarchs became tyrants, and oligarchy and tyranny as constitutions outside law stood in opposition to democracy, which was lawful (e.g., Aesch. 1.4).³⁵ So in the very formulation of democratic theory, while the three forms of constitution were recognized—the rule of the one, the few, and the many—they were also being played off against each other as binary opposites rather than being theorized as a triangulation of forms, as Pindar had presented them. In many ways this is not surprising, as early Greek philosophical thought had often divided phenomena into diametric opposites, which became the cornerstone of some of the earliest scientific speculations on the nature of the *kosmos*.³⁶

It is Herodotus who presents us with the first extant written attempt to systematize and theorize the three constitutions in the Constitution Debate, which is set in Persia and is concerned with the question of which is the best kind of constitution. While Herodotus sets this as a debate among Persians (and he is adamant that the debate was authentic: 3.80.1, 6.43.3), it is often described as a very Greek discussion about which is the best:

---

32. See M. Ostwald, *Oligarchia: The Development of a Constitutional Form in Ancient Greece*, Historia Einzelschriften 144 (Stuttgart: Steiner, 2000), 21–30.

33. The Old Oligarch is the name given to the author of a work on Athenian democracy by someone who is clearly writing from an oligarchic perspective. It is now thought unlikely that the author of the work was the polymath Xenophon, known from the fourth century BCE, although it has been attributed to him as a work of his youth. It is sophistic in style, in that it argues the contrary case: that democracy can be said to be good in so far as it successfully supports a democratic program and rules in the interests of the δῆμος. See J. L. Marr and P. J. Rhodes, *The "Old Oligarch": The Constitution of the Athenians Attributed to Xenophon* (Oxford: Aris and Phillips, 2008), 6–12.

34. On class division in the Old Oligarch, see Marr and Rhodes, "Old Oligarch," 19–24.

35. See L. Mitchell, "Tyrannical Oligarchs at Athens," in *Ancient Tyranny*, ed. S. Lewis; (Edinburgh: Edinburgh University Press, 2006), 178–87.

36. See, for example, the thinking of Heraclitus, whose theories of unities through opposites was influential on Herodotus, or Pythagoreans, who drew up a table of opposites and were the predecessors of, for example, Archytas of Tarentum, who was influential at Athens in the fourth century. For Heraclitus on opposites, see G. S. Kirk, J. E. Raven, and M. Schofield eds., *The Presocratic Philosophers: A Critical History with a Selection of Texts*, 2nd ed. (Cambridge: Cambridge University Press, 1983), 190–200; for Heraclitus's influence on Herodotus, see, for example, A. B. Lloyd, "Herodotus on Egyptians and Libyans," in *Hérodote et les peuples non-grecs: Entretiens sur l'Antiquité classique: Vandoeuvres-Genève, 22–26 Août*, ed. G. Nenci and O. Reverdin (Geneva: Fondation Hardt 35, 1990), 215–45. For Pythagoras's table of opposites, see Kirk, Raven, and Schofield, *Presocratic Philosophers*, 337–78; for Pythagoreans and Archytas of Tarentum, see C. A. Huffman, *Archytas of Tarentum: Pythagorean Philosopher and Mathematician King* (Cambridge: Cambridge University Press, 2005), 51–57.

the rule of the one, the few, or the many. In general terms, it is a Greek discussion, but as D. Asheri points out, Herodotus is aware that there had been enormous constitutional upheaval in Persia surrounding the end of the reign of Cambyses and the beginning of that of Darius: "he therefore tried to understand the phenomenon within the limits of his own frame of reference: the constitutional changes of the Greek *poleis*."[37] Likewise, C. Pelling has insisted on the *Persian* significance of such a debate, particularly in regard to the Persian interest in tyranny, so that it is presented as a debate that has consequence for Herodotus's Persians as well as for his Greek audience.[38]

Otanes speaks first and begins by attacking monarchy (μουναρχίη) on the basis that Cambyses and the Magus who succeeded him were hybristic (3.80.2), whose lawlessness and atrocities were recounted earlier in book 3 and led directly to the crisis that generated the debate. Among his other impieties and acts of cruelty and madness, Cambyses's advisers were said to have discovered a law that he could invent his own laws (3.31), which effectively put him outside law. In fact, one of the main complaints Otanes makes against monarchy is that the monarch can do whatever he wishes without regulation (ἀνεύθυνος) and that even the best man, out of envy, would not be able to resist succumbing to the temptation of deviating from his accustomed habits. The man who rules alone welcomes slander and is erratic and unpredictable. Most of all, however, he subverts the customary laws (νόμαια πάτρια), rapes women, and kills men without trial (3.80.1–5). Otanes contrasts μουναρχία with the rule of the many (the πλῆθος—so a specific reference to "the masses" rather than a more general one to the assembly), which he says has the "fairest name of all, ἰσονομία." By the end of the fifth century BCE, ἰσονομία seems to have become a slogan and synonym for democracy (though it was also possible to talk about an ὀλιγαρχία ἰσόνομος, an 'isonomic oligarchy': Thucydides 3.62.3). Herodotus says that this constitution appointed magistrates by lot, was accountable, and made all decisions in common council (3.80.6).

These are some of the standard markers of democratic government we find being discussed elsewhere, especially in Euripides's *Suppliants*, which also dates to the 420s BCE. Theseus, the king who establishes the δῆμος as μοναρχία, 'having freed this equal-voting city' (ἐλευθερώσας τήνδ' ἰσόψηφον πόλιν: *Suppl*. 352–353), declares that Athens is not ruled by one man but is free (ἐλευθέρα), and the δῆμος rules taking turns annually by lot (*Suppl*. 404–407).[39] It is significant, however, that Otanes does not discuss rule by the few at all but bases his whole argument on the contrast between the rule of one, which is outside law, and rule of the many, which is inside law. Even in the 420s, democracy is being defined not in relation to oligarchy, but in opposition to monarchy (cf. Euripides, *Suppl*. 429–446).

---

37. D. Asheri in D. Asheri, A. Lloyd, and A. Corcella, *A Commentary on Herodotus Book I–IV* (Oxford: Oxford University Press, 2007), 472–73. As Asheri goes on to note, by giving such a debate to the barbarians and insisting on its authenticity, he is further breaking down the barriers between Greeks and barbarians, one of the prevailing aims of the work.

38. C. Pelling, "Speech and Action: Herodotus' Debate on the Constitutions," *Proceedings of the Cambridge Philological Society* 48 (2002): 123–58. For another discussion of this passage in the current volume, see the essay by W. Oswald ("Oligarchy, and Democracy in the Constitutional Debate in Herodotus and in 1 Samuel 8)".

39. The insistence on selection by lot in rotation is significant. In his Funeral Oration, Pericles explicitly denies the importance of the lot and emphasizes the meritocratic nature of Athenian political procedure (Thucydides 2.37.1). This disagreement about the importance of the lot seems to be linked to another important debate in Athenian democracy concerning the nature of equality: was democratic equality based on everyone having the same, or was it based on merit, so that those who contributed more received more? See further below.

Megabyzus, on the other hand, rejects the rule of the πλῆθος in favor of ὀλιγαρχίη (the first appearance of the term in Greek literature: 3.81.1). His argument picks up on the opposition between the rule of one man and rule of the many: on the one hand, the πλῆθος should not rule because it acts like a stupid and brutal mob, whereas a τύραννος at least knows what he is doing (3.81.1–2). It is important that Otanes's denunciation of rule by one man is re-introduced by Megabyzus through his use of the term τύραννος. The point here is that such tyrannical rule would be better than rule by the mob.

His argument for oligarchy, however, is separate: the best people (among whom the seven conspirators involved in the debate themselves belong) should rule because they make the best decisions (3.81.3). This argument was obviously current at the end of the fifth century BCE; it also recurs in Thucydides in the context of political disquiet in Syracuse, where the claim has been made that the best people (οἱ βέλτιστοι) rule best (ἄρχειν ἄριστα) (6.39.1). It also is implied in the Old Oligarch, which dates also to the 420s, especially at 1.5: "In the whole world the best element (τὸ βέλτιστον) is opposed to democracy; for among the βέλτιστοι there is least licentiousness and injustice, and the most scrupulousness in regard to what is important, but among the δῆμος there is the most ignorance, disorderliness and worthlessness."

Darius's argument, on the other hand, is framed rather differently, and unlike the other two speakers, he returns openly to the three constitutions. However, he argues that both oligarchy and democracy would inevitably degenerate into monarchy because factionalism and corruption only can be resolved by one man (3.82.2–4). He makes the proposition that even if the three constitutions were the best of their kinds, the best democracy, the best oligarchy, and the best μούναρχος, monarchy would be the best: "for nothing could seem better than the best man" (3.82.3). Though made explicit here for the first time, being the "best man" had long been the implicit legitimization of one-man rule in Greece,[40] and as a theoretical position, the monarchic rule of the best man was to become a golden thread through political thinking about monarchy in the fourth century BCE; in fact, the monarch could be so good that he could become divine.[41] For Darius, however, his crowning—and ironic—argument is that rule by one man, as exemplified through Cyrus the Great, who represented the ancestral constitution, the πάτριοι νόμοι, brought freedom (ἐλευθερίη) to the Persians (3.82.5).[42]

The Constitution Debate engages with a number of questions current in Greek political and sophistic thought at the end of the fifth century: Who is best to rule? What are the consequences of nature (φύσις)? What is the role of custom? Importantly, the Constitution Debate as a whole shows that there could be good and bad forms of constitution, though ironically, monarchy finally trumps rule of the πλῆθος because monarchy for the Persians, when they are ruled by the best man, brings freedom. Indeed, the debate is framed in terms

---

40. See Mitchell, *Heroic Rulers*, esp. 57–90.

41. For Xenophon, it is superior virtue that makes men willing to be ruled (e.g., *Cyr.* 8.1.21–22); the ability to create willing obedience is a divine virtue (*Oec.* 21.9–12). In Plato, the positive version of the proposition that the strong should rule the weak culminates in the Philosopher King (*Resp.* 473c–e), an individual so aligned with divinity and orderliness that he becomes as divine and orderly as is humanly possible (*Resp.* 500c–e; note esp. c–d). Aristotle also explores the idea of rule of the best man, but he must be a man of such surpassing virtue, then no one could rule him (for that would be like ruling Zeus: *Pol.* 3, 1284b30–34). However, Aristotle, like Plato before him, doubts there could ever be any such man.

42. See L. Mitchell, "Herodotus' Cyrus and Political Freedom," in *Perceptions of Iran: History, Myths and Nationalism from Medieval Persia to the Islamic Republic*, ed. A. Ansari (London: I.B. Tauris, 2014), 111–31.

of monarchy, and specifically Persian monarchy. It begins with a rejection of the monarchy of Cambyses and ends with praise of the monarchy of Cyrus. So it *is* a Persian debate after all.

3. A Plurality of Constitutions

In the fourth century BCE, the exploration of the proposition that there could be good and bad forms of constitution drives the constitutional debate. The starting point seems to have been discussion of positive and negative forms of monarchy. Tyranny as a negative type had become well-developed by the end of the fifth century, especially at Athens, as we have noted, as a foil for democracy. Nevertheless, as well as these negative images of monarchy, out of an anti-democratic discourse at Athens there developed a positive theory of kingship (βασιλεία),[43] and the king (βασιλεύς) was contrasted with the τυραννίς. This contrast is already implicit in Herodotus and Thucydides but is worked out more systematically by Xenophon, who is interested in developing a positive model for rule by one man. For example, in the *Cyropaedia*, when Cyrus has to choose between remaining in Media and returning to Persia, Cyrus's mother, Mandane, compares the court of the Medish king to that of the Persian in terms of kingship at the Persian court (τὸ βασιλικόν) and tyranny (τὸ τυραννικόν) at the court of his Medish grandfather (1.3.18).[44]

As well as positive and negative forms of monarchy, there could also be positive and negative forms of other constitutions, as the Constitution Debate had already suggested. In the *Republic*, Plato suggests that there are five basic kinds of constitutions (aristocracy—which for him primarily meant rule of the best man—timocracy, oligarchy, democracy and tyranny: 543c–545c). These constitutions by nature degenerate from the best type (rule by the best man, the Philosopher King) to rule by the worst (rule by the tyrant). In the *Politicus*, on the other hand, Plato starts again from the three constitutions, but this time concludes (because by this point he is more pessimistic about achieving a Philosopher King in reality) that there are in fact six constitutions, divided primarily between those within law and those outside law: monarchy and tyranny; aristocracy and oligarchy; and finally democracy, which has two forms as the others, but only one name (291d–292a, 302c–303b). Nevertheless, he ultimately rejects all these constitutions in favour of the "best" constitution in which the statesman, the πολιτικός man, rules not according to law but according to reason (293e–294b).[45] In this way, the three constitutions provide for Plato a framework for elaborating why "real" constitutions fall so far short of the ideal.

Aristotle, on the other hand, who rejects rule by one man because no man could be so virtuous and passionless as to be law,[46] thinks law should rule and that this, along with self-interest, is what divides constitutions:

> Since πολιτεία (constitution) signifies the same thing as "civic body" (πολίτευμα), the civic body is sovereign (τὸ κύριον) in the cities, and it is necessary for the sovereign body

---

43. See C. Mossé, *Alexander: Destiny and Myth*, trans. J. Lloyd (Edinburgh: Edinburgh University Press, 2004), 124–32; Mitchell, *Heroic Rulers*, 156–63.

44. Xenophon, however, had a sophisticated idea of tyranny and was willing to develop through his *Hieron* the idea of the benevolent tyrant.

45. See C. J. Rowe, "Killing Socrates: Plato's Later Thoughts on Democracy," *JHS* 121 (2001): 63–76.

46. W. R. Newell, "Superlative Virtue: The Problem of Monarchy in Aristotle's *Politics*," in *Essays on the Foundation of Aristotelian Political Science*, ed. C. Lord and D. O'Connor (Berkeley: University of California Press, 1991), 191–211. See also C. A. Bates, Jr., *Aristotle's "Best Regime": Kingship, Democracy and the Rule of Law* (Baton Rouge: Louisiana State University Press, 2003), 183–87.

to be either one, few (ὀλίγοι), or many (πολλοί). When the one, the few, or the many rule for the advantage of the commonality (τὸ κοινόν), these constitutions are necessarily right (ὀρθαί), but when they rule for the private interests (τὸ ἴδιον) of the one, the few, or the multitude, they are perversions. For either we must say that those who do not share in the constitution are not citizens, or it is necessary for them to have a part in the benefits. We are accustomed to call, of the monarchical forms, the one that looks to the common interest βασιλεία, of the few (ὀλίγοι) (but more than one) ἀριστοκρατία … and whenever the πλῆθος is ruled according to the common interest the name common to all constitutions, πολιτεία … The perversions of the constitutions that have been named are: tyranny from kingship, oligarchy from aristocracy, and democracy from πολιτεία. For tyranny is a monarchy that benefits the man who is ruling, oligarchy benefits those with money (εὔποροι), and democracy benefits those without money (ἄποροι).[47] (*Pol.* 1279a25–39, 1279b4–10)

Aristotle goes on to refine further his division of constitutions and to assert that it is not number that matters, but class, so that in oligarchy it is not so much the few that rule but the rich, and in democracy, it is not so much the many as the poor (*Pol.* 1279b34–1280a6, 1290a30–1290b7).

Nevertheless, even the six constitutions can be further sub-divided, and it becomes evident that some constitutions can be mixtures of the various types. For example:

In our discussion of kingship (βασιλεία) we distinguished two forms of tyranny (τυραννίς) and said that they were closely connected to kingship in the nature of their power because both were according to law. (There are some among the βάρβαροι who choose absolute monarchs (αὐτοκράτορες μόναρχοι), and long ago among the ancient Greeks there were some monarchs in the same way, who were called αἰσυμνῆται). There are some differences between these two forms, but they are "kingly"(βασιλικαί) because they are according to law and because they rule monarchically over the willing, but also "tyrannical" (τυραννικαί) because they rule despotically (τὸ δεσποτικῶς ἄρχειν) according to their own opinions. But there is a third kind of tyranny that seems especially to be a tyranny and is the opposite to absolute kingship (παμβασιλεία). This kind of tyranny is necessarily μοναρχία, which rules without any kind of accountability (ἀνυπεύθυνος) over all his equals (ὅμοιοι) or superiors (βελτίονες) and for its own interest, but not in the interests of those who are ruled. For this reason, it is rule over the unwilling. For none willingly of those who are free (ἐλεύθεροι) will endure such a constitution. (*Pol.* 1295a7–23)

As he himself tells us at the end of *Nicomachean Ethics*, Aristotle was trying to draw up typologies of constitution based on his studies of real constitutions (cf. *Pol.* 1289b27–1290a13).[48] Yet, as is clear, the three constitutions still form the general framework, together with their opposites (cf. *Pol.* 1289.26–38). Furthermore, any of the right forms of constitutions are acceptable if they concern themselves with the pursuit of virtue (ἀρετή) (*Pol.* 1280b5–25), though the deviant forms will always be problematic. Even if they are formed according to law, it will necessarily be bad law.[49] That is not to say that Aristotle was not interested in abstractions: the concern of the political life, for Aristotle, is justice

---

47. At *Rhet.* 1.8, however, Aristotle says there are four constitutions: democracy, oligarchy, aristocracy, and monarchy.
48. Aristotle's school compiled around 158 *politeiai*: see Rhodes, *Commentary* 1–2.
49. Balot, *Greek Political Thought*, 260–61.

in the common interest, which consists in equality for all (*Pol.* 1282b16–17),[50] and which he formulated in his ideal city, the city "according to prayer."[51]

4. The Mixed Constitution

Aristotle, however, like other political theorists, thought that stable government could most readily be achieved through a "mixed" constitution. Thucydides was the first to refer to a mixed constitution as the "reasonable blend (μετρία ξύγκρασις) in the interests of the few (οἱ ὀλίγοι) and the many (οἱ πολλοί)" (8.97.2), which he saw realized in the Constitution of the Five Thousand, the moderate oligarchy established at Athens in 411 BCE.[52] There is some doubt over the precise nature of what Thucydides meant by his blend of the few and the many.[53] However, that Thucydides could associate the hoplite assembly of the Five Thousand with "the many" has been controversial, since the poorest class, the rowers in the fleet (the ναυτικὸς ὄχλος, Thucydides 8.72.2) whom the Old Oligarch had associated with the δῆμος, were excluded from this constitution. As a result, it was only a blending of the few and the many in the sense that a limited assembly shared power with an executive council. Nevertheless, in theoretical terms, the recognition that there could not just be three (or six) types of constitutions but a mixture and that a mixture could produce good government (εὖ πολιτεύσαντες) was innovative in terms of political thought and had a dramatic impact on the course of political thinking in the fourth century BCE.[54]

---

50. By the late fifth century BCE, the definition of equality itself was contested. It seems that even at the end of the fifth century, there were those who thought that democratic equality where all received the benefits of ruling was not fair or intelligent (Thucydides 6.39.1). In response to this democratic sense of equality, another definition of equality was developed that argued that equality was about "fairness" and that those who contributed the most should receive the greatest rewards. Both Plato and Aristotle are quite explicit about the two kinds of equality and their consequences (Plato, *Leg.* 757a–e, Aristotle, *Pol.* 1301b29–39; cf. Isocrates, *Areop.* 21–22). Aristotle thinks of arithmetic equality as democratic and proportionate equality as oligarchic, but proportionate equality became the basis of kingship theory as developed in the fourth century BCE (e.g., Isocrates, *To Nicocles,* 14–16), and it had other applications as well. Notably (and strikingly), Pericles's Funeral Oration, often taken as the *locus classicus* for a definition of democracy, says that δημοκρατία is rule in the interests not of the few but the many, and while all have a share in the laws, public preferment depends on merit (not the lot) (Thucydides 2.37.1), which seems to suggest that there were some at Athens in the late fifth century BCE who were arguing for a definition of democracy based on proportionate equality that rewarded merit rather than the traditional arithmetic meaning of equality, which was the rule by all (cf. Thucydides 6.39.1). Cf. F. D. Harvey, "Two Kinds of Equality," *Classica et Mediaevalia* 26 (1965): 101–46; idem. "Corrigenda," *Classica et Mediaevalia* 27 (1966): 99–100. Note also Huffman, *Archytas of Tarentum*, 211–15.

51. See R. T. Long, "Aristotle's Egalitarian Utopia: The *polis kat' euchen*," in *The Imaginary Polis*, Acts of the Copenhagen Polis Centre, vol. 7 ed., ed. M. H. Hansen (Copenhagen: Museum Tusculanum, 2005), 164–96.

52. It is significant that there is no mention of "the one" in Thucydides's mixed constitution, especially in light of his comments about Pericles and democracy at 2.65.9: "What in theory was δημοκρατία was in fact rule by the first man."

53. On the relationship between the account of Thucydides and that of the Aristotelian *Athenaion Politeia* (29–32), see P. J. Rhodes, "The Five Thousand in the Athenian Revolution of 411 BC," *JHS* 92 (1972): 115–27, though note also the more recent suggestions of E. Harris, "The Constitution of the Five Thousand," *Harvard Studies in Classical Philology* 93 (1990): 243–80.

54. See now D. E. Hahm, "The Mixed Constitution in Greek Thought," in *A Companion to Greek and Roman Political Thought*, ed. R. Balot (Malden, MA: Wiley-Blackwell, 2009), 178–98.

The importance of the mixed constitution was that it would bring stability by giving something to everybody.[55] In the *Laws*, Plato has the Athenian argue that there are only two mother constitutions, monarchy and democracy, and that to achieve freedom (ἐλευθερία) and friendship with judgment, it is imperative for there to be a mixing (μεταλαβεῖν) of the two (693d–e). He then goes on to say that the Spartans and Cretans have been more successful than others at finding the mean (τὰ μέτρια) between the two. Further, while elsewhere in the *Laws* he has Megillus say that he cannot categorize the Spartan constitution (712d), when he has the Athenian talk about Spartan kingship, he has him say that its success and the success of the constitution as a whole was a result of the "blending (σύμμεικτος) of the right elements," which acted as a check and balance on each other and, in particular, the power of the kings (691e–692a). While as S. Hodkinson points out, this description of the Spartan Constitution is not really a mixing of the various elements,[56] the idea that the constitutional elements should work together by acting as a check on each other was influential into the early modern period and the work of political theorists such as Montesquieu.

It is Aristotle who develops furthest the idea of the 'mixture' (μίξις) of constitutions, which for him is exemplified by the constitution he calls πολιτεία. However, for Aristotle, it is not the mixing of democracy and tyranny that is important, but the mixing between democracy and oligarchy (*Pol.* 1293b33–35: "Πολιτεία, put simply, is a mix (μίξις) of democracy and oligarchy.") There are three ways by which such a mixing can be achieved (*Pol.* 1294a35–1294b13): either through a mixing of oligarchic and democratic laws; or to use the mean (τὸ μέσον) between the two (for example, in relation to property qualifications); or to combine elements of both oligarchic and democratic practice. For Aristotle, Sparta is a good example of such a constitution, because it contains elements that are democratic (such as the common mess) and elements that are oligarchic (such as the use of the vote rather than the lot) (*Pol.* 1294b18–34). Elsewhere, however, he concedes that some think the Spartan constitution is the best constitution, which he does not—although he thinks it is the best example of his πολιτεία because it contains a mixture of all elements: monarchy, oligarchy and democracy (*Pol.* 1265b31–1266a1).

5. Constitutional Theorizing and the Three Constitutions

The idea of the three constitutions, as well as their perversions and their variants, was central to Greek political thought of the fifth and fourth centuries BCE and had an impact on medieval, Enlightenment, and early American political thought.[57] However, there was often a significant gap between political thought and political practice, and classifying real-world constitutions in terms of the three constitutions was not straightforward. Sparta, as we have seen, was identified at different times and by different authors as an oligarchy and a mixed constitution (the mean between democracy and monarchy, the mix of oligarchy and democracy, and a mix of monarchy, oligarchy and democracy). In the fourth century BCE, the Athenian Isocrates even made a case in the *Areopagiticus* for Sparta being a democracy.

---

55. See P. Cartledge, "Greek Political Thought: The Historical Context," in *The Cambridge History of Greek and Roman Political Thought*, ed. C. Rowe and M. Schofield (Cambridge: Cambridge University Press, 2005), 11–22 (19–20).

56. S. Hodkinson, "The Imaginary Spartan *Politeia*," in *The Imaginary Polis*, Acts of the Copenhagen Polis Centre, vol. 7, ed. M. H. Hansen (Copenhagen: Museum Tusculanum, 2005), 222–82 (230–31); cf. Hahm, "Mixed Constitution," 180–85.

57. W. Nippel, *Mischverfassungstheorie und Verfassungsrealität in Antike und früher Neuzeit* (Stuttgart: Klett-Cotta, 1998).

The Athenians, on the other hand, had oligarchic elements in the election by vote rather than by lot of the generals (*Athenaion Politeia* 44.4, 66.1), who, in the fifth century BCE, thereby became the most important magistrates in the state. Furthermore, there was even debate about what made a constitution like the one in Athens a democracy: Was it rule by all (cf. Thucydides 6.39.1)? Was it rule by the lower classes (Old Oligarch 1.2)? Was it rule in the interests of the many (Thucydides 2.37.1)? Was it popular decision-making in the assembly and the jury courts (*Athenaion Politeia* 41.2)? Further, in practice it was not always easy to distinguish between democracy and oligarchy. In 411 BCE, Peisander, the leader of the oligarchic coup, promised the Athenians that what he was offering was "democracy not in the same way" (Thucydides 8.53.1). The reason constitutional theorizing was important was because it provided a framework within which these questions could be asked at all.

The cities that emerged on the Greek mainland and Asia Minor after the collapse of the Mycenean palace economies and the sudden (and striking) drive towards urbanization in the eighth century BCE adopted a number of political forms, although there were features in common. While it is often said that they were essentially republican, it is more accurate to say that they were essentially hierarchical, but that among the elite there was an ethos of "competitive egalitarianism." For this reason there was tension in the community, on the one hand, between the individual members of the elite (or those who had a hold on decision-making for these growing communities) and, on the other, between the elite and the aspiring elite, as prosperity grew and there was an upward push for more members of the community to have access to political power.

In this context there was a desire to create εὐνομία, good order, and to establish "straight justice." In his study of Homeric epic, as a way of understanding the nature of the "political" as distinct from political institutions, D. Hammer has developed the idea of the expanding and contracting "political field" in which political actions and political tensions are performed.[58] As we saw at the beginning of this chapter, there was an awareness, if not necessarily the beginnings, of political thinking in the political reorganization of Sparta in the seventh century BCE. This willingness and ability to think politically and constitutionally is also reflected in Tyrtaeus, the seventh-century Spartan poet, who, in one of his poems, recounts an oracle from Apollo:

> Having heard from Phoebus they brought home from the Pytho both oracles of the god and words of sure fulfilment: the god-honoring kings, for whom the lovely city of Sparta is their care, and the noble elders, are to rule over the council; then the people (δημότας ἄνδρας) obeying straight decrees (εὐθεῖαι ῥῆτραι) are to speak nobly and to do what is just, and not to plot anything against the city; for the multitude of the people (δήμου πλήθει) victory and strength would follow. For thus Phoebus has declared about these things for the city. (Fr. 4 West)

Whether or not this poem is linked to the Great Rhetra, it is probably part of the poem known as *Eunomia*, "Good Order."[59] Just like Solon at Athens fifty or so years later, Tyrtaeus, in exhorting the δῆμος to obey the council so that the city will prosper, is, on the one hand, reflecting on the evident instability within the city, but, on the other, even though

---

58. D. Hammer, *The Iliad as Politics: The Performance of Political Thought* (Norman: University of Oklahoma Press, 2002), esp. 19–48.

59. See H. van Wees, "Tyrtaeus' *Eunomia*: Nothing to do with the Great Rhetra," in *Sparta: New Perspectives*, ed. S. Hodkinson and A. Powell (Swansea: Classical Press of Wales, 1999), 1–41.

his position is very conservative, is also thinking in constitutional terms about how stability could be achieved.[60]

Constitutional thinking, however, also arose out of reflections on the past and was shaped by how that past was remembered. Thus it was that in the fourth century BCE, reflections on the mixed constitution were in part a re-working through the transformative act of re-remembering the Spartan constitution of Lycurgus. Likewise, Athenian democratic theorizing placed at its heart tyranny and the invention of the foundational acts of the tyrannicides through a process of reflection on the Persian attack on Athenian soil and the expulsion of the Peisistratids, who themselves subsequently became tyrants after the type of the Persian King.

It is surely within these contexts that second-order abstracted and analytical constitutional thought emerged. Constitutional thinking was trying to make sense of the variety of constitutional forms but also to create a critical framework within which the variety could be explored and understood. As a result, "governance" became something that could be held up for intellectual scrutiny. That it could be critiqued suggested that it could also be changed. As a consequence, the vitality of political experimentation among the Greek cities in the archaic and classical periods is probably without rival. Thinking in terms of the three constitutions was part of the drive to understand what governance was, the many forms that it had, and the other forms it could take, while still achieving a stable society.

Bibliography

Asheri, D., A. Lloyd, and A. Corcella, eds. 2007. *A Commentary on Herodotus Book I–IV*. Oxford: Oxford University Press.

Balot, R. 2006. *Greek Political Thought*. Malden, MA: Blackwell.

Bates, C. A., Jr. 2003. *Aristotle's "Best Regime": Kingship, Democracy and the Rule of Law*. Baton Rouge: Louisiana State University Press.

Bowra, C. M. 1964. *Pindar*. Oxford: Oxford University Press.

Carey, C. 1981. *A Commentary on Five Odes of Pindar: Pythian 2, Pythian 9, Nemean 1, Nemean 7, Isthmian 8*. New York: Arno.

Cartledge, P. 2009. *Ancient Greek Political Thought in Practice*. Cambridge: Cambridge University Press.

———. 2005. "Greek Political Thought: The Historical Context." In *The Cambridge History of Greek and Roman Political Thought*, edited by C. Rowe and M. Schofield, 11–22. Cambridge: Cambridge University Press.

———. 2002. *Sparta and Lakonia: A Regional History 1300 to 362 BC*. 2nd ed. London: Routledge.

———. 1987. *Agesilaos and the Crisis of Sparta*. London: Routledge.

Chamoux, E. *Cyrène sous la monarchie des Battiades*. Paris: de Boccard, 1953.

Flower, M. A. 2002. "The Invention of Tradition in Classical and Hellenistic Sparta." In *Sparta: Beyond the Mirage*, edited by A. Powell and S. Hodkinson, 191–217. London: Routledge.

---

60. There is debate about the point at which political thinking becomes political thought. Hammer argues that as a publicly performed narrative, the *Iliad* does not so much describe political activity in eighth-century Greece as provide a critical reflection on it, and in this sense is a work of political thought (*The Iliad as Politics*, 4–14). P. Cartledge argues, on the other hand, that epic is pre-political (*Ancient Greek Political Thought in Practice* [Cambridge: Cambridge University Press, 2009], 33), but see K. A. Raaflaub, "Poets, Lawgivers, and the Beginnings of Political Reflection in Archaic Greece," in *The Cambridge History of Greek and Roman Political Thought*, ed. C. Rowe and M. Schofield (Cambridge: Cambridge University Press, 2005), 23–59 (24–34).

Hahm, D. E. 2009. "The Mixed Constitution in Greek Thought." In *A Companion to Greek and Roman Political Thought*, edited by R. Balot, 178–98. Malden, MA: Wiley-Blackwell.

Hammer, D. 2002. *The Iliad as Politics: The Performance of Political Thought*. Norman: University of Oklahoma Press.

Hansen, M. H. 1986. "The Origin of the Term *demokratia*." *Liverpool Classical Monthly* 11: 35–36.

———., ed. 2000. *A Comparative Study of Thirty City-State Cultures*. Copenhagen: Royal Danish Academy.

Harris, E. 1990. "The Constitution of the Five Thousand." *Harvard Studies in Classical Philology* 93: 243–80.

Harvey, F. D. 1966. "Corrigenda." *Classica et Mediaevalia* 27: 99–100.

———. 1965. "Two Kinds of Equality." *Classica et Mediaevalia* 26: 101–46.

Hodkinson, S. 2005. "The Imaginary Spartan *Politeia*." In *The Imaginary Polis*, Acts of the Copenhagen Polis Centre, vol. 7, edited by M. H. Hansen, 222–82. Copenhagen: Museum Tusculanum Press.

———. 1997. "The Development of Spartan Society and Institutions in the Archaic Period." In *The Development of the Polis in Archaic Greece*, edited by L. Mitchell and P. J. Rhodes, 83–102. London: Routledge.

Huffman, C. A. 2005. *Archytas of Tarentum: Pythagorean Philosopher and Mathematician King*. Cambridge: Cambridge University Press.

Khurt, A. 2014. "'Even a Dog in Babylonia is Free.'" In *Legacy of Momigliano*, edited by T. Cornell and O. Murray, 77–87. London: The Warburg Institute; Turin: Nino Aragno Editore.

Kirk, G. S., J. E. Raven, and M. Schofield, eds. 1983. *The Presocratic Philosophers: A Critical History with a Selection of Texts*. 2nd ed. Cambridge: Cambridge University Press.

Lloyd, A. B. 1990. "Herodotus on Egyptians and Libyans." In *Hérodote et les peuples non-grecs: Entretiens sur l'Antiquité classique: Vandoeuvres-Genève, 22–26 Août*, edited by G. Nenci and O. Reverdin, 215–45. Geneva: Fondation Hardt 35.

Long, R. T. 2005. "Aristotle's Egalitarian Utopia: The *polis kat' euchen*." In *The Imaginary Polis*. Acts of the Copenhagen Polis Centre, vol. 7, edited by M. H. Hansen, 164–96. Copenhagen: Museum Tusculanum Press.

Malkin, I. 2008. "Foundations." In *A Companion to Archaic Greece*, edited by K. A. Raaflaub and H. van Wees, 373–94. Malden, MA: Wiley-Blackwell.

Marr, J. L. and P. J. Rhodes. 2008. *The "Old Oligarch": The Constitution of the Athenians Attributed to Xenophon*. Oxford: Aris and Phillips.

Martin, M., III and D. C. Snell. 2005. "Democracy and Freedom." In *A Companion to the Ancient Near East*, edited by D. C. Snell, 419–29. Malden, MA: Blackwell.

Miller, M. C. 1995. "Persians: the Oriental Other." *Source: Notes in the History of Art* 15 (*Special Issue: Representations of the "Other" in Athenian Art, c. 510–400 BC*): 39–44.

Mitchell, B. 2000. "Cyrene: Typical or Atypical." In *Alternatives to Athens: Varieties of Political Organisation and Community in Ancient Greece*, edited by R. Brock and S. Hodkinson, 82–102. Oxford: Oxford University Press.

Mitchell, L. 2014. "Herodotus' Cyrus and Political Freedom." In *Perceptions of Iran: History, Myths and Nationalism from Medieval Persia to the Islamic Republic*, edited by A. Ansari, 111–31. London: I.B. Tauris.

———. 2013. *The Heroic Rulers of Archaic and Classical Greece*. London: Bloomsbury.

———. 2013. "Remembering Cyrus the Persian: Exploring Monarchy and Freedom in Classical Greece." In *Bringing the Past to the Present in the Late Persian and Early Hellenistic Period:*

Images of Central Figures, edited by E. Ben Zvi and D. V. Edelman, 283–92. Oxford: Oxford University Press.

———. 2007. *Panhellenism and the Barbarian in Archaic and Classical Greece*. Swansea: Classical Press of Wales.

———. 2006. "Greek Government." In *A Companion to the Classical Greek World*, edited by K. Kinzl, 367–86. Malden, MA: Blackwell.

———. 2006. "Tyrannical Oligarchs at Athens." In *Ancient Tyranny*, edited by S. Lewis, 178–87. Edinburgh: Edinburgh University Press.

———. 1997. "New Wine in Old Wineskins: Solon, *Aretē* and the *Agathos*." In *The Development of the Polis in Archaic Greece*, edited by L. Mitchell and P. J. Rhodes, 137–47. London: Routledge.

Mossé, C. 2004 *Alexander: Destiny and Myth*. Translated by J. Lloyd. Edinburgh: Edinburgh University Press.

Newell, W. R. 1991. "Superlative Virtue: The Problem of Monarchy in Aristotle's *Politics*." In *Essays on the Foundation of Aristotelian Political Science*, edited by C. Lord and D. O'Connor, 191–211. Berkeley: University of California Press.

Nippel, W. 1998. *Mischverfassungstheorie und Verfassungsrealität in Antike und früher Neuzeit*. Stuttgart: Klett-Cotta.

Ostwald, M. 2000. *Oligarchia: The Development of a Constitutional Form in Ancient Greece*. Historia Einzelschriften 144. Stuttgart: Steiner.

Pelling, C. 2002. "Speech and Action: Herodotus' Debate on the Constitutions." *Proceedings of the Cambridge Philological Society* 48: 123–58.

Raafalub, K. A. 2007. "The Breakthrough of *Dēmokratia* in Mid-fifth-century Athens." In *Origins of Democracy in Ancient Greece*, edited by K. A. Raaflaub, J. Ober, and R. W. Wallace, 105–54. Berkeley: University of California Press.

———. 2005. "Poets, Lawgivers, and the Beginnings of Political Reflection in Archaic Greece." In *The Cambridge History of Greek and Roman Political Thought*, edited by C. Rowe and M. Schofield, 23–59. Cambridge: Cambridge University Press.

———. 2004. *The Discovery of Freedom in Ancient Greece*. Chicago, IL: University of Chicago Press.

———. 1990. "Contemporary Perceptions of Democracy in Fifth–century Athens." In *Aspects of Athenian Democracy (Classica et Mediaevalia. Dissertationes XI)*, edited by W. R. Connor, M. H. Hansen, K. A. Raaflaub, and B. S. Strauss, 33–70. Copenhagen: Museum Tusculanum Press.Previously published in *Classica et Mediaevalia* 40 (1989): 33–70.

Rhodes, P. J. 2000. "Oligarchs in Athens." In *Alternatives to Athens: Varieties of Political Organisation and Community in Ancient Greece*, edited by R. Brock and S. Hodkinson, 119–36. Oxford: Oxford University Press.

———. 1994. "The Ostracism of Hyperbolus." In *Ritual, Finance, Politics: Athenian Democratic Accounts Presented to David Lewis*, edited by R. Osborne and S. Hornblower, 85–98. Oxford: Oxford University Press.

———. 1993. *A Commentary on the Aristotelian Athenaion Politeia*. Rev. ed. Oxford: Oxford University Press.

———. 1992. "The Athenian Revolution." In *Cambridge Ancient History: Volume 5, The Fifth Century*. 2nd ed., edited by D. M. Lewis, J. Boardman, J. K. Davies, and M. Ostwald, 62–95. Cambridge: Cambridge University Press.

———. 1972. "The Five Thousand in the Athenian Revolution of 411 BC." *JHS* 92: 115–27.

Rhodes P. J. and R. Osborne, eds. 2003. *Greek Historical Inscriptions 404–323 BC*. Oxford: Oxford University Press.

Rowe, C. J. 2001. "Killing Socrates: Plato's Later Thoughts on Democracy." *JHS* 121: 63–76.
Snodgrass, A. 1986. "Interaction by Design: The Greek City-State." In *Peer Polity Interaction and Sociopolitical Change*, edited by A. C. Renfrew and J. F. Cherry, 47–58. Cambridge: Cambridge University Press.
Wees, H. van. 1999. "Tyrtaeus' *Eunomia*: Nothing to do with the Great Rhetra." In *Sparta: New Perspectives*, edited by S. Hodkinson and A. Powell, 1–41. Swansea: Classical Press of Wales.

— 13 —

Monarchy, Oligarchy, and Democracy in the Constitutional Debate in Herodotus and in 1 Samuel 8

Wolfgang Oswald

1. Introduction

The aim of this essay is to compare two texts from the ancient world. The first text is well known to most of us, the discussion between Samuel, the last of the so-called judges of Israel, and the elders of Israel about the installation of the monarchy in 1 Sam 8. The second text is from Herodotus's *Histories*, the so-called Constitutional Debate in book 3.80–82. It was the late classicist F. Gschnitzer who, in a lecture at the Heidelberg Academy in 1976 was, to my knowledge, the first to suspect a certain relation between these two texts.[1] He did not elaborate further on that, and so the matter was left untreated for a while. In a seminal article on Herodotus's Constitutional Debate a few years later, J. Bleicken mentioned the hint of Gschnitzer to these alleged parallels but was reluctant to venture an opinion.[2] This article picks up the matter again by applying the classical Aristotelian scheme monarchy, oligarchy, and democracy in order to shed some light on the political theory of 1 Sam 8 and *Hist.* 3.80–82.[3]

2. The Two Texts to be Compared

I would like to begin with the text that is more familiar to us, the scene in 1 Sam 8, which I will refer to as the "deuteronomistic Constitutional Debate." Ever since the work of M. Noth, this chapter has been considered one of the so-called reflective passages that from time to time interrupt the flow of the narrative in the books from Deuteronomy through Kings. These passages regularly display deuteronomistic reasoning; therefore, they are considered creations of the author of the Deuteronomistic History.[4] There is ongoing debate

---

1. F. Gschnitzer, *Die sieben Perser und das Königtum des Dareios: Ein Beitrag zur Achaimenidengeschichte und zur Herodotanalyse*, (Heidelberg: Carl Winter 1977), 35–36.
2. J. Bleicken, "Zur Entstehung der Verfassungstypologie im 5. Jahrhundert vor Christus (Monarchie, Aristokratie, Demokratie)," *Historia* 28 (1979): 148–72.
3. This article is an abridged, reworked, and translated version of my essay, "Die Verfassungsdebatten bei Herodot (3,80–82) und im Samuelbuch des Alten Testaments (1 Sam 8)," *Historia* 62 (2013): 129–54.
4. M. Noth, *Überlieferungsgeschichtliche Studien: Die sammelnden und bearbeiten den Geschichtswerke im*

over the political stance expressed in 1 Sam 8 and over its literary integrity. The classical opinion holds that 1 Sam 8 is critical of monarchy and is a unified deuteronomistic text. In my opinion, this view is appropriate.[5] I consider the following passages to be part of the Deuteronomistic History: the victory over the Philistines (1 Sam 7), the debate over the monarchy (1 Sam 8), the lottery for kingship (1 Sam 10:17–27a), and the farewell speech of Samuel (1 Sam 12).

The story in a nutshell: In 1 Sam 7, Samuel appears as the last and paramount judge of Israel. Due to his prayer and offering, the God of Israel causes terror among the Philistines so that they the Israelites can defeat them. After this event, we are informed that the sons of Samuel do not judge impartially; therefore, the elders of Israel demand from Samuel a king "to govern us like other nations" (1 Sam 8:5). Both Samuel and God dislike this request, but even so, Yahweh commissions Samuel to install a king. But before doing so, Samuel has to tell the people "the ways of the king (משפט המלך) who shall reign over them" (1 Sam 8:9, 11). What follows is a long list of disadvantages and vices of the king. This bad news notwithstanding, the people insist on installing a king over them. So far, the first of the two texts.

Book three of Herodotus's *Histories* relates the campaign of the Persian king Cambyses into Egypt, the revolt of Gaumata, a member of the priestly class of the magoi, and the suppression of the revolt by Darius and his co-conspirators. After the death of the usurper Gaumata, Darius I took the throne, as we know from the history books. But Herodotus knows more. Between the defeat of Gaumata and the accession of Darius, three of the conspirators meet to discuss how to come out of the present interregnum. They engage in a theoretical debate over the best form of government.[6]

The first speaker is Otanes, who equates monarchy with tyranny and advocates democracy. The second speaker is Megabyzos, who opines that democracy tends to decline towards an ochlocracy, the rule of the crowd, and therefore advocates aristocracy. The third and last speaker is Darius, who later becomes king, who claims that aristocracy as well as democracy inevitably lead to stasis, which means rioting; hence, monarchy should be considered the best form of government.

The other co-conspirators who do not partake in the discussion endorse the opinion of Darius, and so Persia remains a monarchy. Finally, by means of deceit Darius gains kingship. This is the story, so far.

Alten Testament, 3rd ed. (Tübingen: Niemeyer, 1967), 5.

5. W. Oswald, *Staatstheorie im Alten Israel: der politische Diskurs im Pentateuch und in den Geschichtsbüchern des Alten Testaments* (Stuttgart: Kohlhammer, 2009), 57–58, 136–39. A different opinion is expressed by G. P. Miller, *The Ways of a King: Legal and Political Ideas in the Bible*, Journal of Ancient Judaism Supplements 7 (Göttingen: Vandenhoeck & Ruprecht, 2011), 244–48. Attempts to discern various layers in 1 Sam 7–8 diachronically are, in my opinion, futile. A methodologically thought out but nevertheless unconvincing diachronic proposal has been forwarded by R. Kessler, *Samuel: Priester und Richter, Königsmacher und Prophet*, Biblische Gestalten 18 (Leipzig: Evangelische Verlagsanstalt, 2007), 73–101, esp. n. 87. The fundamental criticism of the monarchical form of government was not advocated in premonarchic or early monarchic times but rather, after the decline of the monarchy.

6. For another discussion of this passage and its precursors and successors, see the preceding essay by L. Mitchell, "The Three Constitutions in Greek Political Thought."

Herodotus 3.80–83 (excerpts)[7]	1 Sam 8 (and Deuteronomy)

Introduction and presentation of the problem

[3.80.1] After the tumult quieted down, and five days passed, the rebels against the Magi held a council on the whole state of affairs, at which sentiments were uttered which to some Greeks seem incredible, but there is no doubt that they were spoken.

8:1 When Samuel became old, he made his sons judges over Israel. [2] ... [3] Yet his sons did not follow in his ways, but turned aside after gain; they took bribes and perverted justice.

[4] Then all the elders of Israel gathered together and came to Samuel at Ramah, [5] and said to him, "You are old and your sons do not follow in your ways; appoint for us, then, a king to govern us, like other nations." [6] But the thing displeased Samuel when they said, "Give us a king to govern us." Samuel prayed to Yahweh, [7] and Yahweh said to Samuel, "Listen to the voice of the people in all that they say to you; for they have not rejected you, but they have rejected me from being king over them. [8] ... [9] Now then, listen to their voice; only – you shall solemnly warn them, and show them the ways of the king who shall reign over them."

[10] So Samuel reported all the words of Yahweh to the people who were asking him for a king. [11a] He said, "These will be the ways of the king who will reign over you:

Arguments contra monarchy

[2] Otanes was for turning the government over to the Persian people: "It seems to me," he said, "that there can no longer be a single sovereign (μούναρχον) over us, for that is not pleasant or good. You saw the insolence of Cambyses, how far it went, and you had your share of the insolence of the Magus. [3] How can monarchy be a fit thing, when the ruler can do what he wants (τῇ ἔξεστι ἀνευθύνῳ ποιέειν τὰ βούλεται) with impunity? Give this power to the best man on earth (τὸν ἄριστον ἀνδρῶν πάντων), and it would stir him to unaccustomed thoughts. Insolence (ὕβρις) is created in him by the good things to hand, while from birth envy is rooted in man. [4] Acquiring the two he possesses complete evil; for being satiated he does many reckless things, some from insolence, some from envy. And yet an absolute ruler ought to be free of envy, having all good things; but he becomes the opposite of this towards his citizens; he envies the best who thrive and live, and is pleased by the worst of his fellows; and he is the best confidant of slander. [5] Of all men he is the most inconsistent; for if you admire him modestly he is angry that you do not give him excessive attention, but if one gives him excessive attention he is angry because one is a

8:11b He will take your sons and appoint them to his chariots and to be his horsemen, and to run before his chariots; [12] and he will appoint for himself commanders of thousands and commanders of fifties, and some to plow his ground and to reap his harvest, and to make his implements of war and the equipment of his chariots. [13] He will take your daughters to be perfumers and cooks and bakers. [14] He will take the best of your fields and vineyards and olive orchards and give them to his courtiers. [15] He will take one-tenth of your grain and of your vineyards and give it to his officers and his courtiers. [16] He will take your male and female slaves, and the best of your cattle and donkeys, and put them to his work. [17] He will take one-tenth of your flocks, and you shall be his slaves.

[18] And in that day you will cry out because of your king, whom you have chosen for yourselves; but Yahweh will not answer you in that day."

---

7. Translation from Godley, LCL, retrieved from www.perseus.tufts.edu.

flatter. But I have yet worse to say of him than that; he upsets the ancestral ways (νόμαιά τε κινέει πάτρια) and rapes women (καὶ βιᾶται γυναῖκας) and kills indiscriminately (κτείνει τε ἀκρίτους).

Arguments pro democracy

[6] But the rule of the multitude has in the first place the loveliest name of all, equality, and does in the second place none of the things that a monarch does. It determines offices by lot, and holds power accountable, and conducts all deliberating publicly (βουλεύματα δὲ πάντα ἐς τὸ κοινὸν ἀναφέρει). Therefore I give my opinion that we make an end of monarchy and exalt the multitude, for all things are possible for the majority." ...

[Deut. 16:18 You shall appoint judges and officials throughout your tribes, in all your towns that Yahweh your God is giving you, and they shall render just decisions for the people.]

Arguments pro aristocracy

[3.81.3] (Megabyzos speaking) "... Let those like democracy who wish ill to Persia; but let us choose a group of the best men and invest these with the power. For we ourselves shall be among them, and among the best men it is likely that there will be the best counsels." [3.82.1] Such was the judgment of Megabyzus.

[Consider the role of the elders in 1Sam 8:4 and elsewhere.]

Arguments contra aristocracy

[3.82.3] (Darius speaking) "... But in an oligarchy, the desire of many to do the state good service often produces bitter hate among them; for because each one wishes to be first and to make his opinions prevail, violent hate is the outcome, from which comes faction and from faction killing, and from killing it reverts to monarchy, and by this is shown how much better monarchy is. [4] Then again, when the people rule it is impossible that wickedness will not occur; and when wickedness towards the state occurs, hatred does not result among the wicked, but strong alliances; for those that want to do the state harm conspire to do it together.

Decision pro monarchy

[3.82.5] But (to conclude the whole matter in one word) tell me, where did freedom come from for us and who gave it, from the people or an oligarchy or a single ruler (παρὰ [τοῦ] δήμου ἢ ὀλιγαρχίης ἢ μουνάρχου)? I believe, therefore, that we who were liberated through one man should maintain such a government, and, besides this, that we should not alter our ancestral ways that are good; that would not be better." ...

(1 Sam 8:19) But the people refused to listen to the voice of Samuel; they said, "No! but we are determined to have a king over us, [20] so that we also may be like other nations, and that our king may govern us and go out before us and fight our battles." [21] When Samuel had heard all the words of the people, he repeated them in the ears of Yahweh. [22] Yahweh said to Samuel, "Listen to their voice and set a king over them." Samuel then said to the people of Israel, "Each of you return home."

[3.83.1] Having to choose between these three options, four of the seven men preferred the last.

3. The Comparison

The account of Herodotus displays several characteristics that contrast with the narrative context and even the rest of the *Histories*. The Constitutional Debate is loaded with political theory, which is not the case elsewhere in the *Histories*. Some scholars have concluded, therefore, that this passage is a later insertion into the *Histories* or, alternatively, that Herodotus himself incorporated this piece from a separate source.[8] This is interesting, since this provides the first parallel to 1 Sam 8, which, together with 1 Sam 7, is commonly considered to be a deuteronomistic insertion into an otherwise older literary context.

However, more recent studies on Herodotus have challenged this assumption. They claim that the Constitutional Debate is very well integrated in its literary context.[9] This may be so or not; I will not take sides, because this matter does not affect our ability to compare these two texts. The "otherness" of the Constitutional Debate lies on a different level. The text introduces Greek, or more specifically Athenian, political theory into the mouth of Persian nobles. From the standpoint of cultural history, it can be ruled out that these three Persians ever engaged in this kind of philosophical discussion. For this conversation is indeed philosophical, since it is independent from the actual situation in which it is placed. It is not a discussion about the qualities of a certain king or contender for kingship. Only at the onset of the argument is there a short reference to the bad experiences with the late king Cambyses and the usurper Gaumata (*Hist.* 3.80.2). Also, it is not a discussion about experiences with democracy in Persia, since there had never ever been any. The discussion is theoretical in the true sense of the word.

And this is another strong parallel to 1 Sam 8. Together with 1 Sam 7, this chapter is also an anachronistic insertion. It is deuteronomistic—and that means Greek-influenced—political theory in the mouth of an early Iron Age chieftain. And like its Herodotian counterpart, the deuteronomistic Constitutional Debate does not judge certain persons but concepts. The dismissal of monarchy does not have an eye toward Saul or David. The first and the second kings of Israel will not commit any of the offences listed by Samuel. He and God, respectively, do not reject these two figures or any other person, but monarchy as an institution.

In order to achieve their goal, both texts use the same literary device: a catalogue of vices, a negative mirror for princes, so to say. In the case of Herodotus, we find it in the speech of Otanes (3.80.3–5); in case of 1 Sam 8, it is part of Samuel's long address to the people (1 Sam 8:11–17). Herodotus names the following points: wantonness and arbitrariness of the king, blandishments of the courtiers, violence against women, and homicide without litigation. Samuel, on the other hand, focuses on different types of conscripted labor the king will impose on the people and on illegal royal appropriation. Otanes closes his input with the statement: "He [i.e., the king] upsets the ancestral ways" (3.80.5), and this could also have been put in the mouth of Samuel. This statement makes no sense in the mouth of a Persian. From the standpoint of a Persian speaker, monarchy is the ancestral way; only from the standpoint of a Greek writer is monarchy alien to ancestral ways.

---

8. Bleicken, "Verfassungstypologie," 153.

9. C. Pelling, "Speech and Action: Herodotus' Debate on the Constitutions," *Proceedings of the Cambridge Philological Society* 48 (2002): 123–58: "firmly established in its context" (126), similarly D. Asheri, A. B. Lloyd, and A. Corcella, eds. *A Commentary on Herodotus Books I-IV*, (Oxford: Oxford University Press, 2007), 472. R. Thomas, *Herodotus in Context: Ethnography, Science, and the Art of Persuasion* (Cambridge: Cambridge University Press, 2000), 114–17, like Pelling, stresses the point that Herodotus intends to warn his Athenian readership of the Persians as potential democrats: The Persian could introduce democracy and benefit from the advantages of this form of government.

Although monarchy finally prevails in both texts, it is the criticism of monarchy that occupies the most space in each. This striking disproportion is surely due to the personal stances of the authors. The Greek Herodotus certainly had no inclination toward monarchy. In the narrative, he expressed his dismissal of the concpet by including the story about Darius's fraudulent accession to the throne (*Hist.* 3.84–86). On the other hand, the arguments against democracy cannot be denied, so Herodotus can best be characterized as a critical proponent of democracy. Likewise, the author of 1 Sam 8 is no friend of the monarchy, but what is his counterproposal?

This question requires a more in-depth analysis of the terminology used in our texts. Herodotus uses the terms μουναρχία and τυραννίς to designate autocracy, and the term ἰσονομία, literally 'equality before the law', to designate democracy. That is, some of the terminology of later political theory is present, but not all of it. The author of the Deuteronomistic History uses the abstract term המלוכה ('monarchy'), although not in 1 Sam 8 but subsequently, in 1 Sam 10:16, 25 (and passim). The counter concept is not expressed in abstract terminology but is paraphrased. In 1 Sam 8:7, God says about the demand of the people: "They have rejected me from being king over them." In abstract terminology, the counter concept reads "kingship of God," which is literally attested elsewhere in the Hebrew Bible twice: in Ps 22:29 and Obad 21. As a theological and cultic concept we find it in the Psalms, but in the Pentateuch and in the Former Prophets, it is a political concept. F. Crüsemann has used it in the formula, "theocracy as democracy."[10]

In order to understand what is meant by "theocracy as democracy," we have to consider the whole of the Deuteronomistic History and, in particular, the book of Deuteronomy. For our present purpose, it is helpful to have a look at the expression "voice of Yahweh." On several occasions the people are encouraged "to listen to (or to heed) the voice of Yahweh," beginning in Exod 19:5 and extending through 2 Kgs 18:12. In between, there are numerous instances, mainly in Deuteronomy, but also in 1 Samuel. In our text, in 1 Sam 8:19 we read, "But the people refused to listen to the voice of Samuel," which is nothing else but the voice of Yahweh, since the law of the king Samuel has just made known to the people are the words of Yahweh. In 1 Sam 12:14, in the farewell speech of Samuel that is closely connected to our text, God warns the people that even when there is a king, they and the king must heed the voice of Yahweh as a top priority.

What has heeding the voice of Yahweh to do with democracy? According to Deuteronomy, the voice of God says that the Israelites shall only be responsible for keeping the law (of Deuteronomy), not to serving a king nor an aristocracy (Deut 26:16–19 and passim). The voice of God says that the Israelites shall appoint their judges and officers themselves (Deut 16:18). The voice of God says that traditional tribal structures do not constitute Israel; rather, a system of offices under control of the popular assembly does (Deut 1:9–15). The voice of God encourages Israel to initiate and to maintain a form of participatory governance that might be called an early form of democracy.[11]

---

10. F. Crüsemann, "'Theokratie' als 'Demokratie': Zur politischen Konzeption des Deuteronomiums," in *Anfänge politischen Denkens in der Antike: die nahöstlichen Kulturen und die Griechen*, Schriften des Historischen Kollegs: Kolloquien 24, (Munich: R. Oldenbourg 1993), 199–214, but see also F. Crüsemann, *Die Tora: Theologie und Sozialgeschichte des alttestamentlichen Gesetzes* (Munich: Kaiser, 1992), 287. Although there is a certain basic agreement with Crüsemann, the view advocated in this essay departs in many ways from his.

11. For an outline of the political concepts of Deuteronomy, compare S. D. McBride, "Polity of the Covenant People: The Book of Deuteronomy," *Interpretation* 3 (1987): 229–44; J. Berman, "Constitution,

When God says to Samuel, "They have rejected me from being king over them" (1 Sam 8:7), it means that Israel has given up participatory governance: They no longer want to install their judges and officers by themselves; they leave that prerogative to the king. The public law (Deut 31:9–13) is no longer valid for everyone; rather, the king has his own law, which is outlined in the ways of a king, the above-mentioned negative mirror for princes. Thus, the debate in 1 Sam 8 is one between monarchy and democracy (in a broad sense). And this is also the case in Herodotus, where the pro-democratic and pro-monarchic arguments are the most elaborated ones.[12]

Particularly close are the opinions on the appointment of governmental officials. According to Otanes, the advantage of democracy is that the people "determine offices by lot, and hold power accountable, and conduct all deliberating publicly" (*Hist.* 3.80.6). Similarly, Deut 16:18 mandates: "You shall appoint judges and officials throughout your tribes, in all your towns that Yahweh your God is giving you, and they shall render just decisions for the people." As 1 Sam 10:17–27a indicates, the procedure to be used for appointment is supposed to be the casting of lots, as in Herodotus. The accountability of the officers is inculcated in Deut 16:19: "You must not distort justice; you must not show partiality; and you must not accept bribes, for a bribe blinds the eyes of the wise and subverts the cause of those who are in the right." And finally, the public character of all decisions is an overall feature of Deuteronomy.

In Herodotus's Constitutional Debate, the advantages and disadvantages of aristocracy are allowed very little space. Megabyzos merely advances the rather self-serving argument that the very participants of the debate would make up the elite group if an aristocratic government could be realized (3.81.3). Darius argues against him, saying that aristocrats tend to compete among each other, making an orderly government impossible (3.82.3–4). Similarly, in the deuteronomistic Constitutional Debate, the concept of aristocracy is not discussed theoretically. It occurs only in form of the elders who advance the proposal to Samuel. Although there is nowhere a definition of who may be counted among the elders, this group may have consisted of estate-owning, affluent, honorable, and influential persons, which makes them an equivalent to what elsewhere was called aristocrats.[13] The elders play an important role as representatives of the people in other parts of the Deuteronomistic History (including the Deuteronomistic sections in Exodus). But there is no discussion about abuse of power or about internal struggles of the elders, probably because the Deuteronomists themselves were affiliated with the group of the elders.[14]

Hence, the main focus in Herodotus and 1 Sam 8 is on monarchy and democracy. But one should be aware not to misunderstand the role of the concept of democracy in these texts. The point is *not* that both the Deuteronomist of 1 Sam 8 and Herodotus plainly advocate democracy. Neither of them makes such a statement overtly. The crucial point is that in both texts, the form of government is no longer considered to be divinely ordained or determined by tradition. Rather, it is a matter of dispute and decision, and that makes both of these texts extraordinary.

Class, and the Book of Deuteronomy," *Hebraic Political Studies* 1 (2006): 523–48; B. M. Levinson, "The First Constitution: Rethinking the Origins of Rule of Law and Separation of Powers in Light of Deuteronomy," *Cardozo Law Review* 27 (2006): 1853–88.

12. Bleicken, "Verfassungstypologie," 156.
13. For a slightly different assessment of the characteristics of an elder, see the article in this volume by T. Stordalen, entitled "Imagining the Memory of an Elder: Job 29–30."
14. These sorts of problems are thematized, e.g., in Neh 5; Jer 34; 37–38 and elsewhere in the prophetic literature. But this is beyond the scope of this essay.

A. Saxonhouse writes of the Constitutional Debate of Herodotus: "The importance of the passage, as I see it, does not lie in its supposed defence of democracy, but in the presentation of individuals having to decide where to allocate authority ... we see here the institutionalization of politics rather than dependence on personalities."[15] The same is true for the deuteronomistic Constitutional Debate in 1 Sam 8. The best form of government for Israel has become a matter of dispute and a matter of deliberate decision. The question arises: When did these debates on the best form of government take place? And why did it occur in such different circumstances?

4. The Historical Settings of the Two Texts

For Herodotus the case is clear, since here we do not have the problem of dating.[16] Herodotus wrote this part of his work around 430 BCE. The exact date is disputed among specialists, but this is not our concern here. Much more important is the general cultural environment of the Herodotian Constitutional Debate, and this is the emergence of the citizen-state in archaic Greece, "the Greek Discovery of Politics," as C. Meier has put it.[17] The transformation of the Greek society from the rule of aristocrats to participatory government took place in the seventh and sixth centuries BCE and brought with it what Bleicken called a "discontinuity of tradition."[18] In the wake of this radical change, nothing was self-evident anymore. The Constitutional Debate of Herodotus is one testimony to this cultural development, which embraced the whole Mediterranean area.

It seems obvious that such a debate can only take place at a time and in a place where some kind of "discontinuity of tradition" has occurred. But when in the history of Israel did such a "discontinuity of tradition" with respect to government and rulership take place? The narrative says it was before the installation of kingship. But this not a historical report. Historically, the transition to some kind of monarchy in Israel in the tenth century BCE is obscure. We do not even know what was before it.

Historically, we must ask when some erudite Israelites would have begun to contemplate the advantages and disadvantages of the monarchy. When was the concept of a democracy in the guise of a theocracy developed? When was there the need and the possibility to decide on the best form of government? To me, the only period of time possible is the time after the decline of the monarchy in the sixth century BCE. The end of the Davidic monarchy provides the necessary "discontinuity of tradition" without which a theoretical discussion about the best form of government never could have taken place. Thus, the time when the Deuteronomistic History was composed is the time when the debate over the pros and cons of the monarchy arose.

And this again is the time when the Greek form of government, the citizen-state, spread in the Mediterranean area. Cultural contacts between Greeks and Samarians or Judahites, respectively, are attested from the seventh century BCE on. Thus, in Judah in the Babylonian and Persian periods, two conditions for this kind of theoretical discussion were in effect: first, the Judeans had the possibility to learn about the Greek way of political

---

15. A. R. Saxonhouse, *Athenian Democracy: Modern Mythmakers and Ancient Theorists* (Notre Dame, IN: University of Notre Dame Press, 1996), 53.

16. As noted earlier, however, there is onging debate over whether this passage was written by Herodotus, incorporated by him from a source, or added into his work later on.

17. C. Meier, *Die Entstehung des Politischen bei den Griechen*, Suhrkamp Taschenbücher Wissenschaft 427 (Frankfurt: Suhrkamp, 1983).

18. Bleicken, "Verfassungstypologie," 149–51.

organization, and second, the Judeans had lost their traditional monarchy and were urged to reconstitute their society.[19] One attempt to reorganize the life of the people was the promulgation of Deuteronomy along with its narrative context and some time later, the authoring of the Deuteronomistic History.

5. Some Concluding Thoughts on the Deuteronomistic History

The author of the Deuteronomistic History clearly dismissed monarchy, as is obvious not only from 1 Sam 8 but also from Deuteronomy itself. The king of Deut 17:14–20 is not a monarch, nor an autocrat; he is not a king in the traditional ancient Near Eastern sense.[20] He is only the holder of one of the many offices in the state and accountable to the common law, like any other citizen. The disadvantages of the traditional type of monarchy are thoroughly laid out in 1 Sam 8 in a theoretical manner. The assessment does not depend on the personality of a particular king.

In 1 Sam 8 and in the Deuteronomistic History in general, to obey the king and to obey the voice of Yahweh, which means to obey the law of Deuteronomy, are mutually exclusive. There is only one exception to this rule, and this is king Josiah (2 Kgs 22–23). But the Josiah of the Deuteronomistic History, like the king decribed in the king's law in Deut 17:14–20, is not a king in the traditional ancient Near Eastern sense. He subjugates himself to the law (2 Kgs 22:11). And when he makes the covenant, the entire people shares equally in it and its obligations (2 Kgs 23:1–3). He is depicted in an ideal way as a *primus inter pares* according to Deut 17:14–20. Thus, the account of Josiah in 2 Kgs 22–23, the Constitutional Debate, 1 Sam 8, and the king's law in Deut 17:14–20 share the same theoretical anti-monarchic attitude.[21]

Bleicken concluded his essay saying that one could call the Constitutional Debate of Herodotus the first treatise on the political theory of state in world history.[22] I wonder if this crown should be passed over to 1 Sam 8.

Bibliography

Albertz, R. 2001. *Die Exilszeit: 6. Jahrhundert v. Chr.* Biblische Enzyklopädie 7. Stuttgart: Kohlhammer.

Alonso-Núñez, J. M. 1998. "Die Verfassungsdebatte bei Herodot." In *Politische Theorie und Praxis im Altertum*, edited by Wolfgang Schuller, 19–28. Darmstadt: Wissenschaftliche Buchgesellschaft.

---

19. Cf. Oswald, *Staatstheorie*, 86–144.

20. For a detailed discussion of the law of the king in Deut 17, see the article by R. Müller in this volume, entitled "Israel's King as Primus Inter Pares: The "Democratic" Re-conceptualization of Monarchy in Deut 17:14–20."

21. For other discussions of the memory of Josiah and his reign in this volume, see J. M. Bos ("Memories of Judah's Past Leaders Utilized as Propaganda in Yehud"), T. M. Bolin ("At the Hands of Foreign Kings: Divine Endorsement of Foreign Rulers in the Hebrew Bible in the Memory of Persian and Hellenistic Yehud"), and R. Müller, "Israel's King as Primus Inter Pares: The "Democratic" Re-conceptualization of Monarchy in Deut 17:14–20").

22. Bleicken, "Verfassungstypologie," 151: "die erste staatstheoretische Abhandlung der Weltgeschichte." Similar views are advocated by J. M. Alonso-Núñez, "Die Verfassungsdebatte bei Herodot," in *Politische Theorie und Praxis im Altertum*, ed. Wolfgang Schuller (Darmstadt: Wissenschaftliche Buchgesellschaft, 1998), 19; H. Ottmann, *Geschichte des politischen Denkens: Bd. 1 Die Griechen: von Homer bis Sokrates* (Stuttgart: Metzler, 2001), 130; Asheri, Lloyd, and Corcella, *Commentary*, 471–72.

Asheri, D., A. Lloyd, and A. Corcella, eds. 2007. *A Commentary on Herodotus Book I–IV*. Oxford: Oxford University Press.

Bakker, Egbert J., I. J. F. de Jong, and H. van Wees, eds. 2002. *Brill's Companion to Herodotus*. Leiden: Brill.

Berman, J. 2006. "Constitution, Class, and the Book of Deuteronomy." *Hebraic Political Studies* 1 (2006): 523–48.

Bichler, R. 2000. *Herodots Welt: der Aufbau der Historie am Bild der fremden Länder und Völker, ihrer Zivilisation und ihrer Geschichte*. Berlin: Akademie Verlag.

Bleicken, J. 1979. "Zur Entstehung der Verfassungtypen im 5. Jahrhundert vor Christus (Monarchie, Aristokratie, Demokratie)." *Historia* 28: 148–72.

Crüsemann, F. 1993. "'Theokratie' als 'Demokratie': zur politischen Konzeption des Deuteronomiums." In *Anfänge politischen Denkens in der Antike: die nahöstlichen Kulturen und die Griechen*, edited by K. Raaflaub, 199–214. Schriften des Historischen Kollegs: Kolloquien 24. Munich: R. Oldenbourg.

———. 1992. *Die Tora: Theologie und Sozialgeschichte des alttestamentlichen Gesetzes*. Munich: Kaiser.

———. 1978. *Der Widerstand gegen das Königtum: Die antiköniglichen Texte des alten Testamentes und der Kampf um den frühen israelitischen Staat*. WMANT 49. Neukirchen-Vluyn: Neukirchener Verlag.

Demandt, A. 2000. *Der Idealstaat: die politischen Theorien der Antike*. 3rd ed. Köln: Böhlau.

Dewald, C. and J. Marincola, eds. 2006. *The Cambridge Companion to Herodotus*. Cambridge: Cambridge University Press.

Fehling, D. 1971. *Die Quellenangaben bei Herodot – Studien zur Erzählkunst Herodots*. Berlin: de Gruyter.

Forsdyke, S. 2009. "Herodotus, Political History and Political Thought." In *The Cambridge Companion to Herodotus*, 4th ed., edited by C. Dewald and J. Marincola, 224–41. Cambridge: Cambridge University Press.

Gschnitzer, F. 1977. *Die sieben Perser und das Königtum des Dareios. Ein Beitrag zur Achaimenidengeschichte und zur Herodotanalyse*. Heidelberg: Carl Winter.

Hagedorn, A. C. 2004. *Between Moses and Plato: Individual and Society in Deuteronomy and Ancient Greek Law*. FRLANT 204. Göttingen: Vandenhoeck & Ruprecht.

Herodotus. 1961. 4 vols. LCL. Translated by A. D. Godley. Cambridge, MA: Harvard University Press.

Kessler, R. 2007. *Priester und Richter, Königsmacher und Prophet*. Biblische Gestalten 18. Leipzig: Evangelische Verlagsanstalt.

Kratz, R. G. 2000. *Komposition der erzählenden Bücher des Alten Testaments: Grundwissen der Bibelkritik*. Uni-Taschenbücher 2157. Göttingen: Vandenhoeck & Ruprecht.

Levinson, B. M. 2006. "The First Constitution: Rethinking the Origins of Rule of Law and Separation of Powers in Light of Deuteronomy." *Cardozo Law Review* 27: 1853–88.

Maul, S. M. 1998. "Der assyrische König – Hüter der Weltordnung." In *Gerechtigkeit: Richten und Retten in der abendländischen Tradition und ihren altorientalischen Ursprüngen*, edited by J. Assmann, B. Janowski, and M. Welker, 65–77. Munich: Wilhelm Fink.

McBride, D. S. 1987. "Polity of the Covenant People. The Book of Deuteronomy." *Interpretation* 3: 229–44.

Meier, C. 1983. *Die Entstehung des Politischen bei den Griechen*. Suhrkamp Taschenbücher Wissenschaft 427. Frankfurt: Suhrkamp.

Miller, G. P. 2011. *The Ways of a King: Legal and Political Ideas in the Bible*. Journal of Ancient Judaism Supplements 7. Göttingen: Vandenhoeck & Ruprecht.

Moenikes, A. 1995. *Die grundsätzliche Ablehnung des Königtums in der Hebräischen Bibel: ein Beitrag zur Religionsgeschichte des Alten Israel.* BBB 99. Weinheim: Beltz Athenäum.

Nippel, W. 1991. "Politische Theorien der griechisch-römischen Antike." In *Politische Theorien von der Antike bis zur Gegenwart*, edited by H.-J. Lieber, 17–46. Bonn: Bundeszentrale für Politische Bildung.

Noth, M. 1967. *Überlieferungsgeschichtliche Studien: die sammelnden und bearbeitenden Geschichtswerke im Alten Testament.* 3rd ed. Tübingen: Niemeyer.

Oswald, W. 2013. "Die Verfassungsdebatten bei Herodot (3,80-82) und im Samuelbuch des Alten Testaments (1Sam 8)." *Historia* 62: 129–45.

———. 2010. "Early Democracy in Ancient Judah: Considerations on Ex 18–24 with an Outlook on Dtn 16–18." *Communio Viatorum* 52: 121–35.

———. 2009. *Staatstheorie im Alten Israel: Der politische Diskurs im Pentateuch und in den Geschichtsbüchern des Alten Testaments.* Stuttgart: Kohlhammer.

Ottmann, H. 2001. *Geschichte des politischen Denkens: Bd. 1 Die Griechen: von Homer bis Sokrates.* Stuttgart: Metzler.

Otto, E. 2000. "Kodifizierung und Kanonisierung von Rechtssätzen in keilschriftlichen und biblischen Rechtssammlungen." In *La codification des lois dans l'Antiquité: Actes du Colloque de Strasbourg 27–29 novembre 1997*, edited by E. Lévy, 77–124. Travaux du Centre de Recherche sur le Prôche-Orient et la Grèce Antiques 16. Strasbourg: Université Marc Bloch; Paris: Diffusion de Boccard.

Pelling, C. 2002. "Speech and Action: Herodotus' Debate on the Constitutions." *Proceedings of the Cambridge Philological Society* 48: 123–58.

Raaflaub, K. A. 2002. "Philosophy, Science, Politics: Herodotus and the Intellectual Trends of his Time." In *Brill's Companion to Herodotus*, edited by E. J. Bakker, I. J. F. de Jong, and H. van Wees, 149–86. Leiden: Brill.

Saxonhouse, A. 1996. *Athenian Democracy: Modern Mythmakers and Ancient Theorists.* Notre Dame, IN: University of Notre Dame Press.

Thomas, R. 2009. "The Intellectual Milieu of Herodotus." In *The Cambridge Companion to Herodotus,* 4th ed., edited by C. Dewald and J. Marincola, 60–75. Cambridge: Cambridge University Press.

———. 2000. *Herodotus in Context: Ethnography, Science, and the Art of Persuasion.* Cambridge: Cambridge University Press.

Thompson, N. 1996. *Herodotus and the Origin of the Political Community: Arion's Leap.* New Haven, CT: Yale University Press.

Winton, R. 2005. "Herodotus, Thucydides and the Sophists." In *The Cambridge History of Greek and Roman Political Thought*, edited by C. Rowe and M. Schofield, 89–121. Cambridge: Cambridge University Press.

— 14 —

Remembering Samson in a Hellenized Jewish Context (Judges 13–16)

Diana V. Edelman

What sort of associations might the story of Samson in Judg 13–16 have evoked in the minds of Hellenized Jews or other members of the religious community of Israel familiar with some of the folk traditions, legends, or the cult of Herakles that likely became known in the southern Levant, Egypt, and Mesopotamia in the Hellenistic period (332–67 BCE)? Certainly, all Jews within the Seleucid Empire would have been familiar at least with the ubiquitous coins bearing the image of Alexander depicted as Herakles, his claimed forebear, issued by both Alexander himself and then reused by subsequent monarchs of the Seleucid line alongside other images of Herakles.[1] Those in the Ptolemaic Empire would have seen some of these coins during the reign of Alexander and, under the first three Ptolemies at least, would have experienced statues, medallions, and no doubt oral tradition paralleling the written texts in which this royal house traced their ancestry to Alexander and Herakles.[2] The widespread issuance of "Alexanders" in mints in various cities in the

---

1. Whether they knew that the image was meant to depict Alexander as Herakles could be open to discussion. In a Hellenized milieu, however, where Alexander would have been a well-known figure, this is likely. For a study of the use of Herakles iconography in the western Mediterranean that reveals its adoption of imagery already developed by Alexander and continued by his successors, the Antigonids, the Seleucids, and Ptolemies and a growing sense of Hellenistic socio-political identity, see L. M. Yarrow, "Heracles, coinage and the West: Three Hellenistic case-studies," in *The Hellenistic West: Rethinking the Ancient Mediterranean*, ed. J. R. W. Prag and J. C. Quinn (Cambridge: Cambridge University Press, 2013), 348–66. For another useful survey of the coinage, see E. Stafford, *Herakles*, Gods and Heroes of the Ancient World (London: Routledge, 2012), 147–50. The Seleucids emphasized their dynastic connections with Apollo on coins and personal connections with Zeus in image and ritual in addition to connections to Herakles inherited from Alexander (M. P. Canepa, "Seleukid Sacred Architecture, Royal Cult and the Transformation of Iranian culture in the Middle Iranian Period, " *Iranian Studies* 48 [2015]: 71–97 [88–89]). For images within Seleucid artistic media, see R. Fleisher, *Studien zur seleukidischen Kunst: Band I Herrscherbildnesse* (Mainz am Rhein: Von Zabern, 1991).

2. The Ptolemies claimed direct Macedonian descent but appear to have favored Alexander's subsequent claim to be the descendant of Zeus Ammon over his earlier claim to be the descendant of Herakles in depicting themselves wearing the aegis of Zeus in the portraits on the front of their coins. The same imagery was used on some royal statues as well; see for example, C. C. Edgar, "A Statue of a Hellenistic King," *JHS*

Levant, Babylon, around the Black Sea, in parts of Greece, and in Thrace until 150 BCE would have reinforced the familiarity of the image over time and over a wide territory.[3] Thus, a comparison between Samson and Herakles, which was common among the later Church Fathers and in the Middle Ages,[4] which was favored in the nineteenth century,[5] and which remained voiced in the late twentieth century, already might have begun or have been current in the Hellenistic period.[6]

Figures and narratives that form part of a group's social memory remain valued over time only if they continue to help maintain the group's understanding of their present by connecting to the past and the future in a perceived continuum. At the same time, it is important to bear in mind that not all members of a community attach the same associations or value to a memory shared by the entire group. Here I want to focus on those who would have considered the Tanak to play a central role in their self-identification as a member of Israel but who also would have constituted a subgroup that would have embraced or would have been open to Greek cultural influences.

The book of Judges explores the possibilities and failings of leadership within an imagined past setting of the early covenantal community of twelve-tribe Israel. The various stories serve as a platform for their readers and hearers to reflect over what kind of human leadership or stewardship is most successful in the community whose recognized leader is YHWH, what roles are necessary for such a leader, and how long a term of office should last. As the stories of Othniel and Ehud show, such leadership is possible, even if, as the remaining stories demonstrate, it usually fails. In theory, it should not be required beyond the community level if Torah is observed. The need for a military leader to overturn foreign oppression arises because of infidelity to YHWH, summarized as going after other gods, which leads to foreign oppression as a form of divine punishment. Once Israel is freed from that foreign control, the military leader is no longer needed, and the individual, if he or she remains in power, serves as a judge for his/her remaining lifetime, holding the people to the terms of the covenant made at Mount Sinai/Horeb. Hereditary kingship does not fare well as a form of leadership for the religious community in the stories of Gideon and Abimelech (6:1–9:57). Deborah's female leadership is rejected because of an inability to lead militarily, even if the ability to function as a judge in legal matters is strong (3:31–4:24). Jephthah illustrates the problem when the people select their own leader who lacks self-confidence

---

33 (1913): 50–52. D. M. Bailey, however, cites non-numismatic evidence where these three kings emphasized their connection to Herakles as well ("Not Herakles, A Ptolemy," *Antike Kunst* 33 [1990]: 107–10 [109]).

3. See R. A. Bauslaugh, "The Numismatic Legacy of Alexander the Great," *Archaeology* 37 (1984): 34–41.

4. See F. M. Krouse, *Milton's Samson and the Christian Tradition* (New York: Octagon, 1974), cited in G. Mobley, *Samson and the Liminal Hero in the Ancient Near East*, LHBOTS 453 (London: Continuum, 2006), 7 (but unavailable to me).

5. See G. F. Moore, *A Critical and Exegetical Commentary on Judges*, ICC (Edinburgh: T&T Clark, 1895), 364, also cited in Mobley, *Samson*, 7.

6. The date of the composition of the narrative is not determinative for the ensuing discussion. It is interesting to note that in a recent discussion, K. Spronk has suggested the book of Judges is an early Hellenistic composition written to bridge the time span between the existing books of Joshua and Samuel as part of a conscious desire to create a continuous history of Israel from creation to restoration after the Babylonian exile ("The Book of Judges as a Late Construct," in *Historiography and Identity [Re]formulation in Second Temple Historiographical Literature*, ed. L. Jonker, LHBOTS 534 [London: T&T Clark, 2010], 15–28). In his view, the book draws directly on contemporary Hellenistic thought and culture.

(10:6–12:7). What about Samson then?

It is not difficult to see that Samson is not your typical judge. From his miraculous conception to his superhuman strength and strong-willed, self-indulgent ways, he stands out from the other judges raised up, usually by YHWH, as temporary leaders of Israel. Here we have a story of YHWH pre-selecting a candidate to serve as שפט, no longer waiting for the outcry for help, which had not come in 40 years—"a long time." But his mother never appears to have disclosed to his father or to him what the angel conveyed to her about his "destiny": he will begin to deliver the Israelites (13:5). Not knowing what to do with his incredible strength, he uses it for personal defense and to react to emotional distress so that he is not recognized as a divinely selected savior by his fellow Danites or Israelites but rather, is seen as a loose cannon to be turned over to the Philistine overlords so he can stop creating problems. He eventually serves his announced destiny at his death by collapsing the temple of Dagon on himself and many Philistines, but he never has been recognized by Israel as a divinely chosen שפט, even if, in the story world, he is one, but perhaps not in the traditional sense.[7] In 16:23–24 he is the Philistines' sole enemy.[8]

---

7. For various proposals concerning the structure of the Samson narrative, see, for example, J. Blenkinsopp, "Structure and Style in Judges 13–16," *JBL* 82 (1963): 65–76, who argues for a semi-poetic narrative structured by threefold and 3 + 1 repetition and repetition in syntactic variation; J. B. Vickery, "In Strange Ways: The Story of Samson," in *Images of Man and God: Old Testament Short Stories in Literary Focus*, ed. B. O. Long (Sheffield: Almond Press, 1981), 58–73, who argues for a central section about Samson's adult life (14:1–16:19) characterized by threefold repetitions with variations, framed by an opening (ch. 15) and conclusion (16:20–31); J. C. Exum, who sees two sections, chs. 14–15 and ch. 16, which open and close in a similar way ("The Theological Dimension of the Samson Saga," *VT* 33 [1983]: 30–45) and its supplementation by E. Assis, who finds that the four episodes in the narrative share the same structural elements that revolve around tension between physical strength and emotional weakness ("The Structure and Meaning of the Samson Narratives [Jud. 13–16]," in *Samson: Hero or Fool? The Many Faces of Samson*, ed. E. Eynikel and T. Nicklas, Themes in Biblical Narrative 17 [Leiden: Brill, 2014], 1–12 [3–9]). He seems indebted to two additional earlier discussions. J. L. Crenshaw had previously identified a pattern of tension in each of the four episodes, but one based on concealment and search revolving around the tension between filial devotion and erotic attachment (*Samson: A Secret Betrayed, A Vow Ignored* [London: SPCK, 1979], 24–26, 65). K. L. Klein had identified irony in the Samson narrative to derive from the strong man who reveals himself to be the weakest judge because he is a slave to physical passion (*The Triumph of Irony in the Book of Judges*, JSOTSup 68, Bible and Literature Series 14 [Sheffield: Almond Press, 1988], 118). C. Camp identifies the riddle in ch. 14 and the Strange Woman as parallel *mises en abyme* combined with binary oppositions in a trickster tale that reflects over identity (*Wise, Strange, and Holy: The Strange Woman and the Making of the Bible*, JSOTSup 320, Gender and Culture Theory 9 [Sheffield: Sheffield Academic, 2000], 94–143). J. Kim reconstructs three cantos, ten sub-cantos, and thirty canticles employing parallel or symmetrical structuring patterns to produce narrative poetry (*The Structure of the Samson Cycle* [Kampen: Kok Pharos, 1993]), while Y. Amit sees a chronological structure in three periods of life (*The Book of Judges: The Art of Editing*, trans. J. Chipman, BibInt 38 [Leiden: Brill, 1999], 267–75).

8. For a study of the elements of the successful folktale husband in the story, which Samson and Herakles both fail, like the Centaurs and Orion, see D. E. Bynum, "Samson as a Biblical *pher oreskuos*," in *Text and Tradition: The Hebrew Bible and Folklore*, ed. S. Niditch, SBL Semeia Studies (Atlanta, GA: Scholars Press, 1990), 57–73 (64–69). He argues that wild men characters are not destined to become domesticated and reproduce. For the question of Samson as a wild man, see further S. Niditch, "Samson as Culture Hero, Trickster, and Bandit: The Empowerment of the Weak," *CBQ* 52 (1990): 608–24, who hesitates to apply the term (613), and G. Mobley, "The Wild Man in the Bible and the Ancient Near East," *JBL* 116 (1997): 217–33 (228–33). He approves of this term for Samson because he is a composite figure that draws on many character types. Kim, on the other hand, argues that the skillful use of what are generally considered to be folkloristic elements, e.g., killing a lion, scooping honey, asking a

Ben Sira provides a fleeting view of one meaning that was attached to Samson by a teacher of Torah in the Hellenistic period. He apparently lived in Jerusalem and wrote the book now called the Wisdom of Sirach/Ecclesiasticus in Hebrew, probably ca. 180 BCE. While living in Egypt under Ptolemy VIII Euegertes in 132 BCE, his grandson claims to have translated his grandfather's book from Hebrew into Greek. But it has nothing to say about individual judges; Samson is subsumed under a larger meaning assigned all משפט in the book: "The judges also, with their respective names, those whose hearts did not fall into idolatry and who did not turn away from the Lord—may their memory be blessed. May their bones revive from where they lie, and may the name of those who have been honored live again in their sons" (46:11–12).[9]

We might question when Samson's heart turned consciously to YHWH; the deity's spirit stirred in him multiple times (13:25; 14:6, 19; 15:14), but it is only after the fourth occasion, when he massacred a thousand Philistines with the jawbone of an ass at Ramat-Lehi and was thirsty from his exertions, that he first called on YHWH, saying, "You have granted this great victory by the hand of your servant. Am I now to die of thirst, and fall into the hands of the uncircumcised?" Nevertheless, it is the case that he did not worship other gods, though it would seem he violated the vows of a נזיר he was supposed to observe from birth[10] when eating the honey from the unclean lion carcass. There is no explicit mention of the consumption of wine, although it would have been served at his seven-day marriage banquet (17, 14:10) (המשתה), allowing the reader or hearer to fill this gap either by assuming he drank it along with his guests or that he refrained because of this nazirite status.

For those living in a Hellenized environment where Greek legends and worldview would have been readily accessible, many details in the biblical portrayal of Samson would have

---

riddle, and the donkey's jawbone, are more theological and poetic than folkloristic in nature in the story. Samson's long hair is not seen to be an old element from a folk tale where the hair is a source of power. Instead, staircase parallelism demonstrates that YHWH's spirit is the secret of his strength. Samson is not a folklore hero or wild man. But this scholar fails to acknowledge that the final coherence of the four stories centered on Samson in Judg 13–16 reveals very little about any underlying material that has been used taken up and shaped in this particular way (*Structure*, 427–28).

9. There is disagreement as to whether Samson failed or succeeded as a judge; for the first understanding, see, for example, Blenkinsopp, "Structure and Style," 70; B. G. Webb, *The Book of Judges: An Integrated Reading*, JSOTSup 46 (Sheffield: Sheffield Academic, 1987), 170–71; Klein, *Triumph of Irony*, 115–18; Amit, *Book of Judges*, 267. For the latter, see for example, Assis, "Structure," 2; Mobley, *Samson*, 112.

10. The angel says he is to be נזיר (*nezir*) from birth; the mother interprets that to mean his entire life, until his death, when she conveys the angel's words to her husband. It thus remains unclear whether his intended status as נזיר was to last only part of his life or his entire life. Others note that the prohibition against drinking wine or touching anything unclean was imposed on the mother, but not on Samson directly; the angel only imposes on Samson the prohibition to cut his hair; so, e.g., Amit, *Book of Judges*, 299; M. W. Bartusch, *Understanding Dan: An Exegetical Study of a Biblical City, Tribe and Ancestor*, JSOTSup 379 (London: Sheffield Academic, 2003), 161–63. He, like many others, suspects the נזיר status is a secondary addition to the story. Nevertheless, someone reading Judges in a collection of writings where they also knew the restrictions on a נזיר on wine and avoidance of a corpse in Num 6, which likely would have been the case in the Hellenistic period, probably would have assumed these other restrictions applied to Samson as well, and the failure to provide a reason for his decision not to tell his parents the source of the honey in the narrative itself would have led some audience members to think this related to the unclean source of the food that then contaminated the honey as well. The imposition of these other two restrictions on the mother indicates that they were considered to be typical of a נזיר, whenever they became part of the current form of the story.

called to mind Herakles. Which details in particular, and what associations? A number of possible parallels have been proposed with varying degrees of cogency,[11] but a list of motifs or details in the Samson story that I think would resonate with aspects of Herakles within Greek culture would be the association of both characters with: 1) womanizing and feasting; 2) betrayal by a woman;[12] 3) having fought armies;[13] 4) divine and human parentage;[14] 5) superhuman strength,[15] 6) breaking out of bonds;[16] 7) having served others as slaves/servants/prisoners;[17] 8) killing a lion using bare hands;[18] 9) pulling down a house/building single-handedly;[19] 10) pillars that are carried;[20] and 11) suicide.[21] Of these traits, the first,

---

11. For eight proposals to link details in the Samson stories to Greek tradition more generally, which only involve Herakles specifically in a few instances, see a series of four articles by O. Margalith: "Samson's Foxes," *VT* 35 (1985): 224–29; "Samson's Riddle and Samson's Magic Locks," *VT* 36 (1986): 225–34; "More Samson Legends," *VT* 36 (1986): 397–405; "Legends of Samson/Herakles," *VT* 37 (1987): 63–70. He worked on the assumption that there was some sort of oral or literary dependency in which the Iron I Israelites or perhaps specifically the Danites borrowed Herakles imagery and other Greek motifs from the coastal Philistines who dominated them. As rightly point out by Mobley, however, the shape of any Herakles legend that might have existed in the period from ca. 1200–1000 BCE cannot be recovered from the final forms known in Homer from the eighth century and the fifth century and later (*Samson*, 8–9), in forms known from playwrights, and on Greek vase painting. A similar point is made by Stafford, who notes that in Homer and Hesiod, Herakles is introduced with the stock formula, "Herakleian might/mighty Herakles," which indicates knowledge of Herakles in the oral tradition of epic already in the pre-Homeric Dark Age (ca. 1000–750 BCE), but we cannot know what these stories involved or how far back they went (*Herakles*, 11). The same applies for any Hebrew story of Samson.

12. So also, for example, Margalith, "Legends of Samson," 63–65; Bynum, "Samson," 68; Stafford, *Herakles*, 13; Spronk, "Book of Judges," 26.

13. So previously, for example, Spronk, "Book of Judges," 26.

14. So also, for example, Margalith, "More Samson," 401–2; R. Bartelmus, *Heroentum in Israel under seiner Umwelt: Eine traditionsgeschichtliche Untersuchung zu Gen. 6,1–4 und verwandten Texten im Alten Testament und der altorientalischen Literatur*, Abhandlungen zur Theologie des Alten und Neuen Testaments 65 (Zurich: Theologischer Verlag, 1979), 95–97 cited in Mobley, *Samson*, 40 but unavailable to me; Mobley, p. 41 considers it possible but unproven); Camp, *Wise, Strange*, 108–9; Y. Zakovitch, "The Strange Biography of Samson," *Nordisk Judaistik* 24 (2003), 19–36 (23–27, 34); Spronk, "Book of Judges," 26. The idiomatic expression used in v. 6 is בא אל. For those who would argue this need not always involve a sexual act, they cannot rule out the likelihood that this expression was used here specifically for its multivalency, which included the sexual dimension.

15. This is such a commonly acknowledged parallel that citations from secondary literature need not be included.

16. So previously, for example, Stafford, *Herakles*, 13.

17. So also, for example, Spronk, "Book of Judges," 26.

18. So also for example, Marglith, "Legends of Samson," 66–67; Stafford, *Herakles*, 13; Spronk, "Book of Judges," 26.

19. So also, for example, Stafford, *Herakles*, 13. For details relating to the story associated with Herakles, see M. Vickers, "Heracles Lacedaemonius: the political dimensions of Sophocles Trachiniae and Euripides Heracles," *Dialogues d'histoire ancienne* 21 (1995): 41–69 (65). The breaking down of the doorposts of the room where Megara was hiding in a structure associated with the altar of Zeus Eleutherios in Euripides's play, "Heracles," might have evoked in the first instance Samson's toppling of the pillars inside the temple of Dagon (16:27–29) but might also have resonated secondarily with his carrying of the city gate posts of Gaza and their setting up on a hill before Hebron (16:3).

20. So also, for example, Margalith, "Legends of Samson," 68–69; Spronk, "Book of Judges," 26.

21. Crenshaw has noted that his suicide is unusual within biblical terms, containing only two of the four typical elements: he finds himself in desperate circumstances and requests death. Missing are the deity's

second, and third are arguably more generic in nature than they are specific to these two heroic characters, while the fourth, fifth, sixth, and seventh are not specific to these two alone but narrow the pool of such candidates considerably. The final four points, on the other hand, seem to provide unusual overlap that would evoke both Samson and Herakles, which would then be reinforced by points four, five, six, and seven and probably by points one, two, and three as well in the minds of some, once the other eight points had already evoked an identification of the two figures.[22] The degree of overlap in many of the points should become clearer in the ensuing section.

Herakles in Greek Culture

If the aspects from the story of Samson just discussed brought Herakles to the mind of Hellenized Jewish readers or listeners, what meanings and values attached to Herakles in Greek culture might have accompanied this association and have been overlaid onto Samson by such readers? Herakles was a figure that was able to represent Greek culture and values within Greece itself and to outsiders who heard the stories told about him. He was the most popular Greek hero and was known and worshiped throughout Greece;[23] his cult spread west to Italy[24] and east to Asia Minor and Phoenicia.[25]

It can be noted that his distinctive traits only emerged after ca. 650 BCE in visual representations on proto-Corinthian vases; earlier depictions are possible on Late Geometric vases and statuettes and sub-geometric bronze fibulae from Boeotia from ca. 700 BCE, but they remain disputed. After 650 BCE, he appears in familiar roles associated with the stories known from literature on vases produced in Boeotia, Sparta, and Athens in addition to Corinth, especially as an animal tamer/doer of labors or as a hoplite.[26] By the middle of the sixth century, he comes to wear his characteristic lion skin, and his popularity becomes widespread, given the number of depictions known from vases, frieze, metopes, and pediment groups.[27]

---

reasoning with or sustaining the person asking to die and the choice of the desperate person to keep living (*Samson*, 46–48). Both of these elements are found in the account of Herakles's death.

22. Less cogent parallels that have been proposed include the following: 1) both are involved in episodes involving bees and foxes; 2) both are related to wells of water (Spronk, "Book of Judges," 26); and 3) Samson's jawbone is meant to evoke Herakles's club (Margalith, "Legends of Samson," 65). Spronk has not cited where points one and two occur in the Herakles cycle and they are not referenced in discussions I read by classicists. Point three as argued is unconvincing.

23. G. K. Galinsky, *The Herakles Theme: The Adaptations of the Hero in Literature from Homer to the Twentieth Century* (Towota, NJ: Rowman & Littlefield, 1972), 3; H. A. Shapiro, "The Death and Apotheosis of Herakles," *Classical World* 77 (1983): 7–18 (9).

24. For details, see for example, J. Bayet, *Herclé: Étude critique sur les principaux monuments relatifs à l'Hercule* Étrusque (Paris: E. de Boccard, 1926); J. Bayet, *Les origines de l'Hercule Romain*, Bibliotheque des écoles françaises d'Athènes et de Rome 13 (Paris: E. de Boccard, 1926); G. Brandley, "Aspects of the Cult of Hercules in Central Italy," in *Herakles and Hercules: Exploring a Graeco-Roman Divinity*, ed. L. Rawlings and H. Bowden (Swansea: The Classical Press of Wales, 2005), 129–51.

25. See, for example, C. Bonnet, *Melqart: Cultes et mythes de l'Héraclès Tyrien en Méditerranée*, Studia Phoenicia 8 (Leuven: Peeters, 1988), 399–415.

26. So J. Boardman, "For You Are the Progeny of Unconquered Herakles," in *Philolakôn: Lakonian Studies in Honour of Hector Catling*, ed. J. M. Sanders (London: The British School at Athens, 1992), 25–29; M. W. Padilla, *The Myths of Herakles in Ancient Greece: Survey and Profile* (New York: University Press of America, 1998), 4.

27. J. D. Beazley, *The Development of Attic Black-Figure*, rev. ed., ed. D. von Bothmer and M. M. B. Moore (Berkeley: University of California Press, 1986); H. A. Shapiro, "Old and New Heroes: Narrative Com-

Herakles appears in a wide variety of roles, and his myth has been revived and adapted in literature many times in the course of some two and a half millennia.[28] These include the great tragic sufferer, the paragon of superhuman strength and manliness, the ideal nobleman and courtier, the paragon of rhetoric, intelligence, and wisdom, the divine mediator, the exemplar of a life lived that will be rewarded by divinization, a metaphysical struggler, a paragon of virtue (ἀρετή), a romantic lover, a comic, gluttonous, lecherous monster,[29] and as ancestor and ideal ruler.[30] The oldest attribute is probably his unusual strength, which was seen both positively and negatively. Its positive side resulted in his worship as "the averter of evil" in life and his being understood and appealed to as an unbeatable divine helper and champion of culture. At the same time, it moved in another direction, where Herakles's series of labors on behalf of himself and others eventually led to his divinization after death and came to serve as an example of the course an ideal human life should take. This view was particularly emphasized in writings of Pindar and Baccylides in the 470s–460s, under the influence of the "Ionian enlightenment" of the sixth century BCE, and in those of the Stoics and the Cynics.[31] At the same time, in the sixth century BCE, when skepticism became more prominent, the divine side of Herakles could be abandoned while maintaining intact the view that his life served as an ideal example of the human struggle to overcome its limitations and of the untamable human spirit.[32]

In Pindar, the story of Herakles's defeat of Diomedes, who had taught his horses to eat men and so transgress νόμος, portrays the hero as the son of Zeus executing his father's orders but at the same time fighting an enemy who went against "order" or "law" that served as the norm for humanity and the gods (fr. 169 Sn).[33] In addition, he emphasized the superiority of nature (φυή, "inborn traits and qualities") to nurture (training or teaching) in making Herakles's first deed of *arête* his strangling of the snakes as an infant (*First Nemean*).[34] Yet, he also used the story of Herakles's trip to set down his famous pillars in the far west as a symbol of the furthest limit of human ability or capacity, which should not be crossed (*Isthmian* 13; *Ol.* 3.43-44; *N.* 3.19-23). He depicts Herakles as exhibiting an untiring spirit as a human living his difficult life, even though he suffers and experiences setbacks as he pursues his goals.[35] Such an understanding of Herakles certainly could resonate with the life story told of Samson, another strong man who struggled, as most humans do, to pursue his goals.

---

position and Subject in Attic Black Figure," *Classical Antiquity* 9 (1990): 114–48; Padilla, *Myths of Herakles*, 5–6. For a good discussion of the artistic evidence for each of the twelve labors and additional battles, see Stafford, *Herakles*, 30–78.

28. For a convenient summary of relevant early literature of the seventh-fifth centuries BCE, see Padilla, *Myths of Herakles*, 6–18.
29. Galinsky, *Herakles Theme*, 1–2. For his traits as a culture hero in particular, see Padilla, *Myths of Herakles*, 22–25. He includes a survey of the wider traits as well (26–33), as does Stafford, *Herakles*, 30–136, with summaries at 78, 103, 136.
30. Stafford, *Herakles*, 137–70.
31. Galinsky, *Herakles Theme*, 4–5, 23–38, 56, 66, 69, 106.
32. Galinsky, *Herakles Theme*, 6–7. The earliest example of this trend seems to be the *Shield of Herakles*, possibly by Hesiod (17–18).
33. Galinsky, *Herakles Theme*, 34–35.
34. Galinsky, *Herakles Theme*, 36.
35. Galinsky, *Herakles Theme*, 37.

In the fifth century BCE in Athens, Herakles became a character in several tragedies and comedies. The best known tragedies include Aeschylus's *Prometheia*, Sophocles's *Trachinian Women* and *Philoctetes*, and Euripides's *Alcestis* and *Herakles*. They are small in number in comparison to his appearance in satyr plays, where he apparently was the most popular character, farces, and comedies, though the latter group is not as well preserved as the tragedies.

In Aeschylus's *Prometheus Bound*, Herakles is an enlightened culture hero; whereas in Sophocles's *Trachinian Women* (ca. 430 BCE), he reverts to a brutish, uncouth muscle-man driven by lusts and appetites, who violates justice (δίκη) and dies a regular mortal, without any apotheosis. This is a portrayal that might equally resonate quite well with the story of Samson. Yet, in *Philoctetes* (ca. 409 BCE), he serves as the ideal mortal and measuring rod, where nature is more influential than training, as in Pindar. Euripides continues this latter tradition; he portrays Herakles as a tragic figure without "a tragic flaw," whose sufferings do not reflect his character; he is noble in spirit because he bears whatever heaven sends. His labors come to demonstrate internal strength of spirit and conviction rather than external success.[36]

In the satyr plays, Herakles often takes revenge on or punishes an unjust ruler, while in comedies he appears as a monster, a brute, a glutton, and a libertine. The former theme resonated with the Greek dislike of tyrants and barbarian kings in the fifth century BCE.[37] The popularity of the Herakles myth at the end of the fourth century is evidenced by the comparison drawn by Socrates between his own search for the meaning of the Delphic oracle and the wandering and labors of Herakles (*Apol.* 22a) and by references made by Plato to prestigious descent from Herakles (*Theaet.* 175A; *Lysis* 205C).[38]

Isocrates, the most influential representative of rhetoric, which became particularly prominent in the fourth century BCE, recognized the full potential as an ideal that Herakles could offer as a Panhellenic hero not tied to any particular province. He urged Philip of Macedon to unify Greece and not only to use Herakles as a model for this goal, but even to consider himself a bloodline descendant of the hero. It was his son, Alexander, who followed this advice. Even so, he was not the first to trace a royal line to Herakles; the kings of Pergamum claimed descent via a union between Herakles and Auge,[39] the kings of Lydia via Omphale,[40] and the kings of Sparta via Hyllus, the son of Herakles and Deianeira.[41] In addition, the Corinthian founders of Corcyra (Chersikrates) on Corfu, Syracuse (Archias) in Sicily, and Eryx (Dorieus) in Sicily made links to Herakles.[42] It is this royal bloodline

---

36. Galinsky, *Herakles Theme*, 40–75.
37. Galinsky, *Herakles Theme*, 83–84, 81–98.
38. Galinsky, *Herakles Theme*, 78 n. 36.
39. Apollodorus, Library 2.7.4; Diodorus Siculus 4.33.7–12; T. Gantz, *Early Greek Myth: A Guide to Literary and Artistic Sources* (Baltimore: Johns Hopkins University Press, 1993), 428–31; A. Blanshard, *Hercules: A Heroic Life* (London: Granta Books, 2005), xxi, 149–50.
40. Apollodorus, Library 2.6.3; Diodorus Siculus 4.31.5–8; Ovid, *Her.* 55–86; Blanshard, *Hercules*, xxi, 128; B. Brundage, "Herakles the Levantine: A Comprehensive View," *JNES* 17 (1958): 225–36 (233–34); Gantz, *Early Greek Myth*, 439–42; Stafford, *Herakles*, 146.
41. Apollodorus, Library 2.5–5.7; Diodorus Siculus 4.35.1–36.5; Ovid, *Her.* 9; Sophocles, *Trach.*; Gantz, *Early Greek Myth*, 432, 436, 458; Blanshard, *Hercules*, xxi, 151. According to Stafford, two Spartan royal lines, the Agiads and the Eurypontids, claimed descent from two of Herakles great-great-great grandsons, Eurysthenes and Prokles, respectively (*Herakles*, 141).
42. I. Malkin, "The Polis Between Myths of Land and Territory," in *The Role of Religion in the Early Greek*

descent from Herakles, particularly as claimed by Alexander,[43] to which I will return in the final section to consider the impact of reading Samson as a figure representing this particular Macedonian king.

In summary, within the Hellenistic world, Herakles carried with him a widely divergent set of associations. Hellenistic Jews would not have experienced firsthand any performances of the plays mentioned above, but that would not have precluded their portrayals of Herakles to have become disseminated more generically in connection with stories told about this hero-turned-god in a wider Hellenistic milieu. These include, once more, the great tragic sufferer, the paragon of superhuman strength and manliness, the ideal nobleman and courtier, the paragon of rhetoric, intelligence, and wisdom, the divine mediator, the exemplar of a life lived that will be rewarded by divinization, a metaphysical struggler, a paragon of virtue (ἀρετή), a romantic lover, and a comic, gluttonous, lecherous monster. If we return to the list of eleven overlaps at the end of the previous section between Herakles and Samson, we and a Hellenized Jewish audience can and could readily see the paragon of superhuman strength and manliness and the romantic (?) lover. In addition, however, then as well as now, some would likely see a metaphysical struggler if not a great tragic sufferer as well as, to some degree, a crude, gluttonous, lecherous monster, given Samson's self-centered, emotionally driven behavior.

How would any of these overlays affect the reading of the character of Samson in the narrative about him in Judg 13–16 and within the wider context of the book of Samuel? Some have already been explored by biblical scholars in the past decades, but in most cases without acknowledging or being aware that they were traits shared by both Samson and Herakles. These include particularly the romantic lover of foreign women,[44] the metaphysical struggler, where Samson is an allegory for Israel, for example,[45] and the tragic figure,[46] while the crude, lecherous "monster" image is a typical modern understanding of Samson among those who have seen the book of Judges to explore the deficiency in human leader-

---

Polis: Proceedings of the Third International Seminar on Ancient Greek Cult, ed. R. Hägg (Stockholm: Swedish Institute at Athens, 1996), 9–19 (12–13); idem, *A Small Greek World: Networks in the Mediterranean* (Oxford: Oxford University Press, 2011), 121–23. For claims making Hercules a colony founder, see Stafford, *Herakles*, 156–60.

43. For a lengthier discussion of the Macedonian claims, see Stafford, *Herakles*, 143–46.

44. So, e.g., Crenshaw, *Samson*, 129–48; M. Bal, *Lethal Love: Feminist Literary Readings of Biblical Love Stories*, Indiana Studies in Biblical Literature (Bloomington: University of Indiana Press, 1987), 37–67 (41–58); J. C. Exum, *Fragmented Women: Feminist (sub)versions of Biblical Narratives*, JSOTSup 163 (Sheffield: Sheffield Academic, 1993), 61–93; Amit, *Book of Judges*, 280–88; Camp, *Wise, Strange*, 94–143; T. J. Schneider, *Judges*. Berit Olam. (Collegeville, MN: Liturgical Press, 2000), 202–27; Zakovitch, "Strange Biography," 28–34; Assis, "Structure," 1–11.

45. E. Greenstein, "The Riddle of Samson," *Prooftexts* 1 (1981): 237–60.

46. So, e.g., Crenshaw, *Samson*, 121–27; Vickery, "In Strange Ways," 62–63; D. M. Gunn, "The Anatomy of Divine Comedy: On Reading the Bible as Comedy and Tragedy," in *Tragedy and Comedy in the Bible*, ed. J. C. Exum, Semeia 32 (Decatur: Scholars Press, 1984), 115–29 (121–22); F. Landy, "Are We in the Place of Averroes? Response to the Articles of Exum and Whedbee, Buss, Gottwald, and Good," in *Tragedy and Comedy in the Bible*, ed. J. C. Exum, Semeia 32 (Decatur: Scholars Press, 1984), 131–48 (140–43). D. M. Gunn, "Samson of Sorrows: An Isaianic Gloss on Judges 13–16," in *Reading between the Texts: Intertextuality and the Hebrew Bible*, ed. D. N. Fewell, Literary Currents in Biblical Interpretation (Louisville, KY: Westminster John Knox, 1992), 225–53 (225–27; 248–53). Josephus played up the tragic aspect (L. H. Feldman, *Josephus' Interpretation of the Bible* [Berkeley: University of California Press, 1998], 474–75).

ship of the twelve tribes in Israel's collective past.[47] The story details tend to exclude any transferral of the concepts of the ideal nobleman and courtier, the paragon of rhetoric, intelligence, and wisdom, the divine mediator, or the exemplar of a life lived that will be rewarded by divinization, to Samson.[48] If some might argue the concept of mediator could be relevant, it should be noted that in the Greek context, this applies quite frequently to Herakles's killing of unjust tyrants, which is not a situation we encounter with Samson.

It is noteworthy that the values assigned to these shared traits might have differed in Greek culture in comparison to Jewish culture. There is no dangerous value associated with the "foreign" origin of women *per se* in Herakles's unfortunate encounters with his women. The metaphorical struggler is a positive attribute, and interestingly, the view of Samson as a positive role model was assumed by Ben Sira, who lived in the Hellenistic period. In contrast, most current scholars seem to consider him to be a negative figure that fails and cannot be a useful role model except as an example of what not to do. The similar portrayal of Herakles as a glutton, letch, and crude "monster" in the comic tradition served this genre's interests "in interfering with the stability of symbolic hierarchies and in thematizing the desires, consumptions, and activities of the male body" while also using his indestructibility to "affirm the power of the human spirit to persevere."[49]

Alexander and Samson

What remains is to consider any possible additional overlay of meaning that might have come from an equation of Samson with Alexander by Jews living in a Hellenized environment and being sympathetic to its worldview and debates.

Prior to Alexander, there had been great dispute about the best form of political rulership: kingship/tyranny, oligarchy, or democracy, a scheme based on a periodization that has recently been challenged.[50] Alexander's accomplishments eliminated democracy in Athens, its hegemonic domination of other Greek cities through its league, and the reality of the independent Greek polis, even if, in practice, only Athens, Sparta, and Thebes had experienced freedom and independence fully.[51] It should be remembered, however, that

---

47. So, e.g., Klein, *Triumph of Irony*, 109–39; Exum, *Fragmented Women*, 69–72; S. Ackerman, "What if Judges Had Been Written by a Philistine?" *BibInt* 8 (2000): 33–41 (34–35).

48. It can be noted, however, that Josephus, writing in the final quarter of the first century CE, emphasizes Samson's possession of intelligence and wisdom, a trait of Aristotle's "great-souled man," in addition to all the cardinal virtues, and highlights the heroic, erotic, and dramatic interests of his story while downplaying the magical and divine elements. His work exhibits a tendency to add details that highlight the wisdom of biblical heroes, so this is not limited to Samson. He singles out four qualities in Samson' s character he considers admirable: valor, strength, high-spirit/great soul, and wrath (Feldman, *Josephus' Interpretation*, 461–89).

49. M. W. Padilla, "Herakles and Animals in the Origins of Comedy and Satyr-Drama," in *Le bestiaire d'Héraclès*, ed. C. Bonnet, C. Jourdain-Annequin, and V. Pirenne-Delforge (Liège: University Press of Lièges, 1998), 217–30.

50. See L. G. Mitchell, *The Heroic Rulers of Archaic Classical Greece* (London: Bloomsbury Academic, 2013) as well as her article in the present volume, "The Three Constitutions in Greek Political Thought." For another dicsussion in this volume of the traditional three forms of constitution, see the article by W. Oswald, "Monarchy, Oligarchy, and Democracy in the Constitutional Debate in Herodotus and in 1 Samuel 8."

51. P. Garnsey, "Introduction: the Hellenistic and Roman periods," in *The Cambridge Ancient History of Greek and Roman Political Thought*, ed. C. Rowe and M. Schofield (Cambridge: Cambridge University Press, 2005), 403–14 (403–4).

Alexander was Macedonian, not Greek, and by descent and upbringing was a hereditary monarch over a kingdom.[52] With Alexander and his successors, absolute monarchies rather than constitutional monarchies controlled a web of cities and many former city-states that no longer controlled their own foreign and military affairs. These imperial kings tended to rule through the help of a restricted circle of trusted functionaries drawn from friends. As a result, the former debates over political philosophy abated greatly, since they became moot in many ways, but they did not disappear altogether. However, philosophy turned more to examining moral issues than political ones, which had been an integral aspect of the earlier philosophical discussion but now no longer had to be. Absolute kingship became the assumed norm and no longer needed to be weighed against other forms of constitution.[53] A dimension that perhaps was new for Jews was that Hellenistic kings received worship.[54]

In Hellenistic philosophical discourse, the king was to be the ideal man who possessed all the normal virtues, which included traits such as courage, self-control, wisdom, justice, honesty, friendliness, truthfulness, kindness, and in addition, the central trait of love of his subjects (φιλανθρωπία), from which all the other traits would naturally follow. In order to protect his subjects, he needed to possess all the qualities of a military leader, exhibit continual foresight, maintain a sleepless watch over his people, foster worship of the gods and be honored by them, and impose taxes only so that his subjects would benefit and have safeguarded security, not to amass wealth for himself. He needed to choose the right sort of friends and officials whom he would trust explicitly so he would not listen to informers. If a king lived up to these sometimes burdensome ideals, his subjects would be free and the polity would be happy and united. If not, he would slip into tyranny and care only for gaining things that were to his own advantage; he would indulge in sexual vices, a luxurious lifestyle, corrupted justice, and cruelty.[55]

Alexander is remembered to have tried to take on airs of being above his peers and, thus, the tendencies of a tyrant who would not be bound by the law.[56] He specifically is remembered to have tried to impose on the inhabitants of Bactria and his Macedonian peers the practice of *proskynesis* in imitation of what the Persian "king of kings" had required of his subjects, and also to have exhibited lack of self-control in his indulgence in passion and drunkenness.[57] His cutting off of the nose and ears of the Persian King Darius before having his brother murder him and his murder of Kleitos during a symposium were two instances of cruel behavior.[58] At the same time, he claimed descent from Herakles and

---

52. T. A Sinclair, *A History of Greek Political Thought*, 2nd ed. (London: Routledge, 1967), 241–42.

53. Garnsey, "Introduction," 402–5.

54. Garnsey, "Introduction," 405.

55. O. Murray, "Philosophy and Monarchy in the Hellenistic World," in *Jewish Perspectives on Hellenistic Rulers*, ed. T. Rajak *et al.*, HCS 50 (London: University of California Press, 2007), 13–28 (24–25). For a general survey of Hellenistic political thought, see conveniently, Sinclair, *History*, 239–68; G. Klosko, *History of Political Theory: An Introduction* Vol. 1: Ancient and Medieval Political Theory (London: Harcourt Brace, 1993), 153–69.

56. For the concept of tyranny and tyrant in earlier Greek thought, see for example, J. F. McGlew, *Tyranny and Political Culture in Ancient Greece* (Ithaca, NY: Cornell University Press, 1993).

57. P. Alexander and L. Alexander, "The Image of the Oriental Monarch in the Third Book of Maccabees," in *Jewish Perspectives on Hellenistic Rulers*, ed. T. Rajak *et al.*, HCS 50 (London: University of California Press, 2007), 92–109 (100, 108 n. 23). For an earlier lengthy discussion, see L. E. Taylor, "The 'Proskynesis' and the Hellenistic Ruler Cult," *JHS* 47 (1927): 53–62.

58. See conveniently, O. Amitay, *From Alexander to Jesus*, HCS 52 (Berkeley: University of California Press,

heroic stature through his military deeds that equaled the deeds done by Herakles, which in literary tradition is remembered to have led to a discussion of Alexander's earning the right to be divinized.[59] Thus, in retrospect, Alexander was seen to have assumed some of the negative traits of an absolute ruler, a tyrant, instead of exemplifying fully the ideal traits of a true king. In the book of 1 Maccabees, which deals with events that took place in Judea and related areas from 167–134 BCE, the opening lines condemn Alexander; after he had plundered many nations and put to death many kings of the earth, when the earth became quiet before him, he was exalted, and his heart was lifted up (1:1–4).

It is interesting to observe that the same demand for *proskynesis* made by Alexander is made by two kings in the biblical texts. Nebuchadnezzar, who is a cipher for Antiochus IV, in Dan 3, commanded this act of all his subjects before a golden statue (of himself probably), while Ahasuerus/Xerxes commanded this act from his subjects before his appointed official, Haman, in Esth 3.[60] The practice is believed to have been introduced by the imperial Achaemenid court. But given that both compositions are thought to have been written in the Hellenistic period, they may include either an intended oblique condemnation of Alexander or else may have evoked such a secondary association in the minds of a Hellenistic audience. Thus, they might have provided additional negative memory echoes associated with the figure of Alexander among a segment of the Jewish community in the Hellenistic period.

Bearing in mind the negative memory associated with Alexander, the portrayal of Samson as one who acted however he wanted, breaking "Israelite" norms in wanting to marry a Philistine woman and not observing the terms of a נזיר associated with refraining from alcohol and dead bodies, in this case scraping honey from the dead carcass of the lion he killed, becomes germane. He is very much an individual who possesses physical power but who lacks self-control, similar though not identical to a tyrant, who claims for himself absolute power he misuses for selfishly indulgent purposes. Even Samson's personal acts of revenge against the Philistines, which had negative repercussions for his own community so that they eventually handed him over to the Philistines to avoid reprisals from those ruling them, would read as attempts to misuse power for personal ends, not for ἀρετή. So even though Samson is not depicted in the story-world as the recognized leader of Israel by his fellow Israelites, the narrator lets the readers know he was predestined by YHWH to begin to deliver Israel as a judge, just as many of his personal acts are stated to be motivated by YHWH ultimately. He was meant to be the leader but is not recognized as such because of his lack of self-restraint and apparent lack of φιλανθρωπία. His outward acts are not deemed by his compatriots as indicative behavior of a leader or judge.

The larger framing of the story would allow an audience to conceive of Samson as intended leader and so reflect over his misuse of his extraordinary strength for personal gain more often than for the good of his fellow Israelites. And, he is limited in his selfish

---

2010), 32, 35–37. Amitay points out that Alexander is portrayed by Arrian to have felt remorse over the latter act, which is atypical of heroes. For a more detailed discussion of this topic in the current volume, which cites the relevant Greek texts, see the article by B. Ego, entitled "At the Crossroads of Persian and Hellenistic Ideology: The Book of Esther as 'Political Theology.'"

59. For a discussion of the list of comparable deeds between the two that would have reinforced their close association and the literary debate over Alexander's worthiness to be divinized, see Amitay, *From Alexander to Jesus*, 27–38.

60. For a discussion of this passage elsewhere in the current volume, see the article by Ego, "At the Crossroads."

acts by being surrendered to the Philistines by his fellow Israelites. In a similar vein, Alexander's attempt to arrogate powers was challenged and refused by his advisory council. His remembered lack of self-restraint in his sex life and drinking likely would have evoked for some Samson's involvement with three women and in his implied excessive drinking at his marriage המשתה.

An overlay of Alexander's life and accomplishments onto the figure of Samson thus likely would have led some in a Hellenistic environment to the reading of his story as a condemnation of absolute kingship, which tended to breed tyrant-type behavior. Such a reading would have resonated with other negative portrayals of absolute monarchs in biblical texts: Sennacherib, Nebuchadnezzar, Cyrus, Ahasuerus/Xerxes, Darius, Artaxerxes, and Antiochus Epiphanes.[61] In a Hellenistic context, Samson would have resonated most strongly with the Seleucid king Antiochus Epiphanes, who is condemned indirectly as a desecrator and destroyer of the "Second Temple" in the book of Daniel by association with the desecrator/destroyer of the monarchic-era temple, Nebuchadnezzar, and is directly castigated for this action in 1 Maccabees.

Such an equation could have been encouraged further by two associations. First, Samson's reported destruction of the Philistine temple made him a temple destroyer as well, even if in his case he was destroying the temple of a foreign god, which would have been considered a positive act in the story-line. For those living during the reign of Antiochus IV and thereafter, however, an overlay of Alexander-related imagery that evoked and condemned his Seleucid descendant might have led this act of Samson's to have been construed negatively, as one of a tyrant-like individual wrongly interfering with local religion. Second, during the reign of Antiochus IV, the Hellenizing Jewish high priest Jason/Joshua is remembered in 2 Macc 4 to have sent envoys with 300 silver drachmas to be used during the quadrennial Tyrian games to pay for a sacrifice to Herakles when the Seleucid king was present himself. Here, the linkage between Antiochus and Herakles might have reinforced a general association already created through the prior two links to the Herakles-like biblical judge, Samson. Be that as it may, this possible evocation of Antiochus IV in particular would not have eliminated the possibility of Samson's calling to mind any Seleucid or Ptolemaic king who had been perceived to have acted capriciously or self-servingly, like a tyrant.

At the same time, it should be recognized that a Jewish perspective would have differed in its underlying reason for such a rejection of absolute monarchy from a Greek one. The latter tended to object to its abrogation of innate individual liberty, while the former tended to prioritize a divine rather than human king and a divine Torah (teaching) that made obedience incumbent equally on the human king and his subjects.[62] Yet, it should be noted that classical Greek thought had also emphasized the role of law that the elected king should obey, though not a divine origin for law.

Conclusion

In summary, if it had existed in an earlier period, the story of Samson in the book of Judges may have gained new dimensions of meaning when read or heard by Jews living in a Hellenized environment who were open to acculturation and knew stories of both Herakles

---

61. E. Gruen, "Persia through the Jewish Looking-Glass," in *Jewish Perspectives on Hellenistic Rulers*, ed. T. Rajak *et al.*, HCS 50 (London: University of California Press, 2007), 53–75; B. Wright, "Ben Sira on Kings and Kingship," in *Jewish Perspectives on Hellenistic Rulers*, ed. T. Rajak *et al.*, HCS 50 (London: University of California Press, 2007), 76–91 (84).

62. Alexander and Alexander, "Oriental Monarch," 104; Wright, "Ben Sira," 89–90.

and Alexander. If it were added to a pre-existing book or first created as part of the book of Judges in the early Hellenistic period, we will be considering possible meanings evoked by an association of Samson with both Herakles and with Alexander in a more contemporary setting, without having inherited an earlier set of associations in its literary context of Judges. The numerous overlaps between the careers of Samson and Herakles would perhaps highlight the heroic and wild man aspects of the biblical character, as well as a possibly tragic dimension, a metaphysical struggler who could serve as a paragon of virtue (ἀρετή), a romantic lover, and a comic, gluttonous, lecherous monster. Any overlay with Alexander, who claimed direct descent from Herakles, might have raised the specter of the overbearing absolute monarch who was manifesting tyrannical tendencies, considering himself above the law and self-restraints, who was self-indulgent, and who cared nothing for the welfare of his subjects. Both of these figures, Herakles and Alexander, evoked the Greco-Hellenistic world, and it is possible that for some Jews who were part of this world, Samson offered an oblique critique of the excesses of many of the absolute Ptolemaic or Seleucid monarchs who regularly occupied the throne and ignored the ideals of kingship, but perhaps in particular, Antiochus IV Epiphanes.

Bibliography

Ackerman, S. 2000. "What if Judges Had Been Written by a Philistine?" *BibInt* 8: 33–41.

Alexander, P. and Alexander, L. 2007. "The Image of the Oriental Monarch in the Third Book of Maccabees." In *Jewish Perspectives on Hellenistic Rulers*, edited by T. Rajak, S. Pearce, J. Aitken, and J. Dines, 92–109. HCS 50. London: University of California Press.

Amit, Y. 1999. *The Book of Judges: The Art of Editing*. Translated by J. Chipman. BibInt 38. Leiden: Brill.

Amitay, O. 2010. *From Alexander to Jesus*. HCS 52. Berkeley: University of California Press.

Assis, E. 2014. "The Structure and Meaning of the Samson Narratives (Jud. 13–16)." In *Samson: Hero or Fool? The Many Faces of Samson*, edited by E. Eynikel and T. Nicklas, 1–12. Themes in Biblical Narrative 17. Leiden: Brill.

Bailey, D. M. 1990. "Not Herakles, A Ptolemy." *Antike Kunst* 33: 107–10.

Bal, M. 1987. *Lethal Love: Feminist Literary Readings of Biblical Love Stories*. Indiana Studies in Biblical Literature. Bloomington, IN: University of Indiana Press.

Bartelmus, R. 1979. *Heroentum in Israel under seiner Umwelt: Eine traditionsgeschichtliche Untersuchung zu Gen. 6,1–4 und verwandten Texten im Alten Testament und der altorientalischen Literatur*. Abhandlungen zur Theologie des Alten und Neuen Testaments 65. Zurich: Theologischer Verlag.

Bartusch, M. W. 2003. *Understanding Dan: An Exegetical Study of a Biblical City, Tribe and Ancestor*. JSOTSup 379. London: Sheffield Academic.

Bauslaugh, R. A. 1984. "The Numismatic Legacy of Alexander the Great." *Archaeology* 37: 34–41.

Bayet, J. 1926. *Herclé: Étude critique sur les principaux monuments relatifs à l'Hercule Étrusque*. Paris: E. de Boccard.

———. 1926. *Les origines de l'Hercule Romain*. Bibliotheque des écoles françaises d'Athènes et de Rome 13. Paris: E. de Boccard.

Beazley, J. D. 1986. *The Development of Attic Black-Figure*. Rev. ed. Edited by D. von Bothmer and M. M. B. Moore. Berkeley: University of California Press.

Blanshard, A. 2005. *Hercules: A Heroic Life*. London: Granta Books.

Blenkinsopp, J. 1963. "Structure and Style in Judges 13–16." *JBL* 82: 65–76.

Boardman, J. 1992. "For You Are the Progeny of Unconquered Herakles." In *Philolakôn: Lakonian Studies in Honour of Hector Catling*, edited by J. M. Sanders, 25–29. London: The British School at Athens.

Bonnet, C. 1988. *Melqart: Cultes et mythes de l'Héraclès Tyrien en Méditerranée*. Studia Phoenicia 8. Leuven: Peeters.

Brandley, G. 2005. "Aspects of the Cult of Hercules in Central Italy." In *Herakles and Hercules: Exploring a Graeco-Roman Divinity*, edited by L. Rawlings and H. Bowden, 129–51. Swansea: The Classical Press of Wales.

Brundage, B. 1958. "Herakles the Levantine: A Comprehensive View." *JNES* 17: 225–36.

Bynum, D. E. 1990. "Samson as a Biblical *pher oreskuos*." In *Text and Tradition: The Hebrew Bible and Folklore*, edited by S. Niditch, 57–73. SBL Semeia Studies. Atlanta, GA: Scholars Press.

Camp, C. 2000. *Wise, Strange, and Holy: The Strange Woman and the Making of the Bible*. JSOTSup 320. Gender and Culture Theory 9. Sheffield: Sheffield Academic.

Canepa, M. P. 2015. "Seleukid Sacred Architecture, Royal Cult and the Transformation of Iranian Culture in the Middle Iranian Period." *Iranian Studies* 48: 71–97.

Crenshaw, J. L. 1979. *Samson: A Secret Betrayed, a Vow Ignored*. London: SPCK.

Edgar, C. C. 1913. "A Statue of a Hellenistic King." *JHS* 33: 50–52.

Exum, J. C. 1993. *Fragmented Women: Feminist (sub)versions of Biblical Narratives*. JSOTSup 163. Sheffield: Sheffield Academic.

———. 1983. "The Theological Dimension of the Samson Saga." *VT* 33: 30–45.

Feldman, L. H. 1998. *Josephus' Interpretation of the Bible*. Berkeley: University of California Press.

Fleisher, R. 1991. *Studien zur seleukidischen Kunst: Band I: Herrscherbildnisse*. Mainz am Rhein: Von Zabern.

Galinsky, G. K. 1972. *The Herakles Theme: The Adaptations of the Hero in Literature from Homer to the Twentieth Century*. Towota, NJ: Rowman & Littlefield.

Gantz, T. 1993. *Early Greek Myth: A Guide to Literary and Artistic Sources*. Baltimore: Johns Hopkins University Press.

Garnsey, P. 2005. "Introduction: the Hellenistic and Roman periods." In *The Cambridge Ancient History of Greek and Roman Political Thought*, edited by C. Rowe and M. Schofield, 403–14. Cambridge: Cambridge University Press.

Greenstein, E. 1981. "The Riddle of Samson." *Prooftexts* 1: 237–60.

Gruen, E. 2007. "Persia through the Jewish Looking-Glass." In *Jewish Perspectives on Hellenistic Rulers*, edited by T. Rajak, S. Pearce, J. Aitken, and J. Dines, 53–75. HCS 50. London: University of California Press.

Gunn, D. M. 1992. "Samson of Sorrows: An Isaianic Gloss on Judges 13–16." In *Reading between the Texts: Intertextuality and the Hebrew Bible*, edited by D. N. Fewell, 225–53. Literary Currents in Biblical Interpretation. Louisville, KY: Westminster John Knox.

———. 1984. "The Anatomy of Divine Comedy: On Reading the Bible as Comedy and Tragedy." In *Tragedy and Comedy in the Bible*, edited by J. C. Exum, 115–29. Semeia 32. Decatur, GA: Scholars Press.

Kim, J. 1993. *The Structure of the Samson Cycle*. Kampen: Kok Pharos.

Klein, L. R. 1988. *The Triumph of Irony in the Book of Judges*. JSOTSup 68. Bible and Literature Series 14. Sheffield: Almond Press.

Klosko, G. 1993. *History of Political Theory: An Introduction*. Volume 1: Ancient and Medieval Political Theory. London: Harcourt Brace.

Krouse, F. M. 1974. *Milton's Samson and the Christian Tradition*. New York: Octagon.

Landy, F. 1984. "Are We in the Place of Averroes? Response to the Articles of Exum and Whedbee, Buss, Gottwald, and Good." In *Tragedy and Comedy in the Bible*, edited by J. C. Exum, 131–48. Semeia 32. Decatur, GA: Scholars Press.

Malkin, I. 2011. *A Small Greek World: Networks in the Mediterranean*. Oxford: Oxford University Press.

———. 1996. "The Polis Between Myths of Land and Territory." In *The Role of Religion in the Early Greek Polis: Proceedings of the Third International Seminar on Ancient Greek Cult*, edited by R. Hägg, 9–19. Stockholm: Swedish Institute at Athens.

Margalith, O. 1987. "Legends of Samson/Heracles." *VT* 37: 63–70

———. 1986. "More Samson Legends." *VT* 36: 397–405.

———. 1986. "Samson's Riddle and Samson's Magic Locks." *VT* 36: 225–34.

———. 1985. "Samson's Foxes." *VT* 35: 224–29.

McGlew, J. F. 1993. *Tyranny and Political Structure in Ancient Greece*. Ithaca, NY: Cornell University Press.

Mitchell, L. 2013. *The Heroic Rulers of Archaic Classical Greece*. London: Bloomsbury Academic.

Mobley, G. 2006. *Samson and the Liminal Hero in the Ancient Near East*. LHBOTS 453. London: Continuum.

———. 1997. "The Wild Man in the Bible and the Ancient Near East." *JBL* 116: 217–33.

Moore, G. F. 1895. *A Critical and Exegetical Commentary on Judges*. ICC. Edinburgh: T&T Clark.

Murray, O. 2007. "Philosophy and Monarchy in the Hellenistic World." In *Jewish Perspectives on Hellenistic Rulers*, edited by T. Rajak, S. Pearce, J. Aitken, and J. Dines, 13–28. HCS 50. London: University of California Press.

Niditch, S. 1990. "Samson as Culture Hero, Trickster, and Bandit: The Empowerment of the Weak." *CBQ* 52: 608–24.

Padilla, M. W. 1998. "Herakles and Animals in the Origins of Comedy and Satyr-Drama." In *Le bestiaire d'Héraclès*, edited by C. Bonnet, C. Jourdain-Annequin, and V. Pirenne-Delforge, 217–30. Liège: University Press of Lièges.

———. 1998. *The Myths of Herakles in Ancient Greece: Survey and Profile*. New York: University Press of America.

Schneider, T. J. 2000. *Judges*. Berit Olam. Collegeville, MN: Liturgical Press.

Shapiro, H. A. 1990. "Old and New Heroes: Narrative Composition and Subject in Attic Black Figure." *Classical Antiquity* 9: 114–48.

———. 1983. "The Death and Apotheosis of Herakles." *Classical World* 77: 7–18.

Sinclair, T. A. 1967. *A History of Greek Political Thought*. 2nd ed. London: Routledge.

Spronk, K. 2010. "The Book of Judges as a Late Construct." In *Historiography and Identity (Re)formulation in Second Temple Historiographical Literature*, edited by L. Jonker, 15–28. LHBOTS 534. London: T&T Clark.

Stafford, E. 2012. *Herakles*. Gods and Heroes of the Ancient World. London: Routledge.

Taylor, L. E. 1927. "The 'Proskynesis' and the Hellenistic Ruler Cult." *JHS* 47: 53–62.

Vickers, M. 1995. "Heracles Lacedaemonius: the political dimensions of Sophocles Trachiniae and Euripides Heracles." *Dialogues d'histoire ancienne* 21: 41–69.

Vickery, J. B. 1981. "In Strange Ways: The Story of Samson." In *Images of Man and God: Old Testament Short Stories in Literary Focus*, edited by B. O. Long, 58–73. Sheffield: Almond Press.

Webb, B. G. 1987. *The Book of Judges: An Integrated Reading*. JSOTSup 46. Sheffield: Sheffield Academic.

Wright, B. 2007. "Ben Sira on Kings and Kingship." In *Jewish Perspectives on Hellenistic Rulers,* edited by T. Rajak, S. Pearce, J. Aitken, and J. Dines, 76–91. HCS 50. London: University of California Press.

Yarrow, L. M. 2013. "Heracles, coinage and the West: Three Hellenistic case-studies." In *The Hellenistic West: Rethinking the Ancient Mediterranean*, edited by J. R. W. Prag and J. C. Quinn, 348–66. Cambridge: Cambridge University Press.

Zakovitch, Y. 2003. "The Stange Biography of Samson." *Nordisk Judaistik* 24: 19–36.

— 15 —

Judith Maccabee? On Leadership, Resistance, and the Great Deeds of Little People

Anne-Mareike Schol-Wetter

Introduction

In Tolkien's *Lord of the Rings*, the world as Frodo the Hobbit knows it is threatened by unfathomably evil Sauron. This super-human villain plots the ruin of all free peoples of Middle Earth, for no apparent reason except an unquenchable thirst for power. Many have fallen under his dominion, but there are some vestiges of resistance. Elves, dwarfs, and men all meet Sauron's challenge in their own way. Humans put their trust especially in the sword, although the vastness of Sauron's armies suggests that resistance through force of arms is futile.

Parallel to this military resistance, however, another plot develops. Frodo and his dedicated servant Sam set out on a desperate journey right into the heart of Sauron's dominion. They must destroy the only thing Sauron still needs to make his power complete: the "one Ring to rule them all." While Frodo and Sam seek their way between murderous orcs and larger-than-life spiders, war continues to rage in the world-at-large. Valorous deeds are undertaken, and Sauron's forces are—temporarily—held at bay. But the reader knows that victory cannot last unless Frodo's quest succeeds. It is a hobbit, the "unlikeliest creature imaginable" who must destroy evil, not by force but by stealth, and from inside the enemy's territory. All depends on Frodo's willingness to risk everything for this goal and on a strategy based on endurance and tricksterism rather than on conventional instruments of power.

In the end, Sauron is overthrown and his works undone, all due to his inability to perceive a threat that is not clad in military gear, even if it crawls right under his nose. The coronation of Aragorn, exiled descendant of kings and most valiant defender of Middle Earth, ushers in the beginning of a new, peaceful era. Frodo returns to his home in the Shire, where he lives for a few more years, together with his loyal servant, Sam.

By now, the confused reader probably wonders what hobbits, orcs, and Middle-Earth have to do with politics in Second Temple Yehud. Very little, at first sight, yet Tolkien's work seems to share a couple of basic themes and plotlines both with the book of Judith and with 1 Maccabees.[1] I hope that pointing out these themes in the former will help with

---

1. In some instances, Tolkien seems to have taken over details from 1 Maccabees almost literally. One no-

their recognition in the latter and help develop a clearer idea of leadership and resistance as construed in these two apocryphal works of early Judaism.

First Maccabees and the book of Judith, written within a few decades of each other, display a number of similarities.[2] In both texts, Jewish identity is threatened, whether by a military force aiming to destroy the Temple, or by the more subtle menace of assimilation to Hellenistic culture.[3] Both books also harken back to similar literary precursors—especially the patriarchal narratives (e.g., 1 Macc 2:52–53; 2 Macc 1:2), Moses and the Exodus (e.g., 1 Macc 4:8; 2 Macc 2), the book of Judges, and the narrative about David and Goliath.

In view of all these similarities, A. LaCocque concludes that Judith is "not only a David redivivus of sorts, she is Judas Maccabee in the feminine."[4] C. Rakel seems justified in wondering: "Why, if Judith wants to remind the reader of precisely these events, does it choose a female protagonist; why an obviously fictitious genre to relate these events; why names that conceal rather than identify?"[5]

My analysis of both books addresses these and related questions. Why, for example, does Judith return to her home after the Assyrians are routed? Why does 1 Maccabees put so much emphasis on priesthood rather than kingship? And how is the enemy construed in both works? My attempt at an answer follows the route set out by B. Eckhardt, who argues:

> Judith *as a literary text* can be read as an attempt to reclaim biblical language and traditions that were embedded into a discursive, legitimizing framework by Hasmonean propaganda [...] Only in the fictitious space of the narration is it possible to revive or redefine traditional semantics without openly opposing the authorities.[6]

Applying this notion to the issue of leadership and resistance, I suggest that the book of Judith does not oppose Maccabean claims to power by offering a viable alternative to their rule. Its opposition takes place on the level of discourse, by offering an alternative interpretation of biblical traditions, thereby robbing the Hasmonean claims of their seemingly self-evident status. It does not, thereby, attempt to put the Hasmoneans out of office but rather, to persuade its readers that leaning on established leaders is not enough in a situation of crisis. It would lead much too far to interpret the book of Judith as proposing some rudimentary form of "democracy." Nevertheless, the narrative puts more power in the hands of the people than does the monarchy/hierocracy that came into being after the Maccabean revolt.

---

    table example is his description of the "oliphaunts" and their exotic masters during the battle of Minas Tirith (cf. 1 Macc 6:35–37, 45–46).

2. See C. Rakel, *Judith – über Schönheit, Macht und Widerstand im Krieg: eine Feministisch-Intertextuelle Lektüre* (Berlin: de Gruyter, 2003), 267–69 for a detailed enumeration of the textual similarities.

3. Quoting C. Rakel, "The significance of the Temple, the pain and anxiety surrounding its desecration and 'vilification' ... as well as the concern for the house of God as the the religious center of Israel" are central concepts in both books (*Schönheit*, 266; author's own tranlsation).

4. A. LaCoque, *The Feminine Unconventional: Four Subversive Figures in Israel's Tradition* (Minneapolis, MN: Fortress, 1990), 39.

5. Rakel, *Schönheit*, 269; author's own translation. Indeed, Eckhardt claims that the book bearing her name is a case of "'counter-discourse' – which is in no way to be confused with 'counter-propaganda'" against the ideology found in 1 Maccabees ("Reclaiming Tradition: The Book of Judith and Hasmonean Politics," *JSP* 18 [2009]: 243–63 [255]).

6. Eckhardt, "Reclaiming Tradition," 245, 260.

Looking at 1 Maccabees, it is evident which form of government the book envisions: a blend of military, religious, and political leadership, combined in the hands of one man. Although at the beginning of the book, the claim to leadership is based more on the actions and abilities of the sons of Mattathias than on their genealogical descent, it becomes increasingly clear that the envisioned outcome is a full-fledged dynasty. In the course of the narrative, the Maccabean priestly genealogy is amended by a narrative one, linking the Maccabees to a variety of leaders in Israel's past.

The "political" preferences of the author of the book of Judith are much less straightforward. The book paints the religious and political leaders as weak and ineffectual. For this and other reasons, it has been read as a critique of Hasmonean claims to power.[7] However, this conclusion must be nuanced to some extent. The book of Judith certainly takes a different stance on a number of issues than does 1 Maccabees, but government, as such, seems to be largely beyond its scope. The following analysis, therefore, approaches the issue from a different angle: I ask first how Israel's enemies are construed in each book and how they should be dealt with, and only then move on to the question of what kind of leadership this construal necessitates.[8] For both topics, I investigate how biblical texts are used in order to create a specific image of Israel—its enemies, its organization, and its ideal population.

Burning with Zeal—Against Whom?

Let me frame the topic of "the enemy" with a few more words on *Lord of the Rings*. In Tolkien's work, evil has two faces. On the one hand, in the shape of Sauron and the orcs and "fell beasts" that make up his armies, it is monolithic and easy to recognize. The need to resist these foes is self-evident: no one in their right mind could question the legitimacy of killing orcs or trying to hold Mordor at bay. On the other hand, there are those individuals who, by birth, position, and past acts should be grouped among the "good guys," but who have voluntarily or unwittingly joined forces with Sauron. Examples of this type can be found in Saruman, one-time head of the "White Council" who now seeks to possess the Ring himself, and Denethor, a faithful steward, who nevertheless falls prey to Sauron's talent for sowing despair. In their cases, it is much more difficult to determine the right course of action. Does a principally "good guy's" choice for Sauron justify killing him? Last, but not least, there are those groups on the margins of the main plot whose allegiances are uncertain—the Dead Men of Dunharrow, for example, or the Wild Men of Drúadan Forest. Should they be courted in order to win their support in the struggle against Sauron, despite their unflattering reputation as oath-breakers and relics of a more primitive age?

The varied faces of evil in the *Lord of the Rings* help point out the positions taken in the books of Judith and 1 Maccabees. Both works draw a sharp dividing line between "Israel" and "the enemy" as far as this enemy is embodied in the forces of the opposing armies—the orcs, so to speak. But they differ on the question whether there is an "enemy within" as well, and conversely, whether friends can be found outside the ethnic and religious border.

As Eckhardt points out,[9] the different construals of in-and out-groups in the book of Judith and 1 Maccabees can be illustrated with the use of zeal-language in both works. First Maccabees and the book of Judith both employ zeal terminology in contexts in which the

---

7. LaCoque, *Feminine Unconventional*.
8. Cf. Eckhardt, "Reclaiming Tradition," 248: "We should rather turn to two more complex reformulations of religious and political semantics of the time: the idea of resistance and the strategies of defining Judaism and its others."
9. Eckhardt, "Reclaiming Tradition."

legitimacy of violent resistance is at stake.[10] However, each text appeals to a different facet of the social memory of Israel and, consequently, legitimizes different kinds of actions.

In 1 Maccabees, the first and paradigmatic occurrence of ζηλόω is in 2:24–25, where the text reports how Mattathias slays an apostatizing Jew and a royal official. The motivation for this act is given in verse 26:[11]

καὶ ἐζήλωσεν τῷ νόμῳ καθὼς ἐποίησεν Φινεες τῷ Ζαμβρι υἱῷ Σαλωμ	And he burned with zeal for the law, as Phinehas had done to Zimri, the son of Shallum.

The narrative alluded to here is found in Num 25 and reports how Phinehas, a son of Aaron, kills the Israelite Zimri and his Midianite lover. Significantly, the adulterer and apostate Zimri is the leader of a *Simeonite* family (Num 25:14). By taking matters into his own hands, Phineas ends the plague that has haunted the Israelite camp since the men had started to "indulge in sexual immorality with the daughters of the Midianites" (Num 25:1). YHWH praises Phineas for appeasing the divine anger against the Israelites, promising him and his descendants "an eternal covenant of priesthood, because he was zealous for his God and made atonement for the children of Israel" (Num 25:13). It is this eternal covenant that Mattathias implicitly claims for himself as he "burns with zeal" as Phinehas did.

In the book of Judith, on the other hand, ζηλόω is approvingly connected with the name of Simeon (Jdt 9:4)—the forefather of the same Zimri whom Phineas kills for adultery and idolatry. In defiance of the biblical genotext, Judith claims God's active involvement in Simeon's revenge against the Shechemites (9:4), and concludes (9:4–5):

> … And you gave their women over as spoils and their virgins into captivity, and all their spoils to the diversity of the sons beloved by you, who burned with zeal for you (ἐζήλωσαν τὸν ζῆλόν σου) and made detestable the defilement of their blood, and called on you for help—O God, my God, listen to me, a widow, as well!

According to Eckhardt, the intertextual references linking ζηλόω to two very different source narratives in 1 Maccabees and the book of Judith, respectively, imply very different connotations of the concept in the two works. He finds the main difference in the dependence on God exhibited by Simeon and Judith and lacking in Phinehas, the ideological ancestor of the Hasmonean dynasty. However, dependence on God does not appear to be the main point of difference between Phinehas and Mattathias, on the one hand, and Simeon and Judith, on the other. Each protagonist is simply connected to a figure from biblical tradition that acted in similar ways under similar circumstances. In Num 25 and 1 Macc 2:24, the "hero" makes sure that an Israelite/Jew pays with his life for breaching covenant law. In Gen 34 and the book of Judith, the threat is less ideological and more physical: a concrete or metaphorical Israelite woman—Dinah or Jerusalem—is in danger of being violated by an outsider. Although notions of defilement play a role in this context, too, it is not the covenant that is at risk, but the safety of Israel and her sanctuary.

---

10. That such violent resistance is, in fact, legitimate if circumstances so require, seems beyond doubt in both works (cf. Eckhardt, "Reclaiming Tradition"), although Rakel argues "the book of Judith not only places a *woman* opposite Judas Maccabee, but also one who does *not use martial means* to turn the threat away from Israel" (*Schönheit*, 271; author's own translation). However, in view of the belligerent character of Judith's speeches and acts, I tend to side with Eckhardt that "Judith is a warrior who happens to be guided by divine assistance" (Eckhardt, "Reclaiming Tradition," 253), and I would argue that even this divine assistance is questionable enough.

11. Other occurrences are found in 1 Macc 2:26, 27, 50, 54, 58; 8:16.

Rather than posit that Simeon and Judith act in dependence on God while Phinehas and Mattathias do not, I suggest that they illustrate different definitions of what counts as legitimate acts of ζηλόω. More precisely, they deal with different definitions of individuals or groups against whom acts of ζηλόω may legitimately be aimed. J. Dunn construes Phinehas's zeal as concerned with the demarcation and protection of Israel's religious and ethnic borders.[12] However, D. Ortlund argues that the main thrust of Num 25 is the atonement for the covenantal breach by the Israelites: "Phinehas's zeal was *atoning*, and atonement concerned not Israel and foreigners but Israel and God."[13] I agree with Ortlund, and it seems to me that the same reasoning applies to 1 Maccabees. The paradigmatic deed of Mattathias described in 1 Macc 2:24–25 speaks volumes: his first victim is a Jew who fails to live up to Mattathias's ideals of Jewishness. The liquidation of the royal official is described as an afterthought rather than the main event.[14] Like Saruman and Denethor in the *Lord of the Rings*, the "Hellenizers" have invited the evil that is now destroying their world. It is against these Jews, the "enemy within," that the main polemic of 1 Maccabees is aimed.

The conclusion that the book's polemics are aimed more against Israelites who have forsaken their heritage than against religious and ethnic outsiders is confirmed by the many political alliances the Maccabeans contract. Surely, if separation from all things foreign had been the main incentive of the Maccabeans' zeal, alliances with foreign powers would have been out of the question. Yet, starting with Jonathan, they court the Romans and Spartans for their political friendship and smartly play the rivaling Seleucid kings against each other.[15] Of course, "friendship," in this instance, is purely functional. Alliances with Rome, Sparta, and whichever Seleucid king happens to have the upper hand may be convenient to Antiochus Epiphanes and his brutal policy, but their portrayal in the text is not at all complimentary. Flatterers and turncoats, their allegiance is no more certain than that of the Dead Men of Dunharrow (e.g., 1 Macc 10:18–20, 25–45; 11:25–53; 15:27). Nevertheless, 1 Maccabees passes no judgment on the friendships of Jonathan and Simon with religious and ethnic outsiders. Unlike the "sons of lawlessness" who dare to fraternize with the foreign overlords in 1 Macc 1:11, the Maccabean leaders are implicitly applauded for their political astuteness by framing them as latter-day Davids and Solomons,[16] courted by the contemporary equivalents of Hiram of Tyre or the queen of Sheba.

Conversely, in the book of Judith, all acts of zeal are directed against those on the other side of the religious and ethnic border.[17] Interestingly, notions of threatened purity similar

---

12. J. D. G. Dunn, *The New Perspective on Paul*, rev. ed. (Grand Rapids, MI: Eerdmans, 2008), 12, 201, 317, 344, 361, 478. Cf. D. Ortlund, "Phinehan Zeal: A Consideration of James Dunn's Proposal," *JSP* 20 (2011): 299–315.

13. Ortlund, "Phinehan Zeal," 302.

14. Cf. O. Keel, "1 Makk 2 – Rechtfertigung, Programm und Denkmal für die Erhebung der Hasmonäer," in *Hellenismus und Judentum: Vier Studien zu Daniel 7 und zur Religionsnot unter Antiochus IV*, ed. O. Keel and U. Staub, OBO 178 (Göttingen: Universitätsverlag Freiburg, Vandenhoeck & Ruprecht, 2000), 123–33 (125).

15. 1 Macc 10–12; 14:16–24; 15:15–24. Cf. D. J. Harrington, *The Maccabean Revolt: Anatomy of a Biblical Revolution* (Wilmington, DE: Glazier, 1988), 91.

16. See A. Schenker, "Die Zweimalige Einsetzung Simons des Makkabäers zum Hohenpriester," in *Recht und Kult im Alten Testament*, ed. A. Schenker, OBO 172 (Göttingen: Universitätsverlag Freiburg/Vandenhoeck & Ruprecht, 2000), 158–69 for an in-depth comparison of Solomon and Simon Maccabee.

17. Perhaps this could be explained by the relatively milder transgressions of which the Bethulians are guilty; rather than actually sacrifice to idols, they only put their own welfare before the preservation of the

to those in Num 25 and 1 Macc 2 are evoked both in Gen 34 and its appropriation in Jdt 9. Simeon and Levi seem at least as appalled at the idea of an *uncircumcised* stranger having relations with their sister (Gen 34:13, 14) as they are outraged at the involuntary nature of these relations (34:7, 31). Three times the rape is described using the term μιαίνω ('defile', Gen 34:5, 13, 27), a verb with a primarily cultic frame of reference.[18] In her prayer, Judith elaborates on the notion of defilement by adding βεβηλόω ('desecrate', Jdt 9:2, 8) to her description of Dinah's fate, turning Dinah into a metaphor for the fate of Jerusalem, and more specifically, the Sanctuary. As opposed to 1 Maccabees, however, the defilement is blamed entirely on the aggressors from outside.

The text thus forcefully establishes an in-and an out-group, the former consisting of "the children of Israel," and the latter of everybody else, with one exception: Achior. Achior, however, despite his Ammonite roots, is no stranger to Israel's history or her beliefs. His conversion, marked and finalized by his self-circumcision, comes as no surprise. Although his allegiance may not have been to the Israelites from the outset, as Holofernes seems to assume (Jdt 6:5–9), he is gradually and genuinely convinced that the God of Israel is the only one worth serving (Jdt 14:10).

The individual figure of faithful Achior stands in peculiar contrast to the rest of the non-Israelites appearing in the narrative. This out-group has the character of a timeless and overwhelming menace that must be dealt with rigorously and definitively. In the book of Judith, there are no Sarumans, nor is there a possibility of forming alliances with other groups. There is only the Sauron-like figure of Nebuchadnezzar and his emissaries. The generic evil image painted of the Assyrian king and his armies confirms Gerstenberger's observation that from the Persian period onward, "the term 'Assyrian' changed into a cipher for every kind of political, imperial or regional oppression."[19] Not unlike Goliath in 1 Samuel or Haman in the book of Esther, the Assyrian general Holofernes has the dubitable honor of embodying this perpetual "superhuman" and, at the same time, de-humanized enemy, and like his predecessors, he will pay for this honor with his life.

The Ideal Leader: Two Approaches

If Holofernes can be compared to Goliath, what does that make Judith? Is she indeed the "David Redivivus" LaCocque speaks of? Not entirely, I suggest, although David does figure among the biblical figures her story seems to be modeled after. Indeed, both Judith and Judas and his brothers are based on a variety of—partly overlapping—biblical models.

Temple. However, the fact that the Jews in Judith's surroundings are *not* guilty of such gross transgressions underlines my point: in the book of Judith, the dividing lines are not between "good Jews," on the one hand, and "bad Jews and non-Jews," on the other, but between "Jews"—without further qualifications—on the one hand, and "non-Jews," on the other.

18. By far the most occurrences, both relative and absolute, are in Leviticus (32), Ezekiel (29), and Numbers (16). In Leviticus and Numbers, the main emphasis is on matters of cultic pollution (e.g., Lev 11:24, 43; 13:8, 11, 14–15; 15:32; Num 6:7, 9, 12; 19:13, 20). An exception is the enigmatic text about the potentially adulterous wife (Num 5:11–31), where the sin the woman may have committed is described as μιαίνω several times. In Ezekiel, too, notions of cultic and sexual impurity are often linked (e.g., Ezek 20:30; 22:11; 23:7, 17, 30, 38).

19. E. S. Gerstenberger, *Israel in the Persian Period: The Fifth and Fourth Centuries B.C.E.*, Society of Biblical Literature Biblical Encyclopedia Series 8 (Leiden: Brill, 2012), 316. Gerstenberger explains this generalization of the Assyrian threat by positing that "[t]he Assyrian campaigns of conquest ... had a traumatizing effect because of their brutality and remained lodged in the collective memory," over against more recent attacks by other nations.

Differences between the ideals of leadership developed in each text are rooted not only in the biblical figures they allude to *per se*, but also in the manner in which these figures are appropriated. Since a comprehensive analysis of this phenomenon far exceeds the limits of this contribution, I limit myself to a few relevant figures: Phinehas, Simeon, and David.

Phinehas and Simeon are especially interesting, as Mattathias and Judith, respectively, refer to them as "my father" (1 Macc 2:54; Jdt 9:2), implying a large measure of identification with their actions. I have already discussed the "zeal" of Phinehas and Mattathias, on the one hand, and Simeon and Judith on the other, including their different perspectives on who is an enemy and who is not. In a nutshell, Phinehas, the ideological ancestor of the Maccabeans, directs his anger toward a fellow Israelite who had breached covenantal law, while Simeon fights those on the outside who threaten the physical and cultic integrity of Israel. Mattathias and Judith emulate the actions of their respective "fathers" by zealously defending Israel's covenantal relationship (Mattathias) and the physical safety of sanctuary and populace (Judith). However, the Maccabees and Judith emulate more than their claimed ancestors' zeal: the leadership role they take upon themselves is fashioned after the role their "fathers" had played as well.

In the blessing Mattathias bestows on his sons, he explicitly refers to the "covenant of eternal priesthood" (διαθήκη ἱερωσύνης αἰωνίας, 1 Macc 2:54) promised to Phinehas and his descendants in Num 25. The writer thereby stresses the inheritance of an official position: Phinehas is endowed with an office whose timeless validity is secured by God himself: ברית כהנת עולם (Num 25:13). As his genealogical and ideological heirs, Mattathias and his sons can claim the same God-granted, spiritual leadership. For both Phinehas and the Maccabees, leadership extends far beyond the moment of the initial crisis and pertains to more than cultic matters. The set-apart status of God's people must be safeguarded with military(-like) actions; consequently, Judas Maccabee is the leader of the army (ἄρχων στρατιᾶς, 1 Macc 2:66) as well as a priest. His military actions, however, take place within the larger framework of the covenant and the cultic purity required to maintain this special relationship with YHWH. Allusions to Phinehas thus legitimize not only "the combination of priestly and military functions"[20] but also the prolongation of the Maccabean leadership (cf. 14:41).

Turning to David, a similar tendency becomes visible. Addressing his sons before his death, Mattathias produces a whole list of biblical heroes—Abraham, Joseph (incidentally, not Moses!), Phinehas, Joshua, Caleb, David, Elijah, Ananias, Azarias, Misael, and Daniel (1 Macc 2:52–50). A recurring key word is αἰώνιος—eternal. Phinehas receives an eternal priesthood (2:54), David, an "eternal kingdom" (2:57), and the Maccabees themselves, an eternal name (2:51). Indeed, the point does not seem to be that the various biblical models and their individual qualities should be emulated *per se*. Rather, the emphasis is on the reward each of them has received. As R. Tomes puts it: "[T]he point of the stories is not the character of their actions but their outcome."[21] The perpetuation of Maccabean leadership is advertised before it has properly begun by tying Mattathias's sons to biblical models of established leaders—political *and* religious. According to A. van der Kooij, look-

---

20. T. Funke, "Phinehas and the Other Priests in Ben Sira and 1 Maccabees," in *Imagining the Other and Constructing Israelite Identity in the Early Second Temple Period*, ed. E. Ben Zvi and D. V. Edelman, LHBOTS 456 (London: Bloomsbury T&T Clark, 2014), 257–76.

21. R. Tomes, "Heroism in 1 and 2 Maccabees," *BibInt* 15 (2007): 171–99 (178).

ing at the book as a whole, the scales are ultimately tipped towards the side of kingship.[22] He argues convincingly that while Phinehas is connected with Mattathias and his zealous deed, ensuring the reward of "eternal priesthood" for both the ideological and the biological father of the Maccabean dynasty, David acts as "prototype to be imitated"[23] by Judas. The reward, in this case, is the "eternal kingship" promised to David and envisioned for Judas and his descendants.[24]

As already elaborated in the context of "zeal language," Simeon is Phinehas's counterpart in the book of Judith. His actions and leadership are prototypical for Judith's initiative. However, unlike Phinehas, whose actions are interpreted within the framework of covenant and rewarded with an everlasting office, Simon's revenge against the "foreigners who had uncovered the womb of the virgin" (Jdt 9:2) is a one-time-event, with no lasting consequences either for his role or for the organization of the group.

Interestingly, the evaluation of Simeon's deed in the genotext (Gen 34) is ambivalent at best. Jacob reacts negatively to his sons' actions ("You have brought trouble on me," Gen 34:30), because they have made living peacefully with the inhabitants of the land impossible for him and his family. As to God's thoughts on the matter, the reader is left to guess whether he sides with Simeon and Levi or rather shares Jacob's negative evaluation of the events. Judith appreciates Simeon's actions much more positively than does the genotext in Gen 34. His adverse attitude concerning any mingling with the inhabitants of the land fits her ideas about the sharp border between "Israel" and "the rest" well. Significantly, despite Judith's vindication of Simeon's actions, the prolongation or official installation of his leadership is not at stake in either text. Neither God nor human agents endow Simeon with any kind of office. Immediately after the events narrated in Gen 34, he fades back into the relative obscurity allotted to Jacob's less prominent sons. Judith inherits his violent tendencies and aversion against mingling with outsiders but not an official position or role.

Judith explicitly names only Simeon as a model for her actions, but her character and activities also point to a number of other biblical heroes, resulting in a collage of what the ideal leader of God's people at a moment of crisis should look like. Jael, Deborah, and Esther immediately come to mind. But the narrative does not recall only female figures. Although somewhat more remote in terms of plot structure, the Exodus and the figure of Moses also occupy a central place in the intertextual fabric of the book of Judith.[25] Finally, Judith's encounter with Holofernes also shows similarities with David's confrontation with Goliath: the contrast between the awe-inspiring foreign champion/captain and his fragile contender, the removal of the head with the fallen enemy's own sword (1 Sam 17:51; Jdt 13:6–8), and last but not least, the trust in God professed by both David and Judith (1 Sam 17:37; Jdt 8:33) are notable parallels in both narratives. Interestingly, the book of Judith seems to emphasize aspects of the David figure that run precisely contrary to his

---

22. A. van der Kooij, "The Claim of Maccabean Leadership and the Use of Scripture," in *Jewish Identity and Poitics Between the Maccabeans and Bar Kokhba: Groups, Normativity, and Rituals*, ed. Benedikt Eckhardt (Leiden: Brill, 2012), 29–49 (49).

23. van der Kooij, "Claim," 45. Other textual features connecting Judas with David he enumerates are the reference to a lion's whelp (1 Macc 3:4), the explicit mention of David in 1 Macc 30–33, the way Judas is mourned (1 Macc 9:19–21), and the liberation and rededication of the temple.

24. Incidentally, even in the case of David, the text achieves a blend of military and religious aspects by emphasizing that David's eternal kingdom is based on his ἐλεός ('mercy', probably Hebrew חֶסֶד). Compare Tomes, *Heroism*, 178.

25. For details, see T. Craven, *Artistry and Faith in the Book of Judith* (Chico, CA: Scholars Press, 1983).

appropriation in 1 Maccabees. First of all, while Judas Maccabee, the implied ideological "son of David," is called a "giant" (3:3), Judith emphasizes that it was *not* by the hands of giants that Holofernes was overcome (Jdt 16:7). More generally, the text does not allude to David the king but to David the young, unlikely, even feminized[26] hero.[27] In Rakel's words, the allusion to David

> completes … a line of significant leadership personalities occupying central offices of Israel: Moses is present as savior in the Exodus events and as prophet *par excellence*, as is Aaron as holder of the priestly office. [...] This line is now joined by the young David, a protagonist at the beginning of a career that steers towards kingship. However, as opposed to 1 Maccabees, the book of Judith is precisely *not* concerned with offices.[28]

David can certainly be seen as a model of both faith and initiative—two important values in the book of Judith—but he is also by definition connected with kingship, and it seems that the book of Judith has little faith in earthly kings or in anyone occupying an office, for that matter. Rather than explicitly develop the parallel between David and Judith any further, then, the figure of Simeon is put forward and adapted in order to fit the book's requirements for a leader in crisis: like young David, he displays unwavering trust in YHWH and the willingness to use both stealth and violence in order to protect the people and the sanctuary. Unlike David, however, he is unwilling to allow any relations with non-Israelites, sexual or otherwise, and, most importantly, he lacks the ambition (or the talent) to establish his leadership beyond the moment of crisis.

Returning once again to The *Lord of the Rings*, I suggest that 1 Maccabees makes an effort to turn Mattathias and his sons, especially Judas Maccabee, into Aragorn-like figures—descended from a noble line, performers of almost superhuman deeds of valor, and destined to rule their people. They mirror David in his later years—the successful military leader and first real king of the nation. Interestingly, like David, Aragorn is portrayed as a spiritual as well as a military leader. Similarly, leadership in 1 Maccabees is always tied to spiritual leadership—it is a blend of *monarchy* and *hierocracy*.

Judith, on the other hand, displays characteristics of Frodo, or—spoken biblically, of David at the beginning of his career—specifically, an apparent unsuitability for the role of leader and savior, and the willingness to resort to very unorthodox means. At the same time, the book subtly deconstructs the portrayal of the established leaders as "Aragorns," and paints them instead as a combination of Boromir and Denethor—blinded by their belief in the efficacy of conventional weapons, and if weapons fail, prone to despair and despondency. Indeed, especially Simon and Jonathan would rather join forces with the enemy—i.e., seek a political solution—than stop his advances or die trying. Rulers in the book of Judith are weak, undecided, and almost pathetic in their efforts to turn away the

---

26. M. Osherow, "'Naked Against the Enemy': The Feminization of David," in *Biblical Women's Voices in Early Modern England* (Farnham, Surrey, UK: Ashgate, 2009), 111–48

27. Her discussion of grassroots leadership overlaps in some ways with the concept of non-official leadership discussed by K. Berge in his contribution, Mystified Authority: Legitimating Leadership Through "Lost Books." Whereas she emphasizes the use of earlier biblical figures by the author of Maccabees to ground later leadership roles, Berge emphasizes the use in Deuteronomy of the process of mystification to provide unofficial, divine authority for those who teach the Torah, citing anthropological parallels. For another form of non-official leadership, patron-client relationships, see Anne Fitzpatrick McKinley, "Models of Local Political Leadership in the Nehemiah Memoir," in this volume.

28. Rakel, *Schönheit*, 264–65; author's own translation.

enemy by an overkill of ritual display. Instead, the book puts its trust in "the unlikeliest creature imaginable"—a woman. Judith's actions are not pragmatic—considering the odds, she is going on a fool's quest. But then, she is not a politician, just one of the people who refuses to believe that all is lost, and who has no faith in diplomacy.

The books of Judith and 1 Maccabees not only construe their enemies differently, they also meet them in different ways. I would not claim that 1 Maccabees is militaristic and that the book of Judith is not—they seem to enjoy a juicy scene of slaughtering and pillaging equally.[29] However, in 1 Maccabees, force of arms is complemented by political alliances with diverse partners. Jonathan and Simon in particular show a good portion of pragmatism when it comes to the consolidation of the new order. Rather than regard everyone on the other side of the ethnic and religious border as an enemy, they establish diplomatic dealings with them, albeit selectively. In Keel's words: "Der von 1 Makk 2 ins Zentrum gerückte Eifer für das Gesetz mag am Anfang der hasmonäischen Bewegung Bedeutung gehabt haben. Er trat in der Folgezeit zurück und wurde durch das Streben nach politischer Unabhängigkeit abgelöst."[30]

Even Mattathias seems tarred with the same pragmatic brush: confronted with the choice to uphold the Sabbath or defend themselves on the holy day, he and his followers choose the latter option (1 Macc 2:40–41). The book of Judith, on the other hand, is thoroughly unpragmatic. It excludes the possibility of political solutions from the outset: One does not negotiate with orcs—I mean, Assyrians. Instead, it condones measures that would not be considered *bon ton* or suitable advertisement material for respectable military or political leaders, Maccabean or otherwise. For Judith, stealth, trickery, seduction, and even cold-blooded murder are all acceptable means to the end of overcoming the Assyrians.

Summing up, both models of resistance and leadership in Judith and 1 Maccabees can boast biblical forerunners—and intriguingly, in some cases, these forerunners overlap. However, the way they are appropriated differs greatly. The figure of David is a case in point: while in the book of Judith, his dependence on God and his courage in the face of impossible odds seem to figure in the background of Judith's actions, in 1 Maccabees, it is his royalty that is remembered.

Organizing Israel

The apparently apolitical character of Judith's actions leads to the last point I want to address: How is the ideal Israel organized? As a dynasty, a democracy, or something else entirely? It seems no more than logical to connect 1 Maccabees with a preference for dynastic succession and the book of Judith with more democratic tendencies. After all, the Hasmoneans *did* establish a dynasty, of warrior high priests at first, but eventually of kings as well. Judith, on the other hand, leaves her secluded life as a widow only for a one-time rescue mission and the subsequent festivities. She declines the formalization of her leadership (Jdt 16:21).

Nevertheless, a straightforward identification of 1 Maccabees with "dynasty" and of Judith with "democracy" would fail to take account of the specific character of both texts. A better pair of words would be "established leadership" versus "anti-establishment." Within the German context, the development of "green" politician Joschka Fischer from street-fighter to Member of Parliament offers an eloquent analogy. Judith, I suggest, tries to hold on to the Guerilla-mentality that characterizes the Maccabees in their early days and

---

29. Cf. Jdt 15:1–7.
30. Keel, "Rechtfertigung," 131.

to avoid the domestication that invariably pairs up with the consolidation of leadership.

The consolidation of the Maccabee's leadership is a slow process: Although the notion of dynasty is introduced on a discursive level in Mattathias's speech to his sons, it takes an entire book to arrive there on a concrete level. Interestingly, the biblical legitimation of Maccabean leadership provided in 1 Macc 2 is most likely of a later date than the popular avowal of the rule of Jonathan and Simon described in ch. 14.[31] According to van der Kooij, this "honorary decree" is modeled after Hellenistic practices and serves to establish Simon as "both high priest and leader"[32] *vis-à-vis* the priests, the elders, and, significantly, the *demos*. The decree is based on merit rather than ideological or genealogical provenance—"the honours were bestowed on him and his family because of the benefactions done to the people."[33] Even more significantly, it is presented as the explicit wish of the people (9:28–31; 13:7–8; 14:27–49). Although the outcome is a hereditary form of leadership (both cultic and military/political), this leadership is rooted in popular affirmation. Despite Mattathias's grandiose words about "eternal" priesthood and kingship, dynastic succession is not (yet) self-evident. While it may be the end towards which the book is directed—indeed, the last ruler mentioned, John Hyrcanus, seems to get along just fine without popular avowal—the concept cannot be introduced without backing it with elements of "democracy."

Judith, on the other hand, has been read as an "antidynastic figure"[34]—like Frodo, she prefers the quiet of her own house to the palace or the temple, and the fact that she does not remarry and remains childless precludes the founding of a new dynasty. Yet, in her case, too, the dichotomy between "dynasty" and "democracy" is less straightforward than appears at first sight. First of all, the short duration of her leadership could be explained in terms of gender stereotypes rather than political preferences. According to A.-J. Levine, for example, female leadership, even in the book of Judith, is an exception to the rule, tolerable under extraordinary circumstances, but not to be prolonged or formalized once the circumstances have changed.[35] Although Judith's seclusion is presented as her own choice, it is questionable whether the alternative—the formalization of the leadership of a *woman*, a woman, too, with no priestly or royal genealogy—would have been feasible, even within the fantastic world of the story.

Whether the reasons must be sought in personal preference, political ideologies, or practicability, Judith does not introduce the concept of dynasty. But does that make her a democrat? Unlike Judas and his brothers, who are publicly acclaimed as leaders, Judith's leadership is based entirely on her own initiative. As a representative of YHWH, she does not need the elders' permission for her outrageous plans—it is rather the other way around: Judith tells the elders how to deal with the crisis at hand. Her leadership is *dei gratia* to an extraordinary extent: there is no sign, no anointment, no legitimation except her own claim that "the LORD will visit Israel by my hand" (Jdt 8:33). As L. Day astutely observes, "God is

---

31. See, e.g., van der Kooij, "Claim," 29–30. He says that the "Honorary Decree" in 1 Macc 14 is to affirm Simons's rule and is modeled after Hellenistic practices.
32. Van der Kooij, "Claim," 30.
33. Van der Kooij, "Claim," 32.
34. C. Nihan, "Judith," in *Introduction à l'Ancien Testament*, ed. T. C. Römer, J.-D. Macchi, and C. Nihan (Geneva: Labor et Fides, 2004), 622–36.
35. A.-J. Levine, "Sacrifice and Salvation: Otherness and Domestication in the Book of Judith," in *A Feminist Companion to Esther, Judith and Susanna*, ed. A. Brenner (London: T&T Clark, 1995), 208–23.

in essence a nonentity in the events"[36]—he neither acts nor speaks, except through his self-appointed plenipotentiary, Judith. Indeed, the elders are warned not to inquire too closely into her plans (8:34), making Judith as unfathomable as God himself. "Democracy" seems an ill-applied term for this kind of self-asserted and nonetheless incontestable leadership.

Finally, one may wonder whether the a-historical character of the book of Judith precludes reading the book as a political manifesto.[37] The fantastic plot leaves little room for concrete, mundane affairs such as the establishment of dynasties or the organization of some other form of government. Of course, the book is critical of the elders and the Jerusalemite priesthood—both fail to secure the people and the temple against the attacks of the Assyrians. But Judith offers no lasting alternative, at least on the human level. Her complete disregard of established leadership and the apocalyptic tendencies of her psalm rather point in the direction of a very different form of government: theocracy.[38] And despite the Maccabees' professed reliance on God (e.g., 2:61; 4:30–34; 11:71), this is an option that does not seem to have occurred to the author of their story.

Conclusions

"I wish the ring had never come to me. I wish none of this had happened," Frodo says to Gandalf, as he realizes the magnitude of Sauron's threat and of the task ahead of him. Gandalf responds: "So do I, and so do all who live to see such times. But that is not for them to decide. All we have to decide is what to do with the time that is given us."[39]

The book of Judith confronts its readers with a similar choice. One of the issues discussed in the present volume concerns the way in which readers are socialized. And perhaps this socialization is one of the most interesting differences between 1 Maccabees and the book of Judith.

Although the book of Judith has been read as "counter-propaganda" to the Maccabean claim to political and religious leadership, I interpret it differently. Judith does not depose the elders or the high priest, although she criticizes their response to the situation at hand. Neither does she present herself or anyone else as an alternative to their established rule. She does, however, criticize the differentiation between "good" and "bad" Jews suggested by 1 Maccabees. No "Jew" in the book of Judith sacrifices to a foreign God or worships Nebuchadnezzar. Their greatest sin is not apostasy but despair—and pragmatism. Judith demonstrates the necessity of faith, commitment, and courage from the grassroots. The readers of her story have learned to distinguish carefully between insiders and outsiders on the basis of a very simple schema: Israelites on one side and everyone else on the other. These readers have been made to understand that politics and diplomacy are vain in the face of a threat that has lost all human qualities. Last but not least, Judith's example has shown them that it is up to them to resist that threat. She, the widow, demonstrates that in times of crisis, everyone is called upon to take on a role of leadership.

---

36. L. Day, "Faith, Character, and Perspective in Judith," *JSOT* 95 (2001): 92.

37. Cf. C. C. Torrey humorous construal of a modern-day setting of Judith, which captures the spirit of the books exposé: "It happened at the time when Napoleon Bonaparte was king of England and Otto von Bismarck was on the throne in Mexico" (C. C. Torrey, *The Apocryphal Literature: A Brief Introduction* [New Haven: Yale University Press, 1945], 89).

38. Cf. Craven's observation that the book is primarily concerned with the establishment of YHWH's sovereign rule over "all the earth," over against Nebuchadnezzar's claims (*Artistry*, 55).

39. Gandalf's response is taken literally from J. R. R. Tolkien, *The Lord of the Rings* (London: HarperCollins, 1991), 50. Frodo's words are from the film version *The Fellowship of the Ring* (2002).

Conversely, 1 Maccabees depicts an inner struggle between "Judaizers" and "Hellenizers" and a continuously changing political scene on the "global" scale. This situation of inner and outer instability requires a strong man, or preferably, a succession of strong men, who will ensure continuity and a sense of direction on the military, political, and religious plane. The readers of this history are implicitly asked to accept the leadership of the Maccabees—they are turned into followers.

Bibliography

Craven, T. 1983. *Artistry and Faith in the Book of Judith*. Chico, CA: Scholars Press.
Day, L. 2001. "Faith, Character, and Perspective in Judith." *JSOT* 95: 71–93.
Dunn, J. 2008. D. G. *The New Perspective on Paul*. Rev. ed. Grand Rapids, MI: Eerdmans.
Eckhardt, B. 2009. "Reclaiming Tradition: The Book of Judith and Hasmonean Politics." *JSP* 18: 243–63.
Funke, T. 2014. "Phinehas and the Other Priests in Ben Sira and 1 Maccabees." In *Imagining the Other and Constructing Israelite Identity in the Early Second Temple Period*, edited by E. Ben Zvi and D. V. Edelman, 257–76. LHBOTS 456. London: Bloomsbury T&T Clark.
Gerstenberger, E. S. 2012. *Israel in the Persian Period. The Fifth and Fourth Centuries B.C.E.* Society of Biblical Literature Biblical Encyclopedia Series 8. Leiden: Brill.
Harrington, D. J. *The Maccabean Revolt: Anatomy of a Biblical Revolution*. Wilmington, DE: Glazier, 1988.
Keel, O. "1 Makk 2 – Rechtfertigung, Programm und Denkmal für die Erhebung der Hasmonäer." Pages 123–133 in *Hellenismus und Judentum: Vier Studien zu Daniel 7 und zur Religionsnot unter Antiochus IV*. Edited by O. Keel and U. Staub. OBO 178. Göttingen: Universitätsverlag Freiburg, Vandenhoeck & Ruprecht, 2000.
Kooij, A. van der. 2012. "The Claim of Maccabean Leadership and the Use of Scripture." In *Jewish Identity and Poitics Between the Maccabeans and Bar Kokhba: Groups, Normativity, and Rituals*, edited by Benedikt Eckhardt, 29–49. Leiden: Brill.
LaCoque, A. 1990. *The Feminine Unconventional: Four Subversive Figures in Israel's Tradition*. Minneapolis, MN: Fortress.
Levine, A.-J. 1995. "Sacrifice and Salvation: Otherness and Domestication in the Book of Judith." In *A Feminist Companion to Esther, Judith and Susanna*, edited by A. Brenner, 208–223. London: T&T Clark.
Nihan, C. 2004. "Judith." In *Introduction à l'Ancien Testament*, edited by T. C. Römer, J. D. Macchi and C. Nihan, 622–636. Geneva: Labor et Fides.
Ortlund, D. 2011. "Phinehan Zeal: A Consideration of James Dunn's Proposal." *JSP* 20: 299–315.
Osherow, M. 2009. ""Naked Against the Enemy": The Feminization of David." In *Biblical Women's Voices in Early Modern England*, 111–48. Farnham, Surrey: Ashgate.
Rakel, C. 2003. *Judit – über Schönheit, Macht und Widerstand im Krieg: eine Feministisch-Intertextuelle Lektüre*. Berlin: de Gruyter.
Schenker, A. 2000. "Die Zweimalige Einsetzung Simons des Makkabäers zum Hohenpriester." In *Recht und Kult im Alten Testament*, edited by A. Schenker, 158–69. OBO 172. Göttingen: Vandenhoeck & Ruprecht; Universitätsverlag Freiburg.
Tolkien, J. R. R. 1991. *The Lord of the Rings*. London: HarperCollins.
Tomes, R. 2007. "Heroism in 1 and 2 Maccabees." *BibInt* 15: 171–99.
Torrey, C. C. 1945. *The Apocryphal Literature: A Brief Introduction*. New Haven, CT: Yale University Press.

Index of Ancient Sources

HEBREW BIBLE TEXTS

Genesis
 3:8 79
 21:22 180
 34 252, 254, 256
 34:5 254
 34:7 254
 34:13 254
 34:14 254
 34:27 254
 34:30 256
 34:31 254
 41 140

Exodus
 2:2 116
 2:14 62
 5:2 135
 12 134
 13:17 62
 14 134
 14:30 134
 15:18 79
 19:5 224
 19:6 14, 21
 24:1 6, 18
 24:9 18
 24:9–11 6
 25:9 49
 25:40 49
 28 81
 29 81
 29:3 83
 30:7–10 81
 30:17–21 81
 30:30–32 81
 30:39 81
 32:1 81
 32:5 81
 32:6 81–82
 32:7–8 81–82
 32:10 82
 32:11–14 82
 32:17 82
 32:20 81
 32:25 82
 32:28 81

Leviticus
 2:1–3 81
 2:8 81
 2:9 81
 9:24 190, 192
 10:1–2 190
 11:24 254
 11:43 254
 13:8 254
 13:11 254
 13:14–15 254
 15:32 254
 26:4–13 98

Index of Ancient Sources

Numbers
  3:1–10 81
  5:11–31 254
  6 234
  6:7 254
  6:9 254
  6:12 254
  11:16 18
  11:16–17 6
  11:24–25 18
  11:24–30 6
  14:3–4 69
  16 16
  16:36–50 81
  17 81
  18 81
  19:13 254
  19:20 254
  20 80
  20:12 81
  21:27 116
  23:21 79
  25 252–54
  25:1 252
  25:13 252, 254
  25:14 252
Deuteronomy 42–43, 48–53, 57–74, 111
  1–32 71
  1:5 71
  1:9–15 224
  4 44
  4:1 46
  4:6 14
  4:7–8 57
  4:8 57, 71
  4:16–18 49
  4:26 60
  4:32–34 57
  4:38 66
  4:40 60
  4:44 71
  5 72
  5–28 71
  5:1 46
  5:16 60
  5:32 72
  5:32–6:2 72–73
  5:33 60
  6:1 72
  6:1–2 72
  6:2 60, 72
  6:14 66
  7:1 66
  7:3–4 69
  7:17 66
  7:22 66
  8 61
  8:12–14 60–61, 70
  8:18 61
  8:20 66
  9:1 66
  9:4–5 66
  11:9 60
  11:23 66
  12-26 62
  12:2 66
  12:10 66
  12:17 61
  12:20 65
  12:29–30 66
  13:8 66
  13:13–19 18
  14:21 61
  14:23 71
  15:3 61
  16:5 61
  16:18 222, 224–25
  16:18–18:22 58
  16:18aβ 59
  16:19 225
  16:20 59
  17 58–59, 62–69, 72–74
  17:1–13 18
  17:2 59
  17:8–13 58, 73
  17:9 59, 68, 73
  17:10 59
  17:11 71
  17:12 73
  17:14 17, 20, 59, 62–63, 65–67, 70
  17:14–15 59, 64
  17:14–15* 63, 68
  17:14–20 17, 58–59, 64, 227
  17:14–20* 64, 68, 70
  17:14b 70
  17:15 57, 61, 65
  17:15* 65, 68
  17:15a 61, 65–68
  17:15b 61, 65
  17:16 61, 68

17:16–17 61
17:16–17* 65
17:16–17 65
17:16–17* 68
17:16* 69
17:16b 62
17:17 60–61, 69
17:17a 65
17:17aα 69
17:17b 60, 65, 69
17:18 59, 61, 70–71
17:18–19 60–61, 70–71
17:18–20 6–7
17:19 60, 61, 71, 73
17:19–20 72
17:20 60–61
17:20* 68
17:20aα 60, 69–70
17:20aβ 72
17:20aβb 61, 72
17:20b 60
18:1 59
18:1–8 58
18:6–8 65
18:7 59
18:9 59, 66
18:14 66
19:1 66
19:1–13 111, 118
19:12 121
20 73
20:15 66
21:1–9 111, 118, 121
21:10–14 73
21:13 116
21:18–21 111, 118, 120
22:3 61
22:7 60
22:13–21 111, 118, 120
23:21 61
24:5 73
25:5–10 111, 118
25:15 60
25:19 66
26:1 59
26:16–19 57, 224
28 49
28:15–68 16
28:36 59
28:36b 59

28:68 62
29:13–27 16
30:1–5 16
30:17–19 16
30:18 60
30:20 60
31 44, 46, 51, 53
31:1 71
31:3 66
31:9 70
31:9–13 225
31:11–12 46
31:12–13 71, 73
31:20 16
31:24 71
31:24–27 43
31:26 50
31:28 50
32:19–25 16
32:47 60
33:5 57, 59
33:14 116
33:29 57

Joshua
  1:7 49
  1:8 17, 19, 73
  2 156
  21:19 81
  24:11 18

Judges 250
  3:7–31 19
  3:8 66
  3:12 66
  3:31–4:24 232
  4:2 66
  6:1–9:57 232
  8:6 180
  8:22 83
  8:23 83
  8:26 83
  8:27 83
  8:31 61
  8:33–34 83
  8:35 83
  9 18
  9:1 61
  9:2 17–18
  9:7–15 17
  9:22–49 83

9:51–55 83
10:6–12:7 232–33
11:12 66
13–16 234
13:5 233
13:25 234
14 233
14–15 233
14:1–16:19 233
14:6 234
14:10 234
14:17 234
14:19 234
15 233
15:14 234
16 233
16:3 235
16:20–31 233
16:23–24 233
16:27–29 235
17:6 19
19:1 19
20:5 18
21:5 19
21:25 19

1–2 Samuel 16, 22, 57, 64, 99
1 Samuel 254
  7 220, 223
  7–8 220
  7:2 84
  7:3 84
  7:6 84
  7:9–10 84
  7:13–14 85
  8 17, 62–64, 66–69, 219–221, 223–27
  8:1 62, 221
  8:1–3 63, 85
  8:1–5 65
  8:1–6 67
  8:1–22 63
  8:3 66, 67
  8:3–7 221
  8:4 222
  8:4–5 85
  8:5 6, 17, 20, 62–63, 65–67, 220
  8:5–6 66
  8:5a 63, 66–67
  8:5b 67
  8:6 63, 66–67

8:6–18 63–64
8:6a 67
8:6aγ 66
8:7 17, 63, 79, 224–25
8:7–9 85
8:7a 63
8:7b–9a 63
8:9 220
8:9–11a 221
8:9a 63
8:11 65, 68, 220
8:11–17 223
8:11–18 64–65
8:11b–18 221
8:13 65
8:18 67
8:19–20 85
8:19–22 222, 224
8:20 17, 20, 63, 66
9–10 68
9:1–10:16 68
9:8–13 85
9:16 85
10 68
10:5 85
10:16 224
10:17 68
10:17–27 67–68
10:17–27a 220, 225
10:20–23 65, 68
10:20–24 65
10:24 65, 68
10:25 224
11:1–11 68
11:7 68
12 17, 220
12:2 85
12:14 224
15 67
15:1–35 150
16:1 67
16:1–13 67–68, 105
16:4 105
16:12b 67
17:12 MT 105
17:12–31 MT 105
17:15 MT 105
17:37 256
17:51 256
20:6 105

23:11 18
24:9 151
28 105
31:1 17
2 Samuel
  1:2 151
  7 92
  9:6 151
  14 73
  15:4 62, 73
  21:12 18
  23:19 180
  24:15 17
1-2 Kings 16, 17, 57, 64, 99
1 Kings 20
  3 73
  5:6 69
  6:37–38 116
  7:7 73
  8:2 116
  9 69
  10 69
  10:26 LXX 69
  10:28 69
  11 69, 135
  11:2a 69
  11:3 69
  11:6 67
  11:29–32 18
  12 18, 37, 69
  14 135
  14:22–25 135
  14:26 135
  15:26 67
  15:29 137
  17:1 17
  18 190
  18:33–38 190
  22 132
  22–23 35
2 Kings 20, 48, 138, 140
  1:13 151
  15:13 116
  17 37
  17:7–18 135
  17:13 19
  17:23 37
  18–19 134
  18:9–12 133
  18:12 224
  18:35 134
  19:10–13 137
  19:16–17 137
  19:28 134
  19:35–36 140
  20:13 69
  20:16–17 69
  21 37
  21:18 79
  21:24 18
  22–23 44, 46, 227
  22:11 227
  22:19 94
  22:20 133
  23 138
  23:1–3 227
  23:4–25 133
  23:22 17, 20
  23:29 133
  23:30 18
  23:31 92
  23:31–34 93
  23:33–34 18
  24:2–4 135
  24:17 18
  24:18 92
  25:4 79
  25:25 170
Isaiah
  7:6 61
  10 134
  11:1–5 105
  23:22 17
  31:1 69
  32:18 156
  36–37 134
  36:20 134
  37:29 134
  37:36 134
  42:1–7 104
  42:6 15
  44:13 49
  44:24–28 104
  44:28 5
  45 61
  45:1–7 5, 104
  45:4–5 134–35
  45:9–13 104
  51:11 156

52:1–4 186
55:3 21
55:3–5 104
55:3–11 14
56:6–8 171
60:1–3 15
66:21 171
Jeremiah 48
  3:6–10 36
  15:16 47
  17:5 69
  21:5 135
  22:15 101
  22:27–30 35
  23:1–6 99
  23:5 101
  25:9 135
  25:12–14 136
  25:30 93
  26 37
  27:6 135
  29:7 136
  31:33–34 24
  33:14–26 MT 104
  33:15 101
  34 225
  34:22 135
  36 37, 44, 46, 48
  36:2 51
  36:23 51
  37–38 225
  40:11 170
  42:10–22 69
  43:10 135
  44:30 135
  46 135
  46:17 135
  50:5 14
  50:17–19 136
  50:23–24 136
  51:7–8 136
  51:11 136
  51:20–23 136
Ezekiel 48, 53, 89–107
  1–39 97, 103
  1:2 94
  1:26 48
  2–3 43, 46
  2:9–10 47

  3:1–3 47
  4–24 89, 92, 94, 105
  6:9 69
  7:27 103
  8:3 49
  8:10 49
  10:8 49
  12:10 93
  12:12 93
  16 91
  16:44 116
  17 89, 93–95, 104, 106
  17:2–10 93
  17:3–4 93–94
  17:5–10 93
  17:9–21 93
  17:12 94
  17:15 93
  17:16 93
  17:19 93
  17:22–24 89, 92–94, 97, 105
  17:23 94, 106
  17:23b 95
  17:24 95
  19 89, 92, 94–95
  19:1–9 92
  19:2 92
  19:2–10 106
  19:3 92
  19:6 92
  19:7 92–93
  19:8 93
  19:10–14 94
  19:14 93, 94
  20:5–31 91
  20:30 254
  21:30 93
  22:11 254
  22:29 103
  23 91
  23:7 254
  23:17 254
  23:30 254
  23:38 254
  26:7 135
  27 170
  30–32 135
  31:6 95
  33–39 90, 99–100
  34 90, 104–6

34:2–10 91, 99, 104
34:11–15 98
34:11–16 99
34:15 98
34:23–24 100, 105
34:24a 97
34:25 98
34:25–30 98
34:26 98
34:27 98
34:29 98
36–40 91, 99
37 90, 103–6
37:15–28 97, 106
37:16–19 100
37:19 105
37:21 98
37:22 98, 100, 105
37:23 98
37:24 MT 105
37:24–25 105
37:24–27 100
37:24–28 104
37:24b 100
37:24b–25a 106
37:25 105
37:26–27 100
37:26b 100
37:27a 100
37:40–48 97
38–39 91, 98
38:16 98
38:18–22 98
38:23 98
39:1–6 98
39:7 98
39:9 98
39:9–10 98
39:10 98
39:21–22 98
40–42 106
40–48 90, 100–104
40:46 102
42:13–14 102
43:7–9 90, 91, 103–4, 106
43:11 106
44:3 102–3
44:15–16 102
44:30 102
45:4 102

45:7 103
45:7–8a 101
45:9 101
45:9–12 101, 103, 106
45:13–16 102
45:16 102–3
45:17 101–2
45:21–24 102
45:22 103
45:25 102
46:2–3 103
46:3 103
46:8 102
46:9 102–3
46:13–15 102
46:15 102
46:16–18 103
46:17 101
47–48 106
48:7 106
48:21–22 101
48:23 106
Ezekiel L^W 91, 99, 104
Ezekiel LXX 102–3
Ezekiel LXX^A 91, 97
Ezekiel LXX^B 91, 97
Ezekiel p967 91, 97, 99, 104
Ezekiel Syriac 102
Hosea
 2:20 98
 8:13 62
 9:3 62, 69
 10 37
 11:5 69
 11:10 93
 12:14 23
 13 37
Joel
 4:16 93
Amos
 1:2 93
 3:8 93
Obadiah
 21 224
Jonah
 3 141

Index of Ancient Sources

Micah
  4:1–5 19
  5:1 105
  5:1–5 105
Zephaniah
  3:1–5 37
Haggai
  1–8 186
  1:3–6 36
  1:7 36
  2:16 36
  2:23 99
Zechariah
  3:8 99
  6:12 99
  9:9–10 105
  9:10 98
  9:10b 105
  11:8 116
  14:9 17
Malachi
  1 38
Psalms 16, 99
  1 13, 25, 73
  1:2 13
  2:8–9 99
  18:22–23 58
  21:8 58
  22:28–29 151
  22:29 224
  24 79
  45:4–6 99
  46:10 98
  69:13 123
  72 73, 116
  72:8 105
  72:11 151
  76:4 98
  89 92
  89:31–33 58
  93 79
  95:6 151
  96 79
  97 79
  99 79
  99:6 81
  131:1 70
  132:12 58

Proverbs
  8 114
  16:18 70
  18:12 70
Job
  1–2 114, 124
  1–18 112
  1:2 112
  1:2–3 115, 123
  1:3 115
  1:14–19 115
  3 112, 114, 124
  3–28 112–13
  3:6 116
  4 114, 117
  4–28 114
  4:1 112
  5:24 115
  6:1 112
  7:3 116
  8:1 112
  8:22 115
  9:1 112
  11:1 112
  11:14 115
  12:1 112
  12:6 115
  15:1 112
  15:34 115
  16:1 112
  16:7–22 113
  18:1 112
  18:6 115
  18:14–15 115
  18:17 117
  19:1 112
  19:12 115
  20:1 112
  20: 115
  21:1 112
  21:28 115
  22–27/28 112
  22:1 113
  22:23 115
  23:1 113
  23:13–17 113
  24:1–25 113
  25:1 113
  26:1 113
  27:1 113

27:2 113
28 112–13, 114
29 112, 115, 121–22, 124
29–30 6, 111, 112, 114, 116, 118, 120–24
29–31 112, 114, 124
29:1 115, 116
29:1–42:6 113–14
29:2 115–16
29:2–6 117
29:3–6 123
29:4 115–16
29:7 115, 117
29:7–10 115
29:7–25 117
29:9–10 117
29:10–11 121
29:11 115
29:12–17 116–17, 121
29:13 115
29:14 117
29:14–16 117
29:16 116
29:18–20 117
29:21–23 117
29:21–24 116
29:21–25 115
29:23 117
29:24 117
29:24–25 121
29:25 116, 117
30 112, 115, 122
30:1 115, 121, 123
30:2 117, 121
30:2–8 121–24
30:2–9 122
30:5 121
30:8 117, 121
30:9–14 115
30:9–15 121, 123
30:10 123
30:11–14 123
30:15 123
30:16–23 117, 123
30:25 115, 117
30:27 115
30:27–31 123
30:–31 117, 123
31 112, 114, 116
31:31 115
32–42:6 114

32:12 114
34:1 114
35:1 114
36:1 114
38:1 114
39:2 116
40:1 114
40:3 114
40:6 114
42 136
42:1 114
42:7–17 112, 114
47:7–17 124

Ruth
 4 111

Lamentations
 3:14 123

Esther 254
 1:1–2:18 147, 150
 1:1–9 149
 1:8 154
 1:13 154
 1:22 149
 2:5 150
 2:5–7 147
 2:19–23 147, 150
 2:21–23 151
 3 242
 3:1 149, 150
 3:1–5 147, 150
 3:2 151, 156
 3:2–6 149
 3:4 150
 3:5 151
 3:6–15 148
 3:8 154–55
 3:9 149
 3:10 149
 3:12 149
 3:13 149
 3:14 149
 3:15 149
 4:1 149
 4:1–17 148
 4:3 149, 156
 4:14 156
 4:16 156
 5:1–8 148
 5:9–14 148

5:10–14a 149
5:14b 149
6:1–13 148
6:12f 149
6:13 156
7:1–8 148
7:7f 149
7:10 149
8:1–17 148
8:1f.11b 149
8:2a 149
8:8–12 155
8:9–12 149
8:13 149
8:14f 149
8:15 160
8:15a 149
8:16 156
8:17 156, 160
8:17a 149
9:1–16 149
9:1–18 148
9:2 156
9:3b–4 160
9:19 148, 157
9:20–28 148
9:27 160
9:29–32 148
10:1–3 148
10:2–3 155
10:2f 149
16–18 158
Daniel 243
  1–4 140–41
  1–5 141
  1:1–2 139
  2 140
  2:28 140
  2:37 140
  2:45 140
  2:46 140
  2:46–47 140
  3 140, 141, 158
  3:29 140
  3:32–33 140
  4 139, 140
  4:1–3 140
  4:23 [26 ET] 140
  4:27 [30 ET] 140
  4:29 140

  4:34 140
  5 140
  5–6 139
  5:2 141
  5:22 141
  5:23 141
  5:24 141
  6 158
Ezra-Nehemiah 42
  10 22
Ezra
  1 140
  1–6 186
  7–10 171
  8:24 180
  8:25 180
  8:29 180
Nehemiah
  1–6 165
  1:1–7:5 165
  1:1a 166
  1:3 170
  1:11b 166
  2 171
  2:1–6 166
  2:8 178
  2:9 170, 180
  2:11 166
  2:15–18 166
  2:19 178
  3 180–81
  3:4 180
  3:5 182
  3:9 178, 182
  3:9–18 179
  3:12 182
  3:15 180
  3:19 180
  3:28 166
  3:30 180
  4 169, 178
  4:3 168
  4:7 171
  4:7–8 168
  4:22 178
  5 170, 183–84, 225
  5:1–15 178
  5:7 180, 183
  5:10 183

5:10–15 179
5:11 179
5:12 183
5:14–15 179
5:17 184
6:2 171
6:6 178
6:7 171, 178
6:9–12 172
6:15 166
6:17–18 168, 170–71
6:18 180
6:19 170
7:2 165, 180, 184
7:11 179
7:70 180
8 33, 48, 189
8–9 189, 194
8:1–8 186–87
8:9 187
9–10 22
9–13 165
11:1–2 165
11:1–13:31 165
11:3 177
12 165
12:27–43 165
12:31–43 165
13 189
13:4 184
13:4–8 170
13:4–31 165
13:5 170
13:7 170
13:9 170
13:10 184
13:15 185
13:15–16 184
13:15–17 185
13:16 185
13:17 185
13:19 187
13:22 187
13:23 171
1-2 Chronicles 14, 16, 23–24, 54, 99, 137
1 Chronicles
  5:6 137
  5:26 137
  9:1 48

28:11–19 49
2 Chronicles 19
  7:1–3 192
  7:3 151
  9:29 48
  10 18
  16:11 48
  17:7–9 32
  23–24 23
  23:16 23
  23:18–19 23
  24:3 23
  24:12 23
  24:14–16 23
  27:7 48
  28:8–15 23
  28:20 137
  29:29 151
  30:26 17
  32 137
  33–48 96
  33:18 24
  33:25 18
  34 96–100
  34–35 35
  34:23–24 96–97, 100, 105
  34:27 94
  34:28 138
  35 138
  35:4 49
  35:15 49
  35:18 17
  35:21 138
  35:22 138
  36 139
  36:1 18
  36:3–4 18
  36:10 18
  36:17 137
  36:23 140
  37 96–100
  37:15–23 97
  37:22 97
  37:24 97
  37:24–25 96–97, 105
  37:25 97

Other Ancient Near Eastern Texts

Aqhat
  II.v.5–7 121
Elephantine papyri
  TAD 8/9 166
  TAD A.4.7 166, 176
  TAD A.4.9 176
Enuma Elish 134
Tayma
  Tayma 1 175
  Tayma 20 175
Wadi Daliyeh papyri 166
Weidner Tablets
  Tablet B, reverse, l. 38–39 93
  Tablet C, II, l. 17–18 93
Xerxes
  XPh (Daiva inscription)
    4–6 158
    4b, 4d 13

Deuteroncanonical Books

Judith 250–53, 257–58
  3:3 257
  6:5–9 254
  8:33 256, 259
  8:34 260
  9 254
  9:2 254–56
  9:4 252
  9:4–5 252
  9:8–13 254
  13:6–8 256
  14:10 254
  15:1–7 258
  16:7 257
  16:21 258
Sirach 186, 234
  24 114
  46:11–12 234
  48 188
  48:11–12 187
  48:13 187
  49:11–12 188
  49:11–16 186
1 Maccabees 243, 250–54, 257–58, 260
  1:1–4 242
  1:11 253
  1:41–64 155

1:49 155
2 254, 258–59
2:24–25 252–53
2:26 252
2:27 252
2:40–41 258
2:50 252
2:51 255
2:52–50 255
2:52–53 250
2:54 252, 255
2:57 255
2:58 252
2:61 260
2:66 255
3:4 256
4:8 250
4:30–34 260
4:41–58 191
6:35–37 250
6:45–46 250
8:16 252
9:19–21 256
9:28–31 259
10–12 253
10:18–20 253
10:25–45 253
11:25–53 253
11:71 260
13:7–8 259
14 259
14:16–24 253
14:27–49 259
14:41 255
15:15–24 253
15:27 253
30–33 256
2 Maccabees 186, 188–190, 193–94
  1:1 192
  1:2 250
  1:18 188–190
  1:19 189
  1:19–36 188
  1:20 191
  1:20–36 189
  1:21 189–190
  1:23 189
  1:30–33 191
  1:33 189, 193
  1:33–34 191

2 190–92, 250
2:1 193
2:4–8 190
2:8–10 190
2:10 193
2:13 190
2:13–15 189, 193–94
4 243
10:3 190
1 Esdras 193
5:47–50 186

Pseudepigrapha

Jubilees 187
16 171
17 171

Greco-Roman Sources

Aeschylus
1.4 207
Pers.
241–42 204
PV 238
Supp.
398–401 204
604 204
Andocides
1.96–98 205
Apollodorus
Bibl.
2.5–5.7 238
2.7.4 238
Aristophanes
Av.
1072–1074 205
Thesm.
338–339 205
Aristotle
Eth. Nic. 211
Poet.
1453a 132
Pol.
1265b31–1266a1 213
1265b38–40 203
1274b18–23 202
1279a25–39 211
1279b4–10 211
1279b34–1280a6 211
1280b5–25 211
1282b16–17 212
1284a3–22 205
1284b30–34 209
1289.26–38 211
1289b27–1290a13 211
1290a30–1290b7 211
1293b33–35 213
1294a35–1294b13 213
1294b18–34 213
1295a7–23 211
1301b29–39 212
Rh.
1.8 211
Arrian
Anab.
1.357 153
4.10–12 153
Athenaion politeia
3.6 204
8.4 205
22.3 205
22.4 205
22.5 204
25 204
29–32 212
41.2 214
44.4 214
66.1 214
Curtius Rufus
8.5 153
Diodorus Siculus
4.31.5–8 238
4.35.1–36.5 238
11.33.2 205
11.72.2–73.3 206
14.11.3 175
14.22.5 175
15.90.3 175
Euripides 238
Supp.
352–353 208
404–407 208
429–446 208
Hellenica Oxyrhynchia
16.2–4 203
Herodotus
1.7–46 132
1.34 132

1:86 132
1.134 151
3:31 208
3.80–82 18, 219
3.80.1 207, 221
3.80.1–5 208
3.80.2 208, 223
3.80.2–5 221–22
3.80.3–5 223
3.80.5 223
3.80.6 208, 222, 225
3.81.1 207, 209
3.81.1–2 209
3.81.3 207, 209, 222, 225
3.82.1 222
3.82.2–4 209
3.82.3 209
3.82.3–4 222, 225
3.82.5 209, 222
3.83 18
3.83.1 222
3.84–86 224
3.86 152
3.142–43 206
3.439 152
4.150–67 202
4.200–205 202
5.55–65 205
6.43.3 207
6.102 204
6.107 204
6.109 204
7.104.4–5 205
7.136 152

Hesiod
  Op. 201
  [*Sc.*]
    17–18 237

Homer
  Il.
    1 132
    15–16 138
    24 132
  Od.
    6.1–10 202
    6.53–55 202
    8.390–391 202

Isocrates
  Areopagiticus
    21–22 212
  To Nicocles
    14–16 212

Old Oligarch
  1.2 214
  1.2–5 207
  1.5 209

Ovid
  Her.
    9 238
    55–86 238

Pindar 203, 207
  fr. 169 Sn 237
  Isthm.
    13 237
  Nem.
    1 237
    3.19–23 237
  Ol.
    3.43–44 237
  Pyth.
    2.86–88 201

Plato
  Ap.
    22a 238
  Leg.
    691e–692a 213
    693d–e 213
    712d 213
    757a–e 212
  Lysis
    205C 238
  Plt.
    291d–292a 210
    293e–294b 210
    302c–303b 210
  Resp.
    473c–e 209
    500c–e 209
    543c–545c 210
  Tht.
    175A 238

Plutarch
  Alex.
    54 152
  Arist.
    7 205

Index of Ancient Sources

Lyc.
  6 202
  6.1 204
Mor. Her. mal.
  873b 205
Them.
  2.73 152

Polybius
  6 24

Simonides
  XV Page *FGE* 205
  XVII (b) Page *FGE* 205

Sophocles
  Phil. 238
  Trach. 238

Strabo
  Geogr.
    16.1.4 193

Thucydides 202
  2.37.1 208, 212, 214
  2.65.9 212
  3.62.3 208
  3.74.2–3 207
  3.82.1–2 207
  5.85–87 203
  6.39.1 209, 212, 214
  6.53–59 205
  6.60.1 205
  8.53.1 214
  8.72.2 212
  8.97.2 212

Tyrtaeus
  Fr. 4 West 214

Xenophon 11
  An.
    2.513 175
    7.8.15 175

Cyr.
  1.3.18 210
  8.1.21–22 209
  8.6 170, 178
Hell. 22
  3.1.10–15 167, 176
  3.1.13 174
  4.1.3 175
  4.1.12–15 182
  4.1.24 174
Hier. 210
Lac.
  15.7 203
Mem.
  3.5.26 175
Oec.
  4.5 170, 178
  21.9–12 209

Josephus
  Ant.
    9.297–310 158
    11 166
    13.249–53 192
    15.19–21 192
  Contra Apionem
    Book I 44
    1.190–193 159
  War
    1.434 192

RABBINIC/JUDAIC SOURCES

Deuteronomy Rabbah
  5.11 17
Palestinian/Jerusalem Talmud
  y. *Ber.*
    7.2 192
  y. *Naz.*
    5.3 192

Author Index

Aberbach, M. 81
Abraham, K. 177
Achenbach, R. 60, 61, 63, 65, 69–70, 73, 151, 158
Ackerman, S. 240
Ackroyd, P. 165, 168
Adam, K.-P. 67
Adorno, T. 49
Ahlström, G. 166
Ahn, G. 151–52
Albenda, P. 92
Albertz, A. 180
Alden, R. L. 117
Alexander, L. 241, 243
Alexander, P. 241, 243
Allen, L. C. 97, 102
Alonso-Núñez, J. M. 227
Alt, A. 167–68
Altmann, P. 42
Amit, Y. 233–34, 239
Amitay, O. 241–42
Artus, O. 101
Ascough, R. S. 128
Asheri, D. 208, 223, 227
Assis, E. 36, 233–34, 239
Assmann, J. 128, 132

Auld, G. A. 83
Avi Yonah, M. 180–82

Bailey, D. M. 232
Bal, M. 239
Balot, R. 201, 211
Barbour, J. 19, 128
Bardtke, H. 150, 156, 158
Barjamovic, G. 172–73
Barstad, H. 127
Bartelmus, R. 235
Bartusch, M. W. 234
Bates, C. A., Jr. 210
Bauslaugh, R. A. 232
Bayet, J. 236
Beauchamp, P. 96
Beaulieu, P.-A. 139
Beazley, J. D. 236
Begg, C. 93
Ben Zvi, E. 12–15, 21–22, 27, 48–49, 54, 73, 90, 107, 127–28, 194
Benjamin, W. 49
Berg, S. B. 148
Berge, K. 42, 46
Berger, P. L. 136
Bergren, T. A. 188–190, 192–93

Author Index

Berlin, A. 150
Berman, J. 77, 224–25
Berquist, J. L. 43
Bickerman, E. J. 151
Biles, J. 51–52
Blanshard, A. 238
Bleicken, J. 219, 223, 225–27
Blenkinsopp, J. 48, 132, 138, 165, 179, 189, 233–34
Block, D. I. 89–95, 97, 99, 102–3
Boardman, J. 236
Bodi, D. 89
Boe, S. 98
Bolin, T. 130, 141
Bonnet, C. 236
Bos, J. M. 34
Bourdieu, P. 30, 118–120, 122, 124–25
Bousquet, J. 174
Bowra, C. M. 201
Boyer, P. 46–47
Brandley, G. 236
Braulik, G. 71
Brett, M. G. 42
Briant, P. 13, 149, 151, 168, 174–76, 182
Brownlee, W. H. 93
Brundage, B. 238
Bryce, T. R. 173–74
Budde, K. 116
Bultmann, C. 58
Burkert, W. 131, 136
Bush, F. W. 148, 150, 157
Bynum, D. E. 233, 235

Camp, C. 233, 235, 239
Campbell, J. K. 120, 122
Canepa, M. P. 231
Carey, C. 30, 201
Carr, D. M. 46, 129–130
Carter, C. 168
Cartledge, C. 203, 213, 215
Certeau, M. de 52–53
Chamoux, E. 202
Chavalas, M. 12

Chomsky, N. 33
Christian, M. A. 41–43
Clines, D. J. A. 112, 116–17, 121–23, 136, 150
Cohen, A. 43
Colledge, M. A. R. 159
Collins, J. J. 140–41, 188
Cooley, J. L. 30
Corcella, A. 223, 227
Craigie, P. C. 65, 71
Crane, A. S. 97, 99
Craven, T. 256, 260
Crenshaw, J. L. 113, 122, 233, 235–36, 239
Cross, F. M. 166–67
Crouch, C. L. 42
Crüsemann, F. 42, 65, 224
Csordas, T. 52
Cunningham, S. 29–32, 38

Dandamaev, M. A. 158, 173
D'arcy, H. 128
Daube, D. 61
Davies, G. H. 83
Davies, P. R. 4–5, 42, 79, 127–28, 139
Davies, W. D. 158
Day, L. 260
De Castelbajac, I. 83
De Silva, D. 188
Demsky, A. 178, 181
Dhorme, É. 112, 117, 123
Dietrich, W. 63
Dommershausen, W. 150
Driver, S. R. 69, 117
Duguid, I. 89, 96, 101–3
Dunn, J. 253
Dupont-Sommer, A. 177
Durkheim, E. 51

Eckhardt, B. 250–52
Edelman, D. V. 4, 6, 27, 127, 166, 168, 170–71, 180–81, 185–86, 188–190, 193–94
Edgar, C. C. 231–32
Ego, B. 150, 156

Author Index

Eliade, M. 51
Ellul, J. 29, 31, 33
Endris, V. 83
Enenkel, K. A. E. 28, 33
Eskenazi, T. C. 41–42
Eslinger, L. M. 84
Evans, P. S. 134, 137
Evrigenis, I. D. 78
Exum, J. C. 233, 239–240

Fei, X. 118–19, 122, 124
Feldman, L. H. 194, 239–240
Feldman, M. H. 45
Finkelstein, I. 167
Finkelstein, L. 158
Fitzmyer, J. 98
Fitzpatrick-McKinley, A. 166–68, 170–72, 177, 186–89, 194
Fleisher, R. 231
Flower, M. A. 202
Fohrer, G. 116, 123
Forty, A. 52–53
Fox, M. V. 148, 157
Frahm, E. 14, 131
Frankel, D. 81
Frazer, J. 49, 51
Freedman, D. N. 77
Fried, L. S. 129, 172, 174
Friedman, R. E. 79
Funk, R. W. 181
Funke, T. 255

Galinsky, G. K. 236–38
Gallagher, W. R. 134
Gantz, T. 238
García López, F. 60–61
Garcia Martinez, F. 98
Garnsey, P. 240–41
Gell, A. 44–45, 50
George, A. R. 131
Gerleman, G. 150, 156
Gerstenberger, E. S. 254
Gertz, J. C. 59

Given, M. 173
Good, E. M. 116–17, 121–22
Goodman, J. E. 118
Grabbe, L. L. 134, 165, 181, 184, 186, 190
Grainger, J. D. 174
Gray, G. B. 117
Grayson, A. K. 137
Greco, A. 185
Greenberg, M. 47
Greenstein, E. 239
Gruen, E. 243
Gschnitzer, F. 219
Gunn, D. M. 239

Habel, N. C. 112, 114–15, 121
Habicht, C. 154
Hahm, D. E. 212–13
Halbwachs, M. 128
Hamilton, M. 117, 122
Hammer, D. 214–15
Handy, L. K. 139
Hansen, M. H. 204, 206
Hansen, S. 159
Harland, P. A. 128
Harrington, D. J. 253
Harris, E. 212
Hartley, J. E. 116
Harvey, F. D. 212
Hayes, C. 171, 188
Hazony, Y. 9
Herman, E. S. 33
Herzfeld, E. 158
Hesse, F. 117
Hobbes, T. 78
Hobson, R. 134, 136
Hodkinson, S. 202, 213
Hoffman, Y. A. 115
Hoglund, K. 166, 168
Hölscher, G. 116
Houtman, D. 45, 50
Huber Villiet, F. 5
Huffman, C. A. 207, 212

Author Index

Hurowitz, V. 165
Huyssen, A. 49–50

Irwin, B. P. 18

Janzen, J. G. 121
Japhet, S. 137–38
Joisten-Pruschke, A. 176
Jonker, L. 42
Joüon, P. 24
Jowett, G. S. 29
Joyce, P. 89–90, 98, 101, 106
Jursa, M. 4

Keel, O. 92, 253, 258
Keen, A. G. 173
Kellermann, U. 165
Kessler, R. 220
Kim, J. 233
Kirk, A. 27
Kirk, G. S. 207
Klauck, H.-J. 154
Klein, A. 96, 98
Klein, L. R. 83, 233–34, 240
Klein, R. W. 137
Kloppenborg, J. S. 128
Klosko, G. 241
Knauf, E. A. 176, 194
Knobloch, H. 71
Knoppers, G. N. 58
Knowles, M. D. 129
Koch, C. 59
Koch, H. 149
Koch, U. S. 10
Köckert, M. 44
Kohl, P. 184
Kooij, A. van der 256, 259
Kottsieper, I. 176
Kratz, R. G. 59, 158, 160, 166
Kriel, J. R. 157
Kroeker, R. J. 22
Krouse, F. M. 232
Küchler, S. 52–53

Kuhrt, A. 13, 160, 182, 185, 206

Laato, A. 89–90, 97
LaCocque, A. 150, 250–51
Landsberger, B. 131
Landy, F. 239
Laroche, E. 177
Lasswell, H. D. 29
Latour, B. 50
Lebram, J. 188
Lebram, J. C. H. 160
Leith, M. J. W. 167
Lemaire, A. 170
Lemche, N. P. 79, 129–130, 168–69, 179, 181
Lerner, R. 10
Leuchter, M. 42
Levavi, Y. 4
Levenson, J. D. 101–2, 150–51, 156
Levin, C. 57, 61–62
Levin, Y. 179
Levine, A.-J. 259
Levinson, B. M. 58, 77, 225
Lierman, J. 16
Lilly, I. E. 91
Lincoln, B. 13
Lindars, B. 83
Lipschits, O. 4, 129
Liss, H. 106
Liverani, M. 173
Lloyd, A. B. 207, 223, 227
Lo, A. 113
Loader, J. A. 150, 156–57
Loewenstamm, S. E. 81
Lohfink, N. 58, 70
Long, R. T. 212
Lucas, R. E. Jr. 78
Lukonin, V. G. 158, 173
Lundbom, J. R. 42
Lust J. 97, 99
Lynch, G. 52
Lynch, M. 41
Macchi, J.-D. 160

Author Index

Mack, B. L. 188
Malchow, B. V. 116
Malkin, I. 202, 238–39
Mann, T. W. 133
Margaliot, M. 80
Margalith, O. 235–36
Markl, D. 57–59
Marr, J. L. 207
Martin, M., III 206
Martinez-Sève, L. 159
Maul, S. 99
McBride, D. S. 224
McCarter, P. K. 68
McConville, J. G. 77
McEvenue, S. E. 167–68
McGlew, J. F. 241
McNutt, P. 111, 118
Meier, C. 226
Meinhold, A. 150, 155
Melamed, A. 10
Mendels, D. 187
Meshorer, Y. 167
Mettinger, T. 6
Metzger, M. 94–95
Meyer, B. 44–45, 50
Meyers, C. L. 105, 118, 121
Meyers, E. M. 105
Miller, G. P. 77, 220
Miller, M. C. 205–6
Mitchell, B. 202
Mitchell, L. 139, 202–3, 206–7, 209–10, 240
Mobley, G. 233–35
Moore, C. A. 150, 157
Moore, G. F. 232
Morgenstern, M. 77
Mossé, C. 210
Motta, F. 79
Müller, R. 57, 59, 61–68
Murphy, R. E. 115
Murray, O. 241

Nagel, P. 157

Nelson, R. D. 60–61, 65, 73
Neusner, J. 192–93
Newell, W. R. 210
Newsom, C. A. 115–18, 120–22
Nicholas, E. W. 79
Niditch, S. 78, 101, 106, 233
Niehaus, J. J. 79
Niehr, H. 101
Niemann, H. M. 158
Nihan, C. 60–67, 90–91, 94, 96–97, 99, 103–4, 259
Nippel, W. 213
Noll, K. L. 46
Nordh, K. 5
Noth, M. 62, 219

O'Carroll, E. 137
O'Connor, M. 24
O'Donnell, V. 29
Ortlund, D. 253
Osborne, R. 205
Osherow, M. 257
Ostwald, M. 207
Oswald, W. 220, 227
Ottmann, H. 227
Otto, A. 20
Otto, E. 72, 99, 101
Otto, R. 51

Padilla, M. W. 236–37, 240
Parpola, S. 95, 131
Paton, L. B. 150–51
Pearce, L. 177
Pelling, C. 208, 223
Pels, P. 45–46
Perlitt, L. 59, 70
Person, R. F. 137
Pfeijffer, I. L. 28, 33
Pohlmann, K.-F. 94, 96
Pritchard, J. B. 181
Procksch, O. 101
Propp, W. H. 80
Pyysiäinen, I. 46

Author Index

Qedar, S. 167

Raafalub, K. A. 203–4, 215
Rabinowitz, I. 176
Radner, K. 173
Rajak, T. 192
Rakel, C. 250, 252, 257
Raurell, F. 103
Raven, J. E. 207
Redford, D. B. 51
Reich, R. 181
Rhodes, P. J. 204–7, 211–12
Römer, T. C. 16, 61–62
Rose, J. 192–93
Rose, M. 60, 62
Rose, W. 98
Rosenberg, J. 77
Ross, J. C. 44, 46
Rossow, F. C. 157
Rowe, C. J. 210
Rowley, H. H. 115
Rudnig, T. A. 104
Rüterswörden, U. 59–60

Sallaberger, W. 5
Särkiö, P. 62
Sasson, J. M. 81
Saxonhouse, A. 226
Schäfer, P. 158
Schäfer-Lichtenberger, C. 60–61
Schaper, J. 42, 129
Schenker, A. 59, 253
Schloen, J. D. 118
Schmitt, A. 148
Schmitt, H. H. 154
Schneider, T. J. 18, 239
Schneider, W. C. 154
Schofield, M. 207
Schroder, B. 159
Schuman, H. 128
Schwartz, B. 128

Schwartz, D. 188–191, 193
Schweitzer, S. J. 104
Seibert, E. A. 78
Seitz, G. 59
Sekunda, N. 174
Seybold, K. 89
Shapiro, H. A. 236–37
Sharon, D. M. 83
Sherwin-White, S. 160
Silverstein, P. A. 118
Sinclair, T. A. 241
Sinopoli, C. M. 12
Skjærvø, P. O. 13
Śliwa, J. 92
Smith, J. Z. 90, 101
Smith, M. 166
Smith-Christopher, D. L. 181
Smolar, L. 81
Snell, D. C. 206
Snodgrass, A. 206
Sonnet, J.-P. 46, 70
Spangenberg, I. J. J. 122
Sperling, S. D. 77
Spronk, K. 232, 235–36
Squire, M. 132
Stafford, E. 231, 235, 237–39
Steadman, S. R. 44, 46
Steinberg, J. 148
Stern, E. 168, 181
Stern, M. 159
Steuernagel, C. 60–62, 69
Stevenson, K. R. 101
Steymans, H. U. 59
Stökl, J. 135, 139
Stoller, P. 47, 49
Stordalen, T. 111, 113, 117–18
Stott, K. M. 132
Strawn, B. A. 92–93
Strong, J. T. 106
Summerer, L. 182
Swartz, D. 30

Author Index

Tadmor, H. 131
Tal, O. 129
Taussig, M. 48–49, 51
Taylor, L. E. 241
Taylor, P. M. 29
Tellenbach, M. 159
Thapar, R. 182
Thomas, R. 223
Thompson, T. 79
Tolkien, J. R. R. 249, 251, 257, 260
Tomes, R. 255–56
Toorn, K. van der 46, 51
Torrey, C. C. 165, 260
Tuplin, C. 178

Uehlinger, C. 92, 167

Van der Woude, A. S. 98
Van Seters, J. 46, 79
Vanderhooft, D. 129
Vanderkam, J. C. 48
Vásquez, M. A. 44, 52
Veijola, T. 57, 62, 64, 72–73
Vermeylen, J. 62
Vickers, M. 235
Vickery, J. B. 233, 239
Von Kienlin, A. 182

Waerzeggers, C. 177, 179
Wahl, H. M. 150, 157
Walbank, F. W. 154
Wallace-Hadrill, A. 168
Waltke, B. K. 24
Walzer, M. 77
Waterbury, J. 168
Watts, J. W. 79, 81
Webb, B. G. 234

Weber, M. 80, 122
Wees, H. van. 214
Weidner, E. F. 93
Weinfeld, M. 60, 73
Weiser, A. 117
Weiskopf, M. N. 174–76
Westbrook, R. 168–69
Westenholz, J. G. 131
Westermann, C. 112, 123
Wetter, A. M. 156–57
Whitley, C. F. 83
Wieczorek, A. 159
Wiemer, H.-U. 153
Wiesehöfer, J. 149, 151, 177
Wilde, A. de. 112
Willi, T. 149, 155
Willi-Plein, I. 158
Williamson, H. G. W. 165
Willis, T. M. 111, 118
Wilson, I. D. 16, 19
Winter, U. 95
Wolfers, D. 116
Wright, B. 243
Wright, J. 132, 165–66, 178

Yarrow, L. M. 231
Yoffee, N. 9
Young, I. M. 46

Zakovitch, Y. 235, 239
Zeller, D. 154
Zenger, E. 101, 148
Zerubavel, E. 27–28
Zimmerli, W. 92–94, 98, 102
Zorn, J. R. 167
Zucker, H. 180

www.ingramcontent.com/pod-product-compliance
Lightning Source LLC
Chambersburg PA
CBHW082111230426
43671CB00015B/2668